NEW PERSPECTIVES

Microsoft® Windows® 10

COMPREHENSIVE

June Jamrich Parsons
Dan Oja
Lisa Ruffolo

CENGAGE
Learning·

Australia • Brazil • Mexico • Singapore • United Kingdom • United States

CENGAGE
Learning®

New Perspectives Microsoft® Windows® 10
Comprehensive
June Jamrich Parsons, Dan Oja, Lisa Ruffolo

SVP, GM Skills & Global Product Management:
 Dawn Gerrain

Product Director: Kathleen McMahon

Senior Product Team Manager: Lauren Murphy

Product Team Manager: Andrea Topping

Associate Product Manager: Reed Curry

Senior Director, Development: Marah Bellegarde

Product Development Manager: Leigh Hefferon

Senior Content Developer: Kathy Finnegan

Developmental Editor: Jane Pedicini

Product Assistant: Erica Chapman

Marketing Director: Michele McTighe

Marketing Manager: Stephanie Albracht

Senior Production Director: Wendy Troeger

Production Director: Patty Stephan

Senior Content Project Manager: Jennifer Goguen
 McGrail

Art Director: Diana Graham

Text Designer: Althea Chen

Cover Template Designer: Wing-Ip Ngan,
 Ink Design, Inc.

Composition: GEX Publishing Services

Cover image(s): schankz/Shutterstock.com

For product information and technology assistance, contact us at
Cengage Learning Customer & Sales Support, 1-800-354-9706

For permission to use material from this text or product, submit all
requests online at **www.cengage.com/permissions**.
Further permissions questions can be e-mailed to
permissionrequest@cengage.com

Mac users: If you're working through this product using a Mac, some of the steps may
vary. Additional information for Mac users is included with the Data Files for this
product.

Some of the product names and company names used in this book have been used for
identification purposes only and may be trademarks or registered trademarks of their
respective manufacturers and sellers.

Windows® is a registered trademark of Microsoft Corporation. © 2012 Microsoft.
Microsoft and the Office logo are either registered trademarks or trademarks of
Microsoft Corporation in the United States and/or other countries. Cengage Learning is
an independent entity from Microsoft Corporation and not affiliated with Microsoft in
any manner.

Disclaimer: Any fictional data related to persons or companies or URLs used throughout
this text is intended for instructional purposes only. At the time this text was published,
any such data was fictional and not belonging to any real persons or companies.

Disclaimer: The material in this text was written using Microsoft Windows 10 Professional
and was Quality Assurance tested before the publication date. As Microsoft continually
updates the Windows 10 operating system, your software experience may vary slightly from
what is presented in the printed text.

Microsoft product screenshots used with permission from Microsoft Corporation.
Unless otherwise noted, all clip art is courtesy of openclipart.org.

Library of Congress Control Number: 2016934472
ISBN: 978-1-305-57938-5

Cengage Learning
20 Channel Center Street
Boston, MA 02210
USA

Cengage Learning is a leading provider of customized learning solutions
with employees residing in nearly 40 different countries and sales in more
than 125 countries around the world. Find your local representative at
www.cengage.com.

Cengage Learning products are represented in Canada by
Nelson Education, Ltd.

To learn more about Cengage Learning, visit **www.cengage.com**

Purchase any of our products at your local college store or at our
preferred online store **www.cengagebrain.com**

Printed in the United States of America
Print Number: 01   Print Year: 2016

TABLE OF CONTENTS

Module 1 Exploring the Basics of Microsoft Windows 10
Investigating the Windows 10 Operating System...... **WIN 1**

Session 1.1 Visual Overview: Windows 10
Desktop . . . . .WIN 2

Introducing Windows 10 . . . . .WIN 4

Starting Windows 10 . . . . .WIN 4

Touring the Desktop . . . . .WIN 6

   Interacting with the Desktop . . . . .WIN 6

   Selecting and Opening Objects. . . . . .WIN 7

   Displaying Shortcut Menus. . . . . .WIN 8

Exploring the Start Menu . . . . .WIN 9

Starting Apps. . . . . .WIN 12

Running Multiple Apps . . . . .WIN 13

   Switching Between Applications . . . . .WIN 14

Manipulating Windows . . . . .WIN 15

Using App Tools . . . . .WIN 18

   Using the Ribbon . . . . .WIN 18

   Using Dialog Boxes. .WIN 19

Closing Apps . . . . .WIN 20

Session 1.1 Quick Check . . . . .WIN 23

Session 1.2 Visual Overview: Working in
File Explorer . . . . .WIN 24

Exploring Your Computer . . . . .WIN 26

   Navigating with File Explorer . . . . .WIN 26

   Changing the View .WIN 27

   Using the Navigation Pane . . . . .WIN 29

Getting Help . . . . .WIN 31

   Using the Get Started App. . . . . .WIN 31

   Getting Help on the Microsoft
   Website. . . . . .WIN 32

   Searching the Windows How-to
   Webpages. . . . . .WIN 33

Turning Off Windows 10 . . . . .WIN 34

Session 1.2 Quick Check . . . . .WIN 36

Review Assignments . . . . .WIN 37

Case Problems. . . . . .WIN 38

Module 2 Organizing Your Files
Managing Files and Folders in Windows 10. . . . . **WIN 41**

Session 2.1 Visual Overview: Files in a
Folder Window . . . . .WIN 42

Preparing to Manage Your Files . . . . .WIN 44

   Understanding the Need for Organizing
   Files and Folders. . . . . .WIN 45

   Developing Strategies for Organizing
   Files and Folders. . . . . .WIN 46

Exploring Files and Folders. . . . . .WIN 48

   Navigating to Your Data Files. . . . . .WIN 52

   Navigating with the Address Bar . . . . .WIN 54

Using the Search Box to Find Files . . . . .WIN 55

Managing Files and Folders . . . . .WIN 56

   Creating Folders . . . . .WIN 57

   Moving and Copying Files and Folders . . . . .WIN 58

   Selecting Files and Folders. . . . . .WIN 61

   Copying Files and Folders . . . . .WIN 61

Session 2.1 Quick Check . . . . .WIN 63

Session 2.2 Customized Folder Window . . . . . . .WIN 64

Naming and Renaming Files and Folders . . . . . .WIN 66

Deleting Files and Folders. . . . . .WIN 67

Working with New Files. . . . . .WIN 68

   Creating a File. . . . . .WIN 68

   Saving a File . . . . .WIN 69

   Opening a File. . . . . .WIN 71

Refining the Organization of Files. . . . . .WIN 72

   Sorting and Filtering Files. . . . . .WIN 73

   Grouping Files. . . . . .WIN 75

Customizing a Folder Window . . . . .WIN 76

Changing the Layout of a Folder
Window . . . . WIN 77

Customizing the File List . . . . WIN 79

Customizing the Navigation Pane . . . . WIN 80

Working with Compressed Files . . . . WIN 81

Restoring Your Settings . . . . WIN 83

Session 2.2 Quick Check . . . . WIN 84

Review Assignments . . . . WIN 85

Case Problems . . . . WIN 86

Module 3 Personalizing Your Windows Environment
Changing Desktop Settings . . . . **WIN 89**

Session 3.1 Visual Overview: Customized
Desktop . . . . WIN 90

Changing Windows Settings . . . . WIN 92

Changing the Desktop Background . . . . WIN 96

Changing Desktop Colors . . . . WIN 98

Personalizing the Lock Screen . . . . WIN 100

Activating a Screen Saver . . . . WIN 102

Selecting Themes . . . . WIN 104

Saving Themes . . . . WIN 105

Changing Display Settings . . . . WIN 106

Changing the Screen Resolution . . . . WIN 107

Changing the Size of Text and
Objects . . . . WIN 108

Personalizing Desktop Icons . . . . WIN 109

Adding Icons to the Desktop . . . . WIN 110

Changing the Appearance of
Desktop Icons . . . . WIN 111

Creating Desktop Shortcuts . . . . WIN 112

Creating a Shortcut to a Drive . . . . WIN 113

Session 3.1 Quick Check . . . . WIN 115

Session 3.2 Visual Overview: Personalized
Start Menu and Taskbar . . . . WIN 116

Modifying the Taskbar . . . . WIN 118

Pinning Apps to the Taskbar . . . . WIN 119

Setting Taskbar Properties . . . . WIN 122

Managing the Desktop with Taskbar Tools . . . . . WIN 123

Arranging Windows with Snap . . . . WIN 123

Keeping Track of Windows with Peek . . . . . . WIN 125

Minimizing and Restoring Windows
with Shake . . . . WIN 127

Using Virtual Desktops . . . . WIN 127

Personalizing the Start Menu . . . . WIN 128

Pinning Tiles on the Start Menu . . . . WIN 129

Organizing Tiles on the Start Menu . . . . WIN 132

Modifying Tiles on the Start Menu . . . . WIN 133

Changing the User Picture . . . . WIN 136

Restoring Your Settings . . . . WIN 138

Session 3.2 Quick Check . . . . WIN 139

Review Assignments . . . . WIN 140

Case Problems . . . . WIN 141

Module 4 Working with the Internet and Email
Communicating with Others . . . . **WIN 147**

Session 4.1 Visual Overview:
Microsoft Edge . . . . WIN 148

Exploring the Internet and the Web . . . . WIN 150

Using Web Browsers . . . . WIN 151

Getting Started with Microsoft Edge . . . . WIN 152

Opening a Page on the Web . . . . WIN 154

Opening a Webpage Using a URL . . . . WIN 154

Navigating with Links . . . . WIN 155

Navigating with Microsoft Edge Tools . . . . . . WIN 158

Managing Webpages in Microsoft Edge . . . . . . WIN 158

Pinning Webpages . . . . WIN 160

Using Cortana to Find Online Information . . . . . WIN 162

Reading and Annotating Webpages . . . . WIN 166

Using the Hub to Revisit Webpages . . . . WIN 169

Creating a Reading List . . . . WIN 169

Using the History List . . . . WIN 170

Adding Webpages to the Favorites List . . . . . WIN 172

Organizing the Favorites List . . . . WIN 175

Printing and Saving Webpage Content. . . . . . WIN 176

Session 4.1 Quick Check . . . . WIN 177

Session 4.2 Visual Overview:
Windows 10 Mail App . . . . WIN 178

Getting Started with Mail . . . . WIN 180

    Examining How Email Works . . . . WIN 180

    Addressing Email . . . . WIN 181

Setting Up Mail . . . . WIN 181

Sending and Receiving Email Using Mail . . . . . . WIN 183

    Creating and Sending Email Messages . . . . . WIN 184

    Receiving and Reading Email
    Messages . . . . WIN 186

    Responding to Email Messages . . . . WIN 187

Attaching a File to a Message. . . . . WIN 188

    Deleting Email Messages . . . . WIN 190

Adding Information to the People App . . . . . . WIN 191

Managing Your Schedule with Calendar. . . . . . WIN 193

    Scheduling Appointments . . . . WIN 194

Restoring Your Settings. . . . . WIN 196

Session 4.2 Quick Check. . . . . WIN 197

Review Assignments . . . . WIN 198

Case Problems. . . . . WIN 199

Module 5 Protecting Your Computer
Managing Computer Security. . . . . **WIN 205**

Session 5.1 Visual Overview:
Windows 10 Security Tools . . . . WIN 206

Using Windows 10 Security Tools . . . . WIN 208

    Managing Windows Firewall. . . . . WIN 210

Setting Up Windows Update . . . . WIN 214

Protecting Your Computer from Malware. . . . . WIN 218

Defending Against Spyware . . . . WIN 220

    Scanning Your Computer with Windows
    Defender. . . . . WIN 221

    Setting Windows Defender Options . . . . . . WIN 223

Defending Against Email Viruses . . . . WIN 225

Session 5.1 Quick Check . . . . WIN 225

Session 5.2 Visual Overview: Microsoft Edge
Security Features. . . . . WIN 226

Managing Microsoft Edge Security. . . . . WIN 228

    Checking Websites with the SmartScreen
    Filter . . . . WIN 228

    Downloading Files Safely . . . . WIN 231

    Blocking Malware . . . . WIN 232

    Blocking Pop-Up Windows. . . . . WIN 233

Selecting Microsoft Edge Privacy
Settings . . . . WIN 234

    Protecting Your Privacy with InPrivate
    Browsing . . . . WIN 237

    Requesting Tracking Protection . . . . WIN 238

Setting Up User Accounts. . . . . WIN 240

    Selecting a User Name and Password . . . . . WIN 241

    Creating a Local-Only User Account . . . . . . WIN 242

    Changing Sign-in Options. . . . . WIN 244

Controlling Access to Your Computer. . . . . WIN 249

Startup and App Security Features. . . . . WIN 250

Restoring Your Settings. . . . . WIN 250

Session 5.2 Quick Check. . . . . WIN 251

Review Assignments . . . . WIN 252

Case Problems. . . . . WIN 253

Module 6 Searching for Information
Finding Apps, Settings, Files, and Information . . . **WIN 257**

Session 6.1 Visual Overview:
Searching for Files. . . . . WIN 258

Developing Search Strategies. . . . . WIN 260

Using Cortana to Search for Apps and
Information . . . . WIN 261

Searching for Settings. WIN 264

Searching for Files. . . . . WIN 267

    Finding Files by Name and Contents . . . . . . WIN 267

Searching by File Type . . . . WIN 270

Filtering the Search Results by Size . . . . WIN 272

Filtering Search Results by Date
Modified . . . . WIN 274

Examining the Search Results. . . . . WIN 275

Saving a Search . . . . WIN 276

Using Tags and Other Properties . . . . WIN 278

Adding Tags to Files . . . . WIN 279

Session 6.1 Quick Check . . . . WIN 281

Session 6.2 Visual Overview:
Searching the Internet . . . . WIN 282

Using Advanced Search Criteria . . . . WIN 284

Combining Criteria When Searching File
Contents . . . . WIN 285

Combining Boolean Filters and File
Properties . . . . WIN 288

Searching the Web . . . . WIN 288

Searching for Web Information with
Cortana . . . . WIN 288

Searching the Web with
Microsoft Edge . . . . WIN 291

Narrowing Your Search . . . . WIN 292

Choosing Search Engines . . . . WIN 296

Restoring Your Settings. . . . . WIN 298

Session 6.2 Quick Check . . . . WIN 299

Review Assignments . . . . WIN 300

Case Problems. . . . . WIN 301

Module 7 Managing Multimedia Files
Working with Graphics, Photos, Music,
and Videos . . . . WIN 305

Session 7.1 Visual Overview:
Creating Graphics in Paint. . . . . WIN 306

Exploring Computer Graphics . . . . WIN 308

Creating Graphics in Paint. . . . . WIN 310

Opening a Graphic in Paint. . . . . WIN 312

Saving a Graphics File. . . . . WIN 314

Copying and Pasting to Create a Graphic. . . . WIN 315

Modifying Graphics in Paint . . . . WIN 317

Resizing the Canvas and Moving
an Image . . . . WIN 317

Adding Text to a Graphic . . . . WIN 320

Drawing Shapes . . . . WIN 325

Moving Part of a Graphic . . . . WIN 327

Resizing and Rotating Graphics . . . . WIN 330

Deleting Part of a Graphic . . . . WIN 332

Changing Colors . . . . WIN 334

Copying an Image. WIN 335

Cropping a Graphic . . . . WIN 337

Session 7.1 Quick Check . . . . WIN 339

Session 7.2 Visual Overview:
Editing Photos . . . . WIN 340

Working with Photos . . . . WIN 342

Acquiring and Importing Photos . . . . WIN 342

Viewing and Organizing Photos . . . . WIN 344

Playing a Simple Slide Show . . . . WIN 348

Editing a Photo . . . . WIN 349

Sharing Photos. . . . . WIN 352

Sharing Photos from the Photos App. . . . . . WIN 352

Sharing Photos Using OneDrive . . . . WIN 354

Finding and Playing Music. . . . . WIN 359

Finding Music Files . . . . WIN 359

Playing Music Files . . . . WIN 361

Creating a Playlist . . . . WIN 362

Working with Videos . . . . WIN 364

Restoring Your Settings. . . . . WIN 365

Session 7.2 Quick Check . . . . WIN 365

Review Assignments . . . . WIN 366

Case Problems. . . . . WIN 368

Module 8 Connecting to Networks with Mobile Computing
Accessing Network Resources . . . . **WIN 375**

Session 8.1 Visual Overview:
Mobile Computing Settings . . . . WIN 376

Managing Mobile Computing Devices . . . . WIN 378

Using Windows Mobility Center . . . . WIN 379

    Setting Speaker Volume . . . . WIN 380

    Displaying the Battery Status . . . . WIN 381

    Selecting a Power Plan . . . . WIN 384

Customizing Power Options . . . . WIN 386

    Modifying a Power Plan . . . . WIN 389

    Selecting Other Power Options . . . . WIN 393

Presenting Information to an Audience . . . . . . WIN 394

    Preparing a Computer for a Presentation . . . . WIN 394

    Displaying Information on an External
    Display Device . . . . WIN 396

Exploring Network Concepts . . . . WIN 398

    Setting Up a Small Office or Home
    Network . . . . WIN 400

Managing Network Connections . . . . WIN 401

    Connecting to a Wireless Network . . . . WIN 402

Session 8.1 Quick Check . . . . WIN 405

Session 8.2 Visual Overview:
Sharing Resources . . . . WIN 406

Using a Windows Homegroup . . . . WIN 408

    Creating a Homegroup . . . . WIN 408

    Adding Other Computers to
    a Homegroup . . . . WIN 411

    Sharing Files with a Homegroup . . . . WIN 412

    Sharing a Printer with a Homegroup . . . . . . WIN 415

Accessing Offline Files . . . . WIN 415

    Setting Up a Computer to Use
    Offline Files . . . . WIN 416

    Making a File or Folder Available Offline . . . . WIN 418

Synchronizing Folders . . . . WIN 419

Using Sync Center . . . . WIN 420

    Resolving Synchronization Conflicts . . . . WIN 421

Using Remote Desktop Connection . . . . WIN 422

Restoring Your Settings . . . . WIN 426

Session 8.2 Quick Check . . . . WIN 427

Review Assignments . . . . WIN 428

Case Problems . . . . WIN 429

Module 9 Maintaining Hardware and Software
Managing Software, Disks, and Devices . . . . **WIN 433**

Session 9.1 Visual Overview:
Managing Data and Software . . . . WIN 434

Backing Up and Restoring Files . . . . WIN 436

    Setting Up File History . . . . WIN 437

    Selecting the Backup Location . . . . WIN 438

    Selecting Folders to Back Up . . . . WIN 438

    Backing Up Files . . . . WIN 439

    Changing Backup Options . . . . WIN 440

    Restoring Files and Folders . . . . WIN 446

Managing System Software . . . . WIN 448

    Creating a System Recovery Drive . . . . WIN 449

    Creating a System Restore Point . . . . WIN 450

    Resetting and Recovering a System . . . . WIN 454

Managing Application Software . . . . WIN 456

    Installing Apps from the Windows Store . . . . . WIN 456

    Uninstalling Software . . . . WIN 458

    Setting Up a Program for Compatibility . . . . . WIN 459

    Exploring Windows To Go . . . . WIN 461

Session 9.1 Quick Check . . . . WIN 461

Session 9.2 Visual Overview:
Managing Hardware . . . . WIN 462

Maintaining Hard Disks . . . . WIN 464

    Viewing Hard Disk Properties . . . . WIN 464

    Checking for Partitions . . . . WIN 466

    Deleting Unnecessary Files with Disk
    Cleanup . . . . WIN 468

Checking a Hard Disk for Errors . . . . WIN 469

Defragmenting a Disk. . . . . WIN 472

Working with Devices and Drivers . . . . WIN 476

Understanding Device Resources. . . . . WIN 478

Understanding Device Drivers . . . . WIN 479

Installing a Device. . . . . WIN 479

Enabling and Disabling Devices . . . . WIN 479

Installing and Updating Device Drivers . . . . . WIN 482

Rolling Back a Driver to a Previous
Version. . . . . WIN 484

Safely Removing Devices . . . . WIN 484

Maintaining Your Display Device. . . . . WIN 484

Adjusting the Screen Refresh Rate . . . . WIN 485

Selecting Color Settings. . . . . WIN 486

Installing and Setting Up a Printer . . . . WIN 488

Installing a Local Printer . . . . WIN 488

Restoring Your Settings. . . . . WIN 490

Session 9.2 Quick Check . . . . WIN 491

Review Assignments . . . . WIN 492

Case Problems. . . . . WIN 493

Module 10 Improving Your Computer's Performance
*Enhancing Your System and Troubleshooting
Computer Problems* . . . . **WIN 497**

Session 10.1 Visual Overview:
Tracking System Performance. . . . . WIN 498

Improving System Performance . . . . WIN 500

Displaying Basic System Information . . . . . . WIN 500

Reviewing Detailed System Information. . . . WIN 503

Optimizing Visual Effects . . . . WIN 505

Using Task Manager to Examine System
Information . . . . WIN 506

Monitoring System Performance . . . . WIN 512

Using Resource Monitor . . . . WIN 517

Generating a System Diagnostics Report . . . . WIN 519

Increasing Memory Capacity. . . . . WIN 520

Using ReadyBoost to Increase Memory
Capacity . . . . WIN 522

Session 10.1 Quick Check . . . . WIN 525

Session 10.2 Visual Overview:
Solving System Problems . . . . WIN 526

Responding to Notifications . . . . WIN 528

Finding Troubleshooting Information . . . . WIN 529

Using Troubleshooters to Find and Fix
Computer Problems . . . . WIN 531

Searching the Microsoft Community . . . . . . WIN 534

Troubleshooting Printing Errors . . . . WIN 536

Recovering from Software Errors . . . . WIN 538

Reporting and Solving Software
Errors. . . . . WIN 538

Viewing the Reliability History . . . . WIN 540

Viewing Details About System
Events . . . . WIN 543

Recovering the Operating System . . . . WIN 545

Using the Steps Recorder . . . . WIN 547

Requesting and Managing Remote
Assistance . . . . WIN 549

Requesting Remote Assistance . . . . WIN 550

Restoring Your Settings. . . . . WIN 553

Session 10.2 Quick Check . . . . WIN 554

Review Assignments . . . . WIN 555

Case Problems. . . . . WIN 556

INDEX . . . . **REF 1**

OBJECTIVES

Session 1.1
- Start Windows 10
- Explore the Start menu
- Start and close apps
- Run apps, switch between them, and close them
- Identify and use the controls in windows and dialog boxes

Session 1.2
- Navigate your computer using File Explorer
- Change the view of the items in your computer
- Get help when you need it
- Turn off Windows 10

Exploring the Basics of Microsoft Windows 10

Investigating the Windows 10 Operating System

Case | *For Pet's Sake*

For Pet's Sake is a nonprofit pet-adoption agency in Glencoe, Illinois, dedicated to placing adoptable companion animals in suitable homes and educating the public about responsible pet ownership. The agency depends on its volunteers to help with daily operations, pet care, and fundraising. As the volunteer coordinator at For Pet's Sake, Ashley Cramer recruits, trains, and manages volunteers. Some of her training sessions involve teaching volunteers how to perform their daily tasks using the agency's computers.

Ashley recently hired you as her assistant. She has asked you to lead the upcoming training sessions on the fundamentals of the Microsoft Windows 10 operating system. As you prepare for the sessions, she offers to help you identify the topics you should cover and the skills you should demonstrate while focusing on the new features in Windows 10.

In this module, you will start Windows 10 and practice some fundamental computer skills. You'll tour the desktop, start applications, and then navigate a computer using File Explorer. Finally, you'll find and use help topics and turn off Windows 10.

Note: With the release of Windows 10, Microsoft is taking a new approach to software publication called "Windows as a Service." With this approach, Microsoft is constantly providing updates to Windows instead of releasing new versions periodically. This means that Windows features might change over time, including how they look and how you interact with them. The information provided in this text was accurate at the time this book was published.

STARTING DATA FILES

There are no starting Data Files needed for this module.

Session 1.1 Visual Overview:

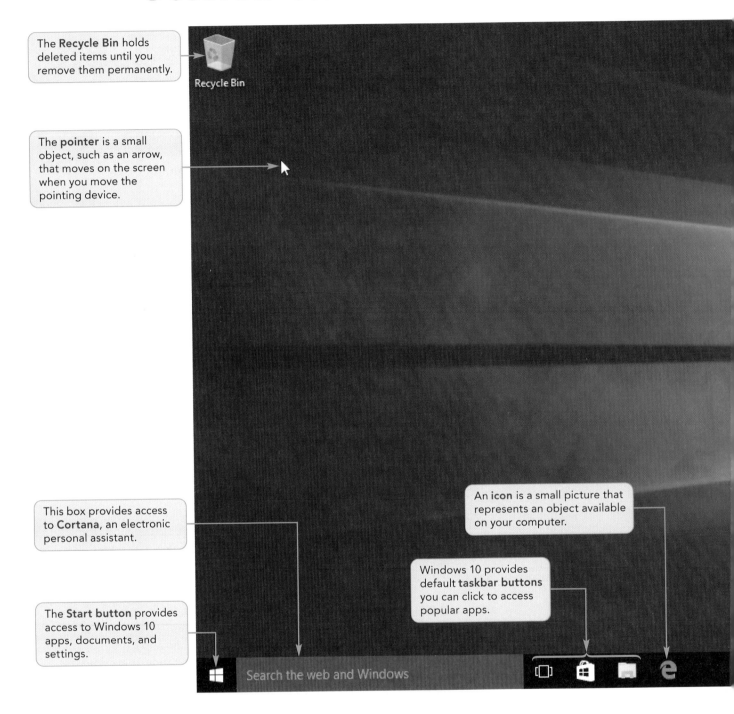

The **Recycle Bin** holds deleted items until you remove them permanently.

Recycle Bin

The **pointer** is a small object, such as an arrow, that moves on the screen when you move the pointing device.

This box provides access to **Cortana**, an electronic personal assistant.

The **Start button** provides access to Windows 10 apps, documents, and settings.

An **icon** is a small picture that represents an object available on your computer.

Windows 10 provides default **taskbar buttons** you can click to access popular apps.

Search the web and Windows

Windows 10 Desktop

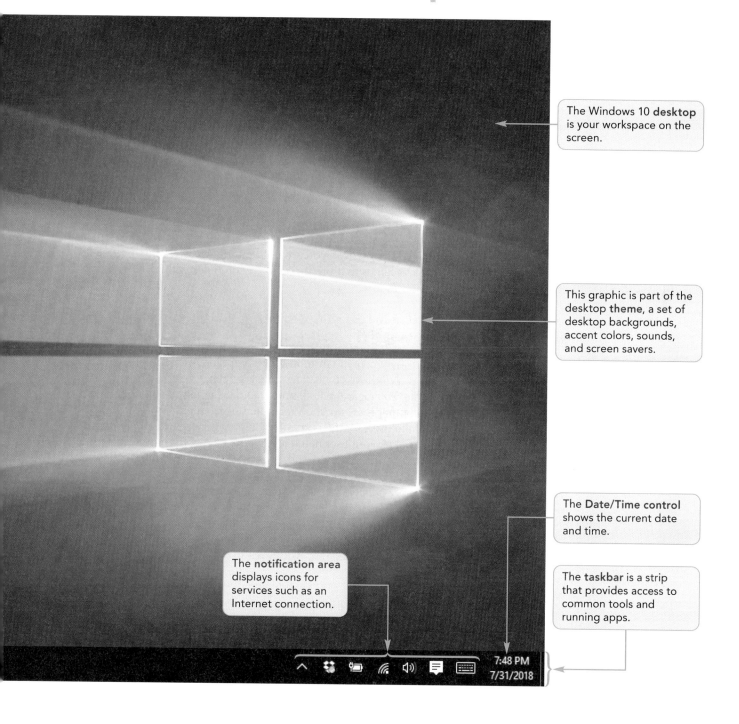

The Windows 10 **desktop** is your workspace on the screen.

This graphic is part of the desktop **theme**, a set of desktop backgrounds, accent colors, sounds, and screen savers.

The **Date/Time control** shows the current date and time.

The **notification area** displays icons for services such as an Internet connection.

The **taskbar** is a strip that provides access to common tools and running apps.

7:48 PM
7/31/2018

Introducing Windows 10

The **operating system** is software that manages and coordinates activities on the computer and helps it perform essential tasks, such as displaying information and saving data. (The term *software* refers to the **programs** a computer uses to complete tasks.) Your computer uses the **Microsoft Windows 10** operating system—**Windows 10** for short. Windows is the name of the operating system, and 10 identifies the version you are using.

The most popular features of Windows 10 include its speed, flexibility, and design. Windows 10 runs software created specifically for Windows 10 and for earlier versions of Windows, such as Windows 7 and 8. This type of software is called an **application**, or **app** for short. You use apps to perform specific tasks, such as writing a document or exchanging messages with another computer user. You can use more than one app at a time and switch seamlessly from one app to another to perform your work efficiently.

Windows 10 is designed to run on computers that use a touchscreen, such as tablets and some laptops, and those that use a keyboard and mouse, such as other laptops and desktop computers. A **touchscreen** is a display that lets you touch areas of the screen to interact with software. To select a button, for example, you touch the button on the tablet display with your fingertip. However, you are not required to use a touchscreen with Windows 10. This book assumes that you are using a computer with a keyboard and pointing device, such as a mouse.

Starting Windows 10

Windows 10 starts automatically when you turn on your computer. After completing some necessary start-up tasks, Windows 10 displays a **lock screen**, which includes a picture, the date, and the time. You clear the lock screen to display the Welcome screen. Depending on how your computer is set up, the Welcome screen might list only your user name or it might list all the users for the computer. Before you start working with Windows, you might need to click your user name and type a password. A **user name** is a unique name that identifies you to Windows, and a **password** is a confidential series of characters that you must enter before you can work with Windows. If you installed Windows yourself, you probably created a user name and password as you set up your computer. If not, the person who created your account assigned you at least a user name and possibly a password. After selecting your user name or entering a password, the Windows 10 desktop appears (as shown in the Session 1.1 Visual Overview).

To begin preparing for your training session, Ashley asks you to start Windows 10.

To start Windows 10:

▶ **1.** Turn on your computer. After a moment, Windows 10 starts and the lock screen appears.

   Trouble? If you are asked to select an operating system, do not take action. Windows 10 should start automatically after a designated number of seconds. If it does not, ask your instructor or technical support person for help.

▶ **2.** Press any key to clear the lock screen and display the Welcome screen.

   Trouble? If the Welcome screen does not appear, click the lock screen, hold down the mouse button, and then drag the lock screen picture up to display the Welcome screen.

▶ **3.** If necessary, click your user name, type your password, and then press the **Enter** key.

The Windows 10 desktop appears, as shown in the Session 1.1 Visual Overview. Your screen might look different.

Trouble? If your user name does not appear on the Welcome screen, try pressing the Ctrl+Alt+Del keys to enter your name. If necessary, ask your instructor or technical support person for further assistance.

Trouble? If a blank screen or an animated design replaces the desktop, your computer might be set to use a **screen saver**, a program that causes a display to go blank or to show an animated design after a specified amount of idle time. Press any key or move your mouse to restore the desktop.

Trouble? If your computer is using a screen resolution other than 1366 × 768, the figures shown in this book might not match exactly what you see in Windows 10 as you work through the steps. Take the screen resolution difference into account as you compare your screen with the figures.

The background area that appears after you sign into Windows 10 is called the desktop because it provides a workspace for projects and the tools you need to manipulate your projects. The desktop displays icons that represent items on your computer, such as apps, files, and folders. A computer **file** is a collection of related information. Typical types of files include text documents, spreadsheets, photos, and songs. A folder is a container that helps you organize the contents of your computer.

Windows gets its name from the rectangular areas called **windows** that appear on your screen as you work, such as those shown in Figure 1-1.

Figure 1-1   **Two windows open on the desktop**

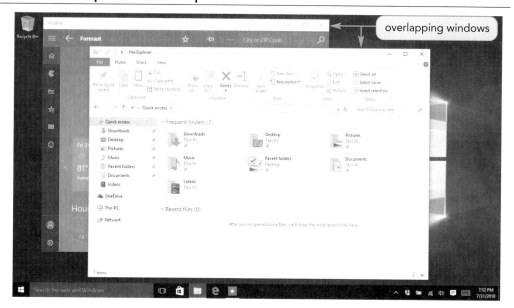

You can open two types of windows in Windows 10: those for Windows apps (also called universal apps), such as the Weather app, and those for traditional desktop applications, such as **File Explorer**, a tool you use to navigate, view, and work with the contents and resources on your computer. You'll explore both types of windows later in the module.

Touring the Desktop

The first time you start a computer after installing Windows 10, the computer uses **default settings**, those preset by the operating system. The default desktop you see after you first install Windows 10, for example, displays a large background image. However, Microsoft designed Windows 10 so that you can easily change the appearance of the desktop. You can, for example, change pictures or add color to the desktop.

Interacting with the Desktop

If you are using a laptop or desktop computer, you use a **pointing device** to interact with the objects on the screen. Pointing devices come in many shapes and sizes. The most common one is called a **mouse**, so this book uses that term. If you are using a different pointing device, such as a trackball or touchpad, substitute that device whenever you see the term mouse. Some pointing devices are designed to ensure that your hand won't suffer fatigue while using them. Most mice work wirelessly and provide access to your computer without being plugged into it. Others are attached directly to your computer by a cable.

You use a pointing device to move the pointer over locations and objects on the screen, or to **point** to them. The pointer is an on-screen object, often shaped like an arrow as shown in the Session 1.1 Visual Overview, though it changes shape depending on its location on the screen and the tasks you are performing. As you move the mouse on a surface, such as a table top, the pointer on the screen moves in a corresponding direction.

When you point to certain objects, such as the objects on the taskbar, a ScreenTip appears near the object. A **ScreenTip** is on-screen text that tells you the purpose or function of the object to which you are pointing.

Ashley suggests that during your class, you introduce For Pet's Sake volunteers to the desktop by viewing ScreenTips for a couple of desktop objects.

To view ScreenTips:

▶ **1.** Point to the **File Explorer** icon ▭ on the taskbar. A ScreenTip identifying the icon appears near the icon, as shown in Figure 1-2.

Figure 1-2 | Viewing a ScreenTip

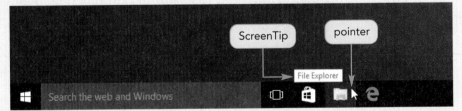

Trouble? If you don't see the ScreenTip, make sure you keep the pointer still for a few seconds.

Clicking refers to pressing a mouse button and immediately releasing it. Clicking sends a signal to your computer that you want to perform an action with the object you click. In Windows 10, you perform most actions with the left mouse button. If you are told to click an object, position the pointer on that object and click the left mouse button, unless instructed otherwise.

Selecting and Opening Objects

TIP

If you are using a device with a touchscreen, a check box appears near an on-screen object when you point to the object. A checkmark appears in the box when you select the object.

You need to select an item, or object, before you can work with it. To **select** an object in Windows 10, you point to or click that object. Windows 10 indicates an object is selected by highlighting it, typically by changing the object's color or displaying a box around it. For example, when you point to the Start button, it changes color. The change shows it is the **active object**. You can interact with active objects by clicking them, for example. When you click the Start button, the Start menu opens. A **menu** is a group or list of commands, and a **menu command** is text that you can click to perform tasks.

The **Start menu** provides access to apps, files, settings, and power options. Ashley suggests you click the Start button to open the Start menu.

To open the Start menu:

▶ **1.** Click the **Start** button ⊞ on the taskbar. The Start menu opens, as shown in Figure 1-3; your Start menu might show different commands.

Figure 1-3	Start menu

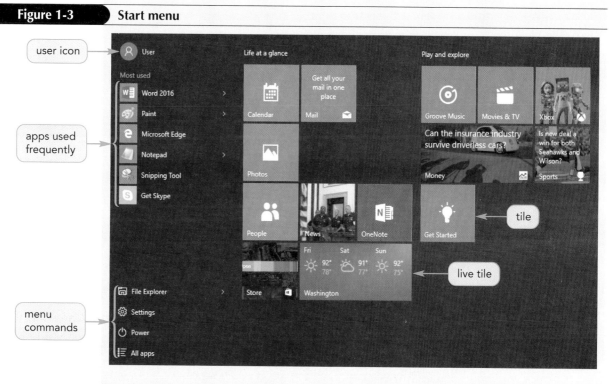

▶ **2.** Click the **Start** button ⊞ on the taskbar to close the Start menu.

Besides menu commands, the Start menu includes colored rectangles called **tiles**, which represent apps. Some tiles display icons, such as the Calendar tile. Other tiles display information that previews the contents of the app, such as the Sports tile, which displays photos and headlines for current sports stories. A tile that displays updated content is called a **live tile**. Tiles such as the Weather tile become live tiles after you open their apps for the first time.

If clicking an object doesn't open its app, you probably need to double-click it. **Double-clicking** means clicking the left mouse button twice in quick succession. For example, you can double-click the Recycle Bin icon to open the Recycle Bin and see its contents. The **Recycle Bin** holds deleted items until you remove them permanently.

Ashley suggests that you have volunteers practice double-clicking by opening the Recycle Bin.

To view the contents of the Recycle Bin:

▶ **1.** Point to the **Recycle Bin** icon, and then click the left mouse button twice quickly to double-click the icon. The Recycle Bin window opens, as shown in Figure 1-4.

Figure 1-4   **Contents of the Recycle Bin**

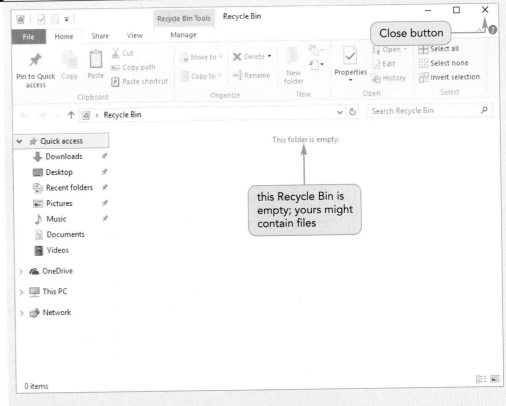

Trouble? If the Recycle Bin window does not open and you see only the Recycle Bin name highlighted below the icon, you double-clicked too slowly. Double-click the icon again more quickly.

Now you can close the Recycle Bin window.

▶ **2.** Click the **Close** button ⊠ in the upper-right corner of the Recycle Bin window.

You'll learn more about opening and closing windows later in this session.

Displaying Shortcut Menus

Your mouse most likely has more than one button. In addition to the left button, the mouse has a right button that you can use to perform certain actions in Windows 10. However, the term *clicking* refers to the left button; clicking an object with the right button is called **right-clicking**. (If your mouse has only one button, you right-click by pressing the right side of the button.)

In Windows 10, right-clicking usually selects an object and opens its **shortcut menu**, which lists actions you can take with that object. You can right-click practically any object—a tile on the Start menu, a desktop icon, the taskbar, and even the desktop itself— to view commands associated with that object. Ashley suggests that when you're not sure what to do with an object in Windows 10, you should right-click it and examine its shortcut menu. Now you can right-click the Recycle Bin icon to open its shortcut menu.

To right-click an object on the desktop:

1. Point to the **Recycle Bin** icon on your desktop, and then right-click the icon to open its shortcut menu. This menu offers a list of actions you can take with the Recycle Bin icon. See Figure 1-5.

| Figure 1-5 | Recycle Bin shortcut menu |

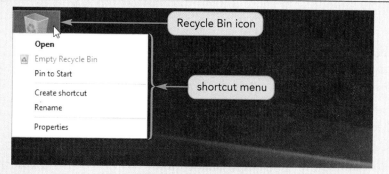

Trouble? If the shortcut menu does not open and you are using a trackball or a mouse with a wheel, make sure you click the button on the far right, not the one in the middle.

2. Click **Open** on the shortcut menu to open the Recycle Bin window again.

3. Click the **Close** button ⊠ in the upper-right corner of the Recycle Bin window.

Now that you've explored the desktop, you can return to the Start menu and use it to start applications.

Exploring the Start Menu

The Start menu is the central point for accessing apps, documents, and other resources on your computer. The Start menu is organized into two **panes**, which are separate areas of a menu or window. See Figure 1-6.

Figure 1-6   Two panes of the Start menu

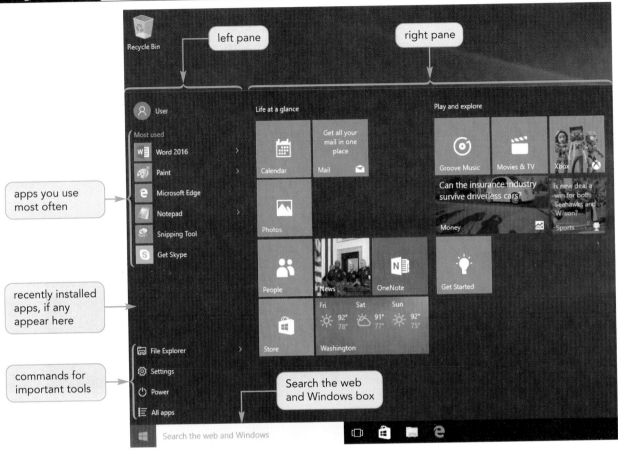

For easy access, the left pane lists the apps you use most often in the Most used list. If you have recently added apps, the left pane also lists those apps in the Recently added list. When you first install Windows 10, the Most used list contains a few apps already installed on your computer. After you use an app, Windows 10 adds it to this list so you can find it quickly the next time you want to use it. The Most used list can contain only a certain number of apps—after that, the apps you have not opened recently are replaced by the apps you used last.

Near the bottom of the left pane are commands for the following important tools:

- File Explorer: Navigate, view, and work with the contents and resources on your computer.
- Settings: Select and change system settings.
- Power: Control the power to the computer by shutting it down, for example.
- All apps: Select from an alphabetic list of all the apps on the computer.

Use the **Search the web and Windows box** to access Cortana, an electronic personal assistant that can search the web, find files, keep track of information, and respond to your questions. You can activate Cortana by typing text or talking. For example, you can ask Cortana to tell a joke, remind you about an appointment, or find a file. See Figure 1-7.

Figure 1-7   Cortana electronic personal assistant

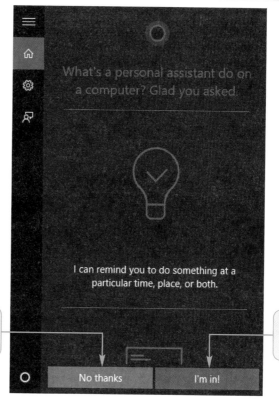

click if you don't want Cortana to track your preferences

click to start working with Cortana

No thanks   I'm in!

INSIGHT

Cortana

Cortana comes from the Halo series of games where she is a smart and powerful character that provides information and helps the master chief complete missions. In Windows 10, Cortana is not a character, but a personalized assistant. The **Notebook** is where Cortana keeps track of what you like, such as your interests and favorite places, and what you want it to do, such as display reminders or information that might interest you. Settings in the People and Maps apps also affect Cortana. For example, if you identify a contact as a friend, Cortana can remind you to call that person. If you identify locations on the map as your home and workplace, Cortana can estimate the time of your commute. As you work, Cortana can take note of your preferences and what you're doing when you ask for information to give personalized answers and recommendations. Because you control the type of information you share with Cortana, the interactions are on your terms and are personalized to your benefit.

From the right pane of the Start menu, you can select tiles for **Windows apps**, or **universal apps**, a type of app that can run on many devices, including laptops, tablets, and mobile phones. You purchase, download, and install Windows apps from the Windows Store, an online resource for games, music, video, and other types of apps, including social and productivity apps. In contrast, many apps in the left pane of the Start menu are **desktop apps**, which run only on personal computers (PCs) such as laptops and desktop computers.

Now that you've explored the Start menu, you're ready to use it to start an app.

Starting Apps

Computers can run two types of software: system software and apps. **System software** is the software that runs a computer, including the operating system. As you know, an app is the software you use to perform tasks, such as writing a screenplay or viewing a webpage. In general, a computer runs system software to perform computer tasks, and you run apps to carry out your work or personal tasks.

REFERENCE

Starting an App

- Click the Start button on the taskbar.
- Click the tile or command for the app you want to start.
- If the app you want does not appear on the Start menu, click All apps, and then click the app you want to start.

or

- In the Search the web and Windows box, type the name of the app until the app appears in the search results on the Start menu; or click the Start button, and then type the name of the app until the app appears in the search results on the Start menu.
- Click the app in the search results.

Ashley suggests that you demonstrate how to start the Calendar app, a Windows app that displays a full-screen calendar where you can schedule appointments and other events.

To start the Calendar app:

1. Click the **Start** button ⊞ on the taskbar to display the Start menu.

2. Click the **Calendar** tile to start the Calendar app. If this is the first time you are starting the Calendar app, click the **Get started** button to set up the calendar. See Figure 1-8.

   Trouble? If a screen appears asking you to let Mail and Calendar access your location, click the No button.

Figure 1-8   **Calendar app**

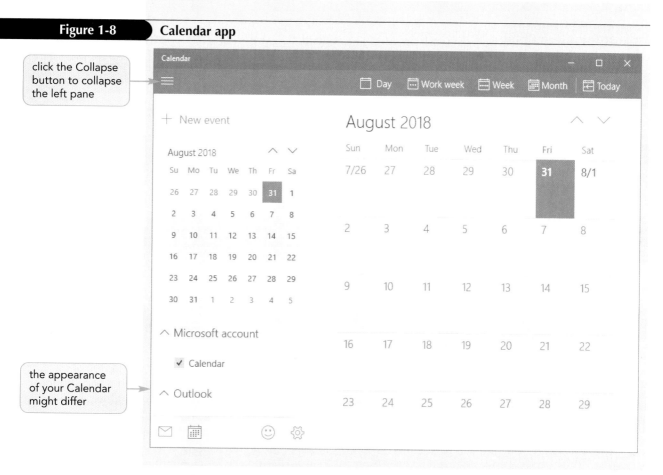

click the Collapse button to collapse the left pane

the appearance of your Calendar might differ

Now that you have started one app, you can start another app and run two at the same time.

Running Multiple Apps

One of the most useful features of Windows 10 is its ability to run multiple programs at the same time. This feature, known as **multitasking**, allows you to work on more than one task at a time and to switch quickly between projects.

To demonstrate multitasking and switching between apps, Ashley suggests that you start Paint, a desktop app you use to draw, color, and edit digital pictures. Paint appears on the Start menu by default.

To run Calendar and Paint at the same time:

1. Click the **Start** button on the taskbar to display the Start menu.

2. In the left pane, click **Paint** to start the app. Now two apps are running at the same time.

   Trouble? If Paint does not appear in the left pane of the Start menu, click All apps, scroll the list of apps, click Windows Accessories, and then click Paint.

3. If the Paint window fills the entire screen, click the **Restore Down** button in the upper-right corner of the Paint window to reduce the size of the window. See Figure 1-9.

Figure 1-9   **Two apps open**

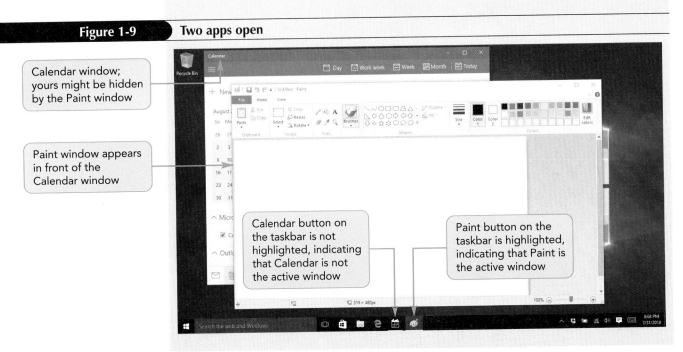

Calendar window; yours might be hidden by the Paint window

Paint window appears in front of the Calendar window

Calendar button on the taskbar is not highlighted, indicating that Calendar is not the active window

Paint button on the taskbar is highlighted, indicating that Paint is the active window

When you start an app, it is said to be open or running. A taskbar button appears on the taskbar for each open app. One taskbar button is highlighted with a background lighter than the other taskbar buttons. This button is for the **active window**, the window you are currently working with—Windows 10 applies your next keystroke or command to the active window. Paint is the active window because it is the one you are currently using. If two or more windows overlap, the active window appears in front of the other windows. Even if the Paint window completely covered the Calendar window, you could still access the Calendar app by using its taskbar button. The taskbar organizes all the open windows so you can quickly make one active by clicking its taskbar button.

Switching Between Applications

Because only one app is active at a time, you need to switch between apps if you want to work in one or the other. The easiest way to switch between running apps is to use the taskbar buttons.

To switch between Calendar and Paint:

1. Click the **Calendar** button 📅 on the taskbar. The Calendar window moves to the front, and the Calendar taskbar button appears highlighted, indicating that Calendar is the active window.

2. Click the **Paint** button 🎨 on the taskbar to switch to the Paint app. The Paint window is again the active window.

TIP

You can also click an inactive window to make it the active window.

Another way to use the taskbar to switch between open apps is to use the Task View button. By default, the Task View button is the first button to the right of the Search the web and Windows box. Click the Task View button to display thumbnails of all running apps. (A **thumbnail** is a miniature version of a larger image, such as a window.) See Figure 1-10.

Figure 1-10	Task view

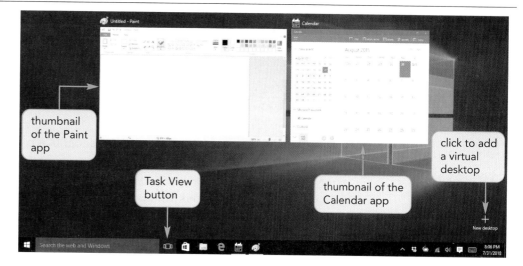

You can switch to one of the running apps by clicking its thumbnail or close it by clicking its Close button. Clicking a thumbnail displays its full window as the active window. To close the Task view, click the Task View button again.

Besides switching apps, you can click the New desktop button in Task view to add a new desktop to the interface, called a **virtual desktop**. For example, you might use the default desktop for school or work projects, and another desktop for entertainment, such as a music player and games.

Another way to switch apps is to bypass the taskbar altogether and use keyboard shortcuts to switch from one open window to another. A **keyboard shortcut** is a key or combination of keys that performs a command. Use the Alt+Tab keyboard shortcut to switch between running apps. To do so, you hold down the Alt key and then press the Tab key to display thumbnails of all running apps, press the Tab key again to select a thumbnail, and then release the Alt key to make that app active. Pressing the Alt+Tab keys displays thumbnails similar to Task view. However, when you release the keys, the thumbnails no longer appear. In Task view, the thumbnails remain on the screen until you select one.

Manipulating Windows

After you open a window, you can manipulate it to display as much or as little information as you need. In most windows, three buttons appear on the right side of the title bar. See Figure 1-11. The first button is the Minimize button, which hides a window so that only its button is visible on the taskbar. Depending on the status of the window, the middle button either maximizes the window or restores it to a predefined size. The last button is the Close button, which closes the window.

Figure 1-11	Window buttons

Paint and Calendar are open on the desktop, so Ashley encourages you to show volunteers how to use their window controls. Start with the Minimize button, which you use when you want to temporarily hide a window but keep the app running.

To minimize the Paint and Calendar windows:

▶ **1.** Click the **Minimize** button — on the Paint title bar. The Paint window shrinks so that only the Paint taskbar button is visible.

Trouble? If the Paint window closed, you accidentally clicked the Close button ☒. Use the Start menu to start Paint again, and then repeat Step 1. If you accidentally clicked the Maximize button ☐ or the Restore Down button ⧉, repeat Step 1.

▶ **2.** Click the **Minimize** button ▬ on the Calendar title bar. The Calendar window is minimized.

You can redisplay a minimized window by clicking the window's taskbar button. When you redisplay a window, it becomes the active window.

To redisplay the Paint window:

▶ **1.** Click the **Paint** button 🎨 on the taskbar to redisplay the Paint window.

The taskbar button provides another way to switch between a window's minimized and open states.

▶ **2.** Click the **Paint** button 🎨 on the taskbar again to minimize the window.

▶ **3.** Click the **Paint** button 🎨 once more to redisplay the window.

The Maximize button enlarges a window so that it fills the entire screen. Ashley recommends that you work with maximized windows when you want to concentrate on the work you are performing in a single app.

To maximize the Paint window:

▶ **1.** Click the **Maximize** button ☐ on the Paint title bar.

TIP

You can also double-click a window's title bar to maximize the window. Double-click the title bar again to restore the window to its previous size.

The Restore Down button reduces the window so that it is smaller than the entire computer screen. This feature is useful if you want to see more than one window at a time. Also, because the window is smaller, you can move it to another location on the screen or change its dimensions.

To restore a window:

▶ **1.** Click the **Restore Down** button ⧉ on the Paint title bar. After a window is restored, the Restore Down button ⧉ changes to the Maximize button ☐.

You can use the mouse to move a window to a new position on the desktop. When you click an object and then press and hold down the mouse button while moving the mouse, you are **dragging** the object. You can move objects on the screen by dragging them to a new location. If you want to move a window, you drag the window by its title bar.

To drag the restored Paint window to a new location:

▶ **1.** Position the pointer on the Paint title bar.

▶ **2.** Press and hold down the left mouse button, and then move the mouse up or down a little to drag the window. The window moves as you move the mouse.

▶ **3.** Position the window anywhere on the desktop, and then release the left mouse button. The Paint window stays in the new location.

▶ **4.** Drag the Paint window near the upper-left corner of the desktop.

You can also use the mouse to change the size of a window. When you point to an edge or a corner of a window, the pointer changes to the resize pointer, which is a double-headed arrow. You can use the resize pointer to drag an edge or a corner of the window and change the size of the window.

To change the size of the Paint window:

▶ **1.** Position the pointer over the lower-right corner of the Paint window. The pointer changes to ⬉. See Figure 1-12.

| Figure 1-12 | Preparing to resize a window |

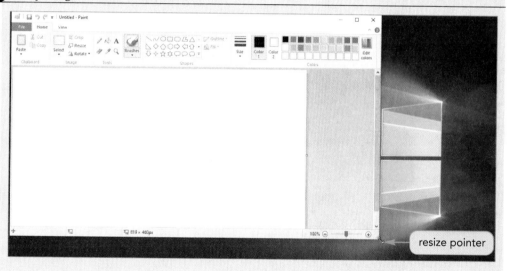

resize pointer

▶ **2.** Press and hold down the mouse button, and then drag the corner down and to the right.

▶ **3.** Release the mouse button. Now the window is larger.

▶ **4.** Practice using the resize pointer to make the Paint window larger or smaller.

You can also use the resize pointer to drag any of the other three corners of the window to change its size. To change a window's size in any one direction only, drag the left, right, top, or bottom window borders left, right, up, or down.

Using App Tools

When you run an app in Windows 10, it appears in a window that contains **controls**, graphical or textual objects used for manipulating a window and for using an app. All apps organize controls in dialog boxes. A desktop application also uses a ribbon to provide controls.

Ashley mentions that Windows 10 comes with a basic word-processing app called WordPad. You use WordPad to create and format basic documents. The WordPad app displays the controls you are likely to see in most windows, including the ribbon, which might be unfamiliar to For Pet's Sake volunteers. Ashley suggests that you start WordPad and identify its window controls during your first training session. You have already started apps using the left and right panes on the Start menu. To start WordPad, you can use the Search the web and Windows box.

As you enter text in the Search the web and Windows box, the Start menu displays search results, including the installed apps, folders, documents, and settings whose names include the text you typed. The search results might also include web search text and Windows Store apps. Two buttons appear at the bottom of the search results: the My stuff button and the Web button. Click the My stuff button to restrict the search to locations on your computer, OneDrive, or network. Click the Web button to start a browser and search the web using the text you entered as the search text.

To start WordPad:

▶ 1. Click the **Start** button ⊞ on the taskbar to display the Start menu. The insertion point appears in the Search the web and Windows box so you can search for an app or other information.

▶ 2. Type **WordPad** to search for the WordPad app and display the results in the Start menu.

▶ 3. Click **WordPad** on the results list to start the app.

▶ 4. Click the **Maximize** button ☐ on the WordPad title bar to maximize the window.

Using the Ribbon

Many desktop apps use a **ribbon** to consolidate features and commands. The ribbon is located at the top of a desktop app window, immediately below the title bar, and is organized into tabs. Each **tab** contains commands that perform a variety of related tasks. For example, the Home tab has commands for tasks you perform frequently, such as changing the appearance of a document. You use the commands on the View tab to change your view of the WordPad window.

To select a command and perform an action, you use a button or other type of control on the ribbon. Controls for related actions are organized on a tab in **groups**. For example, to enter bold text in a WordPad document, you click the Bold button in the Font group on the Home tab. If a button displays only an icon and not the button name, you can point to the button to display a ScreenTip and identify the name or purpose of the button. Figure 1-13 shows examples of the types of controls on the ribbon.

Figure 1-13 Examples of ribbon controls

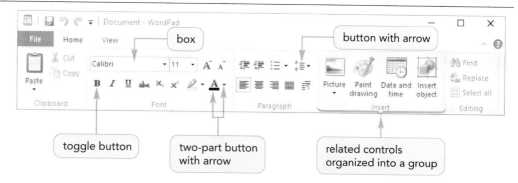

Figure 1-14 describes the types of ribbon controls.

Figure 1-14 Types of controls on the ribbon

Control	How to Use	Example
Button with arrow	Click the button to display a menu of related commands.	
Box	Click the box and type an entry, or click the arrow button to select an item from the list.	
Toggle button	Click the button to turn on or apply a setting, and then click the button again to turn off the setting. When a toggle button is turned on, it is highlighted.	
Two-part button with arrow	If an arrow is displayed on a separate part of the button, click the arrow to display a menu of commands. Click the button itself to apply the current selection.	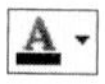

Using Dialog Boxes

When you click some buttons on the ribbon, you open a **dialog box**, a special kind of window in which you enter or choose settings for how you want to perform a task. For example, you use the Print dialog box to enter or select settings for printing a document.

You open dialog boxes by selecting a command on a ribbon tab. For example, the File tab lists commands such as Open, Save, and Print in its left pane. If you point to the Print command, a list of three printing options appears in the right pane, including Print, Quick print, and Print preview. Choose Print to open the Print dialog box, where you can change settings such as the number of copies to print. If you want to print the open document without changing any settings, choose Quick print. Choose Print preview to display the document as it will appear when you print it. If you click the Print command in the left pane without displaying the three printing options, the Print dialog box opens.

Dialog box controls include command buttons, tabs, option buttons, check boxes, and boxes to collect information about how you want to perform a task. Ashley says a good way to learn how dialog box controls work is to open a typical WordPad dialog box, such as the Print dialog box.

To work with a typical Windows 10 dialog box:

▶ **1.** Click the **File** tab on the ribbon, and then click **Print** to open the Print dialog box. See Figure 1-15.

Figure 1-15   **Print dialog box**

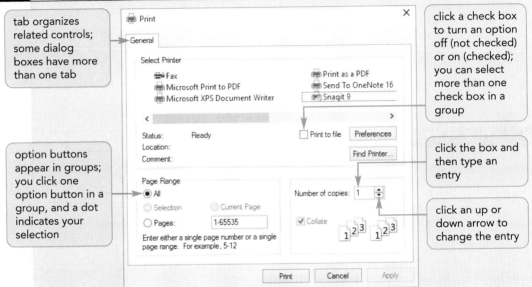

tab organizes related controls; some dialog boxes have more than one tab

click a check box to turn an option off (not checked) or on (checked); you can select more than one check box in a group

option buttons appear in groups; you click one option button in a group, and a dot indicates your selection

click the box and then type an entry

click an up or down arrow to change the entry

▶ **2.** Click the **Pages** option button. You use this control to print only specified pages, not the entire document.

TIP

You can also click an arrow button in the Number of copies box to change the number of copies you want to print.

▶ **3.** Double-click the **Number of copies** box to select the current value, and then type **2**. You use this control to indicate how many copies of the document you want to print.

▶ **4.** Click the **Cancel** button to close the Print dialog box without printing.

If you wanted to print a document with the settings you specified, you would click the Print button instead of the Cancel button. To retain your selections while you perform other tasks in a dialog box, such as setting preferences or finding a printer, you can click the Apply button, complete the other tasks, and then click the Print button.

You're finished working with apps for now, so you should close all open apps.

Closing Apps

You should close an application when you are finished using it. Each application uses computer resources, such as memory, so Windows 10 works more efficiently when only the applications you need are open.

Closing an App

- Click the Close button on the title bar.

  or

- Point to the app's taskbar button to display a thumbnail, point to the thumbnail, and then click the Close button on the thumbnail.

  or

- Click the File tab on the ribbon, and then click Exit.

You can close an app in at least three ways, and you use all three to close the WordPad, Calendar, and Paint apps.

To close WordPad:

▶ **1.** Click the **Close** button ⌧ in the upper-right corner of the WordPad window. WordPad closes while the Paint and Calendar windows remain open. (Recall that the Calendar window is minimized.)

   Trouble? If a dialog box opens with a message asking if you want to save changes, click the Don't Save button.

The Calendar app is still running, though its window is minimized. In this case, the fastest way to close the Calendar app is to use the Close button on the app's thumbnail.

To close Calendar using the thumbnail:

▶ **1.** Point to the **Calendar** button 📅 on the taskbar to display a thumbnail of the Calendar window.

▶ **2.** Point to the thumbnail, and then click the **Close** button ⌧ on the thumbnail. The Calendar app closes and its button no longer appears on the taskbar.

Only the Paint app is still open and running. You can use the Exit command on the File tab to close the Paint window and exit the app.

TIP

You can also right-click the app's taskbar button and then click Close window on the shortcut menu, or click the Task view button, point to a thumbnail, and then click its Close button.

To close Paint using the Exit command:

▶ **1.** Click the **File** tab on the Paint ribbon to display a list of commands for working with Paint files.

▶ **2.** Click **Exit** to close the Paint app.

Trouble? If a message appears asking if you want to save changes, click the Don't Save button.

PROSKILLS

Problem Solving: Working with Apps Efficiently

As you work on your computer throughout the day, you may end up with quite a few apps open and running at the same time. This situation can lead to two common problems that affect your productivity: Finding the information you need becomes more difficult as you switch between apps, and the performance of your computer can slow significantly.

To address both these issues, decide which apps need to be running, and then close the ones you don't need. Closing unnecessary apps allows you to focus on the information you need for the tasks at hand. It also frees up system resources, which makes your computer faster and more responsive and can solve performance problems.

Session 1.1 Quick Check

REVIEW

1. What is the difference between system software and apps?

2. The _____ is the central point for accessing apps, documents, and other resources on your computer.

3. A tile that displays updated content is called a(n) _____.

4. Describe the appearance of the Start menu.

5. Name two tasks you can perform with Cortana.

6. What is a Windows (or universal) app?

7. How can you display an app if its window is minimized?

8. In a desktop app, the _____ is located at the top of the window, immediately below the title bar, and is organized into tabs.

Session 1.2 Visual Overview:

The **Home tab** provides access to commands you perform frequently.

The **Address bar** shows the location of the current window in the Windows hierarchy.

Use the New folder button to create a **folder**, a container for storing and organizing your files.

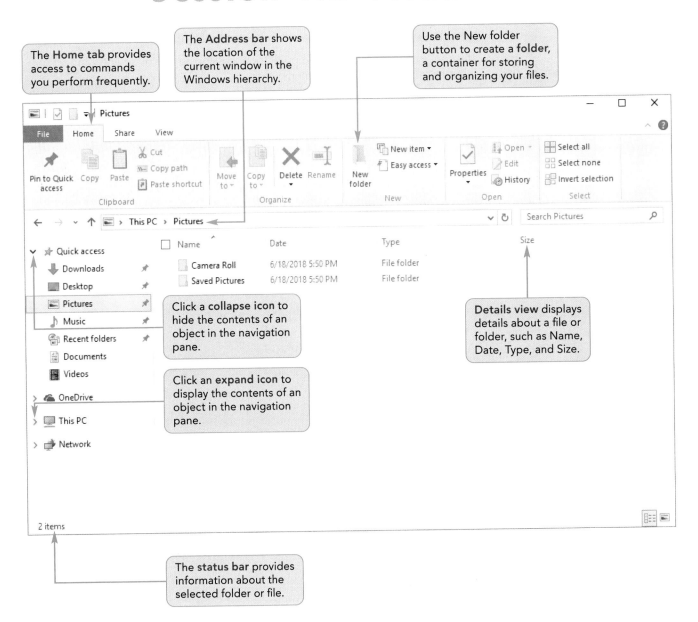

Click a **collapse icon** to hide the contents of an object in the navigation pane.

Click an **expand icon** to display the contents of an object in the navigation pane.

Details view displays details about a file or folder, such as Name, Date, Type, and Size.

The **status bar** provides information about the selected folder or file.

Working in File Explorer

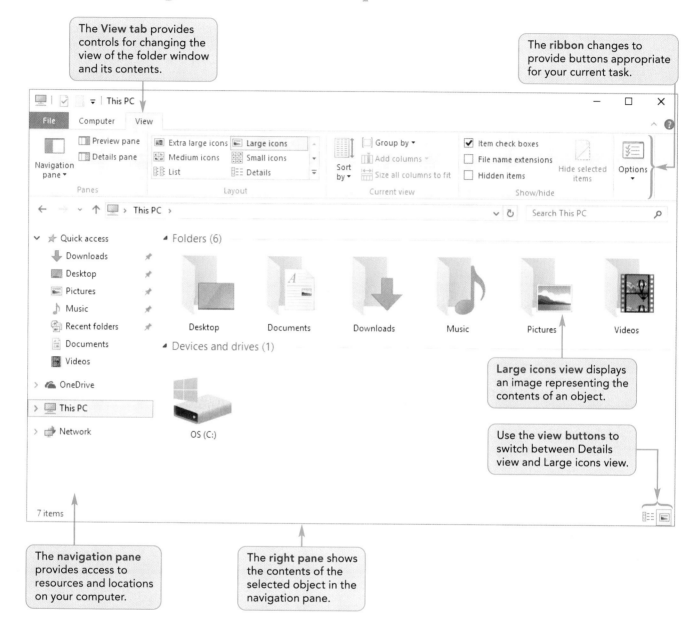

The **View tab** provides controls for changing the view of the folder window and its contents.

The **ribbon** changes to provide buttons appropriate for your current task.

Large icons view displays an image representing the contents of an object.

Use the **view buttons** to switch between Details view and Large icons view.

The **navigation pane** provides access to resources and locations on your computer.

The **right pane** shows the contents of the selected object in the navigation pane.

Exploring Your Computer

To discover the contents and resources on your computer, you explore, or navigate, it. **Navigating** means moving from one location to another on your computer, such as from one file or folder to another, or from one drive to another. In Windows 10, you use File Explorer (as shown in the Session 1.2 Visual Overview) to navigate, view, and work with the contents and resources on your computer.

Navigating with File Explorer

File Explorer is a window that is divided into two panes. The left side of the window is called the navigation pane, which you use to access locations on your computer. The right pane displays the details of the location you navigated to, so you can work with your files, folders, or devices easily. At the top of the window is a ribbon with buttons that let you perform common tasks. A status bar appears at the bottom of the window and displays the characteristics of an object you select in the File Explorer window. You use File Explorer to keep track of where your files are stored and to organize your files.

Ashley Cramer, the volunteer coordinator of For Pet's Sake, is helping you plan a training session for volunteers on the basics of Windows 10. She wants you to start this session by opening File Explorer and exploring the contents of your computer. She suggests exploring the locations in the Quick access list. These locations include standard folders for storing your documents, music, pictures, videos, and other files. In the right pane of the File Explorer window, the standard folders appear in the Frequent folders list. If you have opened files recently, they appear in the Recent files list.

To explore the contents of your computer using File Explorer:

1. If you took a break after the previous session, make sure that your computer is on and Windows 10 is running.

2. Click the **File Explorer** button ▢ on the taskbar. A window opens showing folders in the Quick access list. See Figure 1-16.

| Figure 1-16 | Quick access folders |

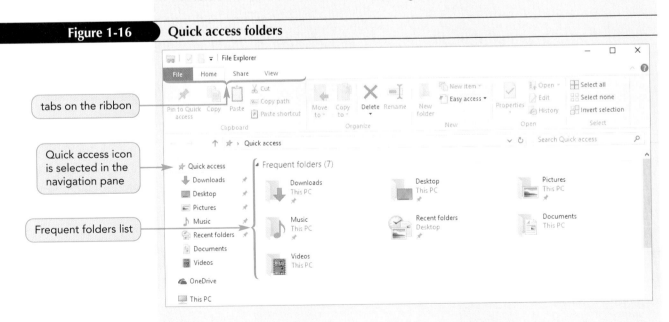

tabs on the ribbon

Quick access icon is selected in the navigation pane

Frequent folders list

▶ **3.** In the navigation pane, click **Pictures**. The right pane of the window shows the contents of the Pictures folder, which is designed for storing your photos and other picture files. The Pictures folder might contain two folders by default: Camera Roll, for saving photos taken with the camera on your device, and Saved Pictures, for storing other images.

▶ **4.** In the right pane, click the **Saved Pictures** folder to select it. See Figure 1-17. Your Pictures folder might contain other files and folders.

| **Figure 1-17** | **Pictures folder in File Explorer** |

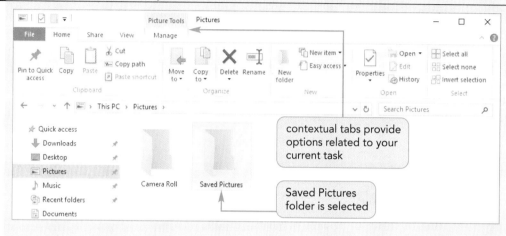

As you open folders and navigate with File Explorer, tabs might appear at the top of the window just above the standard ribbon tabs. For example, the Picture Tools Manage tab appears when you select a file or folder in the Pictures folder. This type of tab is called a **contextual tab**, and it contains options that apply to the object you have selected. For example, the Picture Tools Manage tab contains options for working with pictures.

Ashley mentions that you can change the appearance of most windows to suit your preferences. You'll change the view of the File Explorer window next so you can see more details about folders and files.

Changing the View

Windows 10 provides eight ways to view the contents of a folder: Extra large icons, Large icons, Medium icons, Small icons, List, Details, Tiles, and Content. The default view for the Pictures folder is Large icons view, which provides a thumbnail image of the file contents. (If thumbnails are turned off on your computer, the Large icons view displays a larger version of the file icon.) The default view for other types of folders is Details view, which displays a small icon instead of a thumbnail and lists details about each file. Although only Details view lists all file details, such as the date a photo was taken and its size, you can see some of these details in any other view by pointing to a file to display a ScreenTip.

Selecting a View

INSIGHT

When you display files in Medium icons view or larger, the icon displays a preview of the file's content. The preview images are big and easy to see; however, the window shows fewer files with large icons. When you display files using smaller icons, the window can show more files, but the preview images are not as easy to see. The view you select depends on your preferences and needs.

Changing the Icon View

- In File Explorer, click a view button on the status bar.

or

- Click the View tab on the ribbon.
- In the Layout group, point to a view option to preview its effect in the folder window, if necessary, and then click a view option.

To demonstrate switching from one view to another, Ashley says you can display folders in Details view. To do so, you'll use the Details view button on the status bar.

To change the view of the Quick access window:

1. In the navigation pane, click **Quick access** to display the Frequent folders list in Tiles view, which is the default for this window.

2. Click the **Details view** button 𝄢 on the status bar. The window shows the same folders, but with more details and smaller icons. See Figure 1-18.

Figure 1-18 | **Quick access folders in Details view**

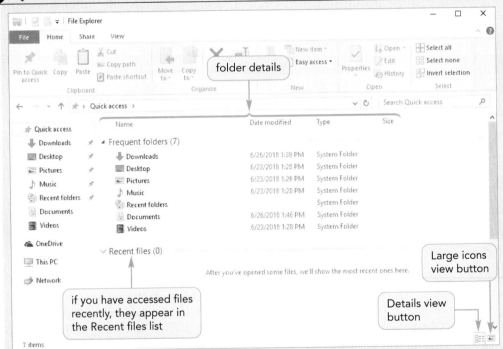

if you have accessed files recently, they appear in the Recent files list

folder details

Large icons view button

Details view button

3. Click the **Large icons view** button 🖾 on the status bar. The window shows the folders with large icons and no details.

Ashley suggests that you now use File Explorer to navigate your computer.

Using the Navigation Pane

To navigate your computer, you use the navigation pane on the left side of the File Explorer window. By default, the navigation pane organizes computer resources into four categories: Quick access (for locations you access frequently), **OneDrive** (for files and folders stored online in your OneDrive folder), This PC (for the folders, drives, and devices on your computer), and Network (for network locations your computer can access).

INSIGHT

OneDrive

File Explorer lists OneDrive as a location in the navigation pane by default. OneDrive is a service from Microsoft that provides 15 GB of free storage space and lets you use software on a **server**, a powerful, high-capacity computer you access using the Internet or other network. You can increase the amount of storage space, if necessary. You use OneDrive to store, synchronize, and share files with people and devices. For example, if you are working on a group project, you can store files in your OneDrive and let other group members read and change the files. Anyone can access OneDrive using a web browser, even if they are using an Apple iPhone, for example, or an Xbox console. However, if you're using Windows 10 (or Windows 8 or 8.1), you can access OneDrive directly from File Explorer. If you are using Microsoft Office 2013 or Office 2016, a suite of productivity apps, you can save and open files directly from most Office apps.

When you move the pointer into the navigation pane, arrows appear next to some icons. A right-pointing arrow, or expand icon, indicates that a folder contains other folders that are not currently displayed in the navigation pane. Click the arrow to expand the folder and display its subfolders. (A **subfolder** is a folder contained in another folder.) A down-pointing arrow, or collapse icon, indicates the folder is expanded, and its subfolders are listed below the folder name. You can click a folder in the navigation pane to navigate directly to that folder and display its contents in the right pane.

Using the navigation pane to explore your computer usually involves clicking expand icons to expand objects and find the folder you want, and then clicking that folder to display its contents in the right pane. To display a list of all the folders on a drive, expand the This PC icon in the navigation pane, and then expand the icon for the drive, such as Local Disk (C:). The navigation pane shows the hierarchy of folders on the drive, so you can use it to find and manage your files and folders.

INSIGHT

Identifying Storage Devices

Each storage device you can access on your computer is associated with a letter. The first hard drive is drive C. (If you add other hard drives, they are usually drives D, E, and so on.) If you have a CD or DVD drive or a USB flash drive plugged in to a USB port, it usually has the next available letter in the alphabetic sequence. If you can access hard drives located on other computers in a network, those drives sometimes (although not always) have letters associated with them as well. Naming conventions for network drives vary. For example, the network drive on a typical computer might have the drive letter Z.

Now you're ready to use the navigation pane to find and open the Documents folder, a convenient place to store text files such as reports, assignments, and other documents. The Documents folder appears in the Quick access list and on This PC by default. You'll navigate to it in two ways.

To open the Documents folder:

▶ **1.** In the navigation pane, click the **Documents** icon in the Quick access list to display the contents of the Documents folder in the right pane. See Figure 1-19. Your Documents folder might contain folders and files.

Figure 1-19   **Contents of the Documents folder**

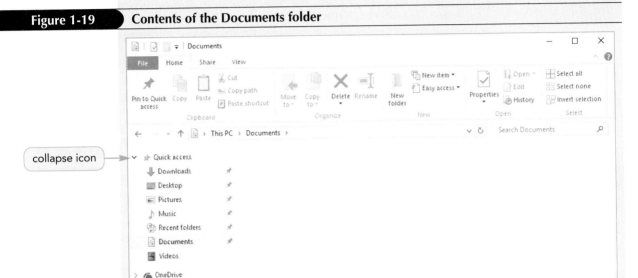

Trouble? If the Documents icon does not appear in the Quick access list, skip Step 1.

If you have opened many folders without opening the Documents folder, the Documents folder might not appear in the Quick access list. You can always open the folder using This PC.

▶ **2.** If necessary, click the **expand** icon ▷ next to This PC in the navigation pane to display locations on your computer. Note that the expand icon changes to a collapse icon ∨.

Trouble? If the expand icon ▷ does not appear next to This PC in the navigation pane, This PC is already expanded. Skip Step 2.

▶ **3.** Click the **Pictures** folder to display its contents in the right pane, and then click the **Documents** folder below This PC in the navigation pane.

The Address bar in File Explorer provides handy shortcuts for navigating to locations on your computer. For example, you can use the Back button to return to the last location you visited. You can use it now to return to the Quick access list.

To return to the Quick access list:

▶ **1.** Click the **Back** button ← on the Address bar to return to your last location: the Pictures folder.

▶ **2.** Click the **Close** button ✕ to close File Explorer.

Getting Help

To get help on using Windows 10, you can use the Get Started app on your computer and Microsoft resources on the web. The Get Started app focuses on features new to Windows 10, including interacting with Cortana, working with apps, using File Explorer, and personalizing your computer.

To access a full library of Windows Help information, visit the How-to webpages for Windows on the Microsoft website. The webpages provide help articles, definitions, and step-by-step instructions for performing Windows tasks. You can also visit the Microsoft Community website to connect with other Windows users and experts to request answers to questions and find solutions to a wide range of problems.

Using the Get Started App

If you are familiar with earlier versions of Windows or want a quick tour of useful features in Windows 10, use the Get Started app.

To start the Get Started app:

▶ 1. Click the **Start** button  on the taskbar to display the Start menu.

▶ 2. Click the **Get Started** tile in the right pane. The Get Started app opens and displays a list of categories and features on the left and an image or information on the right.

  Trouble? If the Get Started tile does not appear on your Start menu, click the All apps command, scroll down the list, and then click Get Started.

▶ 3. Click the **Maximize** button ▢ to maximize the Get Started window.

▶ 4. If necessary, click **Welcome** in the left pane to display the Get to know Windows 10 page. See Figure 1-20. The image on your Get to know Windows 10 page might be different.

| **Figure 1-20** | **Get Started window** |

click to collapse or expand the navigation pane

navigation pane

other Welcome videos

click to play a video introducing you to Windows 10

The Get Started window includes a navigation pane on the left and displays content on the right. When you select Welcome in the navigation pane, you can play one of four videos in the right pane. The Get to know Windows 10 page contains a video that you can play to learn about Windows 10 in general. You can also play videos to explore Microsoft Edge, to gain Start menu tips, and to learn about getting help.

For information about specific features, select an item in the navigation pane to display topic tiles or articles related to that feature. If topic tiles appear in the right pane, click one to display an article related to the topic. After you select an article or topic, a Back button appears on the title bar so you can return to the previous page you viewed.

To view Get Started topics:

▶ **1.** Click **Search and help** in the navigation pane of the Get Started window. Tiles representing articles about searching and getting help appear in the right pane.

▶ **2.** Click the **Search for help** tile. An article describing ways to get help appears in the right pane.

▶ **3.** Scroll down to display the link to Windows support at windows.microsoft.com/support.

While the Get Started app provides an introduction to Windows 10, the Microsoft website includes forums, tutorials, articles, trending topics, and other helpful information about Windows 10.

Getting Help on the Microsoft Website

The Windows webpages on the Microsoft website provide a full range of help topics on using Windows 10. These topics are provided on the How-to webpages for Windows. Most How-to webpages include a link to the Microsoft Community website. If a How-to webpage does not answer your question, you can visit the Microsoft Community site and search for answers and solutions provided to other Windows users.

To access the Microsoft website, you can use **Microsoft Edge**, the default web browser provided with Windows 10. You start Microsoft Edge using its button on the taskbar or by clicking a webpage link in the Get Started app. To go directly to the main How-to page for Windows 10, enter windows.microsoft.com/support in the Microsoft Edge Address bar.

To find a Windows help topic on the Microsoft website:

▶ **1.** In the Get Started app, click the **windows.microsoft.com/support** link at the bottom of the Search and help page. Microsoft Edge starts and opens the How-to page for Windows 10 on the Microsoft website.

Trouble? If the windows.microsoft.com/support link does not appear in the Get Started app, click the **Microsoft Edge** button 🇪 on the taskbar to open the Microsoft Edge browser, click the Address bar, type windows.microsoft.com/support, and then press the Enter key.

▶ **2.** Click the **Maximize** button ☐ to maximize the Microsoft Edge window. See Figure 1-21. The webpage displayed in your Microsoft Edge window might differ.

Figure 1-21	Windows 10 How-to webpage

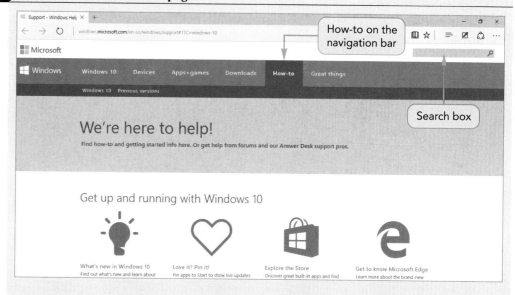

3. Scroll down to review the information on this webpage. In the Categories section, click the **Get started** link. A webpage opens listing Help topics related to new and popular features in Windows 10.

Trouble? If the Get Started link is not listed, click any other link.

The Microsoft website also provides a Search box, a popular way to find answers to your Windows 10 questions.

Searching the Windows How-to Webpages

If you can't find the topic you need by clicking a link or browsing topics, or if you want to quickly find help information related to a particular topic, you can use the Search box on the Windows webpages. Ashley provides a typical example. Suppose you want to know how to close Windows 10, but you don't know if Windows refers to this as exiting, quitting, closing, or shutting down. You can search the Windows How-to webpages to find just the right topic.

To search the How-to webpages for information on exiting Windows 10:

1. Click the **Search** box at the top of the Windows How-to webpage. A blinking insertion point appears.

2. Type **shut down** and then press the **Enter** key. A list of How-to webpages containing the words "shut down" appears in the search results. See Figure 1-22. (Your results might differ.)

Trouble? If a message appears at the bottom of the browser window informing you that only secure content is displayed, click the **Close** button ⊠ to close the message.

TIP

You can also use the Search the web and Windows box on the taskbar to search for information on the web.

Figure 1-22   **How-to search results**

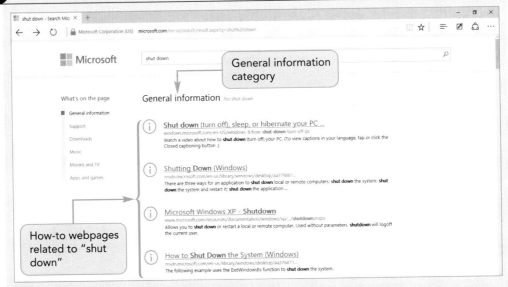

> **3.** Click the **Shut down (turn off), sleep, or hibernate your PC** link. The instructions and a video demonstration appear in the Shut down (turn off), sleep, or hibernate your PC webpage.
>
> If this topic did not answer your question, you could scroll down to the "Need more help?" section and then click the community forums link. Doing so opens the Microsoft Community webpage where you can search for answers to your questions.

> **4.** Click the **Close** button ⊠ to close Microsoft Edge, and then close the Get Started app.

Now that you know how to find help for using Windows 10, Ashley reminds you to use it when you need to perform a new task or want a reminder about how to complete a procedure.

Turning Off Windows 10

TIP

Shutting down does not automatically save your work, so be sure to save your files before selecting the Shut down or Restart option.

When you're finished working in Windows 10, you should always turn it off properly. Doing so saves energy, preserves your data and settings, and makes sure your computer starts quickly the next time you use it.

You can turn off Windows 10 using the Power command on the Start menu. When you click the Power command, you can choose the Sleep, Shut down, or Restart option. If you choose the Sleep option, Windows saves your work and then turns down the power to your display and computer, a condition called **sleep**. A light on your computer case blinks or changes color to indicate that the computer is sleeping. Because Windows saves your work, you do not need to close apps or files before your computer goes to sleep. To wake a computer, you typically press the hardware power button on the computer case. Some computer manufacturers might set the computer to wake when you press a key or move the mouse. After you wake a computer, the screen looks exactly as it did when you put your computer to sleep.

If you choose the **Shut down** option, your computer closes all open programs, including Windows itself, and then completely turns off your computer. Shutting down doesn't save your work, so you must save your files first.

If you select the Restart option, your computer shuts down and then immediately restarts, which you might need to do after installing new programs or hardware.

PROSKILLS

Decision Making: Sign out, Sleep, or Shut Down?

If you are using a computer on the job, your organization probably has a policy about what to do when you're finished working on the computer. If it does not, deciding on the best approach depends on who uses the computer and how long it will be idle. Keep the following guidelines in mind as you make your decision:

- Sign out—If another person might use your computer shortly, sign out of Windows to protect your data and prepare the computer for someone else to use. To sign out of Windows 10, click your user icon on the Start menu and then click Sign out.
- Sleep—By default, Windows 10 is set to sleep after 15–30 minutes of idle time, depending on whether you are using a mobile or desktop computer. If you will be away from the computer for more than 15 minutes but less than a day, you can generally let the computer go to sleep on its own.
- Shut down—If your computer is plugged in to a power outlet and you don't plan to use the computer for more than a day, such as over the weekend, you save wear and tear on your electronic components and conserve energy by turning the computer off. You should also turn off the computer when it is susceptible to electrical damage, such as during a lightning storm, and when you need to install new hardware or disconnect the computer from a power source. If your mobile computer is running on battery power only and you don't plan to use it for more than a few hours, you should also turn it off to save your battery charge.

Ashley suggests that you compare putting your computer to sleep and shutting down Windows 10.

To turn off Windows 10:

▶ **1.** Click the **Start** button ⊞ on the taskbar to display the Start menu.

▶ **2.** Click **Power** to display the Power menu. See Figure 1-23.

Figure 1-23   **Power options**

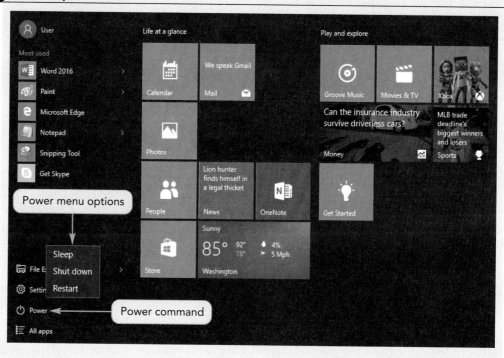

▶ **3.** Click **Sleep**. Windows 10 saves your work and then puts the computer to sleep. The light in the hardware power button changes color or blinks to indicate the computer is in a sleep state.

Trouble? If a Sleep option does not appear when you click the Power command, your computer might be set to go to sleep only automatically. Click Shut down on the Power menu, and skip the remaining steps.

▶ **4.** If the light in the hardware power button changes color or is now blinking, press the hardware power button to wake up the computer. If necessary, clear the lock screen and enter your password. Otherwise, move the mouse or press a key to wake the computer.

▶ **5.** Click the **Start** button ⊞ on the taskbar to display the Start menu.

Trouble? If you are instructed to sign out instead of shut down, click your user icon on the Start menu, and then click Sign out. Skip Step 6.

▶ **6.** Click **Power** and then click **Shut down**. Windows 10 turns off the computer.

Trouble? If the Power button displays the Update and shut down option instead of Shut down, click Update and shut down.

In this session, you learned how to use File Explorer to navigate your computer. You also learned how to change the view of the contents of the File Explorer window. Finally, you learned how to get help when you need it and how to turn off Windows 10. With Ashley's help, you should feel comfortable with the basics of Windows 10 and well prepared to demonstrate the fundamentals of using this operating system.

REVIEW

Session 1.2 Quick Check

1. You use _____ to keep track of where your files are stored and to organize your files.

2. Describe the difference between Details view and Large icons view.

3. In the File Explorer window, what happens when you click the expand icon next to a folder in the navigation pane?

4. In the File Explorer window, what appears in the right pane when you click a folder icon in the navigation pane?

5. The _____ app focuses on features new to Windows 10.

6. What is Microsoft Edge?

7. How would you search for information about shutting down Windows 10 on the Microsoft website?

8. What Power option(s) save(s) your work before turning down the power to the computer?

Review Assignments

There are no Data Files needed for the Review Assignments.

The day before your first Windows 10 training session with For Pet's Sake volunteers, Ashley Cramer offers to observe your tour of the operating system and help you fine-tune your session. You'll start working on the desktop with no apps open. Complete the following steps, recording your answers to any questions according to your instructor's preferences:

1. Start Windows 10 and sign in, if necessary.
2. Record the names and descriptions of each object on the desktop, using the mouse to point to objects as necessary to display ScreenTips.
3. Click the Start button. How many menu commands appear in the left pane of the Start menu?
4. Start the Calendar app.
5. Start Paint and maximize the Paint window. How many apps are running now?
6. Which app is active? How do you know?
7. Minimize the Paint window and then open the Recycle Bin window. Record the number of items it contains, and then drag and resize the Recycle Bin window so that you can see both it and the Calendar window.
8. Close Paint and Calendar. What actions did you take to close each app?
9. Maximize the Recycle Bin window and then click the Home tab. Which buttons are active (not gray)? Use any button on the Home tab to open a dialog box. What dialog box did you open? What do you think this dialog box is used for? Click the Cancel button to close the dialog box, and then close the Recycle Bin window.
10. Start File Explorer. Open the Pictures folder from the navigation pane. List the contents of the Pictures folder. Open a folder in the Pictures library. Explain how you opened the folder and describe its contents.
11. Open This PC from the navigation pane. Change the view of the items displayed in the right pane of the File Explorer window. What view did you select and how did your selection change the appearance of the items? Close File Explorer.
12. Start the Get Started app. Explain how you started the app.
13. Use the Get Started app to learn something new about Windows 10. What did you learn? How did you find this topic?
14. Find information about personalizing your computer. How can you open the Personalization window to change the background picture on the desktop?
15. Find information about Microsoft Edge. Describe one new feature in Microsoft Edge.
16. Close the Get Started app.
17. Turn off Windows 10 by using the Sleep command, shutting down, or signing out.

PRACTICE

APPLY

Case Problem 1

There are no Data Files needed for this Case Problem.

Brandenburg Design Peter Brandenburg is the owner of Brandenburg Design, a graphics design studio in Bloomington, Indiana. Peter hired you to train employees on using their new Windows 10 computers productively. He asks you to show his employees how to determine the contents of their computers, especially media apps. Complete the following steps:

1. Start Windows 10 and sign in, if necessary.
2. Open the Start menu and then examine the tiles in the right pane. Use one to start an app that plays music or videos or displays photos. Which app did you start?
3. Start another media app. Which app did you start?
4. Use the Search the web and Windows box to search for "windows media" apps installed on your computer. Name one app you found.
5. Start an app you found in Step 4. Which app did you start? Is it a Windows app or a desktop app? How can you tell?
6. Start an app you could use to take photos with the camera on your computer. (If asked, do not allow the app to access your location.) Which app did you start? Is it a Windows app or a desktop app?
7. Find apps you can use to record or recognize voice. Which apps did you find?
8. Close all open apps.
9. Start File Explorer, and then navigate to a folder that contains files. Which folder did you open? View the files in Details view. What size is the largest file? (*Hint:* If there are no folders with files on your computer, display the contents of This PC.)
10. Change to Large icons view, and then point to a file to display a ScreenTip. What type of file did you select? What details are provided in the ScreenTip? Close File Explorer.
11. Open the Get Started app, and then find and read a topic about Windows Hello. Explain how to setup Windows Hello.
12. Close all open windows.

Case Problem 2

CHALLENGE

There are no Data Files needed for this Case Problem.

Tools of the Trade After earning a degree in business management and working as a prep cook in a few local restaurants, Erika Alston opened a store called Tools of the Trade in Chicago, Illinois. The store supplies restaurants, cafeterias, and other food service facilities with everything they need from teaspoons to freezers. So that she can concentrate on building her business, Erika hired you to help her perform office tasks. She asks you to start by teaching her the basics of using her computer, which runs Windows 10. She especially wants to know which applications are installed on her computer and what they do. Complete the following steps:

1. Write down the Windows apps listed on the Start menu.
2. Start one of the apps and then describe what it does. Close the app.
3. Use the Windows webpages to search for How-to information on getting apps for your PC. How can you pin an app so its tile appears in the right pane of the Start menu?
⊕ **Explore** 4. Open the Start menu, select the All apps command, scroll down the list to the W category, and then click the Windows Accessories folder to display its apps. List the apps in the Windows Accessories folder.

5. Use the Windows webpages to search for information on one of the apps you examined in the previous step, such as Notepad or the Snipping Tool. List all the How-to topics related to the application you researched in the previous step. How many general information topics are displayed in the results? Select one of these topics and review the Help information. Describe the purpose of the app.

⊕ **Explore** 6. Use the Start menu to start any app you haven't worked with before. Use the Windows webpages to find answers to frequently asked questions (FAQs) about the app. List two FAQs for the app you selected. If no topics provide answers to FAQs, select a general help topic about the app and then list two tasks you can perform with the app.

⊕ **Explore** 7. Use the Search the web and Windows box to learn how to draw a shape in Paint. Describe what you did to find this information and the results of your actions.

8. Close all open windows.

Case Problem 3

There are no Data Files needed for this Case Problem.

Jordan & Phipps Real Estate Alicia Phipps recently joined the Jordan Real Estate firm in Roswell, Georgia, to create a new firm called Jordan & Phipps Real Estate. The firm works with commercial and residential buyers and sellers. Alicia uses her Windows 10 laptop to create listings, contracts, reports, and other documents as required to complete real estate transactions. She uses File Explorer to work with files, but suspects she is not taking full advantage of its features. As a new assistant at Jordan & Phipps, you will be responsible for showing Alicia around the File Explorer window and demonstrating how to customize its appearance. Complete the following steps:

1. Start File Explorer. Click each tab on the ribbon to find out the kind of commands it provides. Write down any commands that seem related to changing the appearance of the folder window.

2. Display the Quick access list, if necessary, and then switch to Large icons view.

⊕ **Explore** 3. Change the view to Content view. (*Hint:* Click the View tab, and then click an option in the Layout group.) Describe the differences between Large icons view and Content view.

4. Open the Pictures folder, select a folder or file in the Pictures folder, and then describe any changes in the ribbon.

⊕ **Explore** 5. Examine the buttons on the Home tab. How can you add a new file to the folder window using a button on the Home tab?

⊕ **Explore** 6. Select a command on the View tab that displays a pane showing the details of the selected folder. What command did you select?

⊕ **Explore** 7. Use a button on the View tab to close the navigation pane. What actions did you perform?

⊕ **Explore** 8. Click the Up one level button next to the Address bar. (*Hint:* Point to a button to display its name in a ScreenTip.) What is now displayed in the File Explorer window?

⊕ **Explore** 9. Close the pane showing the details of the selected folder, and then redisplay the navigation pane. (*Hint:* Perform Steps 6 and 7 again.)

⊕ **Explore** 10. Close File Explorer, and then use the Search the web and Windows box to search for information about changing folder options. Explain how to change folder and search options using the Folder Options dialog box.

11. Close all open windows.

RESEARCH

Case Problem 4

There are no Data Files needed for this Case Problem.

Irving Personal Trainers After earning their certifications as personal trainers specializing in sports medicine, Gabe and Stacy Irving decided to start a service called Irving Personal Trainers. They work with people in their homes to help them meet physical goals through exercise and proper nutrition. They have been using Windows 10 on laptops to schedule client appointments and track client progress, but recently purchased tablet computers to use when they are working with clients face to face. They hired you as a consultant to help them use and maintain their computers. Because Gabe and Stacy learned to use Windows 10 on laptop computers, they anticipate that they might have trouble adapting to tablets. Gabe asks you to help them troubleshoot by researching the skills and techniques they need to use Windows 10 on a tablet. Complete the following:

1. Use the Search the web and Windows box to find information about Tablet mode. What Tablet mode settings can you select?

2. Use the Windows webpages on the Microsoft website to obtain more information about Tablet Mode in Windows 10. Explain how to turn Tablet Mode on and off.

3. Search for information on the touch keyboard, and then watch a video that shows how to use it. Explain how to display the touch keyboard if the computer is using Tablet Mode.

4. Visit the Microsoft Community website and search for information about Tablet Mode in Windows 10. Identify a common Tablet Mode problem discussed on the website.

5. Write one to two paragraphs for Gabe and Stacy explaining the basics of using Windows 10 on a tablet and what problems they might encounter.

OBJECTIVES

Session 2.1
- Develop file management strategies
- Plan the organization of your files and folders
- Find files and folders quickly
- Create folders
- Copy and move files and folders

Session 2.2
- Name and delete files and folders
- Work with new files
- Sort and group files
- Customize a folder window
- Compress and extract files

Organizing Your Files

Managing Files and Folders in Windows 10

Case | *Miami Trolleys*

After moving to Miami, Florida, after college, Diego and Anita Marino started Miami Trolleys, a sightseeing company that provides guided tours of Miami on a hop-on, hop-off trolley. As marketing manager, Diego is in charge of creating resources that describe the tours and sights in Miami. He hired you to help him develop marketing materials and use computer tools to organize photos, illustrations, and text documents to promote the business. For your first task, Diego asks you to organize the files on his new computer. Although he has only a few files, he wants to use a logical organization to help him find his work as he stores more files and folders on the computer.

In this module, you'll work with Diego to devise a strategy for managing files. You'll learn how Windows 10 organizes files and folders, and you'll examine Windows 10 file management tools. You'll create folders and organize files within them. You'll also use techniques to display the information you need in folder windows, and explore options for working with compressed files.

WINDOWS

STARTING DATA FILES

Module2 → **Module**

Budget.txt
City Guide.rtf
Edison.jpg
Logo.png
Miami Beach.jpg
Ocean Drive.jpg
Trolley Tours.rtf
Trolley.jpg

Review

Background.png
Calendar.rtf
Events.xlsx
Skyline.jpg
Walking.rtf
Welcome.jpg

Case1

Advanced Classes.rtf
Beginner Classes.rtf
Designers.txt
Detail.jpg
Intermediate Classes.rtf
Kids Classes.rtf

Lampshade.jpg
Modern.jpg
Round.jpg
Studio.rtf

Case2

Estimate Tips.txt   Planner01.xlsx
Estimate01.xlsx   Planner02.xlsx
Estimate02.xlsx   Planner03.xlsx
Estimate03.xlsx   Project Plans.txt

Case3

Checklist.docx
Client Chart.pdf
Clients.accdb
Clients.pptx
Training.pptx

Session 2.1 Visual Overview:

The **Quick Access Toolbar** contains buttons for viewing the properties of the current file or folder, creating a folder, and customizing the toolbar.

Arrow buttons in the Address bar show the path to the current folder.

The file **path** is a notation that indicates a file's location on your computer.

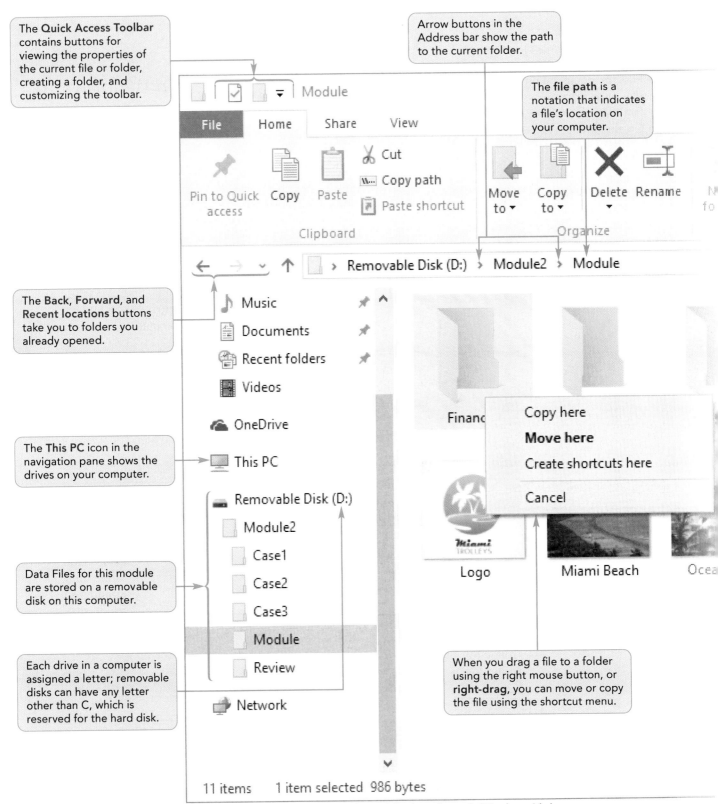

The **Back, Forward,** and **Recent locations** buttons take you to folders you already opened.

The **This PC** icon in the navigation pane shows the drives on your computer.

Data Files for this module are stored on a removable disk on this computer.

Each drive in a computer is assigned a letter; removable disks can have any letter other than C, which is reserved for the hard disk.

When you drag a file to a folder using the right mouse button, or **right-drag**, you can move or copy the file using the shortcut menu.

©iStock.com/Meinzahn, ©iStock.com/Betelgejze, ©iStock.com/bosenok, ©iStock.com/Vladone, ©iStock.com/Ivan Cholakov

Files in a Folder Window

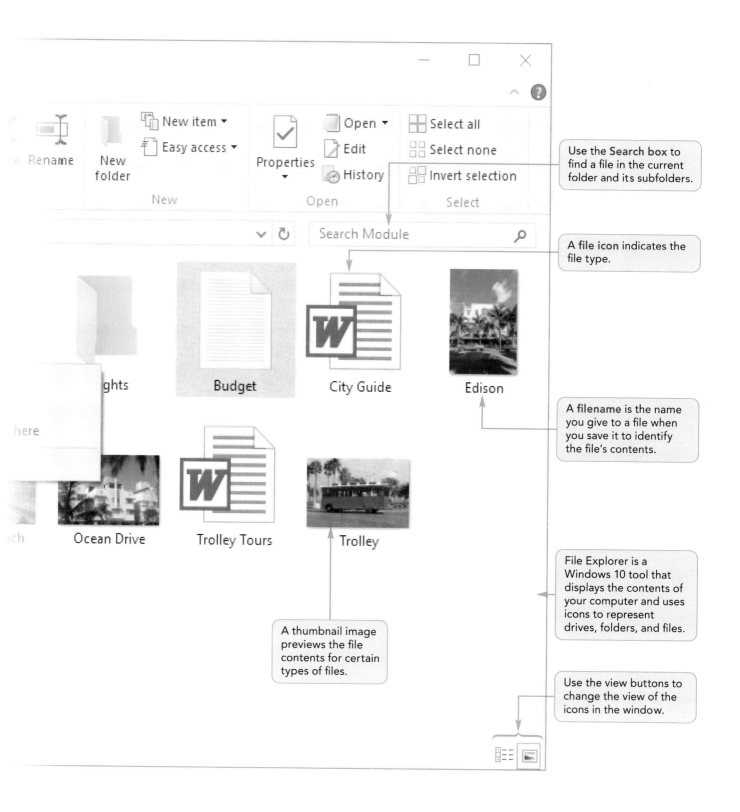

Use the **Search box** to find a file in the current folder and its subfolders.

A **file icon** indicates the file type.

A **filename** is the name you give to a file when you save it to identify the file's contents.

File Explorer is a Windows 10 tool that displays the contents of your computer and uses icons to represent drives, folders, and files.

A **thumbnail image** previews the file contents for certain types of files.

Use the **view buttons** to change the view of the icons in the window.

Preparing to Manage Your Files

Knowing how to save, locate, and organize electronic files makes you more productive when you are working with a computer. After you create a file, you can open it and edit the file's contents, print the file, and save it again—usually with the same application you used to create it. You organize files by storing them in folders. You need to organize files and folders so that you can find them easily and work efficiently.

A file cabinet is a common metaphor for computer file organization. A computer is like a file cabinet that uses a drawer as a storage device, or **disk**. Each disk contains folders that hold documents, or files. To make it easy to retrieve files, you arrange them logically into folders. For example, one folder might contain financial data, another might contain your creative work, and another could contain information you're gathering for an upcoming vacation.

A computer can store folders and files on different types of disks, ranging from removable media—such as **USB flash drives** (also called flash drives, thumbnail drives, or simply USB drives) and digital video discs (DVDs)—to **hard disks**, or fixed disks, which are permanently stored on a computer. Hard disks are the most popular type of computer storage because they provide an economical way to store many gigabytes of data. (A **gigabyte**, or **GB**, is about 1 billion bytes, with each byte roughly equivalent to a character of data.)

To have your computer access a removable disk, you must insert the disk into a **drive**, which is a computer device that can retrieve and sometimes record data on a disk. See Figure 2-1. A computer's hard disk is already contained in a drive inside the computer, so you don't need to insert it each time you use the computer.

Figure 2-1	Computer drives and disks

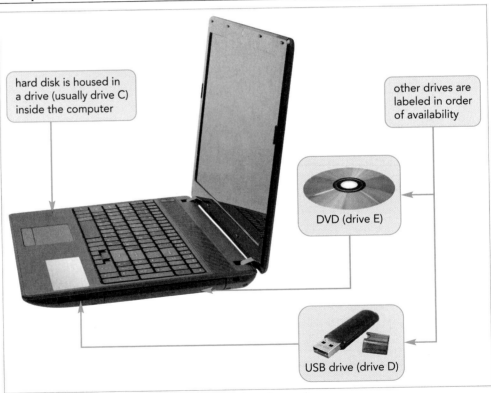

hard disk is housed in a drive (usually drive C) inside the computer

other drives are labeled in order of availability

DVD (drive E)

USB drive (drive D)

©iStock.com/Denis_Dryashkin, ©iStock.com/luminis, ©iStock.com/sassparela

A computer distinguishes one drive from another by assigning each a drive letter. As shown in the Session 2.1 Visual Overview, the hard disk in a computer is assigned to drive C. The remaining drives can have any other letters, but are usually assigned in the order that the drives were installed on the computer—so your USB drive might be drive D, drive E, or drive F.

If you are using a tablet or a recent-model laptop, it might not have drives for removable disks. Instead, you store files on the hard disk or in the **cloud**, a location on a large computer called a server, which you access through the Internet or other network. (A **network** is two or more computers connected together to share resources.) As a Windows 10 user, you probably have OneDrive, a Microsoft service that provides access to a server where you can store your files instead of using a hard disk or removable disk. Your school might also provide a cloud location for storing your files.

INSIGHT

Storing Files on OneDrive

OneDrive provides up to 15 GB of online storage space for your files by default. You can purchase additional storage space if you need it. Because these files are kept online, they take up no storage space on your computer and are available from any computer with an Internet connection, even those not running Windows. To protect the privacy of your files, you can designate which OneDrive users can access them: only you, you and some other users, or anyone. To use OneDrive, you need a free Microsoft account. (You can sign up for a Microsoft account at https://signup.live.com. If you have a Windows phone or use Outlook.com, Xbox Live, or Hotmail, you already have a Microsoft account.)

Understanding the Need for Organizing Files and Folders

Windows 10 stores thousands of files in many folders on the hard disk of your computer. Windows 10 needs these system files to display the desktop, use drives, and perform other operating system tasks. To keep the system stable and to find files quickly, Windows organizes the folders and files in a hierarchy, or **file system**. At the top of the hierarchy, Windows stores folders and important files that it needs when you turn on the computer. This location is called the **root directory** and is usually drive C (the hard disk). The term "root" refers to another popular metaphor for visualizing a file system— an upside-down tree, which reflects the file hierarchy that Windows uses. In Figure 2-2, the tree trunk corresponds to the root directory, the branches to the folders and subfolders, and the leaves to the files.

Figure 2-2   Windows file hierarchy

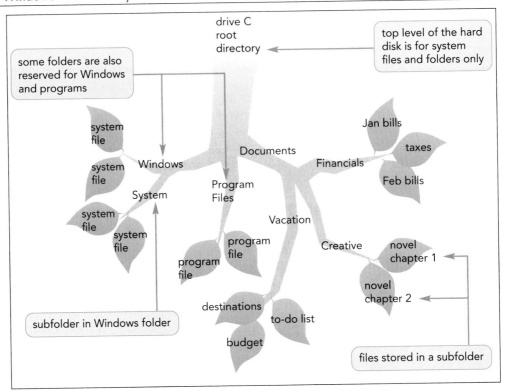

Note that some folders contain other folders. An effectively organized computer contains a few folders in the root directory, and those folders contain other folders, also called subfolders.

The root directory, or top level, of the hard disk is for system files and folders only. You should not store your own work in the root directory because your files could interfere with Windows or an application. (If you are working in a computer lab, you might not be allowed to access the root directory.)

Do not delete or move any files or folders from the root directory of the hard disk; doing so could disrupt the system so that you can't run or start the computer. In fact, you should not reorganize or change any folder that contains installed software because Windows 10 expects to find the files for specific applications within certain folders. If you reorganize or change these folders, Windows 10 can't locate and start the applications stored in those folders. Likewise, you should not make changes to the folder (usually named Windows) that contains the Windows 10 operating system.

Developing Strategies for Organizing Files and Folders

The type of disk you use to store files determines how you organize them. Figure 2-3 shows how you could organize files on a hard disk if you were taking a full semester of business classes. To duplicate this organization, you would open the main folder for your documents, create four folders—one each for the Basic Accounting, Computer Concepts, Management Skills, and Professional Writing courses—and then store the writing assignments you complete in the Professional Writing folder.

Figure 2-3   Organizing folders and files on a hard disk

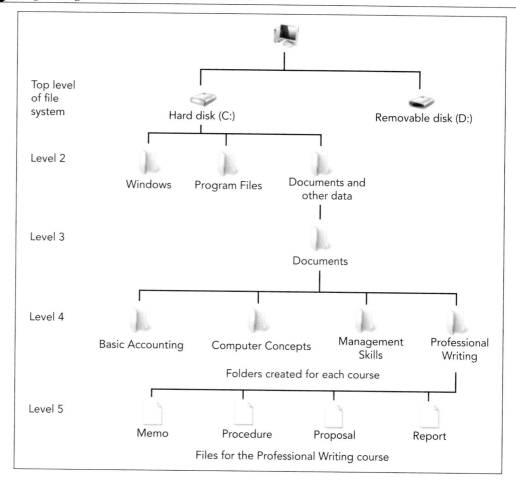

If you store your files on OneDrive or removable media, such as a USB drive, you can use a simpler organization because you do not have to account for system files. In general, the larger the medium, the more levels of folders you should use because large media can store more files and, therefore, need better organization. For example, OneDrive provides a collection of folders such as Documents, Favorites, Music, Pictures, and Public by default. If you were organizing your files on your 15 GB OneDrive, you could create folders in the top-level Documents folder for each course (Basic Accounting, Computer Concepts, Management Skills, and Professional Writing), and each of those folders could contain the appropriate files.

If you were organizing your files on a smaller removable disk, at the top level of the hierarchy you could create folders for each general category of documents you store—one each for Courses, Creative, Financials, and Vacation. The Courses folder could then include one folder for each course (Basic Accounting, Computer Concepts, Management Skills, and Professional Writing), and each of those folders could contain the appropriate files.

PROSKILLS

Decision Making: Determining Where to Store Files

When you create and save files on your computer's hard disk, you should store them in subfolders. The top level of the hard disk is off-limits for your files because they could interfere with system files. If you are working on your own computer, store your files within the Documents folder, which is where many applications save your files by default. When you use a computer on the job, your employer might assign a main folder to you for storing your work. In either case, if you simply store all your files in one folder, you will soon have trouble finding the files you want. Instead, you should create subfolders within a main folder to separate files in a way that makes sense for you.

Even if you store most of your files in the cloud, such as on OneDrive, or on removable media, such as USB drives, you still need to organize those files into folders and subfolders. Before you start creating folders in any location, you need to plan the organization you will use. Following your plan increases your efficiency because you don't have to pause and decide which folder to use when you save your files. A file organization plan also makes you more productive in your computer work—the next time you need a particular file, you'll know where to find it.

Exploring Files and Folders

To explore the files and folders on your computer in Windows 10, you use File Explorer. This tool displays the contents of your computer, using icons to represent drives, folders, and files. When you start File Explorer, it opens to show the contents of the **Quick access list**, which are the folders and files you used frequently and recently, making it easy to find the files you work with often.

A **folder window** refers to any File Explorer window that displays the contents of a folder, drive, or device. It is divided into two sections, called panes. The left pane is the navigation pane, which contains icons and links to locations that your computer can access. The right pane displays the contents of your folders and other locations. If you select a folder in the navigation pane, the contents of that folder appear in the right pane. To display the hierarchy of the folders and other locations on your computer, you select the This PC icon in the navigation pane, and then select the icon for a drive, such as Local Disk (C:) or Removable Disk (D:). If you have a Microsoft account, OneDrive appears as a location in the navigation pane. You can open and explore folders in any drive listed in the navigation pane.

If the navigation pane showed all the folders on your computer at once, it could be a very long list. Instead, you open drives and folders only when you want to see what they contain. If a folder contains undisplayed subfolders, an expand icon appears to the left of the folder icon. (The same is true for drives.) To view the folders contained in an object, you click the expand icon. A collapse icon then appears next to the folder icon; click the collapse icon to hide the folder's subfolders. To view the files contained in a folder, you click the folder icon, and the files appear in the right pane. See Figure 2-4.

Figure 2-4   Viewing files in a folder window

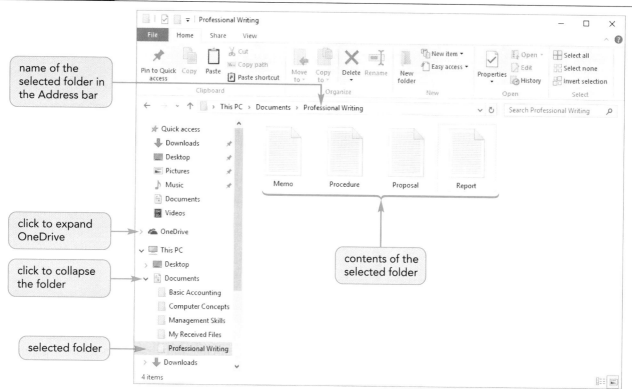

name of the selected folder in the Address bar

click to expand OneDrive

click to collapse the folder

selected folder

contents of the selected folder

Using the navigation pane helps you explore your computer and orients you to your current location. As you move, copy, delete, and perform other tasks with the folders in the right pane of a folder window, you can refer to the navigation pane to see how your changes affect the overall organization.

In addition to using the navigation pane, you can explore your computer from a folder window in other ways. Use the following navigation techniques in any folder window and many dialog boxes:

- Opening drives and folders in the right pane—To view the contents of a drive or folder, double-click the drive or folder icon in the right pane of the folder window. For example, to view the contents of the Professional Writing folder shown in Figure 2-5, you double-click the Professional Writing folder in the right pane.

Figure 2-5   Viewing the contents of a folder

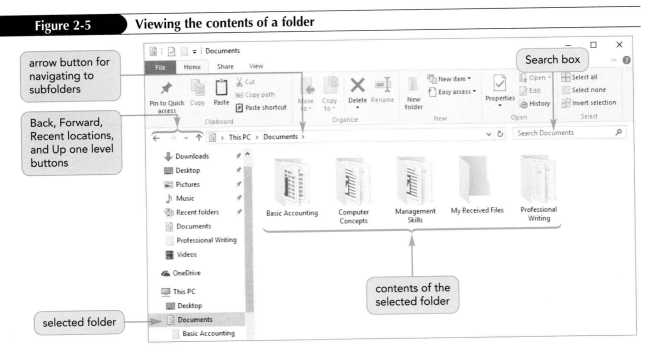

arrow button for navigating to subfolders

Back, Forward, Recent locations, and Up one level buttons

Search box

selected folder

contents of the selected folder

- Using the Address bar—You can use the Address bar to navigate to a different folder. The Address bar displays your current folder as a series of locations separated by arrow buttons. Click a folder name such as Documents or an arrow button to navigate to a different location. You'll explore these controls later in the module.
- Clicking the Back, Forward, Recent locations, and Up one level buttons—Use the Back, Forward, and Recent locations buttons to navigate to other folders you have already opened. After you use the Address bar to change folders, for example, you can use the Back button to return to the original folder. You can click the Recent locations button to navigate to a location you've visited recently. Use the Up one level button to navigate up to the folder containing the current folder. The ScreenTip for this button changes to reflect the folder to which you can navigate. For example, when you are working in a subfolder of the Documents folder, the ScreenTip is Up to "Documents."
- Using the Search box—To find a file or folder stored in the current folder or its subfolders, type a word or phrase in the Search box. The search begins as soon as you start typing. Windows finds files based on text in the filename, text within the file, and other characteristics of the file, such as **tags** (descriptive words or phrases you add to your files) or the author. For example, if you're looking for a document named September Income, you can type *Sept* in the Search box. Windows searches the current folder and its subfolders, and then displays any file whose filename contains a word starting with "Sept," including the September Income document.

Start your work with Diego by showing him how to navigate to the Documents folder using the Quick access list and the This PC icon.

To open the Documents folder:

1. Click the **File Explorer** button 🗖 on the taskbar. The File Explorer window opens, displaying the contents of the Quick access list.

2. Click the **Documents** icon in the navigation pane to display its contents in the right pane. See Figure 2-6. The contents of your computer will differ.

   Trouble? If your window displays icons in a view different from the one shown in the figure, you can still explore files and folders. The same is true for all figures in this session.

Figure 2-6   **Contents of the Documents folder**

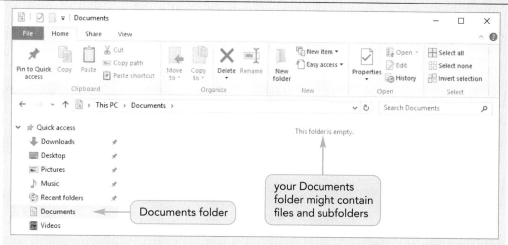

3. In the navigation pane of the open folder window, click the **This PC** icon. The right pane displays the devices and drives on the computer and the locations for storing your work files, including the Documents folder. See Figure 2-7.

Figure 2-7   **Contents of This PC**

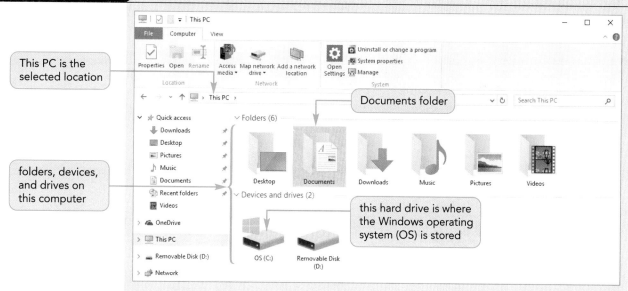

4. In the right pane, double-click the **Documents** folder to display its contents.

The Documents folder is designed to store your files—the notes, reports, spreadsheets, presentations, and other files that you create, edit, and manipulate in an application. The Quick access list and This PC contain other folders that most users open frequently, such as the Pictures folder and the Music folder. Although the Pictures folder is designed to store graphics and the Music folder is designed to store music files, you can store graphics, music, or any other type of file in the Documents folder, especially if doing so makes it easier to find these files when you need them.

Navigating to Your Data Files

TIP

To display the file path in a folder window, click to the right of the text in the Address bar.

To navigate to the files you want, it helps to know the file path. The file path leads you through the folder and file organization to your file. For example, the Logo file is stored in the Module subfolder of the Module2 folder. If you are working on a USB drive, for example, the path to this file might be as follows:

D:\Module2\Module\Logo.png

This path has four parts, with each part separated by a backslash (\ ):

- D:—The drive name followed by a colon, which indicates a drive rather than a folder
- Module2—The top-level folder on drive D
- Module—A subfolder in the Module2 folder
- Logo.png—The full filename, including filename extension

In this example, drive D is the name for the USB drive. (If this file were stored on the primary hard disk, the drive name would be C.) If someone tells you to find the file D:\Module2\Module\Logo.png, you know you must navigate to your USB drive, open the Module2 folder, and then open the Module folder to find the Logo file.

You can keep track of your current location as you navigate between drives and folders using the Address bar, which displays the full file path using arrow buttons instead of backslashes. You can use the open folder window to navigate to the Data Files you need for the rest of this module. Before you perform the following steps, you need to know where you stored your Data Files, such as on a USB drive. The following steps assume that drive is Removable Disk (D:), a USB drive. If necessary, substitute the appropriate drive on your system when you perform the steps.

To navigate to your Data Files:

▶ **1.** Make sure your computer can access your Data Files for this module. For example, if you are using a USB drive, insert the drive into the USB port.

Trouble? If you don't have the starting Data Files, you need to get them before you can proceed. Your instructor will either give you the Data Files or ask you to obtain them from a specified location (such as a network drive). If you have any questions about the Data Files, see your instructor or technical support person for assistance.

▶ **2.** In the open folder window, click the **expand** icon ⟩ next to the drive containing your Data Files, such as Removable Disk (D:). A list appears below the drive name showing the folders on that drive.

▶ **3.** If the list of folders does not include the Module2 folder, continue clicking the **expand** icon ⟩ to navigate to the folder that contains the Module2 folder.

▶ **4.** Click the **expand** icon ⟩ next to the Module2 folder to expand the folder, and then click the **Module2** folder so that its contents appear in the navigation pane and in the right pane of the folder window. The Module2 folder contains the Case1, Case2, Case3, Review, and Module folders, as shown in Figure 2-8. (Because Case Problem 4 does not require any files, the Module2 folder does not include a Case4 folder.) The other folders on your system might vary.

| Figure 2-8 | Navigating to the Module2 folder |

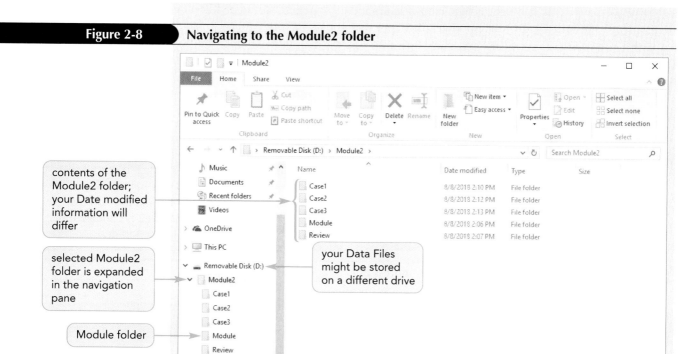

contents of the Module2 folder; your Date modified information will differ

selected Module2 folder is expanded in the navigation pane

Module folder

your Data Files might be stored on a different drive

TIP

If you change the view of one folder, other folders continue to display files in their specified view.

5. In the navigation pane, click the **Module** folder. The files it contains appear in the right pane. To preview the contents of the graphics, you can display the files as medium icons or larger.

6. Click the **View** tab on the ribbon, and then click **Medium icons** in the Layout group. The files appear in Medium icons view in the folder window. See Figure 2-9.

| Figure 2-9 | Files in the Module folder in Medium icons view |

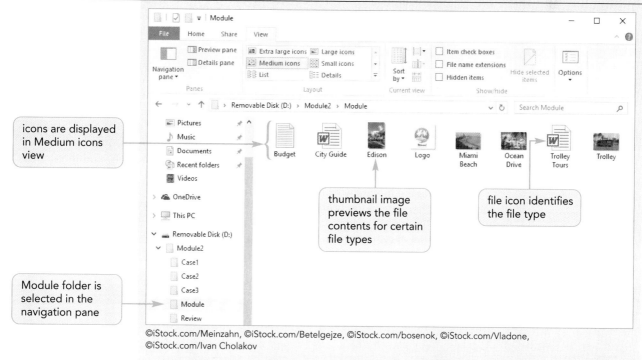

icons are displayed in Medium icons view

Module folder is selected in the navigation pane

thumbnail image previews the file contents for certain file types

file icon identifies the file type

Because the icons used to identify types of files depend on the applications installed on your computer, the icons that appear in your window might be different.

Diego wants to know how to use the Address bar effectively, so you offer to navigate with the Address bar to compare that technique to using the navigation pane.

Navigating with the Address Bar

The Address bar, located at the top of every folder window, displays your current folder as a series of locations separated by arrow buttons. For example, in Figure 2-10, the Address bar shows the Module2 and Module folders separated by an arrow button, indicating that Module is the current folder and it's stored in the Module2 folder. Click the arrow button after the Module2 folder to display a list of subfolders in that folder. The same is true for any location displayed in the Address bar. The first item in the Address bar is Removable Disk (D:), the top level of the removable disk. Module2 is contained in Removable Disk (D:), and the Module folder is contained in the Module2 folder.

Figure 2-10	Navigating with the Address bar

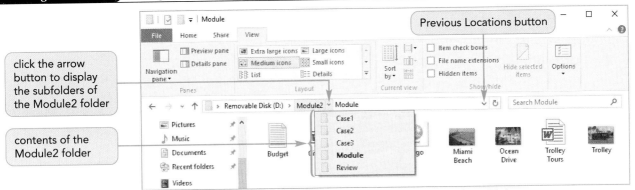

click the arrow button to display the subfolders of the Module2 folder

contents of the Module2 folder

©iStock.com/Meinzahn, ©iStock.com/Betelgejze, ©iStock.com/bosenok, ©iStock.com/Vladone, ©iStock.com/Ivan Cholakov

TIP

To navigate to any location you visited in a folder window, click the Previous Locations button in the Address bar, and then click the location you want to visit.

To change your location, you can click or type a folder name in the Address bar. For example, you can click Module2 to navigate to that folder. You can also type the path to the folder you want, or type the name of a standard, built-in Windows folder, such as the Documents or Pictures folders.

After you navigate to a location by any method, you can click the Back, Forward, and Recent locations buttons to revisit folders you've already opened. For example, if you navigate first to drive D, then to the Module2 folder, and then to the Module folder, you can click the Back button to open your previous location, the Module2 folder. When you do, the Forward button becomes active. You can then click the Forward button to open the next location in your sequence, the Module folder. To navigate to any recent location, click the Recent locations button, and then click a location in the list.

To navigate the hierarchy of folders and drives on your computer, recall that you can use another navigation button: the Up one level button. For example, if you are working in the Module folder, you can click the Up one level button to navigate to the Module2 folder. If you click the Up one level button again, you navigate to the root directory of your removable disk, such as Removable Disk (D:).

To navigate using the Address bar and navigation buttons:

▶ **1.** In the folder window displaying the contents of your Module folder, click the drive containing your Data Files, such as Removable Disk (D:), in the Address bar. The window displays the contents of the drive containing your Data Files.

   Trouble? If the drive containing your Data Files is not listed in the Address bar, click the first arrow button ⟩ in the Address bar, and then click Removable Disk (D:).

   Trouble? If the drive letter of your removable disk is different, substitute the correct drive letter for drive D for the remaining steps.

▶ **2.** Click the **arrow** button ⟩ to the right of Removable Disk (D:) in the Address bar, and then click the name of the **Module2** folder.

▶ **3.** Click the **Back** button ← on the Address bar two times to return to the Module folder.

▶ **4.** Click the **Recent locations** button ⌄ to display a list of locations you visited, and then click **Module2**. The subfolders in your Module2 folder appear in the right pane.

Leave the folder window open so that you can work with other file and folder tools.

Using the Search Box to Find Files

TIP

The name of the Search box reflects the location you are searching. If you select the Documents folder in the left pane, for example, the Search box name is Search Documents.

After you use a computer awhile, you're likely to have hundreds of files stored in various folders. If you know where you stored a file, it's easy to find it—you can use any navigation technique you like to navigate to that location and then scan the file list to find the file. Often, however, finding a file is more time consuming than that. You know that you stored a file somewhere in a standard folder such as Documents or Music, but finding the file might mean opening dozens of folders and scanning many long file lists. To save time, you can use the Search box to quickly find your file.

The Search box appears next to the Address bar in any folder window. To find a file in the current folder or any of its subfolders, you start typing text associated with the file. This search text can be part of the filename, text within the file, tags (keywords you associate with a file), or other file properties. By default, Windows searches for files by examining the names of the files displayed in the folder window and files in any subfolders. If it finds a file whose filename contains a word starting with the search text you specify, it displays that file in the folder window. For example, you can use the search text *guide* to find files named City Guide and Guide to Miami. If you are searching a hard drive, Windows also looks for files that contain a word starting with your search text. If it finds one, it displays that file in the folder window. For example, using *guide* as the search text also finds files containing words such as "guided" and "guidelines." If you are searching a removable drive, Windows searches filenames only by default. However, you can change settings to specify that you want to search other properties, including the contents. The following steps assume you are searching a removable drive.

Diego asks you to find a digital photo of a trolley on his computer. He knows he has at least one photo of a trolley. You can find this file by starting to type *trolley* in the Search box.

To use the Search box to find a file:

▶ **1.** In the folder window displaying the contents of your Module2 folder, click the Search box.

▶ **2.** Type **t** and then pause. Windows 10 examines the files in the Module2 folder and its subfolders, searching for a filename that includes a word starting with "t." The files in the Module2 folder that meet this criterion are displayed in the search results. You can continue typing to narrow the selection.

▶ **3.** Type **ro** after the "t" so that the search text is now *tro*. Only two files have filenames that include a word beginning with "tro." See Figure 2-11. The first three letters in each filename are highlighted. Your files might appear in a different view.

   Trouble? If you are searching a hard drive, you see additional files that contain words beginning with "tro."

Figure 2-11	Searching for a file

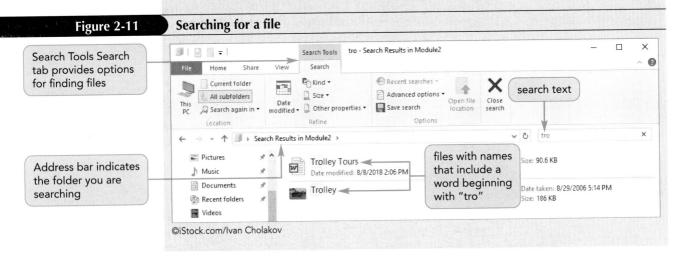

Search Tools Search tab provides options for finding files

Address bar indicates the folder you are searching

search text

files with names that include a word beginning with "tro"

©iStock.com/Ivan Cholakov

When you click the Search box, the Search Tools Search tab appears with options you can use to find your files. You can choose to search the current folder or its subfolders. Clicking the Date modified button displays options such as "today," "yesterday," "two weeks ago," and "last year," which are especially helpful when you can't remember what you named the file, where you stored it, or when you created it.

Using the Search box in a folder window, you found a photo of a trolley for Diego—the Trolley image file.

Now that Diego is comfortable navigating a computer to find files, you're ready to show him how to manage his files and folders.

Managing Files and Folders

After you devise a plan for storing your files, you are ready to get organized by creating folders that will hold your files. You can do so using any folder window. In this module, you create folders in the Module folder, which is probably stored on a USB drive, not a hard drive. When you are working on your own computer, you usually create folders within the Documents folder and other standard folders, such as Music and Pictures. However, Edison, Logo, Miami Beach, Ocean Drive, and Trolley are all graphics files that Diego uses for marketing Miami Trolleys. The City Guide and Trolley Tours files contain descriptions of sights in Miami for customers. The Budget file relates to business finances.

One way to organize these files is to create three folders—one for graphics, one for sights, and another for the financial files. When you create a folder, you give it a name, preferably one that describes its contents. A folder name can have up to

255 characters. Any character is allowed, except / \ : * ? " < > and |. Considering these conventions, you could create three folders as follows:

- Marketing Graphics folder— Edison, Logo, Miami Beach, Ocean Drive, and Trolley files
- Sights folder—City Guide and Trolley Tours files
- Financial folder—Budget file

Before creating the folders, you show your plan to Diego. You point out that instead of creating a folder for the graphics files, he could store them in the Pictures folder that Windows 10 provides for photos, clip art, drawings, and other graphics. However, Diego wants to keep these marketing graphics files separate from any other files. He also thinks storing them in a folder along with the Sights and Financial folders will make it easier to find his business files later.

Guidelines for Creating Folders

Keep the following guidelines in mind as you create folders:

- Keep folder names short and familiar. Long folder names can be more difficult to display in their entirety in folder windows, so use names that are short but clear. Choose names that will be meaningful later, such as project names or course numbers.
- Develop standards for naming folders. Use a consistent naming scheme that is clear to you, such as one that uses a project name as the name of the main folder, and includes step numbers in each subfolder name (for example, 01 Plan, 02 Approvals, 03 First Draft, and so on).
- Create subfolders to organize files. If a file list in a folder window is so long that you must scroll the window, consider organizing those files into subfolders.

Diego asks you to create the three new folders. After that, you'll move his files to the appropriate folders.

Creating Folders

You've already seen folder icons in the windows you've examined. Now, you'll create folders within the Module folder using the ribbon that appears in all File Explorer windows.

Creating a Folder in a Folder Window

- In the navigation pane, click the drive or folder in which you want to create a folder.
- Click the Home tab and then click the New folder button in the New group, or click the New folder button on the Quick Access Toolbar.
- Type a name for the folder, and then press the Enter key.

or

- Right-click a drive or folder in the navigation pane, or right-click a blank area in the folder window, point to New, and then click Folder.
- Type a name for the folder, and then press the Enter key.

Now you can create three folders in your Module folder as you planned—the Marketing Graphics, Sights, and Financial folders. You create these folders in three ways: using the Home tab, shortcut menu, and Quick Access Toolbar.

To create folders:

▶ **1.** Navigate to the **Module2 > Module** folder included with your Data Files.

▶ **2.** Click the **Home** tab, if necessary, and then click the **New folder** button in the New group. A folder icon with the label "New folder" appears in the right pane. See Figure 2-12.

| Figure 2-12 | Creating a subfolder in the Module folder |

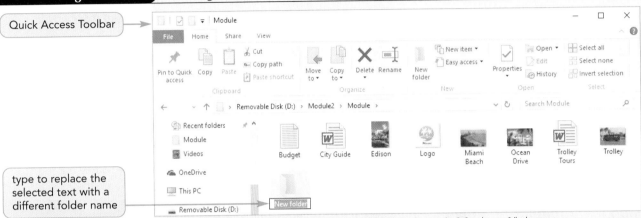

Quick Access Toolbar

type to replace the selected text with a different folder name

©iStock.com/Meinzahn, ©iStock.com/Betelgejze, ©iStock.com/bosenok, ©iStock.com/Vladone, ©iStock.com/Ivan Cholakov

TIP

When you first create a subfolder, it might appear at the end of the file list. When you finish naming the folder, all subfolders appear in the file list according to the sort order.

Trouble? If the "New folder" name is not selected, right-click the new folder, click Rename, and then continue with Step 3.

Windows uses "New folder" as a placeholder, and selects the text so that you can replace it immediately by typing a new name. You do not need to press the Backspace or Delete key to delete the text.

▶ **3.** Type **Marketing Graphics** as the folder name, and then press the **Enter** key. The new folder is now named Marketing Graphics and is the selected item in the right pane. To create a second folder, you can use a shortcut menu.

▶ **4.** Right-click a blank area in the right pane, point to **New** on the shortcut menu, and then click **Folder**. A folder icon appears in the right pane with the New folder text selected.

▶ **5.** Type **Sights** as the name of the new folder, and then press the **Enter** key.

▶ **6.** Click the **New folder** button ▢ on the Quick Access Toolbar, type **Financial**, and then press the **Enter** key to create and name the folder. The Module folder now contains three new subfolders.

After creating three folders, you're ready to organize your files by moving them into the appropriate folders.

Moving and Copying Files and Folders

If you want to place a file into a folder from another location, you can either move the file or copy it. **Moving** a file removes it from its current location and places it in a new location that you specify. **Copying** also places the file in a new location that you specify, but does not remove it from its current location. Windows 10 provides several techniques for moving and copying files. You can drag or right-drag a file with the mouse, use the Clipboard, or select the Move to or Copy to button in the Organize group on the Home tab on the File

Explorer ribbon. (The **Clipboard** is a temporary storage area for files and information that you copy or move from one place and plan to use somewhere else.) The same principles apply to folders: You can move and copy folders using a variety of methods.

REFERENCE

Moving a File or Folder in a Folder Window
- Right-drag the file or folder you want to move to the destination folder.
- Release the mouse button, and then click Move here on the shortcut menu.

or

- Right-click the file or folder you want to move to the destination folder, and then click Cut on the shortcut menu. (You can also click the file or folder and then press the Ctrl+X keys.)
- Navigate to and right-click the destination folder, and then click Paste on the shortcut menu. (You can also click the destination folder and then press the Ctrl+V keys.)

Diego suggests that you move some files from the Module folder to the appropriate subfolders. You'll start by moving the Budget file to the Financial folder using the right-drag technique, which you will learn next.

To move a file using the right mouse button:

1. Point to the **Budget** file in the right pane, and then press and hold the right mouse button.

2. With the right mouse button still pressed down, drag the **Budget** file to the **Financial** folder. When the Move to Financial ScreenTip appears, release the button. A shortcut menu opens as shown in the Session 2.1 Visual Overview.

3. With the left mouse button, click **Move here** on the shortcut menu. The Budget file is removed from the main Module folder and stored in the Financial subfolder.

   Trouble? If you released the mouse button before you dragged the Budget file all the way to the Financial folder and before seeing the Move to Financial ScreenTip, press the Esc key to close the shortcut menu, and then repeat Steps 1–3.

   Trouble? If you moved a file other than the Budget file, press the Ctrl+Z keys to undo the move, and then repeat Steps 1–3.

4. In the right pane, double-click the **Financial** folder. The Budget file is in the Financial folder.

   Trouble? If the Budget file does not appear in the Financial folder, you probably moved it to a different folder. Press the Ctrl+Z keys to undo the move, and then repeat Steps 1–4.

5. Click the **Back** button ⬅ on the Address bar to return to the Module folder.

The advantage of moving a file or folder by dragging with the right mouse button is that you can efficiently complete your work with one action. However, this right-drag technique requires polished mouse skills so that you can drag the file comfortably. When you drag to move files, be sure to verify the destination by waiting for the Move to ScreenTip. Otherwise, you might move the file to an unintended folder and have trouble finding the file later.

Another way to move files and folders is to use the Clipboard. Although the Clipboard does not appear in a folder window, you can use it when working with files and folders. Select a file and use the Cut or Copy command to temporarily store the file on the Clipboard, and then use the Paste command to insert the file elsewhere. Although using the Clipboard takes more steps, some users find it easier than dragging with the right mouse button.

You'll move the City Guide file to the Sights folder next by using the Clipboard.

To move files using the Clipboard:

▶ 1. Right-click the **City Guide** file, and then click **Cut** on the shortcut menu. Although the file icon is still displayed in the folder window, Windows 10 removes the City Guide file from the Module folder and stores it on the Clipboard.

▶ 2. In the right pane, right-click the **Sights** folder, and then click **Paste** on the shortcut menu. Windows 10 pastes the City Guide file from the Clipboard to the Sights folder. The City Guide file icon no longer appears in the folder window.

TIP

As you navigate to folders, Windows displays the folders you use often in the Quick access list.

▶ 3. In the navigation pane, click the **expand** icon ⟩ next to the Module folder, if necessary, to display its contents, and then click the **Sights** folder to view its contents in the right pane. The Sights folder now contains the City Guide file. See Figure 2-13.

Figure 2-13	Moving a file

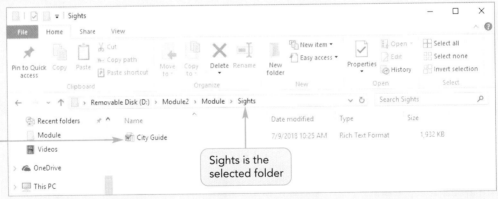

City Guide file now appears in the Sights folder

Sights is the selected folder

Next, you'll move the Trolley Tours file from the Module folder to the Sights folder.

▶ 4. Click the **Back** button ← on the Address bar to return to the Module folder, right-click the **Trolley Tours** file in the folder window, and then click **Cut** on the shortcut menu.

▶ 5. In the navigation pane, right-click the **Sights** folder, and then click **Paste** on the shortcut menu. The file is moved into the Sights folder.

▶ 6. Click the **Forward** button → on the Address bar to return to the Sights folder. The Sights folder now contains the City Guide and Trolley Tours files.

One way to save steps when moving or copying multiple files or folders is to select all the files and folders you want to move or copy, and then work with them as a group. You'll show Diego how to do that next.

Selecting Files and Folders

You can select multiple files or folders using several techniques, so you can choose the most convenient method for your current task. First, you open the folder that contains the files or folders you want to select. Next, select the files or folders using any one of the following methods:

- To select files or folders that are listed together in a folder window, click the first item, hold down the Shift key, click the last item, and then release the Shift key.
- To select files or folders that are listed together in a folder window without using the keyboard, drag the pointer to create a selection box around all the items you want to include.
- To select files or folders that are not listed together, hold down the Ctrl key, click each item you want to select, and then release the Ctrl key.
- To select all of the files or folders, click the Select all button in the Select group on the Home tab.
- To clear the selection of an item in a selected group, hold down the Ctrl key, click each item you want to remove from the selection, and then release the Ctrl key.
- To clear the entire selection, click a blank area of the folder window.

Copying Files and Folders

When you copy a file or folder, you make a duplicate of the original item. You can copy files or folders using techniques similar to the ones you use when moving them.

REFERENCE

Copying a File or Folder in a Folder Window

- Right-drag the file or folder you want to copy to the destination folder.
- Release the mouse button, and then click Copy here on the shortcut menu.

or

- Right-click the file or folder you want to copy to the destination folder, and then click Copy on the shortcut menu. (You can also click the file or folder and then press the Ctrl+C keys.)
- Navigate to and right-click the destination folder, and then click Paste on the shortcut menu. (You can also click the destination folder and then press the Ctrl+V keys.)

You'll copy the five graphics files from the Module folder to the Marketing Graphics folder now.

To copy files using the Clipboard:

1. Using any navigation technique you've learned, return to the Module folder window.

2. Click the **Edison** file, hold down the **Shift** key, click the **Trolley** file, and then release the **Shift** key. Five files are selected in the Module folder window.

3. Right-click the selected files, and then click **Copy** on the shortcut menu. Windows copies the files to the Clipboard.

▶ **4.** Right-click the **Marketing Graphics** folder, and then click **Paste** on the shortcut menu.

▶ **5.** Open the **Marketing Graphics** folder to verify it contains the five files you copied, and then return to the Module folder.

Now that you have copied files using the Copy and Paste commands, you can use the right-drag technique to copy the four photos to the Sights folder. As with moving files, you select the files, point to them, hold down the right mouse button, and then drag the file to a new location. However, when you release the mouse button, you click Copy here (instead of Move here) on the shortcut menu to copy the files.

To copy files:

▶ **1.** Click the **Edison** file, hold down the **Ctrl** key, click the **Miami Beach** file, the **Ocean Drive** file, and the **Trolley** file, and then release the **Ctrl** key. Four files are selected in the Module folder window.

▶ **2.** Right-drag the selected files from the Module folder to the Sights folder.

▶ **3.** Release the mouse button, and then click **Copy here** on the shortcut menu.

▶ **4.** Double-click the **Sights** folder to verify it contains the four photo files, and then return to the Module folder.

TIP

When you move or copy a folder, you move or copy all the files contained in the folder.

You can use another technique to copy or move a file or folder. You can drag the file or folder (using the left mouse button) to another location. Whether the file or folder is copied or moved depends on where you drag it. A ScreenTip appears when you drag a file to a new location—the ScreenTip indicates what happens when you release the mouse button. Figure 2-14 summarizes how to copy and move files and folders by dragging.

Figure 2-14   **Dragging to move and copy files**

Drag a File or Folder:	To:
Into a folder on the same drive	Move the file or folder to the destination folder
Into a folder on a different drive	Copy the file or folder to the destination folder

Although the copy and move techniques listed are common ways to copy and move files and folders, be sure you can anticipate what happens when you drag a file or folder.

REVIEW

Session 2.1 Quick Check

1. _____ is a Windows 10 tool that displays the contents of your computer and uses icons to represent drives, folders, and files.

2. What is the purpose of a file path?

3. Explain why you should not store files in the root directory of a hard disk.

4. Explain how to use a folder window to navigate to a file in the following location: D:\Classes\Digital Literacy\Operating Systems.txt.

5. How can you access a file stored in the Documents folder on your OneDrive?

6. What is the difference between using the Cut and Copy commands when working with files?

7. Describe how to find files using the Search box.

8. What happens if you click the first file in a folder window, hold down the Ctrl key, click the last file, and then release the Ctrl key?

Session 2.2 Visual Overview:

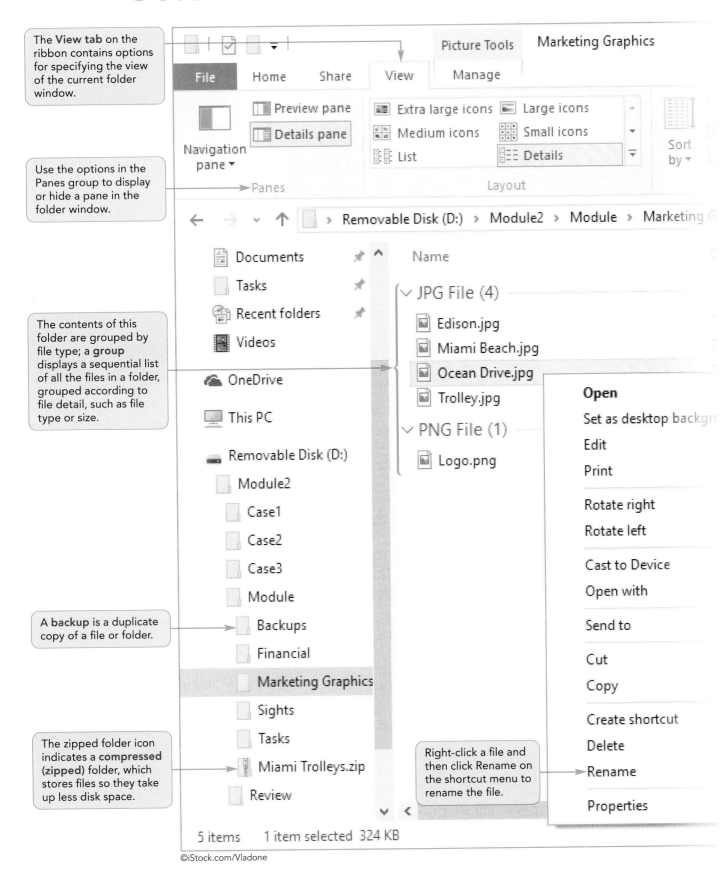

The **View tab** on the ribbon contains options for specifying the view of the current folder window.

Use the options in the Panes group to display or hide a pane in the folder window.

The contents of this folder are grouped by file type; a **group** displays a sequential list of all the files in a folder, grouped according to file detail, such as file type or size.

A **backup** is a duplicate copy of a file or folder.

The zipped folder icon indicates a **compressed (zipped)** folder, which stores files so they take up less disk space.

Right-click a file and then click Rename on the shortcut menu to rename the file.

©iStock.com/Vladone

Customized Folder Window

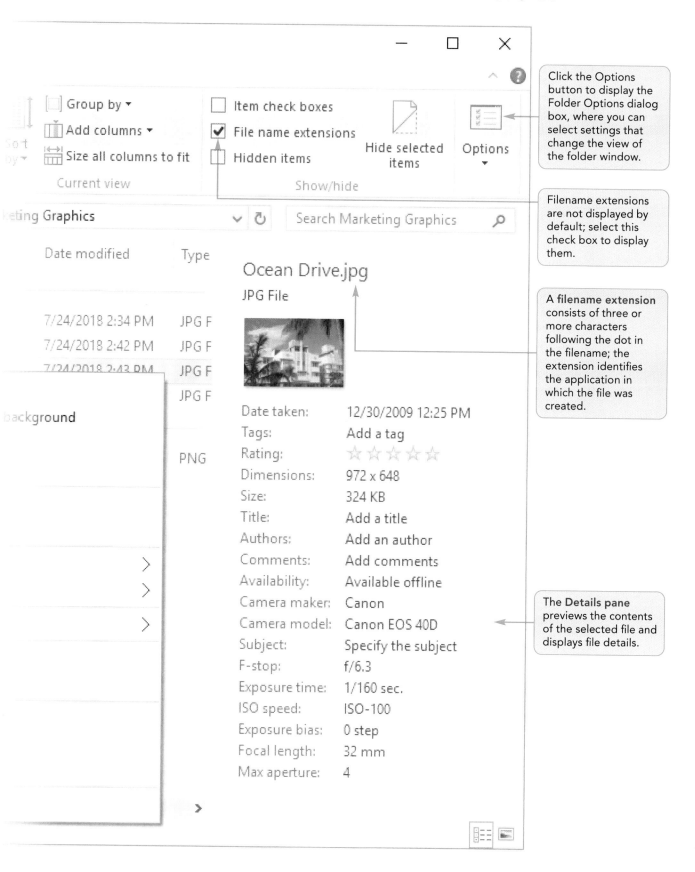

Click the Options button to display the Folder Options dialog box, where you can select settings that change the view of the folder window.

Filename extensions are not displayed by default; select this check box to display them.

A filename extension consists of three or more characters following the dot in the filename; the extension identifies the application in which the file was created.

The **Details** pane previews the contents of the selected file and displays file details.

Naming and Renaming Files and Folders

As you work with files, pay attention to filenames—they provide important information about the file, including its contents and purpose. A filename such as Miami Tours.docx has three parts:

- Main part of the filename—The name you provide when you create a file, and the name you associate with a file
- Dot—The period (.) that separates the main part of the filename from the filename extension
- Filename extension—Usually three or four characters that follow the dot in the filename

The main part of a filename can have up to 255 characters. This gives you plenty of room to name your file accurately enough so that you'll know the contents of the file just by looking at the filename. You can use spaces and certain punctuation symbols in your filenames. Like folder names, however, filenames cannot contain the symbols / \ : * ? " < > or | because these characters have special meanings in Windows 10.

A filename extension indicates the file type. For example, in the filename Miami Tours.docx, the extension .docx identifies the file as one created in Microsoft Word, a word-processing application. You might also have a file called Miami Tours.png—the .png extension identifies the file as one created in a graphics application such as Paint. Though the main parts of these filenames are identical, their extensions distinguish them as different files.

An extension also helps Windows identify what application should open the file. For example, the .txt extension in a file named Brochure.txt indicates that it is a text file and can be opened by applications associated with that extension, such as WordPad, Notepad, and Microsoft Word. You usually do not need to add extensions to your filenames because the application you use to create the file adds the extension automatically. However, although Windows 10 keeps track of extensions, it is not set to display them by default. (You will learn how to show filename extensions later in the module.)

Be sure to give your files and folders meaningful names that will help you remember their purpose and contents. You can, however, rename a file or folder by using the Rename command on the file's shortcut menu.

INSIGHT

Guidelines for Naming Files

The following are best practices for naming (or renaming) your files:

- Use common names. Avoid cryptic names that might make sense now but could cause confusion later, such as nonstandard abbreviations or imprecise names like Stuff18.
- Leave the filename extension as it is. Do not change the filename extension when renaming a file. If you do, Windows might not be able to find an application that can open the file.
- Find a comfortable balance between too short and too long. Use filenames that are long enough to be meaningful, but short enough to be read easily on the screen.

Diego notes that the City Guide file in the Sights folder could contain information about any city. He recommends that you rename that file to give it a more descriptive filename. The City Guide file was originally created to store text specifically about sights on Miami, so you'll rename the file Miami Guide.

To rename the City Guide file:

▶ **1.** If you took a break after the previous session, make sure that a folder window is open, and then navigate to the **Module2** folder included with your Data Files. Click the **Module** folder in the left pane, and change to **Medium icons** view, if necessary.

▶ **2.** Open the **Sights** folder to display its contents.

▶ **3.** Right-click the **City Guide** file, and then click **Rename** on the shortcut menu. The filename is highlighted and a box appears around it.

▶ **4.** Type **Miami Guide** and then press the **Enter** key. The file now appears with the new name.

> **Trouble?** If you make a mistake while typing and you haven't pressed the Enter key yet, press the Backspace key until you delete the mistake and then complete Step 4. If you've already pressed the Enter key, repeat Steps 3 and 4 to rename the file again.

> **Trouble?** If your computer is set to display filename extensions, a message might appear asking if you are sure you want to change the filename extension. Click the No button, and then repeat Steps 3 and 4.

All the files that originally appeared in the Module folder are now stored in appropriate subfolders. You can streamline the organization of the Module folder by deleting the duplicate files you no longer need.

Deleting Files and Folders

You should periodically delete files and folders you no longer need so that your main folders and disks don't get cluttered. In a folder window, you delete a file or folder by deleting its icon. When you use File Explorer to delete a file from a hard disk, including a OneDrive file, Windows 10 removes the file from the folder but stores the file contents in the Recycle Bin. The Recycle Bin is an area on your hard disk that holds deleted files until you remove them permanently. When you delete a folder from the hard disk, the folder and all of its files are stored in the Recycle Bin. If you change your mind and want to retrieve a deleted file or folder, you can double-click the Recycle Bin icon on the desktop, right-click the file or folder you want to retrieve, and then click Restore on the shortcut menu. However, after you empty the Recycle Bin, you can no longer recover the files it contained.

TIP

To rename a file, you can also click the file, pause, click it again to select the filename, and then type to enter a new filename.

TIP

In most cases, a file deleted from a USB drive does not go into the Recycle Bin. Instead, it is deleted permanently when Windows 10 removes its icon, and the file cannot be recovered.

REFERENCE

Deleting a File or Folder

- Click the file or folder you want to delete. (If you want to delete more than one file or folder, select them first.)
- Press the Delete key, and then click the Yes button.

or

- Right-click the file or folder you want to delete. (If you want to delete more than one file or folder, select them first.)
- Click Delete on the shortcut menu, and then click the Yes button.

Because you copied the Edison, Logo, Miami Beach, Ocean Drive, and Trolley files to the subfolders in the Module folder, you can safely delete the original files. As is true for moving, copying, and renaming files and folders, you can delete a file or folder in many ways, including using a shortcut menu or selecting one or more files and then pressing the Delete key or the Delete button in the Organize group on the Home tab on the File Explorer ribbon.

To delete files in the Module folder:

▶ **1.** Use any technique you've learned to navigate to and display the **Module** folder.

▶ **2.** Click **Edison**, hold down the **Shift** key, click **Trolley**, and then release the **Shift** key. All files in the Module folder are now selected. None of the subfolders should be selected.

▶ **3.** Right-click the selected files, and then click **Delete** on the shortcut menu. Windows 10 might ask if you're sure you want to permanently delete these files.

> **Trouble?** If you are working with files on a hard disk, Windows does not ask if you want to permanently delete the files.

▶ **4.** If necessary, click the **Yes** button.

Make sure you have copied the selected files to the Financial, Marketing Graphics, and Sights folders before completing this step.

So far, you've worked with files in folder windows, but you haven't viewed any file contents. To view a file's contents, you open the file. When you double-click a file in a folder window, Windows 10 starts the associated application and opens the file. You'll have a chance to try these techniques in the next section.

Working with New Files

The most common way to add files to a drive or folder is to create new files when you use an application. For example, you can create a text document in a word-processing application, a drawing in a graphics application, or a movie file in a video-editing application. When you are finished with a file, you must save it if you want to use the file again. To work with the file, you open it in an appropriate application; you can usually tell which applications can open a file by examining the filename extension or file icon.

Before you continue working with Diego's files, you decide to create a task list to summarize your remaining tasks. You'll create the task list file, save it, close it, and then reopen it to add some items to the list.

Creating a File

You create a file by starting an application and then saving the file in a folder on your computer. Some applications create a file when you open the application. When you open WordPad, for example, it starts with a blank page. This represents an empty (and unsaved) file. You type and format the document to create it. When you are finished, you save your work using the Save As dialog box, where you can select a location for the file and enter a filename that identifies the contents. By default, most applications save files in a folder such as Documents, Pictures, or Music, which makes it easy to find the files again later.

The task list you want to create is a simple text document, so you can create this file using Notepad, the basic text-editing application that Windows 10 provides.

To create a Notepad file:

▶ **1.** Click the **Start** button 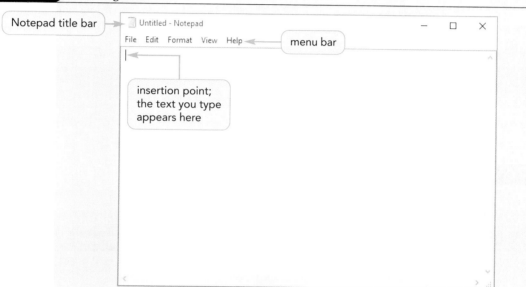 to display the Start menu.

▶ **2.** Type **notep** to insert "notep" in the Search the web and Windows box. The search results include Notepad, a desktop app.

▶ **3.** Click **Notepad** in the search results. The Notepad application window opens on the desktop. See Figure 2-15.

Figure 2-15	Creating a file

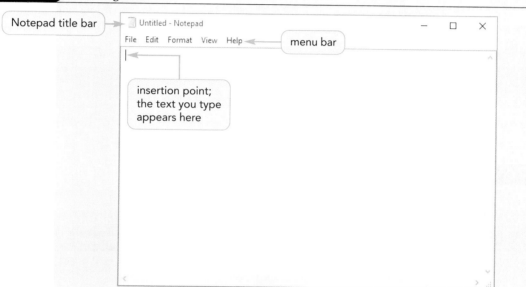

Notepad title bar

menu bar

insertion point; the text you type appears here

▶ **4.** Type the following text in the Notepad window, pressing the **Enter** key at the end of each line, including the last line:

To Do for Diego's Files

1. Sort and filter files.

2. Customize a folder window.

3. Compress and extract files.

The Notepad title bar indicates that the name of this file is "Untitled." To give it a more descriptive name, preserve the contents, and store the file where you can find it later, you must save the file.

Saving a File

As you are creating a file, you should save it frequently so you don't lose your work. When you save a new file, you use the Save As dialog box to specify a filename and a location for the file. When you open a file you've already created, you can use the application's Save command to save the file with the same name and location. If you want to save the file with a different name or in a different location, however, you use the Save As dialog box again to specify the new name or location. You can create a folder for the new file at the same time you save the file.

The Save As dialog box contains the same navigation tools found in a folder window, such as an Address bar, Search box, navigation pane, and right pane displaying folders and files. You can then specify the file location, for example, using the same navigation techniques that are available in all folder windows. In addition, the Save As dialog box always includes a File name box where you specify a filename, a Save as type list where you select a file type, and other controls for saving a file.

If the expanded Save As dialog box covers too much of your document or desktop, you can click the Hide Folders button to collapse the dialog box so it hides the navigation pane, right pane, and toolbar. (The Hide Folders button changes to the Browse Folders button when the dialog box is collapsed.) You can still navigate with the Back, Forward, Recent locations, and Up one level buttons; the Address bar; and the Search box, and you can still use the controls for saving a file, but you conserve screen space.

Now that you've created a task list, you need to save it. A good name for this document is Task List. However, none of the folders you've already created for Diego seems appropriate for this file. It belongs in a separate folder with a name such as Task Documents. You can create the Task Documents folder at the same time you save the Task List file.

To save the Notepad file to a new folder:

▶ **1.** In the Notepad window, click **File** on the menu bar, and then click **Save As**. The Save As dialog box opens. See Figure 2-16.

| Figure 2-16 | Saving a new file |

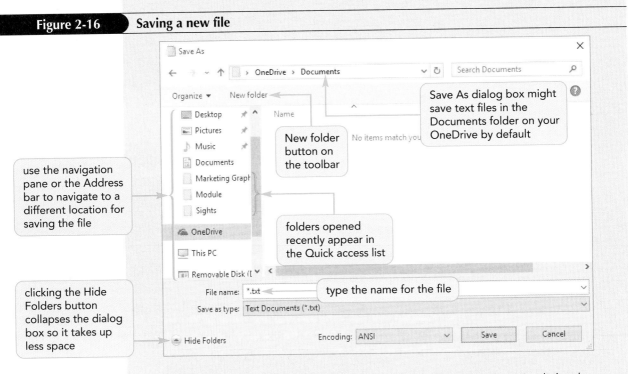

Trouble? If the navigation pane does not appear in the Save As dialog box, click the Browse Folders button.

Your computer might be set up to save Notepad files in the Documents folder on OneDrive or a different location, such as the Documents folder on This PC. You want to create a subfolder in the Module folder for this document.

▶ **2.** In the Save As dialog box, use any technique you've learned to navigate to the **Module2 > Module** folder provided with your Data Files.

▶ **3.** Click the **New folder** button on the toolbar in the Save As dialog box. A new folder appears in the Module folder, with the New folder name highlighted and ready for you to replace.

4. Type **Task Documents** as the name of the new folder, and then press the **Enter** key.

5. Double-click the **Task Documents** folder to open it. Now you are ready to specify a filename and save the task list file in the Task Documents folder.

6. Click the **File name** box to select the *.txt text, and then type **Task List**. Notepad will automatically provide a .txt extension to this filename, so you don't have to type it.

7. Click the **Save** button. Notepad saves the Task List file in the Task Documents folder. The new filename now appears in the Notepad title bar.

8. Click the **Close** button ⊠ to close Notepad.

Next, you can open the file to add another item to the task list.

Opening a File

If you want to open a file in a running application, you use the Open dialog box, which is a folder window with additional controls for opening a file, similar to the Save As dialog box. You use the application's Open command to access the Open dialog box, which you use to navigate to the file you want, select the file, and then open it. If the application you want to use is not running, you can open a file by double-clicking it in a folder window. The file usually opens in the application that you used to create or edit it. If it's a text file with a .txt extension, for example, it opens in a text editor, such as Notepad. If it's a text file with a .docx extension, it opens in Microsoft Word.

Not all documents work this way. Double-clicking a digital picture file usually opens a picture viewing app, which displays the picture. To edit the picture, you need to use a graphics editing application. When you need to specify an application to open a file, you can right-click the file, point to Open with on the shortcut menu, and then click the name of the app that you want to use.

To open and edit the Task List file:

1. In the right pane of the Module folder window, double-click the **Task Documents** folder.

2. Double-click the **Task List** file. Notepad starts and opens the Task List file.

    Trouble? If an application other than Notepad starts, such as WordPad, close the application, right-click the Task List file, point to Open with, and then click Notepad.

3. Press the **Ctrl+End** keys to move the insertion point to the end of the document, and then type **4. Restore system settings.**

    Because you want to save this file using the same name and location, you can use the Save command on the File menu to save your work this time.

4. Click **File** on the menu bar, and then click **Save**. Notepad saves the Task List file without opening the Save As dialog box because you are using the same name and location as the last time you saved the file.

As long as Notepad is still open, you can create another simple text file that describes the photos in the Sights folder.

To create and save another file:

▶ **1.** Click **File** on the menu bar, and then click **New** to open a new, blank document.

▶ **2.** Type the following text in the Notepad window, pressing the **Enter** key at the end of each line:

Sights photos:

Edison: Photo of the Edison hotel

Miami Beach: Photo of Miami Beach and city skyline

Ocean Drive: Photo of an art deco building on Ocean Drive

Trolley: Photo of a company trolley

▶ **3.** Click **File** on the menu bar, and then click **Save**. The Save As dialog box opens because this is the first time you are saving the file.

▶ **4.** Navigate to the **Sights** folder in the Module folder.

▶ **5.** Click in the **File name** box, and then type **Photo Descriptions**.

▶ **6.** Click the **Save** button. Notepad saves the Photo Descriptions file in the Sights folder.

▶ **7.** Click the **Close** button ✕ to close Notepad. (Because Notepad only allows one file to be opened at a time, the application closed the first file for you when you created the new file.)

Now that you've organized Diego's files and then created and saved new folders and files, you're ready to refine the organization of the files.

Refining the Organization of Files

To refine the organization of your files, you can fine-tune the arrangement of your files and folders in a folder window. Changing the order of files in a list can often help you find files and identify those that share common features, such as two versions of the same file. One way to change the view is to sort your files. **Sorting** files and folders means listing them in a particular order, such as alphabetically by name or type, or chronologically by their modification date. You can also **filter** the contents of a folder to display only files and folders with certain characteristics, such as all those you modified yesterday. In short, sorting reorganizes all of the files and folders in a list, while filtering displays only those files and folders that share a characteristic you specify. Both actions change your view of the files and folders, not the items themselves.

Windows 10 provides another way to change the view of your files and folders—grouping. When you group your files by type, for example, Windows separates the files into several groups, such as Microsoft Word documents in one group and photo files in another group.

Problem Solving: Preventing Lost File Problems

Many computer users, even very experienced ones, fall into the trap of saving or moving a file to a folder and then forgetting where it's stored. You can prevent these types of lost file problems by managing your files systematically. To manage files so you know where to find them later, start by formulating a logical plan for organizing your files. Some people sketch a simple diagram of the file structure to help them visualize where to store files. Next, create the folders you need to store the files, and then move and copy your existing files into those folders. As you create files using applications, save them in an appropriate folder and use folder names and filenames that help you identify their contents. If possible, use a similar organization scheme in all of your folders. For example, if you organized the files for one project into subfolders such as Phase 1, Phase 2, Phase 3, and Follow Up, use the same organization for each project. To make it easier to find files, especially in a long file list, you can sort, filter, and group the files in a way that seems logical to you. Performing these basic management tasks helps you keep track of your files so you can easily find information when you need it.

You want to show Diego how to change the view of his files by sorting, filtering, and grouping so he can choose one view that makes the most sense for him or his current task.

Sorting and Filtering Files

When you are working with a folder window in Details view, you can sort or filter the files using the column headings in the right pane of the window. To sort files by type, for example, click the Type column heading. You can sort files in ascending order (A to Z, 0 to 9, or earliest to latest date) or descending order (Z to A, 9 to 0, or latest to earliest date). To switch the order, click the column heading again.

Sorting is often an effective way to find a file or folder in a relatively short file list. By default, Windows 10 sorts the contents of a folder in ascending alphabetic order by filename, with any subfolders listed before the files. A file named April Marketing appears at the top of the list, and a file named Winter Expenses appears at the end. You can change the sort criterion to list files according to any other file characteristic.

If you are working with a longer file list, filtering the list might help you find the file you want. To filter the contents of a folder, you click the arrow button to the right of a column heading, and then click one or more file properties such as a specific filename, created or modified date, author, or file type. Windows displays only files and folders with those properties. For example, if you want to list only music files by a particular artist, you can filter by that artist's name.

Details view always includes column headings corresponding to file details. To sort files in other views that do not display column headings, you can right-click a blank area of the folder window, point to Sort by on the shortcut menu, and then click a file detail such as Type. (You cannot filter files in views without column headings.)

To sort and filter the files in the Sights folder:

▸ **1.** Navigate to the Sights folder and then click the **Details** button 🔳 on the status bar, if necessary, to switch to Details view.

▸ **2.** Click the **Type** column heading to sort the files in ascending order according to file type. A sort arrow appears above the Type column heading label. The sort arrow points up to indicate the column is sorted in ascending order.

   Trouble? If the Type column does not appear in your folder window, right-click any column heading and then click Type. Then complete Step 3.

3. Click the **Type** column heading again to reverse the sort order. The sort arrow now points down, indicating the column is sorted in descending order.

4. Right-click any column heading to display a list of file details. Details with a check mark are displayed in the folder window. If the Date modified column heading does not appear in your folder window, click **Date modified** to display this column. Otherwise, click a blank area of the window. Your folder window should now display only the Name, Date modified, Type, and Size columns.

   Trouble? If your folder window contains columns other than Name, Date modified, Type, and Size, right-click any column heading, and then click the name of the column you want to remove from the folder window. The content of the column is not deleted; it is just no longer visible on-screen.

5. Click the **Date modified** column heading to sort the files in descending chronological order by the date they were modified. See Figure 2-17.

Figure 2-17   Sorting files by date

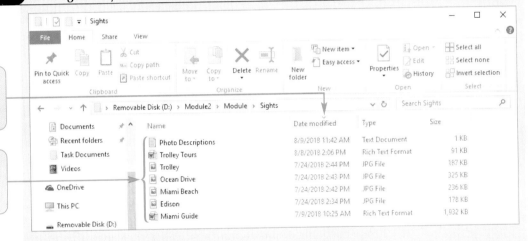

sort arrow points down, indicating the column is sorted in descending order

files are sorted so that the most recently modified files appear first

To compare sorting and filtering, you can filter the files by their modified date to display only the files you modified today.

6. Point to the **Date modified** column heading, and then click its **arrow** button to the right of the column heading to display a list of filtering options.

   Trouble? If the files are sorted in ascending order by Date modified, you clicked the sort arrow. Click the Date modified sort arrow again to sort the files in descending order, and then repeat Step 6.

When you sort files by Date modified with the most recent files on top, you can quickly find the files you modified recently.

7. Click the **Today** check box to select today's date. The folder window displays only the Photo Descriptions file. See Figure 2-18.

   Trouble? If you modified the Photo Descriptions file on a different date, click that date on the calendar.

   Trouble? If you clicked Today rather than the check box, skip Step 8.

| **Figure 2-18** | **Filtering to display files modified today** |

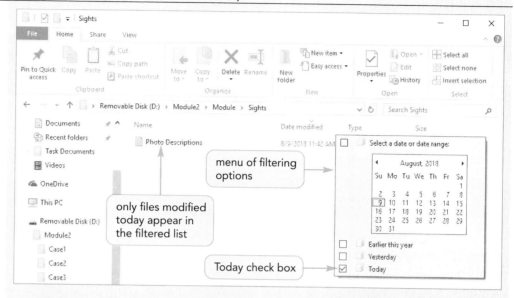

Note that you can filter by two or more properties by selecting the corresponding check boxes.

8. Click a blank area of the window to close the list. A check mark appears next to the Date modified column heading to indicate the file list is filtered by a Date modified detail.

Next, you can group the files in the Sights folder and compare this view to the views displayed when you sorted and filtered the files.

Grouping Files

To change your view of files and folders, you can group them—a technique that is especially effective when you are working with long file lists. You can group files according to any file detail such as Type or Authors. To group files by author, for example, you can right-click a blank area of the window, point to Group by, click More, and then click Authors. Windows divides the folder window into sections, with one section listing files you wrote, for example, and another section for files your colleague wrote.

Before grouping files, you must remove any filters you are using in the folder window. If you don't, you'll rearrange only the files that appear in the filtered list. After removing the filter, you'll group the files in the Sights folder by type using the Group by option in the Current view group on the View tab.

To remove the filter and group the files in the Sights folder:

1. In the Sights folder window, click the **check mark** on the Date modified column heading, and then click the **Today** check box (or the **Select a date or date range** check box if you selected a date on the calendar earlier) to clear the check box. Click a blank area of the folder window. The complete list of Sights files appears in the right pane.

      2. Click the **View** tab on the ribbon, click the **Group by** button in the Current view group, and then click **Type**. Windows arranges all the files in the Sights folder into three groups, one for each file type. See Figure 2-19.

Figure 2-19	Grouping files

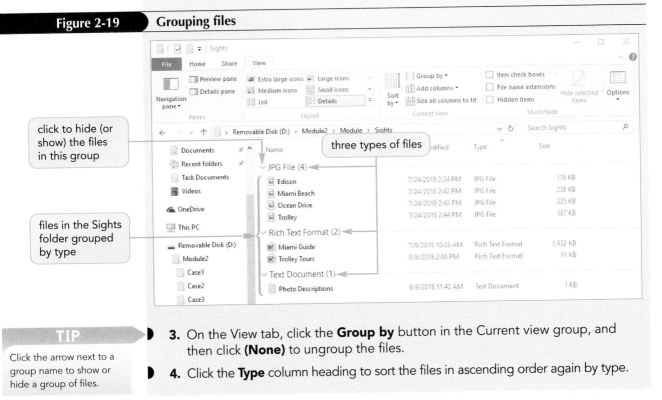

click to hide (or show) the files in this group

three types of files

files in the Sights folder grouped by type

TIP

Click the arrow next to a group name to show or hide a group of files.

      3. On the View tab, click the **Group by** button in the Current view group, and then click **(None)** to ungroup the files.

      4. Click the **Type** column heading to sort the files in ascending order again by type.

Now that Diego knows how to sort, filter, and group files in a folder window, he mentions that he might want to hide or show elements of the folder window itself, such as the navigation pane. You'll show him how to customize the folder window next.

Customizing a Folder Window

As you learned earlier, you can change how you view your files and folders in a folder window, such as changing from large icons to a detailed list. You can make other changes to the layout of your folder windows. For example, you can hide the navigation pane to devote more space to file lists. The View tab includes options you can use to fine-tune the layout of a folder window. You have already used some options in the Current view and Layout groups. Figure 2-20 summarizes all the options on the View tab.

| | **Figure 2-20** | **View tab options** |

Group	Option	Description
Panes	Navigation pane	Show or hide the navigation pane in this window only, and specify whether to expand the navigation pane to the open folder, show all folders, or show libraries, containers for built-in folders such as Documents and Pictures.
	Preview pane	Show or hide the Preview pane. When you select this option, you can preview the contents of a file without having to open an application.
	Details pane	Show or hide the Details pane. When you select this option, you display the most common properties associated with a selected file, such as the author of the file or its type.
Layout	View options	Select one of eight views for displaying the contents of the current folder: Extra large icons, Large icons, Medium icons, Small icons, List, Details, Tiles, Content.
Current view	Sort by	Select a file property to use for sorting, select ascending or descending sort order, and choose one or more columns to display in the current folder window.
	Group by	Group files by a file detail displayed in the current folder window.
	Add columns	Select a file detail to display as a column in the current folder window or choose a file detail not included in the list.
	Size all columns to fit	Change the width of all columns to fit the contents.
Show/ hide	Item check boxes	Show or hide check boxes next to files and folders; use the check boxes to select items.
	File name extensions	Show or hide the extensions for all files in the current folder window.
	Hidden items	Show or hide the files and folders marked as hidden.
	Hide selected items	Hide the selected files or folders.
	Options	Use the Folder Options dialog box to change settings for opening items, file and folder views, and searching.

You'll show Diego how to change the layout of a folder window, and then how to customize the appearance of the folder contents. Finally, you'll demonstrate how to add items to the navigation pane to suit the way he works.

Changing the Layout of a Folder Window

You can change the layout of a folder window by showing or hiding the navigation pane and either the Preview pane or the Details pane. The **Preview pane** appears on the right side of a folder window and displays the contents of a selected picture file and some other types of files. The Details pane also appears on the right and provides information about a selected file, such as the author and file type. Only one of these panes can be open in a folder window. Neither pane appears by default. Figure 2-21 shows a folder window with the Navigation and Preview panes open.

Figure 2-21   Folder window displaying the navigation and Preview panes

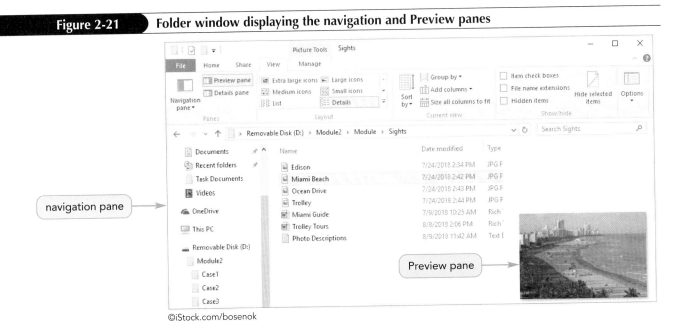

©iStock.com/bosenok

Diego wants to see if he likes having the Details pane in the folder window, so he asks you to display that pane. He is also curious about the Preview pane, so you'll open that for him first. The Sights folder window should currently be open in Details view, with files sorted according to type.

To change the layout of a folder window:

▶ **1.** Click the **Edison** file to select it, click the **View** tab on the ribbon, if necessary, and then click the **Preview pane** button in the Panes group to display the Preview pane.

▶ **2.** On the View tab, click the **Details pane** button in the Panes group to close the Preview pane and display the Details pane. See Figure 2-22. Your file details might vary.

Figure 2-22   Folder window displaying the navigation and Details panes

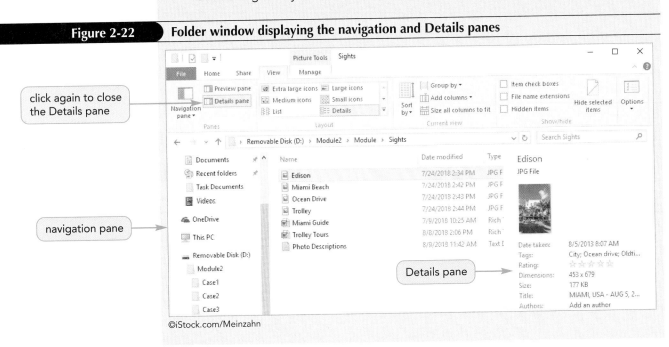

©iStock.com/Meinzahn

You can also use options in the Show/hide group on the View tab to customize the file list.

Customizing the File List

Although Windows 10 refers to a filename extension to identify a file's type, filename extensions are not displayed by default in a folder window. Windows hides the extensions to make filenames easier to read, especially for long filenames. If you prefer to display filename extensions, you can show them in all the folder windows (as you do in the following steps).

Another type of file not displayed by default in a folder window is a **hidden file**. Windows hides many types of files, including temporary files it creates before you save a document. It hides these files so that you do not become confused by temporary filenames, which are similar to the names of the files you save on your computer. By default, Windows 10 also hides system files, which are files the operating system needs to work properly. You should keep these files hidden unless a reliable expert, such as a technical support professional, instructs you to display them. Keep in mind that hidden files still take up space on your disk.

You use the options in the Show/hide group on the View tab to show and hide filename extensions in all windows. To show and hide hidden files, you use the Folder Options dialog box.

To show filename extensions:

1. On the View tab, click the **File name extensions** check box in the Show/hide group to insert a check mark so filename extensions appear in all windows. See Figure 2-23.

Figure 2-23	Folder window showing filename extensions

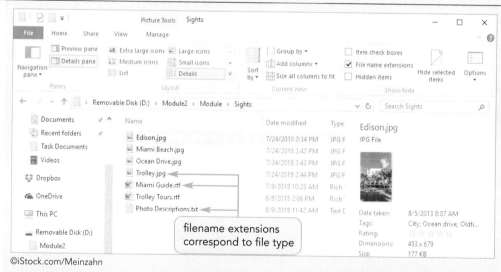

©iStock.com/Meinzahn

2. Click the **Options** button to open the Folder Options dialog box.

3. Click the **View** tab in the Folder Options dialog box. See Figure 2-24. The settings selected on the View tab of your Folder Options dialog box might differ.

Figure 2-24   **Folder Options dialog box**

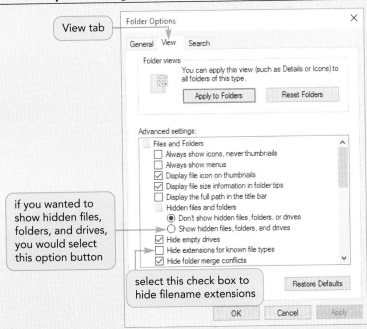

View tab

if you wanted to show hidden files, folders, and drives, you would select this option button

select this check box to hide filename extensions

> **4.** Click the **Hide extensions for known file types** check box to insert a check mark, and then click the **OK** button to hide the filename extensions again.

> **Trouble?** If the Hide extensions for known file types check box already contains a check mark, just close the dialog box.

Next, you can customize the navigation pane by changing its appearance and adding a folder to the Quick access list.

Customizing the Navigation Pane

You can customize the navigation pane by adding, renaming, and removing items in the Quick access list. For example, if you use the navigation pane to open a particular folder, you can drag that folder to the Quick access list to make it one of the locations you access often.

To customize your navigation pane, you'll start by **pinning** the Task Documents folder to the Quick access list so it remains in the list, allowing you to access the folder quickly. Next, you'll rename the actual folder to distinguish it from the Documents folder, which is also listed in the navigation pane. When you do, Windows also renames the pinned folder in the Quick access list so the two names always match. (You cannot rename a pinned item in the Quick access list.) Later, when you restore the settings on your computer, you'll unpin the folder.

TIP

When you unpin a folder from the Quick access list, you remove it from the Quick access list only; you do not delete the folder itself.

To customize the navigation pane:

> **1.** Use any navigation method you've learned to display the folders in the Module folder. Scroll to the top of the navigation pane, if necessary.

> **2.** Drag the **Task Documents** folder from the Module folder to the Quick access icon in the navigation pane. When the Pin to Quick access ScreenTip appears, release the mouse button to pin the Task Documents folder to the Quick access list. See Figure 2-25.

Figure 2-25   Task Documents folder pinned to the Quick access list

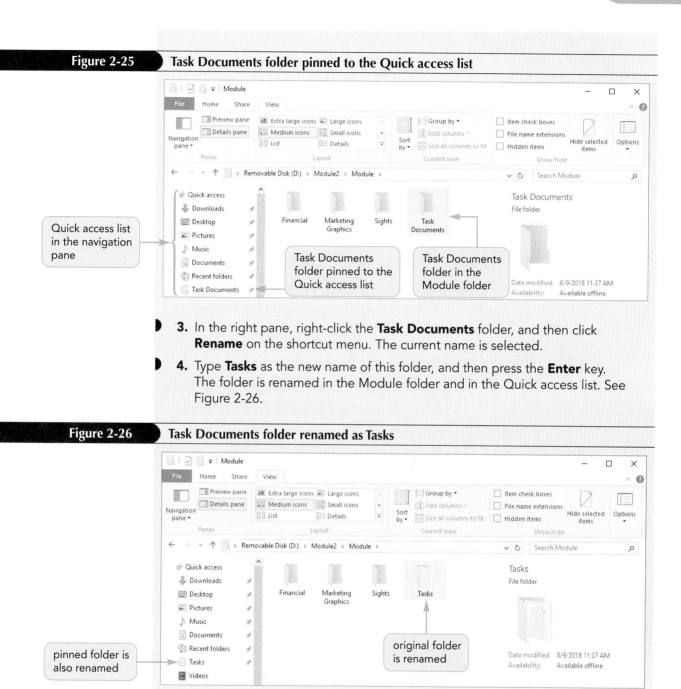

3. In the right pane, right-click the **Task Documents** folder, and then click **Rename** on the shortcut menu. The current name is selected.

4. Type **Tasks** as the new name of this folder, and then press the **Enter** key. The folder is renamed in the Module folder and in the Quick access list. See Figure 2-26.

Figure 2-26   Task Documents folder renamed as Tasks

Now that you've refined your file organization and customized the folder window, you are ready to show Diego two final tasks—compressing and extracting files.

Working with Compressed Files

If you transfer files from one location to another, such as from your hard disk to a removable disk or vice versa, or from one computer to another via email, you can store the files in a compressed (zipped) folder so that they take up less disk space. You can then transfer the files more quickly. If you or your email contacts can send and receive files only up to a certain size, compressing large files might make them small enough to send and receive. When you create a compressed folder using the Windows 10 compression tool, a zipper appears on the folder icon.

You compress a folder so that the files it contains use less space on the disk. Compare two folders—a folder named Photos that contains about 8.6 MB of files, and a compressed folder containing the same files, but requiring only 6.5 MB of disk space. In this case, the compressed files use about 25 percent less disk space than the uncompressed files.

You can create a compressed folder using the Zip button in the Send group on the Share tab of a folder window. Then you can compress additional files or folders by dragging them into the compressed folder. You can open a file directly from a compressed folder, although you cannot modify the file. To edit and save a compressed file, you must extract it first. When you **extract** a file, you create an uncompressed copy of the file in a folder you specify. The original file remains in the compressed folder.

Diego suggests that you compress the files and folders in the Module folder so that you can more quickly transfer them to another location.

TIP

Another way to compress files is to select the files, right-click the selection, point to Send to on the shortcut menu, and then click Compressed (zipped) folder.

To compress the folders and files in the Module folder:

▶ 1. Select all the folders in the Module folder, click the **Share** tab on the ribbon, and then click the **Zip** button in the Send group. After a few moments, a new compressed folder with a zipper icon appears in the Module window with the filename selected.

▶ 2. Type **Miami Trolleys** and then press the **Enter** key to rename the compressed folder. See Figure 2-27.

Figure 2-27   Creating a compressed folder

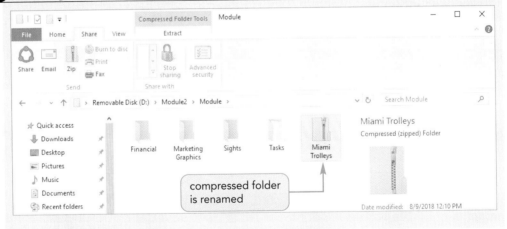

compressed folder is renamed

You open a compressed folder by double-clicking it. You can then copy files and folders from the opened compressed folder to other locations, although you cannot rename the files. More often, you extract all of the files in the compressed folder. Windows 10 then uncompresses and copies them to a location that you specify, preserving the files in their original folders as appropriate.

INSIGHT

Understanding Compressed File Types

Some types of files, such as JPG picture files (those with a .jpg or .jpeg filename extension), are already highly compressed. If you compress JPG (pronounced "jay peg") pictures into a folder, the total size of the compressed folder is about the same as the collection of uncompressed pictures. However, if you are transferring the files from one computer to another, such as by email, it's still a good idea to store the compressed files in a zipped folder to keep them together.

To extract the compressed files:

▶ **1.** Click the **Compressed Folder Tools Extract** tab on the ribbon, and then click the **Extract all** button. The Extract Compressed (Zipped) Folders Wizard starts and opens the Select a Destination and Extract Files dialog box.

▶ **2.** Press the **End** key to deselect the path in the box and move the insertion point to the end of the path, press the **Backspace** key as many times as necessary to delete the Miami Trolleys text, and then type **Backups**. The final three parts of the path in the box should be \Module2\Module\Backups. See Figure 2-28.

| Figure 2-28 | Extracting files from a compressed folder |

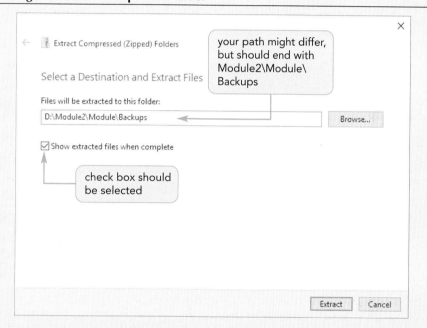

▶ **3.** Make sure the Show extracted files when complete check box is checked, and then click the **Extract** button. Windows extracts the files and then opens the Backups folder, showing the Financial, Marketing Graphics, Sights, and Tasks folders.

▶ **4.** Open each folder to make sure it contains the files you worked with in this module.

▶ **5.** Close the Backups folder window, and then click a blank area of the Module folder window.

In this session, you renamed and deleted files according to your organization plan, and then created a file, saved it in a new folder, and opened and edited the file. Then you refined the organization of the files and folders, customized a folder window, and worked with compressed files. Before you end your Windows 10 session, you should restore your computer to its original settings.

Restoring Your Settings

If you are working in a computer lab or on a computer other than your own, complete the steps in this section to restore the original settings on the computer.

To restore your settings:

▶ **1.** In the Module folder window, click the **View** tab, and then click the **Details pane** button in the Panes group to hide the Details pane in the folder window.

▶ **2.** Right-click the **Tasks** folder in the Quick access list in the navigation pane, and then click **Unpin from Quick access**.

▶ **3.** Close all open windows.

REVIEW

Session 2.2 Quick Check

1. What is the purpose of a filename extension?

2. How can you restore a file that you deleted from the hard disk?

3. If you are using Notepad to edit a text document named Project, how can you save it as a file named Project Steps?

4. Explain the difference between grouping and filtering files.

5. How is sorting a folder window by file type different when using Details view and Medium icons view?

6. What happens to a folder pinned to the Quick access list when you rename the original folder?

7. What is the purpose of compressing a folder?

8. Describe how to extract all the files from a compressed folder.

PRACTICE

Review Assignments

Data Files needed for the Review Assignments: Background.png, Calendar.rtf, Events.xlsx, Skyline.jpg, Walking.rtf, Welcome.jpg

Diego has saved a few files from his old computer on a removable disk. He gives you these files in a single, unorganized folder, and asks you to organize them logically into subfolders. He needs at least one subfolder for files related to a newsletter he is planning. Devise a plan for managing the files, and then create the subfolders you need. Next, rename, copy, move, and delete files, and perform other management tasks to make it easy for Diego to work with these files and folders. Complete the following steps:

1. Use File Explorer to navigate to and open the Module2 > Review folder provided with your Data Files. Examine the six files in this folder and consider possible ways to organize the files.

2. In the Review folder, create three folders: **Business**, **Newsletter**, and **Tours**.

3. To organize the files into the correct folders:
   - Move the Background and Calendar files from the Review folder to the Business folder.
   - Move the Events file to the Newsletter folder.
   - Move the Skyline, Walking, and Welcome files to the Tours folder.

4. Copy the Walking file in the Tours folder to the Newsletter folder.

5. Rename the Calendar file in the Business folder as **2018 Calendar**. Rename the Walking file in the Newsletter folder as **Walking Tours**.

6. Return to the Review folder and use the Search box to find a file whose filename begins with the text "back." Rename this file **Company Banner**.

7. Create a Notepad file that includes the following text:
   When to Visit Miami
   Nov - April: Perfect weather
   Dec - March: High season
   May - Sept: Hot and steamy

8. Save the Notepad file as **When to Go** in the Newsletter folder. Close the Notepad window.

9. Navigate to the Newsletter folder, open the When to Go file, and then add the following line to the end of the document: **Oct: Pleasant**.

10. Save the When to Go file with the same name and in the same location. Open a new document in Notepad, and then type the following text:
    Art Deco Hotels
    Cadillac Hotel
    McAlpin Hotel

11. Save the file as **Art Deco** in the Tours folder. Close Notepad.

12. Navigate to the Tours folder and then perform the following tasks:
    - Sort the files by Date modified. How many files appear in the folder window?
    - Filter the files by today's date (or the date you created the two text files). How many files appear in the folder window?

13. Remove the filter, and then group the files by type. How many types are displayed? How many files are displayed of each type?

14. Navigate to the Newsletter folder, and then display filename extensions in the folder window. Group the files by size. How many files are displayed of each type?

15. Change the layout of the folder window by displaying the Details pane, and then change the grouping to (None).

16. In the Review folder, add the Business folder to the Quick access list in the navigation pane. Rename the folder **MT Business**.

17. Open the MT Business folder, click the Company Banner.png file, and then press the Print Screen key to capture an image of the folder window. (*Hint:* Depending on the type of computer you are using, the Print Screen key might be labeled differently, for example, PrtScn.) Start Paint and then press the Ctrl+V keys to paste this image in a file. Save this file as **Review** in the Module2 > Review folder provided with your Data Files. Close Paint.

18. Restore your computer's settings by hiding the Details pane, hiding filename extensions in the folder window, and unpinning the MT Business folder from the Quick access list in the navigation pane.

19. Create a compressed (zipped) folder in the Review folder named **Miami** that contains all the files and folders in the Review folder.

20. Extract the contents of the Miami compressed folder to a new folder named **Miami Backups** in the Review folder. (*Hint:* The file path will end with \Module2\Review\Miami Backups.)

21. Close all open windows.

Case Problem 1

See the Starting Data Files section at the beginning of this module for the list of Data Files needed for this Case Problem.

APPLY

Art Glass Studio Shannon Beecher started the Art Glass Studio in Lake George, New York, to provide custom stained glass works for residential and commercial buildings. The business also holds classes on stained glass techniques for children and adults. Knowing you are multitalented, Shannon hired you to help her manage the front end of the studio and other parts of her growing business, including electronic business files. Your first task is to organize the files on her new Windows 10 computer. Complete the following steps:

1. In the Module2 > Case1 folder provided with your Data Files, create three folders: **Classes**, **Designs**, and **Marketing**.

2. Move the Advanced Classes, Beginner Classes, Intermediate Classes, and Kids Classes files from the Case1 folder to the Classes folder.

3. Rename the four files in the Classes folder by deleting the word Classes from each name.

4. Move the four JPG files from the Case1 folder to the Designs folder.

5. Copy the remaining two files to the Marketing folder. Also, copy the Designers file to the Designs folder.

6. Delete the Designers and Studio files from the Case1 folder.

7. Open the Recycle Bin folder by double-clicking the Recycle Bin icon on the desktop, and then display the window in Details view. Sort the contents of the Recycle Bin by filename in descending order.

8. Filter the files by their deletion date to display only the files you deleted today. (*Hint:* If you deleted files from the Case1 folder on a different date, click that date on the calendar.) Do the Designers and Studio files appear in the Recycle Bin folder? Explain why or why not. Remove the filter, and then close the Recycle Bin window.

9. Make a copy of the Designs folder in the Case1 folder. The name of the duplicate folder appears as Designs - Copy. Rename the Designs - Copy folder as **Sawyer Designs**.

10. Search for the Advanced file and then copy it to the Sawyer Designs folder. Rename this file **Sawyer Classes**.

11. Compress the four photo files in the Sawyer Designs folder in a new compressed folder named **Photos**, and then move the zipped Photos folder to the Case1 folder.

12. Close all open windows.

Case Problem 2

See the Starting Data Files section at the beginning of this module for the list of Data Files needed for this Case Problem.

Avant Web Design Dante Havens is the owner of Avant Web Design, a new website design company in Austin, Texas. You work as a part-time technology assistant at the company and spend some of your time organizing business files. Dante recently upgraded to Windows 10 and asks you to examine the folder structure and file system on his computer, and then begin organizing the files logically. Complete the following steps:

⊕ **Explore** 1. Open a folder window, click the OneDrive icon in the navigation pane, and then open and identify each folder that appears in the OneDrive folder window.

2. Examine the files in the Module2 > Case2 folder provided with your Data Files. Display the Details pane in the folder window and then select each file to display its details. Based on the filenames and the descriptions displayed in the Details pane, create an organization plan for the files.

3. In the Case2 folder, create the folders you need according to your plan.

4. Move the files from the Case2 folder to the subfolders you created.

5. Rename the spreadsheet files in each subfolder as follows. (*Hint:* If Microsoft Excel is not installed on your computer, Windows displays the .xlsx filename extension as you rename the files.)

   - Estimate01: **Websites**
   - Estimate02: **Costs**
   - Estimate03: **Trade Show**
   - Planner01: **Travel**
   - Planner02: **Kincaid**
   - Planner03: **Sorley**

6. Search for a file in the Case2 folder that contains "estimate" in its filename.

7. Open the text document you found, and then add the following tip at the end of the file: **Estimate technology separately**. Save and close the file.

8. Open the folder window for one of the subfolders you created.

9. Change the view of the folder window to Content. Press the Print Screen key to capture an image of the folder window. (*Hint:* Depending on the type of computer you are using, the Print Screen key might be labeled differently, for example, PrtScn.) Start Paint and then press the Ctrl+V keys to paste this image in a file. Save the image as **Content View** in the Module2 > Case2 folder provided with your Data Files. Close Paint.

⊕ **Explore** 10. In one of the Case2 subfolders, compress all Excel workbooks (that is, all .xlsx files) in a new compressed folder named **Spreadsheets** in the Case2 folder. (*Hint:* After you create the compressed folder, move it to the Case2 folder.)

11. Restore your settings by hiding the Details pane.

12. Close all open windows.

Case Problem 3

CHALLENGE

Data Files needed for this Case Problem: Checklist.docx, Client Chart.pdf, Clients.accdb, Clients.pptx, Training.pptx

Tamada Consulting Haruki Tamada founded Tamada Consulting to help small businesses in Tacoma, Washington, grow and prosper. Haruki recently installed Windows 10 on the company's computers, and now finds that he cannot open some files with any installed application. You offer to help him identify the file types and organize the files. Complete the following:

1. Examine the files in the Module2 > Case3 folder provided with your Data Files. In the Case3 folder, create the subfolders you need to organize the files.
2. Use the View tab on the ribbon to display the filename extensions for all of these files. List the filename extensions not already discussed in this module.
⊕ **Explore** 3. Use your favorite search engine to find information about each file type you listed in Step 2. For example, search for PDF files to learn what type of application can open files with a .pdf extension.
4. Move the files from the Case3 folder to the subfolders you created.
5. Open the Checklist file in an application, read the contents, and then close the application. Based on the contents of the Checklist file, move it to a different folder, if necessary.
⊕ **Explore** 6. Open the Checklist file in its new location. Type your name at the beginning of the file, and then use the Save As dialog box to save the file as a different type, such as .rtf or .txt, but using the same location. (*Hint:* Click the Save as type arrow, and then click a file type.) Close the application.
7. Double-click any other file in a Case3 subfolder and describe what happens.
⊕ **Explore** 8. If an application did not start when you double-clicked the file in Step 7, right-click the file, and then click Open with. If you are connected to the Internet, look for an app in the Windows Store that might open this file. Go to the Windows Store and scroll through apps, looking for one that might open the file. Return to the desktop. Describe what you found.
9. Close all open windows.

Case Problem 4

RESEARCH

There are no Data Files needed for this Case Problem.

Business-Centric Brenda Lindauer owns Business-Centric, a corporate training firm in Minneapolis, Minnesota. Brenda and her staff use Windows 10 laptop and tablet computers when they meet with clients to record their training needs. You are working as a technology intern to teach the staff about using their computers efficiently. One common problem is losing versions of files they have created for clients. Brenda asks you to research this problem so the staff can avoid losing files in Windows 10. Complete the following:

1. Windows 10 provides a feature called File History, which will be very helpful to the company employees. Search Windows websites to find information on File History. What is the purpose of this feature?
2. Search the Windows 10 How-to webpages to learn how to use OneDrive to back up files.
3. Search the Windows 10 How-to webpages to find topics about restoring (or recovering) files. Which Windows 10 tools let you restore (or recover) files?
4. Search the Windows 10 How-to webpages to learn about system image backups. What is a system image and why would you create one?

OBJECTIVES

Session 3.1
- Explore the Settings app and the Control Panel
- Customize the desktop and lock screen
- Change display settings
- Personalize desktop icons
- Create desktop shortcuts

Session 3.2
- Modify the taskbar
- Use taskbar tools
- Personalize the Start menu
- Pin items to the Start menu
- Change the user account picture

Personalizing Your Windows Environment

Changing Desktop Settings

WINDOWS

Case | *Crafted Quilts*

Crafted Quilts is a business based in Springfield, Massachusetts, that sells custom quilts directly to customers through a website and a retail store. Rachel Shearer started the company with Mai Vang about two years ago. Mai now travels throughout the United States to find antique quilts and to contract with quilters, while Rachel runs the website and manages the store in Springfield.

You have been working as the office manager for Crafted Quilts for a few months, providing general assistance to Rachel, Mai, and the staff. Rachel recently upgraded the office computers to Windows 10, and now she asks you to customize those computers so that everyone can access frequently used apps, important files, and computer resources. She also wants the desktop to reflect the image of Crafted Quilts. You will start by personalizing Rachel's computer so she can approve the changes. Later, she will apply the changes to the other office computers.

STARTING DATA FILES

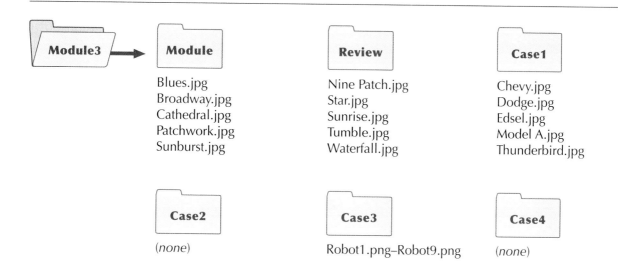

Module3 → Module
Blues.jpg
Broadway.jpg
Cathedral.jpg
Patchwork.jpg
Sunburst.jpg

Review
Nine Patch.jpg
Star.jpg
Sunrise.jpg
Tumble.jpg
Waterfall.jpg

Case1
Chevy.jpg
Dodge.jpg
Edsel.jpg
Model A.jpg
Thunderbird.jpg

Case2
(*none*)

Case3
Robot1.png–Robot9.png

Case4
(*none*)

Session 3.1 Visual Overview:

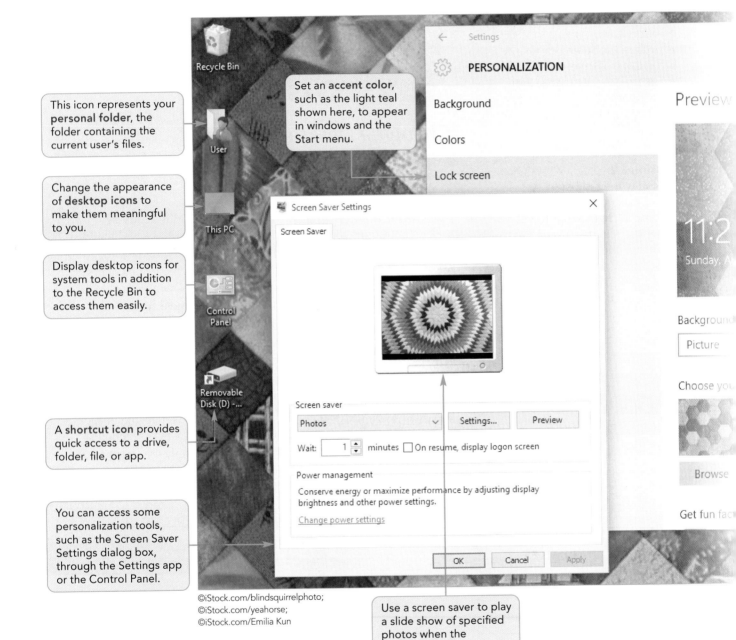

This icon represents your **personal folder**, the folder containing the current user's files.

Change the appearance of **desktop icons** to make them meaningful to you.

Display desktop icons for system tools in addition to the Recycle Bin to access them easily.

A **shortcut icon** provides quick access to a drive, folder, file, or app.

You can access some personalization tools, such as the Screen Saver Settings dialog box, through the Settings app or the Control Panel.

Set an **accent color**, such as the light teal shown here, to appear in windows and the Start menu.

Settings

PERSONALIZATION

Background

Colors

Lock screen

Screen Saver Settings

Screen Saver

Screen saver

Photos   Settings...   Preview

Wait: 1   minutes ☐ On resume, display logon screen

Power management

Conserve energy or maximize performance by adjusting display brightness and other power settings.

Change power settings

OK   Cancel   Apply

Preview

11:2

Sunday, A

Backgroun

Picture

Choose you

Browse

Get fun fac

Use a screen saver to play a slide show of specified photos when the computer is idle.

©iStock.com/blindsquirrelphoto;
©iStock.com/yeahorse;
©iStock.com/Emilia Kun

Customized Desktop

Choose your own picture to display on the lock screen.

Change this setting to **Windows spotlight** to have Windows select lock screen pictures from the bing.com home page.

The background image is part of the desktop **theme**, a collection of settings that determines the appearance of the desktop.

The Personalization window is part of the **Settings app**, a Windows app for changing system settings.

Changing Windows Settings

Windows 10 provides two ways to customize your computer's settings: the Settings app and the **Control Panel**, each with its own user interface. Both are tools you use to customize the computer and select system-wide settings. The settings in the Control Panel affect only the desktop and desktop apps. Because the Settings app is a Windows app, it includes settings that affect only Windows apps. In addition, the Settings app provides settings for customizing the desktop. Because the Settings app runs on all types of Windows devices, including tablets and phones, it provides a touch-friendly interface, so you change many settings using a fingertip if you have a touchscreen.

The Control Panel was originally designed for earlier versions of Windows, so it uses a design familiar to users of desktop and laptop computers without touchscreens. The Control Panel provides access to traditional dialog boxes that let you select or change the **properties**, or characteristics, of an object. For example, you can change the picture displayed for the Recycle Bin icon on the desktop. Both the Control Panel and the Settings app organize settings into similar categories, allowing you to easily change the way Windows looks and behaves to better suit the way you work.

To become acquainted with the difference between the Control Panel and the Settings app, you'll open their main windows, beginning with the Control Panel.

To open the Control Panel:

▶ **1.** Click the **Start** button ▦ to display the Start menu, and then type **Control Panel** to search for the app.

▶ **2.** In the search results, click **Control Panel** to open the Control Panel home page. See Figure 3-1.

| Figure 3-1 | Control Panel home page |

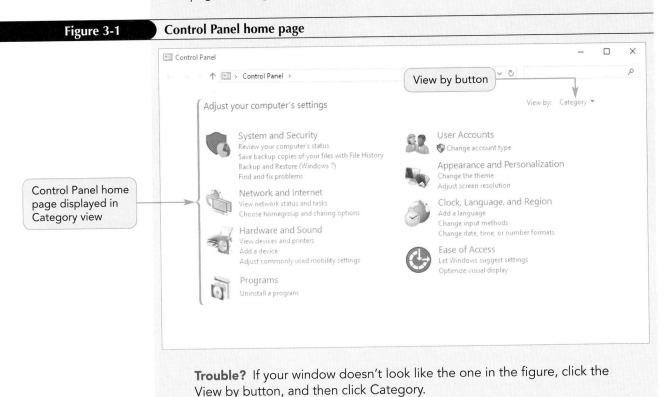

Trouble? If your window doesn't look like the one in the figure, click the View by button, and then click Category.

Trouble? If your icons look slightly different from those in the figure, Microsoft updated the icons, which it does from time to time. The appearance of the icons does not affect the way the Control Panel works.

By default, the Control Panel home page displays tools in Category view, which groups similar tools into eight categories. See Figure 3-2.

Figure 3-2   **Control Panel categories**

Control Panel Category	Typical Tasks
System and Security	Schedule maintenance checks, increase the space on your hard disk, maintain Windows security settings, and keep Windows up to date.
Network and Internet	Set Internet options, view network status, and set up a homegroup to share files and perform other network tasks.
Hardware and Sound	Change the sounds on your computer, and change the settings for your printer, keyboard, mouse, camera, and other hardware.
Programs	Install and uninstall programs and Windows features, and set options for default settings and programs.
User Accounts	Change user account settings and set email options.
Appearance and Personalization	Change the appearance of desktop items, apply a theme or screen saver, and customize the Start menu and taskbar.
Clock, Language, and Region	Change the date, time, and time zone; the language you use on your computer; and the format for numbers, currencies, dates, and times.
Ease of Access	Change computer settings for vision, hearing, and mobility.

For most of the customization settings you change in this module, you can use the Settings app, so you can begin your work for Crafted Quilts by closing the Control Panel, starting the Settings app, and then examining its categories of settings.

To start the Settings app:

1. Close the Control Panel window.

2. Click the **Start** button ⊞ to display the Start menu, and then click **Settings** to start the Settings app. See Figure 3-3.

Figure 3-3   Settings app

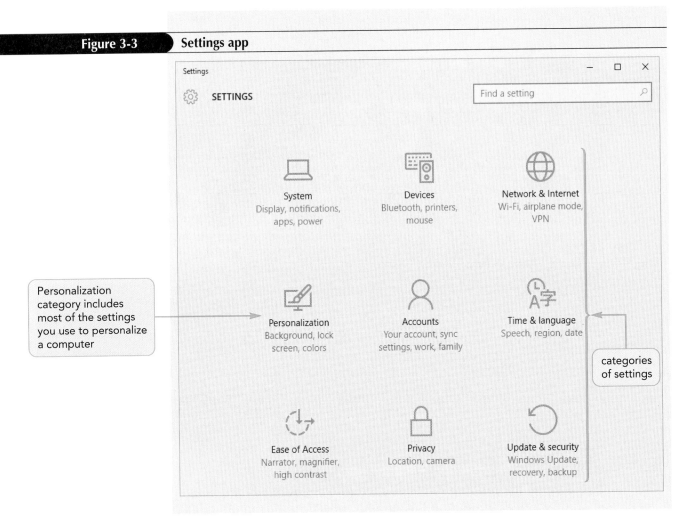

Personalization category includes most of the settings you use to personalize a computer

The main screen of the Settings app is also called the Settings home page. It lists nine categories of settings you can change in Windows. Figure 3-4 describes these categories.

Figure 3-4   Settings app categories

Category	Change Settings for:
System	Display, notifications, apps, power, and system
Devices	Printers and scanners, connected devices, Bluetooth devices, and mouse and touchpad, typing, and AutoPlay behavior
Network & Internet	Wi-Fi, airplane mode, data usage, and network connections
Personalization	Desktop background, system colors, lock screen, themes, and Start menu
Accounts	User accounts, sign-in options, and synchronizing with other Windows devices
Time & language	Date, time, time zone, and the language you use on your computer
Ease of Access	Vision, hearing, and mobility features
Privacy	Privacy options related to location, camera, microphone, Windows apps, and devices
Update & security	Windows updates and computer and data protection

Some of the categories in the Settings app, such as the Ease of Access category, provide the same type of settings as the Control Panel but use a Windows app interface. Other categories, such as Personalization, let you change settings using the Control Panel but are included in the Settings app for convenience.

To change a particular setting, you can select a category to open a category window, which lists the settings you can change. For example, you can open the Personalization window to change the desktop background or to set a theme.

To open the Personalization window:

▌ **1.** On the Settings home page, click **Personalization**. The Personalization window opens, showing the settings related to personalizing your computer's appearance. See Figure 3-5. Your current settings and options might differ.

| Figure 3-5 | Personalization window |

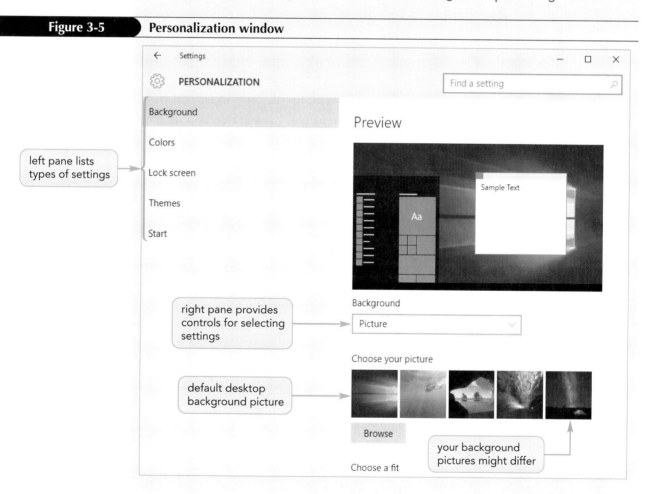

left pane lists types of settings

right pane provides controls for selecting settings

default desktop background picture

your background pictures might differ

The Personalization window, like the other category windows in the Settings app, lists types of settings in the left pane. The right pane is a panel with controls for changing the selected type of setting. Background is selected by default. You use the Background settings in the right pane to change the picture displayed on the desktop background and set other background options.

While Mai is on a buying trip, you'll work with Rachel to customize her computer. She wants the office computers to reflect the image of Crafted Quilts, and she'd like the desktop itself to be more appealing to her and her employees. You'll work with the Settings app to personalize Rachel's desktop.

Changing the Desktop Background

TIP

To display any picture saved on your computer as your desktop background, right-click the picture and then click Set as desktop background.

You can change the desktop background, or its **wallpaper**, to display one of the pictures that Windows provides, or you can select your own picture to use as wallpaper. When you change the background, you are not placing a new object on the desktop; you are only changing its appearance. You can also determine how you want to position the picture—resized to fill the screen, resized to fit the screen, stretched across the screen (which might distort the picture), tiled (repeated across the screen), or centered. If you center the picture on the screen, you can select a color to frame the background picture.

REFERENCE

Changing the Desktop Picture

- Click the Start button and then click Settings.
- Click Personalization and then click Picture in the Background box in the right pane.
- In the Choose your picture section, click a picture to display as the desktop background, or click the Browse button and then select a picture stored on your computer.

In addition to displaying a picture, you can display a solid color as the desktop background or play a slide show of pictures.

If you have more than one device running Windows 8 or later, Windows can synchronize the desktop backgrounds. For example, suppose you are using a tablet at school and a laptop at home, both running Windows 10. If you change the desktop background on the tablet, and then return home and sign into Windows 10 on your laptop, the laptop displays the same desktop background picture as the tablet.

You and Rachel decide to examine the desktop backgrounds that Windows provides to find a suitable picture.

To change the desktop background:

1. If necessary, click **Background** in the left pane of the Personalization window to display the Background settings. Note your current desktop background picture so you can restore it later.

2. Click the **Background** box and then click **Picture**, if necessary.

3. In the Choose your picture section, click the picture of someone swimming underwater. See Figure 3-6. Your Background settings might differ.

Figure 3-6	Background settings

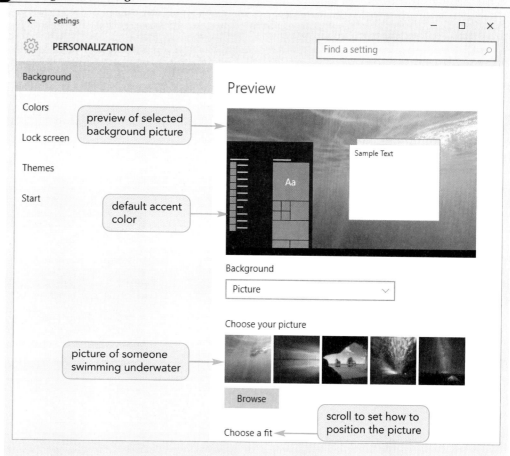

Trouble? If the picture of someone swimming underwater isn't available, choose any picture other than the current one.

▶ **4.** Minimize the Personalization window to see the new background picture.

After examining the desktop, Rachel doesn't think the underwater picture is right for her business. However, she didn't notice other more appropriate pictures in the Choose your picture section of the Background settings. She does have a picture of a quilt that she often uses in promotional materials. You offer to show her how to use that picture as the desktop background.

To use a different picture as the desktop background:

▶ **1.** Make sure your computer can access your Data Files for this module. For example, if you are using a USB flash drive, insert the drive into the USB port.

> **Trouble?** If you don't have the starting Data Files, you need to get them before you can proceed. Your instructor will either give you the Data Files or ask you to obtain them from a specified location (such as a network drive). If you have any questions about the Data Files, see your instructor or technical support person for assistance.

▶ **2.** Click the **Settings** button 🔧 on the taskbar to restore the Personalization window.

▶ 3. Click the **Browse** button to open the Open dialog box.

▶ 4. Navigate to the **Module3 > Module** folder provided with your Data Files.

▶ 5. Click the **Blues** picture file, and then click the **Choose picture** button. The Blues picture appears as the desktop background. See Figure 3-7.

Figure 3-7   **Desktop background with Blues picture**

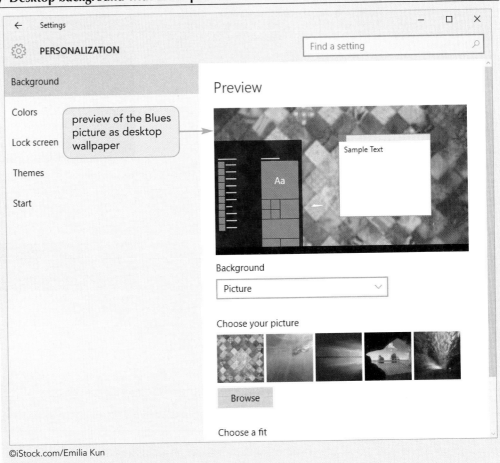

©iStock.com/Emilia Kun

Rachel likes the new picture but comments that she would prefer more colorful windows, preferably using a color that coordinates with the background picture. You'll show her how to change the colors of the desktop.

Changing Desktop Colors

Besides changing the desktop background, you can use the Colors settings in the Personalization window to set the accent, or contrasting, color of windows and the Start menu. Windows uses the accent color in several places to create contrast or visual interest. For example, Windows apps use the accent color for icons and the highlight bar that indicates a selection. The Start menu uses the accent color as a background for icons and tiles.

You can select an accent color from a palette of almost 50 colors or let Windows select an accent color from the background picture.

By default, the Start menu, taskbar, and action center are semitransparent and black. (The **action center** is a panel that keeps track of your notifications.) You can change the Colors settings so that these items show the selected accent color and are opaque rather than transparent.

Rachel wants all the Crafted Quilts computers to apply an accent color to the icons and highlight bar in Windows apps and as a background for icons and tiles on the Start menu.

To change the accent color:

▶ **1.** In the Personalization window, click **Colors** in the left pane to display the Colors settings. See Figure 3-8. Note the current accent color so you can restore it later.

Figure 3-8   **Colors settings**

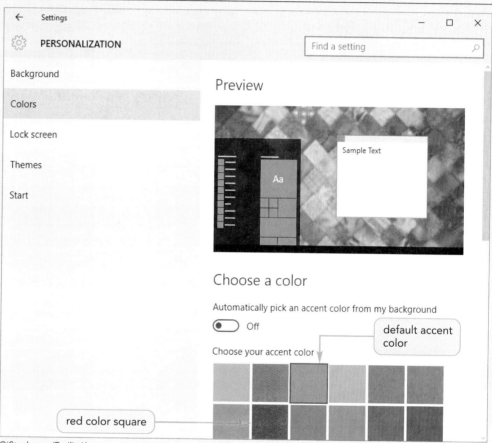

©iStock.com/Emilia Kun

▶ **2.** Click the **red square**, which is in the second column and second row of the accent color palette. The Settings icon and highlight bar change to red.

▶ **3.** On the Choose a color slider, drag the **slider button** from Off to On. Windows changes the red accent color to one it finds in the Blues background picture.

Rachel wants all of the Crafted Quilts computers to use the same accent color, so you'll show her how to select a different one from the color palette.

▶ **4.** On the Choose a color slider, drag the **slider button** from On to Off, and then click the **teal** color square, the color square in the fourth column and third row of the palette. See Figure 3-9.

Figure 3-9   New accent color

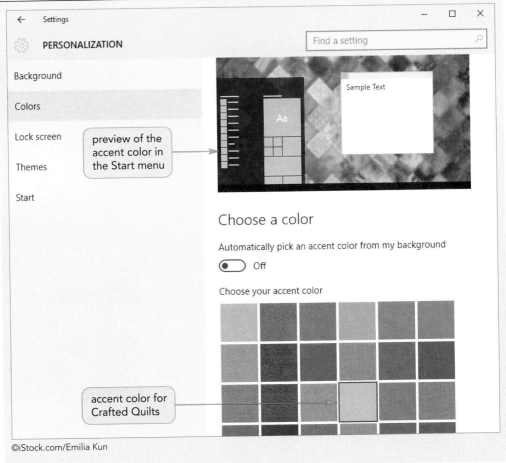

©iStock.com/Emilia Kun

The desktop is now personalized for Rachel and displays the Blues quilt picture and coordinated accent color. You'll show Rachel how to personalize the Windows lock screen next.

Personalizing the Lock Screen

Recall that shortly after you start Windows 10, the lock screen appears to display a picture, the date, and the time. The lock screen also appears when you wake your computer from sleep or hibernation. By default, the lock screen displays Windows spotlight pictures, which are photos from the bing.com home page. (Bing.com is a website you use to search the Internet and is owned by Microsoft.) The lock screen also displays facts, tips, and links related to Windows. You can personalize the lock screen by clicking a link to vote for pictures you like. Windows will select pictures based on your votes and display them on the lock screen.

REFERENCE

Changing the Lock Screen Picture

- Click the Start button and then click Settings.
- Click Personalization, and then in the left pane, click Lock screen.
- Click the Background box, and then click a picture to display as the desktop background, or click the Browse button and then select a picture stored on your computer.

You can also set the lock screen background to display a picture of your choice or play a slide show of pictures. If you want to display a single picture, you can choose one of the built-in lock screen pictures, which are different from the desktop pictures, or you can choose one of your own. For a slide show, select the Pictures folder on your computer to display pictures stored in that folder or add a different Pictures folder, such as the one stored on your OneDrive.

By default, Windows also displays facts, tips, and links on the lock screen pictures and slide shows you select, though you can change this setting to display the pictures only. In addition, you can select apps to provide helpful information on the lock screen. For example, you can display details about today's appointments stored in the Calendar app or a brief overview of the weather in your location.

Instead of using the Windows spotlight images, Rachel wants to display a picture of a different quilt on the lock screen.

To change the lock screen picture:

▶ **1.** In the Personalization window, click **Lock screen** in the left pane to display the Lock screen settings. See Figure 3-10. Your lock screen picture will differ. Note the current settings so you can restore them later.

Figure 3-10	**Lock screen settings**

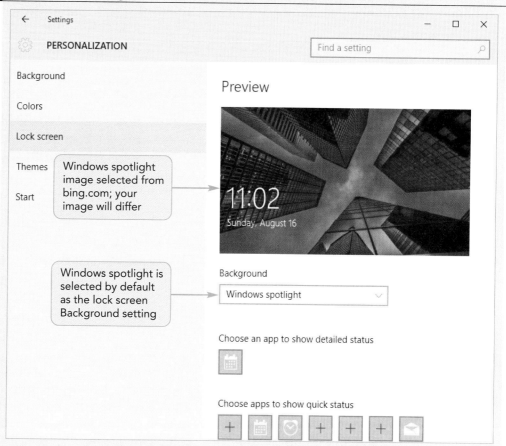

▶ **2.** Click the **Background** box and then click **Picture** to display the options for using a Picture as the lock screen background.

▶ **3.** Click the **Browse** button to open the Open dialog box so you can select a lock screen picture.

▶ **4.** If necessary, navigate to the **Module3 > Module** folder provided with your Data Files.

▶ **5.** Click the **Patchwork** picture file, and then click the **Choose picture** button. The Patchwork picture appears as the lock screen background. See Figure 3-11.

Figure 3-11   **Personalized lock screen picture**

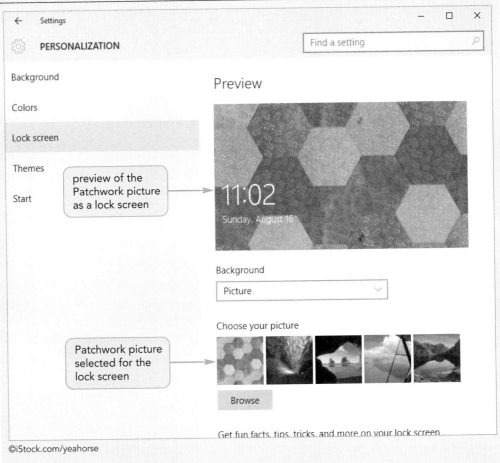

preview of the Patchwork picture as a lock screen

Patchwork picture selected for the lock screen

©iStock.com/yeahorse

The next time the computer starts or wakes up from sleep or hibernation, it will display the new lock screen picture.

Activating a Screen Saver

No matter which lock screen setting you select, you can also set your computer to use a screen saver, a program that clears images from your screen or displays a moving design after the computer has been idle for a specified period of time. Screen savers can be entertaining and handy for hiding your data from others if you step away from your computer. Windows 10 comes with several screen savers. Some show an animated design, whereas another plays a slide show of pictures stored on your computer. When a screen saver is on, you display the lock screen by moving your mouse or pressing a key. You can then return to the desktop the way you normally do.

You can select how long you want the computer to sit idle before the screen saver starts. Most users find settings between 3 and 10 minutes to be the most convenient. You set up a screen saver and specify the idle time using the options in the Screen Saver Settings dialog box.

Using a Screen Saver for Security

To enhance the security of your computer and prevent unauthorized people from accessing your files, take advantage of a security setting available in the Screen Saver Settings dialog box. To have the screen saver request your user name and password before displaying your desktop, select the check box in this dialog box labeled "On resume, display logon screen." This means that only you and other people who know your user name and password can work with your desktop and files.

Rachel wants to examine the screen savers that Windows provides and then choose the most appropriate one for her organization.

To activate a screen saver:

1. Scroll the Lock screen settings, if necessary, to click the **Screen saver settings** link at the bottom of the Personalization window. The Screen Saver Settings dialog box opens. See Figure 3-12. Note the name of the current screen saver so you can restore it later.

   Trouble? If the Screen Saver Settings dialog box opens behind the Personalization window, click the title bar of the dialog box or click the Screen Saver Settings taskbar button 🖼 to make it the active window.

Figure 3-12   Screen Saver Settings dialog box

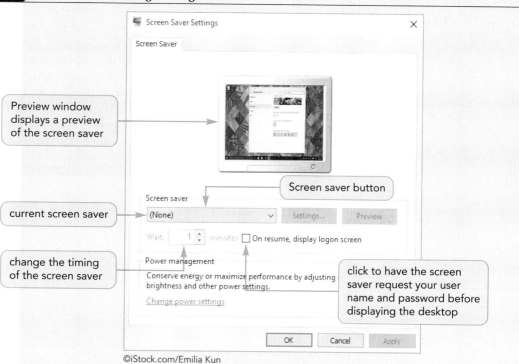

Preview window displays a preview of the screen saver

Screen saver button

current screen saver

change the timing of the screen saver

click to have the screen saver request your user name and password before displaying the desktop

©iStock.com/Emilia Kun

2. Click the **Screen saver** button to display the screen savers installed on your computer.

3. Click **Ribbons**. The animated screen saver plays in the Preview window. Rachel likes that screen saver, but it's not appropriate for her company. You suggest the Photos screen saver, which plays a slide show of the pictures and videos stored in the Pictures folder by default.

▶ **4.** Click the **Screen saver** button, and then click **Photos**. By default, the preview window plays a slide show of the graphics files stored in the Pictures folder, if any.

▶ **5.** To display pictures of quilts, click the **Settings** button to open the Photos Screen Saver Settings dialog box. You use this dialog box to specify which files to include in the slide show and to select other settings, such as the slide show speed.

▶ **6.** Click the **Browse** button. The Browse For Folder dialog box opens.

▶ **7.** Navigate to the **Module3 > Module** folder provided with your Data Files, and then click the **OK** button to indicate you want to include all the pictures in the Module folder in the screen saver slide show.

▶ **8.** Click the **Save** button to close the Photos Screen Saver Settings dialog box. Now only the pictures in the Module3 > Module folder appear in the Preview window.

▶ **9.** Click the **OK** button to close the Screen Saver Settings dialog box.

After your computer is idle for a minute or so, the screen saver will start, playing a slide show of the photos.

Now that Rachel has personalized the desktop, lock screen, and screen saver, you'll show her how to save these settings as a theme.

Selecting Themes

Instead of selecting individual settings for the desktop background and screen saver, you can also personalize the desktop by selecting a theme. When you select a theme, you select one or more desktop background pictures, an accent color, a collection of sounds to signal system tasks, such as shutting down Windows, and a screen saver. Windows themes include collections of high-resolution pictures. Instead of working with separate desktop background pictures, you can select one of the pictures in a theme to display as the desktop background, or you can play a slide show of the pictures and switch from one picture to another after a specified amount of time. Windows also provides a few high-contrast themes, which make the items on your screen easier to see.

REFERENCE

Selecting a Theme

- Click the Start button and then click Settings.
- Click Personalization.
- In the left pane, click Themes.
- In the right pane, click Theme settings.
- Click a theme.

or

- Open the Control Panel and switch to Category view, if necessary.
- Click Appearance and Personalization.
- Click Personalization.
- Click a theme.

Rachel asks you to show her a few desktop themes to see if one would be suitable for Crafted Quilts.

To change the theme:

▶ **1.** In the Personalization window, click **Themes** in the left pane.

▶ **2.** Click **Theme settings** in the right pane to open the Control Panel's Personalization window, which lists many types of themes. See Figure 3-13. Your Personalization window might differ.

| Figure 3-13 | Themes in the Control Panel Personalization window |

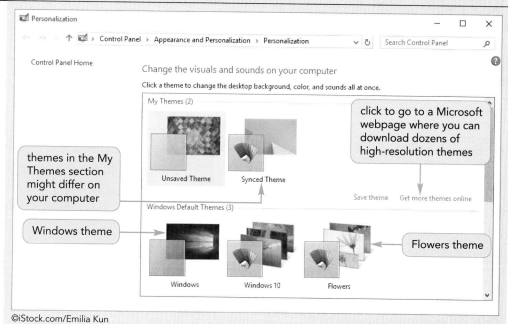

©iStock.com/Emilia Kun

▶ **3.** If necessary, scroll the themes, and then click **Flowers**. The desktop background changes to a picture of a large flower, the taskbar and window borders change color, and a sound plays (if your speakers are turned on). Minimize the Control Panel's Personalization window to see more of the picture, and then restore the window.

   Trouble? If the Flowers theme does not appear in your Personalization window, select any other theme that displays photos.

The Control Panel's Personalization window includes a Get more themes online link, which you can click to start a browser and visit a Microsoft webpage listing themes organized into categories such as Featured, Animals, and Natural wonders. To use an online theme, click the Download link for the theme. When the download is finished, the browser displays a message in which you can click the Open button to add the theme to the Control Panel's Personalization window.

The Flowers theme is not as suitable for Crafted Quilts as the Blues quilt background picture and teal accent color. Windows is keeping track of your customized settings in case you want to save them as a new theme.

Saving Themes

After personalizing the desktop, you can save the settings as a theme. If you save the current settings as a theme, you can apply all of the changes—the Blues picture desktop background, the teal accent color, and the screen saver—at the same time, without selecting the individual settings again. By default, Windows stores the theme files in a system folder. You can create your own theme file—called a **theme pack**—that you can store in a folder of your choice, and then share that theme with other people running Windows 8 or later on their computers. Although you cannot move or copy a theme from a system folder, you can move or copy a theme pack.

If you change settings that affect the desktop appearance, sounds, or screen saver, Windows records the changes in a theme called Unsaved Theme. For example, if you select the Flowers theme and then change the accent color to blue, Windows records that change in the Unsaved Theme. If you want to switch themes but return to the Flowers theme with the blue accent color, you can save the Unsaved Theme as Blue Flowers, for example. The original Flowers theme remains unchanged.

You will save the desktop settings you created for Rachel as a theme and a theme pack, both called Crafted Quilts. Rachel will use the theme pack and the photos in the Module folder to apply the Crafted Quilts theme to other office computers. Before saving a theme, you must select the one you want to save. In this case, you select the Unsaved Theme, which still includes all the settings customized for Rachel.

To save the desktop settings as a theme:

TIP

The Unsaved Theme stores any changes you make to the current theme settings in case you want to save those changes as a new theme.

1. In the My Themes section of the Control Panel's Personalization window, click **Unsaved Theme** to select it as the desktop theme.

2. Click the **Save theme** link to open the Save Theme As dialog box.

3. Type **Crafted Quilts** as the name of this theme.

4. Click the **Save** button. The Crafted Quilts theme now appears in the My Themes section.

5. To save the theme so that others at Crafted Quilts can use it, right-click the **Crafted Quilts** theme in the Personalization window, and then click **Save theme for sharing** on the shortcut menu.

6. In the Save Theme Pack As dialog box, navigate to the **Module3 > Module** folder provided with your Data Files.

7. Click in the **File name** box, if necessary, and then type **Crafted Quilts**. Note that the Save as type is Desktop Theme Pack (*.deskthemepack).

8. Click the **Save** button. Windows saves the Crafted Quilts theme pack file in the Module folder.

9. Close the Personalization windows for the Control Panel and the Settings app.

Next, you can explore the display properties that affect the sharpness of the images on your desktop.

Changing Display Settings

After working with the properties for the desktop background, theme, and screen saver, you're ready to explore the properties that affect the computer display itself. For example, you can set the size of the desktop and choose whether to use more than one display. Windows selects the best settings, including screen resolution and orientation, based on your display hardware. **Screen resolution** is the number of horizontal and vertical pixels on a display screen, which determines the clarity of the text and images on your screen. (A **pixel**, short for "picture element," is an individual point of color.) At higher resolutions, items appear sharper and smaller, so more items fit on the screen. At lower resolutions, fewer items fit on the screen, but they are larger and easier to see. At very low resolutions, however, images might have jagged edges. Selecting the best settings for your display enhances your Windows experience.

INSIGHT

Selecting the Best Settings for Your Display

Laptop and desktop computers have a standard or widescreen liquid crystal display (LCD) screen. Settings for standard LCD display screens typically differ from those for widescreen displays. However, all LCD screens show the sharpest images and clearest text at a particular resolution, which is called their **native resolution**. Screen resolution is measured horizontally and vertically in pixels. For example, many 19-inch standard LCD screens have a native resolution of 1280 × 1024. A 22-inch widescreen LCD screen usually has a native resolution of 1680 × 1050. You can change the resolution to a lower setting, such as 1024 × 768, to make the on-screen objects larger, although the text might not be as clear as text displayed at the native resolution. If you are using a standard display screen, be sure to select a resolution with an aspect ratio of 4:3, such as 1024 × 768. (An **aspect ratio** is the ratio of the width to the height.) If you are using a widescreen display, select a resolution with an aspect ratio of 16:9 or 16:10, such as 1366 × 768.

Changing the Screen Resolution

In the Settings app, you use the Advanced Display Settings window to change the screen resolution. The Resolution box lists the available resolutions for your display screen. Select a setting to increase or decrease the resolution, or sharpness, of the desktop image. You will change the screen resolution from its current setting to 1024 × 768, if that setting is not already selected, and then back to its original setting.

To change the screen resolution:

1. Right-click the **desktop** and then click **Display settings** on the shortcut menu to open the System window in the Settings app with Display selected in the left pane.

2. Scroll down, if necessary, and then click the **Advanced display settings** link to open the Advanced Display Settings window. Note the original setting in the Resolution box so you can restore it later.

3. Click the **Resolution** box to list the settings available for your display. See Figure 3-14. Your settings might differ.

Figure 3-14 **Changing the screen resolution**

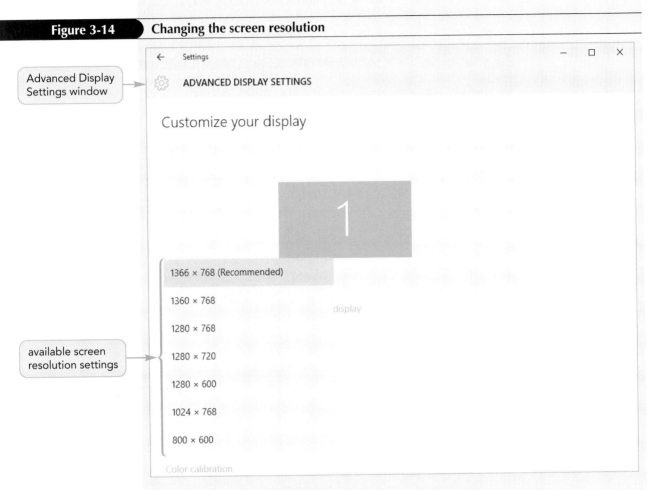

4. Click the **1024 × 768** resolution, if possible.

   Trouble? If your Resolution settings do not include the 1024 × 768 resolution, choose a different resolution.

5. Click the **Apply** button to select the new screen resolution.

6. When Windows asks you to confirm the change, click the **Keep changes** button to change the screen resolution, and then minimize the Advanced Display Settings window to view the change to the desktop.

7. To return to the original resolution, display the Advanced Display Settings window again, click the **Resolution** box, click the original resolution, such as 1366 × 768, click the **Apply** button, and then click the **Keep changes** button.

If you select a screen resolution recommended for your display but find the text and objects are now too large or small, you can adjust the size of the text and objects.

Changing the Size of Text and Objects

Without adjusting your screen resolution, you can change the size of the text and objects, such as icons on your screen. This means you can increase or decrease the size of text and objects while maintaining the native resolution of your monitor. For example, if you use a low screen resolution, such as 1024 × 768, you can make text and objects smaller to display more information on the screen. Conversely, if you use a high resolution, you can make text and objects easier to see by making them larger while retaining the sharpness of the high resolution.

Rachel's computer uses the 100% setting, which is the default for her display. You'll view the other settings to see if they would improve the appearance of her desktop.

To view the display settings:

▶ **1.** In the Advanced Display Settings window, click the **Back** button ⬅ to return to the System window with the Display category selected.

▶ **2.** On the Change the size of text, apps, and other items slider, drag the **slider button** to 125%.

Trouble? If the 125% setting is already selected, drag to the 100% setting.

▶ **3.** Click the **Apply** button to apply the new setting. The text and objects in the Display window are larger and easy to see, but they take up too much space.

Trouble? If a window opens requesting you to sign in again for the best experience, click the Sign out later button.

▶ **4.** On the Change the size of text, apps, and other items slider, drag the **slider button** to your original setting, such as 100% (Recommended), and then click the **Apply** button.

Trouble? If a window opens requesting you to sign in again for the best experience, click the Sign out later button.

▶ **5.** Close the System window.

Personalizing Desktop Icons

As you know, the desktop displays a background picture, the Recycle Bin icon, and the taskbar by default. Your desktop might also include other icons installed by your computer manufacturer or your school.

Because the desktop provides your first view of the computer and its contents, it should contain the items you want to access when you start your computer. You can place icons on the desktop that represent objects you want to access quickly or frequently, such as Windows tools, drives, programs, and documents. Windows provides desktop icons for system tools, such as the Recycle Bin and This PC. You can add or remove these icons according to your work preferences. Figure 3-15 shows the types of icons you can include on the desktop and the objects they represent.

Figure 3-15   Types of desktop icons

Icon	Description
	This PC icon
	Control Panel icon
	Document shortcut icon
	Drive shortcut icon
	Folder shortcut icon
	Network icon
	Program shortcut icon (such as Paint)
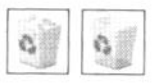	Recycle Bin icon (full and empty)
	User folder icon

Besides the built-in desktop icons for system tools, you can use shortcuts to start an app or access an object. Double-clicking a shortcut on the desktop opens its associated file, folder, device, or app. When you delete a shortcut or desktop icon, you delete only the icon—the file or resource it represents remains in its original location. You typically create shortcuts on the desktop (or elsewhere, such as in a folder) to locations, files, and devices that you use often.

PROSKILLS

Problem Solving: Simplifying Tasks with Shortcuts

If you work with many devices, apps, or folders, it might be difficult to access all of these resources efficiently. One way to solve this problem is to add shortcuts to the desktop. Shortcut icons can simplify tasks you perform regularly. For example, you can create a shortcut icon for a USB drive and then drag files to the shortcut icon to copy them to the removable disk. You also can create a shortcut icon for a desktop app you use often, such as Paint, and then double-click the icon to start the app. Some apps add a shortcut icon to the desktop when you install the app. If you work with a particular folder often, you can add a desktop shortcut to the folder. That way, you can double-click the folder shortcut to open the folder without navigating many folder windows.

You'll show Rachel how to add icons to the desktop for system tools she uses often and how to create a shortcut icon on the desktop to a USB drive.

Adding Icons to the Desktop

Windows provides five standard icons that you can display on the desktop. Besides the Recycle Bin, which appears on the desktop by default, you can display the This PC icon (also called the Computer icon) to provide easy access to the This PC window and therefore the drives and devices connected to your computer. If you display the desktop icon for your personal folder (that is, the folder containing the current user's files), you can quickly find and open the folders containing your documents. Having the Network icon on the desktop gives you access to a window that lists the shared computers and other devices on your network. You can also add the Control Panel icon to the desktop and then use that desktop app to change the way Windows looks and behaves.

Rachel mentions that the Windows tools she plans to use most frequently are her personal folder, This PC, and the Control Panel. You'll add these icons to Rachel's desktop.

To display standard desktop icons:

▶ **1.** Right-click a blank area of the **desktop**, and then click **Personalize** on the shortcut menu. The Settings app starts and opens the Personalization window.

▶ **2.** In the left pane, click **Themes**.

▶ **3.** In the Related Settings section of the right pane, click **Desktop icon settings**. The Desktop Icon Settings dialog box opens. See Figure 3-16. The Recycle Bin check box is already selected, indicating that Windows is displaying the Recycle Bin icon on the desktop.

TIP

Note that the Recycle Bin icon has two appearances: one when it is empty, and another when it contains deleted items.

| **Figure 3-16** | **Desktop Icon Settings dialog box** |

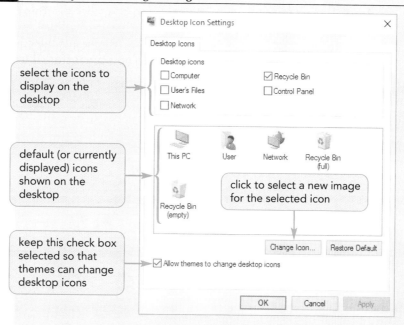

select the icons to display on the desktop

default (or currently displayed) icons shown on the desktop

keep this check box selected so that themes can change desktop icons

Trouble? If you are working in a computer lab, you might not be able to open the Desktop Icon Settings dialog box. In that case, read but do not perform the remaining steps in this section and the next section.

Trouble? If the settings in your Desktop Icon Settings dialog box differ from those in the figure, note the current options so you can restore them later, and then change the options so only the Recycle Bin check box is selected.

4. Click the **Computer**, **User's Files**, and **Control Panel** check boxes.

5. Click the **Apply** button to apply the changes but keep the Desktop Icon Settings dialog box open, and then drag the dialog box to the middle of the desktop so you can see the icons for your personal folder, This PC, and the Control Panel on the left side of the desktop.

Some themes include customized desktop icons. If the Allow themes to change desktop icons check box is checked (which it is by default) in the Desktop Icon Settings dialog box, the icons change when you select a new theme. If you want the desktop icons to always keep their appearance, click to remove the check mark from the check box.

Now that you've added desktop icons for Rachel, you can customize their appearance according to her preferences.

Changing the Appearance of Desktop Icons

You can change the images displayed on the desktop icons using the Change Icon dialog box, which you open from the Desktop Icon Settings dialog box. Change the image to suit your preferences or to display a more accurate image. For example, the This PC icon shows an image of a desktop computer. If you work on a different type of computer, you might want to change this image to match your computer type.

Because Rachel works on an all-in-one computer, with the computer and display screen built in to the same case, she wants to change the image for the This PC icon on the desktop.

To change the image of the This PC icon:

▶ **1.** In the Desktop Icon Settings dialog box, click the **This PC** icon, and then click the **Change Icon** button. The Change Icon dialog box opens to display images you can apply to the icon and highlights the current image. Note the image used for the This PC icon so you can restore it later.

▶ **2.** Click the icon directly below the current icon, as shown in Figure 3-17.

Figure 3-17 ▶ **Changing the default This PC icon**

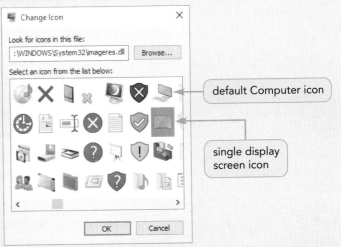

Trouble? If the computer display image shown in the figure does not appear in your Change Icon dialog box, click any other suitable image.

▶ **3.** Click the **OK** button to close the Change Icon dialog box.

▶ **4.** Click the **OK** button to close the Desktop Icon Settings dialog box, and then close the Personalization window. The This PC icon on the desktop now appears as a single display screen.

The standard Windows desktop icons provide quick access to common Windows tools. These are standard tools that Windows provides to simplify or enhance your computer work. However, other items you access often (such as documents, folders, and drives) might be different from the items other users access often. In addition, the folders you use frequently one week might differ from those you use frequently the next week. To personalize your desktop to provide quick access to these items, you can create and use shortcuts.

Creating Desktop Shortcuts

On the desktop, you can create shortcuts to access drives, documents, files, apps, or other computer resources, such as a network folder. For example, you can easily open a document from the desktop by creating a shortcut icon for the document. A shortcut icon for a document works much the same way as a document icon does in a folder window—you can double-click the shortcut icon to open the document in the appropriate program. However, a shortcut icon is only a link to the actual document. If you move the icon, you move only the shortcut, not the document itself. One advantage of using shortcut icons is that if your desktop becomes cluttered, you can delete the shortcut icons without affecting the original documents.

You can also create shortcut icons for the folders, drives, and devices on your computer. This way, you can access your local hard disk, for example, directly from the desktop, instead of having to open a folder window and then navigate to the hard disk.

Windows provides several ways of creating shortcuts on the desktop. Figure 3-18 summarizes the techniques you can use to create shortcuts. The one you choose is a matter of personal preference.

Figure 3-18   Methods for creating shortcuts

Method	Description
Drag (for drives and devices only)	To create a drive shortcut on the desktop, use a folder window to locate the drive icon, and then drag the icon to the desktop.
Right-drag	Use a folder window to locate and select an icon, hold down the right mouse button, and then drag the icon to a new location. Release the mouse button and click Create shortcuts here on the shortcut menu.
Right-click, Create shortcut	Use a folder window to locate an icon, right-click the icon, click Create shortcut on the shortcut menu, and then drag the shortcut icon to a new location.
Right-click, Send to	To create a shortcut on the desktop, use a folder window to locate an icon, right-click the icon, point to Send to, and then click Desktop (create shortcut).

Next, you'll create a shortcut to a USB drive on the desktop. You could use any technique for creating shortcuts, but you'll use the drag method because it involves the fewest steps.

Creating a Shortcut to a Drive

TIP

You can rename a shortcut icon the same way you rename a folder.

To create a shortcut to a drive, you can open the This PC window and then drag the drive icon from the window to the desktop. Windows creates a shortcut icon that looks like a drive icon with a shortcut arrow and includes an appropriate label, such as Removable (D) – Shortcut. If you drag a document icon from a folder window to the desktop, you move the actual document from its original location to the desktop. However, you cannot move a drive, a program, or another computer resource—its location is fixed during installation. Therefore, when you drag a drive icon to the desktop, you automatically create a shortcut.

When you create a shortcut to a USB drive, you can insert the drive in a USB port and then double-click the shortcut to view your Data Files. You can move or copy documents to the drive without having to open a separate folder window.

Rachel regularly copies files from her computer to a USB drive and wants to use a shortcut to simplify the task. You'll show her how to create a shortcut to a USB drive on her desktop.

To create a shortcut to a USB drive:

1. If necessary, insert the USB drive containing your Data Files into a USB port on your computer.

2. Double-click the **This PC** icon on the desktop. If necessary, move or resize the This PC window so you can see the icons along the left side of the desktop. You need to see both the desktop icons and the This PC window to drag effectively.

▶ **3.** Point to the **Removable Disk (D:)** icon in the This PC window, press and hold the left mouse button, and then drag the **Removable Disk (D:)** icon from the This PC window to an empty area of the desktop.

Trouble? If your USB drive has a name other than Removable Disk (D:), substitute the appropriate name and drive on your system as you perform the steps.

▶ **4.** Release the mouse button. A shortcut labeled Removable Disk (D) – Shortcut now appears on the desktop. Click the desktop to deselect the shortcut icon. See Figure 3-19. Your shortcut icon might appear in a different part of the desktop.

Figure 3-19	Shortcut to a removable disk

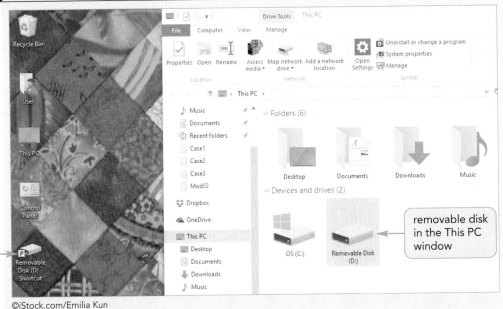

shortcut created on the desktop

removable disk in the This PC window

©iStock.com/Emilia Kun

Trouble? If you dragged with the right mouse button instead of the left, a shortcut menu appears when you release the mouse button. Click Create shortcuts here to add the Removable Disk (D) – Shortcut to the desktop.

▶ **5.** Point to the **Removable Disk (D) – Shortcut** icon to view its ScreenTip, which indicates the permanent location of the drive on your computer.

Rachel wants to copy a picture of a freeform quilt from the Module3 > Module folder on the USB drive to a new folder in the Pictures folder. She expects Mai to send her other pictures of freeform quilts, and she wants them to be available in a central location. Use the shortcut on the desktop to copy the file from the Module3 > Module folder on the USB drive to a new folder in the Pictures folder.

To use the removable disk shortcut:

▶ **1.** In the navigation pane of the This PC window, click **Pictures** to display the contents of the Pictures folder.

▶ **2.** In the New group on the Home tab, click the **New folder** button to create a folder in the Pictures folder.

▶ **3.** Type **Freeform Quilts** as the name of the new folder, and then press the **Enter** key.

▶ **4.** Double-click the **Freeform Quilts** folder to open it.

▶ **5.** Double-click the **Removable Disk (D) – Shortcut** icon on the desktop. A new window opens showing the contents of the USB drive.

▶ **6.** Navigate to the **Module3 > Module** folder provided with your Data Files. Arrange the windows to display the right panes of both windows on the desktop.

▶ **7.** Drag the **Broadway** file from the Module folder to the right pane of the Freeform Quilts folder window. Because you are dragging a file from a removable disk to a folder on a hard drive, Windows copies the Broadway file rather than moving it to the Module folder.

▶ **8.** Close all open windows.

Using a shortcut to a drive saves a few steps when you want to make backup copies of files or transfer files from one computer to another.

Session 3.1 Quick Check

REVIEW

1. How are the Settings app and the Control Panel similar? How are they different?
2. Name two places where the Settings app uses the current accent color.
3. How can you use Windows spotlight to personalize the lock screen?
4. What is the advantage of saving personalization settings as a theme?
5. Explain the difference between low- and high-screen resolutions.
6. What happens when you double-click a shortcut on the desktop?
7. If you display the desktop icon for your _____, you can quickly find and open the folders containing your documents.
8. Which screen saver do you select in the Screen Saver Settings dialog box to play a slide show of pictures as a screen saver?

Session 3.2 Visual Overview:

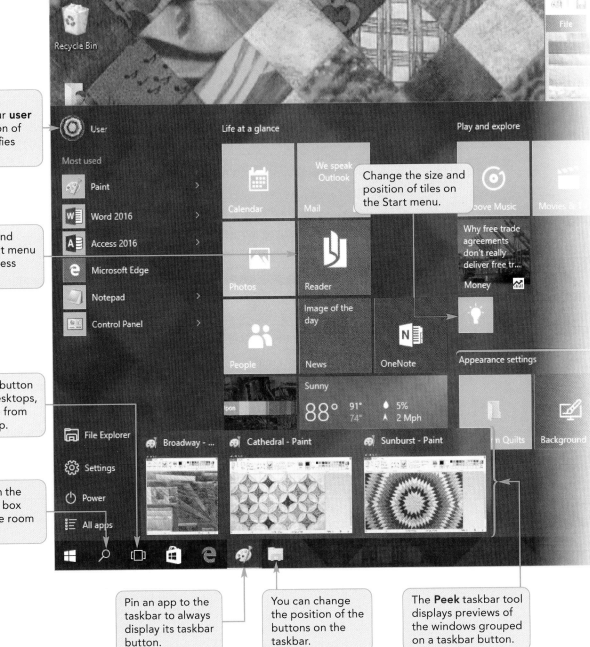

Change the picture associated with your **user account**, a collection of settings that identifies you to Windows.

Pin apps, folders, and settings to the Start menu so that you can access them quickly.

Use the Task View button to create virtual desktops, which are separate from the default desktop.

Change the Search the web and Windows box to an icon to create room on the taskbar.

Change the size and position of tiles on the Start menu.

Pin an app to the taskbar to always display its taskbar button.

You can change the position of the buttons on the taskbar.

The **Peek** taskbar tool displays previews of the windows grouped on a taskbar button.

Personalized Start Menu and Taskbar

Use **Shake** (quickly drag a window by its title bar right and left) to minimize all open windows except the one you are shaking.

Use **Snap** to arrange and resize windows by dragging them to an edge or corner of the desktop.

Organize tiles logically into **groups**, which you can name and move.

Click an icon in the **notification area**, such as the Speakers icon, to adjust a system setting or display system information.

Use the Show hidden icons button to display additional icons for background programs.

The notification area displays icons for **background programs**, programs that Windows uses to provide a service, such as an Internet connection.

Modifying the Taskbar

As you know, the bar that appears by default at the bottom of the desktop is the taskbar. In Windows 10, the taskbar is divided into the following four sections:

- Start and Cortana search area: This section, which begins at the left side of the taskbar, contains the Start button and Search the web and Windows box.
- Pinned items: This section contains the Task View, File Explorer, Windows Store, and Microsoft Edge icons by default.
- Middle section: This section displays taskbar buttons for desktop apps currently running.
- Notification area: On the right side of the taskbar is the notification area, this section shows icons for system tools and the current date and time.

In the middle section of the taskbar, Windows displays buttons for each Windows and desktop app that is running. Each button is identified by an icon, not a text label, to conserve space. If you open another file in one of these apps, Windows groups the buttons for that app into a single button. A few windows might be grouped on the Paint button, for example. The Paint icon would appear on top, and the outlines of the open windows would be stacked behind it.

When you point to a taskbar button, Windows displays a thumbnail preview of the corresponding window. The preview is designed to help you identify a window by more than the title alone. If a window is playing a video or an animation, the video or animation also plays in the preview. When you point to a grouped taskbar button, Windows arranges the thumbnail previews in a row above the taskbar. You can click a thumbnail to open a window. Recall that to close a window, you can point to a thumbnail until a Close button appears in the upper-right corner of the thumbnail, and then you click the Close button.

You can personalize the taskbar to suit your preferences. For example, you can reorder the taskbar buttons by dragging them to a new location. You can also change the appearance of taskbar buttons by displaying button labels and specifying when buttons should be grouped together. To further customize the taskbar, you can change the size and position of the taskbar or hide it altogether.

PROSKILLS

Decision Making: Monitoring the Notification Area

The icons in the notification area of the taskbar let you access certain computer settings, such as the system time. The icons also communicate the status of programs running in the background. Background programs are those programs that Windows runs to provide a service, such as an Internet connection. The notification area displays only a few icons, which are usually determined by your computer manufacturer and the programs installed on your computer. The New notifications icon is for the action center. When you click the New notifications icon, a panel opens with notification messages from apps and Windows listed in the upper part of the panel and quick actions (settings for some background programs) in the lower part of the panel.

You can also point to any icon in the notification area to display its status or name. (You might need to click the Show hidden icons button (an up arrow) on the taskbar to display all of the icons in the notification area.) For example, if you're having trouble hearing sounds on your computer, point to the speaker icon to determine whether you need to turn up the volume. (The name of the speaker icon varies depending on the hardware manufacturer.)

Now you can personalize the taskbar on Rachel's computer. You'll start by showing her how to pin items to the taskbar.

Pinning Apps to the Taskbar

Task View, File Explorer, Windows Store, and Microsoft Edge are pinned to the taskbar by default. If you use another Windows or desktop app often, you can also pin that app to the taskbar. Pinning an app to the taskbar increases your efficiency because the pinned app is always visible as you work on the desktop, and you can start the app with a single click. (You need to double-click desktop shortcut icons for programs.) You can rearrange the buttons for pinned and running apps on the taskbar to suit your preferences.

REFERENCE

Pinning Apps to the Taskbar

- If the app is already running, right-click the taskbar button, and then click Pin this program to taskbar on the shortcut menu.

or

- If the app is not running, open the Start menu, locate and right-click the app's tile or command on the Start menu or All apps menu, and then click Pin to taskbar on the shortcut menu.

Because Rachel frequently uses Paint, you suggest that she pin Paint to the taskbar.

To pin Paint to the taskbar:

▶ 1. Click the **Start** button ⊞ to display the Start menu, and then click **Paint**.

   Trouble? If Paint does not appear on the Start menu, type "Paint" in the Search the web and Windows box, and then click Paint in the search results.

▶ 2. Right-click the **Paint** button 🖌 on the taskbar, and then click **Pin this program to taskbar** on the shortcut menu.

▶ 3. To confirm that Paint is pinned to the taskbar, close the Paint window. The Paint button remains on the taskbar.

   Trouble? If a dialog box appears asking if you want to save changes to an image, click the Don't Save button.

TIP

You can use the same technique to pin Windows apps to the taskbar.

In addition to starting an app from the taskbar, you can use a pinned item to open favorite and recent files from that program. To do so, you use a **Jump List**, a list of recently or frequently opened files, folders, or websites. When you right-clicked the Paint button in the previous steps, you displayed the Paint Jump List at the top of the shortcut menu. If you opened any picture files in Paint, such as the Broadway quilt picture, one or more of them might have appeared on the Jump List. To make sure you can always access one of those files, you can pin it to the Jump List. To open a pinned file, right-click the Paint button on the taskbar to display the Jump List, and then click the recent or favorite file you want to open in Paint.

Rachel plans to use the picture of the Broadway quilt often, so you'll show her how to pin the file to the Paint Jump List and then open the file from the taskbar. First, you'll open two files in Paint to make sure you have pictures to display in the Jump List.

To pin a file to the Paint Jump List:

1. Click the **Paint** button ![icon] on the taskbar, click the **File** tab on the ribbon, and then click **Open** to open the Open dialog box.

2. Navigate to the **Module3 > Module** folder provided with your Data Files, and then double-click the **Blues** picture to open it. Next, open a second picture in Paint.

3. Click the **File** tab, click **Open** to open the Open dialog box, and then double-click the **Broadway** picture to open it.

4. Close Paint. Now you are certain to see recent files in the Paint Jump List.

5. Right-click the **Paint** button on the taskbar to display the Jump List.

6. Point to **Broadway**, and then click the **Pin to this list** icon ![icon] to pin the Broadway picture file to the Jump List. See Figure 3-20. The items in your Paint Jump List might differ.

| Figure 3-20 | File pinned to the Paint Jump List |

©iStock.com/Emilia Kun

TIP

To unpin a file, open the Jump List, point to the filename, and then click the Unpin from this list icon.

7. To open the Broadway file in Paint, click **Broadway** on the Jump List. Paint starts and opens the Broadway picture file.

8. Close the Paint window.

Rachel mentions that she would also like to adjust the position of the taskbar buttons. She uses the File Explorer button frequently, so she asks you to move the File Explorer button to the right of the Paint button for easy access.

To move a taskbar button:

1. Point to the **File Explorer** button ![icon] on the taskbar, and then drag it to the right.

2. When the File Explorer button appears to the right of the Paint button, release the mouse button. See Figure 3-21.

Figure 3-21 Moving a taskbar button

File Explorer is now to the right of the Paint button

©iStock.com/Emilia Kun

You can move any taskbar button, even those for programs that are not pinned to the taskbar. When you do, you move the entire button group so the open files remain grouped on a program button.

The taskbar is starting to look cluttered with buttons and icons. To create room for other items, you can change the Search the web and Windows box to an icon.

To change the Search the web and Windows box to an icon:

TIP

You can also use the taskbar shortcut menu to hide or show the Task View button.

1. Right-click a blank area of the taskbar, and then point to **Search** on the shortcut menu to display a list of options for the Search the web and Windows box. You can hide the box, show an icon instead of the box, or continue showing the box.

   Trouble? If Cortana is activated on your computer, point to Cortana on the shortcut menu instead of Search.

2. Click **Show search icon** on the menu to display an icon instead of a box. All of the icons on the taskbar move to the left. See Figure 3-22.

Figure 3-22 Search icon on the taskbar

icon displayed instead of a box

©iStock.com/Emilia Kun

Trouble? If Cortana is activated on your computer, click Show Cortana icon instead of Show search icon. The Cortana icon appears on the taskbar instead of the search icon.

Now that you've shown Rachel how to customize the icons on the taskbar, you'll show her how to change the taskbar itself.

Setting Taskbar Properties

You can set taskbar properties using the Taskbar and Start Menu Properties dialog box. Using this dialog box, you can increase the amount of screen space available for open windows by hiding the taskbar. In this case, the taskbar is not closed, removed, or minimized, but instead hidden under the border of the desktop or the app windows open on the desktop. The taskbar still remains active and accessible—you can point to the area of your screen where the taskbar would be located to redisplay the taskbar when you need to use it.

You can also use the Taskbar and Start Menu Properties dialog box to determine whether to display small icons on the taskbar, group similar taskbar buttons, and change the location of the taskbar to another position on the screen.

You'll show Rachel how to increase the amount of screen space on the desktop by hiding the taskbar and using small icons.

To set taskbar properties:

▶ **1.** Right-click a blank area on the taskbar, and then click **Properties** on the shortcut menu. The Taskbar and Start Menu Properties dialog box opens. See Figure 3-23. Your settings might differ.

Figure 3-23   **Taskbar and Start Menu Properties dialog box**

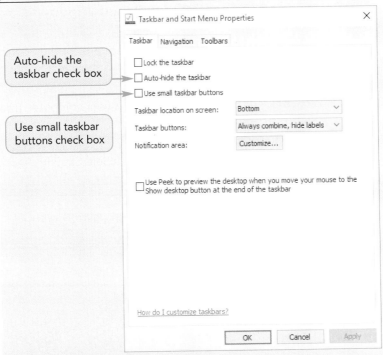

Note the options currently selected in this dialog box so you can restore them later.

▶ **2.** Click to select the **Auto-hide the taskbar** check box, and then click the **Apply** button. Windows hides the taskbar.

▶ **3.** Point to the bottom of the desktop to redisplay the taskbar. Pointing away from the taskbar hides it again.

4. In the Taskbar and Start Menu Properties dialog box, click the **Auto-hide the taskbar** check box to remove the check mark, and then click the **Apply** button. The taskbar appears in its default position at the bottom of the desktop.

5. Click to select the **Use small taskbar buttons** check box, and then click the **Apply** button. The taskbar icons shrink and the height of the taskbar decreases accordingly.

6. Click the **Use small taskbar buttons** check box to remove the check mark, and then click the **Apply** button to display the taskbar icons at their default size.

7. Make sure the options in the Taskbar and Start Menu Properties dialog box are in their original state, and then click the **OK** button to close the dialog box.

Managing the Desktop with Taskbar Tools

Windows 10 includes three taskbar tools you can use to manage the windows on your desktop: Snap, Peek, and Shake. You can also use the Task View button on the taskbar to create and use virtual desktops, which are desktops you can add to the Windows user interface, separate from the default desktop.

Arranging Windows with Snap

With Snap, you can drag the title bar of an open window to the top of the desktop to maximize the window. To restore the window to its original size, drag the title bar away from the top of the desktop. You can also use Snap to arrange two windows side by side and arrange four windows in each corner of the desktop. You can also use a feature called **Snap Assist** to list the thumbnails of open windows as you snap a window into place. Instead of dragging, you can click the thumbnail you want to snap into an empty part of the desktop.

To use Snap, you first turn on the feature in the Settings app. Your screen resolution must also be high enough (at least 1366 × 768) to snap windows. Turning on Snap activates two other settings. One adjusts the size of the snapped windows so they each take up an equal amount of the desktop. The other setting turns on Snap Assist. You can turn on Snap, but turn off the other two settings according to your preferences.

To turn on Snap:

1. Click the **Start** button ⊞ to display the Start menu, and then click **Settings** to start the Settings app.

2. Click **System** to display the System settings.

3. In the left pane, click **Multitasking** to display multitasking features, including Snap, in the right pane.

4. If the first slider is set to Off, click the **slider button** to change the Snap from Off to On. By default, you also activate the other two Snap settings. See Figure 3-24.

TIP
To find the Snap settings quickly, you can start the Settings app and then type "Snap" in the Find a setting box.

| **Figure 3-24** | **Turning on Snap** |

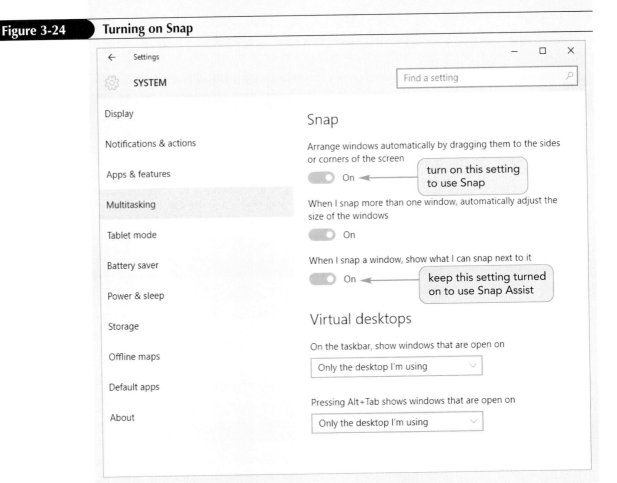

Trouble? If the Snap settings are unavailable, your screen resolution might be too low to use Snap. Read but do not perform the next two series of steps.

Rachel sometimes needs to work with two windows open as she examines images and manages her files and folders. You offer to show her how to quickly arrange windows side by side using Snap and Snap Assist. The System window is already open. You'll open the Broadway picture in Paint and then snap the windows.

To arrange windows side by side with Snap:

▶ 1. Right-click the **Paint** button ✏ on the taskbar to display its Jump List, and then click **Broadway** to open the Broadway picture in Paint.

   Trouble? If the Paint window opens as maximized, click the Restore Down button ☐ to resize the window.

▶ 2. Click the **title bar** of the Paint window, and then drag it to the left side of the desktop until a translucent outline of the window appears. Make sure the outline takes up half of the desktop.

▶ 3. Release the mouse button to snap the Paint window to the left side of the desktop and display a thumbnail of the System window. See Figure 3-25.

| Figure 3-25 | Arranging windows with Snap and Snap Assist |

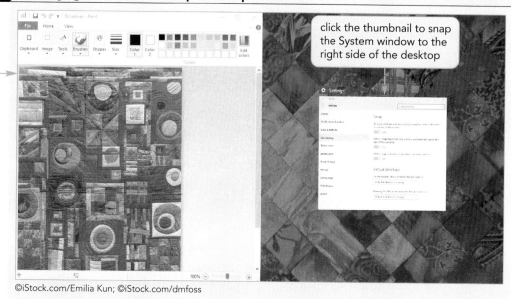

Paint is snapped to the left side of the desktop

click the thumbnail to snap the System window to the right side of the desktop

©iStock.com/Emilia Kun; ©iStock.com/dmfoss

Trouble? If the Paint window is maximized, you dragged the window to the upper-center part of the desktop. Click the Restore Down button 🗗 and then repeat Steps 2 and 3.

▶ **4.** Click the **thumbnail** of the System window to snap it to the right side of the desktop.

Instead of arranging windows side by side, you can arrange up to four windows in each corner of the desktop. If your screen resolution is higher than 1366 × 768, you can snap one window to a corner of the desktop and then use Snap Assist to display thumbnails of the remaining windows to snap.

Keeping Track of Windows with Peek

Peek helps you manage open windows. To quickly minimize all open windows, you click the Show desktop button on the far right side of the taskbar. To preview open windows without leaving your current window, you point to a taskbar button to display thumbnails of open files, and then point to a thumbnail. Any open windows fade to reveal the selected window and then reappear when you move the pointer away from the thumbnail. To open the window you're previewing, you click the thumbnail.

When Rachel has many windows open, she often has to stop working with a document or an image to manage those windows. For example, she might open a few more image files and then decide to copy other files to a USB drive. She'd like to quickly view the desktop to verify that it contains a shortcut to the removable disk so she can copy the files using the shortcut icon. She also wants to know how to briefly display a particular window to view its contents. You'll show her how to use Peek to perform both tasks.

To use Peek:

▶ **1.** Click the **Show desktop** button on the far right side of the taskbar (to the right of the date and time) to minimize all of the open windows. See Figure 3-26.

Figure 3-26	Displaying the desktop with Peek

©iStock.com/Emilia Kun

▶ 2. Double-click the **Removable Disk (D)** shortcut icon on the desktop to display the contents of the removable disk, and then navigate to the **Module3 > Module** folder provided with your Data Files.

▶ 3. Right-click the **Cathedral** file, point to **Open with** on the shortcut menu, and then click **Paint** to open the Cathedral picture file in Paint.

▶ 4. Minimize the new Paint window.

▶ 5. Right-click the **Sunburst** file, point to **Open with** on the shortcut menu, and then click **Paint** to open the Sunburst picture file in Paint.

▶ 6. Minimize the new Paint window.

▶ 7. Point to the **Paint** button 🎨 on the taskbar to display thumbnail previews of the three pictures open in Paint. See Figure 3-27.

Figure 3-27	Previewing windows with Peek

©iStock.com/Emilia Kun; ©iStock.com/dmfoss; ©iStock.com/Jewelee; ©iStock.com/blindsquirrelphoto

Trouble? If a list of filenames appears instead of thumbnails when you point to the Paint taskbar button, the thumbnails feature is probably disabled on your computer. Read but do not perform Steps 8 and 9.

TIP

To restore the desktop when you're previewing a window, move the pointer away from the thumbnail.

▶ 8. To preview the Sunburst picture, point to the **Sunburst** thumbnail. The File Explorer window fades so that the Sunburst window is the only one open on the desktop.

▶ 9. Click the **Sunburst** thumbnail to display the Sunburst picture in Paint and make it the active window. The File Explorer window is also redisplayed, but it is not the active window.

Minimizing and Restoring Windows with Shake

Shake is another handy tool for managing windows. Use Shake to quickly minimize all open windows on the desktop except the one you want to focus on—you don't have to minimize the windows one by one. Click and hold the title bar of the window you want to keep open, and then shake it by quickly dragging the window to the right and left. When you do, you minimize all of the other open windows. To restore the minimized windows, shake the open window again.

Rachel mentions that when she needs to focus on the contents of a window, she likes to minimize all of the other open windows. You suggest she use Shake to do so.

To use Shake:

▶ 1. Point to the **Paint** button ◉ on the taskbar, and then click the **Broadway** thumbnail to open the Broadway picture in Paint.

▶ 2. Point to the **Paint** button ◉ on the taskbar again, and then click the **Cathedral** thumbnail to open the Cathedral picture in Paint.

▶ 3. Point to the **title bar** of the Cathedral window, hold down the mouse button, and then quickly drag the window about an inch to the right and left to shake it. The Cathedral window remains open while all of the other open windows are minimized.

▶ 4. To restore the minimized windows, shake the **Cathedral** window again.

▶ 5. Click the **Show desktop** button on the far right side of the taskbar to minimize all open windows.

You have used the taskbar to manage open windows. Next, you'll learn how to use the taskbar to manage multiple desktops.

Using Virtual Desktops

If your desktop quickly becomes cluttered or you want to keep certain apps open or pinned to the taskbar depending on your task, you can create one or more virtual desktops. For example, you might use the default desktop for work-related tasks and open apps such as Calendar, WordPad, and File Explorer. At the end of the day or during a break, you can switch to a second desktop and catch up on the weather or explore the Windows Store. If an app is open on one desktop but you need it in a different one, you can move the window from one desktop to another.

Rachel thinks virtual desktops will help her be more productive, so you'll show her how to create and use a second desktop. First, you'll open a window on the default desktop so you can easily distinguish between the default and virtual desktops.

To use a virtual desktop:

▶ 1. Point to the **Paint** button ◉ on the taskbar, and then click **Cathedral** to display the Cathedral picture in a Paint window on the default desktop.

▶ 2. Click the **Task View** button ◻ on the taskbar, and then click **New desktop** in the lower-right corner of the desktop. Desktop 2 opens as a duplicate of Desktop 1 (the default desktop) except that Desktop 2 does not include any open apps. See Figure 3-28.

Figure 3-28	New virtual desktop

©iStock.com/Emilia Kun; ©iStock.com/Jewelee

▶ **3.** Click the **Desktop 2** thumbnail to switch to Desktop 2.

▶ **4.** Click the **Start** button ⊞ and then click **Weather** to start the Weather app and open its window on Desktop 2.

▶ **5.** Click the **Task View** button ⊡ and then right-click the **Weather** thumbnail on the desktop.

▶ **6.** Point to **Move to** on the shortcut menu, and then click **Desktop 1** to move the Weather window to the default desktop. The Weather window no longer appears on Desktop 2.

▶ **7.** Point to the **Desktop 1** thumbnail to display the windows open on the default desktop: Weather, three Paint windows, and one File Explorer window.

▶ **8.** Point to the **Desktop 2** thumbnail to display a Close button on the thumbnail, and then click the **Close** button ⊠ to close Desktop 2.

▶ **9.** Click a blank area of the desktop, and then close all open windows.

Besides customizing the taskbar to suit your preferences and work habits, you can do the same to the Start menu.

Personalizing the Start Menu

Most of the items on the Start menu are created for you by Windows 10 or by the apps you install. Windows 10 personalizes the left pane of the Start menu as you work to show the apps you use most frequently. However, you can also determine the content and appearance of your Start menu. For example, you can pin tiles for apps, settings, and folders to the Start menu and organize the Start menu to use it most effectively. Because the Start menu is the gateway to the apps on your computer, it should display the apps you use most often, organized in a way that makes sense for how you work.

To personalize the Start menu, you can add tiles for apps you use often and remove tiles for the apps you don't use. Like the shortcut icons on the desktop, each tile is a shortcut, providing a quick way to perform an action such as starting an app. Besides shortcuts for apps, you can add shortcuts for folders such as the Documents folder and settings such as the Background settings.

The Start menu initially contains two groups of tiles by default: a Life at a glance group, for apps you are likely to use every day, and a Play and explore group for entertainment apps. If you add a new tile or drag one near the bottom of the right pane in the Start menu, you can create a new group. For example, you might want to pin a few settings to the Start menu and organize them into a Settings group.

If the Start menu becomes cluttered with tiles, you can display it as a full-screen menu. To do so, start the Settings app, select Personalization, select the Start category, and then turn on the "Use Start full screen" setting. Because the Start menu background is transparent by default, you can still see the desktop when you display the Start menu full screen.

Problem Solving: Adding Apps to Work Productively

In addition to the default apps that come with Windows 10, you can purchase and install apps using the Windows Store, a Microsoft website accessible from the taskbar and Start menu. The Windows Store provides apps created by Microsoft and other developers. It organizes apps by categories, such as Social, Productivity, Tools, and Security. If you're looking for a specific app, you can use Cortana or the Search the web and Windows tool to search for the app by name. Most of the default apps are designed for entertainment and connecting with your contacts. The Windows Store includes Windows and desktop apps to help you work productively, such as dictionaries, eBook readers, antivirus software, and even the latest version of Microsoft Office. Signing in to Windows 10 makes you eligible to purchase, download, and install apps from the Windows Store. Microsoft and other developers frequently post new apps in the Windows Store, so you should visit the site occasionally to see whether new productivity apps are available.

Rachel wants to change the Start menu on her computer to include a tile for a new Windows app and for settings she uses often. You'll show her how to pin these items as tiles on the Start menu.

Pinning Tiles on the Start Menu

To pin an app, setting, folder, or device on the Start menu, you find the command or icon for the item, right-click it, and then select the Pin to Start command. The tiles on the Start menu are pinned items because they remain on the Start menu until you unpin them. When you unpin an item, Windows removes the tile from the Start menu, but it doesn't remove the app from your computer.

Pinning an App on the Start Menu

- Click the Start button and then click All apps.
- Right-click an app in the All apps list, and then click Pin to Start on the shortcut menu.

Rachel mentions that she often receives reports and other documents as **PDF files**, which are files in the Portable Document Format. Reader is a Windows app that lets you read and navigate PDF documents. Because Rachel thinks she will use Reader often, she wants to add a tile for the app to the Start menu. She also plans to use the Background settings and the Lock screen settings often, and she wants quick access to the Freeform Quilts folder.

You'll show Rachel how to pin tiles for Reader, Background settings, Lock screen settings, and the Freeform Quilts folder on the Start menu.

To pin Reader on the Start menu:

▶ **1.** Click the **Start** button ⊞ to display the Start menu, and then click **All apps** to display an alphabetic list of apps installed on your computer.

▶ **2.** Click a letter, such as A, to collapse the All apps list, click **R**, and then right-click **Reader** to display its shortcut menu. See Figure 3-29. Your All apps list might contain different apps.

Figure 3-29 Pinning an app to the Start menu

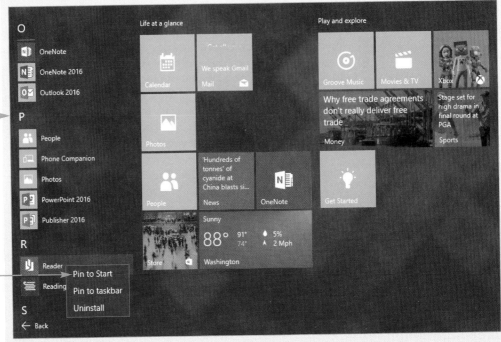

All apps list is sorted alphabetically

click to pin the Reader app to the Start menu

©iStock.com/Emilia Kun

3. Click **Pin to Start** on the shortcut menu. A Reader tile appears on the Start menu while a Reader icon remains on the All apps list.

Trouble? If the Reader app is not installed on your computer, right-click any other app that does not appear in the right pane, such as the Reading List app, and then click Pin to Start on the shortcut menu.

You can also pin apps to the taskbar the same way: right-click the app on the All apps list, and then click Pin to taskbar on the shortcut menu.

Next, you can add tiles for the Background and Lock screen settings to the Start menu.

To pin the Background and Lock screen settings to the Start menu:

1. At the bottom of the All apps list, click the **Back** button to return to the Start menu, and then click **Settings** to start the Settings app.

2. Click **Personalization** to open the Personalization window, which includes the Background and Lock screen settings.

3. In the left pane, right-click **Background** and then click **Pin to Start** on the shortcut menu.

4. Right-click **Lock screen** in the left pane, and then click **Pin to Start** on the shortcut menu.

5. Close the Personalization window, and then click the **Start** button ⊞ to display the Start menu with the new pinned tiles. See Figure 3-30.

Figure 3-30 | Settings pinned to the Start menu

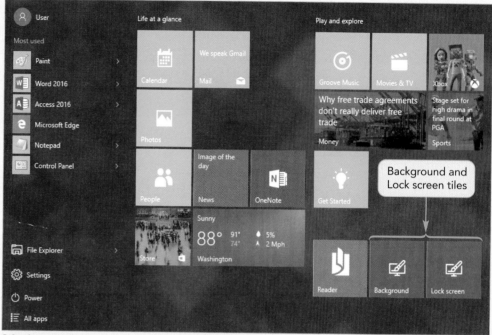

©iStock.com/Emilia Kun

▶ **6.** Click a blank area on the desktop to close the Start menu.

The last tile to add to the Start menu for Rachel is one for the Freeform Quilts folder.

To pin the Freeform Quilts folder to the Start menu:

▶ **1.** Click the **File Explorer** button 🗔 on the taskbar, and then display the contents of the Pictures folder.

▶ **2.** Right-click the **Freeform Quilts** folder, and then click **Pin to Start** on the shortcut menu.

▶ **3.** Close the File Explorer window.

You can test the four new tiles on the Start menu to make sure each opens the appropriate app, settings, or folder.

To test the new tiles on the Start menu:

▶ **1.** Click the **Start** button 🔳 to display the Start menu with four new tiles.

▶ **2.** Click the **Reader** tile on the Start menu to start Reader. When the app starts, it might display a document explaining how to convert PDF files into Word documents or it might display a Browse button, which you can click to find a PDF file to open.

▶ **3.** Close the Reader window, and then click the **Start** button 🔳 to display the Start menu again.

▶ **4.** Click the **Background** tile on the Start menu. The Personalization window opens and displays the Background settings.

▶ **5.** Click the **Start** button ⊞ and then click the **Lock screen** tile. The Personalization window changes to display the Lock screen settings.

▶ **6.** Click the **Start** button ⊞ again, scroll down, if necessary, and then click the **Freeform Quilts** tile to open the folder window on the desktop.

▶ **7.** Close all open windows.

Now that you've pinned apps to the Start menu, you can organize them to make the tiles easier to find.

Organizing Tiles on the Start Menu

If you continue to pin items to the Start menu, you will eventually have an unmanageable number of tiles on the Start menu. One way to organize tiles is by grouping them so that similar tiles appear together. You can assign a name to the group, which helps you quickly find the tile you want. Another way to organize the tiles is to modify their appearance. For example, you can reduce the size of tiles to fit more on the Start menu and turn live tiles on or off. If you're not using a tile, you can remove it from the Start menu, which helps to keep the Start menu uncluttered. You can still use the All apps list or the Search the web and Windows tool to start and use the app.

You pinned four new tiles on the Start menu for Reader, Background settings, Lock screen settings, and the Freeform Quilts folder. All of these new tiles appear together in their own group. You can start organizing the tiles by moving the Reader tile into one of the default groups, such as the Life at a glance group. Next, you can create a group for the Freeform Quilts, Background, and Lock screen tiles. Rachel plans to occasionally update the appearance settings on the company computers and will use these tiles when she does.

To organize the new tiles on the Start menu:

▶ **1.** Click the **Start** button ⊞ to display the Start menu.

▶ **2.** Drag the **Reader** tile to a blank area in the Life at a glance group of tiles. The other three new tiles remain together in a group, which you can name to identify them.

▶ **3.** Point above the three new tiles until "Name group" appears, and then click **Name group** to display a box for naming the group. See Figure 3-31.

| Figure 3-31 | Naming a group of tiles |

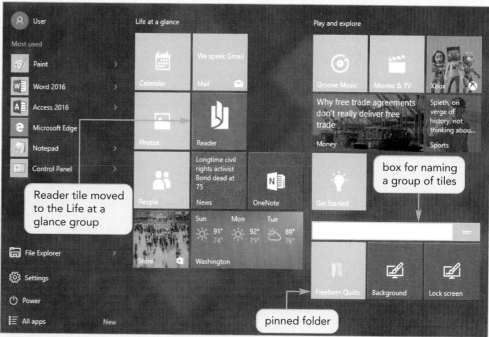

©iStock.com/Emilia Kun

▶ **4.** Type **Appearance settings** and then press the **Enter** key to name the group.

To keep your Start menu clean and uncluttered, you can remove tiles to display only those you use often. To remove a tile, right-click it, and then click Unpin from Start on the shortcut menu. Keep in mind that when you remove a tile, you are only unpinning the item, not deleting an app or a folder.

Modifying Tiles on the Start Menu

Besides rearranging, grouping, and removing the tiles on the Start menu, you can also change their size. For example, if you need to scroll to display tiles, you can reduce the size of large tiles to display more tiles in the same space. You can display tiles as small, medium, wide, or large. You can also modify tiles by making them live tiles, which change to display the contents or updated information for an app. For example, if you make the Photos tile a live tile, it displays a slide show of photos and other images.

Turning on Live Tiles

Some tiles on the Start menu are live tiles by default—they display the latest information from apps including Store, News, Weather, Money, and Sports. To turn on live tiles for other apps, such as Mail, People, and Photos, you need to set up an account or add information to the app. For example, after you use Mail to set up an email account, the Mail tile becomes a live tile and displays recent email messages. For the People app, you need to add contact information, including pictures. If a live tile becomes too distracting, you can right-click the tile and then click Turn live tile off on the shortcut menu to change the tile to a static one.

To display images in the live Photos tile, first make sure you have stored photos in a location the Photos app can access, such as the Pictures folder in This PC or on OneDrive, or add a location to the Photos app. You can then have the Photos tile display photos from your collection. You can also display a single photo in the Photos tile instead of a changing series of images.

Rachel asks you to reduce the size of a tile so she can see how to display more tiles on the Start menu. She also wants to display the Broadway quilt picture in the Photos tile to see if she likes the result.

To change the size of Start menu tiles:

TIP

To change the size of the Start menu itself, drag its top or right border.

1. On the Start menu, right-click the **Money** tile, point to **Resize** on the shortcut menu, and then click **Medium** to change its size setting from Wide to Medium.

   Trouble? If the size setting for the Money tile is already Medium, keep the setting by clicking Medium as instructed in Step 1.

2. Right-click the **Get Started** tile, point to **Resize** on the shortcut menu, and then click **Small** to change its size. See Figure 3-32.

Figure 3-32   Changing the size of tiles

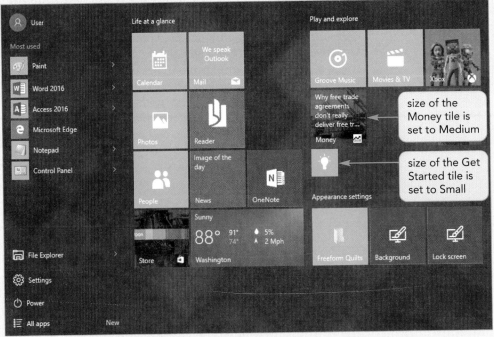

©iStock.com/Emilia Kun

Next, you can start the Photos app to select the Freeform Quilts folder as a source for photos to display in the tile and make the Photos tile a live tile on the Start menu.

To make the Photos tile a live tile:

▶ **1.** Right-click the **Photos** tile, point to **More**, and then click **Turn live tile on** on the shortcut menu.

   Trouble? If the Turn live tile off option appears on the shortcut menu instead of the Turn live tile on option, the Photos tile is already a live tile. Skip Step 1.

▶ **2.** Click the **Photos** tile to start the Photos app, which might display a collection or album of photos stored on your computer or in your OneDrive.

▶ **3.** In the upper-left corner of the Photos window, click the **Menu** button ≡ to display a list of options.

▶ **4.** Click **Settings** on the Photos menu to display the settings for the app. See Figure 3-33.

Figure 3-33 Settings for the Photos app

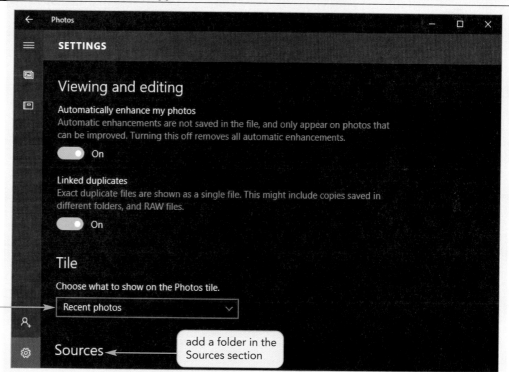

keep this setting to display recently viewed photos on the live Photos tile

add a folder in the Sources section

▶ **5.** In the Sources section, click the **Add a folder** button to open the Select folder dialog box.

▶ **6.** Navigate to the **Pictures > Freeform Quilts** folder, and then click the **Add this folder to Pictures** button to add this folder as a source of pictures to display on the Photos tile on the Start menu.

▶ **7.** Close the Photos app and then open the Start menu. The Photos tile becomes a live tile displaying photos from the sources listed in the Photos app, including the Broadway quilt photo, which might take a few seconds. See Figure 3-34.

Figure 3-34	Live Photos tile

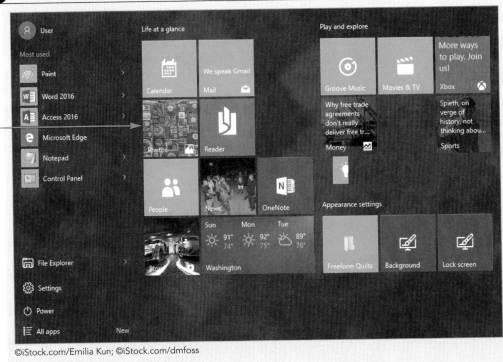

Broadway picture displayed on the Photos tile; your tile might display a different picture

©iStock.com/Emilia Kun; ©iStock.com/dmfoss

Now the live Photos tile reflects the mission of the Crafted Quilts organization.

Changing the User Picture

Windows displays a generic icon as the default user account picture, but you can change this picture to display a photo of yourself or anything else that identifies you. If your computer includes a built-in camera, you can use the camera to take a photo and display it as your user account picture. Otherwise, you can use any image file stored in a location your computer can access, such as the Pictures folder. Your user picture represents your user account, which is a collection of information specifying how you can use the computer and its apps and includes appearance settings such as your Start menu background and color.

Rachel wants to use the photo of a Sunburst quilt as her user picture. You'll show her how to replace the generic user icon on the Start menu with a more meaningful photo.

To change the user account picture:

▶ 1. Click the **user icon** on the Start menu, and then click **Change account settings** on the shortcut menu to open the Accounts window displaying settings for your user account. See Figure 3-35. Your account information will differ.

Figure 3-35	Changing the account picture

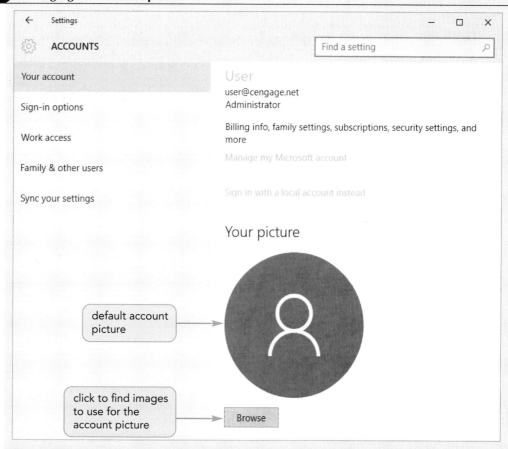

2. Click the **Browse** button to open the Open dialog box, and then navigate to the **Module3 > Module** folder.

3. Click the **Sunburst** file to select it.

4. Click the **Choose picture** button to select the Sunburst picture as the account picture.

5. Close the Accounts window and then open the Start menu, which now includes the new account picture.

To create an image of the Start menu that displays many of the changes you made, you can take a screenshot of the Start menu. Rachel can use that image for reference as she customizes the other Crafted Quilts computers.

To create a screenshot of the Start menu:

1. Press the **Print Screen** key to capture an image of the Start menu and save the image on the Clipboard. Depending on the type of computer you are using, the Print Screen key might be labeled differently (for example, PrtScn).

2. Click the **All apps** icon on the Start menu, scroll the list, click **Windows Accessories**, and then click **WordPad** to start WordPad and open a new, blank document.

3. Type your name followed by **Customized Start menu**, and then press the **Enter** key.

TIP

You can also press the Windows+Print Screen keys to create a screenshot named Screenshot (1), for example, which Windows stores in a folder named Screenshots in the Pictures folder.

▶ **4.** Press the **Ctrl+V** keys to paste the Start menu image into the new WordPad document.

▶ **5.** Click the **Save** button ▣ on the Quick Access Toolbar, navigate to the **Module3 > Module** folder provided with your Data Files, type **Start menu** as the name of the file, and then click the **Save** button to save the file in the Module folder.

Trouble? If necessary, click the default name in the File name box to select it before typing a new file name. WordPad will automatically add the file extension .rtf.

▶ **6.** Close WordPad.

You've finished personalizing the Windows 10 desktop on Rachel's computer, so you should restore your computer to its original settings.

Restoring Your Settings

Complete the steps in this section to restore the original settings on your computer.

To restore your settings:

▶ **1.** Click the **Start** button ⊞ to display the Start menu.

▶ **2.** Right-click the **Reader** tile (or the tile for the other app you pinned), and then click **Unpin from Start** on the shortcut menu to unpin the app from the Start menu. Repeat this step to remove the Freeform Quilts, Background, and Lock screen tiles from the Start menu. Windows removes the group name when you remove the tiles.

▶ **3.** Right-click the **Money** tile on the Start menu, point to **Resize** on the shortcut menu, and then click your original size setting. Right-click the **Get Started** tile on the Start menu, point to **Resize** on the shortcut menu, and then click your original size setting.

▶ **4.** Right-click the **Photos** tile on the Start menu, and then click **Turn live tile off** on the shortcut menu.

▶ **5.** Click the **user icon** on the Start menu, click **Change account settings** to open the Accounts window, and then click your original user picture.

Trouble? If you were using the original generic user picture that appeared when you installed Windows, and this picture is not provided in the Accounts window, click the Browse button and then enter C:\ProgramData\Microsoft\ User Account Pictures in the Address bar of the Open dialog box to navigate to the location of the generic pictures. Click the user picture, and then click the Choose picture button.

▶ **6.** Click the **Start** button ⊞ and then click the **Photos** tile to start the app. In the Photos window, click **Settings**. In the Sources section, click the **Close** button ☒ for the Pictures > Freeform Quilts folder, click the **Remove Folder** button, and then close the Photos app.

7. Right-click the **desktop**, and then click **Personalize** on the shortcut menu to display the Personalization settings. In the left pane, click **Themes**. In the right pane, click **Theme settings**, and then click your original theme, such as **Windows**, to restore your original desktop background, window color, screen saver (which might be "None"), and desktop icons.

8. Right-click the **Crafted Quilts** theme, and then click **Delete theme** on the shortcut menu. If necessary, click the **Yes** button to confirm the deletion. Close the Control Panel's Personalization window.

9. In the right pane of the Personalization window for the Settings app, click **Desktop icon settings**. Click the check boxes to restore the original settings. By default, only the Recycle Bin appears on the desktop. Click the **OK** button to close the Desktop Icon Settings dialog box.

10. In the left pane of the Personalization window, click **Lock screen**, click the original lock screen picture, click the **Background** box, and then click your original background setting. Close the Personalization window.

11. Open the Pictures folder, and then move the **Freeform Quilts** folder to the **Module3 > Module** folder provided with your Data Files. Close all open windows.

12. Click the desktop **shortcut icon** that you created in this module, and then press the **Delete** key to delete the shortcut. If necessary, click the **Yes** button to confirm the deletion.

13. Right-click the **Paint** button 🖌 on the taskbar, point to **Broadway**, and then click the **Unpin from this list** icon 📌.

14. On the Paint shortcut menu, click **Unpin this program from taskbar**.

15. Drag the **File Explorer** button 🗔 on the taskbar to its original location to the left of the Microsoft Edge button on the taskbar.

16. Right-click the **Search the web and Windows** button 🔍 on the taskbar, point to **Search** on the shortcut menu, and then click **Show search box** to redisplay the Search the web and Windows box on the taskbar.

    Trouble? If you have activated Cortana, point to Cortana on the shortcut menu, and then click Show search box.

Session 3.2 Quick Check

REVIEW

1. How do you change the position of taskbar buttons?
2. Why would you pin a file to a taskbar button's Jump List?
3. You can use a feature called _____ to list the thumbnails of open windows as you snap a window into place.
4. How can you quickly minimize all open windows on the desktop?
5. Explain how to create a virtual desktop.
6. Name two ways you can change the appearance of a tile on the Start menu.
7. What can you do with the Reader app?
8. Explain how to personalize the user icon on the Start menu.

PRACTICE

Review Assignments

See the Starting Data Files section at the beginning of this module for a list of Data Files needed for the Review Assignments.

Crafted Quilts keeps a computer in its conference area for any staff member to use when needed. Rachel asks you to customize that computer so it is appropriate for the company. Rachel recently received photographs of new quilts that Mai found and wants to make the photos available to staff members to use in promotional materials for an upcoming quilt show. As you perform the following steps, note the original settings of the desktop and other items so you can restore them later. Complete the following steps:

1. Change the desktop theme to any other theme that displays photographs.
2. Change the lock screen to display the Star picture in the Module3 > Review folder provided with your Data Files.
3. Change the screen saver to play a slide show of the pictures in the Module3 > Review folder.
4. Change the desktop icon settings on your computer to display the This PC and Control Panel icons in addition to the default Recycle Bin icon. Change the image for the This PC icon so that it displays any other appropriate image.
5. With the USB drive or other removable media containing your Data Files in the appropriate drive, create a shortcut to this drive on the desktop. Use **Review Removable Disk Shortcut** as the name of the shortcut.
6. Use the Review Removable Disk Shortcut on the desktop to copy the five picture files in the Module3 > Review folder provided with your Data Files to a new folder in the Pictures folder. Use **Classic Quilts** as the name of the new folder.
7. Complete the following steps to open and work with Paint:
   - Use Paint to open the Tumble picture in the Classic Quilts folder, and then pin Paint to the taskbar.
   - Pin the Tumble picture file to the Paint Jump List.
   - Close the File Explorer and Personalization windows.
8. Use Snap to align the Paint window on the right side of the desktop.
9. Move the Paint button so it appears directly to the right of the Task View button.
10. Open the Screen Saver Settings dialog box again. (*Hint*: Double-click the Control Panel shortcut icon on the desktop, click Appearance and Personalization, and then click Change screen saver in the Personalization category.) Close the Control Panel window, and then position the Screen Saver Settings dialog box to the left of the Paint window.
11. Press the Print Screen key to capture an image of the desktop. In Paint, open a new file. (*Hint*: Click File on the menu bar, and then click New.) Press the Ctrl+V keys to paste the image in the Paint file. Save the file as **Review Desktop XY**, where XY are your initials, in the Module3 > Review folder provided with your Data Files. Close Paint and the Screen Saver Settings dialog box.
12. Pin the following items to the Start menu:
    - Maps app
    - Classic Quilts folder (which you created in Step 6)
    - Themes settings
13. Complete the following tasks on the Start menu:
    - If the Maps tile is a live tile, turn the live tile off.
    - Resize the Maps tile to the Large setting.
    - Arrange the Themes and Classic Quilts tiles directly to the right of the Maps tile.
    - Use **Quilt Show** as the name of the new group of tiles.
14. Change the user picture to display one of the pictures stored in the Classic Quilts folder.

15. Complete the following tasks to create a screenshot of your Start menu:
    - Display the Start menu, scroll to show the entire Quilt Show group, and then press the Print Screen key to capture an image of the Start menu.
    - Start Paint, and then press the Ctrl+V keys to paste the image in the Paint file.
    - Save the file as **Review Start XY**, where XY are your initials, in the Module3 > Review folder provided with your Data Files.
    - Close Paint.
16. Complete the following tasks to restore the settings on your computer:
    - Make the Maps tile on the Start menu a live tile.
    - Unpin the Maps, Themes, and Classic Quilts files from the Start menu.
    - Restore the default image for the user picture.
    - Change the desktop theme to its original theme, which is Windows by default.
    - Display the original set of icons on the desktop.
    - Unpin the Tumble picture file from the Paint Jump List, and then unpin Paint from the taskbar.
    - Delete the Classic Quilts folder in the Pictures folder.
    - Delete the Review Removable Disk Shortcut icon from the desktop.
17. Close any open windows.

Case Problem 1

See the Starting Data Files section at the beginning of this module for a list of Data Files needed for this Case Problem.

Retro Motors Chad Bachman started Retro Motors as a place for classic car enthusiasts to buy and sell their cars. When he is not traveling to auto shows and private dealers to test drive vintage vehicles, Chad manages 10 employees in a showroom and office in Tempe, Arizona. He has hired you to help him run the office. Because he just installed Windows 10, he asks you to personalize the Start menu and desktop on his computer to focus on tools he can use in his business. As you perform the following steps, note the original settings of the Start menu and desktop so you can restore them later. Complete the following steps:

1. Change the desktop theme to any other theme (including an online theme) that seems appropriate for Retro Motors. (*Hint*: If you choose an online theme, click the Open button when the download is complete to add the theme to the Control Panel's Personalization window.) Close Microsoft Edge or other browser, if necessary. Close the Control Panel's Personalization window.
2. Complete the following tasks to add desktop icons to the desktop:
    - Change the desktop icon settings on your computer to display the Computer, Network, and Control Panel icons in addition to the default Recycle Bin icon.
    - Change the image for the Network icon so that it displays any other appropriate image.
3. Change the accent color to orange (first square in the color palette).
4. Insert the USB drive or other removable media containing your Data Files in the appropriate drive, and then create a shortcut to this drive on the desktop. Use **Case1 Removable Disk Shortcut** as the name of the shortcut.
5. Use the Case1 Removable Disk Shortcut on the desktop to copy the five picture files in the Module3 > Case1 folder provided with your Data Files to a new folder in the Pictures folder. Use **Retro** as the name of the new folder.
6. Complete the following tasks to customize the Start menu:
    - Unpin the News and Xbox tiles.
    - Pin the Calculator and Camera apps.
    - Pin the Retro folder (which you created in Step 5).

- Resize the Calculator and Camera tiles to the Wide setting, and then stack them on top of one another.
- Name the group containing the Calculator, Camera, and Retro tiles as **Business**.
- Change the user picture to display one of the pictures stored in the Pictures > Retro folder.

7. Display the Start menu, scroll down to display the entire Business group, and then press the Print Screen key to capture an image of the Start menu. Start Paint and then press the Ctrl+V keys to paste the image in the Paint file. Save the file as **Case1 Start XY**, where XY are your initials, in the Module3 > Case1 folder provided with your Data Files.

8. Complete the following tasks to set up a screen saver:
   - Open the Screen Saver Settings dialog box, and select the Photos screen saver.
   - Change the settings so the screen saver displays pictures from the Retro folder.
   - Move the dialog box so that some or all of the desktop items are clearly visible.
   - Use a taskbar tool to minimize other open windows.

9. Press the Print Screen key to capture an image of the desktop. Make Paint the active window, and then press the Ctrl+V keys to paste the image in the Paint file. Save the file as **Case1 Desktop XY**, where XY are your initials, in the Module3 > Case1 folder provided with your Data Files.

10. Complete the following tasks to restore the settings on your computer:
    - Close the Screen Saver Settings dialog box without saving your changes.
    - Unpin the Calculator, Camera, and Retro tiles from the Start menu.
    - Pin the News and Xbox apps to the Start menu, and then drag each to its original group.
    - Restore the default image for the user picture.
    - Restore the original theme, which is Windows by default.
    - If you downloaded a theme from the Microsoft website, delete the theme. (*Hint*: Right-click the theme, click Delete theme on the shortcut menu, and then click the Yes button.)
    - Display the original set of icons on the desktop (which is only the Recycle Bin icon by default).
    - Delete the Retro folder in the Pictures folder.
    - Delete the Case1 Removable Disk Shortcut icon from the desktop.

11. Close any open windows.

Case Problem 2

There are no Data Files needed for this Case Problem.

Clarity Weather Services Kiera and Will Moore own Clarity Weather Services, a company in Bethesda, Maryland, that provides weather information to businesses that need accurate, constantly updated forecasts. You are the office manager for the company and work with the staff and clients to help them use the company's resources. After installing Windows 10 on all of the office computers, Kiera asks you to personalize the desktop on her computer to reflect the company image. As you perform the following steps, note the original settings of the Start menu and desktop so you can restore them later. Complete the following steps:

1. Change the desktop theme to any other theme (including an online theme) that seems appropriate for Clarity Weather Services. (*Hint*: If you choose an online theme, click the Open button when the download is complete to add the theme to the Control Panel's Personalization window.) Close Microsoft Edge or other browser, if necessary. Close the Control Panel's Personalization window.

2. Complete the following tasks to add desktop icons to the desktop:
   - Change the desktop icon settings on your computer to display the This PC and Network icons in addition to the default Recycle Bin icon.
   - Change the image for the Recycle Bin (full) icon so that it displays a picture of a folder with contents.
   - Change the image for the Recycle Bin (empty) icon so that it displays a picture of a folder with no contents.

CHALLENGE

3. Change the accent color to one Windows picks from the desktop background picture.

Explore 4. Show the color on the Start menu, taskbar, and action center. (*Hint*: In the Colors category of the Personalization window, use a slider in the Choose a color section.)

5. Save the current desktop settings as a theme for sharing. Name the theme **Clarity**, and store it in the Case2 folder.

Explore 6. Pin the Weather app to the taskbar.

Explore 7. In the Lock screen category of the Personalization window, show detailed status for the Weather app. (*Hint*: Use a button in the "Choose an app to show detailed status" section.)

8. Change the screen saver to Mystify. Leave the Personalization window open, but close any other open windows.

9. Create a virtual desktop and then switch to it. Open the Weather app on the new desktop.

10. Switch to Desktop 1 and then display thumbnail images of both desktops.

11. Press the Print Screen key to capture an image of the desktops. Start Paint on Desktop 1, and then press the Ctrl+V keys to paste the image in the Paint file. Save the file as **Case2 Desktop XY**, where XY are your initials, in the Module3 > Case2 folder provided with your Data Files.

12. Complete the following tasks to work with the two desktops:

   • Close the Screen Saver Settings dialog box on Desktop 1.

   • Move the Weather app from Desktop 2 to Desktop 1.

   • Close Desktop 2.

13. Snap the Weather app to the right side of the desktop, and then snap the Personalization window to the left side of the desktop.

Explore 14. Complete the following steps to customize the Start menu:

   • Pin the following items to the Start menu: Alarms & Clock app, Cortana app, and File Explorer. (*Hint*: Use the File Explorer command on the Start menu.)

   • Move each new tile into a blank space in the Life at a glance group.

15. With the Start menu open, press the Print Screen key to capture an image of the Start menu. Start Paint, and then press the Ctrl+V keys to paste the image in the Paint file. Save the file as **Case2 Start XY**, where XY are your initials, in the Module3 > Case2 folder provided with your Data Files. Close Paint.

16. Complete the following tasks to restore the settings on your computer:

   • Unsnap the two windows on the desktop. (*Hint*: Drag the title bar of each window.)

   • Unpin the Alarms & Clock, Cortana, and File Explorer tiles from the Start menu.

   • Unpin the Weather app from the taskbar, and then close the Weather window.

   • Restore the original app used to show detailed status on the Lock screen.

   • Restore the original screen saver.

   • Restore the original theme, which is Windows by default.

   • If you downloaded a theme from the Microsoft website, delete the theme. (*Hint*: Right-click the theme, click Delete theme on the shortcut menu, and then click the Yes button.)

   • Display the original set of icons on the desktop (which is only the Recycle Bin icon by default).

   • Restore the default images for the Recycle Bin icons.

   • Turn off the setting that shows color on the Start menu, taskbar, and action center.

17. Close any open windows.

CHALLENGE

Case Problem 3

See the Starting Data Files section at the beginning of this module for a list of Data Files needed for this Case Problem.

Pottery Works Allison Markos is the manager of Pottery Works in Asheville, North Carolina. Allison provides clay and studio space in which customers can sculpt clay or choose a piece of pottery and then paint or glaze it. Allison finishes the piece by firing it in a kiln. For inspiration, Allison provides sample designs. The most popular of these are robot pictures that customers paint on plates and other pottery with flat surfaces. Allison recently hired you as an assistant to provide customer service and general back-office support. She has a visual impairment and asks you to customize her computer so she can use it more effectively. As you perform the following steps, note the original settings of the desktop and other items so you can restore them later. Complete the following steps:

1. Insert the USB drive or other removable media containing your Data Files in the appropriate drive, and then create a shortcut to this drive on the desktop. Use **Case3 Removable Disk Shortcut** as the name of the shortcut.

2. Use the Case3 Removable Disk Shortcut on the desktop to copy the nine picture files in the Module3 > Case3 folder provided with your Data Files to a new folder in the Pictures folder. Use **Robots** as the name of the new folder.

3. Pin the following items to the Start menu: Paint app, Ease of Access settings, Display settings, Personalization settings, and the Robots folder.

Explore 4. Complete the following steps to use the Personalization tile to change the desktop background:
   - Play a slide show on the desktop background.
   - Choose the Robots folder (which you created in Step 2) as the source of the pictures.
   - Change the picture every minute.
   - Choose the Fit setting for the desktop pictures.

Explore 5. Display the Start menu as a full-screen menu. (*Hint*: Use the Start category of settings in the Personalization window.) Close the Personalization window.

6. Complete the following tasks to rearrange the tiles on the Start menu:
   - Unpin two medium tiles from the Start menu. (Note which tiles you remove so you can pin them later.)
   - Resize two medium tiles in the Life at a glance group to large. (Note which tiles you resize so you can restore them to their original size later.)
   - Move tiles in the Life at a glance group into blank spaces in the group. (Note the original configuration so you can restore it later.)
   - Rename the new group, which contains the Paint, Ease of Access, Display, Personalization, and Robots tiles, as **Pottery Works**.

7. With the Start menu open, press the Print Screen key to capture an image of the desktop. Start Paint, and then press the Ctrl+V keys to paste the image in the Paint file. Save the file as **Case3 Start XY**, where XY are your initials, in the Module3 > Case3 folder provided with your Data Files.

Explore 8. Complete the following tasks to make the taskbar easier for Allison to use:
   - Pin Paint to the taskbar.
   - Use Paint to open three pictures of your choice in the Robots folder. Pin each picture to the Paint Jump List, and then minimize the Paint window.
   - If necessary, unlock the taskbar. (*Hint*: Right-click the taskbar and if the Lock the taskbar option is checked, click Lock the taskbar to deselect the option.)
   - Increase the height of the taskbar to make it about twice its original height. (*Hint*: Drag the top of the taskbar to resize it.)
   - Use the Ease of Access tile on the Start menu to display the Ease of Access settings.
   - Turn on Magnifier.

- When the Magnifier icon appears, increase the magnification to 200%. (*Hint*: Click the Magnifier icon, if necessary, to display the Magnifier title bar and toolbar, and then click the Zoom In button.)
- Right-click the Paint button to display its Jump List.

⊕ **Explore** 9. Press the Print Screen key to capture an image of the desktop. Reduce the magnification to 100%. (*Hint*: Click the Magnifier icon, and then click the Zoom out button.)

10. Make Paint the active window, and then press the Ctrl+V keys to paste the image in the Paint file. Save the file as **Case3 Desktop XY**, where XY are your initials, in the Module3 > Case3 folder provided with your Data Files. Minimize the Paint window.

⊕ **Explore** 11. Turn off the Magnifier, and then close the Ease of Access window.

12. Change the desktop icon settings on your computer to display the This PC and Control Panel icons.

⊕ **Explore** 13. Use the desktop shortcut menu to change the view of the desktop so it displays large icons. (*Hint*: Right-click the desktop, point to View, and then click Large icons.)

14. Press the Print Screen key to capture an image of the desktop. Make Paint the active window, and then press the Ctrl+V keys to paste the image in the Paint file. Save the file as **Case3 Icons XY**, where XY are your initials, in the Module3 > Case3 folder provided with your Data Files. Close Paint.

15. Complete the following tasks to restore the settings on your computer:
- Delete the Case3 Removable Disk Shortcut icon from the desktop.
- Change the view of the desktop so it displays Medium icons.
- Display the original set of icons on the desktop, which is only the Recycle Bin by default.
- Change the taskbar to its original height.
- Restore the original theme, which is Windows by default.
- Unpin the three robot pictures from the Paint Jump List, and then unpin Paint from the taskbar.
- Unpin the Paint, Ease of Access, Display, Personalization, and Robots tiles from the Start menu.
- Resize the two large tiles in the Life at a glance group to medium.
- Pin the two tiles you removed from the Start menu.
- Return all the tiles to their original positions.
- Turn off the setting that displays the Start menu full screen.
- Delete the Robots folder in the Pictures folder.

16. Close all open windows.

Case Problem 4

There are no Data Files needed for this Case Problem.

Choi Graphics After training to be a graphic designer, Jin Choi decided to start his own company in Santa Clara, California, providing illustrations and animations to electronic game companies. Jin recently upgraded all of the computers at Choi Graphics to Windows 10 and then hired you to manage the office. After working with a client in San Jose, Jin shows you a screenshot of that client's Start menu and another of his desktop. See Figure 3-36. He thinks the design of the Start menu and desktop would be appropriate for the computers at Choi Graphics, and he asks you to create something similar on your computer.

Figure 3-36   Model Start menu and desktop for Choi Graphics

1. Complete the following steps to customize the desktop:
   - Download an online theme in the Art (illustrative) or Games category. The one shown in the figure is called "Giving Heroes." (*Hint*: If you choose an online theme, click the Open button when the download is complete to add the theme to the Control Panel's Personalization window.)
   - Set Windows to automatically pick an accent color from the desktop background.
   - Choose the Ribbons screen saver.
   - Minimize the Personalization window, if necessary.
2. Capture an image of the desktop with the Screen Saver Settings dialog box open, and then save the image in a Paint file named **Case4 Desktop XY**, where XY are your initials, in the Module3 > Case4 folder provided with your Data Files.
⊕ Explore 3. Complete the following steps to customize the Start menu:
   - Display the Start menu full screen. (*Hint*: Use the Start category of settings in the Personalization window.)
   - Show color on the Start menu, taskbar, and action center. (*Hint*: In the Colors category of the Personalization window, use a slider in the Choose a color section.)
   - Resize the Xbox tile to the Large setting.
4. Capture an image of the Start menu, and then save the image in a Paint file named **Case4 Start XY**, where XY are your initials, in the Module3 > Case4 folder provided with your Data Files.
5. Restore the original settings, and then close all open windows.

Working with the Internet and Email

Communicating with Others

OBJECTIVES

Session 4.1
- Open, view, and navigate webpages in Microsoft Edge
- Find online information with Cortana
- Annotate webpages
- Read and revisit webpages
- Organize links to your favorite webpages

Session 4.2
- Explain how email works
- Send, receive, reply to, and delete email with Mail
- Attach a file to an email message
- Add a contact using People
- Create appointments with Calendar

Case | *Step Up*

Kent Arneson is the director of Step Up in Salt Lake City, Utah, a career coaching agency that provides job counseling services to recent graduates, residents returning to the workforce, and professionals interested in changing careers. Step Up focuses on opportunities in Salt Lake City and surrounding areas and offers workshops on general career development topics. One of the organization's most popular workshops teaches participants how to research jobs and find reliable, up-to-date occupation information. Although Kent has been focused on running the company, he wants to teach a few workshops to keep in touch with clients. He is also organizing a three-day conference on career opportunities in Salt Lake City for people from out of state. In preparation, he wants to learn about using online resources to find quick answers to questions about living and working in Salt Lake City. As his project assistant, you regularly use Microsoft Edge to gather information for Step Up on the World Wide Web. You also use the Windows 10 Mail app to exchange email with Step Up's clients. Kent has asked you to get him up to speed on using these apps.

In this module, you'll explore how the Internet and the web work and use Microsoft Edge to visit and organize webpages. You'll examine email technology and use Mail to send, receive, and reply to email messages. You'll also use two Windows apps to manage your contacts and your schedule.

STARTING DATA FILES

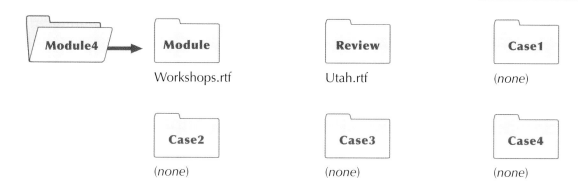

Module4 → Module
Workshops.rtf

Review
Utah.rtf

Case1
(*none*)

Case2
(*none*)

Case3
(*none*)

Case4
(*none*)

Session 4.1 Visual Overview:

The **Favorites bar** contains links to pages you view often.

The **uniform resource locator (URL)** of the webpage indicates its location.

A hyperlink text (or hypertext) document on the web is called a **webpage**.

The **navigation bar** includes tools for navigating and managing websites you visit.

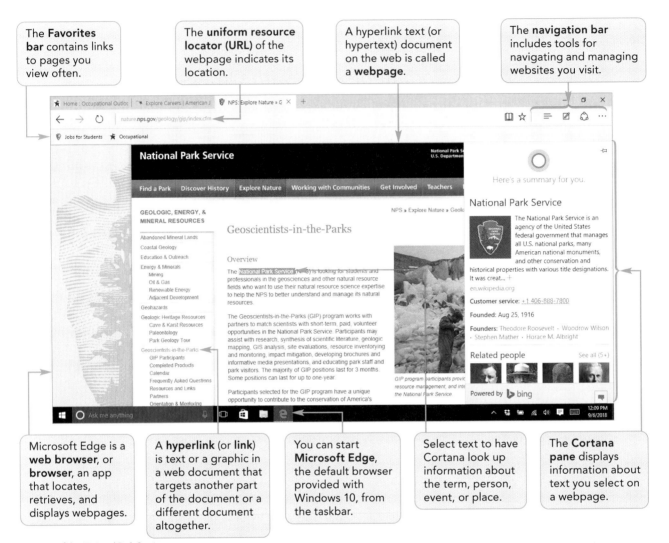

Microsoft Edge is a **web browser**, or **browser**, an app that locates, retrieves, and displays webpages.

A **hyperlink** (or **link**) is text or a graphic in a web document that targets another part of the document or a different document altogether.

You can start **Microsoft Edge**, the default browser provided with Windows 10, from the taskbar.

Select text to have Cortana look up information about the term, person, event, or place.

The **Cortana pane** displays information about text you select on a webpage.

Courtesy of the National Park Service

Microsoft Edge

Use the **Make a Web Note** tools to annotate a webpage.

Use **tabbed browsing** to open more than one webpage in a single browser session.

The **Favorites list** displays links to webpages you plan to visit often.

The **Reading list** contains links to webpages you designate for later reading.

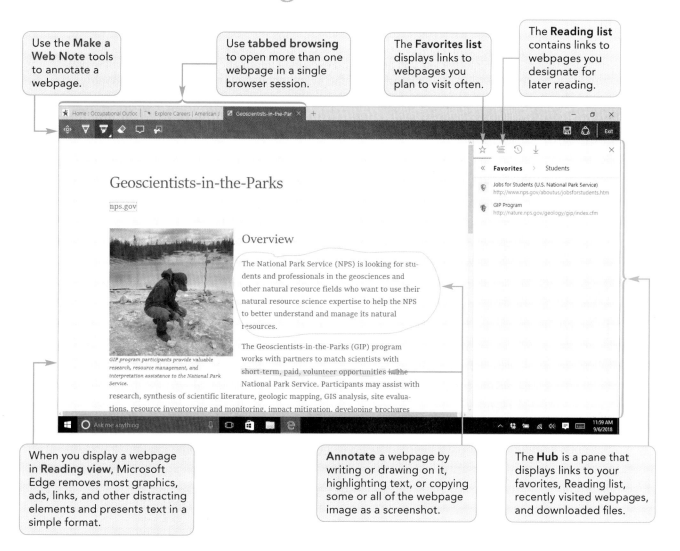

When you display a webpage in **Reading view**, Microsoft Edge removes most graphics, ads, links, and other distracting elements and presents text in a simple format.

Annotate a webpage by writing or drawing on it, highlighting text, or copying some or all of the webpage image as a screenshot.

The **Hub** is a pane that displays links to your favorites, Reading list, recently visited webpages, and downloaded files.

Exploring the Internet and the Web

When you connect two or more computers to exchange information and resources, they form a network. You can connect networks to each other to share information across a wide area. The worldwide, publicly accessible collection of networks is called the **Internet**, and it consists of millions of computers linked to networks all over the world. The Internet lets you access and exchange information via electronic mail (email), online newsgroups, file transfer, and the linked documents of the **World Wide Web**, better known as the **web**. See Figure 4-1.

Figure 4-1   **Connecting computers to the Internet**

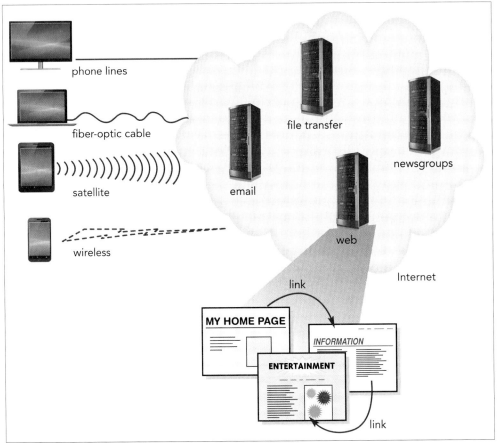

©iStock.com/CostinT, ©iStock.com/scanrail

The web is a service that you access via the Internet. While the Internet is a collection of networks connected by communication media such as fiber-optic cables and wireless connections, the web is a collection of documents connected by hyperlinks. You click a link to display the targeted information. For example, as shown in Figure 4-2, you can click links on the first Library of Congress web document to display related documents.

Figure 4-2   **Library of Congress webpage with links to other webpages**

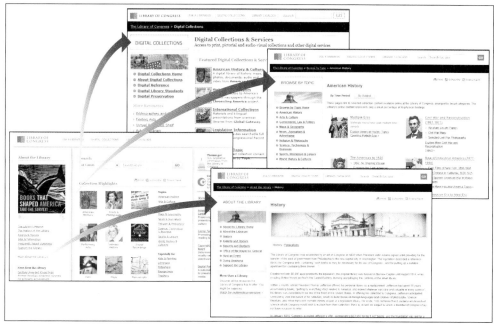

Courtesy of the Library of Congress

Webpages are stored on Internet computers called **web servers**. A **website** is a collection of webpages that have a common theme or focus, such as all pages containing information about the Library of Congress. The web is appealing because it generally displays up-to-date information in a colorful, lively format that can use images, text, sound, video, and animation.

When you want to find information on the web, you typically use a **search engine**, which is a program that conducts searches to retrieve webpages. To work with a search engine, you enter a word or an expression as the search criteria. The search engine lists links to webpages that fit your criteria. General search engines include Google and Bing.

A popular innovation in web technology is called **cloud computing**, which refers to providing and using computer tools, such as software, via the Internet (or the cloud). With cloud computing you can use your web browser to access and work with software. You do not need to purchase and install a complete app. Instead, you use the software services you need for free or for a usage fee. For example, when you use a web mapping service, such as MapQuest or Google Maps, to find directions from one location to another, you are using cloud computing. The software and data for the maps are not stored on your computer—they're on the cloud at the mapping service's website. This software is known as a **web app**. For example, Microsoft Office Online is a suite of web apps provided on the cloud as simplified versions of the programs provided in Microsoft Office, such as Word and Excel.

Using Web Browsers

You use a web browser, or browser, to visit websites around the world; interact with webpages by clicking links; view multimedia documents; transfer files, images, videos, and sounds to and from your computer; conduct searches for specific topics; and run programs on other computers. The browser included with Windows 10 is called Microsoft Edge.

When you attempt to view a webpage, your browser locates and retrieves the document from the web server and displays its contents on your computer. The server stores the webpage in one location, and browsers anywhere in the world can display it.

For your browser to access the web, you must have an Internet connection. In a university setting, your connection might come from your campus network. If you are working on a home computer, you have a few options for connecting to the Internet. Most likely, you are using a **broadband connection**, a high-capacity, high-speed medium for connecting to the Internet. Popular broadband technologies include a **digital subscriber line (DSL)**, which is a high-speed connection through your telephone line, and **digital cable**, which uses a cable modem attached to cable television lines. A **wireless connection** uses infrared light or radio-frequency signals to communicate with devices that are physically connected to a network or the Internet. Home connections also require an account with an **Internet service provider (ISP)**, a company that sells Internet access. The ISP provides instructions for connecting your computer to one of its servers, which is connected to the Internet. You can then use your browser to visit websites and access other Internet services.

Getting Started with Microsoft Edge

Microsoft Edge (or Edge for short) is the default web browser in Windows 10 and lets you communicate, access, and share information on the web. Microsoft Edge has a clean, modern design that lets you focus on webpage content instead of browser controls. As a Windows app, it can run on a variety of Windows 10 devices ranging from desktops and laptops to tablets and smartphones. Because it integrates with other Windows 10 apps such as Cortana, Microsoft Edge does not run on earlier versions of Windows. To maintain compatibility with older websites, Windows 10 still includes Internet Explorer, the default browser provided with earlier versions of Windows.

When you start Microsoft Edge, it opens to a **home page**, which is the webpage that a browser is set to open at startup. The default home page for Microsoft Edge is the Start page, which displays a changing gallery of personalized news images, weather information, sports, and games collected from websites. Your computer manufacturer or school might have set up a different home page.

Your first task in showing Kent how to research career information for Step Up clients is to start Edge. You must be connected to the Internet to perform all of the steps in this session. Mute your speakers, if necessary, so the sounds that certain webpages play do not disturb others.

To start Microsoft Edge:

▶ **1.** Click the **Microsoft Edge** button e on the taskbar. Microsoft Edge opens to its home page.

>   **Trouble?** If a Network Connection dialog box opens, enter your user name and password, and then click the Connect button. If you do not know your user name or password, ask your instructor or technical support person for help. You must have an Internet connection to complete the steps in this module.

TIP

To change the home page, start Microsoft Edge, click the More button, click Settings, and then select an option in the Open with section.

▶ **2.** Click the **Maximize** button ☐ to maximize the Microsoft Edge window, if necessary. Figure 4-3 shows the Start page in Microsoft Edge. Your Start page will differ, or you might have a different home page.

| Figure 4-3 | Microsoft Edge default home page |

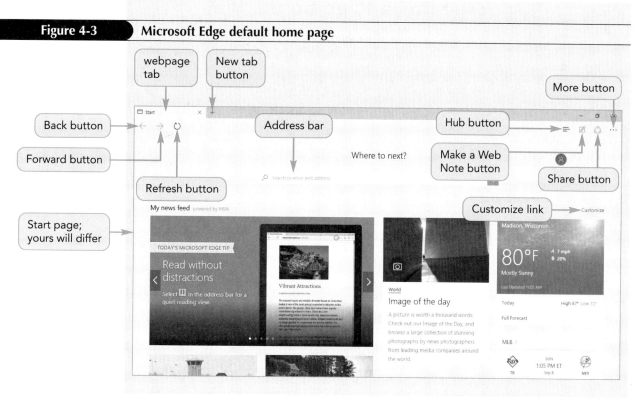

When you start Microsoft Edge, it displays a navigation area at the top of the window. The navigation area includes the following tools:

- Tabs—Display the webpages you open on separate tabs so you can switch from one webpage to another.
- Back and Forward buttons—Browse to the previous or next webpage in a sequence of opened pages.
- Refresh button—Refresh the contents of the webpage.
- Hub button—Access webpages you've identified as favorites and view other personalized information, such as your browsing history.
- Make a Web Note button—Click this button to use a pointing device, stylus, or fingertip to write and draw directly on a webpage. (A **stylus** is a pen-shaped digital tool for selecting and entering information on a touchscreen.) The Make a Web Note button is not active on the Start page.
- Share button—Share webpages with others through apps such as Mail. The Share button is not active on the Start page.
- More button—Manage the current webpage, and select settings for Microsoft Edge. For example, you can click the More button, and then click New window to open the current webpage in a new window.
- Address bar—View the address of the webpage; you can also type the address of a webpage you want to visit.

The main part of the Start page displays your **news feed**, a collection of live headlines, images, and information from six categories of websites: autos, entertainment, lifestyle, money, news, and sports. You can click the Customize link on the Start page to display websites from fewer than six categories, such as only news and sports.

Now you're ready to use Microsoft Edge to open and view a webpage.

Opening a Page on the Web

To find a particular webpage among the billions stored on web servers, your browser needs to know the uniform resource locator (URL) of the webpage. URLs are also called web addresses because they indicate the location of a webpage. As shown in Figure 4-4, a URL can consist of the following four parts:

- Protocol to use when transferring the webpage
- Address of the web server storing the page
- Pathname of the folder containing the page
- Filename of the webpage

Figure 4-4	Parts of a URL

The URL for most webpages starts with http, which stands for **Hypertext Transfer Protocol**, the most common way to transfer information around the web. (A **protocol** is a standardized procedure computers use to exchange information.) When the URL for a webpage starts with http://, the web browser uses Hypertext Transfer Protocol to retrieve the page.

The server address indicates the location of the web server storing the webpage. In www.loc.gov, the www indicates that the server is a web server, loc is the name the Library of Congress chose for this website, and .gov means that a government entity runs the web server. Other common types of web servers in the United States are .com (commercial), .net (network service providers or resources), .org (not-for-profit organizations), and .edu (educational institutions). The server address in a URL corresponds to an Internet Protocol (IP) address, which identifies every computer on the Internet. An **IP address** is a unique number that consists of four sets of numbers from 0 to 255 separated by periods, or dots, as in 216.35.148.4. Although computers can use IP addresses easily, they are difficult for people to remember, so domain names were created. A **domain name** identifies one or more IP addresses, such as loc.gov. URLs use the domain name in the server address part of the URL to identify a particular website.

In addition, each file stored on a web server has a unique pathname, just like files stored on a disk. The pathname in a URL includes the names of the folders containing the file, the filename, and its extension. A common filename extension for webpages is .html, sometimes shortened to .htm. For example, the pathname might be library/index.html, which specifies a file named index.html stored in a folder named library.

Not all URLs include a pathname. If you don't specify a pathname or filename in a URL, most web browsers open a file named index.html or index.htm, which is the default name for a website's main page.

Opening a Webpage Using a URL

One way to open a webpage in Microsoft Edge is to enter a URL in the Address bar. You can often find URLs in advertisements, in informational materials, and on the web so that you can gain quick access to specific information.

In most cases, URLs are not case sensitive, so you can enter a URL using all lowercase or all uppercase text. However, if the web server storing a webpage uses the UNIX operating system, the URL might be case sensitive. For mixed-case URLs, it's safer to enter them using the mixed case exactly as printed.

The first webpage you want to open for Kent is the home page of the U.S. Bureau of Labor Statistics, which provides information about employment throughout the United States.

To open a page on the web using a URL:

▶ **1.** Click in the **Address bar**. On the Start page, the Address bar displays "Search or enter web address." Microsoft Edge removes this text when you begin to type a web address. If Microsoft Edge is using a home page other than the Start page, clicking the Address bar selects the current web address. If the contents of the Address bar are not selected, drag to select the entire address.

▶ **2.** Type **bls.gov** in the Address bar. As you type, Microsoft Edge displays the names of other webpages you've opened that have URLs starting with the same characters, a feature called **AutoComplete**. Also, you can omit the http:// and www when you type a web address. Edge recognizes the entry in the Address bar as a URL.

▶ **3.** Press the **Enter** key. Edge opens the main, or home, page for the Bureau of Labor Statistics website. See Figure 4-5.

   Trouble? If the home page of the Bureau of Labor Statistics website does not open, you might have typed the URL incorrectly. Repeat Steps 1–3, making sure that the URL in the Address bar matches the URL in Step 2. If you still receive an error message, ask your instructor or technical support person for help.

Figure 4-5	Opening the Bureau of Labor Statistics home page

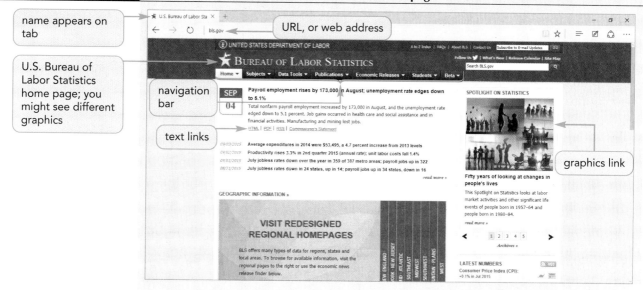

Because web content changes frequently, the webpages you open might differ from the figures in this module.

A home page on the web can have at least two meanings. It can be the webpage a browser is set to open by default, and it can also be the main page for a website that provides links to other webpages with related information.

Navigating with Links

The home page for a typical website includes plenty of links to help you navigate to its webpages, and those pages also include links you can click to navigate from one page to another. Links can be text, images, or a combination of both. Text links are usually colored and underlined, though the exact style can vary from one website to another.

To determine whether something on a webpage is a link, point to it. If the pointer changes to 🖑, the text or image is a link you can click to open a webpage. A ScreenTip displaying the URL of the link appears at the bottom of the window.

Step Up's clients are interested in the outlook for particular occupations so they can pursue jobs in fields that are expected to grow or be in high demand. For example, many clients are interested in the technology field and often ask about jobs as a computer support specialist. You'll show Kent how to find the occupational outlook for computer support specialists on the Bureau of Labor Statistics website.

To navigate a website using links:

▶ 1. Point to **Publications** in the site's navigation bar. The pointer changes to 🖑 and a menu of links in the Publications category appears below the navigation bar. See Figure 4-6.

Figure 4-6	Pointing to a link

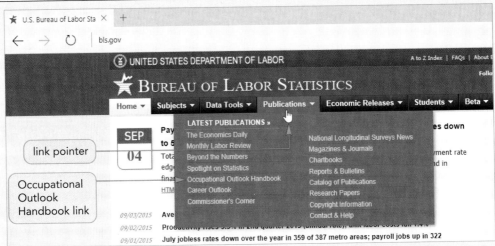

Trouble? If the current Bureau of Labor Statistics home page does not include a Publications link, point to any other link in the navigation bar and substitute that link when you perform Step 2.

Trouble? If a window opens asking for your feedback, close the window.

▶ 2. Click **Occupational Outlook Handbook** in the Publications menu to open the Occupational Outlook Handbook webpage.

▶ 3. In the OCCUPATION GROUPS list on the left, click **Computer and Information Technology** to open the Computer and Information Technology Occupations page, which lists occupations, summarizes the jobs, identifies the education required for an entry-level position, and provides the median pay in a recent year.

Trouble? If the webpage does not include a Computer and Information Technology link, read but do not perform the remaining steps in this section.

▶ 4. Scroll to display the Computer Support Specialists link. See Figure 4-7. The webpage you opened might look different.

| Figure 4-7 | Computer and Information Technology Occupations webpage |

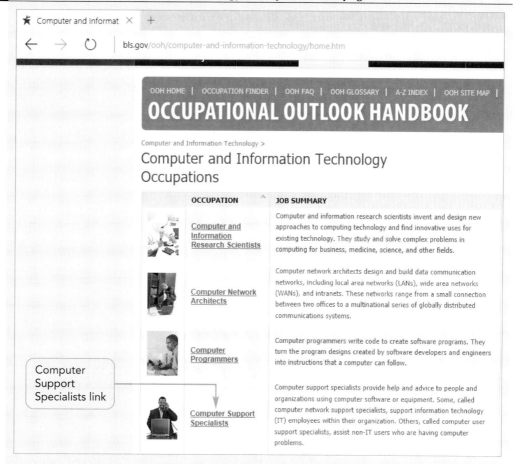

5. Click the **Computer Support Specialists** link to open the Computer Support Specialists page, which provides detailed information about the occupation.

Besides clicking links to navigate from one webpage to another, you can use tools that Edge provides.

Displaying Webpages in Internet Explorer

Microsoft Edge is designed for modern websites and apps that use contemporary technology. However, many websites use older technology such as Silverlight videos or ActiveX controls. (**Silverlight** is a web technology that creates interactive media experiences. **ActiveX controls** are small programs that enhance your browsing activities or help with tasks such as installing software. Both technologies are **deprecated**, meaning that developers are discouraged from using them because newer technologies have been created to take their place.) When you open a webpage that depends on these types of older technologies, it usually displays a message indicating that you need to install or use a **browser plug-in**, software that extends the capabilities of a browser. Because Microsoft Edge does not support plug-ins, you can use Internet Explorer in Windows 10 when you need to visit a webpage that uses plug-ins. If you encounter such a webpage while using Microsoft Edge, you can click the More button and then click Open with Internet Explorer. To start Internet Explorer on its own, open the Start menu and type "Internet Explorer," or click the All apps command on the Start menu, scroll the list, click the Windows Accessories folder, and then click Internet Explorer.

Navigating with Microsoft Edge Tools

Recall that when you use File Explorer, you can click the Back and Forward buttons to navigate the devices and folders on your computer. Microsoft Edge includes similar buttons you can use to navigate from one webpage to another, and it keeps track of the pages you visit. To return to the previous page, you can click the Back button to the left of the Address bar. After you navigate to a previous page, you can click the Forward button to continue to the next page in the sequence.

To return to previously viewed webpages:

▶ 1. To the left of the Address bar, click the **Back** button ← to return to the Computer and Information Technology Occupations page.

▶ 2. Click the **Forward** button → to return to the Computer Support Specialists page.

   Trouble? If you opened different webpages in the previous set of steps, substitute the names of the pages as appropriate in Steps 1 and 2.

Next, you want to show Kent how to use tabs to open other webpages without closing the Computer Support Specialists page.

Managing Webpages in Microsoft Edge

If you want to open a new webpage without closing the one you're currently viewing, you can use tabbed browsing to open more than one webpage at a time. To use tabbed browsing, you open a tab for each new page you want to view. You can open a new tab in three ways: click the New tab button at the top of the Microsoft Edge window, press the Ctrl key as you click a link on a webpage, or right-click the link and then click Open in new tab on the shortcut menu. You can then switch from one webpage to another by clicking the tabs at the top of the Microsoft Edge window. Each tab displays the title of its webpage so you can quickly identify the page you want to display. To close a tab, you click its Close tab button.

Now that you've explored a few pages on the Bureau of Labor Statistics website, you can compare that information to information on the American Job Center website, which provides resources for job seekers and people who want to explore career options. You'll show Kent how to open a new tab in Microsoft Edge and then use it to open the American Job Center home page.

To open other webpages on new tabs:

TIP

To customize the New tab, click the Customize link, and then choose whether you want the New tab to display top sites and your news feed, top sites only, or a blank page.

1. Click the **New tab** button ⊞ at the top of the Microsoft Edge window to open the New tab, which provides an Address bar and tiles representing popular websites.

2. Click in the **Address bar**, type **jobcenter.usa.gov**, and then press the **Enter** key. The American Job Center home page opens on the new tab. See Figure 4-8. The webpage you open might look different.

Figure 4-8   American Job Center home page

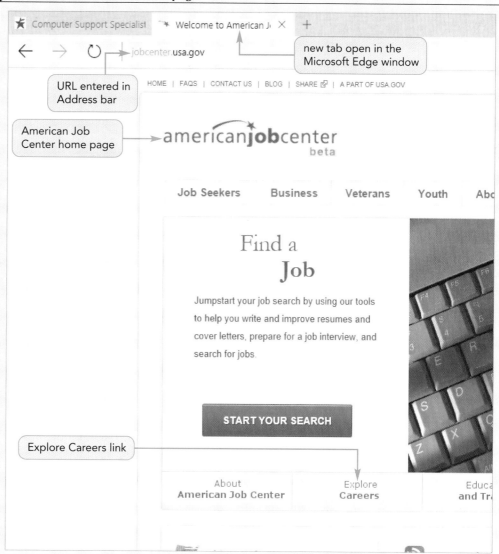

3. Right-click the **Explore Careers** link on the webpage, and then click **Open in new tab** on the shortcut menu. The Explore Careers webpage opens in a new tab, although the page is not visible yet. You need to display the tab for that page.

Trouble? If the Explore Careers link does not appear on the current webpage, right-click a different link on the page.

4. Click the **Explore Careers** tab to display the webpage. Now three tabs are displayed in Microsoft Edge for the open webpages. See Figure 4-9.

Figure 4-9	Tabs for the open webpages

three tabs open in Microsoft Edge

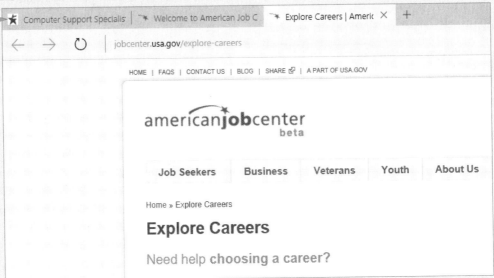

5. Click the **Welcome to American Job Center** tab to display that webpage.

TIP

Point to an undisplayed tab to see a thumbnail of the webpage.

Kent will return often to the home pages for the Bureau of Labor Statistics and American Job Center websites. To make it easy for him to reopen the webpages, you'll show him how to pin the webpages to the Start menu.

Pinning Webpages

When you find a website that you'll return to often, you can pin the site to the Start menu. Windows organizes the pinned sites into a group, which you can name. If you have an account on a website that displays messages or other account information, such as Twitter or Facebook, you can make the pinned site a live tile so it displays messages on the tile.

Because Kent wants to access the home pages for the Bureau of Labor Statistics and American Job Center websites quickly, you'll pin the sites to the Start menu.

To pin websites to the Start menu:

1. Click the **More** button ⋯ in the navigation bar, click **Pin this page to Start**, and then click the **Yes** button to pin the page to the Start menu.

2. Click the **Computer Support Specialists** tab to display its webpage. Kent wants to pin the home page for the Bureau of Labor Statistics to the Start menu, so you need to open the home page in a new tab.

▶ **3.** Press and hold the **Ctrl** key, and then click the **Bureau of Labor Statistics** link at the top of the webpage to open the Bureau of Labor Statistics home page in a new tab.

▶ **4.** Click the **U.S. Bureau of Labor Statistics** tab to display the webpage.

▶ **5.** Click the **More** button ⋯ in the navigation bar, click **Pin this page to Start**, and then click the **Yes** button to pin the page to the Start menu.

▶ **6.** Click the **Close** button ✕ to close Microsoft Edge. When a dialog box opens asking if you want to close all tabs, click the **Close all** button.

Trouble? If a dialog box asking if you want to close all tabs does not open, someone has already selected the Always close all tabs check box. All tabs close when you close Microsoft Edge.

▶ **7.** Click the **Start** button ⊞ to display the Start menu, which now includes the two tiles for the pinned sites. See Figure 4-10. The tiles on your Start menu might appear in a different place.

Figure 4-10 **Pinned sites on the Start menu**

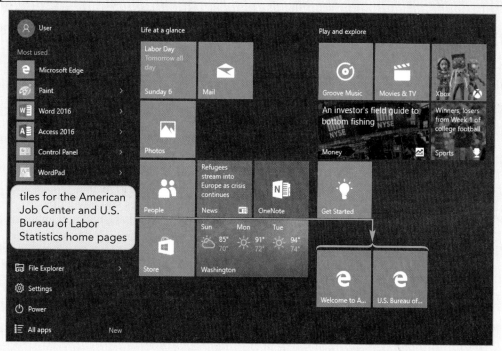

Trouble? If you can't see the two tiles for the pinned sites, you might need to scroll the Start menu.

▶ **8.** Click the **Welcome to American Job Center** tile to open the site in Microsoft Edge.

▶ **9.** Click the **Start** button ⊞ and then click the **U.S. Bureau of Labor Statistics** tile to open the home page for the Bureau of Labor Statistics website on a new tab.

Now that Kent knows the basics of opening and navigating webpages, he wants to learn how to search for a webpage. You'll show him how to use Cortana without leaving Microsoft Edge to find webpages.

Using Cortana to Find Online Information

Recall that Cortana is an electronic personal assistant designed to help you find files, search the web, keep track of information, and answer your questions. Cortana is integrated with Microsoft Edge to find answers and information on the web. When you enter a search term or ask a question in the Address bar, Edge displays search suggestions, search terms you've used before, and in some cases, the result or answer from Cortana, saving you the extra step of navigating to a search engine. For example, if you enter "Salt Lake City weather" in the Address bar, Cortana opens a highlighted bar below the Address bar to display the current weather conditions in Salt Lake City, Utah. Because the answer appears as you are typing the search term, the answer is called an instant result.

REFERENCE

Using Cortana to Find Online Information

- In Microsoft Edge, enter a question about weather, sports, finance, or other category in the Cortana Notebook to display instant results.

or

- Select text on a webpage.
- Right-click the selection, and then click Ask Cortana on the shortcut menu.

or

- Click the Cortana icon in the Address bar.

You can also use Cortana to learn more about a topic displayed on a webpage. Right-click a word, link, or selected text, and then click Ask Cortana to find out more information about the topic. Cortana opens a pane called the Cortana pane in Microsoft Edge to display the results so you don't have to leave the current webpage. For example, if you're viewing a webpage about things to do in Salt Lake City, you can select text on the page and use the Ask Cortana feature to display details about the Arches National Park, including opening and closing times and travel tips.

For some webpages that contain an address, phone number, or other location information, the Cortana icon ◯ appears in the Address bar. You can click the icon to have Cortana display detailed information about the place in the Cortana pane. For example, if you visit the website for a restaurant, Cortana displays a map identifying the restaurant's location, lists reviews, shows photos, provides the restaurant's phone number and hours, and presents links to directions and menus.

Cortana is turned off by default. If you have a Microsoft account, you can activate Cortana, which involves agreeing to let it collect information about you. If you use more than one Windows device, Cortana uses the information you provide to keep the devices in sync.

In the following steps, you activate Cortana if you haven't already activated it.

To activate Cortana:

▶ 1. Click in the **Search the web and Windows** box on the taskbar. Cortana opens and displays some of the tasks it can do for you. See Figure 4-11.

   Trouble? If your taskbar has an Ask me anything box instead of a Search the web and Windows box, Cortana is already activated. Skip ahead to the "To find an instant result" steps on the next page.

   Trouble? If your screen does not match the one in Figure 4-11, click the Try Cortana button ◉ in the left pane.

Figure 4-11 Activating Cortana

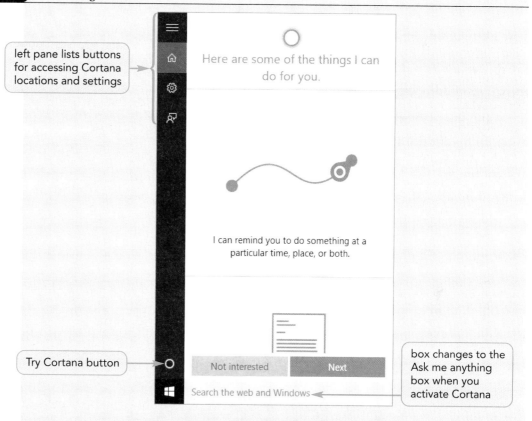

left pane lists buttons for accessing Cortana locations and settings

Here are some of the things I can do for you.

I can remind you to do something at a particular time, place, or both.

Try Cortana button

Not interested | Next

Search the web and Windows

box changes to the Ask me anything box when you activate Cortana

▶ **2.** Click the **Next** button. A notice appears explaining that Cortana will collect and use information and store it in its Notebook. (Recall that the Notebook keeps track of what you like, such as your interests and favorite places, and what you want it to do, such as display reminders or information that might interest you.)

▶ **3.** Click the **I agree** button. Cortana asks for a name to use when addressing you.

▶ **4.** Type your first name and then click the **Next** button. Cortana displays a few starter interests, webpages, and search text that might suit you based on information in your Microsoft account.

▶ **5.** Click the **Got it** button. Cortana stores the webpage information and search text in your Notebook.

Step Up is organizing a conference on job opportunities in Salt Lake City to attract people to the area from out of state. Kent is planning an event at the conference center to welcome participants the day they arrive. Many of the conference participants will fly through Denver on their way to Salt Lake City, and Kent wants to track the flights to check their status. You'll show him how to use Microsoft Edge and Cortana to find the status of a popular flight as an instant result.

To find an instant result:

▶ **1.** Click the **New tab** button ⊞ at the top of the Microsoft Edge window to open the New tab.

▶ **2.** In the Address bar, type **frontier 579** to search for the status of Frontier Airline's flight 579. Cortana displays the current status of the flight. See Figure 4-12.

Trouble? If you pressed the Enter key after typing the text in the Address bar, click the Back button ← and then repeat Step 2, making sure you do not press the Enter key.

Trouble? If no flight information appears, the flight number has probably changed. Continue to Step 3.

Figure 4-12	Instant search results

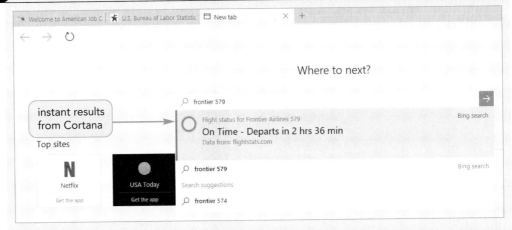

3. Click a blank spot on the New tab to close the results.

Kent knows that many people considering a move to Salt Lake City want to know about nearby outdoor activities. In fact, Utah has five national parks, many of them near Salt Lake City. You'll show Kent how to find a webpage about Utah's national parks and then use Cortana to display details about one of the parks.

To find a webpage and display details about a topic:

1. On the New tab, select the text in the Address bar, and then type **utah national park** to display search suggestions for the text you entered. See Figure 4-13.

Figure 4-13	Search suggestions on the New tab

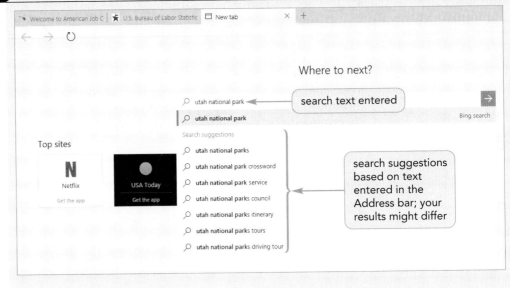

2. In the search suggestions, click **utah national park service** to display the search results in Bing, the Microsoft search engine.

   Trouble? If "utah national park service" does not appear in the search results, continue typing to add "service" to the search text, and then press the Enter key.

3. Scroll as necessary to display a result from the U.S. National Park Service, and then click that result. For example, click **Utah (U.S. National Park Service)**. (The specific wording of your result might vary.) A webpage on the National Park Service website (nps.gov) opens displaying information about the national parks in Utah.

   Trouble? If "Utah (U.S. National Park Service)" does not appear in the search results, type "nps.gov/state/ut/index.htm" in the Address bar, and then press the Enter key.

4. Scroll as necessary to display information about Bryce Canyon, right-click the **Bryce Canyon** link, and then click **Ask Cortana** on the shortcut menu. The Cortana pane opens on the right side of the Microsoft Edge window to display information about Bryce Canyon National Park, including photos, a map, and a description. See Figure 4-14.

Figure 4-14	Cortana providing details about a webpage topic

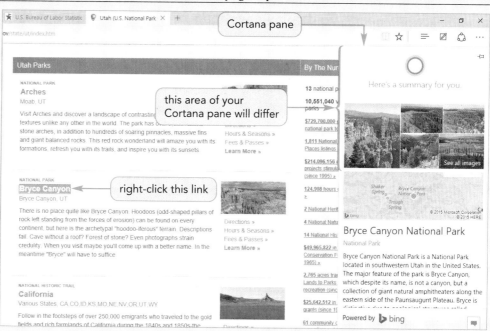

5. Scroll down to review the information, and then click a blank area of the webpage to close the Cortana pane.

The National Park Service (NPS) often employs people living in Salt Lake City and other parts of Utah, especially students looking for summer jobs and internships. Kent wants to explore employment resources on the NPS website next. As he does, you'll show him how to use two popular features in Microsoft Edge: Reading view and Make a Web Note.

Reading and Annotating Webpages

When you find a webpage containing information you want to focus on, you can use the Reading view button on the Address bar to switch to Reading view, which removes most graphics, ads, links, and other distracting elements and presents webpage text in a simple format. Reading view is especially helpful when you are browsing information-rich webpages, such as articles or studies, and pages that are cluttered with extra, nonessential content. You can also set your preferences for how the webpage appears in Reading view. For example, you can display the page with a light or dark background and change the size of the text.

Microsoft Edge can display many, but not all, webpages in Reading view. If the Reading view button on the Address bar is active—that is, it is no longer grayed, or dimmed, and displays a ScreenTip when you point to it—you can display the current webpage in Reading view.

On pages containing information you want to refer to quickly, you can use the Make a Web Note button to annotate the webpage by writing or drawing on it, highlighting text, or copying some or all of the webpage image as a screenshot. You can also save the annotated webpage and share it with others.

Kent thinks he will use Reading view frequently because he is often distracted by graphics, ads, and other extraneous information when viewing webpages. As you look for student employment information on the National Parks Service website, you'll show Kent how to use Reading view and set his preferences for using it.

To display a webpage in Reading view and change settings:

▶ **1.** Scroll to the top of the Utah webpage in the National Park Service website, click **About Us** in the navigation bar, and then click **Work With Us**. The Work with Us (U.S. National Park Service) webpage opens showing an overview of NPS employment information.

▶ **2.** In the list of links on the left, click **Jobs for Students**.

Trouble? If the list of links does not include Jobs for Students, click any other link in the list.

▶ **3.** Scroll to display the list of opportunities, and then click **Geoscientists-in-the-Parks Internships** to display a webpage describing this program.

▶ **4.** Click the **Reading view** button 📖 on the Address bar to switch to Reading view. See Figure 4-15.

| Figure 4-15 | Webpage in Reading view |

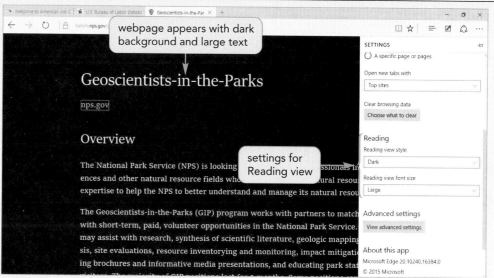

page appears with most of the graphics and links removed

Reading view button

your page in Reading view might display a photo or differ in other ways

5. Click the **More** button […] in the navigation bar, and then click **Settings** to display the Settings pane.

6. Scroll to display the Reading section, click the **Reading view style** box to display the styles, and then click **Dark**. The webpage appears with a black background and white text.

7. Click the **Reading view font size** box, and then click **Large** to change the font size of the webpage text. See Figure 4-16.

| Figure 4-16 | Changing Reading view settings |

The current settings might work well in sunny conditions, but you might not need them in normal indoor lighting. For now, you can return the settings to their defaults.

> **8.** In the Settings pane, click the **Reading view style** box, and then click **Default**.

> **9.** Click the **Reading view font size** box, and then click **Medium**.

> **10.** Click a blank spot on the webpage to close the Settings pane.

Now you can show Kent how to use annotations on the current webpage. He wants to highlight information of interest to potential applicants.

To annotate a webpage:

> **1.** Click the **Make a Web Note** button 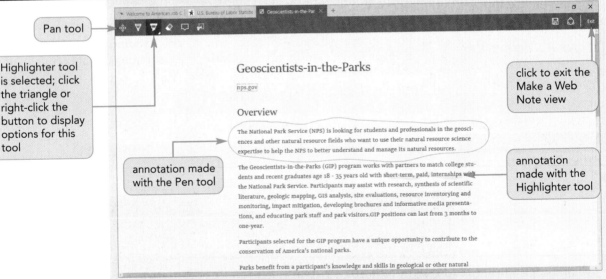 to display the Make a Web Note tools at the top of the webpage. The Pan tool is active by default, allowing you to drag the webpage to display content out of view. Panning is typically more useful on a regular webpage than one in Reading view.

> **2.** Click the **Pen** button on the toolbar, and then drag to draw a circle around the first paragraph after the "Overview" heading. Release the mouse button when the circle is complete.

> **3.** Click the **Highlighter** button on the toolbar, and then drag to highlight **short-term, paid, internships** in the next paragraph. See Figure 4-17.

Figure 4-17 **Annotated webpage**

Pan tool →

Highlighter tool is selected; click the triangle or right-click the button to display options for this tool

Geoscientists-in-the-Parks

nps.gov

Overview

The National Park Service (NPS) is looking for students and professionals in the geosciences and other natural resource fields who want to use their natural resource science expertise to help the NPS to better understand and manage its natural resources.

The Geoscientists-in-the-Parks (GIP) program works with partners to match college students and recent graduates age 18 - 35 years old with short-term, paid, internships with the National Park Service. Participants may assist with research, synthesis of scientific literature, geologic mapping, GIS analysis, site evaluations, resource inventorying and monitoring, impact mitigation, developing brochures and informative media presentations, and educating park staff and park visitors.GIP positions can last from 3 months to one-year.

Participants selected for the GIP program have a unique opportunity to contribute to the conservation of America's national parks.

Parks benefit from a participant's knowledge and skills in geological or other natural

annotation made with the Pen tool

click to exit the Make a Web Note view

annotation made with the Highlighter tool

The Make a Web Note toolbar includes three other buttons you can use to annotate a webpage. Use the Eraser tool to erase a mark you made with the Pen or Highlighter tool. (Be aware that the Eraser removes all the annotation marks). Select the Add a typed note button to write a short note, which you can leave open or collapse so the note appears only as a numbered icon. Select the Clip button to take a screenshot of some or all of the webpage and store the image temporarily on the Clipboard. You can then start an app such as Paint to paste the image in a new file and save it.

Now that you've annotated the webpage for Kent, he wants to save the annotations. You can do so by saving it to the Microsoft Edge Reading list, which is part of the Hub. The next section explains both of these features.

Using the Hub to Revisit Webpages

Microsoft Edge provides a central location for tracking, storing, and finding webpages you've already visited and files you downloaded from websites. This feature is called the Hub, a pane that displays links to webpages you've identified as your favorites (your Favorites list), webpages you've designated for reading later (your Reading list), webpages you visited recently (the **History list**), and a list of files you downloaded recently.

Creating a Reading List

Both the Favorites list and the Reading list provide quick access to webpages you want to revisit. The difference between the two tools is how you plan to use the webpages. Use the Favorites list for webpages you plan to return to often. For example, if you frequently use an online dictionary while preparing assignments or reports, add the home page of the online dictionary to your Favorites list. Use the Reading list for webpages you plan to return to once or twice so you can read the information at a convenient time. For example, if you are reading an in-depth article on a news site but don't have time to finish it, save the article to your Reading list so you can finish it later.

You can add annotated webpages to the Favorites list or the Reading list. When you do, Microsoft Edge saves the annotations along with the webpage. (You can also send the annotated webpage to OneNote, a Windows app for collecting and organizing your digital information.) Edge removes the annotations when you close the webpage, so you lose the annotations if you don't save them.

You'll show Kent how to save the current webpage, including annotations, to the Reading list.

To save an annotated webpage to the Reading list:

1. Click the **Save Web Note** button 💾 on the toolbar to display a list of places you can save the annotated webpage.

2. If necessary, click **Reading list** to display an image of the page and a box where you can enter a name. See Figure 4-18.

Figure 4-18   Adding a webpage to the Reading list

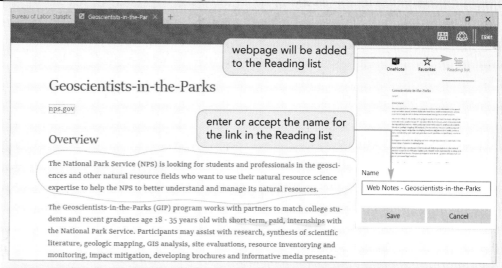

The suggested name is short and accurate, so you can accept it as the name to use in the Reading list.

TIP

You can add a webpage to the Reading list with or without annotations and save it in Reading view or regular webpage view.

3. Click the **Save** button to add the webpage and its annotations to the Reading list.

4. Click **Exit** on the toolbar to exit the Make a Web Note view and return to the current webpage without annotations.

   To make sure that Microsoft Edge saved a link to the annotated page, you can display the Reading list in the Hub.

5. Click the **Hub** button ≡ in the navigation bar, and then click the **Reading list** button 🗏 to display the contents of the Reading list. See Figure 4-19.

Figure 4-19   Reading list

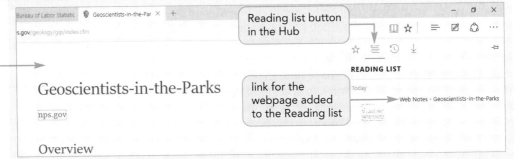

webpage might display a photo after you exit the Make a Web Note view

Reading list button in the Hub

link for the webpage added to the Reading list

6. Click a blank area of the webpage to close the Reading list.

7. Click the **Close** button ✕ to close Microsoft Edge. When a dialog box opens asking if you want to close all tabs, click the **Close all** button.

Another way to revisit a webpage you've already opened is to use the History list.

Using the History List

To open any webpage you've recently visited, you can use the History list, which is available in the Hub. The History list includes the websites you visited today, last week, and up to three weeks ago by default. You can also clear all history, which removes all the webpages in the History list. You should clear the History list after you visit websites that use confidential information, such as banking sites, so that unauthorized users cannot access the site and any passwords or other private information you might have entered.

Kent wants to return to the webpage on the American Job Center website that provides information about exploring careers. Because you already closed Edge, you can't use the Back button to return to that page. You'll use the History list to revisit the Explore Careers webpage.

To use the History list:

1. Click the **Microsoft Edge** button 🅔 on the taskbar to start Microsoft Edge.

2. Click the **Hub** button ≡ in the navigation bar to open the Hub and display the Reading list, the last location you used in the Hub.

Be sure to pin the Hub to the Edge window so you can work with its features efficiently.

3. Click the **Pin this pane** button 📌 at the top of the Hub to keep the Hub open on the right side of the Edge window.

   Trouble? If the Pin this pane button 📌 does not appear in your Hub, the Hub is already pinned to the Microsoft Edge window. Skip Step 3.

4. Click the **History** button 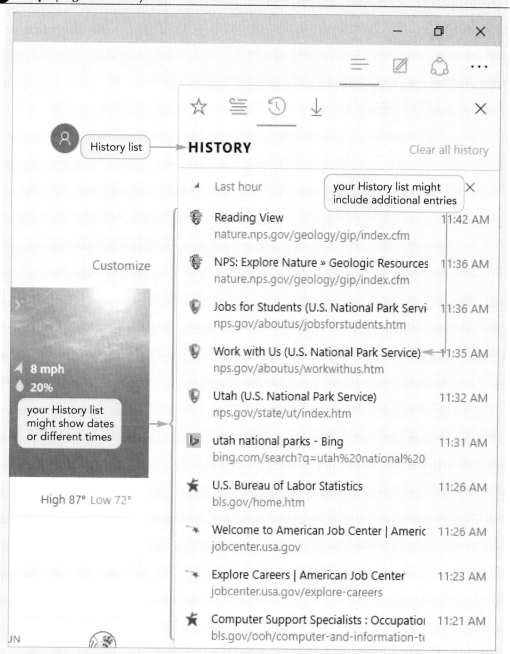 to display the History list. See Figure 4-20.

Figure 4-20   Displaying the History list

High 87° Low 72°

HISTORY   Clear all history

⊿   Last hour   your History list might
                       include additional entries   ✕

⚜   Reading View   11:42 AM
    nature.nps.gov/geology/gip/index.cfm

⚜   NPS: Explore Nature » Geologic Resources   11:36 AM
    nature.nps.gov/geology/gip/index.cfm

    Jobs for Students (U.S. National Park Servi·   11:36 AM
    nps.gov/aboutus/jobsforstudents.htm

    Work with Us (U.S. National Park Service)←──11:35 AM
    nps.gov/aboutus/workwithus.htm

    Utah (U.S. National Park Service)   11:32 AM
    nps.gov/state/ut/index.htm

    utah national parks - Bing   11:31 AM
    bing.com/search?q=utah%20national%20

★   U.S. Bureau of Labor Statistics   11:26 AM
    bls.gov/home.htm

⁻★ Welcome to American Job Center | Americ   11:26 AM
    jobcenter.usa.gov

⁻★ Explore Careers | American Job Center   11:23 AM
    jobcenter.usa.gov/explore-careers

★   Computer Support Specialists : Occupatioɪ   11:21 AM
    bls.gov/ooh/computer-and-information-tɛ

History list

your History list might show dates or different times

5. If necessary, click **Last hour** or click **Today** in the History list to expand the list and display the most recent webpages you've visited.

6. Click **Jobs for Students (U.S. National Park Service)**. The corresponding webpage opens in Edge. See Figure 4-21.

| Figure 4-21 | Revisiting a webpage from the History list |

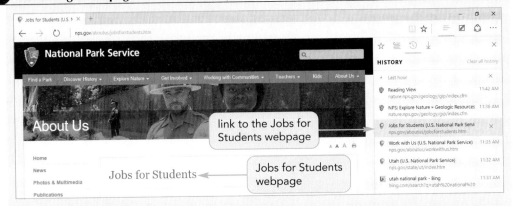

7. Click the **New tab** button ➕ to open the New tab.

8. In the History list, click **Explore Careers | American Job Center** to open that webpage on the new tab.

9. Click the **New tab** button ➕ and then click **Home : Occupational Outlook Handbook** in the History list to open the webpage on a new tab.

Although the History list helps you access webpages you opened recently, the Favorites list helps you organize webpages you open often, which you'll show Kent next.

Adding Webpages to the Favorites List

As you explore the web, you'll find pages that are your favorites—those you visit frequently. When you use Microsoft Edge, you can save the location of your favorite webpages in the Favorites list. When you want to revisit one of your favorite webpages, you can click its link in the Favorites list and display the page in your browser. As you add links or your list of favorite pages grows, you can organize the links into folders. For example, you could create a Favorites folder for travel websites and another for news websites.

REFERENCE

Adding a Webpage to the Favorites List

- Open the webpage in Microsoft Edge.
- Click the Add to favorites or reading list button in the Address bar.
- Click the Favorites button, if necessary.
- Enter a new name for the webpage and select a folder, if necessary.
- Click the Add button.

To add a webpage to the Favorites list, you access the page in Microsoft Edge, and then you use the Add to favorites or reading list button in the Address bar. By default, Microsoft Edge adds the new page to the end of the Favorites list. If you organize the webpages into folders, you can add a webpage to one of the folders. You can store the page using the title of the webpage as its name, or you can change the name so it is more descriptive or meaningful to you.

If you created favorites in another browser such as Internet Explorer or Chrome, you can import the favorites to Microsoft Edge. You do so by using the Import favorites link in the Favorites list to display a list of browsers installed on the computer. Select the browser with the favorites you want to import to have Microsoft Edge add them to the Favorites list.

The Favorites list includes one folder at first: the Favorites Bar folder. This folder is for links you want to display on the Favorites Bar, a separate location for links to webpages you visit often. Microsoft Edge does not display the Favorites bar by default. If you change a setting to display it, the Favorites bar appears as a horizontal bar below the navigation bar.

The three open webpages provide the kind of information Kent will refer to often when preparing workshops for Step Up. You'll add the pages to the Favorites list.

If you are working on a school network, you might not be able to change the content of the Favorites list. In that case, read the following steps and examine the figures, but do not perform the steps.

TIP

To display the Favorites bar, click the More button in the navigation bar, click Settings, click the View favorites settings button, and then click the slider button for the Show the favorites bar setting from Off to On.

To add webpages to the Favorites list:

▶ **1.** With the Occupational Outlook Handbook page displayed in Microsoft Edge, click the **Add to favorites or reading list** button ☆ on the Address bar. A window opens where you choose to add a link to the Favorites list or the Reading list.

   Trouble? If you clicked the Favorites button in the Hub, the History list switched to the Favorites list. Click the Add to favorites or reading list button ☆ in the Address bar above the Hub to add a webpage to the Favorites list.

▶ **2.** Click the **Favorites** button in the window to indicate that you want to add a link to the Favorites list. The Name box displays the name of the webpage, and the Save in box displays the location, such as "Favorites" for the Favorites list. If you wanted to save the link in a folder, you could click the Create new folder link and enter a folder name. In the Name box, you can change the name of the webpage, but the default name here makes the page easy to identify.

▶ **3.** With Home Occupational Outlook Handbook displayed in the Name box, click the **Add** button to add the webpage to the Favorites list. The Add to favorites or reading list button is yellow, indicating that the webpage is a favorite.

▶ **4.** Click the **Explore Careers | American Job Center** tab to display the webpage, and then click the **Add to favorites or reading list** button ☆ on the Address bar.

▶ **5.** Click the **Add** button to add the webpage to the Favorites list using the name suggested in the Name box.

   Kent wants to keep the Jobs for Students link separate from the others in the Favorites list, so you'll create a folder as you add the webpage to the Favorites list.

▶ **6.** Click the **Jobs for Students (U.S. National Park Service)** tab, and then click the **Add to favorites or reading list** button ☆ on the Address bar.

▶ **7.** Click the **Create new folder** link, and then type **Students** as the folder name.

8. Click the **Add** button to add a link to the webpage to the Students folder in the Favorites list. See Figure 4-22.

Figure 4-22 **Links to webpages in the Favorites list**

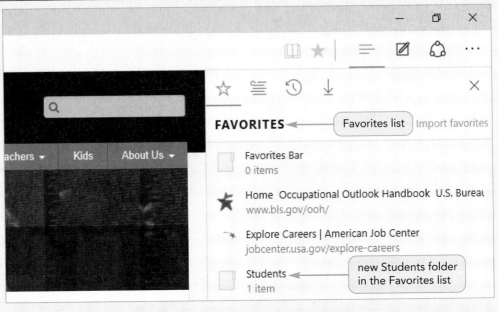

Kent realizes that many students will be interested in the NPS Geoscientists-in-the-Parks program and now wants to add that page to the Favorites list. You'll use the History list to open the page on a new tab, and then save a link to the webpage in the Students folder in the Favorites list.

To add a webpage to a folder in the Favorites list:

1. Click the **New tab** button ⊞ at the top of the Microsoft Edge window to open the New tab.

2. In the Hub, click the **History** button 🕔 to display the History list.

3. Click the **Geoscientists-in-the-Parks** link to open the Geoscientists-in-the-Parks webpage on the new tab.

4. Click the **Add to favorites or reading list** button ☆ in the Address bar to display the window for adding the webpage to the Favorites list.

   You can rename the webpage and add it to the Students folder at the same time.

5. In the Name box, type **GIP Program** to rename the link.

6. Click the **Save in** box, click **Students**, and then click the **Add** button to add the GIP Program link to the Students folder.

7. In the Hub pane, click the **Favorites** button ☆ to display the Favorites list.

8. Click the **Students** folder to display the links you saved as favorites.

TIP

To add a link to the Favorites bar instead of the Favorites list, select the Favorites Bar folder as the Save in location.

Next, you can organize the Favorites list to make the links easy to find.

Organizing the Favorites List

As you add more items to the Favorites list, you can organize its links by renaming or deleting some links and moving others to new folders. Using folders is an excellent way to organize your favorite webpages.

REFERENCE

Organizing the Favorites List

- Click the Hub button and then click the Favorites button to open the Favorites list.
- To move a link into a new folder, right-click the link and then click Create new folder on the shortcut menu. Type the folder name and then press the Enter key.
- To move a link into a Favorites folder, drag the link to the folder.
- To remove a link or folder from the Favorites list, right-click the item and then click Delete on the shortcut menu.
- To rename a link or folder, right-click the item and then click Rename on the shortcut menu. Type the name and then press the Enter key.

Kent sees the value of storing related links in a folder and now wants to move the links to the Explore Careers and Occupational Outlook Handbook webpages into a folder. He also wants to rename a link to shorten it.

To organize the Favorites list:

▶ 1. Click the **Favorites** button to return to the main Favorites list.

▶ 2. Right-click the **Home Occupational Outlook Handbook U.S. Bureau of Labor Statistics** link, and then click **Rename** on the shortcut menu.

▶ 3. Type **Occupational Outlook Handbook** as the new name, and then press the **Enter** key.

▶ 4. Right-click the **Explore Careers American Job Center** link, and then click **Create new folder** on the shortcut menu. A new folder appears in the Favorites list with the placeholder name, New folder, selected.

▶ 5. Type **U.S. Gov** as the new folder name, and then press the **Enter** key.

▶ 6. Drag the **Occupational Outlook Handbook** link to the U.S. Gov folder to move the link.

▶ 7. Drag the **Explore Careers American Job Center** link to the U.S. Gov folder to move the link.

▶ 8. Click the **U.S. Gov** folder in the Favorites list to verify that both links are now stored in the folder, and then click **Favorites** to return to the main Favorites list.

Now the Favorites list is organized so that Kent can easily access his favorite webpages.

Using the Downloads List

In addition to the Favorites list, Reading list, and History list, the Hub includes a Downloads list. Many websites provide files you can download to your computer. For example, you can visit the Downloads webpage on the Microsoft website to download desktop themes. Microsoft Edge keeps track of the downloaded files in the Downloads list. If you need to access a downloaded file, you can display the Downloads list and then click a filename to open the file or run an installation program. You can also click the Open folder link in the Downloads list to display the file in File Explorer so you can move or delete it. (By default, Microsoft Edge saves downloaded files in the Downloads folder.) To remove a filename from the Downloads list, click the Clear button for the file. Clearing a filename from the Downloads list does not delete the downloaded file.

Printing and Saving Webpage Content

If you find a page on the web and want to refer to it when you don't have computer access, you can print the webpage. Sometimes, webpages include a Printer-Friendly Format link or other similar link for printing a webpage, indicating that the website formats the page for a standard size sheet of paper before printing. However, not all webpages provide such an option. Therefore, you should preview the page before you print it to see how it will look when printed. To print a webpage in Microsoft Edge, click the More button in the navigation bar, and then click Print to open the Print dialog box, which displays a preview of how the content will appear on the printed page. If the webpage requires more than a single page to print, you can view each page before printing. Click the Print button to print the webpage.

Decision Making: Determining Whether to Save Webpage Content

Using a browser, you can easily save webpage content on your computer, including the graphic images displayed on the page, files the webpage provides (such as text or music files), and the webpage itself. However, doing so is not always legal or ethical. Before you save any webpage content on your computer, you need to determine whether you have the legal right to do so. This consideration is especially important when you want to save and use images, video, and other media for work projects because commercial use of such content is often prohibited.

Web content such as software, video, music, and images is easy to copy in its digital form. However, if this material is protected by copyright, you usually are not allowed to copy or share it unless you receive permission from the owner. The term **copyright** refers to the originator's exclusive legal right to reproduce, publish, or sell works he or she creates. If you copy someone else's work without giving that person credit, you are committing plagiarism, and you may also be violating copyright laws.

Before you copy or save content from websites that you visit, you need to find out if and how you can use the materials. If you want to use material you find on a website, first get permission from the owner of the site. Often, websites include links to their copyright and permission-request information on their main pages. Even if you think the information or material you found is not copyrighted, you should always request permission to use it and give credit to any website that you use in your work or school projects.

Kent does not want to print or save any information you found for Step Up because he can access it quickly using Edge tools. You can exit Edge.

To close the Hub and exit Edge:

▶ **1.** Click the **Close this pane** button ☒ in the upper-right corner of the Favorites list to close the Hub.

▶ **2.** Click the **Close** button ☒ on the Microsoft Edge title bar.

▶ **3.** Click the **Close all** button in the dialog box to close all tabs.

So far, you have learned about the structure of the Internet and the web and how to use Microsoft Edge to open, navigate, and organize webpages. In the next session, you'll use another service the Internet provides—email.

REVIEW

Session 4.1 Quick Check

1. A(n) _____ is a program that locates, retrieves, and displays webpages.

2. What are two definitions for the term "home page"?

3. What is the purpose of a webpage tab?

4. How can you use Cortana to learn more about a topic you find on a webpage?

5. When you find a webpage containing information you want to focus on, you can switch to _____, which removes most graphics, ads, links, and other distracting elements and presents text in a simple format.

6. Explain how to draw a circle around a paragraph on a webpage.

7. What is the difference between the Reading list and the Favorites list?

8. What is the difference between the History list and the Favorites list?

Session 4.2 Visual Overview:

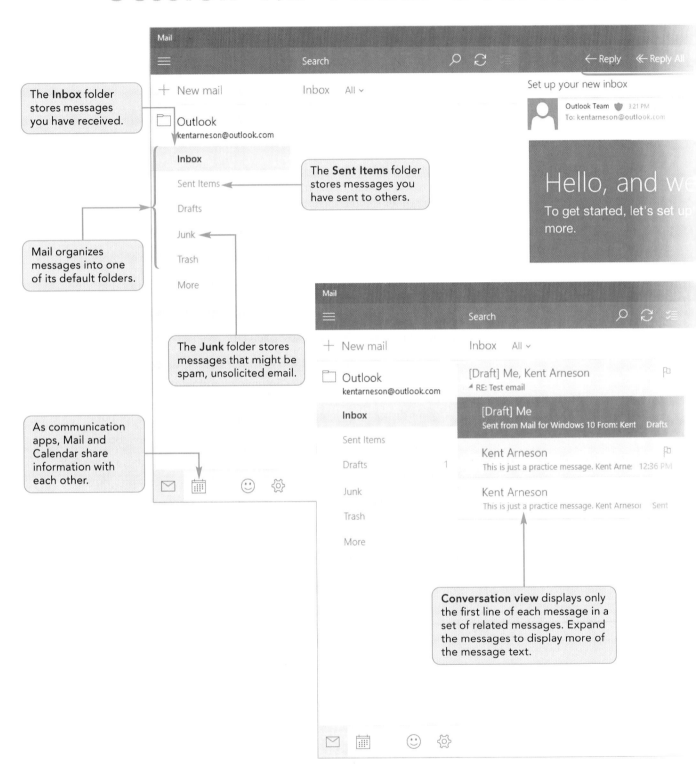

The **Inbox** folder stores messages you have received.

The **Sent Items** folder stores messages you have sent to others.

Mail organizes messages into one of its default folders.

The **Junk** folder stores messages that might be spam, unsolicited email.

As communication apps, Mail and Calendar share information with each other.

Conversation view displays only the first line of each message in a set of related messages. Expand the messages to display more of the message text.

Windows 10 Mail App

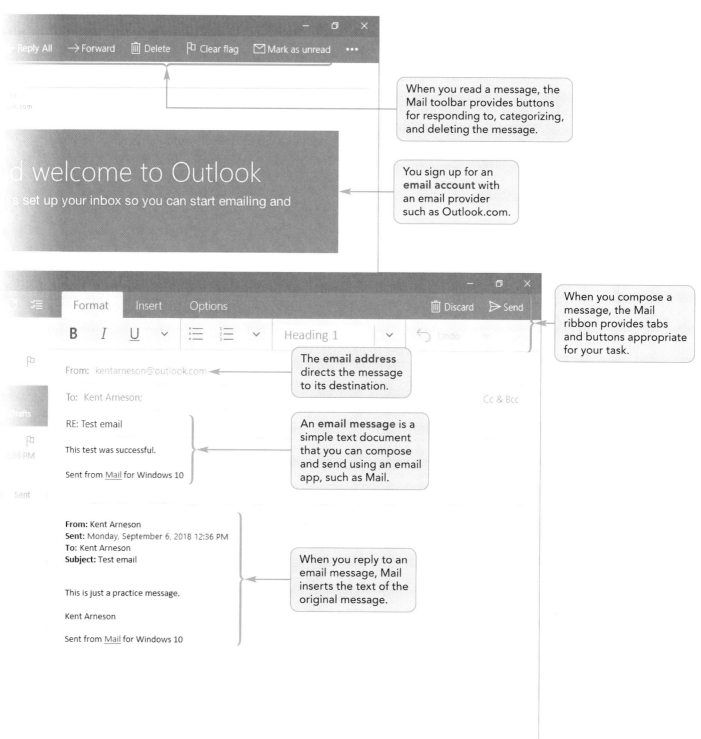

When you read a message, the Mail toolbar provides buttons for responding to, categorizing, and deleting the message.

You sign up for an **email account** with an email provider such as Outlook.com.

When you compose a message, the Mail ribbon provides tabs and buttons appropriate for your task.

The **email address** directs the message to its destination.

An **email message** is a simple text document that you can compose and send using an email app, such as Mail.

When you reply to an email message, Mail inserts the text of the original message.

Reply All   → Forward   🗑 Delete   🏳 Clear flag   ☑ Mark as unread   •••

d welcome to Outlook
's set up your inbox so you can start emailing and

Format   Insert   Options   🗑 Discard   ▷ Send

B   *I*   U   ⌄   ☰   ☰   ⌄   Heading 1   ⌄   ↶ Undo

From: kentarneson@outlook.com

To: Kent Arneson;   Cc & Bcc

RE: Test email

This test was successful.

Sent from Mail for Windows 10

From: Kent Arneson
Sent: Monday, September 6, 2018 12:36 PM
To: Kent Arneson
Subject: Test email

This is just a practice message.

Kent Arneson

Sent from Mail for Windows 10

Getting Started with Mail

As you learned, the web is a service that the Internet provides. Another service is electronic mail, or email. Windows 10 includes Mail, an **email app** that you use to send, receive, and manage email. If you're like most computer users, you exchange many email messages every day with friends, family, colleagues, and other contacts. You probably also receive newsletters, coupons, offers, and other types of messages from companies and organizations. You might start your email app as soon as you turn on your computer and leave it running until you shut down at the end of the day. In short, email is a central part of your computing activities.

Using Mail, you can send email to and receive email from anyone in the world who has an email address, regardless of the operating system or type of computer the person is using. Although this module provides steps for using the Mail app, the concepts and activities the module covers apply to any email application, including Microsoft Outlook and Outlook.com.

Examining How Email Works

An email message is a simple text document that you can compose and send using an email app, such as the Windows 10 Mail app. When you send a message, it travels from your computer, through a network, and arrives at a computer called an **email server**. The email server stores the email messages until the recipients request them. Then the server forwards the messages to the appropriate computers. Typically, the system administrator of your network or ISP manages the email server.

Email uses **store-and-forward technology**, which means you can send messages to anyone on the Internet or a network, even if a recipient's computer isn't turned on. When it's convenient, your recipients connect to the Internet or network and use their email apps to receive and read their messages. Figure 4-23 illustrates the process of sending and receiving email messages.

Figure 4-23	Sending and receiving email

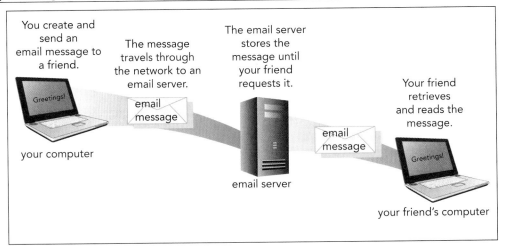

To send and receive email, you must be able to access an email server on the network. If your computer is part of a network at a college or university, for example, you sign in to the network to access its services. An email server provides mail services to faculty, staff, and students who have access to the network. When someone sends you a message, it is stored on your email server until you sign in to the network and use an email app to check your mail. The email server then transfers new messages to your electronic mailbox. You use an email app to open, read, print, delete, reply to, forward, and save the mail.

If your computer is not part of a network, you can access an email server on the Internet. To do so, you open an email account with a service that provides Internet access. For example, email accounts are included as part of the subscription fee for most ISPs. Email accounts are also provided free of charge by advertiser-supported websites, such as Outlook.com and Google. After you establish an email account, you can connect to the Internet to send and receive your email messages.

Addressing Email

Just as you must address a piece of ordinary mail, you need to supply an address for an email message. The email address you enter directs the message to its destination. Your email address is included in the message as the return address so your recipients can easily respond to your message. Anyone who has an email address can send and receive electronic mail. If you work for a company or attend a school that provides email, a system administrator probably assigns an email address to you. Other times, you create your own email address, though it must follow a particular format. See Figure 4-24.

| Figure 4-24 | Typical format of an email address |

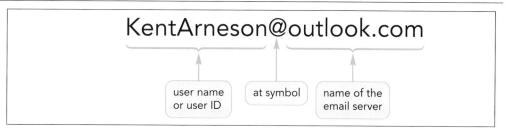

The **user name**, or **user ID**, is the name entered when your email account is set up. The @ symbol (read as "at sign") signifies that the email server name is provided next. For example, "KentArneson" is the user name and "outlook.com" is the email server.

The easiest way to learn a person's email address is to ask the person what it is. You can also look up an email address in a network or Internet directory. Most businesses and schools publish a directory listing email addresses of people who have email accounts on their network. Many websites also provide email directories for people with email accounts on the Internet, such as Yahoo! People Search at people.yahoo.com.

When you sign up for an email account, you can send your new email address to friends, colleagues, and clients. If your email address changes, such as when you change email services, you can subscribe to an email forwarding service so you don't miss any mail sent to your old address.

Setting Up Mail

To use email, you need an Internet connection, an email app, and an email address. Make sure you have an Internet connection and email address before performing the steps in this section. Having an email address means you have an email account, which is space on an email server reserved for your messages. You set up an account with an email service provider, which can be an ISP, an employer or school, or a web service such as Outlook.com or Gmail.

You can set up the following types of email accounts in Mail:

- Outlook—Microsoft offers Outlook.com as a free web-based email service.
- Exchange—This type of account can be an Exchange or Office 365 account (also offered by Microsoft). Organizations such as a business or school typically offer Exchange accounts, which reside on an Exchange server. Home users usually do not have Exchange accounts.

- Google—Google provides Gmail, a free web-based email service.
- YahooMail—Yahoo provides YahooMail, a free web-based email service.
- iCloud—Apple provides iCloud, a free web-based email service.
- Other account—Accounts provided by ISPs, including Post Office Protocol (POP) accounts and Internet Message Access Protocol (IMAP) accounts.

If you already have one of these types of email accounts, you can set up Mail to send and receive email by starting Mail and then entering the user name and password you use for the account. If you use more than one of these email accounts, you can add them to Mail.

If you do not have any of these types of email accounts, you can set up a free Outlook.com or Gmail account. To set up an Outlook.com account, use a browser to go to Outlook.com. Sign up for a Microsoft account by providing your name and other information and then selecting an account name (which is the same as a user name) and a password. You can also set up a Gmail account in a similar way. Use a browser to go to mail.google.com, provide your name and other information, and then select a user name and password.

INSIGHT

Using a Microsoft Account

A Microsoft account provides access to online services such as OneDrive for file storage and Outlook.com for email. You can sign in to a Microsoft account on any device connected to the Internet. When you do, you can read and respond to your Outlook.com email messages or access files stored on OneDrive. If you access Outlook.com on a public computer, for example, and then return to your Windows 10 home computer, your email messages and responses also appear in Mail. Your Microsoft account synchronizes Outlook.com and Mail so your messages are up to date in either place.

Kent has an Outlook.com account, but he hasn't set up Mail to use it yet. Because this is the first time you're starting Mail on his Windows 10 computer, you'll show Kent how to set up Mail to use his Outlook.com account. The following steps assume that you have a Microsoft account.

To set up Mail:

1. Click the **Start** button ⊞ to display the Start menu.

2. Click the **Mail** tile to start the Mail app. The Mail app starts and opens the Welcome window.

   Trouble? If a dialog box opens asking if you want Mail to be your default mail program, click the Yes button only if you are using your own computer and want to use Mail as your mail program. If you are using a school or institutional computer, click the No button or ask your technical support person for assistance.

3. Click the **Get started** button to display the Accounts window.

4. If the Accounts window displays an email account you want to use in Mail, click the account name and then click the **Ready to go** button. You can skip the remaining steps. Otherwise, click the **Add account** button to display the Choose an account window in which you select an account type.

5. Click an account type, such as **Outlook.com**. The Add your Microsoft account window opens.

 Trouble? If you select an account type other than Outlook.com, the remaining steps might differ. Follow the on-screen instructions to finish setting up your email account.

 Trouble? If you want to use a Microsoft account but don't have one, click the No account? Create one! link, and then follow the on-screen instructions to set up the account.

6. Click in the **Email or phone** box, and then enter the email address or phone number for your Microsoft account.

7. Click in the **Password** box, and then enter the password for the account.

8. Click the **Sign in** button. If this is the first time you are signing in to Mail, the app connects to your Outlook.com account and displays messages received in that account.

Now you can show Kent how to send and receive email.

Sending and Receiving Email Using Mail

You can use the Mail app to compose, send, and receive email messages. After you set up an email account, you're ready to start using Mail to manage your email.

To start Mail:

1. Start Mail if necessary (click the **Mail** tile on the Start menu), and then maximize the window. Figure 4-25 shows the Mail window. The email account shown in the figures in this module belongs to Kent Arneson. Your screens will look different from the figures. For example, the background color or design might differ.

Figure 4-25   Mail app

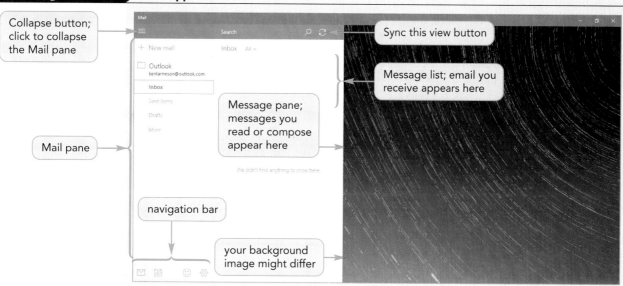

TIP

You can display the Junk and Trash (or Deleted Items) folders in the Mail pane by clicking the More link, right-clicking an unpinned folder, and then clicking Add to Favorites.

The Mail app includes the following tools and components:

- Mail pane—This part of the Mail window lists your email accounts at the top followed by the default Mail folders, including the Inbox, Sent Items, and Drafts folders. These folders are pinned to the Mail pane as favorites so that they are always available in that pane. Click the More link in the Mail pane to pin additional folders as favorites, including Junk and Trash. (Your folder might be called Deleted Items, depending on the type of email account.) Mail organizes your email into these folders automatically.
- Message list—This area displays the email messages you have sent or received.
- Message pane—This area displays the email message you are composing or reading.
- Navigation bar—The navigation bar provides buttons for starting the Calendar app, providing feedback, and displaying settings.

Creating and Sending Email Messages

An email message uses a format similar to a standard memo, which typically includes Date, To, and Subject lines, followed by the content of the message. The To box indicates who will receive the message. The Subject line, although optional, alerts the recipient to the topic of the message. You should always include a Subject line because people often delete messages without reading them if they do not contain subjects. Finally, the message area contains the content of your message. You can also include additional information, such as a Cc line, which indicates who will receive a copy of the message. Mail automatically supplies the date you send the message (as set in your computer's clock).

REFERENCE

Creating and Sending an Email Message

- Click the New mail button in the Mail pane.
- Enter the email address of the recipient in the To box.
- Click in the Subject box, and then type the subject of the message.
- Click in the message area, and then type the content of the message.
- Click the Send button.

To send an email message, you first compose the message and then click the Send button on the message window. Mail sends the message from your computer to your email server, which routes it to the recipient.

INSIGHT

Using the Cc and Bcc Lines

In the To box, restrict the email addresses to those of your primary recipients. Use the Cc (courtesy copy) box for secondary recipients who should receive a copy of the message. If you want to hide the names or email addresses of any recipients, enter their email addresses in the Bcc (blind courtesy copy) box. Mail sends individual copies of the message to each person listed in the Bcc box but displays only the recipient's and sender's email addresses. To display the Cc and Bcc boxes, click the Cc & Bcc link in the message window.

Mail includes a built-in spelling dictionary. As you type the text of a message, Mail corrects any words it flags as misspelled according to its dictionary. When a red line appears under a word, it means that the word is not in Mail's spelling dictionary.

You can right-click the word to display a shortcut menu of spelling suggestions and an option to add the word to the dictionary.

TIP

To personalize the appearance of the Mail app, click the Settings button in the navigation bar, and then click Personalization.

When you create or reply to an email message, Mail inserts a signature line by default. A **signature line** identifies the sender of the message. You can change the signature line to include your name, for example, by clicking the Settings button at the bottom of the Mail pane, clicking Options on the Settings menu, and then changing the text in the Signature box.

Now you can show Kent how to create and send an email message using Mail by sending a practice email to yourself.

To create and send an email message:

1. Click the **New mail** button in the Mail pane. The window for composing a new message opens. See Figure 4-26. Maximize the Mail window, if necessary.

Figure 4-26   Composing a new message

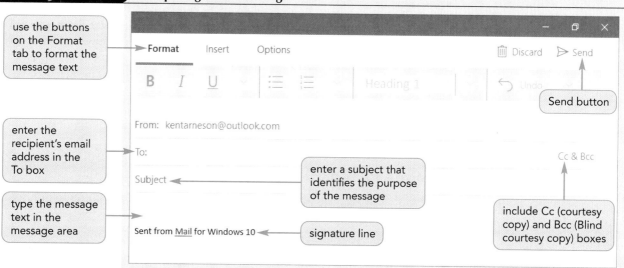

- use the buttons on the Format tab to format the message text
- enter the recipient's email address in the To box
- type the message text in the message area
- enter a subject that identifies the purpose of the message
- signature line
- Send button
- include Cc (courtesy copy) and Bcc (Blind courtesy copy) boxes

TIP

Mail might suggest the complete email address (or a list of possible email addresses) after you type a few characters in the To box.

2. Type your email address in the To box. When you finish, Mail converts the email address to the display name, such as Kent Arneson, and adds a semicolon after the name in case you need to enter another email address.

   Trouble? If you're not sure what email address you should enter, check with your instructor or technical support person.

3. Click in the **Subject** box, and then type **Test email** as the subject.

4. Click in the message area, and then type **This is just a practice message.** as the message content.

5. Press the **Enter** key twice, and then type your name.

6. Click the **Send** button on the toolbar. Mail sends the message to your email server and then places a copy of the sent message in the Sent Items folder. To make sure your message has been sent, you can open the Sent Items folder to see all of the messages you have sent.

7. In the Mail pane, click **Sent Items**. Your message appears in the Message list.

   Trouble? If your message does not appear in the Message list, and you entered your email address correctly in the original message, then Mail is not configured to send messages immediately. In that case, click the Sync this view button on the toolbar to send your message, which Mail saved in the Drafts folder.

When you composed the new message, you might have noticed that the window displayed the Format tab, Insert tab, and Options tab on the Mail ribbon. Use the tabs and buttons for formatting the text, inserting content such as tables and pictures, and using options such as checking the spelling.

Receiving and Reading Email Messages

Mail automatically checks to see if you've received email whenever you start the program and periodically after that. (Every 30 minutes is the default.) Mail also checks for received email when you click the Sync this view button on the toolbar. Email you receive appears in your Inbox. By default, the Inbox shows the **message header** for each message, which includes the name of the sender, the subject, the first line of the message, and the date or time you received the message. Mail you have received but have not read yet appears in bold. To read a message, you click the message in the list to open the message window.

By default, Mail displays messages in Conversation view, which collapses related messages into a single entry in the message list. To display all of the related messages, click the expand icon (a triangle) next to the main entry. For example, if you receive an email message and then reply to it, one main entry appears in the message list. Click to expand the main entry and display two messages: the original message you received and the reply you sent to that message. If you prefer to list each message separately in the message list, you can turn off Conversation view by clicking the Settings button in the navigation bar, clicking Options in the Settings pane, scrolling down to View Settings, and then clicking the slider button for the Show messages arranged by conversation from On to Off.

You'll show Kent how to read the email message you just sent.

To receive and read the Test email message:

▶ **1.** In the Mail pane, click **Inbox** to display the contents of the Inbox folder in the Message list.

▶ **2.** If necessary, click the **Sync this view** button 🔁 to retrieve your messages from your email server, route them to your Inbox, and display them in the Message list. Your Inbox folder might contain additional email messages from other people.

Trouble? If the message you sent doesn't appear in the Inbox, wait a few minutes, and then click the Sync this view button 🔁 again.

▶ **3.** If necessary, click the **Test email** message to display the message. See Figure 4-27.

| Figure 4-27 | Reading a message |

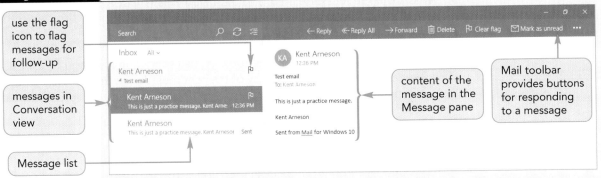

use the flag icon to flag messages for follow-up

messages in Conversation view

Message list

content of the message in the Message pane

Mail toolbar provides buttons for responding to a message

The flag icons on each message are for setting a reminder to follow up on the message. When you click a flag icon, it turns red by default, making it easy to find the message.

Next, you'll show Kent how to perform another common email task—responding to the messages you receive.

Responding to Email Messages

Some of the email you receive might ask you to provide information, answer questions, or confirm decisions. Instead of creating a new email message, you can reply directly to a message that you receive. When you reply to a message, Mail inserts the email address of the sender and the subject into the proper places in the message window and includes the text of the original message.

You can respond to messages by using the Reply or Reply all command. If the original message was sent to more than one person, use the Reply command to respond to only the original sender. Use the Reply all command to respond to all other recipients as well. Use the Reply all command carefully so that the only messages people receive from you are those they need to read. You can also use the Forward command to create a message with the original message text, and then you can send the message to someone other than the original senders.

You will show Kent how to reply to an email message.

To reply to the Test email message:

▶ **1.** With the Test email message displayed in the Mail window, click the **Reply** button on the toolbar. The window displays the text of the original message, inserts the email address of the original recipient in the To box, and displays RE: before the original subject text. It also marks the reply message you are writing as a draft because it's in progress. See Figure 4-28.

Figure 4-28	Replying to a message

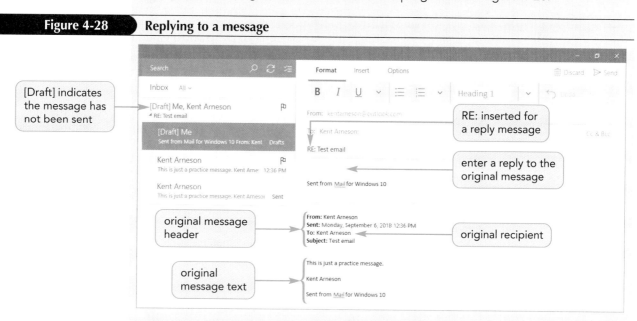

▶ **2.** In the message area, type **This test was successful.** and then click the **Send** button on the toolbar.

▶ **3.** When the RE: Test email message appears in your Inbox, click it, if necessary, to display the content of the four related messages: the original message with the "This is just a practice message." text, the copy of that message that appears in the Sent Items list, the reply with the "This test was successful." text, and the copy of the reply that appears in the Sent Items list. See Figure 4-29.

Trouble? If the message doesn't appear in the Inbox folder, click the Sync this view button 🔄.

Figure 4-29	Displaying the contents of related messages

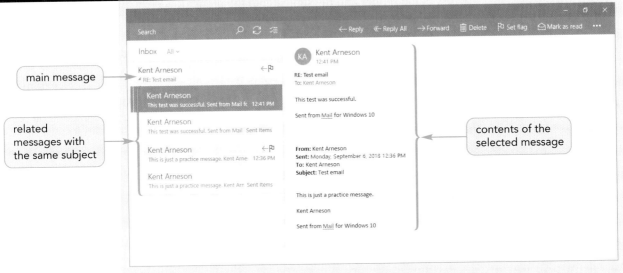

Kent mentions that clients often request a list of upcoming career information workshops, which he stores in a Word document. You'll show him how to attach a file to an email message so he can reply to people and provide the information they request.

Attaching a File to a Message

Besides sending email to others, you can also transfer files to them by attaching the files to messages. You can send any kind of file, including documents, pictures, music, or videos. Check the size of the files you attach before you send a message. If you attach a large file to an email message, it might take a long time for your recipient to download your message. Most email servers limit the size of the files you can attach; some allow files no larger than 3 MB. Check with your correspondents before sending large file attachments to find out about size restrictions and set up a convenient time to send the attachment.

You'll show Kent how to send and open an email message that includes an attachment. As before, you'll create a test message and send it to yourself.

To create and send a message with an attachment:

▶ **1.** Make sure your computer can access your Data Files for this module. For example, if you are using a USB drive, insert the drive into the USB port.

▶ **2.** In the Mail pane, click the **New mail** button.

▶ **3.** Type your email address in the To box.

▶ **4.** Click in the **Subject** box, and then type **Workshop list you requested** as the message subject.

▶ **5.** Click in the message area, click the **Insert** tab on the Mail ribbon, and then click the **Attach** button to display the Open dialog box.

▶ **6.** Navigate to the **Module4 > Module** folder provided with your Data Files, click the **Workshops** file, and then click the **Open** button. Mail attaches the file to the message and displays the filename and size next to the file icon.

▶ **7.** In the message area, type **This is a test email message with a file attachment.**

▶ **8.** Click the **Send** button on the toolbar.

▶ **9.** If necessary, click the **Sync this view** button 🔄 on the toolbar to send and receive the message.

When you receive a message that contains an attachment, you can choose to save or open the attached file. You should open files only after scanning them with antivirus software. Some people spread harmful software, called viruses, in email attachments. Before you open the file, you need to make sure the app used to create the attachment is installed on your computer. If it's not, you can sometimes use a text editor, such as WordPad or Notepad, to open and read the attached file.

To receive and open a message with an attachment:

▶ **1.** When the Workshop list you requested message appears in your Inbox, click the message to expand it, and then click the first message below it, which is the message you received, to display the entire message.

▶ **2.** Right-click the **Workshops.rtf** file icon to display a shortcut menu, which lets you open or save the attachment.

▶ **3.** Click **Open** on the shortcut menu. The file opens in a desktop word-processing program, such as Word or WordPad. You could save the document now if necessary.

▶ **4.** Close the word-processing program.

Written Communication: Observing Email Etiquette

Because email is a widespread form of communication, you should follow standard guidelines and common sense when using it. For example, use language appropriate for the purpose of your message and your recipients. Following are a few guidelines to keep in mind when you are composing email messages so that you can communicate effectively, without offending or annoying your correspondents:

- Be concise and direct. As a courtesy to your correspondents and to make sure your message is read, get right to the point and keep your messages short.
- Include your response first. When you reply to an email, you can include text from the original message. If you do, make sure that your response is at the top of the message so your recipients can find it easily. If you respond to questions or insert comments in the original message, use a contrasting font color so your recipients can identify your additions.
- Don't email sensitive or confidential information. Email is not private, and your recipients can forward your message to others, either intentionally or accidentally. Be professional in your tone and careful about what you say to and about others.
- Avoid abbreviations. Although you should strive to be brief, don't overcompensate by using nonstandard abbreviations. Stick to the abbreviations that are common in business writing, such as FYI and ASAP.
- Don't use all capital letters. Using all capital letters, as in "SEND ME THE REPORT TODAY," can be difficult to read and misconstrued as shouting.
- Check your spelling and grammar. The accuracy and quality of your writing in an email message is as important as in any piece of communication you send. Use the spelling tool available in your email app, and proofread for grammatical accuracy.

Kent might want to delete the email messages he's read. You'll show him how to do so next.

Deleting Email Messages

After you read and respond to your messages, you can delete any message you no longer need. When you delete a message, it moves to the Trash folder (also called the Deleted Items folder in some types of accounts). Messages remain in the Trash folder until you delete them. You can delete a message by selecting the message and then clicking the Delete button on the toolbar, by pointing to the message and then clicking the Delete this item icon 🗑, or by right-clicking the message and then clicking Delete on the shortcut menu. If the Trash (or Deleted Items) folder isn't listed in the Mail pane, click the More button and then click Trash.

To select messages before you delete them or perform any other task with them, you can click the Enter selection mode button on the toolbar to display a check box next to each message. You click the check box to select the corresponding message. If you have only one or two messages, you can point to a message to display a Delete this item icon, and then click the icon to delete the message.

To delete the Test email messages:

1. Point to the main message in the Message list, and then click the **Delete this item** icon 🗑 to delete the message. A Delete message and icon appear briefly at the bottom of the Mail window, and the message is moved to the Trash or Deleted Items folder.

INSIGHT

Dealing with Junk Email

Junk email, or **spam**, is unsolicited email, often containing advertisements, fraudulent schemes, or legitimate offers. Mail includes a junk email filter that analyzes the content of the email messages you receive and moves suspicious messages to the Junk folder, where you can examine and manage them as necessary. To reduce the amount of junk email you receive, avoid posting your email address on websites or other public areas of the Internet. If a website requests your email address, read its privacy statement to make sure it doesn't disclose your email address to others. Finally, never respond to junk email—you're likely to receive even more spam. Be sure to open your Junk folder often to review the messages it contains, and then delete the spam messages, which are often from senders you don't recognize.

You're finished working with Mail for now, so you can close the app. You should also delete the test email messages you worked with in this session.

To delete messages and close Mail:

▶ **1.** Point to the message in the message list for the Inbox, and then click the **Delete this item** icon 🗑 to delete the message.

▶ **2.** In the Mail pane, click **Sent Items**.

▶ **3.** Point to the main messages in the message list, and then click the **Delete this item** icon 🗑 to delete each message.

▶ **4.** Click the **Close** button ✕ to close Mail.

Two Windows apps are designed for use with Mail: People and Calendar. You'll explore the People app next.

Adding Information to the People App

Another communication app in Windows 10 is the People app, which you use to keep track of your contacts, including email correspondents. You can also use People on its own to save information about people and organizations. In addition to storing email addresses, you can store related information such as street addresses, home phone numbers, and personal information, such as anniversaries and birthdays. When you create an email message to someone stored in the People app, Mail suggests the complete email address after you type a few characters in the To box.

REFERENCE

Adding a Contact in People

- Click the Start button and then click the People tile.
- Click the Add button in the Contacts pane.
- Enter contact information.
- Click the Save button.

You can add contact information to People by importing the information from an email app or from social networking sites where you maintain contacts, such as Google, LinkedIn, and Twitter. If you import the same contact information from two or more sources, the People app detects the duplicate contacts and combines them into a single entry called a linked contact. You can also create a new contact and then enter as much information as you want about that contact, including a photo.

If you import contact information from your accounts on social networking sites, People maintains a connection to those accounts so it can display updated contact information. If the People tile is a live tile on the Start menu, it also displays updated information as it becomes available.

If you have more than one account set up in the Mail app, you must choose an account in which you want to save your new contacts the first time you start People. For example, the accounts might include your Microsoft account and an Outlook.com account. If you choose the Microsoft account, you can access the contacts on any device for which you sign in using a Microsoft account. The name of the window you use to add a contact reflects the account you select. For example, the window might appear with the title New Outlook Contact.

Kent doesn't want to import his contacts from other services, so you'll show him how to use People to add a new contact.

To add a contact:

1. Click the **Start** button ⊞ to display the Start menu, and then click the **People** tile to start the People app.

    Trouble? If the People tile does not appear on your Start menu, type "People" in the Ask me anything box after you click the Start button, and then click the People app in the results.

2. If this is the first time you are starting the People app, a window opens listing sources of contacts, such as your Microsoft account. Click the account in which you want to store your contacts.

3. Click the **Add** button ➕ in the Contacts pane to display a window for adding a new contact. The type of online account you are using, such as Outlook, appears in the Save to box.

4. Click in the **Name** box, if necessary, and then type **Kent Arneson**.

5. Click in the **Mobile phone** box, and then type **(801) 555-1100**. To change the box label, click the Phone down arrow to display the Change label menu, and then click the label you want—for example, Work.

6. Click in the **Personal email** box, and then type **KentArneson@outlook.com**. You can change the type of email from Personal to Work, for example, by clicking the Personal email arrow to display the Change label menu.

7. Click **Other** to display the Add a field menu with a list of other contact details, and then click **Company** to add the Company box to the window.

8. Type **Step Up** in the Company box.

9. Click the **Save** button 💾 on the toolbar in the upper-right part of the window.

10. If the contact information for Kent Arneson does not appear in the right pane, click **Kent Arneson** in the Contacts pane to display his contact information. See Figure 4-30.

TIP

You can click the Add a field button (plus icon) below a box to enter phone numbers, email addresses, addresses, or other information for a contact.

Figure 4-30   New contact in People

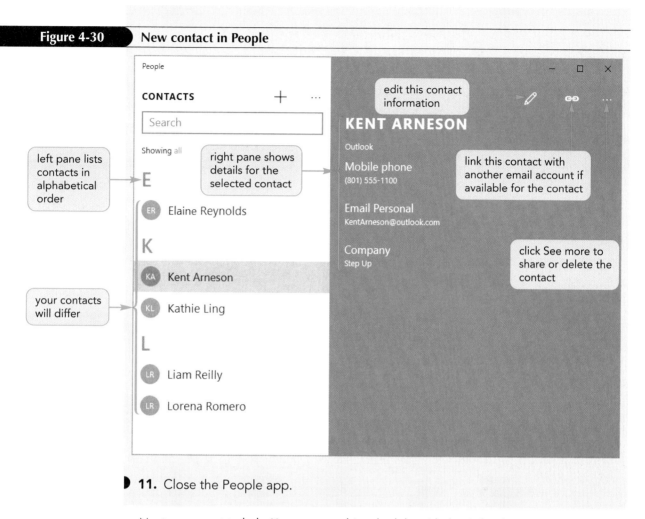

left pane lists contacts in alphabetical order

your contacts will differ

right pane shows details for the selected contact

edit this contact information

link this contact with another email account if available for the contact

click See more to share or delete the contact

▶ **11.** Close the People app.

Next, you want to help Kent manage his schedule with the Calendar app.

Managing Your Schedule with Calendar

Calendar is another app that works with Mail. You use it to schedule appointments, track tasks, and stay on top of deadlines. Calendar also lets you schedule recurring events, such as weekly staff meetings, and set reminders so you don't miss an important appointment. When you schedule an event, Calendar blocks out the time in your schedule, helping you avoid scheduling conflicts. If the event is a meeting, you can invite contacts stored in the People app to attend the meeting. You can also adjust the Calendar view to display scheduled events in the Day, Week, or Month format. The Day format shows you the events for today and tomorrow.

Calendar actually includes more than one calendar. The Main calendar displays your user name and is designed for scheduling all of your appointments and events. Other calendars include Birthday, Personal, Holidays, and Work. If you want to keep your personal appointments separate from work events, for example, you can maintain two calendars—Personal and Work. On the Birthday calendar, add birthdays of your contacts and other people. Calendar will remind you about the upcoming birthday in a notification message as you are working anywhere in Windows 10. The same is true for the Holidays calendar. If you list national and personal holidays in the calendar, Calendar will remind you about each one.

Because Kent works so often at his computer, he is ready to use an electronic calendar. You'll show him how to start Calendar.

To start Calendar:

TIP

When you're working in the Mail app, click the Calendar button in the navigation bar to start the Calendar app.

▶ **1.** Click the **Start** button ⊞ to display the Start menu, and then click the **Calendar** tile. The Calendar app opens, showing a calendar for the current day, week, or month.

> **Trouble?** If this is the first time you are starting Calendar, a Welcome screen appears. Click the Get started button to display a list of email accounts. Click your email account and then click the Ready to go button.

▶ **2.** If the calendar shows the day or week view, click the **Month** button on the toolbar at the top of the window to display your schedule for the month.

▶ **3.** If necessary, widen the window until the horizontal scroll bar no longer appears.

The first time you start Calendar, a window opens asking you to add your email accounts. If you already entered accounts in Mail, they are listed in this window for confirmation.

Now that you've opened Calendar, you can use it to schedule appointments.

Scheduling Appointments

In Calendar, you can schedule appointments such as meetings that occur for part of a day. You can also schedule events that last 24 hours or longer. An appointment appears as a colored block in your calendar, while a day-long event appears in a banner at the beginning of a day. When you schedule appointments, you can specify that they are recurring, such as training that takes place once per week, meetings scheduled once per month, or birthdays and other annual events. If you set a reminder for an event, a notification appears as you're working on another task in Windows 10, such as browsing the Internet.

You can add events in two ways: directly on the calendar or using the Details pane. The first method is faster because you enter only a few event details. However, you cannot select settings such as status, reminders, and recurrence. To select those settings and enter more event details, click the New event button to collapse the left pane and open the Details pane.

The first appointment Kent wants to schedule is for a staff meeting later today, which is usually 30 minutes long. He wants to be reminded about the meeting 30 minutes before it begins so he has time to prepare.

To schedule an appointment:

▶ **1.** In the left pane, click today's date, if necessary, to select it, and then click the **New event** button. The left pane collapses and a Details pane opens on the right, displaying the details you can enter for the new appointment, such as the name, location, and start time.

▶ **2.** In the Event name box, type **Staff meeting** as the event name.

▶ **3.** Click in the **Location** box, and then type **West conference room**.

▶ **4.** Click the **arrow button** for the Start time, and then click a time about two hours from now, such as **1:30 pm**.

> **Trouble?** If the Start time box is gray and unavailable, click the All day check box to remove the checkmark, and then perform Step 4.

TIP

To invite people to an event or meeting, use the People pane.

▶ **5.** Click in the **Event description** box, and then type **Check the status of accounts and workshops.** to enter a description.

▶ **6.** Click the **Reminder** box on the toolbar, and then click **30 minutes** on the menu to set the reminder time. You can accept the current selection for the Calendar box. See Figure 4-31.

Figure 4-31   **Scheduling an appointment**

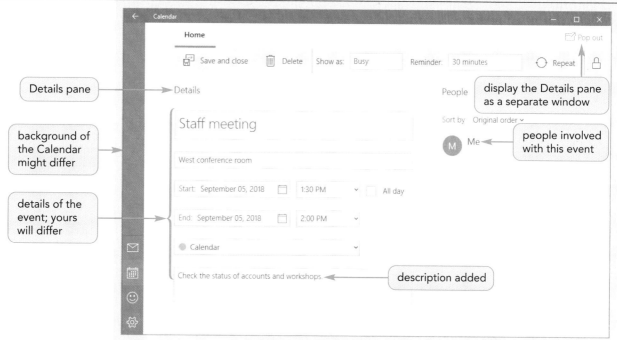

▶ **7.** Click the **Save and close** button on the toolbar. The calendar in the right pane displays an entry for the event.

▶ **8.** Close the Calendar app.

TIP

To edit an appointment already scheduled in the Calendar, double-click the appointment.

You've created an appointment for Kent's weekly staff meeting. Recall that when you set options for the lock screen, you could choose an app to show its detailed status on the lock screen. By default, the Calendar app shows your appointment details on your lock screen so you see them as soon as you turn on your computer or return to it after being away awhile. You can verify that the lock screen shows details from the Calendar app using the Settings app, which you've used in previous modules.

To display Calendar details on the lock screen:

▶ **1.** Click the **Start** button ⊞ to display the Start menu, and then click **Settings** to start the Settings app.

▶ **2.** Click **Personalization** to display the Personalization window.

▶ **3.** In the left pane, click **Lock screen** to display the settings for the lock screen.

▶ **4.** Scroll down to the Lock screen apps section. In the Choose an app to show detailed status section, click an icon to display apps that can show detailed information on the lock screen. See Figure 4-32.

| Figure 4-32 | Selecting Calendar as a lock screen app |

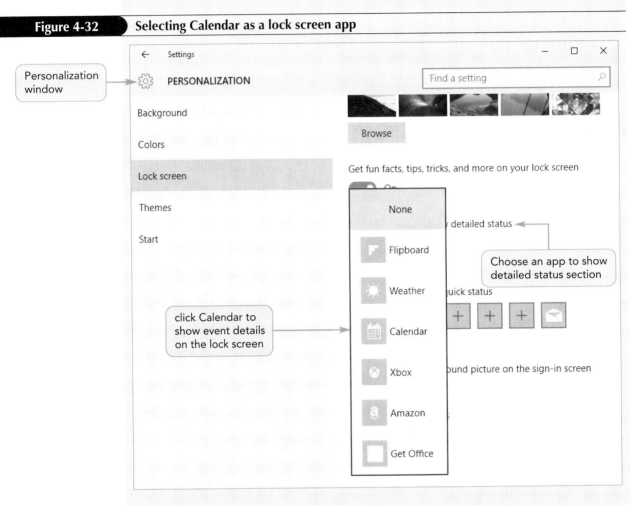

Personalization window

click Calendar to show event details on the lock screen

Choose an app to show detailed status section

▶ **5.** If Calendar is not selected, click **Calendar** and then close the Personalization window.

▶ **6.** Hold down the **Windows** key ⊞ and then press the **L** key to display the lock screen. Today's event appears on the lock screen. Press the **Enter** key and then sign in to Windows the way you usually do.

Now that you've finished exploring the Internet and email on Kent's computer, you should restore the computer to its original settings.

Restoring Your Settings

If you are working in a computer lab or using a computer other than your own, complete the steps in this section to restore the original settings on the computer.

To restore your settings:

▶ **1.** Start Microsoft Edge, click the **Hub** button 📑 in the navigation bar, click the **History** button 🕒, click **Clear all history**, click the **Browsing history** check box to select it (if necessary), deselect the other check boxes, and then click the **Clear** button.

▶ 2. Click the **Hub** button ☰ and then click the **Favorites** button ☆ to display the Favorites list.

▶ 3. Right-click the **U.S. Gov** folder, and then click **Delete** on the shortcut menu to delete the folder.

▶ 4. Right-click the **Students** folder in the Favorites list, and then click **Delete** on the shortcut menu to delete the folder.

▶ 5. Click the **Reading list** button ▤ to display the contents of the Reading list.

▶ 6. Right-click the first link in the Reading list, and then click **Delete** on the shortcut menu to delete the link.

▶ 7. Close Microsoft Edge.

▶ 8. Click the **Start** button ⊞ to display the Start menu, right-click the **Welcome to American Job Center** tile, and then click **Unpin from Start** to remove the tile from the Start menu.

▶ 9. Right-click the **U.S. Bureau of Labor Statistics** tile, and then click **Unpin from Start** to remove the tile from the Start menu.

▶ 10. Start Mail, click the **No** button if a message appears asking if you want to set Mail as your default email app, click **Trash** (or **Deleted Items**) in the Mail pane or click **More** and then click **Trash** (or **Deleted Items**). Click the first message, and then hold down the **Delete** key to delete all the messages. Close the Mail app.

▶ 11. Click the **Start** button ⊞ and then click the **People** tile (or search for it using the Ask me anything box). Right-click **Kent Arneson** in the list of contacts, click **Delete** on the shortcut menu, and then click the **Delete** button to confirm. Close the People app.

▶ 12. Click the **Start** button ⊞ and then click the **Calendar** tile. Right-click the appointment you added to the calendar, and then click **Delete** on the shortcut menu. Close the Calendar app.

▶ 13. Close all apps and windows.

REVIEW

Session 4.2 Quick Check

1. Before you can have an email address, you must sign up for an email _____ with an email service.

2. Where does Mail display the email messages you have sent or received?

3. Identify the user name and the email server name in the following email address: CoraPatel@mymail.net.

4. When composing an email message, what information do you enter in the To box?

5. The _____ for an email message includes the name of the sender, the subject, the first line of the message, and the date or time you received the message.

6. If you set a reminder for a scheduled event, how does Calendar remind you?

7. Describe how the Mail app and the People app can work together.

Review Assignments

Data File needed for the Review Assignments: Utah.rtf

You already showed Kent how to conduct research on career development resources to prepare for his workshops at Step Up. He also needs information about the attractions of Utah for out-of-state people thinking of relocating to Salt Lake City. He is interested in information about state parks, especially the activities and attractions for visitors. You'll use Microsoft Edge to research information for Kent. Complete the following steps:

1. Start Microsoft Edge and then use the Address bar to search for websites with information about Utah state parks.
2. Open the first webpage listed on a new tab. Explore the webpage and then click any link that might provide more information about activities or things to do in the state parks.
3. Pin the webpage about Utah state park activities to the Start menu.
4. Return to the search results to find a link to another webpage about Utah state parks. Open that webpage on a new tab.
5. Explore the new webpage and then click any link that might provide more information about activities or things to do in the state parks. Pin the second webpage about Utah state park activities to the Start menu.
6. Return to the search results, and then open any other webpage on a new tab. If the Reading view button is available, keep the webpage open. If the Reading view button is not available, close the tab, return to the search results, and then open a different webpage on a new tab.
7. When you find a webpage available in Reading view, switch to Reading view, and then scroll to display all of its information.
8. Use a Make a Web Note tool to highlight a heading or other text on the page.
9. Display the Start menu, scroll if necessary to display the pinned tiles, and then press the Print Screen key to capture an image of the screen. Start Paint, paste the screen image in a new file, and then save the file as **Reading view** in the Module4 > Review folder provided with your Data Files.
10. Exit from Make a Web Note and Reading view.
11. Return to the search results, and then search for information about Bear Lake state park. Find a webpage about Bear Lake state park, open it on a new tab, and then display the webpage.
12. Display the Favorites bar in the Microsoft Edge window. (*Hint*: Click the More button, click Settings, click the View favorites settings button, and then click the slider button for the Show the favorites bar setting from Off to On.)
13. Add the webpage about Bear Lake state park to the Favorites bar. (*Hint*: As you are creating the favorite, click the Save in box and then click Favorites Bar.)
14. Ask Cortana about Bear Lake state park.
15. Press the Print Screen key to capture an image of the Microsoft Edge window. In Paint, paste the screen image in a new file, and then save the file as **Bear Lake** in the Module4 > Review folder provided with your Data Files.
16. Close Paint and Microsoft Edge.
17. Start Mail and create an email message. Enter your email address and your instructor's email address in the To box and **Utah state parks** in the Subject box.
18. In the message area, write a message describing one activity or attraction Kent should mention to out-of-state visitors, based on your research.
19. Attach the **Utah** file from the Module4 > Review folder to the message, and then send the message.
20. Add your email address and your instructor's email address to the People app.
21. Add an appointment to the Calendar for a 30-minute meeting with Kent today to discuss his upcoming presentation.

22. Complete the following tasks to restore your computer to its original settings:
    * In Microsoft Edge, clear the History list, remove the webpage you added to the Favorites bar (*Hint*: Right-click the link and then click Delete on the shortcut menu), and then hide the Favorites bar.
    * Close Microsoft Edge.
    * On the Start menu, delete the tiles for the pinned webpages.
    * In Mail, delete the emails you sent and received, and then delete the messages from the Trash (or the Deleted Items) folder.
    * In People, delete yourself and your instructor from the contacts list.
    * In Calendar, delete the appointment you created.
23. Close all open windows and apps.

Case Problem 1

There are no Data Files needed for this Case Problem.

Wild Weather   Joseph Lafleur is the publisher of *Wild Weather*, a magazine for students interested in weather and meteorology, in Lincoln, Nebraska. Joseph runs a summer school program on tornadoes, which is especially popular with students in all grades. He wants to take advantage of the tornado information posted on the web by national weather organizations and use it in his program. Recently, Joseph hired you to help administer the program. He asks you to find online information about tornados, especially information involving students. Complete the following steps:

1. Start Microsoft Edge and then go to the home page for the National Oceanic and Atmospheric Administration website at **noaa.gov**.
2. Using the tools on this page, look for information about tornados. (*Hint*: You might need to search for this information.) Open one of the pages you found.
3. On a new tab, open the National Weather Service webpage at **weather.gov**.
4. On a new tab, use the Address bar to search for **Smithsonian tornados**, and then open the first webpage in the search results.
5. On a new tab, use the Address bar to search for **JetStream weather school**, and then open the first webpage in the search results.
6. Pin the Favorites list to the Microsoft Edge window, and then add the four webpages to the Favorites list in a new folder named **Tornados**.
7. Display the favorites in the Tornados folder.
8. On one of the webpages, use the Make a Web Note tool to circle basic information about tornados, such as the definition of a tornado or when tornados are likely to occur.
9. Press the Print Screen key to capture an image of the screen. Start Paint, paste the screen image in a new file, and then save the file as **Tornados** in the Module4 > Case1 folder provided with your Data Files.
10. Exit from the Make a Web Note view.
11. Display the JetStream webpage and then add it to the Reading list with the name Microsoft Edge suggests.
12. Display the Smithsonian tornado webpage, and then add it to the Reading list with the name Microsoft Edge suggests.
13. Display the Smithsonian tornado webpage in Reading view.
⊕ **Explore** 14. Use Cortana and the Address bar to define "tornado." (*Hint*: Type **define tornado** in the Address bar without pressing the Enter key to have Cortana display the definition.)
15. Press the Print Screen key to capture an image of the screen. Start Paint, paste the screen image in a new file, and then save the file as **Definition** in the Module4 > Case1 folder provided with your Data Files.

16. Exit from Reading view.

17. On the open webpages, look for information about tornado warnings. Ask Cortana to display information about a tornado warning.

18. Press the Print Screen key to capture an image of the screen. Start Paint, paste the screen image in a new file, and then save the file as **Warning** in the Module4 > Case1 folder provided with your Data Files.

19. Close Microsoft Edge and Paint.

20. Start Mail and create an email message. Enter your email address and your instructor's email address in the To box, and enter **Ideas for tornado program** as the subject of the message.

21. In the message area, write a message describing the tornado information provided on one of the webpages you found. Send the message.

22. Restore your computer by completing the following tasks:

   • In Microsoft Edge, clear the History list, delete the Tornados folder you added to the Favorites list, and then delete the links in the Reading list. Close Microsoft Edge.

   • In Mail, delete the email you sent, and then delete the messages from the Trash (or Deleted Items) folder.

23. Close all open windows and apps.

Case Problem 2

APPLY

There are no Data Files needed for this Case Problem.

Artifact   Phoebe Carver owns a shop called Artifact in Harrisburg, Pennsylvania. The shop acquires rights to reproduce archaeological artifacts from museums and universities. Phoebe and her staff create replicas of figurines, statues, plaques, coins, and other objects found at archaeological sites. Phoebe is expanding her offerings of fossils and miniature replicas of dinosaurs. She recently hired you as a research assistant and wants you to focus on learning about the dinosaur collections at American natural history museums, which you can do by using Microsoft Edge. Complete the following steps:

1. Start Microsoft Edge, and then go to the Smithsonian National Museum of Natural History website at **mnh.si.edu**.

2. On additional tabs, open the home pages for the following websites:

   • Field Museum: **fieldmuseum.org**
   • American Museum of Natural History: **amnh.org**

3. Use the links on each website and the tools available in Microsoft Edge to find information on dinosaurs or dinosaur exhibits.

4. Pin the three dinosaur webpages to the Start menu.

5. Open the Start menu, and then press the Print Screen key to capture an image of the screen. Start Paint, paste the screen image in a new file, and then save the file as **Dinosaurs** in the Module4 > Case2 folder provided with your Data Files.

6. Display the home page for the Smithsonian National Museum of Natural History.

7. Use the links on the website and Microsoft Edge tools to find information about location and hours at the museum. (*Hint*: Look for a "Plan Your Visit" link.)

8. Add the page you found to the Reading list using the name that Microsoft Edge suggests. Pin the Hub to the Microsoft Edge window.

9. Return to the Field Museum home page. (*Hint*: Use the History list.) Use the navigation bar to explore the Science topic. Find a page that shows images of fossils, and then add the page to the Reading list using the name that Microsoft Edge suggests.

10. On the American Museum of Natural History website, find a page showing information about dinosaur discoveries. Display the page in Reading view.

⊕ **Explore** 11. Send the webpage to your instructor by sharing it with Mail. (*Hint*: Click the Share button in the Microsoft Edge navigation bar, and then click Mail.)

12. Add the Dinosaur Discoveries page to the Reading list.

13. Press the Print Screen key to capture an image of the desktop. In Paint, paste the screen image in a new file, and then save the file as **Reading List** in the Module4 > Case2 folder provided with your Data Files.

14. Close Reading view. On any open webpage, find the name of a dinosaur—for example microraptor. Ask Cortana to find information about the dinosaur you found.

15. Press the Print Screen key to capture an image of the desktop. In Paint, paste the screen image in a new file, and then save the file as **Cortana** in the Module4 > Case2 folder provided with your Data Files.

16. Restore your computer by completing the following tasks:

   • In Microsoft Edge, clear the History list and then delete the links you added to the Reading list.
   • Unpin the tiles from the Start menu.
   • Close Microsoft Edge.
   • In Mail, delete the email you sent, and then empty the Trash (or Deleted Items) folder.

17. Close all open windows and apps.

CHALLENGE

Case Problem 3

There are no Data Files needed for this Case Problem.

Concierge Atlanta   Belinda Washington started Concierge Atlanta to provide personal assistant services to companies, residents, and visitors in Atlanta, Georgia. Belinda and her staff make restaurant reservations, secure tickets to events, organize travel, order gifts, and perform other personal services. Belinda recently hired you as a junior concierge and asked you to begin by researching requested information on the Internet. Complete the following steps:

1. Start Microsoft Edge, and then use the Address bar to search for information about the best restaurants in Atlanta.

⊕ **Explore** 2. Find a restaurant listed as one of the top ten restaurants in Atlanta and then go to the home page of the restaurant's website. Use the Make a Web Note tools to capture an image of the restaurant's hours and copy it to the Clipboard. Start Paint, paste the screen image in a new file, and then save the file as **Hours** in the Module4 > Case3 folder provided with your Data Files.

3. Exit Make a Web Note view, and then navigate the restaurant's website to display a menu.

4. Use the Make a Web Note tools to highlight a menu item that sounds appealing to you.

5. Save the annotated menu page in the Reading list using the name Microsoft Edge suggests, and then exit Make a Web Note view.

⊕ **Explore** 6. Navigate to a webpage that displays the name of the restaurant. If Cortana appears in the Address bar, click the Cortana icon to display information about the restaurant.

   If Cortana does not appear in the Address bar, select the name of the restaurant and then ask Cortana to display information about it.

7. Press the Print Screen key to capture an image of the desktop. In Paint, paste the screen image in a new file, and then save the file as **Restaurant** in the Module4 > Case3 folder provided with your Data Files.

8. Use the Address bar to search for a calendar of classical music events in Atlanta. Select an event that appeals to you, and then add the details to the Calendar app.

⊕ **Explore** 9. Switch to Day view, and then navigate to the day and time of the event. (*Hint*: Click the date in the left pane, and then scroll the right pane.)

10. Add the webpage to the Reading list using the name that Microsoft Edge suggests.

11. Arrange the Calendar window over the Microsoft Edge window so the Reading list is visible, and then press the Print Screen key to capture an image of the screen. Start Paint, paste the screen image in a new file, and then save the file as **Calendar** in the Module4 > Case3 folder provided with your Data Files.

12. Minimize the Calendar window, and then use the Address bar to search for information about the Georgia Aquarium. Open the home page of the Georgia Aquarium, and then click a link to display webpages about experiencing the aquarium.

⊕ **Explore** 13. Find a description of a tour, and then use the Share button in the navigation bar to send an email message about the tour to your instructor.

⊕ **Explore** 14. On the Georgia Aquarium website, find a video or webcam displaying images of the wildlife at the aquarium. Display the webpage in Internet Explorer. (*Hint*: Click the button in the navigation bar to find the appropriate command.)

15. When the Internet Explorer window opens, maximize the window, and then press the Print Screen key to capture an image of the screen. Start Paint, paste the screen image in a new file, and then save the file as **Internet Explorer** in the Module4 > Case3 folder provided with your Data Files.

16. Close Internet Explorer.

17. Restore your computer by completing the following tasks:
    - In Microsoft Edge, clear the History list, and then delete the links in the Reading list.
    - Close Microsoft Edge.
    - In Calendar, remove the event you added. (*Hint*: Click the event and then click the Delete button on the toolbar.)
    - Close Calendar.
    - In Mail, delete the email you sent, and then empty the Trash (or Deleted Items) folder.

18. Close all open windows and apps.

Case Problem 4

There are no Data Files needed for this Case Problem.

WLAX Boosters   WLAX Boosters is an organization in Chestnut Hill, Massachusetts, that supports and promotes women's lacrosse teams at colleges and universities in the United States. Jen Dickerson, the director of the organization, recently hired you as a part-time assistant. You help Jen write the monthly newsletter and organize promotional events. Jen wants you to visit college websites periodically to make sure the colleges are promoting their women's lacrosse teams. Complete the following steps:

1. Start Microsoft Edge and go to the home page for the National College Athletics Association (NCAA) website at ncaa.com, and then find the webpage for women's lacrosse.

2. Display the current rankings in NCAA women's lacrosse.

3. On additional tabs, open the following webpages:
   - Maryland Terrapins Athletics home page: umterps.com
   - University of North Carolina Tar Heels Official Athletic home page: goheels.com
   - Syracuse University Athletics home page: cuse.com

4. On each of the three university athletic home pages, explore links to find a webpage for women's lacrosse. (*Hint*: Look for a Sports link on each page.)

5. Click links and use Microsoft Edge tools to find at least one webpage from each site that shows the schedule for the recent or upcoming season.

6. Pin the three webpages you found to the Start menu.

⊕ **Explore** 7. Use a link on one of the university sport webpages to print that school's schedule.

⊕ **Explore** 8. Use a link to email a schedule to yourself. Start Mail and display the Inbox with the message you received containing a link to the schedule.

9. Display the Start menu and then press the Print Screen key to capture an image of the screen. Start Paint, paste the screen image in a new file, and then save the file as **Schedule** in the Module4 > Case4 folder provided with your Data Files.

10. From the ncaa.com page, navigate to **ncaapublications.com**, the home page for NCAA manuals, rule books, scorebooks, and other publications.

11. Point to the COMPLIMENTARY link, and then click Records Books to display a list of NCAA record books. Find a publication appropriate for WLAX Boosters, and then click the link to the publication.

⊕ **Explore** 12. Use the links on the page to download a free PDF of the publication. When the download is finished, right-click the webpage, and then click Save As on the shortcut menu. Save the webpage as a PDF file named **NCAA** in the Module4 > Case4 folder provided with your Data Files. (Recall that PDFs, or Portable Document Format files, contain text and images that you can often download from a website and read with Windows Reader.) Close the webpage with the download.

13. In Mail, create an email message addressed to you and your instructor. Enter **NCAA publication** as the subject.

14. In the message area, write a message identifying the type of publication you downloaded, such as a rule book.

15. Attach the NCAA file to the message, and then send the message.

⊕ **Explore** 16. On the website for any of the three colleges, find a webpage showing the results of a recent season. Share the results with OneNote. (*Hint*: Click the Share button in the navigation bar).

⊕ **Explore** 17. Start OneNote from the Start menu, and then display the information you shared from the women's lacrosse website. Press the Print Screen key to capture an image of the screen. Start Paint, paste the screen image in a new file, and then save the file as **OneNote** in the Module4 > Case4 folder provided with your Data Files.

18. Restore your computer by completing the following tasks:
    - In Microsoft Edge, clear the History list.
    - On the Start menu, delete the tiles for the pinned webpages.
    - In Mail, delete the emails you sent and received, and then empty the Trash (or Deleted Items) folder.
    - In the left pane of OneNote, right-click the page containing the link to lacrosse results, and then click Delete Page on the shortcut menu. Click the Delete Page button to confirm you want to delete the page.

19. Close all open windows and apps.

Protecting Your Computer

Managing Computer Security

OBJECTIVES

Session 5.1
- Manage Windows Firewall
- Set up Windows Update
- Protect your computer from viruses and other malicious software
- Use Windows Defender to protect against spyware
- Examine Mail security

Session 5.2
- Manage Microsoft Edge security
- Protect privacy with InPrivate Browsing
- Set up user accounts
- Control access to your computer
- Examine other built-in security features

Case | *Snap Home Automation*

A few years ago, Lamar Jefferson founded Snap Home Automation in Santa Clara, California. Snap Home Automation (or Snap for short) designs and installs systems that keep homes safe, manage energy consumption, and control electronic devices using a smartphone. Snap works with homeowners and businesses throughout California and other parts of the West Coast. Recently, Lamar has become concerned with the security of Snap's computers. Many of Lamar's system designers work at client sites using mobile computers, including laptops and tablets, running Windows 10. Although the designers can access the Internet with their computers, they can't usually connect to the Snap network, where an administrator oversees security. Instead, they must take advantage of the security tools in Windows 10 to prevent problems stemming from viruses, spyware, and other types of harmful software. Lamar hired you to support the system design staff. One of your first duties is to investigate the security features in Windows 10 and show Lamar how to use them to address security threats.

In this module, you'll explore the security tools in the Control Panel's System and Security category, including Windows Firewall, and those provided through the Settings app, including Windows Update and Windows Defender. You'll learn how to set up Windows 10 to work with antivirus software and how to implement other security measures, including setting up user accounts. You will also examine Microsoft Edge security settings so that you can use the Internet safely.

STARTING DATA FILES

There are no starting Data Files needed for this module.

Session 5.1 Visual Overview:

The **Security and Maintenance window** is a Control Panel tool that helps you manage security if Windows detects a security problem.

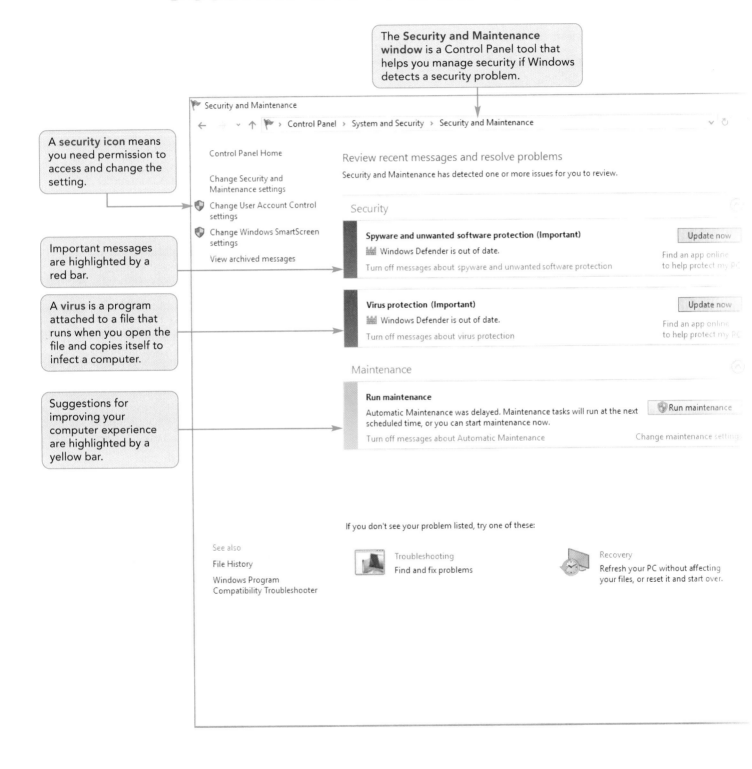

A **security icon** means you need permission to access and change the setting.

Important messages are highlighted by a red bar.

A **virus** is a program attached to a file that runs when you open the file and copies itself to infect a computer.

Suggestions for improving your computer experience are highlighted by a yellow bar.

Security and Maintenance

← → ↑ 🚩 > Control Panel > System and Security > Security and Maintenance

Control Panel Home

Change Security and Maintenance settings

Change User Account Control settings

Change Windows SmartScreen settings

View archived messages

Review recent messages and resolve problems

Security and Maintenance has detected one or more issues for you to review.

Security

Spyware and unwanted software protection (Important)   Update now

Windows Defender is out of date.

Turn off messages about spyware and unwanted software protection   Find an app online to help protect my PC

Virus protection (Important)   Update now

Windows Defender is out of date.

Turn off messages about virus protection   Find an app online to help protect my PC

Maintenance

Run maintenance   Run maintenance

Automatic Maintenance was delayed. Maintenance tasks will run at the next scheduled time, or you can start maintenance now.

Turn off messages about Automatic Maintenance   Change maintenance settings

See also

File History

Windows Program Compatibility Troubleshooter

If you don't see your problem listed, try one of these:

Troubleshooting
Find and fix problems

Recovery
Refresh your PC without affecting your files, or reset it and start over.

Windows 10 Security Tools

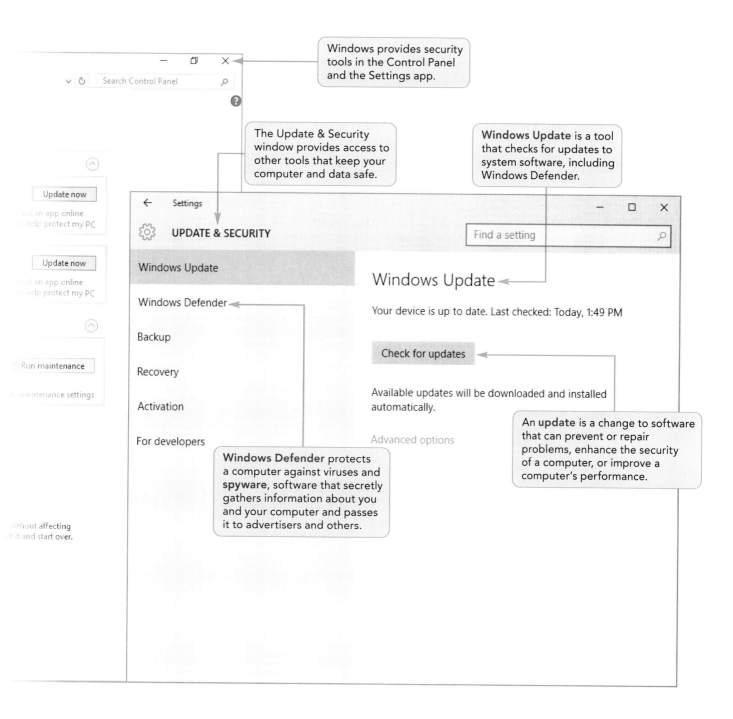

Windows provides security tools in the Control Panel and the Settings app.

The Update & Security window provides access to other tools that keep your computer and data safe.

Windows Update is a tool that checks for updates to system software, including Windows Defender.

Windows Defender protects a computer against viruses and **spyware**, software that secretly gathers information about you and your computer and passes it to advertisers and others.

An **update** is a change to software that can prevent or repair problems, enhance the security of a computer, or improve a computer's performance.

Settings

UPDATE & SECURITY

Windows Update

Windows Defender

Backup

Recovery

Activation

For developers

Find a setting

Windows Update

Your device is up to date. Last checked: Today, 1:49 PM

Check for updates

Available updates will be downloaded and installed automatically.

Advanced options

Search Control Panel

Update now

Find an app online to help protect my PC

Update now

Find an app online to help protect my PC

Run maintenance

maintenance settings

without affecting
it and start over.

Using Windows 10 Security Tools

Windows 10 provides security tools that help to keep your computer safe from threats such as harmful software, unsolicited email, and invasions of your privacy. When you connect to the Internet, send and receive email, or share your computer or files with others, your computer is vulnerable to harm from people who might attempt to steal your personal information, damage your files, or interrupt your work. You should use the Windows 10 security tools and other techniques to defend against these threats.

Harmful software, referred to as **malicious software**, or **malware**, includes viruses. By copying itself and triggering computer code, a virus can infect your computer. The damage a virus causes can range from changing your desktop settings to deleting or corrupting files on your hard disk. Viruses are often spread by email and run when you open an email attachment or the email message itself. Files you download from websites can also contain viruses that run when you save the files on your computer.

People who create and send malware are called **hackers**, a generic term that refers to anyone who intends to access a computer system without permission. (Hackers with criminal intent are sometimes called **crackers**, or black hat hackers.) Hackers can also invade your privacy by accessing your computer via the Internet to find information such as passwords and financial account numbers. Hackers sometimes access your computer using spyware, software that secretly gathers information about you and your computer actions, including sensitive information.

If you are working on a computer connected to a network, a network administrator probably defends the network against security threats such as malware, viruses, spyware, and hackers. Otherwise, if you are working on a home computer, for example, you should take advantage of the security features that Windows 10 provides.

You'll start by showing Lamar the security features provided in Windows 10.

To open the Security and Maintenance window:

1. Click in the **Ask me anything** box on the taskbar, and then begin typing **Security and Maintenance** until Security and Maintenance appears in the search results.

   Trouble? If Cortana is not activated, turn on Cortana, or click in the Search the web and Windows box on the taskbar.

2. In the search results, click **Security and Maintenance** to open the Security and Maintenance window in the Control Panel.

   Trouble? If Security and Maintenance does not appear in the search results, delete the text you typed, and then type "Control Panel." Click Control Panel in the search results, click System and Security, and then click Security and Maintenance.

3. If necessary, click the **expand** button ⊙ to expand the Security section, as shown in Figure 5-1.

| Figure 5-1 | Security and Maintenance window |

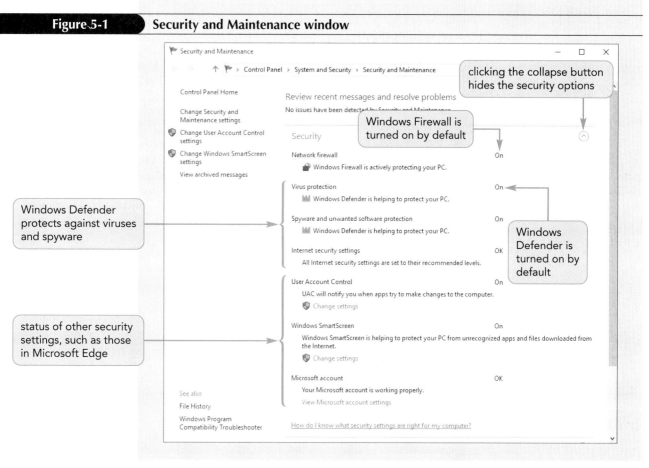

Figure 5-2 describes the security features listed in the Security and Maintenance window.

| Figure 5-2 | Security features |

Security Feature	Description
Network firewall	This feature uses Windows Firewall by default to monitor and restrict communication with the Internet, which helps protect your computer from hackers. Before an app can send or receive information via the Internet, Windows Firewall must allow it to do so.
Virus protection	Antivirus software is your best protection against viruses, worms, and other types of harmful software. If you have antivirus software, Windows reminds you to use it regularly to scan your computer for virus infections and to monitor email. If you do not have antivirus software, Windows Defender runs automatically to defend your computer against malware.
Spyware and unwanted software protection	Antispyware software, such as Windows Defender, prevents some types of malware from infecting your system.
Internet security settings	Security and Maintenance checks that your web browser is using appropriate security settings to block malware from being installed on your system when you visit websites.
User Account Control (UAC)	This service displays a dialog box requesting your permission to install software or open programs that could harm your computer.
Windows SmartScreen	This tool protects your computer from unrecognized apps and files you download from the Internet.
Microsoft account	This tool keeps track of your account settings and alerts you if an unauthorized user tries to change them.

Most of the features listed in Figure 5-1 and Figure 5-2 are considered essential—all of these security features should be turned on to keep your computer secure. If Windows detects a problem with one of these essential security features, Windows displays an **alert message** near the Notifications icon 📧 in the notification area of your taskbar. For example, you might see the following alert message, "Solve PC issues: 1 message." You can click the alert message to open the Security and Maintenance window and find out how to address the problem. You can also see if the Security and Maintenance window lists any new messages by pointing to the Notifications icon. The ScreenTip for this icon changes depending on whether you have new notifications. If you do, the ScreenTip appears as "New notifications." Otherwise, the ScreenTip appears as "No new notifications."

Some features display a security icon next to the Change settings link (as shown in the Session 5.1 Visual Overview). This icon indicates that you might need permission to access and change the setting. You indicate that you have permission by entering an administrator password. Requiring a user to enter a password to change system settings is another way to protect your computer.

Managing Windows Firewall

Windows Firewall is software that serves as a barrier between your computer and a network or the Internet. As shown in Figure 5-3, Windows Firewall checks information coming from the network or the Internet and either blocks it from your computer or allows it to pass, depending on your settings. In this way, Windows Firewall prevents unauthorized users from accessing your computer and is the first line of defense against malware. Many antivirus programs include a firewall that works in a similar way.

| Figure 5-3 | How Windows Firewall protects your computer |

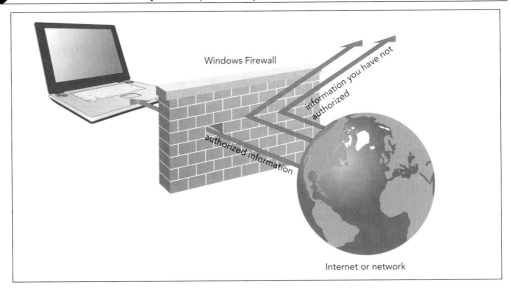

A firewall defends against malware trying to gain access to your computer by monitoring your network and Internet connections. However, a firewall does not scan email, so it cannot detect viruses sent in email messages (a common way to spread viruses). Neither can a firewall detect viruses in files you download from the web. Furthermore, a firewall can't protect you from email scams, called **phishing**, that try to deceive you into revealing private information such as passwords. To protect against viruses in email and downloaded files, use antivirus software. To minimize phishing attempts, use the Windows SmartScreen Filter. (Both topics are covered later in this module.)

Windows Firewall is turned on by default, so it doesn't allow communications with most programs via the Internet or a network. However, your computer manufacturer or someone else might turn off Windows Firewall, so you should verify that it is running. Typically, Windows Firewall is turned off only if another firewall, which might be provided by other security software or your network, is protecting your computer.

Using Windows Firewall, you can customize four settings for each type of network location, including **private networks**, which are those you use at home or work involving people and devices you trust, and **public networks**, those in public places such as airports and libraries. You'll show Lamar how to find these Windows Firewall settings.

To turn on Windows Firewall:

▶ **1.** In the Security and Maintenance window, click **System and Security** in the Address bar to display the System and Security window.

▶ **2.** Click **Windows Firewall** to open the Windows Firewall window.

▶ **3.** If necessary, click the **expand** icons ⓥ to expand the Private networks and the Guest or public networks sections. See Figure 5-4.

Figure 5-4	Windows Firewall window

Trouble? If a different firewall is installed on your computer and is managing the firewall settings, your Windows Firewall window will look different from the figure, and you might not be able to expand the sections or change the settings. In that case, read but do not perform Steps 4–6.

▶ **4.** Click the **Turn Windows Firewall on or off** link in the left pane.

Trouble? If a User Account Control dialog box opens requesting an administrator password or your permission to continue, make sure you have permission to change Windows Firewall settings (check with your instructor, if necessary), and then enter the password or click the Yes button.

▶ **5.** In the Customize Settings window, click the first **Turn on Windows Firewall** option button (the one for Private network settings) if it is not already selected. See Figure 5-5.

Figure 5-5	Customize Settings window

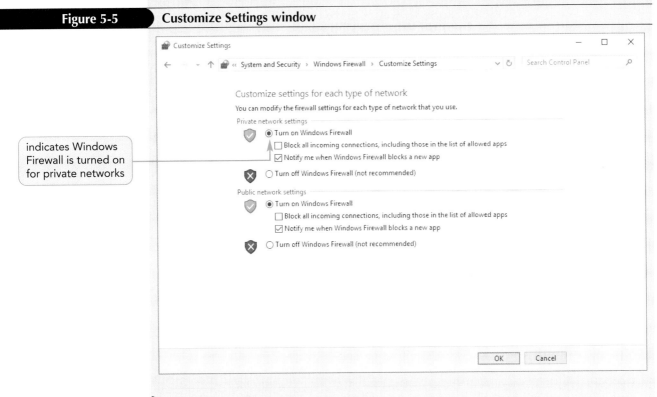

indicates Windows Firewall is turned on for private networks

▶ **6.** Click the **OK** button.

When Windows Firewall is turned on and an unknown app tries to connect to your computer from the Internet, Windows Firewall blocks the connection. Instead of turning off Windows Firewall every time you want to use a blocked app, you can customize the firewall by adding apps to its allowed list so that it maintains a level of security that's right for you.

In the Customize Settings window, you can specify the following firewall settings for each type of network location that you use:

• Turn on Windows Firewall—This setting is selected by default, meaning that most apps are blocked from communicating through the firewall.
• Block all incoming connections, including those in the list of allowed apps—When you connect to a public network, such as in a hotel or an airport, you might want to select this setting. Windows blocks all apps, even those in the allowed apps list.
• Notify me when Windows Firewall blocks a new app—When you select this check box, Windows Firewall informs you when it blocks a new app, giving you the option of adding the app to the allowed apps list.
• Turn off Windows Firewall (not recommended)—The only time you should select this setting is when another firewall is running on your computer.

Lamar often sets up entertainment networks in client homes so they can play their favorite music and videos in any room, even those that don't have a computer. To provide this service, he uses Windows Media Player, an app you can use to store, organize, and play media files such as music and videos. By default, Windows Media Player is blocked from sending or receiving media on a network. You'll show Lamar how to add the Windows Media Player app to the allowed programs list so he can use and test this app on the entertainment networks he sets up.

If you are performing the following steps in a computer lab, you might not be able to change the allowed apps. Check with your instructor or technical support person to determine whether you can specify Windows Media Player as an allowed app in Windows Firewall. If you cannot, read but do not perform the following steps.

To add an app to the allowed apps list:

▶ **1.** In the left pane of the Windows Firewall window, click the **Allow an app or feature through Windows Firewall** link to open the Allowed apps window.

   Trouble? If the Allow an app or feature through Windows Firewall link is inactive in the Windows Firewall window, click the Back button ⬅ to return to the System and Security window, and then click the Allow an app or feature through Windows Firewall link.

   Trouble? If a dialog box opens requesting an administrator password or your permission to continue, make sure you have permission to change the Windows Firewall settings (check with your instructor, if necessary), and then enter the password or click the Yes button.

▶ **2.** Scroll the list, which is sorted alphabetically, to display the Windows Media Player check box. See Figure 5-6. Your apps might differ.

| Figure 5-6 | Allowed apps window |

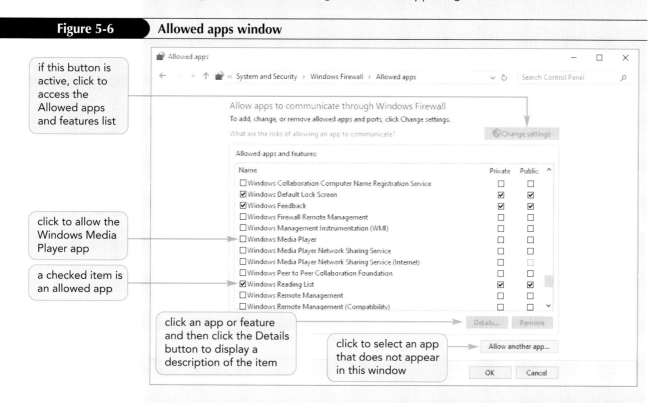

> **3.** Click the **Windows Media Player** check box to select it. A checkmark appears in the Private column, indicating that Lamar will be able to connect to the device within a private network.
>
> **Trouble?** If you cannot select an app in the list, click the Change settings button, and then repeat Step 4.
>
> **Trouble?** If you are not allowed to change the allowed apps in Windows Firewall, click the Cancel button in the Allowed apps window, and then skip Step 5.
>
> **Trouble?** If Private is not selected, click the check box in the Private column to insert a checkmark, and then click the check box in the Public column to remove the checkmark, if necessary.
>
> **4.** Click the **OK** button to add Windows Media Player to the allowed apps list for private networks and to return to the Windows Firewall window.
>
> **5.** Click the **Back** button ← to return to the System and Security window, and then minimize it.

Keep in mind that when you add an app to the Windows Firewall allowed apps list, you are making your computer easier for apps to access and therefore more vulnerable to malware infection. You should allow an app only when you really need it, and never allow an app that you don't recognize—it could be a virus or a worm. Finally, be sure to remove an app from the allowed apps list when you no longer need it.

Setting Up Windows Update

An **update** is a change to software that can prevent or repair problems, enhance the security of a computer, or improve a computer's performance. Microsoft regularly releases updates to Windows 10 and provides them for download from its website. You can look for, download, and install these updates any time you visit the Microsoft website. However, because updates often include critical security repairs and enhancements, Microsoft also makes them available to you through the Windows Update feature. Windows Update makes sure your operating system and its tools have the most recent software improvements and security enhancements.

Windows Update periodically checks for updates to the operating system from Microsoft, including security updates, critical updates, and service packs. (When Microsoft combines many updates in one package, the collection of updates is called a **service pack** and is often abbreviated as **SP**.) If an update is available, Windows Update downloads the software and installs it for you. Windows downloads the updates in the background as long as you're connected to the Internet. If you are disconnected from the Internet before Windows finishes downloading, Windows continues downloading the next time you connect to the Internet.

You can also check for updates yourself at any time using the Check for updates button in the Windows Update window. If updates are available, Windows downloads and installs them.

Some updates restart the computer when they finish installing the updated files, usually because they are replacing a file that Windows requires and runs in the background. To advise you that an update with a required restart is scheduled, a notification appears when you sign in to Windows or as you are working on the desktop. By default, Windows downloads and installs the update as you work on your computer, but waits until you save data to restart. If you prefer not to be interrupted as you are using the computer, you can schedule the restart for a more convenient time. If you are using a version of Windows other than Windows Home, you can defer downloading and installing the update until a later date that you specify.

To view your current update status and settings for Windows Update, you open the Update & Security window in the Settings app. You can also use this window to access advanced options and review your update history.

Windows 10 updates automatically because Microsoft offers Windows as a Service rather than a software package. The Windows-as-a-Service approach means that after you install Windows on a device, Microsoft keeps it up to date for as long as the device is running. One reason that Microsoft adopted this approach is to keep Windows secure from hackers.

INSIGHT

Windows Update and Metered Internet Connections

A **metered Internet connection** is one for which your ISP sets a limit on the amount of data your device sends and receives. If you exceed the limit, you might be charged extra for the data usage or your connection speed might be slower until the end of the billing cycle. Metered Internet connections are common on mobile devices such as cell phones. If you are using a metered Internet connection, Windows Update downloads only priority updates, which are those Microsoft considers necessary to maintain the security and reliability of Windows. If you access the Internet through a mobile broadband network, which provides high-speed Internet access for cell phones and other portable devices, Windows sets your Internet connection to metered by default. If you are using a different type of network with a metered connection, you can set your computer to use a metered connection. To check the setting, start the Settings app and then select Network & Internet. With Wi-Fi selected in the right pane, click Advanced options in the right pane. In the Metered connection section, click the slider button to turn on the Set as metered connection setting.

Although Lamar will update automatically most of the time, he wants to know how to schedule a restart after an update has been downloaded and installed. He sometimes keeps his computer running all night to test systems that he is about to install. After Windows notifies him about an update, he can schedule a restart so it doesn't interrupt his testing.

As you perform the following steps, note your original settings so you can restore them later.

To set up Windows Update:

TIP

To check for updates manually, click the Check for updates button in the right pane.

1. Click the **Start** button ⊞ to display the Start menu, and then click **Settings** to start the Settings app.

2. In the Settings home page, click **Update & security**. The Update & Security window opens with Windows Update selected in the left pane. See Figure 5-7. Your settings might differ.

Figure 5-7   Update & Security window

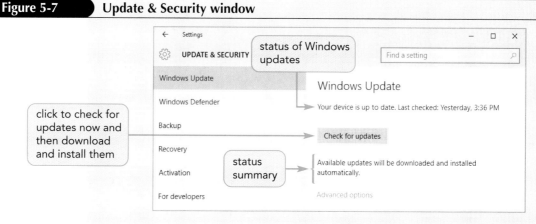

▶ **3.** In the right pane, click the **Advanced options** link. The Advanced Options window opens. See Figure 5-8.

Figure 5-8	Advanced Options window

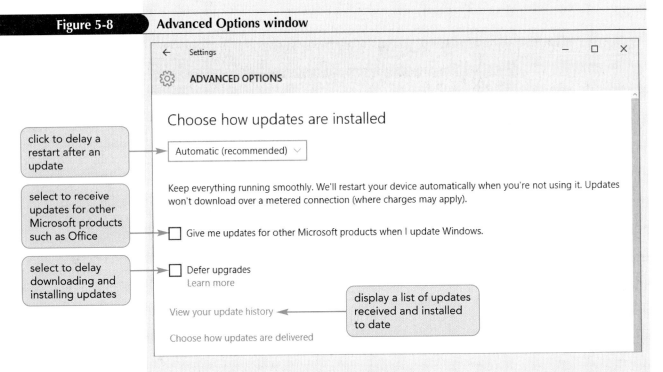

click to delay a restart after an update

select to receive updates for other Microsoft products such as Office

select to delay downloading and installing updates

display a list of updates received and installed to date

▶ **4.** Click the **Automatic (recommended)** box in the Choose how updates are installed section.

Trouble? If the box in the Choose how updates are installed section is labeled "Notify to schedule restart," click the box and continue with Step 5.

▶ **5.** Click **Notify to schedule restart** to select the option.

The next time an update with a required restart is available, open the Update & security window to view your options. Windows indicates an update is ready and that it will restart the computer when you usually don't use it, such as at 3:30 am. As shown in Figure 5-9, you can click the Select a restart time option button to select the date and time of the restart.

Figure 5-9 Selecting a restart time

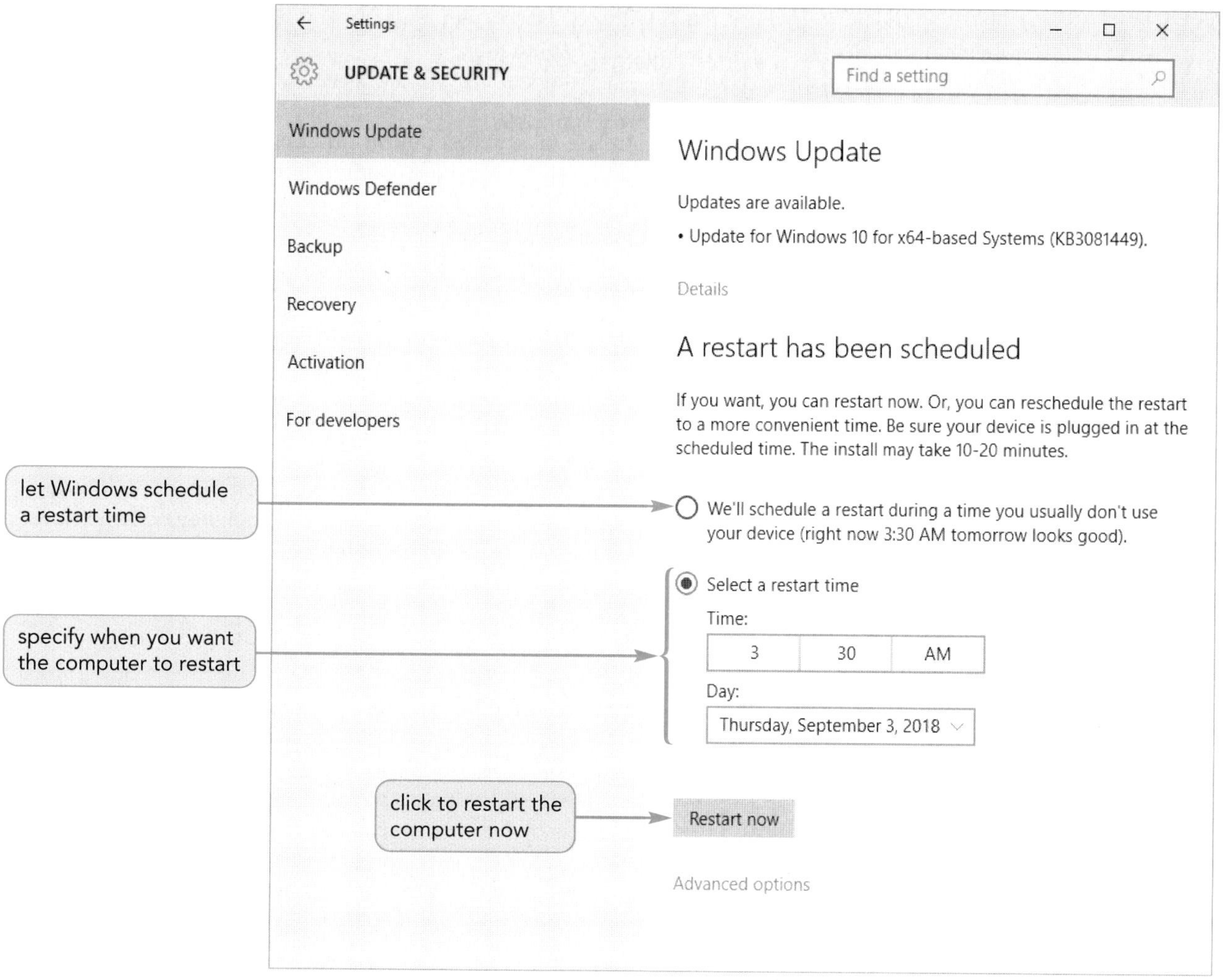

Settings

⚙ **UPDATE & SECURITY**

Find a setting

Windows Update

Windows Defender

Backup

Recovery

Activation

For developers

Windows Update

Updates are available.
• Update for Windows 10 for x64-based Systems (KB3081449).

Details

A restart has been scheduled

If you want, you can restart now. Or, you can reschedule the restart to a more convenient time. Be sure your device is plugged in at the scheduled time. The install may take 10-20 minutes.

let Windows schedule a restart time ————→ ○ We'll schedule a restart during a time you usually don't use your device (right now 3:30 AM tomorrow looks good).

⦿ Select a restart time

Time:

specify when you want the computer to restart ————→

| 3 | 30 | AM |

Day:

Thursday, September 3, 2018 ∨

click to restart the computer now ————→ Restart now

Advanced options

Windows also keeps track of the updates it installed. You can display the list of updates to determine whether the update was successfully installed. If it wasn't, you can try to install it again. If you or a technical support specialist suspects a problem with an update, you can also uninstall the update to see if that solves the problem. You'll show Lamar how to display the update history on his computer.

To view your update history:

▶ **1.** In the Advanced Options window, click the **View your update history** link to display the View Your Update History window, which lists recent updates. The Update history list includes the name of the update, whether it was installed successfully, and when the installation was attempted or completed.

▶ **2.** Click the **Back** button ⬅ to return to the Advanced Options window.

▶ **3.** Click the **Back** button ⬅ again to return to the Update & Security window, and then close the window.

Now that you know Lamar's copy of Windows 10 is up to date, you can turn to protecting his computer from viruses and other types of malware.

Protecting Your Computer from Malware

Your best protection against malware is to use the current version of your antivirus software to scan email messages, attachments, and other files on your computer for viruses, worms, and other types of malware. Antivirus software locates a virus by comparing identifying characteristics of the files on your computer to the characteristics of a list of known viruses, which are called **virus definitions**. When it finds a virus, or any type of malware, the antivirus software notifies you about the virus.

INSIGHT

Recognizing Types of Malware

Recall that a virus is a program that replicates itself and attaches to files or programs, usually affects your computer's performance and stability, and sometimes damages or removes files. Viruses are often transmitted through email attachments or downloaded files, but they don't spread until you open the infected attachment or file. In contrast, a **worm** is harmful computer code that spreads without your interaction. A worm slips from one network connection to another, replicating itself on network computers. As it does, a worm consumes network resources, overwhelming computers until they become slow or unresponsive. Another type of malware is a **Trojan horse**, which hides inside another program, such as a photo-viewing program you download from the web. When you install the program, the Trojan horse infects the operating system, allowing a hacker to access your computer. Trojan horses can't spread on their own; they depend on programs, including viruses and worms, to proliferate. If hackers access your system through a Trojan horse, they might install a **rootkit**, malware that gains administrator-level, or root-level, access to a computer or network without the system administrators or users detecting its presence. Hackers use rootkits to monitor keystrokes (to learn passwords, for example), modify files, disable or alter tools that might detect the rootkit, and attack other devices on the network. Common symptoms of malware are when your computer runs much slower than normal, messages appear unexpectedly, programs start or close on their own, or Windows shuts down suddenly.

When you buy a new computer, most likely it comes with antivirus software already installed as a trial version so you can test it for a limited time. (Look for the antivirus software on the All apps list.) Windows Defender is automatically installed with Windows 10 to make sure the computer is protected from malware. To determine whether you should continue running the preinstalled antivirus software or Windows Defender, you should compare their features and read reviews from security experts to learn how well each app protects against viruses, spyware, Trojan horses, rootkits, and other malware.

Windows 10 can detect whether you have antivirus software installed on your computer. If you do not, Windows runs Windows Defender to protect your computer from malware. If you have antivirus software installed on your computer but the subscription has expired, Windows reminds you to renew the subscription, activate Windows Defender, or select another antivirus program from the Windows Store. If you have antivirus software installed and it's up to date, do not also run Windows Defender to scan for viruses because only one antivirus app should be running on your computer at any time.

Most vendors of antivirus software offer fee-based subscription services that provide regular updates for current virus definitions. You can refer to the antivirus software's help system to learn how to run the software and receive regular updates, or you can use the Security and Maintenance window to check for updates. Besides Windows Defender, Windows recognizes most types of antivirus software and displays their status in the Security and Maintenance window. In most cases, you can use the

Security and Maintenance window to determine whether your antivirus software needs to be updated and then run the updating program. Windows Update keeps Windows Defender and its virus definitions up to date. Keeping the virus definition list current helps to protect your computer from new attacks. If your list of viruses is out of date, your computer is vulnerable to new threats.

Although Lamar is certain that antivirus software is installed on his computer, he asks you to make sure it is up to date and that virus scanning is turned on.

To check for virus protection on your computer:

▶ **1.** In the Control Panel, open the System and Security window, and then click **Security and Maintenance** to return to the Security and Maintenance window. If necessary, click **Security** to expand the Security section.

▶ **2.** Examine the settings in the Virus protection section, which should report if an installed antivirus program is protecting your computer. In Figure 5-10, the Security and Maintenance window reports that the antivirus program is out of date.

   Trouble? If the Security and Maintenance window reports that your virus protection is up to date and is protecting your computer, skip Step 3.

| Figure 5-10 | Antivirus software needs to be updated |

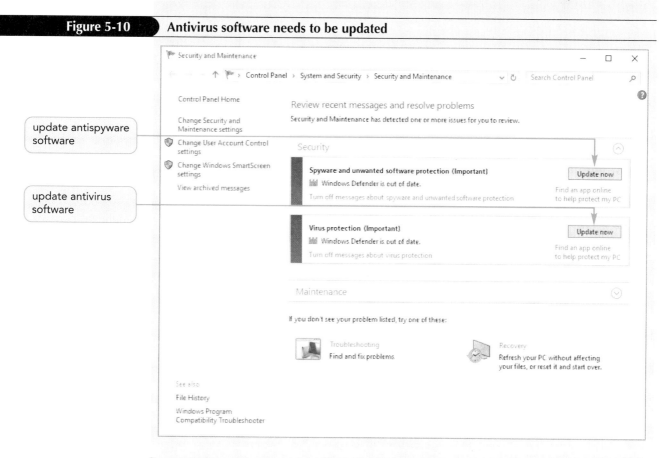

▶ **3.** If necessary, click the **Update now** button. Your antivirus software starts and checks for updates on its manufacturer's website. When it is finished updating, close the antivirus software window, if necessary.

▶ **4.** Close the Security and Maintenance window.

Problem Solving: Avoiding and Removing Viruses

One of the most difficult computer problems to solve is removing a virus from your system. To avoid this problem, you can defend against viruses in the following ways so that they do not infect your computer:

- Do not open unexpected email attachments. If the message containing the attachment is from a trusted source, send an email to that person asking about the file and what it contains.
- Regularly scan your hard drive with an antivirus program. Most antivirus software includes an option to schedule a complete system scan. You only need to make sure your computer is turned on to perform the scan.
- Set your antivirus program to scan all incoming email.
- Keep your antivirus software up to date. New viruses are introduced frequently, and your antivirus software needs to use the latest virus definitions to protect your computer.
- Create backups of your work files periodically. Viruses can corrupt or destroy data files, which are the most valuable files on your computer.

When you notice symptoms such as your computer running slowly or turning off on its own, suspect a virus. You can try to remove a virus in the following ways:

- Update your antivirus software. Look for an update feature that connects with the website of your antivirus software developer to download the latest virus definitions.
- Use the antivirus software to scan your entire computer. The software might be able to remove the virus for you or identify the virus by name.
- Use an online scanner. If your antivirus software does not find or report a virus, visit the Microsoft website (www.microsoft.com) and search for "Windows security software providers." In the search results, look for a link to vendors that provide free online virus scanners to help you find and remove the virus.
- Search for instructions on removing the virus. If your antivirus software or online scanner identifies but does not remove the virus, search an antivirus vendor's website to find information about removing the virus.

Another security concern is spyware, which can also affect your computing experience.

Defending Against Spyware

Spyware can install itself or run on your computer without your consent or control. It's called spyware because it monitors your computing actions, usually while you are online, to collect information about you. Spyware can change system settings, interrupt programs, and slow your computer's performance. Spyware might infect your computer when you visit a certain website or download a free program, such as a screen saver or search toolbar. Less frequently, spyware is distributed along with other programs on a CD, DVD, or other type of removable media. Spyware might also pass information about your web browsing habits to advertisers, who use it to improve their products or websites. Other times, a special type of spyware called **adware** changes your browser settings to open **pop-up ads**, which are windows that appear while you are viewing a webpage and advertise a product or service. Pop-up ads interrupt your online activities and can be difficult to close; they can also be vehicles for additional spyware or other types of malware.

Because spyware can download, install, and run on your computer without your knowledge or consent, it's often difficult to know if spyware is infecting your computer. If you are experiencing any of the following symptoms, they are most likely due to spyware:

- New toolbars, links, or favorites appear in your web browser unexpectedly.
- Your home page, pointer, or search engine changes without your consent.
- When you enter a URL for a website, such as a search engine, you go to a different website without notice.
- Pop-up ads interrupt you, even when you're not on the Internet.
- Your computer suddenly restarts or runs slowly.

Be sure to scan your computer with a program, such as Windows Defender, to detect and remove any spyware on your computer.

Scanning Your Computer with Windows Defender

To protect your computer against spyware, you can run an up-to-date **antispyware** (or **antimalware**) **program**, such as Windows Defender, to check for both spyware and viruses. Windows Defender helps prevent malware from installing itself and running on your computer, and it periodically scans your computer to detect and remove malware.

REFERENCE

Performing a Quick Scan with Windows Defender

- Click in the Ask me anything box or the Search the web and Windows box, and then type Windows Defender.
- Click Windows Defender in the search results.
- Click the Quick option button on the Home tab.
- Click the Scan now button.

You need to keep the malware definitions in the antimalware up to date. Windows Defender refers to the definitions to determine whether software it detects is a virus or spyware. When you update your computer, Windows Update installs any new virus and spyware definitions. You can also set Windows Defender to check for updated definitions before scanning your computer.

You'll show Lamar how to start Windows Defender and scan for malware. You can run a quick scan, a full system scan, or a custom scan. A quick scan checks the locations on your computer that spyware is most likely to infect. A full scan checks all your files and programs, but it takes longer and can make your computer run slowly. With a custom scan, you select the locations you want Windows Defender to check.

TIP

You can find Windows Defender in the Windows System category in the All apps list or in the Update & security window from the Settings home page.

To start Windows Defender and perform a quick scan:

1. Click in the **Ask me anything** box on the taskbar, type **Windows Defender**, and then click **Windows Defender** in the search results. The Windows Defender window opens on the desktop. See Figure 5-11, which shows that Windows Defender is up to date. Your settings might differ.

   Trouble? If Windows Defender is turned off, click the Turn on button.

Figure 5-11   Windows Defender

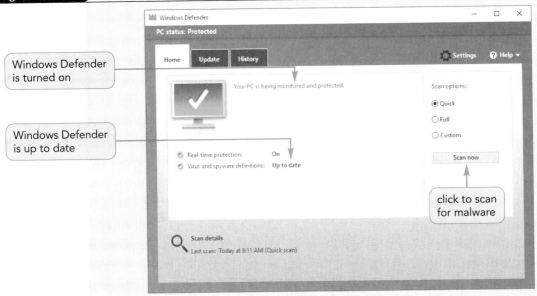

Windows Defender is turned on

Windows Defender is up to date

click to scan for malware

2. If the virus and spyware definitions are not up to date, click the **Update** tab, and then click the **Update** button. Windows Defender checks for program and malware definition updates, downloads and installs any updates, and then reports the update status.

3. If necessary, click the **Home** tab, click the **Quick** option button (if necessary), and then click the **Scan now** button. Windows Defender scans your computer, displaying first its progress and then the results of the scan. Depending on the number of programs on your computer, your scan might take a few minutes. Wait for the scan to finish and for Windows Defender to display the results before continuing.

TIP

Most antivirus programs quarantine suspicious files so you can choose to restore or delete them.

If Windows Defender finds suspicious files, it alerts you that these files have been **quarantined**, which means Windows Defender moved them to another location on your computer to safely segregate them from other files. Quarantined files cannot run, so they cannot harm your computer. You can review all quarantined files to determine what to do with them. Open the History page in Windows Defender, click the Quarantined items option button, and then click the View details button to display a list of quarantined files. The file list includes the filename, alert level, and date of quarantine. The alert level can help you decide whether to remove or restore a file. Remove files with a Severe or High alert level. If you do not recognize or trust the publisher of files with Medium or Low alert levels, search the web for information on those files to determine whether it is safe to restore them.

Windows Defender occasionally identifies a file as potential malware when the computer actually needs the file. If your computer has experienced problems since quarantining those files, go to the Microsoft Support webpage (https://support.microsoft.com) to contact a Microsoft support person and determine what to do with the files. If you haven't had any computer problems since Windows Defender quarantined the files, you can remove the files or leave them in the quarantine location.

To remove a quarantined file:

▶ **1.** In the Windows Defender window, click the **History** tab to display the History page, click the **Quarantined items** option button, if necessary, and then click the **View details** button to display details about quarantined items. See Figure 5-12.

Trouble? If a dialog box opens requesting an administrator password or your permission to continue, enter the password and then click the Yes button.

Trouble? If Windows Defender did not quarantine any items after its quick scan, or if you do not have permission to work with quarantined items, read but do not perform Step 2.

Figure 5-12	Quarantined item in Windows Defender

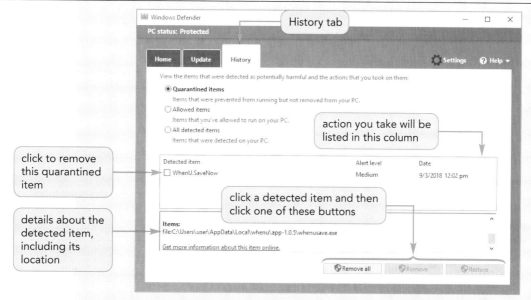

The quarantined item, WhenU.SaveNow, has a Medium alert level. Lamar does not recognize the publisher of this program, so you will remove it.

▶ **2.** In the Quarantined items list, click **WhenU.SaveNow** (or another item with a Severe, High, or Medium alert level and a publisher you do not recognize), and then click the **Remove** button.

Trouble? If a dialog box opens requesting an administrator password or your permission to continue, enter the password or click the Yes button.

Now that you've scanned Lamar's computer and handled the items Windows Defender found, you can set an option to make sure Windows Defender runs effectively and then learn how to turn Windows Defender on and off.

Setting Windows Defender Options

To turn Windows Defender on or off, you use an option in the Settings app. If you have been using Windows Defender and then install different antimalware software, you should turn Windows Defender off so it doesn't interfere with the other antivirus or antispyware program. If you remove other antimalware software or do not renew an antimalware subscription, Windows Defender runs automatically. To make sure your computer is being protected, you can verify Windows Defender's status in the Settings app and make sure it is set to use **Real-time protection**. This setting is selected by default, which means Windows Defender is set to constantly monitor your computer for virus and spyware activity. Windows Defender then alerts you when suspicious software attempts to install itself or to run on your computer, and notifies you when programs try to change important Windows settings. As with a scan, when Windows Defender detects suspicious software using Real-time protection, it assigns an alert level to the software and then displays a dialog box where you can choose one of the following actions:

- Quarantine—Quarantine the software. Windows Defender prevents the software from running and allows you to restore it or remove it from your computer.
- Remove—Permanently delete the software from your computer.
- Allow—Add the software to a list of allowed items so the software can run on your computer. Windows Defender does not alert you to risks that the software might pose to your privacy or your computer unless you remove the program from the Allowed items list.

Other Windows Defender settings you can select include **Cloud-based protection**. When this option is turned on, Windows sends information about potential security problems to Microsoft, which can use the information to better identify malware and remove it. If you do not want Windows Defender to scan specific files, folders, file types, or processes—which are parts of computer programs—you can add that item to the **Exclusion list**. Keep in mind that Windows Defender does not scan any item you add to the Exclusion list, which can make your computer more vulnerable to malware.

You'll show Lamar how to make sure Windows Defender is turned on and using Real-time protection.

To verify Windows Defender options:

▶ **1.** In the Windows Defender window, click the **Settings** link to display the Update & Security window in the Settings app. See Figure 5-13.

Figure 5-13   **Windows Defender settings**

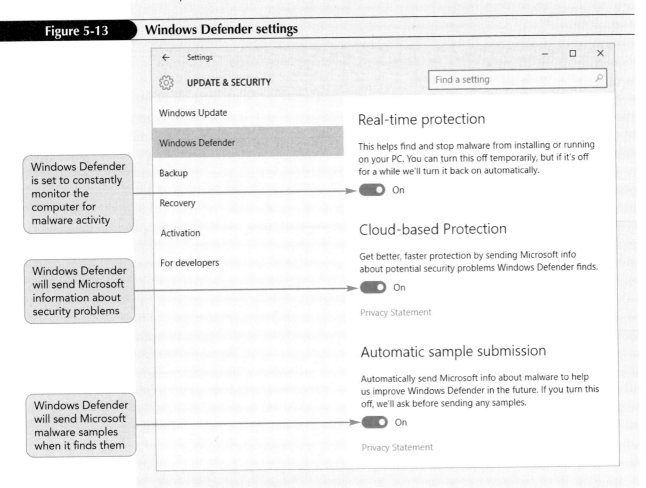

Windows Defender is set to constantly monitor the computer for malware activity

Windows Defender will send Microsoft information about security problems

Windows Defender will send Microsoft malware samples when it finds them

▶ **2.** In the Real-time protection section, click the **slider button**, if necessary, to change the Windows Defender setting from Off to On.

▶ **3.** Scroll down to view the other settings.

▶ **4.** Close all open windows.

Defending Against Email Viruses

TIP

Viewing a picture in a junk email message might validate your email address and result in your receiving more junk email.

An annoying and potentially dangerous type of privacy invasion is **spam**, or junk email, messages offering products and services that are sometimes fake or misleading. Some users receive thousands of spam messages a day; the volume alone makes spam a nuisance. In addition, spam can be a vehicle for malware. Communicating via email is one of the most popular activities on the Internet, and email is the most common way for computer viruses to spread. Viruses and other security threats are often contained in email attachments, especially files with filename extensions such as .exe, .bat, and .js.

To help prevent spam and potentially offensive material, Mail does not download graphics with messages sent in HTML format. People sending spam (called **spammers**) often use graphics to access your email address. Spammers can also take advantage of vulnerabilities in your computer to use it to send spam to other computers without your permission, a practice known as an **email relay**. This lets spammers work without being detected and can seriously downgrade the performance of your computer.

Phishing (pronounced *fishing*) is an attempt to deceive you into revealing personal or financial information when you respond to an email message or visit a website. A typical phishing scam starts with an email message that looks like an official notice from a trusted person or business, such as a bank, credit card company, or reputable online merchant. The email message asks you to reply with sensitive information, such as an account number or password, or directs you to a fraudulent website that requests this information. Phishers often use the information for identity theft.

To combat these threats, Mail blocks email attachments, graphics, and website links that might be harmful, notifying you when it does. Mail also helps prevent spammers from using your computer for email relays, and catches obvious spam messages and moves them to the built-in Junk folder.

REVIEW

Session 5.1 Quick Check

1. What is Windows Firewall?

2. Harmful software is called malicious software or _____.

3. Why might you want to view your update history?

4. What is a virus definition?

5. How do you use Windows Defender to check only the locations on your computer that spyware is most likely to infect?

6. If Windows Defender finds files that might be spyware, it _____ the files, which means it moves them to another location on your computer and prevents them from running until you remove or restore the files.

7. What is phishing?

Session 5.2 Visual Overview:

If a website is safe for an online transaction, the website name is green and a lock icon appears in the Address bar.

✓ Endpoint, Cloud, Mobile ✕ ＋

← → ↻ 🔒 Symantec Corporation [US]   symantec.com/index.

If the InPrivate button appears next to the tabs, InPrivate Browsing is in effect.

⊞ InPrivate   ▶ Bing   ✕ ＋

← → ↻ ⊞ bing.com   📖 ☆

IMAGES   VIDEOS   MAPS   NEWS   EXPLORE   SEARCH HISTORY

▶ bing

InPrivate Browsing opens a separate Microsoft Edge window for private browsing.

The **Pop-up Blocker** limits most pop-up windows and displays a notification when it blocks a pop-up.

Only secure content is displayed.

Microsoft Edge Security Features

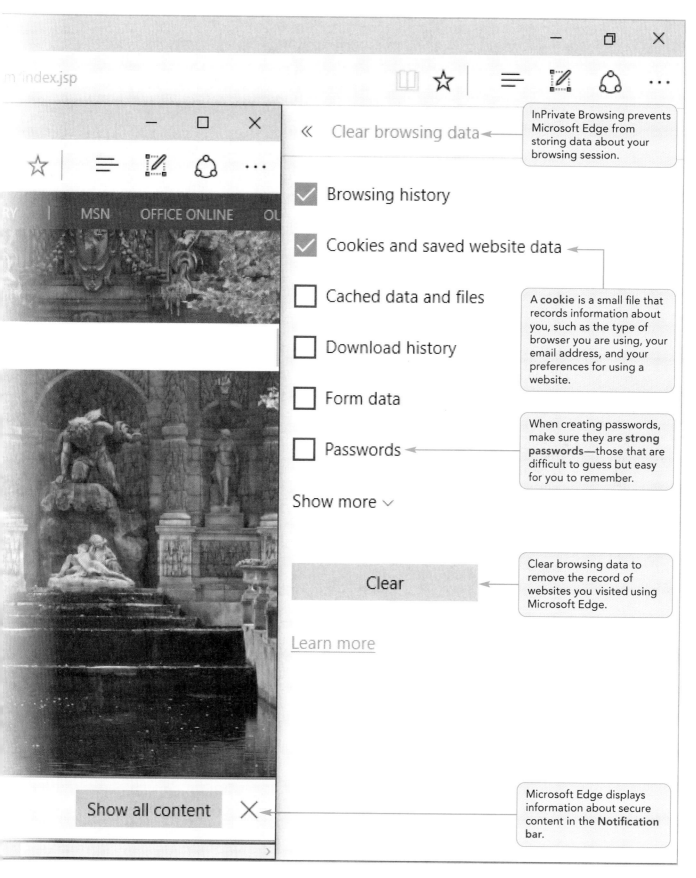

《   Clear browsing data ◄

InPrivate Browsing prevents Microsoft Edge from storing data about your browsing session.

☑ Browsing history

☑ Cookies and saved website data ◄

☐ Cached data and files

A **cookie** is a small file that records information about you, such as the type of browser you are using, your email address, and your preferences for using a website.

☐ Download history

☐ Form data

When creating passwords, make sure they are **strong passwords**—those that are difficult to guess but easy for you to remember.

☐ Passwords ◄

Show more ⌄

Clear browsing data to remove the record of websites you visited using Microsoft Edge.

Clear

Learn more

Microsoft Edge displays information about secure content in the **Notification bar**.

Show all content   ✕ ◄

Managing Microsoft Edge Security

Your computer is most vulnerable to security threats when you are connected to the Internet. You should therefore take advantage of the security settings in Microsoft Edge to help protect your computer by identifying viruses and other security threats that are circulated over the Internet, making your computer and personal information more secure. As a Windows app, Microsoft Edge is designed to resist online threats. For example, Microsoft Edge does not support ActiveX controls, which are small, self-contained programs. Older websites might use ActiveX controls to make it easier to perform tasks, such as submitting information to websites. Other ActiveX controls can harm your computer and files. Microsoft Edge blocks ActiveX controls and similar types of add-on or plug-in programs. Microsoft Edge always runs in a protected environment called a **sandbox** to guard against websites trying to save files or install malware on your computer.

In addition, Microsoft Edge uses the security features provided in the following list:

- SmartScreen Filter—This feature helps detect online scams, such as websites that try to trick you into revealing financial account information. The SmartScreen Filter also helps detect and block unknown and potentially malicious programs in files that you download from websites.
- Pop-up Blocker—This tool allows you to limit or block most pop-up windows.
- Digital signatures—Microsoft Edge can detect and display **digital signatures**, which are electronic security marks added to files to verify their authenticity.

Checking Websites with the SmartScreen Filter

Recall that phishing is an attempt to deceive you into revealing personal or financial information when you respond to an email message or visit a website. Microsoft Edge can protect you from online scams by detecting possible phishing websites. The SmartScreen Filter helps to protect you from phishing attacks, online fraud, and spoofed websites. (A **spoofed website** is a fraudulent site posing as a legitimate one.) The SmartScreen Filter operates in the background to analyze a website you visit by comparing its address to a list of reported phishing and malicious software websites, a practice called **reputation checking**. If the SmartScreen Filter finds that the website you're visiting is on the list of known malware or phishing sites, Microsoft Edge does not display the suspicious website. Instead, it shows a blocking webpage where you can choose to bypass the blocked website and go to your home page instead. If you are certain the blocked website is safe, you can continue to the site, though Microsoft does not recommend it.

If a spoofed site has not been reported as possibly malicious, the SmartScreen Filter will not detect it as a site to avoid. Commonly spoofed websites are those where you perform financial transactions, such as online banking or shopping sites. They often use phony web addresses to mislead you into thinking you are visiting a legitimate site. When you visit a site that requests personal or financial information, look in the Address bar for the web address. Microsoft Edge displays the true domain you are visiting. For example, you might do your online banking at an Accounts webpage with the address www.bank.com/accounts. If you visit the Accounts webpage but notice that the Address bar displays the address www.phony.com/accounts, you are visiting a spoofed site and should close the webpage, and then report it as a possible phishing site. The Microsoft support team will investigate the site and add it to the list of known phishing sites as appropriate.

INSIGHT

Protecting Yourself from Phishing Attempts

In addition to using the SmartScreen Filter, use the following guidelines to protect yourself from online phishing:

- Never provide personal information in an email, an instant message, or a pop-up window.
- Do not click links in email and instant messages from senders you do not know or trust. Even messages that seem to be from friends and family can be faked. Therefore, check with the sender to make sure he or she actually sent the message (especially if the message contains only a link to a website).
- Only use websites that provide privacy statements or indicate how they use your personal information.

The SmartScreen Filter is turned on by default so that it checks websites and files automatically as you browse. You'll show Lamar how to make sure the SmartScreen Filter is protecting his computer when it is connected to the Internet.

To turn on the SmartScreen Filter in Microsoft Edge:

▶ **1.** Click the **Microsoft Edge** button 🅔 on the taskbar to start the browser.

▶ **2.** Click the **More** button ⋯ in the navigation bar, and then click **Settings** to display the Settings pane.

▶ **3.** Scroll the Settings pane and then click the **View advanced settings** button in the Advanced settings section to display the Advanced settings options.

▶ **4.** Scroll the Advanced settings options to display a section titled Help protect me from malicious sites and downloads with SmartScreen Filter. See Figure 5-14. This option is turned on by default.

TIP

You can also set SmartScreen Filter options by clicking Change Windows SmartScreen settings in the left pane of the Security and Maintenance window.

| **Figure 5-14** | **SmartScreen Filter setting in Microsoft Edge** |

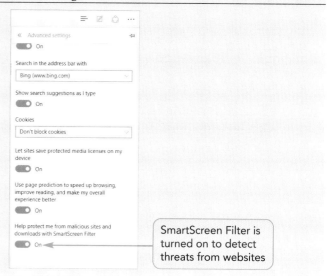

SmartScreen Filter is turned on to detect threats from websites

▶ **5.** If SmartScreen Filter is not turned on, click the **slider button** to change the setting from Off to On.

If you want to check an individual website to determine whether it has been reported as a potentially unsafe site, you must switch to Internet Explorer. You can also report websites to Microsoft using Internet Explorer. You'll show Lamar how to perform both tasks.

To check and report a website:

1. Click a blank area of the Start page (or a webpage), click in the **Address bar**, type **microsoft.com**, and then press the **Enter** key to go to the Microsoft website.

2. To switch to Internet Explorer, click the **More** button ⋯ in the navigation bar, and then click **Open with Internet Explorer**.

3. Maximize the Internet Explorer window, if necessary, click the **Tools** button ⚙ in the navigation bar, point to **Safety**, and then click **Check this website**. The SmartScreen Filter dialog box opens and explains that the site has not been reported to Microsoft for containing threats. The message tells you to check the address to make sure it is a site you trust, and if you suspect that the site it unsafe, you can report it to Microsoft.

   Trouble? If the SmartScreen Filter dialog box does not open, you or another user chose not to display the message again. Skip Step 4.

4. Click the **OK** button to close the SmartScreen Filter dialog box.

5. To see how to report a possible phishing site, click the **Tools** button ⚙ in the navigation bar, point to **Safety**, and then click **Report unsafe website**. The Microsoft Report a website webpage opens so you can report information about the website. See Figure 5-15.

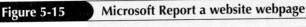

Figure 5-15   Microsoft Report a website webpage

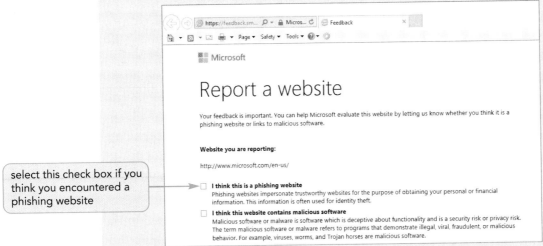

select this check box if you think you encountered a phishing website

6. Close the Microsoft Report a website webpage and Internet Explorer.

As you visit websites, Microsoft Edge checks their certificates. A **certificate** is a digital document (similar to a digital signature) that verifies the security of a website you visit. Microsoft Edge can detect certificate errors, which are signs that you are visiting a phishing site or one that uses spyware or other malware. If Microsoft Edge detects a certificate error or other security problem, it identifies the problem type in the Address bar. For example, a certificate error message might appear in the Address bar. You can click the error message to learn about the problem. See Figure 5-16.

| **Figure 5-16** | **Security message in Microsoft Edge** |

red Unsafe website message indicates a problem with this site's certificate

detailed message about the potentially unsafe website and the recommended action

close the tab to avoid security threats

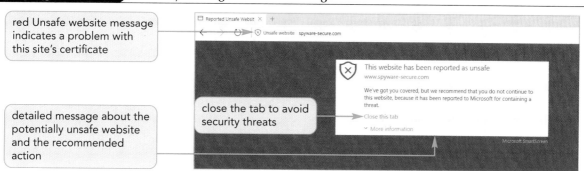

The color of the website message in the Address bar also indicates the type of error or problem. Red means the certificate is out of date, is invalid, or has an error. Yellow signals that the certificate cannot be verified, which sometimes happens with a suspected phishing site. White means the certificate is normal, and green indicates sites that have high security, such as those for financial transactions.

Downloading Files Safely

The SmartScreen Filter also works with the Microsoft Edge Downloads list to manage downloaded files. Recall that you can click the Downloads button in the Hub to list the files you download from the Internet, keep track of where they're stored on your computer, and pause, open, run, delete, or save the downloaded files. The SmartScreen Filter analyzes files you want to download similar to how it analyzes websites. When you select a file to download from a website, the SmartScreen filter refers to a list of files known to be malicious. If the file you want to download is on that list, the SmartScreen Filter blocks the download and explains the file is unsafe. If the file is not on the list of malicious files, the SmartScreen Filter refers to a list (kept by Microsoft) of programs downloaded by a significant number of other Microsoft Edge and Internet Explorer users. The SmartScreen Filter displays an Open file – Security Warning dialog box to notify you if the file is not on the list of commonly downloaded files. In that case, you should not open or install the file unless you trust its publisher and the website that provided the file. You can use the Downloads list to delete the program or run it if you know the file is safe.

If you download a file and find that it is unsafe, such as a file quarantined after a scan, you can right-click the file in the Downloads list, and then click Report that this download is unsafe on the shortcut menu to report the file to Microsoft, which adds the file to the SmartScreen Filter list of malicious files.

You'll show Lamar how to use Microsoft Edge to display a list of downloaded files. Lamar also wants to know where the Downloads list stores downloaded files on his computer. If he suspects a downloaded file contains malicious software, he can quickly find the file and delete it using File Explorer. He can also use the Downloads list to test, delete, and report suspicious files.

To display and locate downloaded files:

▶ **1.** Click the **Hub** button ≡ in the navigation bar, and then click the **Downloads** button ↓ to display the Downloads list. See Figure 5-17. The list of downloaded files on your computer will differ.

Figure 5-17	Downloads list

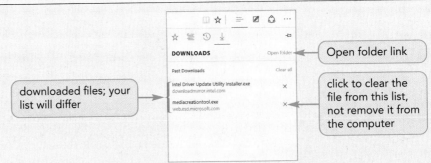

2. Click the **Open folder** link to open the folder window displaying the location of the downloaded files. By default, Windows 10 uses the Downloads folder for downloaded files.

3. Close the Downloads folder window.

If you want to remove all downloaded files in the Downloads list, you can click the Clear all link in the Downloads list. To remove a single file, click its Clear button. Removing the file from the Downloads list does not delete the file from your computer. You must navigate to the Downloads folder and then delete the file to remove it from your computer.

Blocking Malware

To install or run programs on your computer, hackers often take advantage of web programming tools, such as scripts, that are designed to enhance your online experience. A **script** is programming code that performs a series of commands and can be embedded in a webpage. For example, a website designer might use a script to verify that you've completed all the necessary fields in an online form. In contrast, hackers use scripts on a webpage to automatically download programs to your computer that can collect and transmit information about you without your knowledge or authorization.

A common way for hackers to distribute adware and spyware is to include the malware with other content or programs. If the files lack digital signatures, meaning the files are unverified, Microsoft Edge blocks them and displays a message that only secure content is shown. Recall that a digital signature is an electronic security mark that can be added to files, similar to a certificate added to websites. A digital signature identifies the publisher of a file and verifies that the file has not changed since it was signed.

INSIGHT

Digital Signatures

Microsoft Edge and other programs, including Windows 10, can detect whether a file has a digital signature. A file without a valid digital signature might not be from the stated source or might have been tampered with (possibly by a virus) since it was published. Avoid opening an unsigned file unless you know for certain who created it and whether the contents are safe to open. However, even a valid digital signature does not guarantee that the contents of the file are harmless. When you download a file, determine whether to trust its contents based on the identity of the publisher and the site providing the file.

To protect against malicious scripts and unsafe content, Microsoft Edge runs in a protected environment that makes it difficult for hackers to install malware on your computer. If a webpage tries to install any type of software or run a script, Microsoft Edge displays a dialog box warning you about the attempt. If you trust the program, you can allow it to run once or always. If you are not familiar with the program or don't want to run it, you can deny it once or always.

Next, you'll show Lamar how to use the Pop-up Blocker to limit or block most pop-up windows when he visits websites.

Blocking Pop-Up Windows

A pop-up ad is a small web browser window that appears when you visit a website and advertises a product or service. Many legitimate advertisers use pop-up ads because they effectively get your attention and provide information or services that might interest you. However, some pop-up ads are annoying because they repeatedly interrupt your online activities, are difficult to close, or display objectionable content. Other pop-up ads are dangerous because they can download spyware or **hijack** your browser—meaning they seize control of the browser, opening many more new windows each time you close one pop-up window until you have to close your browser or restart your computer.

To avoid the nuisance and danger of pop-up ads, Microsoft Edge includes the Pop-up Blocker, which warns you about or blocks pop-up ads. The Pop-up Blocker is turned on by default, meaning that Microsoft Edge blocks most pop-up windows. Not all pop-up windows are ads. If a pop-up window opens as soon as you visit a website, it probably contains an ad. However, many websites use pop-up windows to display tools such as calendars or verification notices. For example, if you visit a travel website to make flight or hotel reservations, the site might provide a calendar in a pop-up window so you can select your travel dates. If you click a link or button to open the pop-up window, Microsoft Edge does not block it by default. However, it does block pop-up windows that appear automatically if you have not clicked a link or button.

Lamar has had problems with pop-up ads before, so he wants to verify that Microsoft Edge is blocking pop-ups.

To verify the pop-up settings in Microsoft Edge:

1. In Microsoft Edge, click the **More** button ⋯ in the navigation bar, and then click **Settings** to display the Settings pane.

2. Scroll the Settings pane, and then click the **View advanced settings** button. See Figure 5-18.

Figure 5-18 ❯ **Block pop-ups setting**

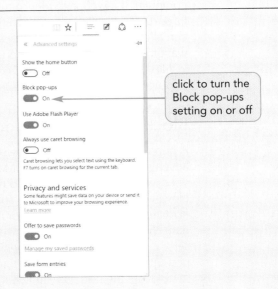

click to turn the Block pop-ups setting on or off

Trouble? If the Block pop-ups setting is turned off, then click the slider button to change the setting from Off to On.

❯ **3.** Leave the Settings pane open for the next set of steps.

Now that you have explored the security settings in Microsoft Edge, you can turn your attention to its privacy settings.

Selecting Microsoft Edge Privacy Settings

In addition to security protection, Microsoft Edge includes the following tools and features to protect your privacy:

- Privacy settings and alerts—These settings specify how to handle identifying information when you're online and alert you when a website you're visiting doesn't meet your criteria.
- InPrivate Browsing—This feature helps prevent Microsoft Edge from storing data about your browsing session by opening a separate InPrivate Browsing Microsoft Edge window to keep your browsing actions private.
- Do Not Track requests—This feature helps prevent website content providers from collecting information about sites you visit.
- Secure connections—Microsoft Edge informs you when it is using a secure connection to communicate with websites that handle sensitive personal information.

REFERENCE

Selecting Privacy Settings

- In Microsoft Edge, click the More button.
- Click Settings.
- Click the View advanced settings button.
- Scroll to the Privacy and services section, and then change the settings using the slider buttons.

One privacy concern is cookies, which many websites store on your computer when you visit them. A cookie is a small file that records information about you, such as the type of browser you are using, your email address, and your preferences for using a website. Like other web tools, cookies can enhance your online experience by helping trusted websites customize their service to you. However, they can also pose a security risk—hackers can retrieve cookies to search for private information such as passwords, or use cookies to track the websites you visit. In Microsoft Edge, you can specify privacy settings to either allow websites to save cookies on your computer or prevent them from doing so.

One way to protect your privacy with Microsoft Edge is to block cookies on some or all of the websites you visit. You should be selective about which websites you allow to store cookies on your computer. Blocking all cookies keeps your website visits private but might also limit your experience or prove annoying. Allowing all cookies might compromise your privacy. Some users find that the Block only third party cookies setting provides a good balance because it allows most **first-party cookies**, which are generated from the websites you visit and contain information the website reuses when you return. For example, to keep track of products you add to an electronic shopping cart or wish list, a website saves a first-party cookie on your computer. In contrast, this setting blocks most **third-party cookies**, which are generated from website advertisers, who might use them to track your web use for marketing purposes.

Lamar often visits his business clients' websites for research as he prepares to develop automation systems for them. He wants to protect the privacy of Snap Home Automation and his clients by blocking third-party cookies.

As you perform the following steps, note your original settings so you can restore them later.

To change privacy settings for saving cookies:

▶ **1.** Scroll the list of Advanced settings, and then click the box in the Cookies section to display options for blocking and allowing cookies. See Figure 5-19.

Figure 5-19   **Blocking or allowing cookies**

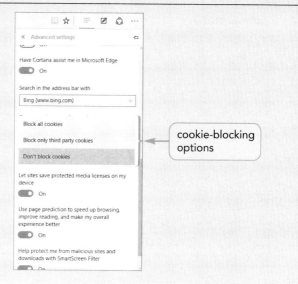

Trouble? If you are working in a computer lab, you might not have permission to change the Privacy and services settings. In that case, read but do not perform Step 2.

▶ **2.** Click **Block only third party cookies**. When you select this setting, Microsoft Edge blocks cookies except for some first-party cookies and those created by websites you identify.

▶ **3.** Click a blank area of the webpage to close the Settings pane.

Microsoft Edge will block most cookies except for first-party cookies on Lamar's computer from now on. However, if websites stored cookies on his computer before you changed the privacy setting, they will remain there until you delete them. You can delete cookies by clearing your browsing history. In addition to cookies, Microsoft Edge stores cached data and files, form data, a history of the websites you've visited, information you've entered in the Address bar, and web passwords you've saved. **Cached data and files** are copies of webpages, images, and other media that Microsoft Edge stores on your computer so it can download content faster the next time you visit a website. Microsoft Edge also stores media licenses, pop-up exceptions, and permissions you've granted to websites. Usually, maintaining this history information improves your web browsing because it can fill in information that you would otherwise have to retype. If you have particular privacy concerns, however, such as when you are using a public computer, you can clear some or all of your browsing history to delete this information.

Lamar wants to delete all of the cookies and the list of websites he has visited.

To clear cookies and your browsing history:

▶ **1.** Click the **Hub** button ▤ in the navigation bar, and then click the **History** button ⟲, if necessary, to display the History list.

▶ **2.** Click the **Clear all history** link to display a list of browsing information you can clear.

▶ **3.** Click the **Show more** button, if necessary, to display the complete list. See Figure 5-20. Your settings might differ.

Figure 5-20   **Clearing browsing data**

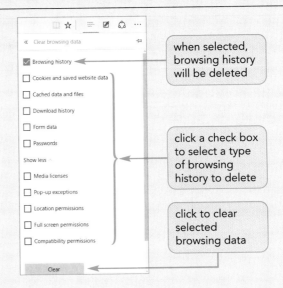

Trouble? If you are working in a computer lab, you might not have permission to clear your browsing history. In that case, read but do not perform Steps 4–6.

▶ **4.** If necessary, click the **Browsing history** check box to insert a check mark and indicate you want to delete the list of websites you have visited.

▶ **5.** If necessary, click the **Cookies and saved website data** check box to insert a checkmark and indicate you want to delete all of the cookies stored on your computer.

▶ **6.** Click the **Clear** button to delete cookies and your browsing history. It takes a few moments for Microsoft Edge to clear the browsing history and cookies.

▶ **7.** When Microsoft Edge is finished, click a blank area of the webpage to close the Hub.

Another privacy feature of Microsoft Edge is InPrivate Browsing, which you'll explore next.

Protecting Your Privacy with InPrivate Browsing

If you want to keep information about your web browsing private, you can use InPrivate Browsing. This feature prevents Microsoft Edge from storing data about your browsing session. If you are searching online for a gift, for example, or want to prevent another user from retracing your steps to a website containing your financial information, use InPrivate Browsing to hide the history of the webpages you visited. When you do, Microsoft Edge opens a new window and displays InPrivate on the title bar. As you work in the InPrivate window, Microsoft Edge protects your privacy. To end your InPrivate Browsing session, close the browser window.

Keep in mind that InPrivate Browsing does not make you anonymous on the Internet. Websites might still be able to identify you through your web address. They can still record and save any forms you complete and selections you make. You will show Lamar how an InPrivate Browsing session works.

To turn on InPrivate Browsing:

▶ **1.** Click the **More** button ⋯ in the navigation bar, and then click **New InPrivate window** to start an InPrivate Browsing session. Maximize the window, if necessary. See Figure 5-21.

Figure 5-21 | **InPrivate window**

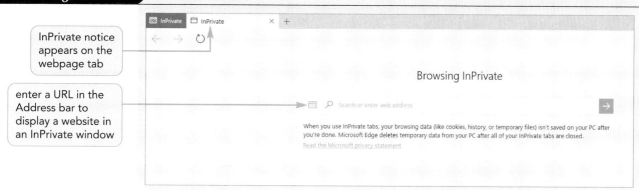

InPrivate notice appears on the webpage tab

enter a URL in the Address bar to display a website in an InPrivate window

Browsing InPrivate

When you use InPrivate tabs, your browsing data (like cookies, history, or temporary files) isn't saved on your PC after you're done. Microsoft Edge deletes temporary data from your PC after all of your InPrivate tabs are closed.
Read the Microsoft privacy statement

▶ **2.** Click in the **Address bar**, type **www.whitehouse.gov**, and then press the **Enter** key. The home page for the White House website appears in the InPrivate browser window.

▶ **3.** Point to the **Briefing Room** link near the top of the page, and then click the **Your Weekly Address** link in the From the Press Office section.

Trouble? If the Your Weekly Address link does not appear on the webpage you are viewing, click any other link.

▶ **4.** Click the **Hub** button ☰ in the navigation bar, and then click the **History** button 🕔, if necessary, to display the History list. Note that the White House webpages you visited during your InPrivate Browsing session are not included in the History list. When you close the InPrivate window, the list of recent webpages in the regular Microsoft Edge window will not include any of the White House pages either.

▶ **5.** Close the InPrivate window.

▶ **6.** Click the **Hub** button ☰ in the navigation bar, and then click the **History** button 🕔, if necessary, to display the History list. Expand the list to show the webpages you visited in the last hour or today, which includes pages you visited recently except for those you visited during your InPrivate Browsing session.

▶ **7.** Click a blank area of the webpage to close the Hub.

Microsoft Edge includes another privacy feature—Do Not Track requests—which you'll learn about next.

Requesting Tracking Protection

Many webpages use content such as ads, maps, or web analysis tools that count the number of visitors to the website. This content is typically supplied by other websites called content providers or third-party websites. When you visit a website with third-party content, information that identifies your computer is sent to the content provider. For example, the content provider can learn your browser type, operating system, web address, and screen resolution. If you visit many websites that the same content provider uses, the content provider can create a profile of your browsing preferences. The profile can be used to target ads that are likely to appeal to you, for example.

Web tracking tools, such as visitor counters, sometimes appear as visible content, but not always. For example, **web beacons** are transparent images that invisibly track website usage. Web analysis tools often contain scripts that can track information such as the pages you visit and the selections you make. To control the information sent to content providers, you can have Microsoft Edge send Do Not Track requests to the websites.

By blocking content, the Do Not Track requests can protect your privacy on the web. However, content providers often pay for website content that you can view or use for free. Refusing to be monitored can make webpages load slowly and prevent websites you like from earning income they need. However, if you notice that you consistently have trouble displaying webpages when a content provider's address appears in the status bar, that content provider is probably tracking your browsing actions, and you can turn on the Do Not Track option in Microsoft Edge. This option is turned off by default.

Lamar notices that when webpages are slow to open, the ads.doubleclick.net web address appears in the status bar. You suggest he set Microsoft Edge to send Do Not Track requests to see if that improves his browsing experience.

To send Do Not Track requests:

▶ **1.** Click the **More** button ⋯ in the navigation bar, and then click **Settings** to display the Settings pane.

▶ **2.** Scroll the Settings pane and then click the **View advanced settings** button in the Advanced settings section to display the Advanced settings options.

▶ **3.** Scroll the list of Advanced settings, if necessary, and then click the **slider button** for the Send Do Not Track requests setting from Off to On.

▶ **4.** Click a blank area of the webpage to close the Advanced settings.

▶ **5.** Close Microsoft Edge.

Besides using the security tools provided in Microsoft Edge, use common sense when visiting websites, especially when sharing private information.

PROSKILLS

Decision Making: Deciding Whether to Trust a Website

Your decision about whether to trust a website should be based on who publishes the website, what information the publisher wants from you, and what you want from the site. To make your web browsing more efficient and productive, consider the following guidelines when deciding whether to trust a website with confidential information:

- Ensure you have a secure connection to the website. Look in the Address bar for a website address that begins with "https" rather than "http." Also, look for a security icon such as a padlock in the Address bar or status bar, which indicates that the website is secure.
- Confirm that you are familiar with the organization that sponsors the website. If you are a satisfied customer of a business that provides products in a physical location, you can probably trust its website. Read the website's privacy or terms of use statement to make sure you are comfortable with the terms. Avoid websites that require you to accept email offers or advertising from the website.
- Check to see if the website is certified by an Internet trust organization. An Internet trust organization verifies that a website has a privacy statement and gives you a choice about how it uses your information. Approved websites display one or more privacy certification seals, usually on their home page or order forms. However, unscrupulous websites sometimes fraudulently display these trust logos. You can contact the trust organization to see if the website is registered with it. Reputable trust organizations include TRUSTe (www.truste.com), the Better Business Bureau or BBBOnLine (www.bbb.org/online), and webTrust (www.webtrust.org). On the website of each trust organization, you can display a list of certified websites.
- Stay away from sites that unnecessarily request confidential personal information. Provide personal or confidential information such as credit card numbers only when necessary and only on a secure form. Make sure you are using a secure connection when completing the form. Also, look for a message explaining that your information will be encrypted for security.
- Avoid sites that use untrustworthy ways to contact you. Untrustworthy websites are often referred to you through an email message from someone you don't know. Stay away from websites making offers that seem too good to be true.

Now that you have thoroughly explored the privacy and security settings in Microsoft Edge, you can show Lamar another way to protect his company's computers—by using user accounts.

Setting Up User Accounts

In Windows, a **user account** is a collection of information that indicates the files and folders you can access, the types of changes you can make to the computer, and your preferred appearance settings (such as your desktop background or color scheme). If you have a user account on a computer that you share with other people, you can maintain your own files and settings separate from the other users.

REFERENCE

Setting Up a User Account

- Click the Start button and then click Settings.
- Click Accounts.
- In the left pane, click Family & other users.
- In the right pane, click the Add someone else to this PC button.
- Click the I don't have this person's sign-in information link.
- Click the Add a user without a Microsoft account link.
- Enter a user name, password, and password hint, and then click the Next button.

You can create two types of accounts in Windows 10:

- **Microsoft account**—This type of account provides access to Microsoft cloud computing services, such as Outlook.com for email, OneDrive for file storage, and Xbox for games. With this type of user account, you can use Windows 10 and some Windows apps to access files and other data stored in your online Microsoft account. For example, if you keep albums of photos on your OneDrive, you can use the Photos app to display those photos on your PC. If you run Windows 10 on more than one PC, you can also **synchronize**, or **sync**, (that is, to make sure data on the two devices match) your settings, preferences, and some apps so that all your PCs are set up the same way. The advantage of a Microsoft account is that you provide one user name and one password to connect to the cloud and to sync settings. Most likely, you created a Microsoft account when you set up Windows 10.
- **Local-only user account**—This type of account accesses only resources on your computer. If you want to allow family members or other people to use your computer occasionally, you can set up a local-only user account for those users.

In addition, a Microsoft account or a local-only user account is a Standard account or an Administrator account, which determines how much control the user has over the computer:

- **Standard account**—A Standard account is designed for everyday computing and can protect your computer and data by preventing users from changing settings that affect all users. To make changes such as installing software or changing security settings, Windows requests permission or a password for an Administrator account. Microsoft recommends that every regular user on a computer have a Standard account.
- **Administrator account**—An Administrator account is created when Windows 10 is installed and provides full access to the computer. The administrator can access the files of any user, install software, and change any settings. The intention is that when you install Windows 10, you first sign in to the computer as the administrator, and then create a Standard user account for yourself and for each person who will use the computer.

When you install Windows 10, the setup program guides you through the steps of creating an Administrator account. During that process, you choose whether you want to use your Microsoft account or a local-only user account as the Administrator account. If you don't have a Microsoft account, you can create one as you install Windows.

After completing the installation, you can set up Standard accounts using the Settings app. Any accounts you create after the initial Administrator account are Standard accounts by default. Standard accounts can be Microsoft or local-only user accounts.

Selecting a User Name and Password

When you create an Administrator account or a Standard account, Windows asks for your user credentials, which are a user name and a password. If you have a Microsoft account, you can provide the user name and password you use for that account. If you don't have a Microsoft account, you can create one as you set up a new Administrator or Standard account. To use a Microsoft account, you provide your email address and a password as your user credentials.

INSIGHT

Synchronizing Accounts

If you use your Microsoft account credentials for your user account on a Windows 10 laptop, for example, you can synchronize settings, preferences, and some apps that you use on other computers, such as a Windows 10 tablet. No matter which computer you use, the desktop will look the same and you'll have access to the same apps.

Before you can synchronize accounts, you need to trust each computer you use. (**Trusting** a computer means you verify that you have an account on that computer.) To trust a computer, open the Settings app and then select Accounts. With Your account selected in the left pane, click the Verify link in the right pane. (If the Verify link does not appear, the PC is already a trusted device in your Microsoft account.) Enter the password to your Microsoft account, and then click the OK button. Choose how you want to receive a security code for verification, such as a text or email message, and then click the Next button. Wait to receive the security code, enter it, and then click the Submit button. The PC is now a trusted device and will sync settings and data automatically.

If you set up a new Administrator or Standard account as a local-only user account, you must provide a user name, but the password is optional. However, Microsoft strongly recommends that you use a password for all accounts, which is one of the most effective ways you can keep your computer secure. When your computer is protected with a password, only someone who knows the password can sign in to Windows.

A **text password** is a series of letters, numbers, spaces, and symbols that you provide to access your files, applications, and other resources on the computer. Windows passwords are case sensitive, so LaJffson18 is different from lajffson18. Passwords strengthen computer security because they help to make sure that no one can access the computer unless he or she is authorized to do so. Therefore, you should not give your passwords to others or write them in a place where others can see them.

When creating a text password, make sure you devise a strong password—one that is difficult to guess but easy for you to remember. Strong text passwords have the following characteristics:

- Contain at least eight characters
- Do not include your user name, real name, or company name
- Are not words you can find in the dictionary
- Are significantly different from your previous passwords
- Contain characters from each of the following categories: uppercase letters, lowercase letters, numbers, and symbols (not including spaces)

For any account that has a text password, you can also set up a four-digit **personal information number (PIN)**, a picture password, or Windows Hello to protect the account. Similar to a PIN you use for banking transactions, you can use a PIN for a

Windows account as a fast way to sign in. (Keep in mind, however, that a PIN does not meet the requirements for a strong password.)

A **picture password** involves an image and gestures, and is easiest to provide on a touchscreen device. You select a photo or another graphic stored in a location your computer can access, and then draw three gestures (that is, circles, lines, and taps or clicks) on the picture to create a password. You must remember the size, position, and direction of the gestures and the order you make them so you can repeat the gestures to gain access to your account.

If your device has a fingerprint reader or a high-quality camera, you can sign in using **Windows Hello**, a feature that accepts a fingerprint or facial scan instead of a password. When you set up Windows Hello, you might be asked to enter a PIN to associate with your fingerprint or facial scan. Windows Hello is a form of **biometric security**, a way to verify your identity based on physical characteristics. Microsoft considers Windows Hello the most secure way to sign in to Windows.

At times, Windows requests your text password or fingerprint or facial scan, such as when you want to change system settings. At other times, you can use a PIN or picture password, such as to sign in to your account.

Creating a Local-Only User Account

Lamar has a Microsoft Administrator account on his PC, but wants to set up a separate Standard account on the same computer to prevent anyone from using it to change system settings or install unauthorized software. He can then let his assistants use his PC by signing in to the Standard account when they are working at a client site. Because he also wants to prevent his assistants from downloading and installing apps from the Windows Store, he wants the Standard account to be a local-only user account, which means it is restricted to his PC only.

To create a Standard local-only user account on Lamar's computer, you provide a user name and password. You can also set up a PIN so he can sign in quickly and create a picture password as an alternate method for signing in to Windows. He also wants to investigate Windows Hello to determine whether the camera on his PC is compatible with this feature.

You must be signed in using an Administrator account to perform the following steps. If you do not have access to an Administrator account, read but do not perform the following steps.

To create a Standard local-only user account:

▶ **1.** Click the **Start** button ⊞ to display the Start menu, and then click **Settings** to start the Settings app.

▶ **2.** Click **Accounts** in the Settings home page to display the Accounts window, which includes your account information.

Trouble? If a message appears on your account screen about trusting the PC, disregard the message. You don't need to sync settings now.

▶ **3.** In the left pane, click **Family & other users** to display options for setting up accounts for your family or other people. See Figure 5-22.

Figure 5-22   Family and other users settings

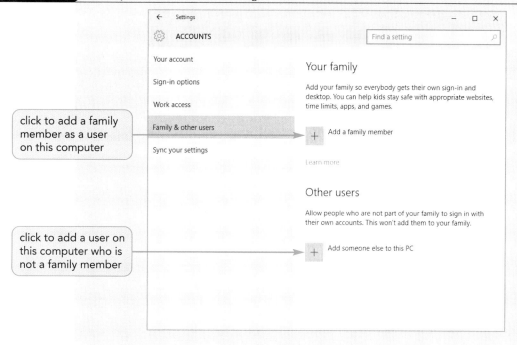

click to add a family member as a user on this computer

click to add a user on this computer who is not a family member

4. Click the **Add someone else to this PC** button to display a window asking how this person will sign in. See Figure 5-23.

Figure 5-23   Choosing how the new user will sign in

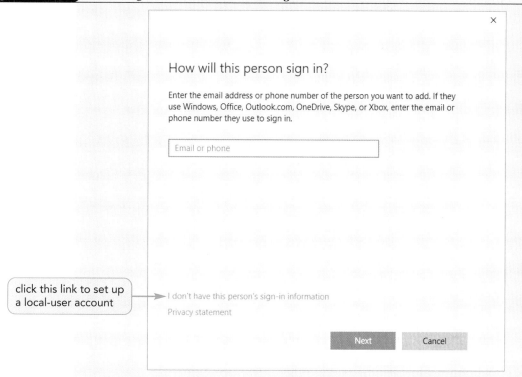

click this link to set up a local-user account

5. Click the **I don't have this person's sign-in information** link to continue creating a local-only user account.

▶ **6.** Near the bottom of the Let's create your account window, click the **Add a user without a Microsoft account** link to display the Create an account for this PC window. See Figure 5-24.

Figure 5-24 Create an account for this PC window

Create an account for this PC

If you want to use a password, choose something that will be easy for you to remember but hard for others to guess.

Who's going to use this PC?

enter a user name, such as a first and last name → | User name |

Make it secure.

enter a password and a password hint → | Enter password |
| Re-enter password |
| Password hint |

Back   Next

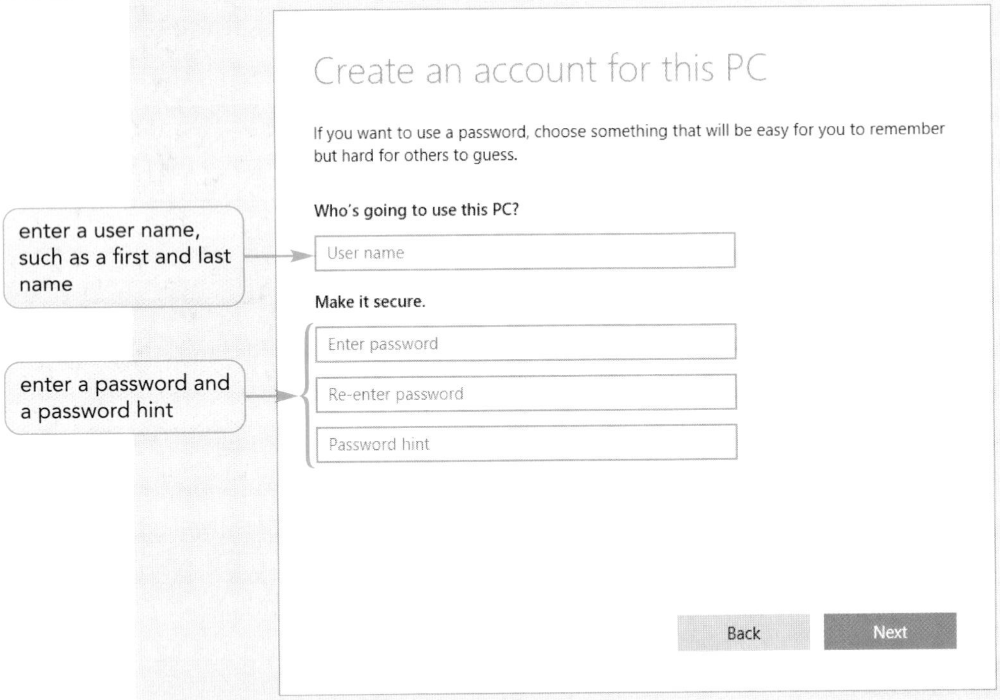

▶ **7.** Click in the **User name** box, enter **Lamar**, press the **Tab** key, and then enter **SHA_jeff01** as the password.

▶ **8.** Click in the **Re-enter password** box, and then enter **SHA_jeff01** again.

▶ **9.** Click in the **Password hint** box, enter **Mother's first name** as the password hint, and then click the **Next** button to finish creating the account.

▶ **10.** Close the Accounts window.

If you forget your password and you're using a local account, use your password hint as a reminder. You can also ask someone with an Administrator account on your computer to change the password for you.

Changing Sign-in Options

After you create an account, you can switch to the account and then change the sign-in options to change your text password, if necessary, create a PIN and a picture password, and set up Windows Hello if your computer has a fingerprint reader or camera that supports Windows Hello. You'll use the sign-in options in the Accounts window to set up a PIN, picture password, and Windows Hello, if possible, for Lamar. Before setting up Windows Hello, you must create a PIN for the account and compatible hardware must be installed on the computer.

To switch accounts:

▶ **1.** Click the **Start** button ⊞ to display the Start menu.

▶ **2.** Click the **user icon** at the top of the Start menu, and then click **Lamar** to switch to the new account. Windows signs out of your account and displays the sign-in screen.

▶ **3.** Type **SHA_jeff01** in the Password box, and then press the **Enter** key to sign in. Windows takes a few minutes to set up the new account.

Next, you can create a PIN. Lamar wants to use 5412 as the PIN, the date he founded the company.

To create a PIN:

▶ **1.** On the desktop for the new account, click the **Start** button ⊞ to display the Start menu, click **Settings** to start the Settings app, and then click **Accounts** to display the Accounts window for the Lamar account.

▶ **2.** In the left pane, click **Sign-in options** to display the sign-in options in the right pane.

▶ **3.** In the PIN section, click the **Add** button to display a window where you verify your account password.

▶ **4.** Type **SHA_jeff01** in the Password box, and then click the **OK** button to verify the password. The Set up a PIN window opens. See Figure 5-25.

| Figure 5-25 | Create a PIN |

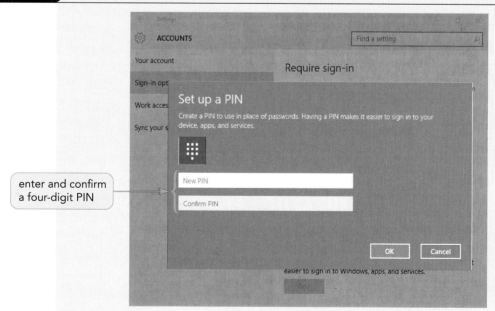

enter and confirm a four-digit PIN

▶ **5.** Enter **5412** in the New PIN box.

6. Click in the **Confirm PIN** box, type **5412**, and then click the **OK** button to create the PIN.

If your computer is equipped with the hardware required for Windows Hello, the Windows Hello options are now available in the Accounts window. Scroll to display the Windows Hello option. See Figure 5-26. The computer in this figure has a fingerprint reader. If your computer has a camera compatible with Windows Hello, the Windows Hello option is different.

Trouble? If the Windows Hello option does not appear in the Accounts window, your computer does not have the hardware required to use Windows Hello.

| **Figure 5-26** | **Windows Hello option for fingerprint verification** |

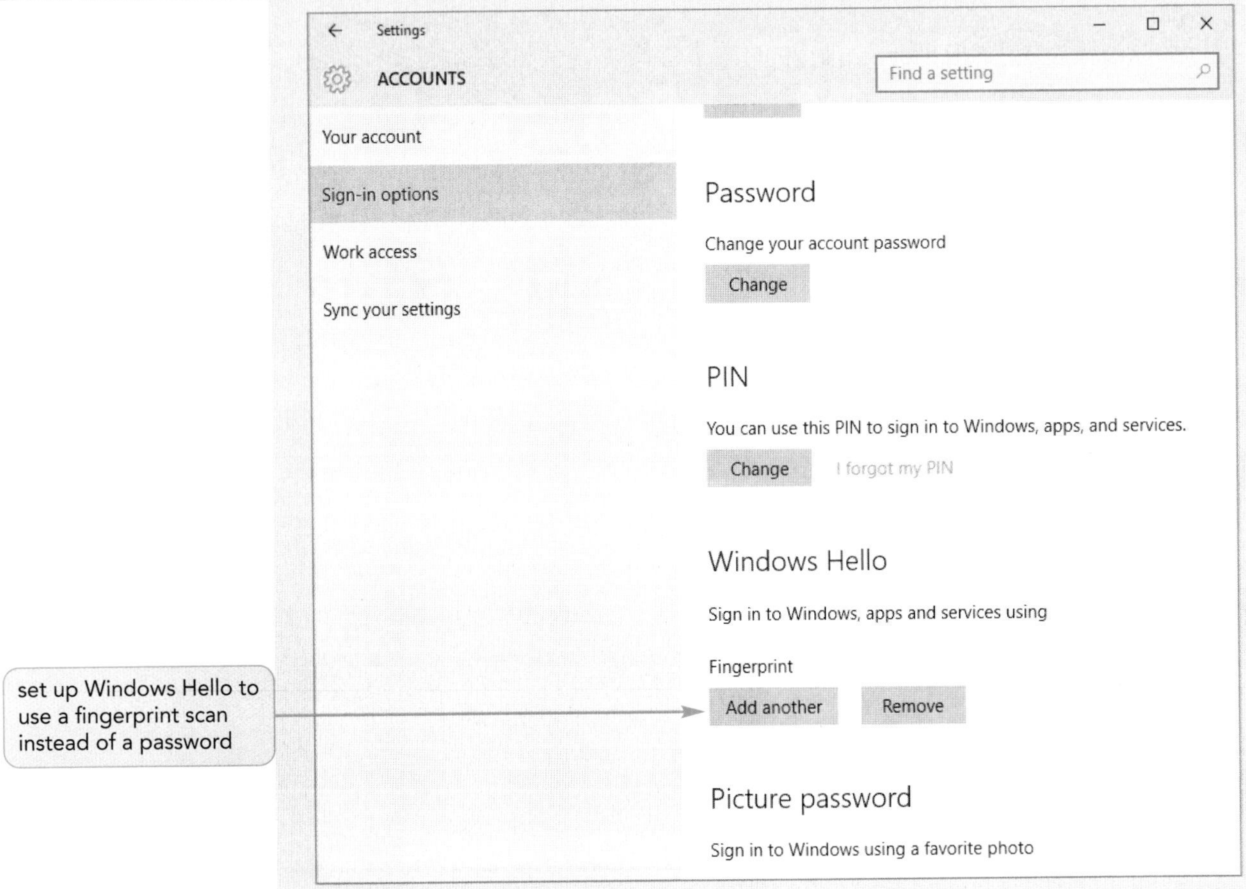

set up Windows Hello to use a fingerprint scan instead of a password

Next, you can set up Windows Hello to sign in to Windows with a fingerprint scan. If your computer has a camera compatible with Windows Hello or does not have hardware that works with Windows Hello, read but do not perform the following steps.

To set up Windows Hello:

1. In the Windows Hello section of the Accounts window, click the **Add another** button below the Fingerprint text to display the Windows Hello setup window, which introduces Windows Hello.

2. Click the **Get started** button to display a window requesting your PIN to verify your identity.

3. In the PIN box, type **5412** to display a window showing how to scan your index finger on the fingerprint reader for your computer.

4. Follow the on-screen instructions to scan your fingerprint a few times so that Windows recognizes it. See Figure 5-27.

Figure 5-27  **Scanning your fingerprint**

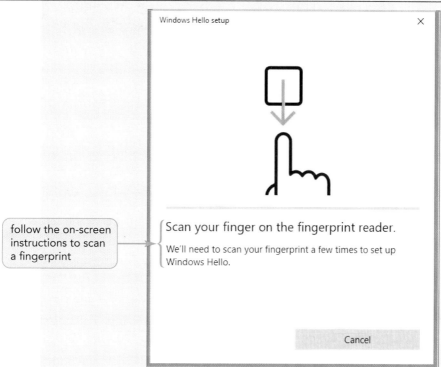

follow the on-screen instructions to scan a fingerprint

5. When the All set! window opens, click the **Close** button.

The next time you sign into the Lamar account, you can do so with a fingerprint scan. Next, you can create a picture password for Lamar's account. First, you'll take a screenshot of the Bing home page and then use that image for the picture password.

To create a picture password:

1. Start Microsoft Edge, maximize the window, and then navigate to the Bing website at **www.bing.com**.

2. When the Bing home page is displayed, press the **Print Screen** key to capture an image of the screen, and then close Microsoft Edge.

3. Start Paint.

4. Press the **Ctrl+V** keys to paste the screen image in a new Paint file.

5. Click the **Save** button 🖫 on the Quick Access Toolbar, and then save the screen image as a PNG file named **Bing** in the Pictures folder. Close Paint.

6. In the Accounts window, click the **Add** button in the Picture password section.

7. Type **SHA_jeff01** in the Password box, and then click the **OK** button to verify the password and display the Picture password window. See Figure 5-28.

Figure 5-28 Picture password window

click to select a picture

sample picture

visual hint about how to draw a circle on this screen

> **8.** Click the **Choose picture** button, and then click the screenshot you saved in the Pictures folder.

> **9.** Click the **Use this picture** button. The Set up your gestures screen appears.

> **10.** Draw three gestures on the picture as described in the left pane of the screen. Select objects on the picture and use gestures you can remember easily.

> **11.** When the Confirm your gestures screen appears, repeat the gestures in the same order you used in Step 10.

> **Trouble?** If the "Something's not right" message appears, click the Try again button and repeat Step 11, carefully redrawing the gestures you created. If you are still having trouble, click the Start over button and repeat Steps 10 and 11, but make sure you use simple gestures (for example, draw a line under a word or picture) and note their placement on the screen.

> **12.** Click the **Finish** button, and then close the Accounts window.

To perform the remaining steps in the module, you need to sign out of the Standard account and sign in with your original (that is, Administrator) account.

To switch accounts:

> **1.** Click the **Start** button ⊞ to display the Start menu, click the **Lamar** user icon, and then click your user name. Windows signs out of your account and displays the sign-in screen.

> **2.** Enter your password and then press the **Enter** key.

Now you and Lamar can show all of the Snap Home Automation employees how to create accounts and passwords on their computers.

Controlling Access to Your Computer

One way to manage access to your computer is to take advantage of **User Account Control (UAC)**, a feature that is turned on by default and can help prevent unauthorized changes to your computer. As you performed previous steps in this module, you might have seen UAC at work, asking for permission by providing an administrator password before performing actions that could affect your computer's settings. A User Account Control dialog box usually opens when a program or an action is about to start. The dialog box requests an administrator password as permission to start the program. By notifying you, UAC can help prevent malware from installing itself on or changing your computer without permission. Make sure the name of the action or program in the User Account Control dialog box is one that you intended to start. The dialog box indicates whether the program or action is part of Windows, is not part of Windows, is unidentified, or is blocked by the administrator. The dialog box also indicates whether the program has a digital certificate. If you are working on a computer on which you've set up an Administrator account and one or more Standard accounts, the User Account Control dialog box asks for an administrator password so that software can be installed only with the administrator's knowledge or permission.

The UAC feature is turned on by default and should not be turned off. You'll show Lamar how to make sure UAC is turned on for all of the Snap computers.

> **To verify that User Account Control is turned on:**
>
> ▶ **1.** Click in the **Ask me anything** box on the taskbar, type **Security and Maintenance**, and then click **Security and Maintenance** in the search results to open the Security and Maintenance window in the Control Panel.
>
> ▶ **2.** Click the **Change User Account Control settings** link. The User Account Control Settings window opens. See Figure 5-29.

Figure 5-29	User Account Control Settings window

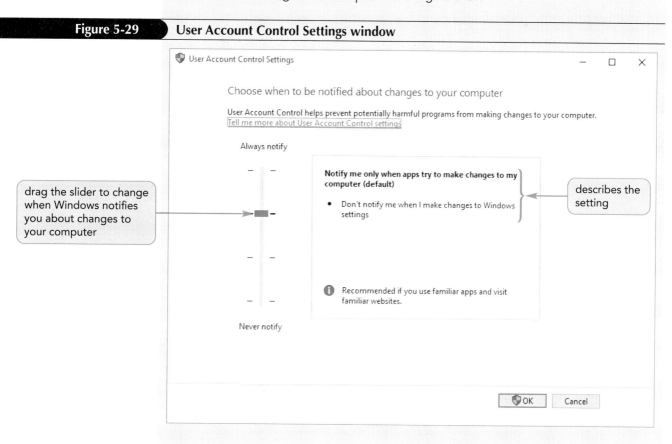

drag the slider to change when Windows notifies you about changes to your computer

describes the setting

▶ **3.** Drag the slider up and down to examine each setting, drag the slider to the **Notify me only when apps try to make changes to my computer (default)** setting, and then click the **OK** button.

Trouble? If a User Account Control dialog box opens asking if you want to allow the program to make changes to this computer, click the Yes button.

Besides controlling access to your computer with passwords and UAC, you should be aware of security features that Windows provides at startup when installing apps.

Startup and App Security Features

Besides the tools and features covered so far in this module, Windows provides behind-the-scenes security protections that don't require your intervention. One of these is a boot method called **Unified Extensible Firmware Interface (UEFI)**.

When you turn on the power to a computer, it performs a series of steps and checks as it loads the operating system and prepares for you to use it. This startup process is called **booting** the computer. A computer with UEFI boots faster and in a more secure way than previous methods. Some malware is designed to start as the operating system loads. The computer is vulnerable at this point because antivirus software hasn't started yet. Rootkits in particular can interfere with operating system files and start before antivirus software can detect them. The Secure Boot feature in UEFI makes Windows 10 resistant to this type of malware. **Secure Boot** can detect when a file has interfered with the operating system and prevent that file from loading so it doesn't interfere with the operating system again.

After the operating system loads, the next application that starts is antivirus software. Malware sometimes tampers with antivirus software as it loads so it appears to be running but is in fact disabled. Windows 10 detects any tampering with the antivirus software and restores the unmodified version so it protects against malware.

Computers are also vulnerable to attack when you install new software. Malware can attach itself to legitimate files posted for download on websites, for example. When you download a new app, you might also be downloading a virus or worm. This scenario is very unlikely with apps you download from the Windows Store. Microsoft rigorously screens apps posted for download on the Windows Store to make sure they are free from malware. Microsoft provides a digital signature to verify the app is safe, and Windows tools such as the SmartScreen Filter and Windows Defender read the digital signature to make sure the file was not intercepted and changed during the download. Windows 10 also runs apps so they have only limited access to other resources on your computer, which minimizes the damage any malware could cause.

Restoring Your Settings

If you are working in a computer lab or on a computer other than your own, complete the steps in this section to restore the original settings on the computer. If a User Account Control dialog box opens requesting an Administrator password or confirmation after you perform any of the following steps, enter the password or click the Yes button.

To restore your settings:

▶ **1.** Display the Control Panel home page in Category view, click **System and Security**, and then click **Windows Firewall**.

2. In the left pane of the Windows Firewall window, click the **Allow an app or feature through Windows Firewall** link, and then click the **Change settings** button.

3. Click the **Windows Media Player** check box to remove the check mark, and then click the **OK** button.

4. Start the Settings app, click **Update & security**, and then click the **Advanced options** link. Click the **Notify to schedule restart** button, and then click **Automatic (recommended)**. Close the Advanced Options window.

5. Start Microsoft Edge, click the **More** button [···] in the navigation bar, and then click **Settings** to display the Settings pane. Click the **View advanced settings** button and then click the **slider button** to turn the Send Do Not Track requests setting from On to Off.

6. In the Cookies section, click the **Block only third party cookies** box, and then click your original setting.

7. Click the **chevron** button [≪] at the top of the Advanced settings pane to display the Settings pane, and then click the **Choose what to clear** button to display the list of browsing data you can clear. Click the check boxes as necessary to restore the original settings. Close Microsoft Edge.

8. In the Windows Firewall window, return to the Control Panel home page, click **User Accounts**, and then click **Remove user accounts**. Click the **Lamar** icon for the local user account you created, click **Delete the account**, click the **Delete Files** button, and then click the **Delete Account** button. Click the **Yes** button to confirm you want to remove the account. Close the Control Panel window.

9. Close all open windows.

REVIEW

Session 5.2 Quick Check

1. A(n) _____ is an electronic security mark added to a file to verify its authenticity.

2. Explain how the SmartScreen Filter uses reputation checking to find potentially harmful websites.

3. How can you check an individual website to determine whether it has been reported as a potentially unsafe site?

4. What happens when you remove a file from the Downloads list in Microsoft Edge?

5. What threats do some pop-up ads pose?

6. A(n) _____ is a collection of information that indicates the files and folders you can access, the types of changes you can make to the computer, and your preferred appearance settings.

7. In Microsoft Edge, you can use _____ to hide the history of the webpages you visited.

8. What is Windows Hello?

PRACTICE

Review Assignments

There are no Data Files needed for the Review Assignments.

Lamar recently bought a new Windows 10 computer for you to share with Christie Chen, one of his project managers. Christie often transfers photos of client homes and businesses to her computer using a wireless camera. She is also preparing to visit a client in Oakland, California, and is concerned about the security of her computer during the visit. You'll show Christie how to keep the new computer secure. Complete the following steps, noting your original settings so you can restore them later:

1. Open the Windows Firewall window, and then perform the following tasks:
   a. Choose to allow an app through Windows Firewall.
   b. Change the settings to add Wireless Portable Devices to the allowed apps list on private networks.
   c. If the Allowed apps window is maximized, click the Restore Down button to resize it.

2. Start the Settings app, and then display the Advanced Options window for Windows Update. Display your update history.

3. Arrange the Allowed apps window and the View Your Update History window to display the setting you changed for Windows Firewall. Press the Print Screen key to capture an image of the screen. Open Paint or WordPad, and then press the Ctrl+V keys to paste the image in a new file. Save the file as **Review Settings** in the Module5 > Review folder provided with your Data Files.

4. Close all open windows. Start Windows Defender and then use it to perform a quick scan on your computer.

5. With the Windows Defender window open on your desktop and displaying the scan results, press the Print Screen key to capture an image of the window. Open Paint or WordPad, and then press the Ctrl+V keys to paste the image in a new file. Save the file as **Defender** in the Module5 > Review folder provided with your Data Files. Close all open windows.

6. In Microsoft Edge, open a webpage in your Favorites list or go to the home page of a popular search engine, such as Google (www.google.com) or Bing (www.bing.com). Open the webpage with Internet Explorer, and then arrange the Internet Explorer and Microsoft Edge windows side by side. In Internet Explorer, use the SmartScreen Filter to verify this website is not a phishing website.

7. Make sure the Pop-up Blocker in Microsoft Edge is turned on, and then visit a website that uses pop-up windows such as www.movies.com. Enter a search term (for example, spider man) to display a Notification bar explaining that only secure content is displayed. Press the Print Screen key to capture an image of the desktop. Open Paint or WordPad, and then press the Ctrl+V keys to paste the image in a new file. Save the file as **Blocked** in the Module5 > Review folder provided with your Data Files.

8. Close the Notification bar in Microsoft Edge, close the SmartScreen Filter dialog box in Internet Explorer, and then close Internet Explorer.

9. In Microsoft Edge, turn on InPrivate Browsing and then perform the following tasks:
   a. Visit the California state website at www.ca.gov.
   b. Click the Visit & Play tab.
   c. Click the Activities & Events link.

10. In the original Microsoft Edge window you used in Step 7 (that is, the movie website), pin the Hub to the window, display the History list, and then click the Last hour or the Today link, if necessary, to display websites you visited today except for those visited during your InPrivate Browsing session.

11. Perform the following tasks to capture an image of the windows:

    a. Resize the InPrivate Browsing window so it appears next to the window displaying the History list.

    b. Press the Print Screen key to capture an image of the desktop.

    c. Open Paint or WordPad, and then press the Ctrl+V keys to paste the image in a new file.

    d. Save the file as **InPrivate** in the Module5 > Review folder provided with your Data Files.

    e. Close all open windows.

12. Create a PIN for your user account using **6695** as the number.

13. With the Set up a PIN window open, press the Print Screen key to capture an image of the screen. Open Paint or WordPad, and then press the Ctrl+V keys to paste the image in a new file. Save the file as **Pin** in the Module5 > Review folder provided with your Data Files.

14. To restore the settings on your computer, remove Wireless Portable Devices from the Windows Firewall allowed apps list.

15. Close all open windows.

Case Problem 1

There are no Data Files needed for this Case Problem.

Rockwell Accounting   Nicole Rockwell runs a small business in Windsor, Connecticut, called Rockwell Accounting, which helps small businesses manage their finances and plan for growth. Nicole uses a laptop computer running Windows 10 to create most of her business plans and other documents, which she develops while visiting clients. She is concerned about maintaining security as she researches competitors for her clients. In particular, she has experienced problems with pop-up ads and spyware and wants to know how to block pop-ups in Microsoft Edge. You'll help her use the Windows 10 security settings to protect her computer. Complete the following steps, noting your original settings so you can restore them later:

1. Open the Windows Firewall window, and then add File and Printer Sharing to the Windows Firewall allowed apps list for private and public networks. Leave the Allowed apps window open.

2. Start Windows Defender and then use it to perform a quick scan on your computer.

3. Arrange all windows to show the settings you changed, and then press the Print Screen key to capture an image of the desktop. Open Paint or WordPad, and then press the Ctrl+V keys to paste the image in a new file. Save the file as **File Security** in the Module5 > Case1 folder provided with your Data Files. Close all open windows.

4. In Microsoft Edge, display the pop-ups setting, and then set Microsoft Edge to block pop-ups, if necessary. Press the Print Screen key to capture an image of the dialog box. Open Paint or WordPad, and then press the Ctrl+V keys to paste the image in a new file. Save the file as **Popups** in the Module5 > Case1 folder provided with your Data Files.

5. Set Microsoft Edge to clear browsing data for your browsing history, cookies, and saved website data. Press the Print Screen key to capture an image of the window. Open Paint or WordPad, and then press the Ctrl+V keys to paste the image in a new file. Save the file as **Browsing** in the Module5 > Case1 folder provided with your Data Files. Close Microsoft Edge.

6. Start a Windows app and then capture the screen. Save the image as a file named **Windows App** in the Pictures folder. Close the Windows app.

7. Create a picture password for your user account using the Windows App picture. Enter the required three gestures.

8. Before you confirm the three gestures, press the Print Screen key to capture an image of the screen. Open Paint or WordPad, and then press the Ctrl+V keys to paste the image in a new file. Save the file as **PicPassword** in the Module5 > Case1 folder provided with your Data Files. Confirm the gestures and then close the Picture password window.

9. Restore the settings on your computer. Remove File and Printer Sharing from the Windows Firewall allowed apps list. Change the Pop-up Blocker setting to its default setting, if necessary. Remove the picture password from your user account, and then delete the Windows App file from the Pictures folder.

10. Close all open windows.

Case Problem 2

There are no Data Files needed for this Case Problem.

Shorewood Health Center   Kelly Robson is the director of the Shorewood Health Center, a clinic in Shorewood, Wisconsin. The Shorewood Health Center has three mobile walk-in clinics that Shorewood residents can visit to receive flu shots and vaccinations, and request other health services. Because the Health Center computers are not part of the municipal network, Kelly uses Remote Desktop to connect to other computers in the city, and regularly uses Microsoft Edge to run the organization. She has experienced problems with spyware and viruses, and wants to know when to trust websites she visits. You'll help her use the Windows 10 security settings to protect her computer. Complete the following steps, noting your original settings so you can restore them later:

1. Change the settings to add Windows Remote Management to the Windows Firewall allowed apps list for private and public networks. Capture an image of the Allowed apps window, and then save it in a Paint file named **Firewall** in the Module5 > Case2 folder provided with your Data Files.

⊕ **Explore** 2. In Windows Update, check for updates. When Windows Update finishes checking, capture an image of the Update & Security window, and save it as a Paint file named **Update Check** in the Module5 > Case2 folder provided with your Data Files. Close all open windows.

3. In Microsoft Edge, open a webpage in your Favorites list or go to the home page of a popular search engine, such as Google (www.google.com) or Bing (www.bing.com). Open the webpage with Internet Explorer and then maximize the Internet Explorer window. Use the SmartScreen Filter to verify this website is not a phishing website. Capture an image of the Internet Explorer window and SmartScreen Filter dialog box, and then save it in a Paint file named **Filter** in the Module5 > Case2 folder provided with your Data Files.

⊕ **Explore** 4. Close the SmartScreen Filter dialog box, click the Tools button in the navigation bar, and then click Internet options to open the Internet Options dialog box. On the General tab in the Browsing history section, click the Delete button to display the browsing data you can delete in Internet Explorer. Capture an image of the dialog box, and then save the image as a Paint file named **Delete** in the Module5 > Case2 folder provided with your Data Files.

⊕ **Explore** 5. Click the Cancel button to close the Delete Browsing History dialog box. Click the Privacy tab, and then click the Advanced button to open the Advanced Privacy Settings. Change the settings to accept all first-party cookies and prompt you for all third-party cookies. Capture an image of the dialog box, and then save the image as a Paint file named **IE Cookies** in the Module5 > Case2 folder provided with your Data Files.

6. Click the Cancel button to close the Advanced Privacy Settings dialog box, close the Internet Options dialog box, and then close Internet Explorer. Close Microsoft Edge.

⊕ **Explore** 7. Open the Control Panel and then display a window that lets you change your account type. Start the Settings app and then use it to display your account information. With both windows open, capture an image of the desktop, and then save the image as a Paint file named **Accounts** in the Module5 > Case2 folder provided with your Data Files.

8. Restore the settings on your computer. Remove Windows Remote Management from the Windows Firewall allowed programs list. Change the Advanced Privacy Settings for accepting all first-party cookies and prompting you for all third-party cookies to their original settings.

9. Delete browsing history and close all open windows.

Case Problem 3

There are no Data Files needed for this Case Problem.

Beowulf Books   Cliff Gervase owns Beowulf Books in Oxford, Mississippi, and has designed the bookstore as a casual gathering place for the neighborhood. Besides selling books and hosting readings, Cliff offers Internet connections and computers to customers who want to use them. His school-age son often visits him in the bookstore and uses the computers to do homework. Cliff is particularly concerned about the security of the computers when customers access the Internet and check email. You'll help him use the Windows 10 security settings to protect a public computer. Complete the following steps, noting your original settings so you can restore them later:

Explore 1. In Windows Firewall, block all incoming connections for private and public networks. (*Hint*: Select options in the Customize Settings window.)

Explore 2. Set Windows Defender to perform a custom scan of your removable disk or any disk other than your hard disk. Keep the Windows Defender dialog box open showing the drive you selected to scan.

3. Capture an image of the screen. Save the image as a Paint file named **Scan** in the Module5 > Case3 folder provided with your Data Files. Close all open windows.

Explore 4. In Microsoft Edge, start an InPrivate Browsing session. Select options to clear browsing data that includes passwords, media licenses, and location permissions. Clear any other selected options. Capture an image of the desktop, and then save it as a Paint file named **Private** in the Module5 > Case3 folder provided with your Data Files.

5. Clear browsing history and then close all open windows.

Explore 6. Start Mail. Use the Settings button to display the Trust Center settings. Capture an image of the desktop, and then save it in a Paint file named **Trust** in the Module5 > Case3 folder provided with your Data Files. Close Mail.

Explore 7. Begin to set up an account for a family member. (*Hint*: Open the Accounts window in the Settings app, select Family & other users, and then click the Add a family member button.)

8. With the Add a child or an adult dialog box open on the desktop, capture an image of the desktop, and then save it as a Paint file named **Family** in the Module5 > Case3 folder provided with your Data Files. Click the Cancel button to close the dialog box, and then close the Settings app.

9. Restore the settings on your computer. Restore the original settings in Windows Firewall so you are not blocking all incoming connections. Restore Windows Defender to scan using its original settings.

10. Close all open windows.

RESEARCH

Case Problem 4

There are no Data Files needed for this Case Problem.

Rodriguez Engineering   Paco Rodriguez is the president of Rodriguez Engineering, a firm in Towson, Maryland, that performs environmental clean-up on building sites. Paco wants to protect the computers his staff uses against security threats. To do so, he first wants to understand who typically attacks computers and their data. He also wants to learn more about the types of attacks people use to access computers, and how much damage such attacks have caused. He asks you to research these topics and report your findings. Complete the following steps:

1. Use your favorite search engine to find information about the types of people behind attacks on desktop computers. (Attacks on networks are in a separate category.) Search for information about the following types of attackers:
   a.   White hat hackers
   b.   Black hat hackers
   c.   Blue hat hackers
   d.   Script kiddies
2. Use your favorite search engine to find information about the techniques attackers use to exploit a computer. Search for information about the following types of techniques:
   a.   Smurf attacks
   b.   Password cracking
   c.   Social engineering
   d.   Spoofing or phishing attacks
   e.   Vulnerability scanners
3. Use a word processor to summarize your findings in one or two pages. Be sure to define any new terms and cite the websites where you found your information. Save the document as an RTF file named **Attacks**.
4. Clear browsing history and then close all open windows.

WINDOWS

Session 6.1
- Develop search strategies
- Find information on your computer using Cortana
- Search for apps and settings
- Find files by name, type, and category
- Filter the search results

Session 6.2
- Use Boolean filters in advanced searches
- Search the web using Cortana and Microsoft Edge
- Use search engines
- Narrow searches using advanced search features
- Add a search engine to Microsoft Edge

Searching for Information

Finding Apps, Settings, Files, and Information

Case | *Ithaca Imports*

A few years ago, Howard Brandt opened Ithaca Imports, a shop in Ithaca, New York, that imports prints, crafts, and other artistic goods from around the world. The shop then sells pieces to gift shops, home décor stores, and the general public. Recently, Howard received a shipment of prints of European paintings and photos of sculptures, which he wants to post on the shop's website. He hired you to assist him with the website and at the shop. Your duties include taking digital photos of the imports, organizing them logically, and finding items to feature on the website to keep it up to date.

In this module, you'll learn how to develop strategies for finding apps, data, files, folders, and settings on your computer and the web and to use the Windows 10 search tools in that pursuit. You'll refine your searches by using advanced techniques such as Boolean filters and multiple criteria. You'll also learn how to apply these search strategies when using Cortana to find information on your computer and when using Microsoft Edge to find information on the web.

STARTING DATA FILES

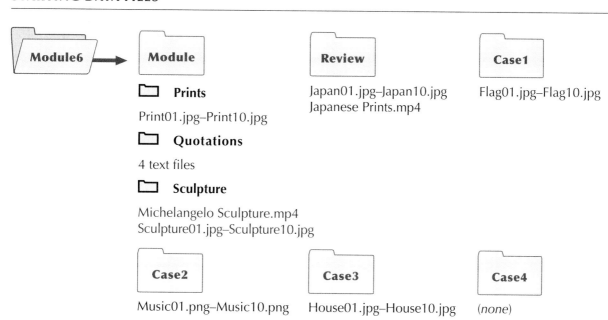

Module6 → Module

   📁 **Prints**
Print01.jpg–Print10.jpg

   📁 **Quotations**
4 text files

   📁 **Sculpture**
Michelangelo Sculpture.mp4
Sculpture01.jpg–Sculpture10.jpg

Review
Japan01.jpg–Japan10.jpg
Japanese Prints.mp4

Case1
Flag01.jpg–Flag10.jpg

Case2
Music01.png–Music10.png

Case3
House01.jpg–House10.jpg

Case4
(*none*)

Session 6.1 Visual Overview:

Use the Search Tools Search tab in a folder window to work with search results.

A **search filter** narrows a search to files that share a specified detail.

Select a condition when you use a search filter.

Click the Save search button to save the search criteria.

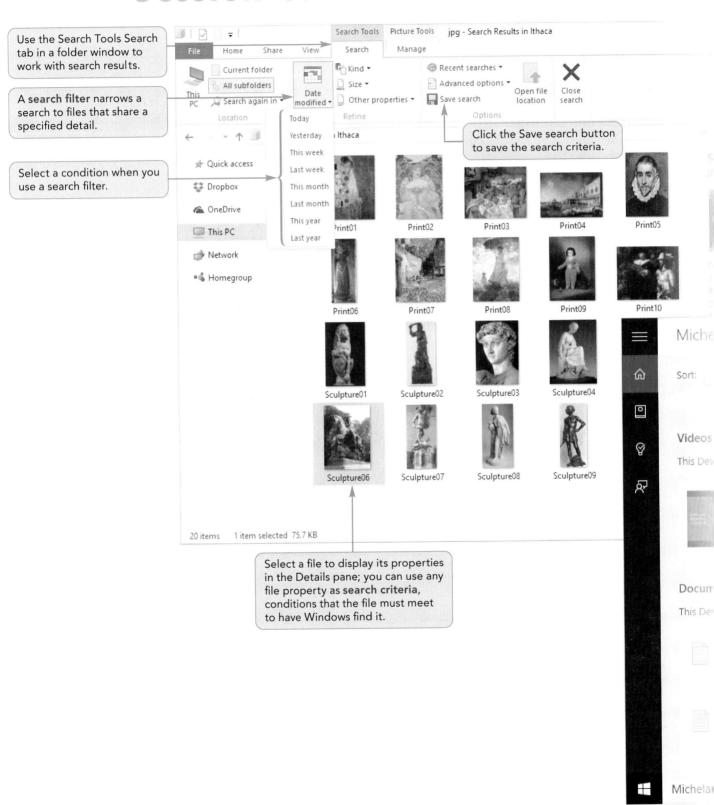

Select a file to display its properties in the Details pane; you can use any file property as **search criteria**, conditions that the file must meet to have Windows find it.

Searching for Files

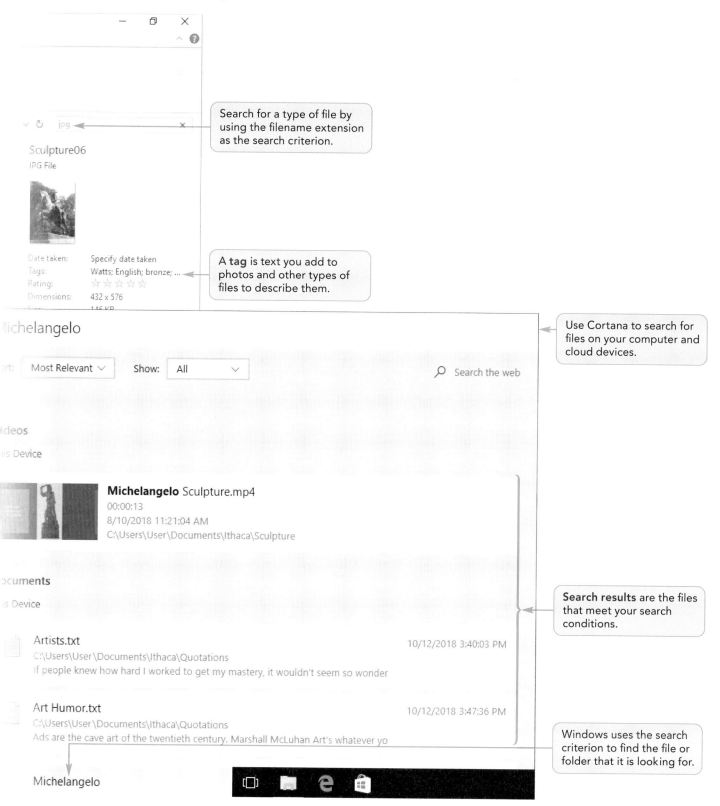

Search for a type of file by using the filename extension as the search criterion.

Sculpture06
JPG File

Date taken: Specify date taken
Tags: Watts; English; bronze; ...
Rating: ☆ ☆ ☆ ☆ ☆
Dimensions: 432 x 576

A **tag** is text you add to photos and other types of files to describe them.

Michelangelo

Sort: Most Relevant ∨   Show: All   ∨   🔎 Search the web

Use Cortana to search for files on your computer and cloud devices.

Videos

This Device

Michelangelo Sculpture.mp4
00:00:13
8/10/2018 11:21:04 AM
C:\Users\User\Documents\Ithaca\Sculpture

Documents

This Device

Search results are the files that meet your search conditions.

Artists.txt   10/12/2018 3:40:03 PM
C:\Users\User\Documents\Ithaca\Quotations
If people knew how hard I worked to get my mastery, it wouldn't seem so wonder

Art Humor.txt   10/12/2018 3:47:36 PM
C:\Users\User\Documents\Ithaca\Quotations
Ads are the cave art of the twentieth century. Marshall McLuhan Art's whatever yo

Windows uses the search criterion to find the file or folder that it is looking for.

Michelangelo

Developing Search Strategies

As you install apps and store data on your computer, the number of files and folders you have grows, making it harder to locate a particular item. Using an efficient organization scheme helps you find files and folders when you need them. Knowing your way around the Start menu and the desktop makes it easier to find apps and settings. However, if pinpointing an item means browsing dozens or hundreds of files and folders, or if you don't know where to look, you can use a Windows 10 search tool. You have already used the Search the web and Windows box and the Ask me anything box (Cortana) to find apps and the Search box in a folder window to find files. Figure 6-1 offers recommendations on when to choose one search tool over another.

Figure 6-1	Choosing a search tool

Search Tool	What to Find	What You Know	Technique to Use
Cortana	App	Some or all of the app name	Enter some or all of the app name
	Setting	Some or all of the setting name	Enter some or all of the setting name
	File anywhere on the computer, including system files	Some or all of the filename or a file detail	Enter some or all of the filename or enter a detail, an operator, and a filter
	Information on the web	Word or phrase appropriate for the information	Enter some or all of the word or phrase
Search text box in a folder window	File in the current folder or its subfolders	Some or all of the filename	Enter some or all of the filename
		Word or phrase in the file	Enter some or all of the word or phrase
		Details listed below the Search text box	Select a detail, such as size, and then select a filter, such as Large
		Details not listed below the Search text box	Enter a detail, an operator, and a filter
	File anywhere on the computer	Name, contents, or details	Expand the search, such as to other folders or the entire computer
Search text box in a Settings or Control Panel window	Setting or system tool	Some or all of the name	Enter some or all of the name, description, or keyword

To develop a search strategy, you need to know what you are looking for and you need to have some information about the item. Start by identifying what you want to find or what task you want to perform. Cortana can help you find apps, settings, and files on your computer and information on the web, so you can use Cortana to search for any of these items. Folder windows also include a Search box to help you find files. Likewise, the Settings and Control Panel windows include a Search box for finding settings and system tools. For example, if you want to start Notepad, a text-editing application, to open a text file named Maps.txt, you use Cortana. If you want to find the Maps.txt file, you can use the Search box in a folder window. If you want to set the default app for displaying maps, you can use Cortana or the Search box in the Settings window.

Next, you need to identify what you already know about the item you want to find. This information becomes your search criteria, which are conditions that the app, setting, or file must meet to have Windows find it. These conditions help you define and narrow your search so you can quickly find the item you want. For example, if you are searching for an app and using "explore" as the search condition, Windows locates and displays every app that matches that condition—in other words, all apps whose names contain a word starting with "explore," such as Internet Explorer and File Explorer. Note that case doesn't matter—you could type explore, Explore, or even EXPLORE to include Internet Explorer and File Explorer in the search results.

When you know what you want to find and what information you have about the item, you can choose the search tool that best fits your needs, and then use search criteria that are most likely to find the item. For example, suppose you want to find a photo that you took last New Year's Eve and stored somewhere in the Pictures folder. Because you know the location of the photo, you can use the Search box in the Pictures folder window. You also know when you took the photo, so you can search for files created on 12/31/2017.

Using Cortana to Search for Apps and Information

You have already used the Search the web and Windows box to find apps installed on your computer. After you activated Cortana, the label for this box became "Ask me anything." This module uses Cortana as a major search tool in Windows 10, and therefore assumes that you have already activated Cortana, which was covered in an earlier module. If you have not activated Cortana, you will be able to perform some, but not all, of the steps in this module. Some of the explanations that refer to Cortana do not apply to the Search the web and Windows box.

If you want to find an app, click the Start button or the Ask me anything box and start typing the name of the app. The text appears in the search box on the taskbar. As you type, Cortana displays a pane with the search results, which are separated into categories, such as apps installed on your computer, apps available in the Windows Store, settings, folders, websites, and files. Files might be further categorized as music, photos, videos, or documents. For example, if you click in the Ask me anything box and begin to type *photo*, the results include apps whose names contain a word starting with the text you typed, including Photos, an app that comes with Windows 10, and Photo Editor, which is available in the Windows Store. The results might also include settings for choosing a default photo viewer, a folder named Vacation Photos, and a file named American photography.docx.

The search results display the name and icon associated with the item so you can identify it. For some items, Cortana also displays the source or location. For example, when Windows apps that come with Windows 10, such as Calendar and Weather, are displayed in the search results, they include the text "Trusted Windows Store app." This notation indicates that they are available in the Windows Store and have been verified as safe apps by their vendor.

When the item you want appears in the search results, you can stop typing and then click the item to access it. For example, you can click an app's name to start the app, click a document name to open it in its default app, or click a setting to open it in the Settings app or Control Panel.

Howard often works with an art dealer in Amsterdam, the Netherlands, to buy and sell prints of artwork. He needs a quick way to convert the price of a print from U.S. dollars to euros when he's selling a print, and to convert from euros to U.S. dollars when he's buying a print. He asks you to find tools on his Windows 10 computer that let him perform these tasks.

You know that one app Howard can use to convert currencies is the Calculator app. You'll show him how to use Cortana to find the Calculator app.

To search for an app:

▶ **1.** Click in the **Ask me anything** box, and then type **cal** to search for apps whose name contains a word starting with "cal." See Figure 6-2. Your search results will differ but should include the Calculator app.

Figure 6-2   App search results

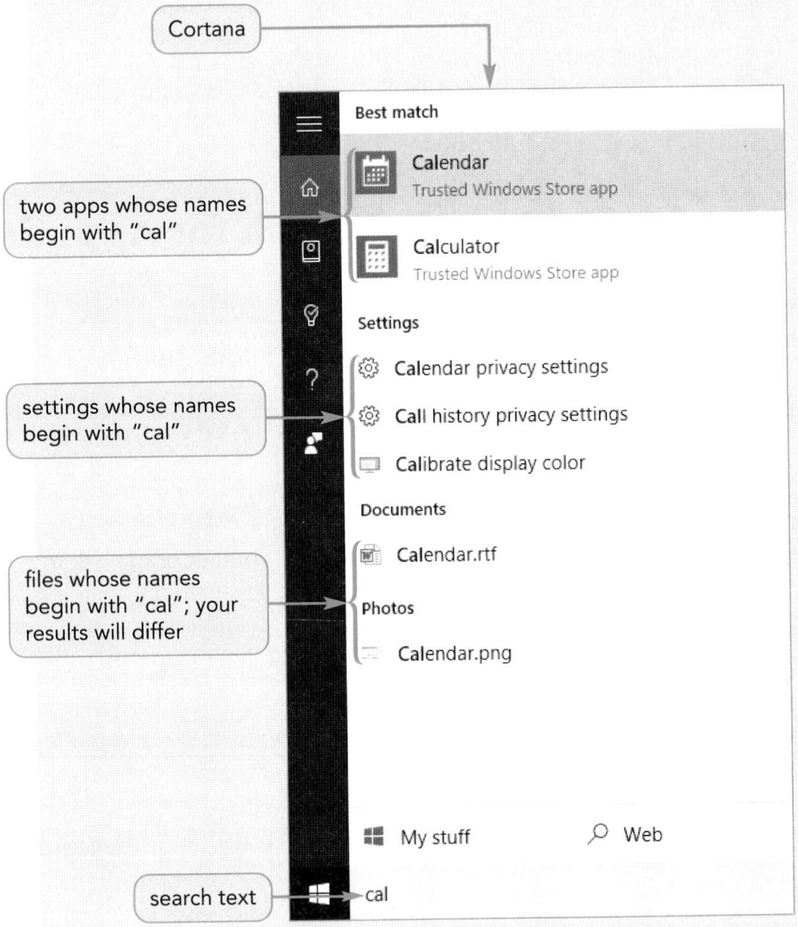

2. In the search results, click **Calculator** to start the Calculator program.

Howard has a print that he usually sells for $25 and wants to calculate the cost in euros. Before he can do that, he needs to know how many euros are equivalent to $1. You'll show him how to use Cortana to find up-to-date currency information.

To use Cortana to search for information:

▶ **1.** Click in the **Ask me anything box**, and then type **$1 is how many euros**. Cortana retrieves the latest currency conversion information from the web and then displays the results. See Figure 6-3. Your results might differ.

Trouble? If you pressed the Enter key, your browser probably opened. Close the browser and then repeat Step 1, making sure not to press the Enter key.

| Figure 6-3 | Cortana displaying currency conversion |

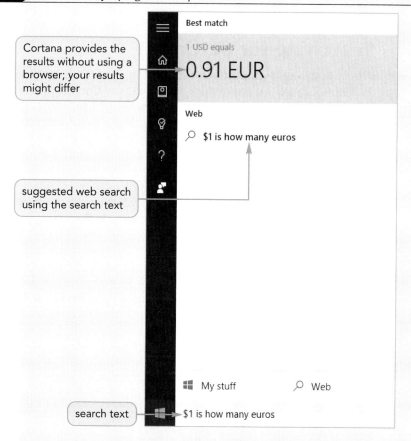

Cortana provides the results without using a browser; your results might differ

suggested web search using the search text

Best match

1 USD equals

0.91 EUR

Web

$1 is how many euros

My stuff   Web

search text $1 is how many euros

▶ **2.** Click a blank area of the desktop to close the search results.

Now you and Howard know that $1 currently equals 0.91 euros. You'll use the Calculator to determine the cost in euros of the $25 print.

To use the Calculator to convert dollars to euros:

▶ **1.** Click in the Calculator window to make it the active program, if necessary.

TIP

Instead of typing the equation, you can use the Calculator keypad.

▶ **2.** Type **25*.91** and then press the **Enter** key to display the results: 22.75.

▶ **3.** Click the **Close** button ☒ to close the Calculator app.

Howard wonders if Cortana could do the complete conversion so he doesn't need to use the Calculator app. You'll use Cortana again to find how many euros equal $25.

To use Cortana to find more detailed information:

▶ **1.** Click in the **Ask me anything box**, and then type **$25 equals how many euros**. Cortana retrieves the latest currency conversion information from the web, performs the calculation, and then displays the results: 22.67 EUR. Your results might differ.

▶ **2.** Click a blank area of the desktop to close the search results.

Besides converting between euros and dollars, Howard wants to display a clock that shows the current time in Amsterdam. You'll use Cortana to look for such a tool on Howard's computer.

Searching for Settings

Windows settings include items in the Settings app, such as Windows Update, and in the Control Panel, such as themes. When you use Cortana to search for settings, the search results begin with the Best match section, those settings that include the search text in their name. For example, if you use *theme* as the search text, the Best match section includes "Change the theme" and "Themes and related settings." In the search results, a Settings app item appears with a Settings icon ⚙ and identifies its location as "System settings." A Control Panel tool with an icon identifying the tool, such as the Personalization icon 🖼, identifies its location as "Control panel."

After the Best match section, Cortana lists Settings followed by other items such as Folders, Files, or Store. If the results do not include the setting you want, you can click the My stuff button to conduct a more detailed search on your computer and other connected drives, such as OneDrive. The detailed search results are also organized into categories, including Settings. The settings are any that might be related to your search term. For example, if you search for "theme" and then click the My stuff button, the Settings category in the search results includes "Change the theme," as in the original results, and "Choose your accent color," which is related to the theme but does not include the word "theme" in its name.

To find a tool that displays a clock in a different time zone for Howard, you can use *clock* as the search text.

To search for a setting:

▶ **1.** Click in the **Ask me anything box**, and then type **clock** to search for apps, settings, files, and web search terms that contain the word "clock," which is bold in the search results. See Figure 6-4. Your results might differ.

Figure 6-4	Searching for a setting

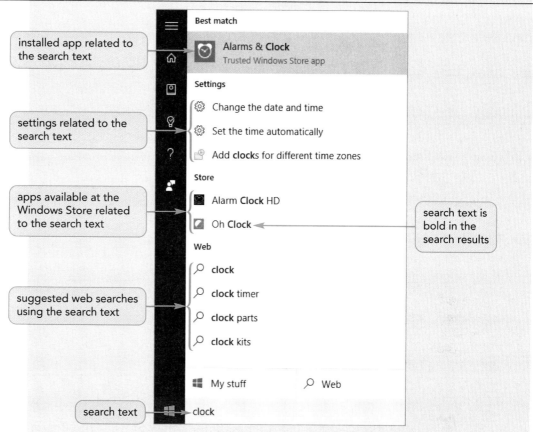

installed app related to
the search text

settings related to the
search text

apps available at the
Windows Store related
to the search text

search text is
bold in the
search results

suggested web searches
using the search text

search text

The results include an app in the Best match section, a few settings in the
Settings section, followed by apps at the Store and popular search terms
containing the word "clock." The "Add clocks for different time zones" setting
seems the most promising.

2. Click **Add clocks for different time zones** to display the Date and Time
dialog box, which is open to the Additional Clocks tab. See Figure 6-5.

Windows | Module 6 Searching for Information

Figure 6-5	Date and Time dialog box

click the Show this clock check box to add the first additional clock

Select time zone button

enter a name for the additional clock

Date and Time ✕

Date and Time   Additional Clocks   Internet Time

Additional clocks can display the time in other time zones. You can view them by clicking on or hovering over the taskbar clock.

☐ Show this clock

Select time zone:

(UTC-06:00) Central Time (US & Canada)

Enter display name:

Clock 1

☐ Show this clock

Select time zone:

(UTC-06:00) Central Time (US & Canada)

Enter display name:

Clock 2

[OK]   [Cancel]   [Apply]

▶ **3.** Click the first **Show this clock** check box to select it. The current time zone is selected for the additional clock, so you need to change it to show the time zone in Amsterdam.

▶ **4.** Click the **Select time zone** button, and then click **(UTC + 01:00) Amsterdam, Berlin, Bern, Rome, Stockholm, Vienna** to select the time zone for Amsterdam.

▶ **5.** Select the text in the Enter display name box, and then type **Amsterdam** to name the clock.

▶ **6.** Click the **OK** button to close the Date and Time dialog box.

▶ **7.** Point to the date and time control in the notification area of the taskbar to display the local time and the current time in Amsterdam.

Howard is confident he will use the additional clock frequently when communicating with the art dealer in Amsterdam.

To try the same search with a different tool, you can use the Search box in the Settings app.

To search in the Settings app:

▶ **1.** Click the **Start** button ⊞ and then click **Settings** to open the Settings app.

▶ **2.** Click in the **Find a setting** box, and then type **clock** to search for settings related to the search text. The Search Results window displays a few settings, including "Add clocks for different time zones."

▶ **3.** Close the Search Results window.

Searching the Control Panel works in the same way—you open the Control Panel window and then enter search text in the Search box. Now you can use more than one method to find settings when you need them.

Searching for Files

You can search for files using Cortana or the Search box in a folder window. Cortana looks for files stored anywhere on your computer or locations in the cloud you use to store files, such as OneDrive. The Search box looks for files in the current folder or one of its subfolders. The tool you choose depends on your current task. If you are working on the desktop or in an app, use Cortana. If you are working in a folder window, use the Search box.

When you search for files using either tool, you can conduct a basic search or an advanced search. If you use text from the filename or the file contents as search criteria, you are conducting a basic search. If you use other properties such as tags or file size as search criteria, you are conducting an advanced search. The other properties you can use as search criteria include any detail you can display as a column in a folder window. (Recall that you can display additional columns in a folder window by right-clicking any column heading, and then clicking a detail on the shortcut menu. If the detail you want to display does not appear on the shortcut menu, click More to open the Choose Details dialog box.) Figure 6-6 describes common criteria you can use when you conduct basic and advanced searches to find a file.

| Figure 6-6 | Typical search criteria |

File Property	Description	What to Find	Search Criterion
Basic Searches			
Filename	All or part of the filename	File named April sales.docx	Apr or sales
File type	Filename extension	All of your photos	jpg
Contents	Text the file contains	File that uses "European Paintings" as a heading	European Paintings
Advanced Searches			
Date	Date the file was modified, created, or accessed	Document edited on May 15, 2018	datemodified:5/15/2018
Size	Size of the file	Files larger than 3 MB	size>3 MB
Tag	Word or phrase in the file properties	Photo with "winter," "vacation," and "ski" as tags	tag:winter vacation ski
Author	Name of the person who created the file	Document that Howard created	author:Howard

When you combine criteria, such as to find a file named Agenda that you created last Monday, you are also conducting an advanced search. You'll learn how to combine search criteria later in the module.

Finding Files by Name and Contents

Suppose you want to start working with a spreadsheet file named Poster Prices as soon as you sign in to Windows. Click in the Ask me anything box and then start typing a word in the filename, such as "poster," to display files on your hard disk with filenames or contents that include a word beginning with the letters you typed. Performing this type of basic search using Cortana or a folder window is the most common way to find files on a Windows 10 computer.

A sales clerk for Ithaca Imports created a short video that showcases prints of Michelangelo's sculpture. Howard knows this video is stored somewhere on his computer, but isn't sure of the exact location or the complete filename. He does know that the filename includes the word "Michelangelo." You'll show him how to use Cortana to find the file.

First, however, you'll copy the Data Files for this module to the Documents folder on your hard disk. The Module6 > Module folder includes three subfolders: Prints, Quotations, and Sculpture. The Prints folder includes images of paintings, and the Sculpture folder contains files related to the shop's collection of prints showing sculpture. The Quotations folder contains text documents of quotations from authors, artists, and other people on various subjects. Howard likes to include at least one quotation on the shop's website.

To copy files and search for files by name:

1. Open File Explorer, open the Documents folder, and then create a folder named **Ithaca** in the Documents folder.

2. If necessary, insert the USB flash drive containing your Data Files into a USB port on your computer.

Be sure to copy the folders to the subfolder of the Documents folder so you can search for files and contents.

3. Right-click the **File Explorer** button ▭ on the taskbar, and then click **File Explorer** to open a second folder window. Display the contents of the Module6 > Module folder provided with your Data Files. Copy the **Prints**, **Quotations**, and **Sculpture** folders from the Module folder to the Ithaca folder.

4. Close the Module folder window (the second window displaying the USB flash drive), but leave the Ithaca folder window open.

5. Click in the **Ask me anything** box, and then type **michela** to search for files and other items with a name starting with the text "michela," the first few letters in "Michelangelo." See Figure 6-7. Your results might differ.

Trouble? If the Michelangelo Sculpture.mp4 file doesn't appear in the search results, click in a blank area in the folder window, and then make sure the contents of the Ithaca folder are displayed in the right pane of the File Explorer window before repeating Step 5.

| Figure 6-7 | Using Cortana to find files |

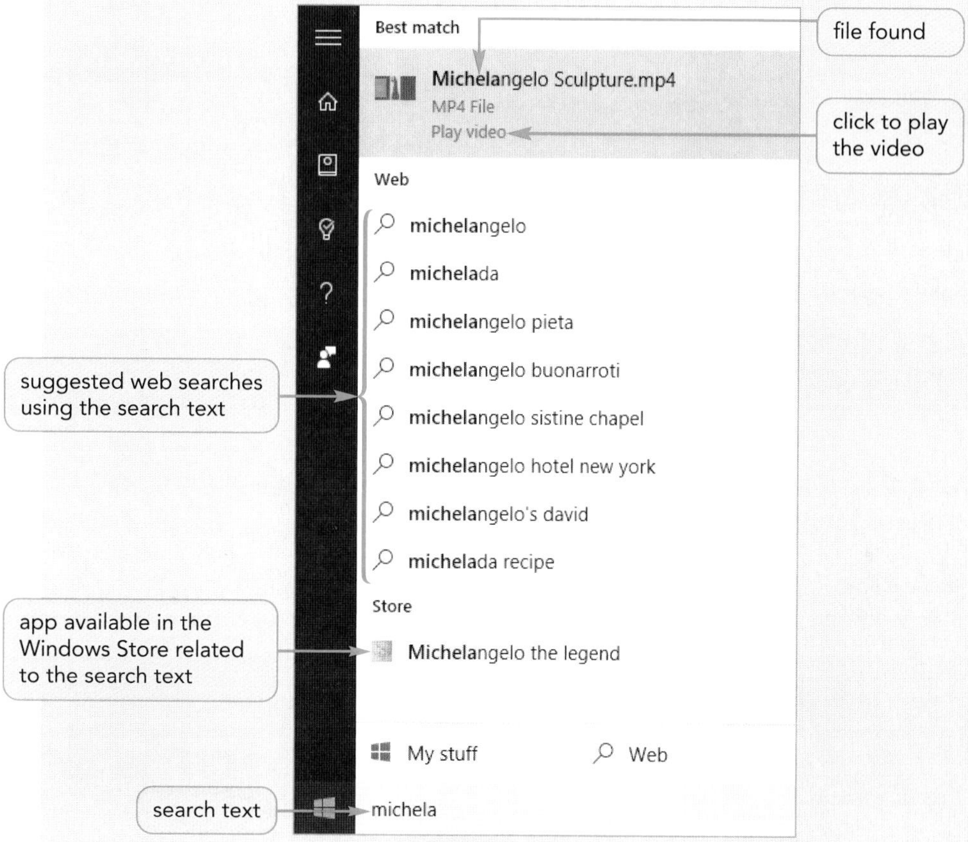

6. In the search results, right-click **Michelangelo Sculpture.mp4** and then click **Open file location** on the shortcut menu. Windows opens the Sculpture folder in the Ithaca folder and selects the Michelangelo Sculpture file.

7. Close the Sculpture window.

TIP

To open the file in its default app, click the file in the search results.

Howard plans to provide the Michelangelo Sculpture video on the Ithaca Imports website. When he does, he wants to include a quotation by or about Michelangelo. If one of the text files in the Quotations folder had a filename containing a word that starts with "michela," the text file would have appeared in the previous search results. To find a quotation by or about Michelangelo, you need to search the file contents. You can use Cortana to search file contents by using the My stuff button.

To search for files by contents:

1. Click in the **Ask me anything** box, and then type **michela** to conduct the same search as in the previous steps.

2. Click the **My stuff** button to display files whose filenames or contents include a word starting with "michela." See Figure 6-8.

Figure 6-8	Searching file contents

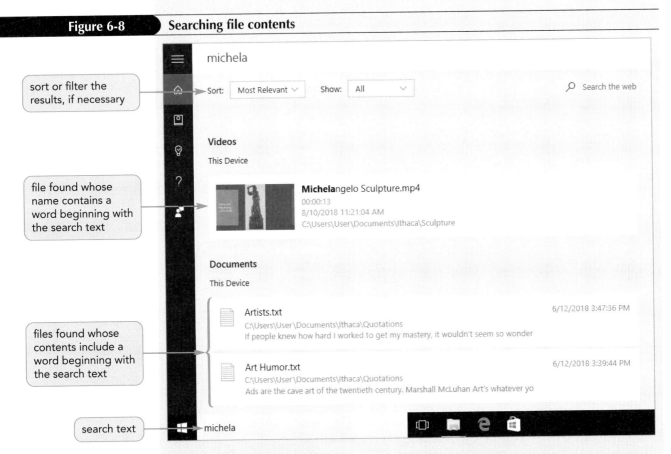

3. Point to **Artists.txt** in the Documents section to display the file contents. The ScreenTip displays the contents without line breaks, which is difficult to read.

4. Click the **Artists.txt** text file to open it in Notepad. This file contains quotations from artists.

5. Press the **Ctrl+F** keys to open the Find dialog box, type **michela** in the Find what box, and then click the **Find Next** button. Notepad selects the first instance of "michela" in the Artists file, the name "Michelangelo" following a quotation about carving marble. This quotation is perfect for Howard's needs. When he's ready, he can return to the Artists file in the Quotations folder to copy and paste the quotation on the Ithaca Imports website.

6. Close the Find dialog box and then close Notepad.

Although the Artists and Art Humor filenames do not include a word starting with "michela," the file contents do. When you search files stored on a hard disk, Windows includes the file contents in the search. However, if you search files stored on a removable disk, such as a USB drive, Windows searches only the filenames, not the contents, by default.

Searching by File Type

Using the Search box in a folder window to find files based on their filenames and contents is similar to using Cortana. You type text in the Search box, and Windows displays only those files in the current folder or its subfolders that match the criterion—files whose contents or filename include a word starting with the text you typed.

You can also use a filename extension as the search criterion to find files by type. For example, you could enter *jpg* to find files with a .jpg extension (image files called JPGs, pronounced *Jay Peg*), which are usually photo files. When you search for files by type, you can enter the filename extension on its own (*jpg*) or use an asterisk and a dot before the filename extension (**.jpg*). In this case, the asterisk is a **wildcard**, a symbol that stands for one or more unspecified characters in the search criterion.

Using a wildcard is a good idea if you want to search for certain types of files, such as those with a DOC extension. Suppose some of your filenames include words that start with the extension text, such as "Doctor Visit," "June Docket," or "Howard Docs." In this case, using a wildcard and a dot makes it clear that you are searching by filename extension only and produces more accurate search results.

Howard is creating webpages and printed marketing materials that feature prints of notable European paintings and sculptures in the shop's collection. He has been taking photos of these prints and saving the photos on his computer. First, he wants to know how many photos of paintings and sculpture he has saved. Because all of these photos are stored in two subfolders, you can provide the information Howard wants by conducting a basic search in a folder window using the filename extension .jpg as the search criterion.

To search for files by type:

1. In the File Explorer window, display the contents of the Ithaca folder in the Documents folder, if necessary.

2. Click in the **Search Ithaca** box, and then type **jpg**. Windows displays only the files with a .jpg extension in the search results.

3. If necessary, click the **Large Icons** button in the status bar to display the search results in Large icons view. See Figure 6-9. Your files might appear in a different order. Note that the status bar indicates that the search results include 20 files.

Figure 6-9	Searching for files with a .jpg filename extension

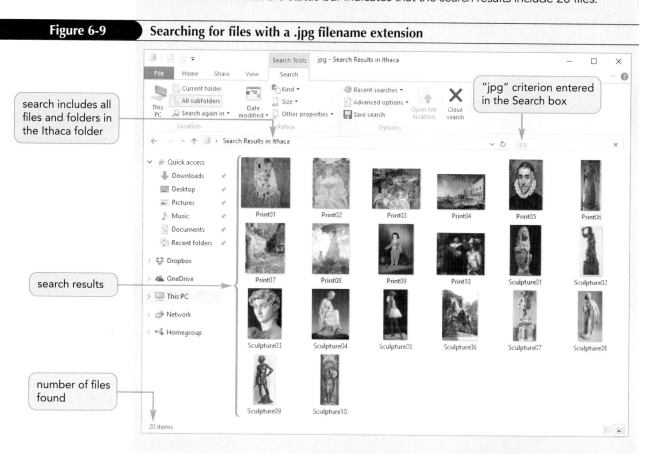

search includes all files and folders in the Ithaca folder

"jpg" criterion entered in the Search box

search results

number of files found

Decision Making: Searching vs. Sorting, Filtering, or Grouping

Recall that instead of using the Search box, you can often quickly find files by sorting, filtering, or grouping files using the column headings or the View menu in a folder window. The method you choose depends on the number of files you want to search, the location of the files, and their names. For example, suppose you need to find JPG files. If you want to search the current folder and its subfolders, use the Search box—the other options find files only in the current folder.

If you're searching a single folder, the Search box is also preferable if the folder contains similar filenames (because sorting would list many files that start with the same text) or many types of files (because grouping would produce many groups). If you want to find a particular file in a very large folder, it is often easier to use the Search box rather than dealing with a long file list; however, if the folder doesn't contain too many files, then sorting, grouping, or filtering is usually a more efficient method.

Now that you found the number of photos Howard took of paintings and sculpture, he wants you to research the items so he can provide accurate information in the webpages and printed brochure. Some of the JPG files you found have filenames starting with "Print" followed by a number, such as Print01 and Print02. The other JPG files have filenames starting with "Sculpture" followed by a number. Howard set his digital camera to assign these names so he could take the photos quickly. The camera used Print01 for the first photo Howard took of a print and then automatically added 1 to the number each time he took another photo until he finished photographing the prints. The camera used the same process to name the sculpture photos. Although this filenaming scheme worked well to save the photo files quickly, it poses challenges for your research because the filenames do not reveal anything about the content except that they show paintings or sculpture.

Filtering the Search Results by Size

Besides simply typing a few characters in the Ask me anything box or the Search box, you can also conduct more advanced searches using Cortana or a folder window. To search for files modified on a certain date or files of a certain size, for example, you can add a filter to narrow a search to files that share a specified detail. (Recall that a filter displays only files with a certain characteristic you specify.)

Filtering Search Results

- Open the folder or drive you want to search.
- Enter text in the Search box.
- To specify a filter, click a button in the Refine group on the Search Tools Search tab, and then click a criterion.

When you enter text in the Search box of a folder window, Windows displays the results in the right pane and opens the Search Tools Search tab on the ribbon. You use the buttons in the Refine group to narrow the results. For example, if you are searching the Pictures folder for photos you took last week, you can click the Search box in the Pictures folder and then type jpg to display all the photos stored in the Pictures folder. To narrow the results to display only the photos you took last week, click the Date modified button in the Refine group on the Search Tools Search tab, and then click Last week. Windows displays only the files in the Pictures folder that meet your criteria.

When you select a search filter, Windows automatically adds a file property name, a colon, and the criterion to the Search box. The file property name is shorthand for the detail you want to use to narrow the search. The criterion determines how to narrow the search. For example, when you click the Date modified button on the Search Tools Search tab and then click Last week, Windows inserts "datemodified:last week" in the Search box.

To conduct an advanced search using Cortana, you use more natural language. For example, to find photos you took last week, enter *find photos from last week* in the Ask me anything box, and then click the My stuff button. Cortana searches files on your hard disk and other connected drives, such as OneDrive.

Howard photographed one of the prints using a high resolution, which makes the image sharp and clear even when printed. He wants to use this photo in a printed brochure. However, he can't recall which photo has the high resolution. He mentions that high-resolution images are usually large files, often more than 1 MB in storage size. You can use this information to find the file Howard wants. Conducting a basic search using the jpg extension as the search text finds all the JPG files in the Prints and Sculpture folders. To narrow the search to large files only, you'll refine the results.

To narrow a search using a search filter:

▶ **1.** In the folder window displaying the results of the previous search, click the **Search Tools Search** tab, if necessary, and then in the Refine group, click the **Size** button to display a list of size options. See Figure 6-10.

   Trouble? If the folder window open on the desktop does not display the results of the previous search, type "jpg" in the Search box.

Figure 6-10	Selecting a search filter

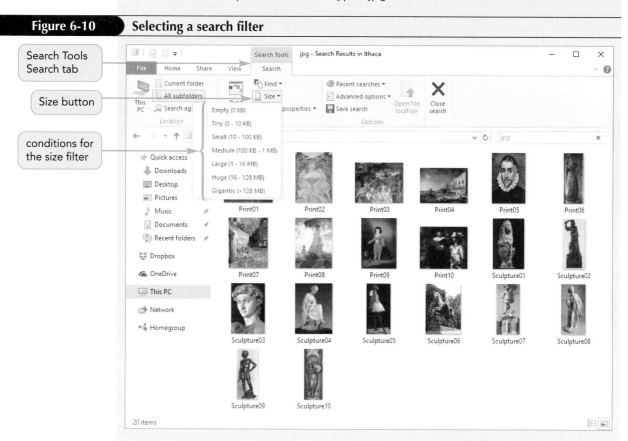

▶ **2.** Click **Large (1–16 MB)** in the Size options list. Windows reduces the search results to files that meet both criteria—large JPG files.

Only one file meets the search criteria: Print07, which is a high-resolution photo of a Van Gogh painting of a café at night.

Filtering Search Results by Date Modified

Howard usually photographs an imported item as soon as he receives it. On the shop's website, Howard wants you to display photos of imported items he acquired recently, which are those photos taken after August 31, 2018. To find these files, you can start with the same criterion you used to find all the JPG files, and then narrow the results by specifying the date condition. When you use the Date modified button in the Refine group on the Search Tools Search tab, you can select only predefined options such as Today, This week, or Last year. To use a specific date, you select one of these criteria and then click the Search box to display a calendar where you can select a date or date range.

To find JPG files taken after August 31, 2018:

▶ 1. In the folder window, click the **Back** button ← until you return to the Ithaca window.

▶ 2. Click in the **Search** box and then type **jpg**. Windows displays all the JPG files in the search results.

▶ 3. In the Refine group on the Search tab, click the **Date modified** button, and then click **Today** to select a date option. No results appear, so you need to modify the date further.

▶ 4. Click in the text "today" in the Search box to display a calendar control. See Figure 6-11.

Figure 6-11   **Using a date modified search condition**

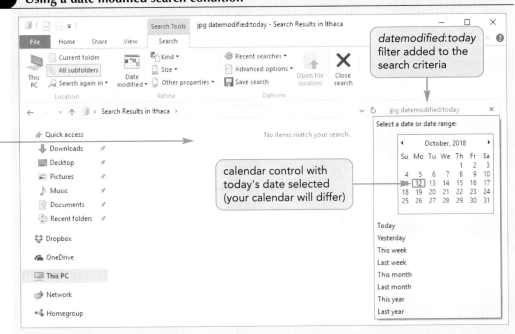

no files appear in the search results because no JPG files were modified today

datemodified:today filter added to the search criteria

calendar control with today's date selected (your calendar will differ)

▶ 5. Use the calendar controls to display the August 2018 page. To change the month (and eventually the date), click the left arrow and right arrow buttons. When the calendar page for August, 2018 appears, click **31**.

No files appear in the search results because no files in the Ithaca folder were modified on August 31, 2018. You want to find files that were modified after that date. To do so, you use the greater than (>) operator. You can use the greater than operator with any property in the Search box. For example, to find files that are larger than 500 KB, enter *size:>500KB*. (You can include a space after the colon or omit it—the space does not affect the search results.) You can also use the less than (<) operator in the same way. To find files less than 500 KB, enter *size:<500KB*. To find files modified after August 31, 2018, you use the greater than operator to enter *datemodified:>8/31/2018* in the Search box.

To modify the search criteria:

▶ **1.** Click in the **Search** box.

▶ **2.** Move the insertion point after the colon (:) in datemodified, and then type >. Seven files appear in the search results.

To make sure you find the files you need or to expand a search, you should examine the search results.

Examining the Search Results

After you enter search criteria using the Search box, Windows filters the view of the folder window to display files that meet your criteria. These are your search results. Figure 6-12 shows the results of the search performed in the preceding set of steps—JPG files modified after August 31, 2018.

Figure 6-12	Search results

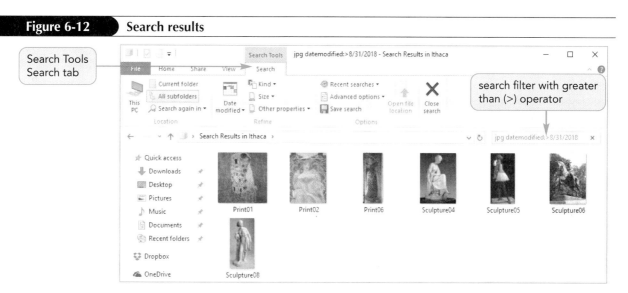

Search results windows provide extra tools and information to help you work with the files you found. The title bar displays the search criteria. In Details view, the search results display the name, location, date modified, size, and other available properties of each file. If the results include text files, they preview their first two lines of text to help you identify the file contents.

Besides the buttons in the Refine group, the Search Tools Search tab contains other groups of controls to help you find the files or information you need. The Location group and Options group provide other search tools that you can use to broaden or narrow your search. Using the buttons in the Location group, you can change the default search location on your computer (that is, the current folder and all of its subfolders), or you can search the Internet using your default web browser (such as Microsoft Edge) and search engine, which is a program (such as Google or Bing) a website uses to conduct the search using keywords. The Recent searches button in the Options group stores a history of the criteria for your last eight searches. The Advanced options button in this group allows you to change how Windows uses the criteria entered to search for files using an exact match setting, for example. To speed up a search, you can set Windows to search an indexed location, such as the Documents folder or Pictures folder on your hard disk, so Windows searches the file contents. (An **indexed location** is one or more folders that Windows indexes so it can search them quickly. Folders and other locations that contain your personal files—not system files—are indexed locations.) The Save search button provides access to tools for saving the criteria and folder location of a search. Use the Open file location button to open the location of the selected file.

Howard occasionally works with files stored on a removable disk, so you want to show him how to search filenames and contents in that location.

To search for files on a removable disk:

▶ **1.** If necessary, insert the USB flash drive containing your Data Files into a USB port on your computer.

▶ **2.** Navigate to and display the contents of the **Module6 > Module** folder on the USB flash drive.

▶ **3.** Type **michela** in the Search box to display folders and files with names that contain a word beginning with **michela**.

▶ **4.** In the Options group on the Search Tools Search tab, click the **Advanced options** button and then click **File contents** under the In non-indexed locations section (which includes a USB drive). Windows adds the two text files that contain a word beginning with "michela" to the search results.

Trouble? If File contents is already selected, a JPG and two text files are already displayed in the results for Step 3. Do not click File contents; this will deselect the option. Press the Esc key to close the list of advanced options.

In addition to the extra tools provided in a search results window, you can use the standard folder window tools to open, move, copy, rename, or delete a file.

Saving a Search

If you conduct a successful search that you are likely to conduct again, especially one that uses two or more criteria, you might want to save the search. Saving a search preserves your original criteria and folder location so you can perform the search again without reconstructing the criteria. By default, Windows saves the search in the Searches folder, which is stored in your personal folder (the one whose name is the same as your user name). You can double-click a saved search to use the same criteria in a new search. The search results display the most current files that match the original conditions, so the results might differ from other times when you conducted the same search.

To save a search and perform it again:

TIP

Click in the Search box to display the recent searches, and then click jpg datemodified:>8/31/2016.

1. In the search results window, click the **Back** button ← to navigate back to the results of the jpg datemodified:>8/31/2018 search.

   Trouble? If a new folder window opened when you inserted the USB drive containing your Data Files, close that window and return to the one showing the results of the jpg datemodified:>8/31/2018 search.

2. Click the **Save search** button in the Options group on the Search Tools Search tab. The Save As dialog box opens, providing jpg datemodified8-31-2018 as the filename. (Windows doesn't include the colon and greater than symbol because they are not allowed in filenames; Windows also replaces any forward slashes with dashes for the same reason.) See Figure 6-13.

Figure 6-13	Saving a search

by default, Windows saves your searches in the Searches folder in your personal folder

suggested name for saved search without the colon or greater than sign

Be sure to save the search so you can use it again.

3. Change the filename to **JPG Sept**, and then click the **Save** button to save the search in the Searches folder.

4. To view the saved search, click **Searches** in the Address bar of the folder window. The JPG Sept search appears in the Saved Search list.

5. To test the search, double-click **JPG Sept**. Windows conducts the search again and finds the JPG files modified after August 31, 2018.

Howard asks if using tags would help him find and identify files. In fact, one of the most useful properties when searching for files is a file tag, which is one or more descriptive words you store with a file to help identify its purpose or contents. You are sure that adding tags to the photo files would save you and Howard a lot of time when searching for photos. You'll show him how to do so next.

Using Tags and Other Properties

As you know, properties are characteristics of files, such as names and sizes. When you create or modify a file, you automatically set some file properties, including the filename, location, and date created or modified. You can add other properties later, including tags, ratings, titles, and authors. Tags are often the most useful properties because they make finding similar files easier.

To add properties to a file, you can use the Details pane in a folder window or the file's Properties dialog box. (You can use the Details pane to add or modify the properties of only some types of files, such as Microsoft Office documents, but not TXT or RTF files.) As you recall, to open the Details pane in a folder window, you click the Details pane button in the Panes group on the View tab. Figure 6-14 shows the Details pane when the Print01 file is selected in the Prints folder.

Figure 6-14   **File properties in the Details pane**

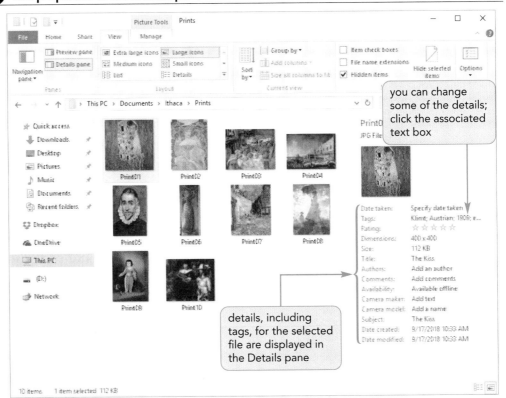

you can change some of the details; click the associated text box

details, including tags, for the selected file are displayed in the Details pane

Properties you can add using the Details pane vary by file type. For photos, you can specify date taken, tags, and other properties by using the appropriate box in the Details pane. You can also rate photos by clicking a star in a series of five stars. If you click the first star, you apply a one-star rating. If you click the fourth star, you apply a four-star rating.

If you want to specify file properties other than the ones that appear in the Details pane by default, you can open the Properties dialog box for a file. To do so, you right-click the file and then click Properties on the shortcut menu. On the Details tab, you can add or modify dozens of properties. Figure 6-15 shows the Properties dialog box for the Print01 file.

Figure 6-15 File details in the Properties dialog box

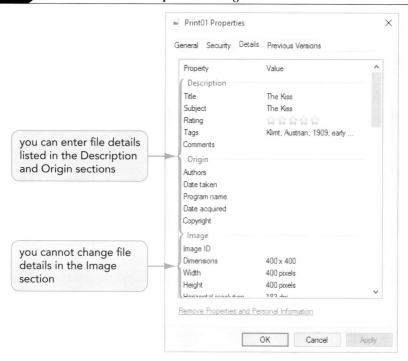

you can enter file details listed in the Description and Origin sections

you cannot change file details in the Image section

Adding Tags to Files

You can add a tag to a file by using the Save As dialog box when you save the file, or by using the Details pane or the file's Properties dialog box after you save the file. To use the Details pane, you select the file, click the Tags box in the Details pane, and then type a word or phrase that will help you find the file later. To add more than one tag, separate each word or phrase with a semicolon (;). For example, if you have a photo of yourself on the peak of the Blackrock Mountain in Virginia, you could use Blackrock; mountain; Virginia as tags.

REFERENCE

Adding Tags to Files

- In a folder window, click the file to which you want to add a tag.
- In the Panes group on the View tab, click the Details pane button to display the Details pane.
- Click the Tags box in the Details pane, and then type a tag. To enter another tag, type a semicolon (;) and then type the next tag.
- Click the Save button on the Details pane.

Howard has already added tags to some of the photo files in the Prints and Sculpture folders, but two recent files still need tags. Howard asks you to add descriptive tags to these files.

To add tags to files:

1. Open the Sculpture folder in the Documents > Ithaca folder on your hard disk, and then switch to Details view. Maximize the window, if necessary.

2. Click the **View** tab on the ribbon, and then in the Panes group, click the **Details pane** button to display the Details pane.

3. Display the Tags column, if necessary, by right-clicking any column heading and then clicking **Tags** on the shortcut menu.

4. Click the **Size all columns to fit** button in the Current view group to display all of the columns in the window.

5. Click each file in the file list to examine its properties in the Details pane. Note that Michelangelo Sculpture, Sculpture09, and Sculpture10 do not have any tags. Michelangelo Sculpture is a video, so it's easy to identify that file without tags.

6. Click **Sculpture09** to display its image and boxes for file details, such as Tags, in the Details pane. Howard knows that this sculpture is called *David* and the sculptor is Verrocchio.

7. Click in the **Tags box** in the Details pane, and then type **David** as the first tag. Windows inserts an ending semicolon for you. Click after the ; (semicolon), and then type **Verrocchio; 1473** as the second and third tags. See Figure 6-16.

Figure 6-16	Adding tags to a file

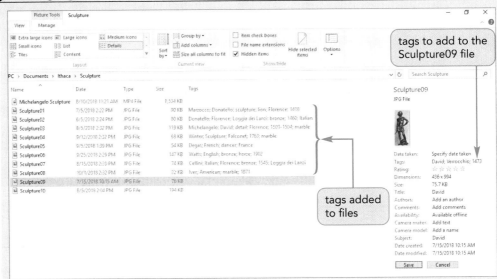

8. Click the **Save** button in the Details pane. Windows saves the tags you added. Because you modified the file by adding a tag, the date in the Date column changes to today's date.

TIP

If Windows suggests tags as you begin to type, click the tag you want.

9. Click the **Sculpture10** file, add the tags **Sibyl; Ghiberti; 1425**, and then click the **Save** button. Note that after you save a tag in one file, that tag appears in the list of suggested tags for other files.

10. Close all open windows.

When entering multiple tags, you don't need to click after the semicolon automatically entered; it is replaced as you type a series of tags.

INSIGHT

Selecting Tags for Files

To create tags that will help you find files later, keep the following guidelines in mind:
- Include the obvious. Use words or phrases that describe the overall purpose or content of the file. For photo files, use tags that list the people in the picture, the location of the photo, and the occasion. For documents, describe the type of document, such as a proposal or report, and its subject.
- Consider the sample tags. If you are working with files on a hard disk, you can find typical tags by typing a letter in the Tags box in the Details pane. For example, type *p* to find sample tags that start with the letter *p*, such as people, pet owners, pets, and photography.
- Use complete words and phrases. Avoid abbreviations and codes because you might not remember them later. Assign complete words or use phrases to be as clear as possible. Feel free to use text that appears in the filename; doing so might help you find other related files with the same tag but a different filename.

You've already explored many ways to search for files on your computer. You conducted basic searches by searching filenames and contents. You also conducted advanced searches by using properties to filter the search results. In the next session, you'll build on these techniques by searching tags and combining criteria using shorthand notation and Boolean filters. You'll apply these new skills to search for information in Windows 10 apps and on the Internet.

REVIEW

Session 6.1 Quick Check

1. What are search criteria?
2. Name two ways you can search for settings.
3. When you use Cortana to search for apps, what does the notation "Trusted Windows Store app" mean in the search results?
4. You can use Cortana to search file contents by using the _____ button.
5. Explain how to search for DOCX files in a folder window.
6. How can you search for files larger than 1 MB in a folder window?
7. Why might you want to save a search?

Session 6.2 Visual Overview:

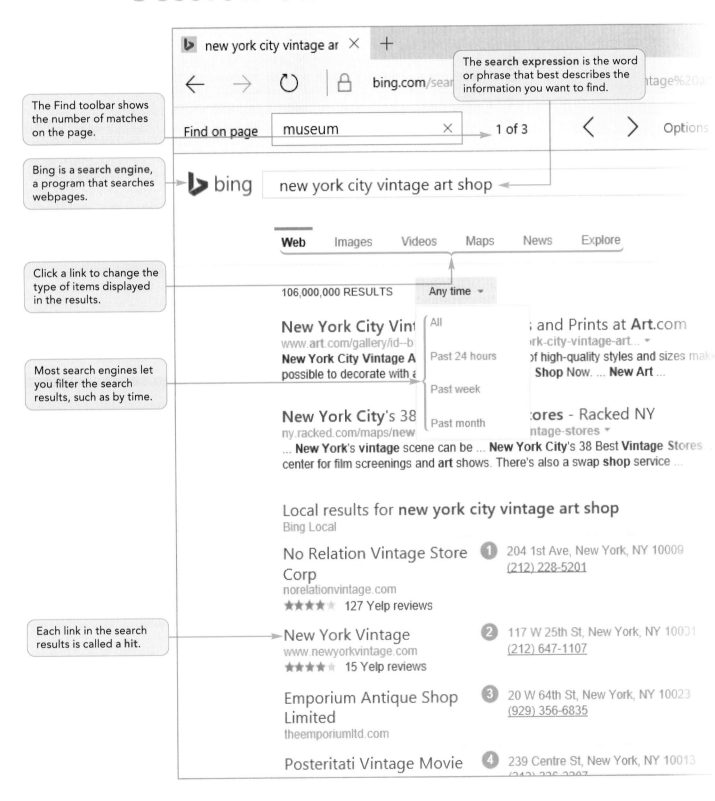

The Find toolbar shows the number of matches on the page.

The search expression is the word or phrase that best describes the information you want to find.

Bing is a search engine, a program that searches webpages.

Click a link to change the type of items displayed in the results.

Most search engines let you filter the search results, such as by time.

Each link in the search results is called a hit.

new york city vintage ar ✕ ＋

← → ↻ 🔒 bing.com/sear ...ntage%20a...

Find on page | museum ✕ | 1 of 3 ‹ › Options

b bing | new york city vintage art shop

Web Images Videos Maps News Explore

106,000,000 RESULTS | Any time ▾

All
Past 24 hours
Past week
Past month

New York City Vint... ; and Prints at **Art**.com
www.art.com/gallery/id--b... ...rk-city-vintage-art... ▾
New York City Vintage A... of high-quality styles and sizes mak...
possible to decorate with a... Shop Now. ... **New Art** ...

New York City's 38 ...tores - Racked NY
ny.racked.com/maps/new ...ntage-stores ▾
... **New York**'s **vintage** scene can be ... **New York City**'s 38 Best **Vintage Stores** ...
center for film screenings and art shows. There's also a swap **shop** service ...

Local results for **new york city vintage art shop**
Bing Local

No Relation Vintage Store Corp
norelationvintage.com
★★★★☆ 127 Yelp reviews
① 204 1st Ave, New York, NY 10009
(212) 228-5201

New York Vintage
www.newyorkvintage.com
★★★★☆ 15 Yelp reviews
② 117 W 25th St, New York, NY 1000...
(212) 647-1107

Emporium Antique Shop Limited
theemporiumltd.com
③ 20 W 64th St, New York, NY 10023
(929) 356-6835

Posteritati Vintage Movie
④ 239 Centre St, New York, NY 1001...

Searching the Internet

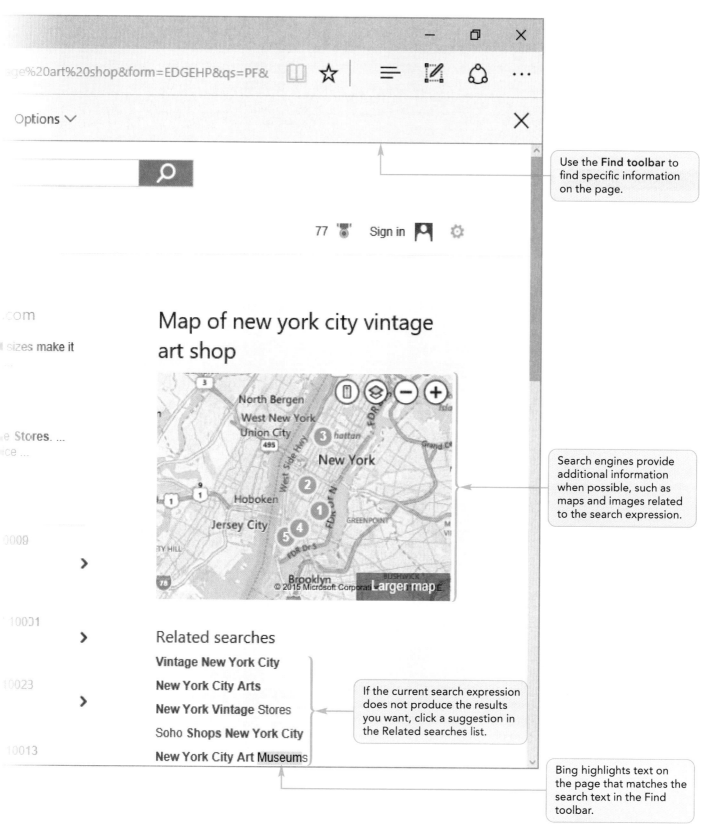

Use the **Find toolbar** to find specific information on the page.

Search engines provide additional information when possible, such as maps and images related to the search expression.

If the current search expression does not produce the results you want, click a suggestion in the Related searches list.

Bing highlights text on the page that matches the search text in the Find toolbar.

Using Advanced Search Criteria

In addition to searching for files using common properties such as file type or size, you can use the Search box in a folder window to search for other properties, including tags, title, and subject. To use any property as a criterion, you specify the property using the following shorthand notation: *property name:criterion*. (You can include or omit the space after the colon.) For example, if you want to search for files that include the word "Ithaca" as a tag, you could enter *tag:ithaca*. (The properties are not case sensitive, so you could also enter *Tag:Ithaca*.) The properties you can use as search criteria include any detail you can display as a column in a folder window. Figure 6-17 provides examples of the shorthand notation you can use to specify file properties as search criteria.

Figure 6-17   Examples of using file properties as search criteria

Property	Example	Finds
Name	Name:city	Files and folders with names that contain a word beginning with "city"
Date modified	DateModified:10/28/2018	Files and folders modified on October 28, 2018
	DateModified:<10/28/2018	Files and folders modified before October 28, 2018
Date created	DateCreated:>10/28/2018	Files and folders created after October 28, 2018
	DateCreated:2018	Files and folders created during the year 2018
Size	Size:200KB	Files with a size of 200 KB
	Size:>1MB	Files larger than 1 MB
Type	Type:docx	Files with a .docx filename extension
Tags	Tag:French	Files that include "French" as a tag
Authors	Author:Howard	Files that specify "Howard" as the author
Artists	Artist:Elvis	Files that specify artists with "Elvis" in their names, such as Elvis Presley and Elvis Costello
Rating	Rating:4 stars	Files with a rating of four stars

Being able to include any file detail as a search criterion is especially useful when you are working with photos, music, and videos because they have special properties for their file types, such as album artists, album, rating, and length.

When searching in a folder window, you can use the Other properties button in the Refine group on the Search Tools Search tab to display a list of properties you can use in a search, such as Authors, Tags, and Title. In each case, when you click a property on the Other properties list, Windows inserts the property name and a colon in the Search box. Using the Other properties button can help you create advanced criteria using the proper shorthand notation. If you know the correct shorthand notation, you can enter it directly in the Search box.

For the updates Howard is planning for the Ithaca Imports website, Howard wants to show French art. Howard inserted the nationality of the artist as a tag for the photos in the Prints and Sculpture folders. You can search the tags of the files in the Ithaca folder to find art photos Howard can use.

To find files by specifying a property in the Search box:

▶ **1.** Open the Ithaca folder in the Documents folder on your hard disk, if necessary.

▶ **2.** Click in the **Search Ithaca** box, and then type **tag:french**. As you type, Windows filters the view of the files in the folder window, and then displays three files that contain the text "french" in their Tags property: Print03, Print08, and Sculpture05.

▶ **3.** Click **Print03** and examine the information in the Details pane. This is a photo of *The Kitchen Table*, a painting by Cezanne, a French painter, created from 1880–1890.

▶ **4.** Click **Print08** and examine its details. This is a photo of *Woman with a Parasol*, a painting by Monet, also a French painter, created in 1875.

▶ **5.** Click **Sculpture05** and examine its details. This is a photo of *Young Dancer*, a sculpture by Degas, a French artist, created in 1881.

By searching for text in the Tags property, you found three photos to display on the Ithaca Imports website.

Combining Criteria When Searching File Contents

TIP

When you use two or more words as a search condition, Windows searches as if the condition includes the AND Boolean filter.

To perform a precise search, you can combine criteria in the Search box. For example, suppose you store your financial documents on your computer and need to find a list of charitable donations you made in 2018. You don't recall where you've stored this information, and scanning the filenames in your Financial folder doesn't reveal the file. If you search the contents of the files using *donation* as the search criterion, you'll find lists of donations for many years as well as other documents, including those with text such as "Thanks for your support! Every donation helps." If you search the contents of files using *2018* as the search criterion, you'll find dozens of documents that mention that year. To pinpoint your search, you can combine the criteria to find files that contain the word "donation" and the year "2018." When you search file contents, you can use **Boolean filters**, which are filters that let you search for specific information using the words AND, OR, and NOT to combine search criteria. You can use quotation marks and parentheses to refine the search conditions further. Figure 6-18 describes how to use AND, OR, and NOT along with quotation marks and parentheses when combining search criteria.

Figure 6-18 | Combining search criteria

Word or Punctuation	Examples	When to Use
AND	donation AND 2018 donation 2018	To narrow the search to files that contain "donation" and "2018" even if the words are not next to each other
OR	donation OR 2018	To broaden the search to files that contain "donation" or "2018"
NOT	donation NOT 2018	To restrict the search to files that contain "donation" but not "2018"
"" (quotation marks)	"donation 2018"	To pinpoint the search to files that contain the exact phrase "donation 2018"
( ) (parentheses)	(donation 2018)	To open the search to files that contain both items next to each other in any order

When you use the words AND, OR, and NOT, you must enter them using all uppercase letters.

One of your ongoing projects for Ithaca Imports is maintaining an archive of quotations, which Howard uses on the shop's website. Howard, employees, and customers provide these quotations in various ways, such as in a word-processing document or an email message. You store the quotations in TXT documents to make sure anyone at the shop can use the documents. However, this means that you cannot add tags or other properties to the files; you can add these details only to Microsoft Office documents.

Along with the photos of French art, Howard wants to include at least one quotation about art collecting. You can use Boolean logic to combine search criteria and search the contents of the Quotations folder to find suitable quotations.

INSIGHT

Preparing to Combine Search Criteria

Before you combine search criteria, select the search text, select the filter you plan to use, if any, and then select the condition. For example, choose *.txt as the search text to find text files. If you want to find text files modified after a certain date, use the datemodified: filter, and then select the appropriate date, such as >8/31/2018. Next, determine whether you should use AND, OR, or NOT to combine the criteria, and whether you need quotation marks or parentheses to find the files you want. For example, if you want to find files that use "Ithaca" as a tag and have "Howard" as the author, you use the AND filter, whether you insert AND or not. In other words, *tag:Ithaca AND author:Howard* is the same as *tag:Ithaca author:Howard*.

If you want to find either text files or Word documents, you need to insert OR, as in *.txt OR *.doc*. (The search condition *.doc* finds Word documents that have a .doc or a .docx filename extension.) To determine the best criteria, test each method in order, starting with AND. Keep in mind that AND narrows the search results, whereas OR broadens the results. For example, if you search for files that are photos and use "Ithaca" as a tag, you find fewer files than searching for files that are photos or use "Ithaca" as a tag.

Although you want to find quotations about art collecting, using *art* and *collecting* as search criteria won't find quotations that include "collection" or "collector" or even "collect," which might be appropriate quotations. A good rule of thumb when specifying search text is to use the root of the word; for example, use *collect* to find documents containing "collecting," "collection," "collector," and "collect." Using the root of a word is also called **stemming**. For Howard's search, you can use *art* and *collect* as search criteria.

Next, determine the best way to combine the criteria, as shown in the following list:

- *Art collect* (or *art AND collect*) finds documents that include both words.
- *Art OR collect* finds documents that include at least one of the words.
- *Art NOT collect* finds documents that include "art" but not those that include "collect."
- *"Art collect"* finds documents that include the exact phrase "art collect."
- *(Art collect)* finds documents that include the exact words "art" and "collect" consecutively in either order.

Because the phrase *art collect* will produce the results you want, you'll use it as your search criteria to find quotations about art collecting.

To find files using AND criteria:

1. Click the **Close search** button on the Search Tools Search tab to return to the Ithaca folder in the Documents folder.

2. Click in the **Search Ithaca** box, and then type **art collect**. As you type, Windows searches filenames and file contents that meet your criteria and finds one file. See Figure 6-19.

Figure 6-19   Finding files that contain *art* AND *collect*

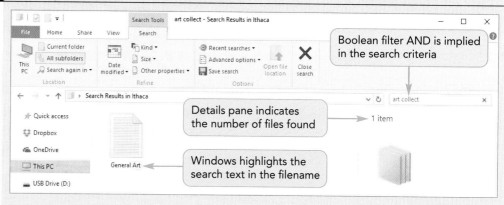

- Boolean filter AND is implied in the search criteria
- Details pane indicates the number of files found → 1 item
- Windows highlights the search text in the filename

3. To verify this file contains a quotation you can use, double-click **General Art** to open it in a text-editing program such as Notepad.

4. Press the **Ctrl+F** keys to open the Find dialog box, type **collect** in the Find what box, click the **Find Next** button until you find a quotation Howard can use, and then close the Find dialog box and Notepad.

Try your search again, this time using the Boolean filter OR to find files that contain either "art" or "collect."

To find files using OR criteria:

1. Display the contents of the Ithaca folder again.

2. In the search box, modify the criterion to **art OR collect**. Now Windows finds four files that contain the word "art" or "collect." See Figure 6-20.

Figure 6-20   Finding files that contain *art* OR *collect*

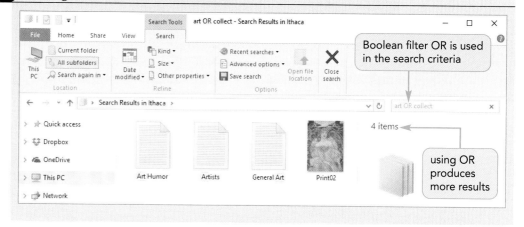

- Boolean filter OR is used in the search criteria
- 4 items
- using OR produces more results
- Art Humor, Artists, General Art, Print02

To pinpoint what you want to find and to refine your search criteria, you can combine Boolean filters and file properties.

Combining Boolean Filters and File Properties

When you search files by file property, you can use Boolean filters to combine criteria. For example, suppose Howard is working on the website and requests a photo of Italian art from the 1400s. You can search the tags of the photo files to find those that contain this text. To search efficiently, you can use the Boolean filter AND to combine the criteria and use an asterisk (*) wildcard to search for photos that include the tags "Italian" and "14*." (If you used the Boolean filter OR, you would find photos of Italian art, but not necessarily art from the 1400s, and photos of art from the 1400s that are not necessarily Italian.) If you use *tag: Italian 14**, Windows searches for files that include "Italian" as a tag and a number whose first two digits are 14 (including 140, 1499, and 14,500) in any property, including the Size property. To restrict the search to tags only, enclose the criteria in parentheses.

To find files by combining file property criteria:

▶ **1.** Display the contents of the Ithaca folder.

▶ **2.** Click in the **Search Ithaca** box, and then type **tag: (Italian 14*)**. Windows finds two files that meet your criteria. See Figure 6-21.

| **Figure 6-21** | **Combining Boolean filters with file properties** |

▶ **3.** Close File Explorer.

You now know many expert techniques to search for files, so you can turn your attention to searching for information on the web.

Searching the Web

The web provides access to a wealth of information; the challenge is to find the information you need or want. You have already learned how to develop search strategies and specific criteria to find files on your computer. You can use many of the same search strategies to find information on the Internet. The first place to start is Cortana, which provides some information from the web. If Cortana can't find what you're seeking, you can click the Web button in Cortana to conduct the same search using Microsoft Edge.

Searching for Web Information with Cortana

You have already used Cortana to search for information from the web when you converted euros to dollars earlier in the module. When you asked Cortana to tell you how many euros equal one dollar, Cortana found the current rate for the currency conversion on the web to use in the calculation. In fact, all of the instant results Cortana provides for calculations, conversions, definitions, flight information, stocks, sports scores, weather, and restaurant information involve gathering information from the web.

INSIGHT

Cortana Voice Search

Instead of typing search text in the Ask me anything box, you can set up Cortana to respond to your voice and use spoken words as search text. You need a microphone attached to or built into your computer to use voice search. To set up Cortana, you click the microphone icon in the Ask me anything box and then complete a wizard (a series of dialog boxes) so that Cortana can detect a microphone and learn to recognize your voice and how you speak. (Cortana is available only in certain regions and recognizes certain languages, including English, Chinese, French, Italian, German, and Spanish.) After you set up Cortana, you can click the microphone icon in the Ask me anything box and then start speaking. Cortana recognizes your speech and uses it as search text. To skip clicking the microphone icon altogether, set up Cortana to respond when you say "Hey, Cortana." Click the Ask me anything box, click the Notebook icon, and then click Settings. Click the slider button to turn the Hey Cortana setting from Off to On to activate it.

Howard is traveling to New York City in a few days to attend a conference for small businesses in the import/export field. He wants to know what kind of weather to expect in New York. For a presentation he will make at the conference, he also needs to find a few facts. For example, he needs to know the population of New York City. You'll show him how to use Cortana to find this information. Unlike searching for files using the Search box in a folder window, with Cortana, you can provide search text using more natural language.

To find weather and flight information with Cortana:

▶ 1. Click in the **Ask me anything** box on the taskbar. Cortana opens in a pane on the desktop.

▶ 2. Type **What's the weather forecast for New York** to display the results in Cortana. See Figure 6-22. Your results might differ.

Figure 6-22 | **Finding weather information with Cortana**

The search results show the current conditions in New York. Cortana can also display the forecast for the next few days.

3. In the search results, click **what's the weather forecast for new york** to display a more detailed forecast for the week in Bing, the Microsoft search engine. See Figure 6-23. Your results might differ.

Trouble? If Cortana displays the forecast instead of opening Edge, click the See more results in Bing.com link.

Figure 6-23   Weather search results in Bing

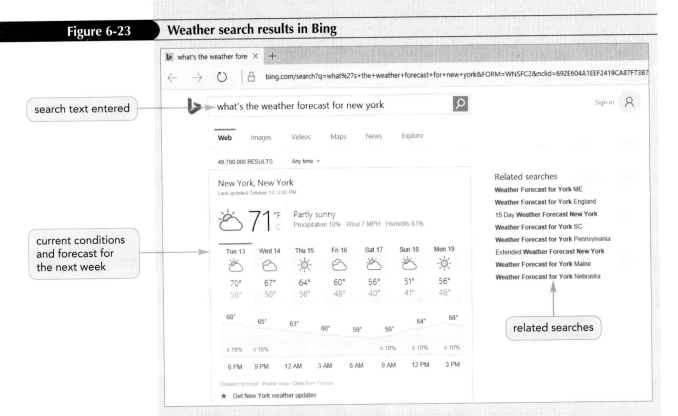

search text entered

current conditions and forecast for the next week

related searches

4. Close Microsoft Edge. Next, you can ask Cortana about the population of New York City.

5. Click in the **Ask me anything** box, and then type **population nyc** to display the results in Cortana, which is about 8.5 million people. Howard also wants to know the size of New York city in square miles.

TIP

To select the text quickly in the Ask me anything box, click the beginning of the text on the left side of the box.

6. Select the text in the Ask me anything box, and then type **how big is nyc** to display the results in Cortana, which is about 470 square miles.

7. To compare the results to Bing, click **how big is nyc** in the Web section of the search results to start Microsoft Edge and display the same results in Bing.

Cortana is designed to make your computing experience enjoyable, so you can ask Cortana to tell you a joke, sing a song, or answer a trivia question.

Searching the Web with Microsoft Edge

Instead of using Cortana to search the web, you can use the more full-featured search tools provided in Microsoft Edge, including the Address bar and a search engine.

The terminology that you use when searching the web with a browser is slightly different from the terminology you use to search for files or settings on your computer. As shown in the Session 6.2 Visual Overview, the word or phrase you use to search the web is typically called a search expression. Each word in the search expression is called a **keyword**. After you enter a search expression in the Microsoft Edge Address bar or the search engine's Search box, Microsoft Edge displays the results, which are links to webpages that meet your criteria. You can click these links, or hits, to access webpages that contain the keywords in your search expression.

When you enter a search expression in the Address bar of Microsoft Edge, it uses a search engine such as Bing or Google. Because searching all of the webpages on the Internet to find those that contain your search expression would take a prohibitive amount of time, search engines typically search a database of indexed webpages. These databases are updated periodically, though not often enough to keep all of the indexed webpages up to date. This is why a page of search results might include inactive or broken links.

Website designers and owners can make their webpages easier for search engines to find by **optimizing** the site. In its webpage headings, an optimized site lists keywords and phrases that you and other web users are likely to use to find the information on the webpages. Conversely, you are more likely to find the webpages you want if you are aware of the types of keywords web designers often use.

PROSKILLS

Problem Solving: Searching the Web Effectively

Because the web provides access to a vast amount of information, finding the information you need can be a problem. Conducting a search that finds millions of results is inefficient, even if search engines list the webpages most relevant to your search first. To work effectively, you need to use search techniques that provide a few high-quality results. Keep the following guidelines in mind to search the Internet efficiently:

- Be specific. If you search for general categories, you'll find an overwhelming number of pages. Searching for specific terms or details is more likely to provide results you can use. For example, instead of searching for "desserts," search for "pear cake recipe."

- Form a question. Think of your search expression as a question you want answered, such as "Which restaurants in the Denver area serve vegetarian food?" Eliminate the articles and common words to form a workable search expression, such as "restaurants Denver vegetarian."

- Modify the search expression. Add keywords to a search expression to reduce the number of pages to review. For example, suppose you search for "pear cake recipe" and find many thousands of results. If you want a recipe similar to the one your Swedish grandmother made, you can add "Swedish" to your search expression.

Now that you've found some general information Howard can use during his trip to New York, he wants to find more specific information. He wants to expand into vintage posters and prints that include travel and movie posters, and he plans to visit a few shops in New York that carry these types of pieces. You offer to search the web to find shops that specialize in vintage art. You'll start the search by using *New York City vintage art shop* as the search expression to find webpages describing shops that specialize in vintage art in New York City.

Because webpages and search indexes change frequently, the search results you find when you perform the steps in this section will differ from those shown in the figures. The following steps use Bing as the search engine. If you are using a different search engine, your results will differ.

To search using a search expression:

▶ **1.** In Microsoft Edge, select the text in the Address bar, type **New York City vintage art shop**, and then press the **Enter** key. Bing looks for webpages containing the search expression you entered, and then displays the results. See Figure 6-24.

| Figure 6-24 | Search results for the search expression *New York City vintage art shop* |

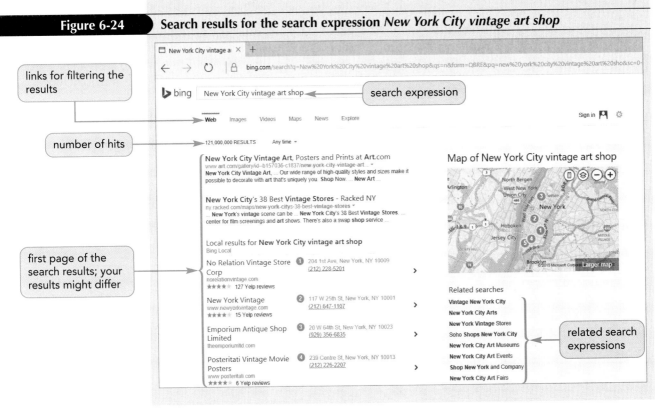

Using "New York City vintage art shop" as the search expression produced about 121 million results, which is not unusual and can change daily. You need to narrow your search to find more useful webpages.

Narrowing Your Search

You can narrow your web search by modifying your search expression or by limiting the kinds of webpages you want in your results. One way to modify your search expression in most search engines is to use quotation marks to search for specific phrases. If you enclose a phrase in quotation marks, you restrict the results to webpages that contain that exact phrase. For example, using a search expression such as *vintage art shop* finds webpages that include those three words anywhere on the page. If you enclose a search expression in quotation marks, as in "vintage art shop," you find only webpages that include the exact text in the specified order.

Another way to modify your search expression is to use the advanced search features that search engines typically offer. Figure 6-25 shows the Advanced Search page from Google, a popular search engine.

Figure 6-25   **Google Advanced Search page**

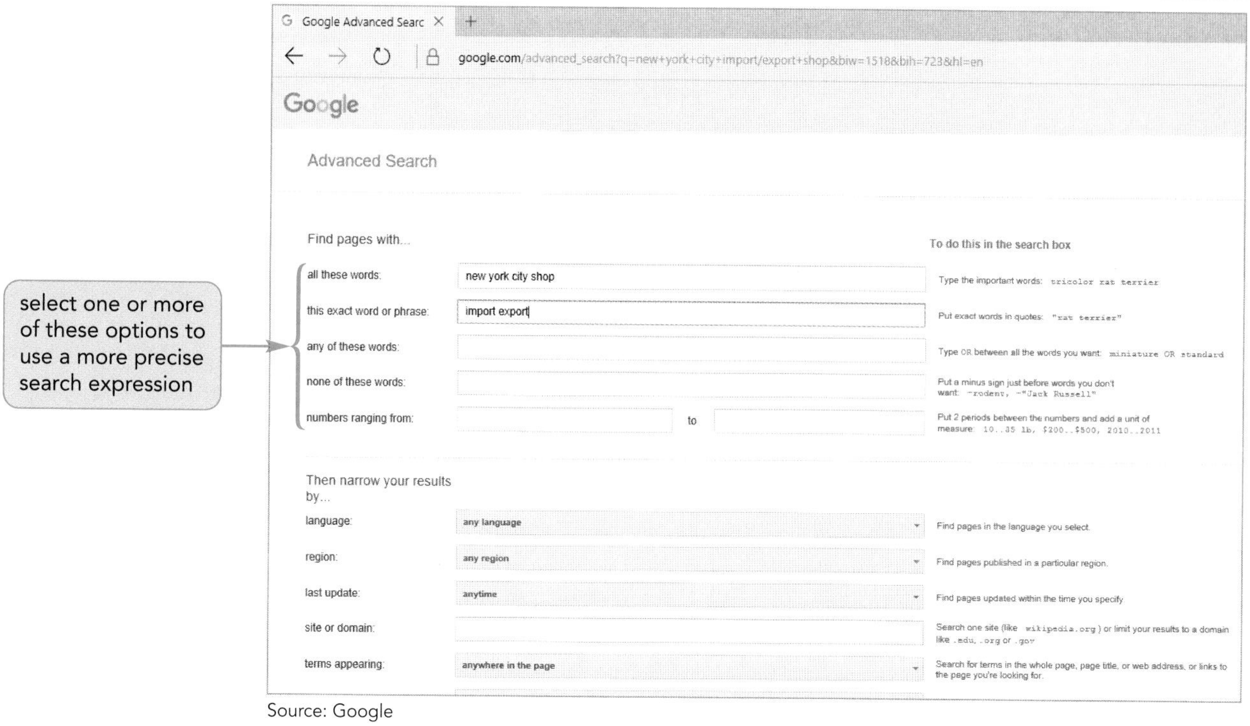

select one or more of these options to use a more precise search expression

Source: Google

Although Bing does not have an Advanced Search page, you can use the same advanced search tools that let you specify and combine search conditions. Most advanced search tools provide the following types of options:

- Find pages that include all of the words. This is the default for most search engines.
- Limit the results to pages that match the exact phrase. This is the same as using quotation marks to enclose an expression.
- Find pages that include at least one of the words in the search expression. This is the same as using OR between each search term.
- Specify keywords that you do not want included on the webpage. This is the same as inserting NOT or a hyphen before the keyword to exclude.

Search engines often provide extensive help information. For example, enter a search term in Google, click the Options button, and then click Search help to display the Search Help webpage, which provides links to basic search information and more advanced tips for searching. In Bing, click the Help link at the bottom of the Bing home page to display the Bing Help page.

Besides providing an advanced search page for narrowing your search expression, most search engines include tabs or links that specify the kind of results you want. For example, the Bing results page shown earlier includes a navigation bar near the top of the page with links such as Web, Images, Videos, and Maps. By default, Bing displays webpages in the results. If you are searching for images, such as photos and drawings, you can click the Images link before or after you enter a search expression to restrict the results to pages including images that meet your criteria.

When you search for *New York City vintage art shop*, many of the results are for vintage clothing shops in New York. Because Howard has time to visit only a couple of shops, he wants to refine the search to exclude vintage clothing stores. To specify this kind of search condition, you can insert a hyphen, or minus sign, before the keyword you want to exclude from the search results. Using NOT before a keyword has the same effect. For Howard, you want to search for vintage art shops in New York City, but not those that sell clothing.

To narrow a search by excluding keywords:

▶ **1.** On the search results page, click in the search box at the top of the page.

▶ **2.** Edit the text so it appears as **New York City vintage art shop -clothing** and then press the **Enter** key. This time, you find many fewer results, some of which are promising for Howard.

INSIGHT

Evaluating Webpages in the Search Results

Although a webpage might be listed at the top of the search results, that doesn't guarantee the page provides reliable and up-to-date information that will meet your needs. On a search engine's webpage, the search results are usually organized into sections. At the top or in another prominent location on the page are sponsored links; companies pay to have these links appear when certain keywords are used in a search expression. The companies pay an additional fee when you click one of their sponsored links. Using sponsored links helps search engines offer their services free to the public. However, that doesn't mean a sponsored link will lead to the information you want. Before using a webpage or citing it as a source, review the content with a critical eye. At the bottom of the webpage, look for the author's name and evidence of the author's credentials. Look for links to the original source of quoted information, which tends to validate the information on a webpage. Also look for signs of bias, such as unsubstantiated claims or extreme points of view.

Howard wonders if you can quickly show examples of vintage art available in New York. To fulfill his request, you can use the Images link on the navigation bar. Google and other search engines include a similar tool. First, however, you should edit the search expression. If you click the Images link now, the results would show images of art shops, not art itself.

To display images of vintage art:

▶ **1.** On the search results page, click in the search box at the top of the page.

▶ **2.** Edit the text so it appears as **New York City vintage art** and then press the **Enter** key. The results include a section that previews images of vintage art, most of them using New York City as the subject. This isn't exactly what Howard was looking for, but the results might help him find the kind of vintage travel art he is seeking.

▶ **3.** In the navigation bar, click the **Images** link. At the top of the search results, Bing displays suggested keywords for narrowing the search and a toolbar of buttons for filtering the results by image size or color, for example. In the main part of the page, Bing displays many images that meet the search criteria, whereas, at the bottom, it displays images that other users search for after searching for "New York City vintage art." See Figure 6-26. Your results might differ.

| Figure 6-26 | Displaying images in the search results |

Images selected for image search

ways to narrow the search results

images that meet the search criteria

images that other users search for after using the search expression

Howard thinks that his clientele would be interested in vintage postcards of New York City.

4. In the search results, click an image of a vintage postcard of New York City, such as the first image shown in Figure 6-26. Instead of displaying a webpage, Bing displays a larger version of the image and related information, including the webpage that displays the image. See Figure 6-27. Your image might differ.

| Figure 6-27 | Displaying image information |

selected image

select other images in the search results

information about the selected image

From here, Howard can explore other vintage New York City postcards, view and possibly purchase the postcard at a commercial website, or search for other types of vintage New York City images.

Choosing Search Engines

In Microsoft Edge, you can choose which search engine you want to use when you enter keywords in the Address bar to search for information on the Internet. Microsoft Edge uses Bing by default; however, you can change the default to use a different search engine to increase your searching options. Microsoft Edge includes search engines only if they use Open Search technology, so it might not support your favorite search engine. Open the home page of the search engine's website and then change the Microsoft Edge settings to select a default search engine. If Microsoft Edge lists the search engine whose home page you displayed, you can use it as the default search engine.

Keep in mind that you can use a search engine's website, such as google.com, to perform a search even if it is not selected as your search engine.

REFERENCE

Adding a Search Engine

- In Microsoft Edge, navigate to the website of the search engine you want to use.
- Click the More button in the navigation bar, and then click Settings.
- Click the View advanced settings button.
- Click the Change button in the Search in the address bar with section.
- Click a search engine and then click the Set as default button.

You and Howard often use Wikipedia, an online encyclopedia, to search for information. Microsoft Edge lets you use Wikipedia as a search engine, which is handy if you want to look up factual information about a topic. You'll set Wikipedia as the default search engine so you can use Wikipedia for your next search.

To change the default search engine:

1. Click in the **Address bar**, type **en.wikipedia.org**, and then press the **Enter** key to display the main Wikipedia page.

2. Click the **More** button ⋯ in the navigation bar, and then click **Settings** to display the Settings pane.

3. Scroll the Settings pane and then click the **View advanced settings** button.

4. Scroll the Advanced settings list, click the **Change** button in the Search in the address bar with section to display search engines, including Wikipedia. See Figure 6-28.

   Trouble? If Wikipedia is not listed, close Microsoft Edge, and then repeat Steps 1–4 to allow Microsoft Edge to detect Wikipedia. If it still does not detect Wikipedia, click the webpage to close the Change search engine pane.

| Figure 6-28 | Setting the default search engine |

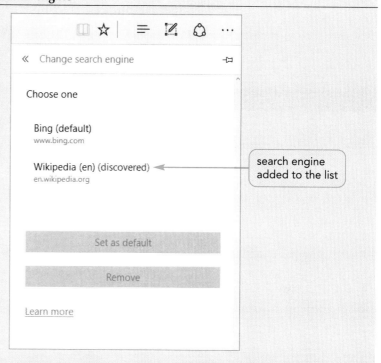

5. Click **Wikipedia (en) (discovered)** and then click the **Set as default** button to make Wikipedia the default search engine.

   Trouble? If you selected Wikipedia as a search engine before performing these steps, the Change search engine pane lists the search engine as Wikipedia (en).

6. Close Microsoft Edge.

One of Ithaca Imports' most popular prints is *Woman with a Parasol* by Claude Monet. Customers often ask about Monet's biography, especially his period in Giverny, where he created *Woman with a Parasol* and his famous water lily paintings. Howard would like you to write a short biography of Monet to post on the Ithaca Imports website. You can use Wikipedia as the search engine to find a summary of Monet's life and works. When you are displaying a webpage, you can use the Find toolbar in Microsoft Edge to find specific information on the page. After you find suitable biographical information about Claude Monet, you'll show Howard how to search for information about Monet's life in Giverny using the Find toolbar in Microsoft Edge.

To use Wikipedia as the search engine:

1. Start Microsoft Edge, click in the **Address bar**, type **claude monet**, and then press the **Enter** key. Microsoft Edge uses Wikipedia as the search engine and finds a Wikipedia entry for Claude Monet.

   Trouble? If you could not select Wikipedia as the search engine in the preceding set of steps, click in the Address bar to select the text, type "en .wikipedia.org," and then press the Enter key. Click in the Search box on the Wikipedia page, type "claude monet," and then press the Enter key.

2. Press the **Ctrl+F** keys to display the Find toolbar at the top of the Microsoft Edge window.

3. In the Find on page box, type **giverny**. Microsoft Edge highlights all instances of "giverny" and displays the number of matches on the page. Your number might differ. See Figure 6-29.

Figure 6-29   **Using the Find toolbar**

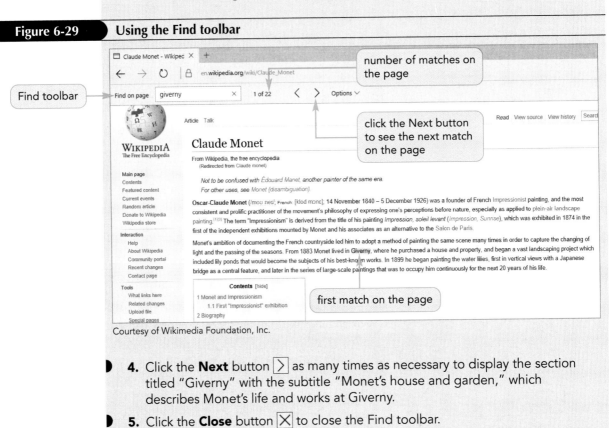

Courtesy of Wikimedia Foundation, Inc.

4. Click the **Next** button ⟩ as many times as necessary to display the section titled "Giverny" with the subtitle "Monet's house and garden," which describes Monet's life and works at Giverny.

5. Click the **Close** button ✕ to close the Find toolbar.

6. Close Microsoft Edge.

Howard plans to provide biographies on other artists, so you can use Wikipedia as a search engine to find information about their lives and works.

Restoring Your Settings

If you are working in a computer lab or on a computer other than your own, complete the steps in this section to restore the original settings on the computer.

To restore your settings:

1. Open File Explorer, navigate to the **Users > user name** folder (where *user name* is your user name), and then open the **Searches** folder.

2. Move the **JPG Sept** saved search to the Ithaca folder in the Documents folder.

3. Click in the **Search Ithaca** box to display the Search Tools Search tab, click the **Advanced options** button in the Options group, and then click **File contents** under the In non-indexed locations section to remove the checkmark.

4. Move the **Ithaca** folder to the Module6 > Module folder provided with your Data Files.

5. Close the Details pane in the folder windows, and then close File Explorer.

6. Start Microsoft Edge, click the **More** button ⋯ in the navigation bar, and then click **Settings** to display the Settings pane. Click the **View advanced settings** button, click the **Change** button in the Search in the address bar with section, click **Bing (www.bing.com)**, and then click the **Set as default** button. Close Microsoft Edge.

7. Click the **Start** button ⊞, type **clock**, click **Add clocks for different time zones**, click the first **Show this clock** check box to remove the checkmark, and then click the **OK** button to close the Date and Time dialog box.

8. Close any open windows.

Session 6.2 Quick Check

REVIEW

1. What shorthand notation would you use to find files that include the word "artist" in the Title property?

2. If you use tag: French OR 1900 as search criteria, what files would you find?

3. Explain how you can quickly find weather conditions in Los Angeles.

4. The word or phrase you use to search the web is typically called a(n) _____.

5. If you enclose a phrase in quotation marks in a search expression, how does that affect the results?

6. After using a search expression to search the web, how can you specify that you want to display only news stories in the results?

7. Explain what happens if you use Wikipedia as the search engine in Microsoft Edge and use Michelangelo as the search expression.

PRACTICE

Review Assignments

Data Files needed for the Review Assignments: Japan01.jpg–Japan10.jpg, Japanese Prints.mp4

Ithaca Imports purchased a collection of Japanese prints, and you are now working with Howard on developing and showcasing the collection. You have taken photographs of the Japanese prints and created a video featuring a few of the prints. Howard wants you to help him search for apps that can play video and find Japanese prints for the shop's website. Just for fun, he also wants to include a joke on the home page. Complete the following steps:

1. In the Documents folder on your hard disk, create a folder named **Prints**. Move all of the files in the Module6 > Review folder provided with your Data Files to the Prints folder.

2. Use Cortana to search for a file that contains the word "Japanese" in its filename. Select a media file and then play the file.

3. Press the Print Screen key to capture an image of the screen, and then paste the image in a new Paint or WordPad file. Save the file as **Video App** in the Module6 > Review folder provided with your Data Files. Minimize Paint or WordPad, and then close the Movies & TV app.

4. Search for an app you can use to play media files, and then start the app. (*Hint*: If a dialog box opens where you can select initial settings, click the Recommended settings option button, and then click the Finish button.) Click Videos in the left pane of the app window, drag the Japanese Prints video stored in the Prints folder to the app's window, and then click the Play button to play the video.

5. Press the Print Screen key to capture an image of the screen, and then paste the image in a new Paint or WordPad file. Save the file as **Media App** in the Module6 > Review folder provided with your Data Files. Close the media app. Minimize Paint or WordPad.

6. Search for a setting on your computer related to AutoPlay settings for media files, and then display the setting for using AutoPlay for all media and devices. Press the Print Screen key to capture an image of the window, and then paste the image in a new Paint or WordPad file. Save the file as **AutoPlay** in the Module6 > Review folder provided with your Data Files. Close the window with the AutoPlay settings. Minimize the Paint or WordPad window.

7. Search for all of the JPG files in the Prints folder.

8. Add the following tags to Japan03: **Mt. Fuji; landscape; Japan**. Change the filename to **Mountain Landscape**.

9. Add the following tags to Japan04: **woodblock; traditional; Japan**. Change the filename to **Kimono**.

10. In the Prints folder, search for JPG photos that have *woodblock* as a tag. Save the search as **JPG woodblock**. Move the JPG woodblock file to the Prints folder.

11. Move the files you found to a new subfolder named **Woodblocks** in the Prints folder.

12. In the Prints folder, find a photo that has *watercolor* and *zen* as tags. Change the name of this file to **Zen**. Close File Explorer. Minimize the Paint or WordPad window, and then close all other open windows.

13. Ask Cortana to tell you a joke. Press the Print Screen key to capture an image of the search results, and then paste the image in a new Paint or WordPad file. Save the file as **Joke** in the Module6 > Review folder provided with your Data Files.

14. Start Microsoft Edge and use Bing to find webpages providing information about traditional Japanese prints. Narrow the search to find images of traditional Japanese woodblock prints. (*Hint*: Click the Images link on the navigation bar.) Press the Print Screen key to capture an image of the first screen of search results, and then paste the image in a new Paint or WordPad file. Save the file as **Traditional** in the Module6 > Review folder provided with your Data Files.

15. Use a search engine other than Bing to search for Hiroshige woodblock prints. (Hiroshige is a Japanese artist.) Press the Print Screen key to capture an image of the search results, and then paste the image in a new Paint or WordPad file. Save the file as **Hiroshige** in the Module6 > Review folder provided with your Data Files.

16. Restore your computer by restoring Bing as the default search engine in Microsoft Edge. Move the Prints folder from the Documents folder on your hard disk to the Module6 > Review folder provided with your Data Files. Close the Details pane in the folder window, and then close all open windows.

APPLY

Case Problem 1

Data Files needed for this Case Problem: Flag01.jpg–Flag10.jpg

Sister Cities Association   Richard and Debra Cowen run the Sister Cities Association in York, Pennsylvania. The organization is devoted to promoting international goodwill and educating Americans about other countries by forming sister city relationships between their city and a city in another country. You work as an all-around assistant to Richard and Debra. Currently, they want you to help them find graphics for their webpages using flags of the world. They also want to back up their files online, and ask you to find information about apps they can use to do so. Complete the following steps:

1. Search for an app you can use to read news stories. Start the app, maximize the window, and then click a link to display technology news.

2. Press the Print Screen key to capture an image of the app, and then paste the image in a new Paint or WordPad file. Save the file as **News App** in the Module6 > Case1 folder provided with your Data Files. Close the app.

3. Search for a setting on your computer related to backups. Display the setting or tool for backing up using File History.

4. Press the Print Screen key to capture an image of the tool, and then paste the image in a new Paint or WordPad file. Save the file as **Backups** in the Module6 > Case1 folder provided with your Data Files. Close the window.

5. Use Cortana to find the current time in Arles, France, which is the sister city to York, Pennsylvania. Press the Print Screen key to capture an image of the result, and then paste the image in a new Paint or WordPad file. Save the file as **Time** in the Module6 > Case1 folder provided with your Data Files.

6. Open File Explorer and then review the tags and other properties already assigned to the files in the Module6 > Case1 folder. Add a tag to the Flag04 and the Flag09 files based on information in the other properties.

7. Using the Details pane, add **Liz Kerr** as the author of the following images: Flag06, Flag07, and Flag10.

8. Use the Search box to find a photo that includes the tag *2018* and has C Maki as the author. Rename the file **2018**.

9. Start Microsoft Edge and use Bing to find webpages providing information on Arles, France. Narrow the search to find images of the city. Press the Print Screen key to capture an image of the screen, and then paste the image in a new Paint or WordPad file. Save the file as **Arles** in the Module6 > Case1 folder provided with your Data Files.

🌐 **Explore** 10. If necessary, set Google as the default search engine in Microsoft Edge, and then use Google to search for information about Arles, France. Display a map of the city. (*Hint*: Click the Maps button near the top of the webpage.) Press the Print Screen key to capture an image of the screen, and then paste the image in a new Paint or WordPad file. Save the file as **Arles Map** in the Module6 > Case1 folder provided with your Data Files.

11. Restore your computer by restoring the original default search engine in Microsoft Edge. Close all open windows.

CHALLENGE

Case Problem 2

Data Files needed for this Case Problem: Music01.png–Music10.png

Sonoma Chamber Orchestra   Isabel Williams is the marketing director of the Sonoma Chamber Orchestra in Sonoma, California. She is developing new print brochures to make available at ticket windows and throughout the orchestra hall during concerts. As an intern at the Sonoma Chamber Orchestra, you help Isabel prepare promotional materials. She asks you to help her find and organize images that will fit within the design of the new brochure and to research general information about composers and orchestral music. Isabel is also interested in information about music-playing apps that she can use to listen to music. Complete the following steps:

Explore 1. Search for an app you can use to play music. Start the app, maximize the window, and then click a link to get music in the Store.

Explore 2. In the Store window, scroll to the bottom of the page, and then select Classical as the genre. Press the Print Screen key to capture an image of the music app and the Store, and then paste the image in a new Paint or WordPad file. Save the file as **Music Store** in the Module6 > Case2 folder provided with your Data Files. Close the Store window and the music app.

3. Search for a setting that lets you adjust the system volume. Open the setting window, and then press the Print Screen key to capture an image of the window. Paste the image in a new Paint or WordPad file. Save the file as **System Volume** in the Module6 > Case2 folder provided with your Data Files. Close the volume setting window.

4. Using the Details pane, add a Date taken of **11/14/18** to the following files in the Module6 > Case2 folder: Music01, Music06, and Music09.

Explore 5. Using the Details tab in the Properties dialog box, add a Date taken of **10/24/18** to the following files: Music02, Music04, and Music05. (*Hint*: Right-click the file and then click Properties on the shortcut menu to open the Properties dialog box for the file.)

Explore 6. Using **dimensions** as the property name in the Search box, find files in the Module6 > Case2 folder that have 600 pixels as one of their dimensions. Move the file(s) to a new folder named **Dim 600** in the Module6 > Case2 folder provided with your Data Files.

Explore 7. Using **size** as the property name in the Search box, find files In the Module6 > Case2 folder that are larger than 100 KB in size. (*Hint*: Add KB to the search text.) Move the files to a new folder named **Large** in the Module6 > Case2 folder provided with your Data Files.

Explore 8. Start Microsoft Edge and use Bing to find webpages providing information on classical music styles. Select a link listed in the "Related searches for classical music styles" list. Press the Print Screen key to capture an image of the screen, and then paste the image in a new Paint or WordPad file. Save the file as **Classical Music** in the Module6 > Case2 folder provided with your Data Files.

9. Explore at least one of the links in the results and then select a classical music genre.

10. Use any other search engine to conduct a search for information on the classical music genre you selected. Open a page displaying information about this topic. Use the Find toolbar to find information on the page about a composer. Press the Print Screen key to capture an image of the screen showing the Find toolbar, and then paste the image in a new Paint or WordPad file. Save the file as **Composer** in the Module6 > Case2 folder provided with your Data Files. Close all open windows.

11. Restore the original default search engine, and then close all open windows.

Case Problem 3

Data Files needed for this Case Problem: House01.jpg–House10.jpg

Great House Walking Tour   Dwight Payton is an America architect living in London, England. Wanting to combine his two major enthusiasms—British great houses and walking for fitness—Dwight started a small travel business that conducts walking tours to great houses throughout Great Britain. Dwight publishes an online newsletter to attract travelers to his tours. He has a collection of images of the great houses he tours and needs to organize them. He also wants to find a new app he can use for his online newsletter. He's heard about Flipboard and wants to know if that app would be suitable. As his editorial assistant, you offer to help him find this information and organize the images for the newsletter. Complete the following steps:

1. Search for Flipboard and then start the app. Press the Print Screen key to capture an image of the app. Paste the image in a new Paint or WordPad file. Save the file as **Flipboard** in the Module6 > Case3 folder provided with your Data Files.

2. Use the app to select Travel as a category of content to include. Press the Print Screen key to capture an image of the opening window showing your selection. Paste the image in a new Paint or WordPad file. Save the file as **Travel** in the Module6 > Case3 folder provided with your Data Files. Close Flipboard.

3. Working in the Module6 > Case3 folder, add **Yorkshire** as a tag to the House01 and House03 files. Add the tag **Wales** to the House02 file and the tag **Scotland** to the House05 file.

4. Conduct a search in the Case3 folder to find files with the word "palace" in any of the properties. Move the files you found into a new folder named **Palaces** in the Module6 > Case3 folder.

5. Conduct a search in the Case3 folder to find files with "park" in any of the properties. Move the files you found into a new folder named **Parks** in the Module6 > Case3 folder.

6. Conduct another search in the Case3 folder to find files with "Yorkshire" as a tag. Copy the files you found into a new folder named **Yorkshire** in the Module6 > Case3 folder. (*Hint*: Be sure to copy rather than move the files.)

7. Start Microsoft Edge and conduct a search to produce results similar to those shown in Figure 6-30.

Figure 6-30   **Google search results**

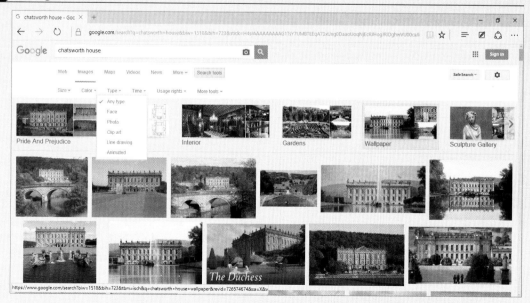

8. Press the Print Screen key to capture an image of the first screen of search results, and then paste the image in a new Paint or WordPad file. Save the file as **Chatsworth** in the Module6 > Case3 folder provided with your Data Files.

9. Close all open windows.

Case Problem 4

There are no Data Files needed for this Case Problem.

Sabota Reference   Tanya and Gary Sabota are starting a company called Sabota Reference. They plan to provide research services for businesses and others, especially those who need demographic information for marketing research. They hired you as an assistant and want you to investigate the types of information available on the web, including tools that search engines provide. Complete the following steps:

1. Start Microsoft Edge and use any search engine to research the following terms:

   Web 2.0

   Web 3.0

   Keyword search engines

   Blog search engines (provide examples)

2. Use WordPad or another word-processing program to create a document that lists these terms and provides a definition for each one. Save the document as **Research** in the Module6 > Case4 folder.

3. Search engines such as Google and Bing offer tools for marketing research. For example, Bing has a collection of tools called Bing solutions that help businesses reach more customers. Google has the AdWords, AdSense, and Analytics tools for business. Research one of these tools to learn its purpose and how it works.

4. In the Research document, describe the Bing or Google business tool you researched and then explain how Sabota Reference or another business might use it. Save the document.

OBJECTIVES

Session 7.1
- Explore computer graphics
- Create and edit graphics in Paint
- Add text to a graphic
- Apply color and draw shapes in an image

Session 7.2
- Acquire, view, and share photos
- Find, play, and organize music files
- Play a slide show with music
- Play video files

Managing Multimedia Files

Working with Graphics, Photos, Music, and Videos

Case | *FreeSail Boat Club*

Shawn Graham and Oscar Aragon own the FreeSail Boat Club in Seattle, Washington, which offers memberships to people in the Seattle area who want to enjoy sailing without the commitment of owning and maintaining a boat. As an intern at the business, you work with customers to select boats and memberships, arrange for sailing lessons, and help the front-desk staff with sales and billing. Because you have a special interest in graphic design, you are also working with the marketing manager to create graphics the club can use to market and sell its services. Your first projects are to create a logo for the club's website and email stationery, and to assemble a multimedia presentation to showcase the boats available to members.

In this module, you'll learn how to create, acquire, and modify multimedia files, including graphics, photos, music, and videos. You'll also explore how to organize and play audio files. Finally, you'll learn how to share media files with others and set up a multimedia slide show.

STARTING DATA FILES

Module
Frame.png
Lifesaver.png
Sail01.jpg–Sail10.jpg
Sailboat.png
Sailing Lessons.mp4
Sailing.mp3
Waves.mp3

Review
Anchor.png
Frame.png
Piano1.mp3
Piano2.mp3
Sailboat Parts.png
Shipwheel.png
Sight1.jpg–Sight7.jpg

Case1
Class1.jpg–Class8.jpg
Design.png
Drums.mp3
Swing.mp3

Case2
Chicago.png
Game01.png–Game10.png
Mystery.mp3

Case3
Costume1.jpg–Costume5.jpg
Mask.jpg
Prelude.mp3

Case4
Banner.png
Green.png
Seed.png
Tree.png

Session 7.1 Visual Overview:

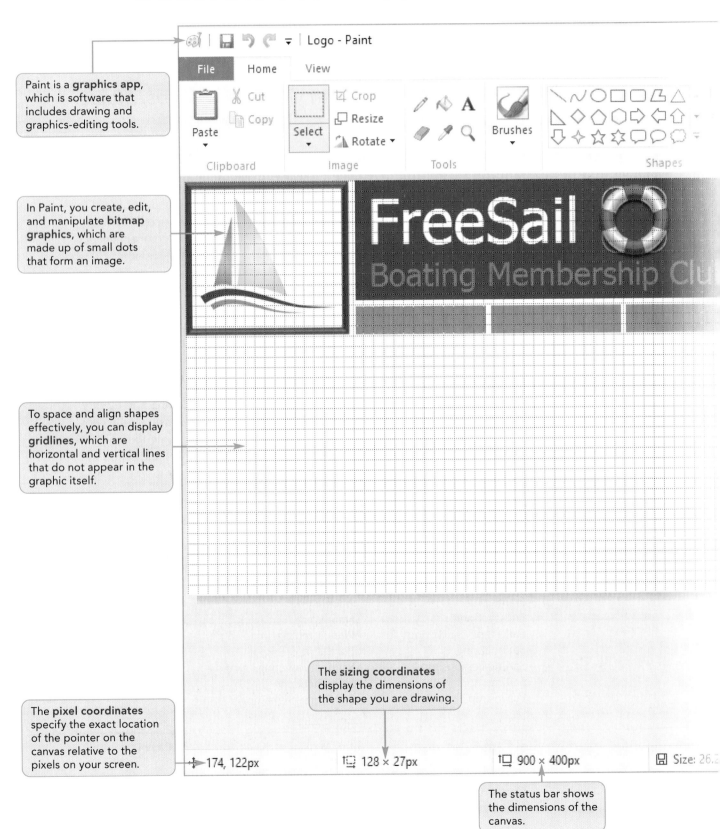

Paint is a **graphics app**, which is software that includes drawing and graphics-editing tools.

In Paint, you create, edit, and manipulate **bitmap graphics**, which are made up of small dots that form an image.

To space and align shapes effectively, you can display **gridlines**, which are horizontal and vertical lines that do not appear in the graphic itself.

The **pixel coordinates** specify the exact location of the pointer on the canvas relative to the pixels on your screen.

The **sizing coordinates** display the dimensions of the shape you are drawing.

The status bar shows the dimensions of the canvas.

Logo - Paint

File   Home   View

Paste   Cut   Copy   Clipboard

Select   Image   Crop   Resize   Rotate

Tools   Brushes

Shapes

FreeSail
Boating Membership Clu

174, 122px   128 × 27px   900 × 400px   Size: 26.2

Creating Graphics in Paint

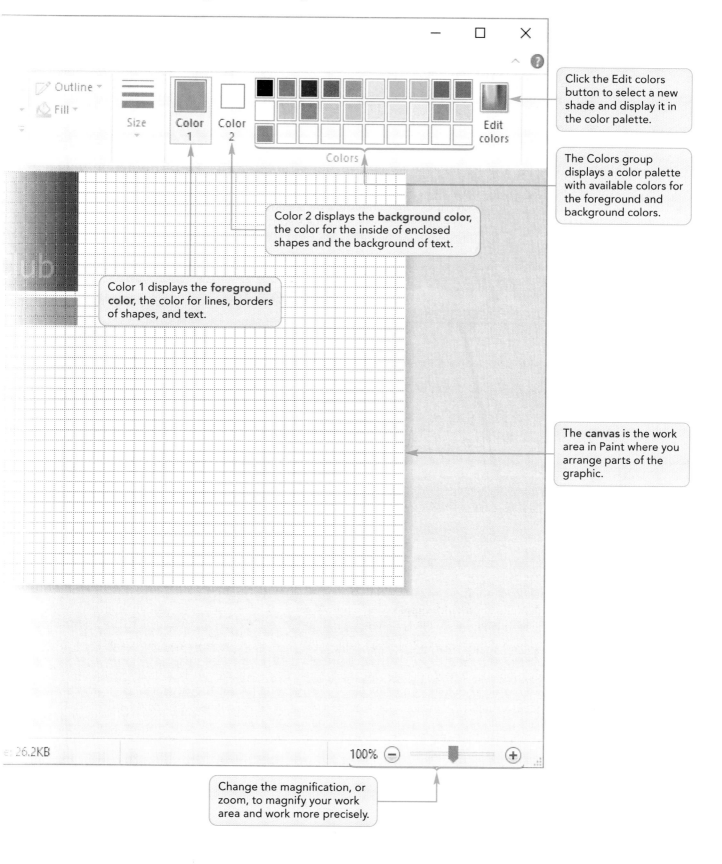

Click the Edit colors button to select a new shade and display it in the color palette.

The Colors group displays a color palette with available colors for the foreground and background colors.

Color 2 displays the **background color**, the color for the inside of enclosed shapes and the background of text.

Color 1 displays the **foreground color**, the color for lines, borders of shapes, and text.

The **canvas** is the work area in Paint where you arrange parts of the graphic.

Change the magnification, or zoom, to magnify your work area and work more precisely.

Exploring Computer Graphics

Pictures and other images enhance your experience of working on a computer and make the documents you produce more appealing and engaging. Pictures on a computer are called **graphics images**, or **graphics**. A computer graphic is different from a drawing on a piece of paper because a drawing is an actual image, whereas a computer graphic is a file that displays an image on a computer screen. Computer graphics come in two fundamental types: bitmap and vector.

When you manipulate a bitmap graphic, you work with a grid of dots, called pixels. A bitmap graphic (or bitmap for short) is created from rows of colored pixels that together form an image. The simplest bitmaps have only two colors, with each pixel being black or white. Bitmaps become more complex as they include more colors. Photographs or pictures with shading can have millions of colors, which increases file size. Bitmaps are appropriate for detailed graphics, such as photographs and the images displayed on a computer monitor. See Figure 7-1. Typical types of bitmap file formats include PNG, JPG, GIF, and BMP. (You'll learn more about graphics file formats later.) You create and edit bitmaps using graphics apps such as Adobe Photoshop and Windows Paint. Bitmap-editing programs are also called painting programs.

Figure 7-1	Bitmap graphics

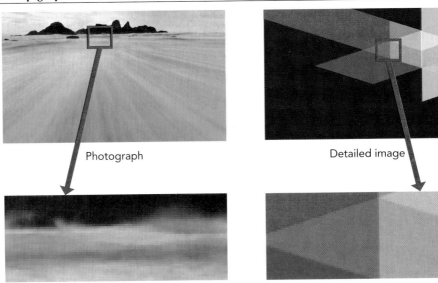

Photograph   Detailed image

Pixels in bitmapped images

In contrast, a **vector graphic** is created by mathematical formulas that define the shapes used in the image. When you work with a vector graphic, you interact with a collection of lines. Rather than a grid of pixels, a vector graphic consists of shapes, curves, lines, and text that together make a picture. While a bitmap image contains information about the color of each pixel, a vector graphic contains instructions about where to place each component. Vector images are appropriate for simple drawings, such as line art and graphs, and for fonts. See Figure 7-2. Typical types of vector file formats include WMF, SWF, and SVG, a standard for vector images on the web. You use drawing programs such as Adobe Illustrator to create and edit vector images.

Figure 7-2 | **Vector graphics**

Aa Bb Cc

Aa Bb Cc

Fonts are a kind of vector image

A vector shape is a collection of
points, lines, and curves

Edges stay smooth when a vector image is enlarged

Decision Making: Selecting Bitmap or Vector Graphics

If you're designing materials that include graphics, such as a webpage or flyer, one of your first decisions is whether to use bitmap or vector graphics. Keep the following guidelines in mind as you make this decision:

- In general, a bitmap file is much larger than a similar vector file, making vector files more suitable for displaying graphics on webpages.
- Avoid resizing bitmap graphics significantly because resolution (the number of pixels in an image) affects their quality. If you enlarge a small bitmap graphic, it often looks jagged because you are redistributing the pixels in the image. If you reduce the size of a large bitmap graphic, its features might be indistinct and fuzzy. On the other hand, you can resize vector graphics without an effect on quality because vectors redraw their shapes when you resize them.
- To edit vector graphics, you often need to use the same drawing program that was used to create them. Before you acquire vector graphics from various sources, make sure you have the program that created them in case you need to edit them. In contrast, most painting programs can open many types of bitmapped graphic formats.
- Bitmaps are suitable for photographs and photorealistic images, while vector graphics are more practical for typesetting or graphic design.

You can add graphics files to your computer in a few ways. One way is to use a **scanner**, which is a device that converts a paper image into an electronic file that you can open and work with on your computer. Another popular method is to use an external or built-in digital camera to take photos and then store the images on your computer. You can also capture images displayed on your computer screen and save them as graphics. You have already captured screen images using the Print Screen key on your keyboard. In addition, Windows 10 provides the Snipping Tool as an accessory. Instead of capturing the full screen, you can use the Snipping Tool to capture a window, Start menu tile, or any other part of the screen. Software and websites also provide graphics you can use, often as **clip art**, or completed pictures and symbols you can add to electronic documents. The clip art images websites provide are usually line drawings and, therefore, vector images. Many websites maintain online catalogs of drawings, images, and photographs that are available for download. Some of these sites charge a membership fee, some charge per image, and others provide copyright-free images that are also free of charge.

To edit a graphic or create one from scratch, you use a graphics app. Windows 10 includes a basic graphics app called Paint, which lets you create, edit, and manipulate bitmap graphics, though not vector graphics. Many programs designed for Windows 10, including Microsoft Office, include tools for creating and editing vector graphics such as charts, flowcharts, and other drawings in a document or worksheet, for example. Shawn wants to combine two images to create the FreeSail logo; because they are both bitmap graphics, you can use Paint for this project.

Creating Graphics in Paint

As you already know, Paint is a Windows 10 app that you can use to create and modify bitmap graphics. Using Paint, you can draw shapes, add and change colors, insert text, remove parts of a picture, and copy and paste images, including those you capture on your computer screen. Shawn is ready to learn about Paint, so you can start the app and introduce him to its graphic tools.

To start Paint:

▶ 1. Click in the **Ask me anything** box on the taskbar, and then type **Paint** to search for the Paint app.

▶ 2. Click **Paint** in the search results to start Paint. If necessary, resize the Paint window to display all of the tools on the Home tab.

When you start Paint without opening a picture, the Paint window is mostly blank, providing many tools for drawing and painting. The white area in the Paint window is the canvas, where you work with your graphic. Above the canvas is the ribbon, which opens to the Home tab by default. The status bar at the bottom of the window provides information about the tools you select and about the location of the pointer when it's in the canvas. See Figure 7-3.

Figure 7-3   Paint window

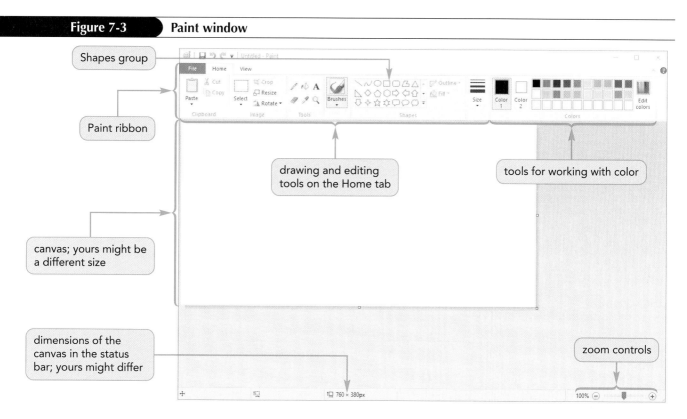

Figure 7-4 describes the tools on the Home tab that you can use to create and edit graphics.

Figure 7-4   Paint tools

Tool	Icon	Description
Clipboard Group		
Paste		Insert an image from the Clipboard or one stored on your computer.
Cut	X Cut	Remove some or all of the image and store it on the Clipboard.
Copy	Copy	Copy some or all of the image and store it on the Clipboard.
Image Group		
Select	Select	Select a rectangular or free-form part of an image.
Crop	Crop	Remove part of an image from its sides.
Resize	Resize	Make some or all of an image larger or smaller, or change the slant of an image horizontally or vertically by degrees.
Rotate	Rotate ▾	Rotate or flip some or all of an image.
Tools Group		
Pencil		Draw a free-form line or one pixel at a time.
Fill with color		Fill an enclosed area with the selected color.
Text	A	Add text to an image.
Eraser		Erase a part of an image.
Color picker		Pick up a color in an image to set the current foreground or background color.
Magnifier		Change the magnification and zoom into or out of an image.
Brushes	Brushes	Paint free-form lines and curves using a brush in a variety of styles.
Shapes Group		
Shapes gallery	n/a	Draw various shapes, including lines, rectangles, and ellipses (circles).
Outline	Outline ▾	Select a style for the line or border as you draw.
Fill	Fill ▾	Select a style for the fill (inside area) as you draw.
Size	Size	Select a width for the line or border as you draw.
Colors Group		
Color 1	Color	Select the foreground color (the color for lines, borders of shapes, and text).
Color 2	Color	Select the background color (the color for the inside of enclosed shapes and the background of text).
Color palette	n/a	Select a color to change the foreground or background color.
Edit colors	Edit colors	Select a color that does not appear on the palette.

Opening a Graphic in Paint

You open a graphic in Paint the same way you open a file in any Windows 10 program—
use the Open dialog box to navigate to where you store the image file, select the file,
and then open it. Paint can keep only one graphic open at a time, similar to the way
Notepad handles files. If you are working with a graphic and then try to open another
one, Paint closes the first graphic and gives you a chance to save your changes before
opening the new graphic. If you want to work with a second image at the same time as
the first image, you can start another session of Paint and open the second image.

Shawn asks you to show him how to open the two PNG files he found so you can discuss how to combine them to create a single image.

To open the two image files:

1. Click the **File** tab on the ribbon, and then click **Open**. The Open dialog box opens.

2. Navigate to the **Module7 > Module** folder provided with your Data Files.

3. Click **Sailboat** in the list of files, and then click the **Open** button. The sailboat image opens in the Paint window. See Figure 7-5.

| Figure 7-5 | Sailboat image open in Paint |

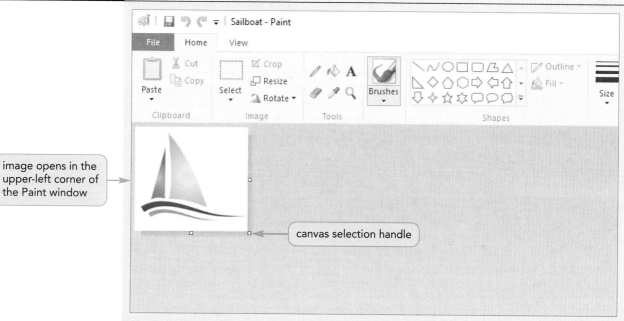

image opens in the upper-left corner of the Paint window

canvas selection handle

4. To examine the second image, click the **File** tab, navigate to the **Module7 > Module** folder if necessary, and then click **Open**.

5. In the file list, click **Frame** and then click the **Open** button. Paint closes the sailboat image so only the frame image appears in the Paint window.

Now that you've seen the two images Shawn wants to use, you can plan the logo graphic. Clearly, the best way to combine these images is to insert the sailboat image inside the frame. You also need to add the text "FreeSail Boating Membership Club" to the graphic. After making a few sketches, you and Shawn agree on the design shown in Figure 7-6.

| Figure 7-6 | Design for the logo |

blue frame

sailboat image

colored background

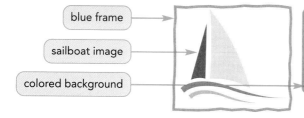

FreeSail
Boating Membership Club

To start creating this design, you need to add the sailboat image to the center of the frame. You'll show Shawn how to do this shortly. Before you do, you should save the Frame file with a new name in case you need the original again in its unchanged state.

Saving a Graphics File

When you save a graphics file with a new name, you use the Save As dialog box, as you do in other Windows apps. In the Save As dialog box, you select a location for the file, provide a filename, and select a file type, or format, if necessary. Paint can save and open images in many bitmap formats, and each format has its pros and cons. To work effectively with graphics, you should understand the basics of the most popular Paint file bitmap formats: PNG, JPG, GIF, and BMP. A fifth file format—TIF—is useful if you are creating images for print. PNG is the default format in Windows 10.

When you create a graphics file, you choose its format based on what you intend to do with the image and where you want to display it. If you want to use the image on a website or send it via email, for example, you need an image with a small file size. In this case, you should choose a file format that compresses color information. For example, if a picture has an area of solid color, it doesn't need to store the same color information for each pixel. Instead, the file can store an instruction to repeat the color until it changes. This space-saving technique is called **compression**. Some compression methods save space without sacrificing image quality, and others are designed to save as much space as possible, even if the image is degraded. Figure 7-7 summarizes the pros and cons of five bitmap graphics formats.

| Figure 7-7 | Graphics file formats |

File Format	Advantages	Disadvantages	Use for
Graphics Interchange Format (GIF)	Compresses images without losing quality and allows animation	Not suitable for photographs	Graphics such as logos, line drawings, and icons
Joint Photographic Experts Group (JPG or JPEG)	Efficiently compresses photographic images	Can reduce quality	Photographs and images with fine detail
Portable Network Graphics (PNG)	Compresses images without losing quality	Does not allow transparency	Nonphotographic images designed for the web
Tagged Image File Format (TIF or TIFF)	Maintains image quality in print and on screen	Some web browsers cannot display TIF images	Images used in desktop publishing, faxes, and medical imaging
Windows Bitmap (BMP)	Simplest way to store a bitmapped graphic	Can waste large amounts of storage space	Basic shapes and images with few colors

TIP

To save a file as a different type, point to Save as and then click a different file type, such as JPEG picture.

The Frame and Sailboat files are both PNG files, which is an appropriate file format for displaying graphics on a webpage or distributing graphics via email. You'll save a copy of the Frame file as a PNG file. However, if you need to provide a graphic in a different file format, you can convert it in Paint by choosing that format when you save the file.

To save the Frame image with a new name:

1. Click the **File** tab and then click **Save as**. The Save As dialog box opens.

2. If necessary, click the **Browse Folders** button to open the navigation pane, and then navigate to the **Module7 > Module** folder provided with your Data Files.

3. In the File name box, type **Logo**. The file type is already displayed as PNG (*.png) in the Save As dialog box. See Figure 7-8.

| Figure 7-8 | Saving the Frame file with a new name |

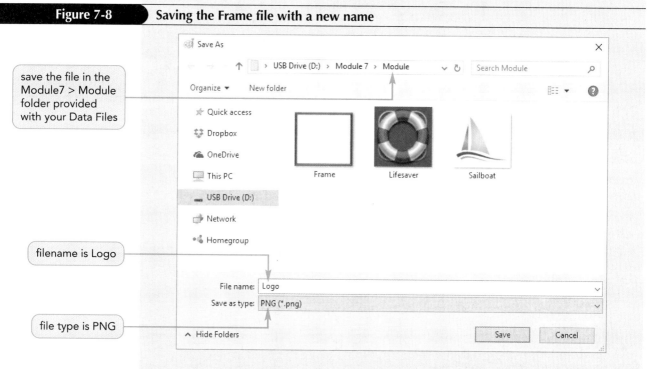

save the file in the Module7 > Module folder provided with your Data Files

filename is Logo

file type is PNG

4. Click the **Save** button. Paint saves a copy of the frame image as a file named Logo.

Trouble? If a dialog box opens explaining that any transparency will be lost if you save the image, click the OK button.

Saving a Bitmap Graphic in a Different File Type

INSIGHT

In general, you cannot improve the quality of a compressed image by saving it in a different file format. For example, suppose you convert a JPG graphic, which omits some color information to compress the file, to a format such as TIF, which doesn't sacrifice quality to reduce file size. The colors from the original JPG file remain the same, but the file size increases because the TIF file provides an expanded color palette that includes colors not used in the image.

Now you are ready to create the FreeSail logo by combining the picture of the sailboat with the frame image.

Copying and Pasting to Create a Graphic

One way to insert the sailboat image inside the frame is to open the Sailboat file again, select the entire image, cut or copy it, open the Logo file with the frame image, and then paste the sailboat image in the frame. To reduce the number of steps you need to perform, Paint provides a shortcut method—the Paste from command on the Paste button. You can use this command when you want to copy an entire image from another file and paste it in your current image.

To paste the sailboat image in the Logo file:

▶ **1.** On the Home tab, in the Clipboard group, click the **Paste button arrow**, and then click **Paste from**. The Paste From dialog box opens, which has the same controls as the Open dialog box.

> **Trouble?** If the Paste From dialog box did not open, you probably clicked the Paste button instead of the Paste button arrow. Repeat Step 1.

▶ **2.** In the file list, click **Sailboat** and then click the **Open** button. The sailboat image appears in the upper-left corner of the logo picture in a selection box. See Figure 7-9.

Figure 7-9   **Pasting the sailboat image in the Logo file**

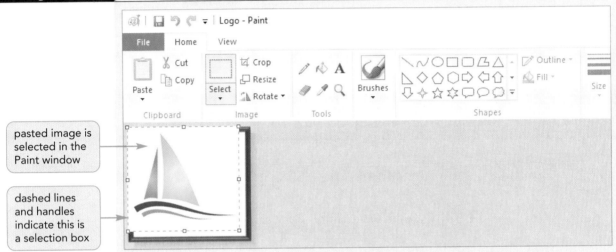

pasted image is selected in the Paint window

dashed lines and handles indicate this is a selection box

Because you need to move the sailboat image, do not click anywhere in the Paint window. If you do, you remove the selection box from the sailboat image and its pixels replace the ones from the logo picture underneath it.

> **Trouble?** If you clicked in the Paint window and removed the selection box from the sailboat image, click the Undo button 🔄 on the Quick Access Toolbar, and then repeat Steps 1 and 2.

If you make a mistake while working in Paint, click the Undo button on the Quick Access Toolbar. You can reverse up to your last three actions. A best practice is to save frequently, always making sure the changes you've made are what you want.

The selection box around the sailboat image indicates that you can manipulate the image by moving, copying, resizing, or deleting it. You can think of the selected image as floating on top of the frame picture because any changes you make to the sailboat image do not affect the Logo file until you click to remove the selection box. You want to show Shawn how to move the sailboat image to the center of the frame. You can do so by dragging the selected sailboat image.

To move the selected sailboat image:

▶ **1.** Point to the selected sailboat image. The pointer changes to ✛.

▶ **2.** Drag the sailboat image to the center of the frame as shown in Figure 7-10, taking care not to cover any part of the frame, and then release the mouse button. The sailboat image is still selected, but it now appears in the middle of the frame.

| Figure 7-10 | Moving the sailboat image |

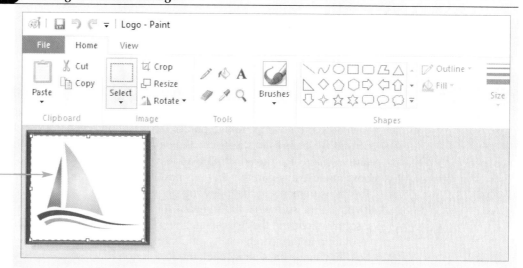

move the sailboat image to the center of the frame

▶ **3.** Click anywhere outside of the selected image to remove the selection box. The sailboat image is now part of the Logo file.

Now that you have created the first major part of the graphic, you should save the Logo file so you don't inadvertently lose your changes.

To save the Logo graphic:

▶ **1.** Click the **Save** button 🔲 on the Quick Access Toolbar. Paint saves the current image using the same name and location you used the last time you saved the graphic.

Next, you need to add text describing the business to the graphic to make it a true logo. According to your sketch, the text should appear in a colored rectangle that extends to the right of the frame. Right now, there's not enough room in the graphic to accommodate this rectangle. You need to modify the graphic by resizing the canvas and then moving the image to create space for the logo text.

Modifying Graphics in Paint

After you create and save an image in Paint, you can modify it by adding graphic elements, such as lines, shapes, and text; changing colors; and cropping, or removing, parts of the graphic. According to your sketch for the FreeSail logo, you need to add a text box to the right of the framed sailboat image. To provide enough work space for creating the text box, you should first resize the canvas.

Resizing the Canvas and Moving an Image

When you open a graphic, it fills the canvas if the graphic is the same size as or larger than the canvas. If the graphic is smaller than the canvas, you can resize the canvas to fit snugly around the image. Doing so reduces file size and eliminates a border around your picture. Reducing the width or height of the canvas is one way to crop, or remove, a row or column of pixels from an edge of a graphic. You can also resize the canvas if you want to make it larger than the image so you can add more graphic elements to the picture. When you enlarge the canvas, the image remains in the upper-left corner of the Paint window as you drag a selection handle on the canvas to make it longer, wider, or both.

After increasing the size of the canvas, you often need to move the image to provide room to work or so that the image fits more aesthetically within the enlarged space. To move all or part of an image in Paint, you first select the image using the Rectangular selection tool or the Free-form selection tool. With the Rectangular selection tool, you draw a selection box around the area you want to select. With the Free-form selection tool, you draw a line of any shape around the area. To select the entire graphic, you can click the Select button arrow in the Image group on the Home tab, and then click Select all.

When you move a graphic, part of the selection box can extend past the edges of the canvas. Because Paint saves only the part of the graphic that appears on the canvas, make sure all parts of a moved graphic appear on the canvas before you remove the selection box. You lose any part that extends past the canvas when you remove the selection box. The measurements in the following steps depend on a screen resolution of 1366 × 768. If you are not sure what the screen resolution is on your computer or need to change the resolution, click in the Ask me anything box, type "resolution," click Change the screen resolution in the search results, and then look at the setting displayed in the Resolution box. To change the setting, click the Resolution box, select 1366 × 768, and then click the Apply button. Close the Advanced Display Settings window.

To resize the canvas and then move the logo graphic:

▶ **1.** Point to the selection handle on the lower-right corner of the canvas so that the pointer changes to ⬂, and then begin to drag down and to the right, watching the dimensions in the middle of the status bar. See Figure 7-11.

| Figure 7-11 | Resizing the canvas |

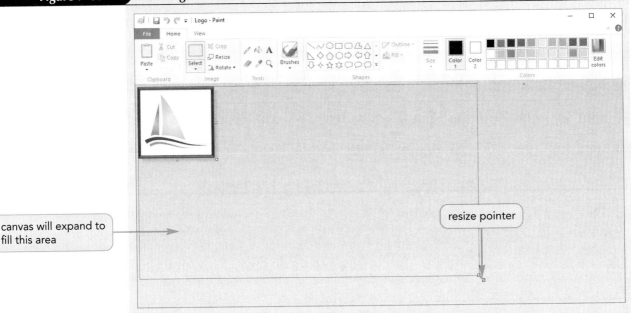

canvas will expand to fill this area

resize pointer

▶ **2.** When the dimensions are about 900 × 400px, release the mouse button.

▶ **3.** On the Home tab, in the Image group, click the **Select button arrow**, and then click **Select all** to select the entire graphic.

▶ **4.** Drag the graphic down and to the right as shown in Figure 7-12 to create room to work on the logo.

Figure 7-12   Moving the graphic

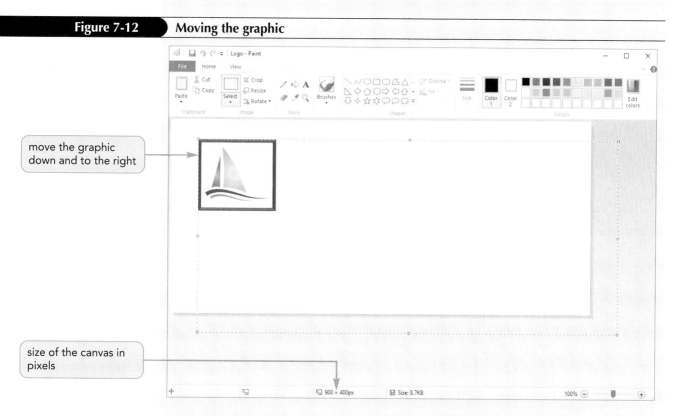

move the graphic down and to the right

size of the canvas in pixels

▶ **5.** Click any part of the window outside of the selected image to remove the selection box.

You can resize the canvas to any dimensions you need for your graphic, including those that extend beyond the boundaries of the Paint window. If you do, you can scroll horizontally and vertically to display the entire graphic or you can enlarge the Paint window. When you are working with a large canvas and plan to print the graphic, be sure to use Print Preview to see how the graphic will look when printed. To do so, click the File tab, point to Print, and then click Print preview. Click the Page setup button in the Print group on the Print Preview tab to open the Page Setup dialog box, where you select print settings such as page orientation and paper size. If you want to print the graphic on a single page, be sure the Fit to option button is selected and is set to 1 by 1 pages.

As you've already noticed, Paint helps you identify and control your location while you are drawing shapes or dragging selections. The pixel coordinates in the status bar specify the exact location of the pointer on the canvas relative to the pixels on your screen. Paint displays the pixel coordinates in an (x,y) format (x represents the horizontal location and y represents the vertical location). Pixel coordinates of 150 × 25, for example, indicate that the center of the pointer is 150 pixels from the left edge of the screen and 25 pixels from the top. Using these coordinates helps you position a shape or an image on the canvas, and position graphic elements in relation to one another. In addition, when you draw a shape, you can use the sizing coordinates, which appear immediately to the right of the pixel coordinates, to determine the size of the shape you are dragging. For example, when you draw a text box, you might start at pixel coordinates 15 × 15 and drag to sizing coordinates of 300 × 30—so your text box is long and narrow and appears in the upper-left corner of the graphic.

Resizing the canvas and moving the image provides plenty of room to work as you perform the next step—adding the logo text to the graphic.

Adding Text to a Graphic

To add words to a graphic in Paint, you use the Text tool. You first use the Text tool to create a text box, and then you type the text in this box. When you select the Text tool, the Text Tools Text tab opens on the ribbon, so you can select a font, a size, and attributes for the text. If your text exceeds the length and width of the text box, you can drag the sizing handles to enlarge the box.

REFERENCE

Adding Text to a Graphic

- On the Home tab, in the Tools group, click the Text tool and then drag a text box on the canvas.
- On the Text Tools Text tab, in the Font group, select a font, a font size, attributes, and background options.
- Type the text in the text box, and use the sizing handles to resize the text box, if necessary.
- Adjust the font, font size, and attributes, as necessary.
- Click outside the text box.

When you add text to a graphic, Paint displays black text on a white rectangle, by default. If you want to change the colors, you should do so before you use the Text tool. (Changing colors after you complete your work with the Text tool is tricky.) You can change the Color 1 (foreground) and Color 2 (background) colors, which appear to the left of the color palette in the Colors group on the Home tab. Paint uses Color 1 for lines, borders of shapes, and text. Paint uses Color 2 for the background of text rectangles and the inside, or fill, color of enclosed shapes. To set a color, you click the Color 1 or Color 2 button, and then click a color in the palette. If the color palette does not contain a color you want to use, you can select one from your image using the Color picker tool. Click the Color picker tool in the Tools group on the Home tab, and then click a color in the image to change Color 1 to the color you clicked. Do the same with the right mouse button to change Color 2.

REFERENCE

Magnifying a Graphic

- To zoom in, click the Magnifier tool in the Tools group on the Home tab, and then click the graphic one or more times, or drag the magnification slider to the right to increase the magnification.
- To zoom out, click the Magnifier tool in the Tools group on the Home tab, and then right-click the graphic one or more times, or drag the magnification slider to the left to decrease the magnification.

TIP

You can also change the magnification by clicking the View tab and then clicking the Zoom in or Zoom out button in the Zoom group.

According to your sketch, "FreeSail Boating Membership Club" should appear on two lines in a colored rectangle to the right of the frame. The word "FreeSail" should be in a large white font on one line and the words "Boating Membership Club" should appear in medium blue on the next line. To match the font and style that Shawn and Oscar use for other promotional materials, you'll use Tahoma as the font of the text. You suggest picking a color from the sailboat image as the background color of the text box and using white as the foreground color for the first line of text. When you use the Color picker tool to change a color, it is often helpful to zoom in, or increase the magnification of the image, so you can see the pixels of color more clearly. To do so, you can use the Magnifier tool in the Tools group on the Home tab or you can use the magnification control on the status bar. Increase the magnification by dragging the slider to the right or by clicking the Zoom in button. You can decrease the magnification, or zoom out, by dragging the slider to the left or by clicking the Zoom out button.

To zoom in and pick a color:

1. On the Home tab, in the Tools group, click the **Magnifier** tool 🔍, and then click the center of the sailboat image twice to increase the magnification to 300% and center the Paint window on the sailboat. See Figure 7-13.

Figure 7-13   **Changing the magnification of the image**

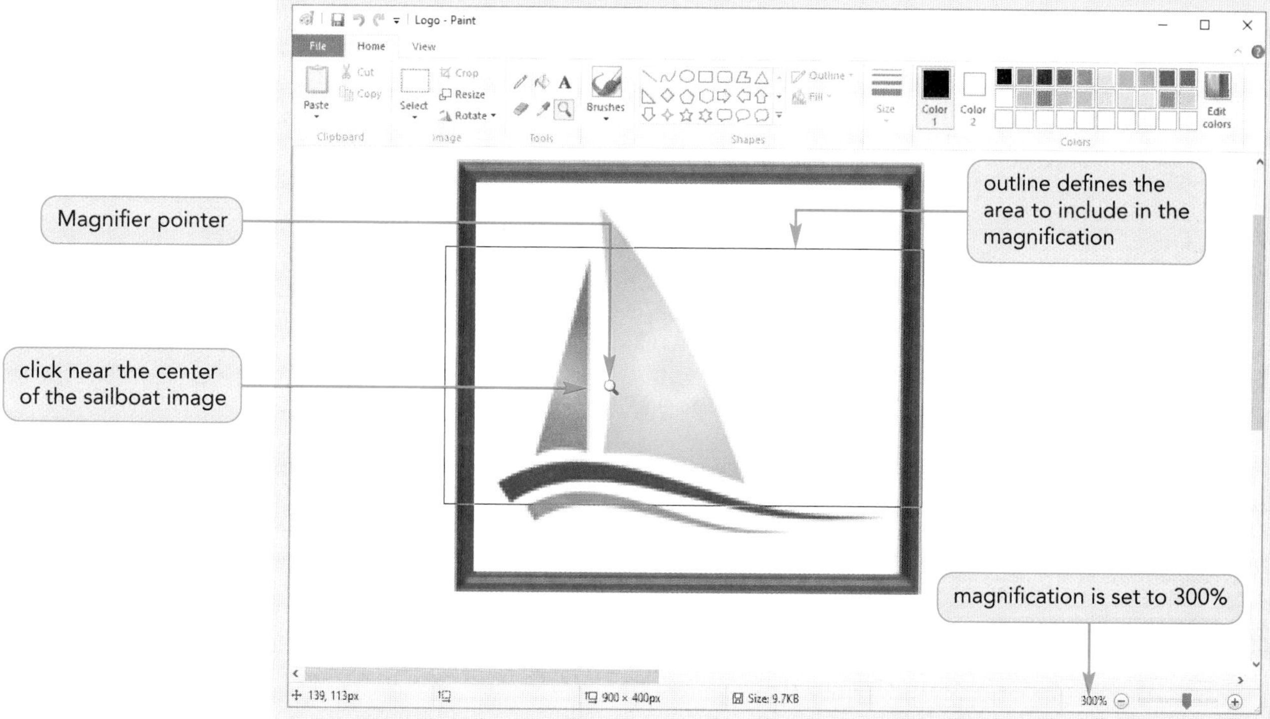

Magnifier pointer

click near the center of the sailboat image

outline defines the area to include in the magnification

magnification is set to 300%

Trouble? If you magnified a different area of the graphic, use the scroll bars to display the center of the sailboat as shown in Figure 7-13.

2. In the Tools group, click the **Color picker** tool 🖉, and then right-click a **dark-blue pixel** in the sailboat image. The Color 2 button displays the color you clicked.

Trouble? If you clicked the dark-blue pixel with the left mouse button instead of the right, repeat Step 2.

3. In the Colors group, click the **Color 1** button if necessary, and then click the **white color square** in the color palette (middle row, first column). The Color 1 button displays white. These settings mean that white is the foreground color and dark blue is the background color, so the text will be white on a dark-blue background.

4. Click the **Zoom out** button ⊖ on the status bar twice so the graphic appears at 100% zoom.

Now you are ready to use the Text tool to add the logo text to the graphic. To avoid making mistakes in the current graphic, you'll create the text box below the framed sailboat and then move it to a more precise position later. To make sure that the text appears on the background color you chose, select the Opaque button in the Background group on the Text Tools Text tab. If Opaque is not selected, Paint uses the Transparent setting instead, allowing the colors of the image to show through. If you use the current settings and then click the Opaque button before drawing a text box below the framed sailboat, white text appears on a dark blue background. If you use the current settings and then click the Transparent button, the white text appears on the white canvas, making it invisible.

Besides using the colors and background settings you specify, the text you type will appear with the font, size, and attributes shown on the Text Tools Text tab. The font size of the letters is measured in points, where a single point is 1/72 inch. That means a one-inch-tall character is 72 points, and a half-inch-tall character is 36 points. Attributes are characteristics of the font, including bold, italic, underline, and strikethrough. You can change the font, size, and attributes before you type, after you select the text you type, or as you edit the text. When you are satisfied with the text and its appearance, you click outside the text box so that Paint anchors the text into place, making it part of the bitmap graphic. After the text is anchored in a graphic, you can change the font or its attributes only by deleting the text and starting over with the Text tool.

To add text to the graphic:

▶ 1. In the Tools group, click the **Text** tool $\boxed{A}$.

▶ 2. Below the sailboat image on the canvas, drag the I beam pointer $\overline{I}$ to create a text box about 400 pixels wide by 75 pixels tall. Refer to the left-middle part of the status bar for the size coordinates. Then release the mouse button. The Text Tools Text tab appears on the ribbon.

   Trouble? If the text box you created is not about 400 × 75 pixels, click outside of the selected text box, and then repeat Steps 1 and 2.

▶ 3. On the Text Tools Text tab, in the Background group, click the **Opaque** button to display the blue fill in the text box. See Figure 7-14.

| Figure 7-14 | Creating a text box |

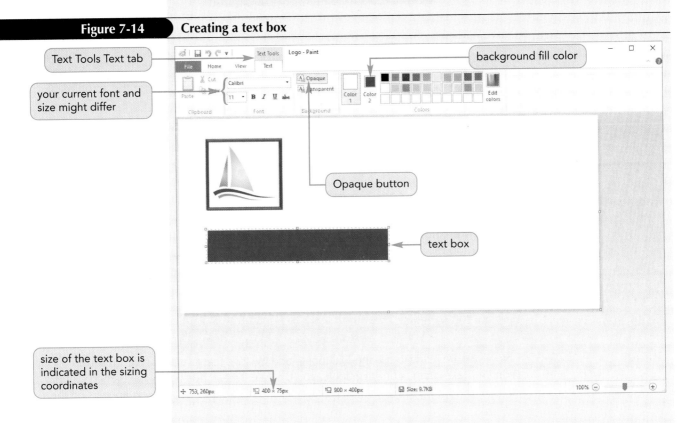

Text Tools Text tab

background fill color

your current font and size might differ

Opaque button

text box

size of the text box is indicated in the sizing coordinates

Make sure you select Tahoma so your text fits in the text box and matches the figures in this module.

▶ **4.** In the Font group, click the **Font family button arrow** `Calibri ▾`, scroll the fonts list as necessary, and then click **Tahoma**.

▶ **5.** In the Font group, click in the **Font size** `11 ▾` box, type **46**, and then press the **Enter** key.

▶ **6.** Click in the text box, press the **spacebar** to insert a space, and then type **FreeSail**. See Figure 7-15.

| **Figure 7-15** | Adding text with the Text tool |

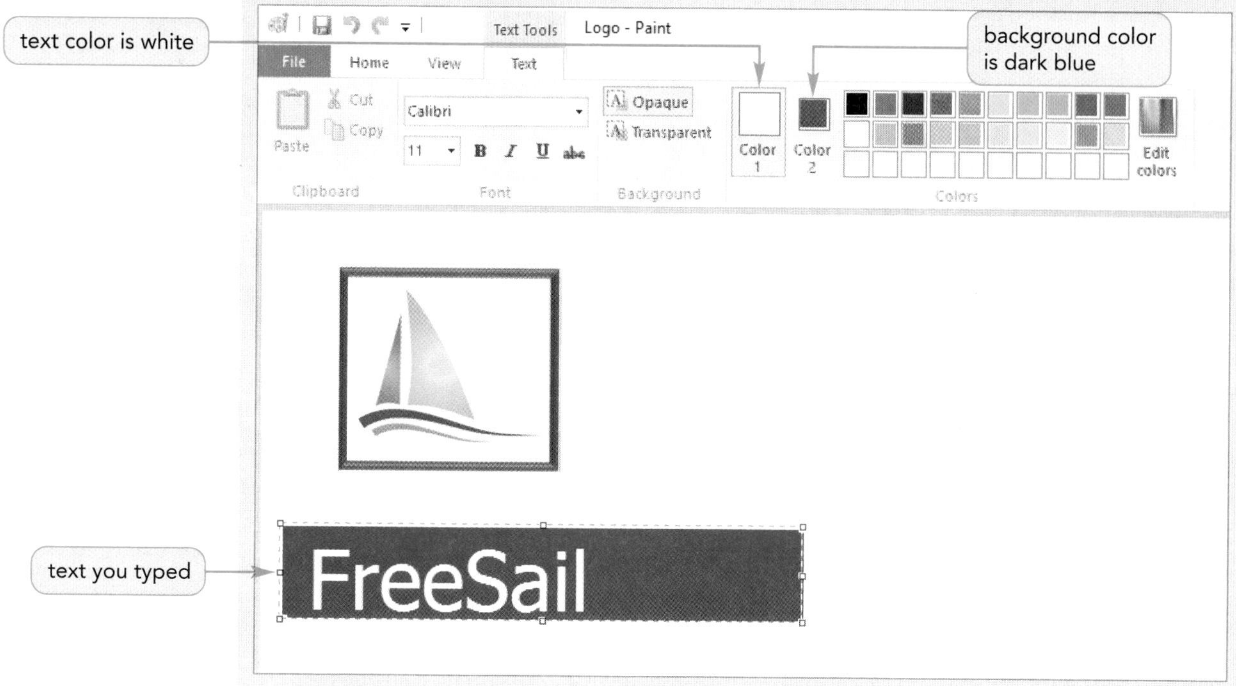

text color is white

background color is dark blue

text you typed

FreeSail

Trouble? If the text wraps within the text box or does not fill the text box as shown in the figure, drag the lower-right sizing handle to increase the size of the text box.

▶ **7.** Click a blank area of the canvas outside the text box to anchor the text.

▶ **8.** Click the **Save** button 🖫 on the Quick Access Toolbar to save your work.

Now you need to use the same techniques to create a text box with a dark-blue background and lighter blue text that displays the rest of the logo text. This time, however, you'll use the Color picker tool to select dark blue as the foreground color, and then edit the color to make it a lighter shade of blue. Later, you will move this text below the "FreeSail" text you just created.

To add a second line of text to the graphic:

▶ **1.** On the Home tab, in the Tools group, click the **Color picker** tool 🖉 and then click the background of the text box. Both the Color 1 button and the Color 2 button display dark blue.

▶ **2.** In the Colors group, click the **Edit colors** button to open the Edit Colors dialog box.

▶ **3.** To select a lighter shade of blue, click the **narrow bar** on the right side of the Edit Colors dialog box to change the foreground color. Click the narrow bar several times, if necessary, to display the correct values for the lighter color, as shown in Figure 7-16.

| Figure 7-16 | Selecting a shade of blue in the Edit Colors dialog box |

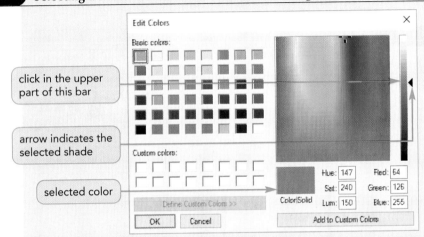

▶ **4.** Click the **OK** button to change Color 1 to medium blue. Now the text you add to the graphic will appear in medium blue with a dark-blue background.

▶ **5.** In the Tools group, click the **Text** tool **A** and then click to the right of the "FreeSail" text to insert a text box about the same size as the first text box.

Trouble? If the text box appears too far to the right, use the move pointer ⊕ and drag the text box closer to the other text box.

▶ **6.** On the Text Tools Text tab, in the Font group, click the **Font size button arrow** 11 ▼ and then click **24** to change the font size.

▶ **7.** Click in the new dark blue text box, press the **spacebar** to insert a space, and then type **Boating Membership Club**. See Figure 7-17.

Figure 7-17 **Adding a second line of text**

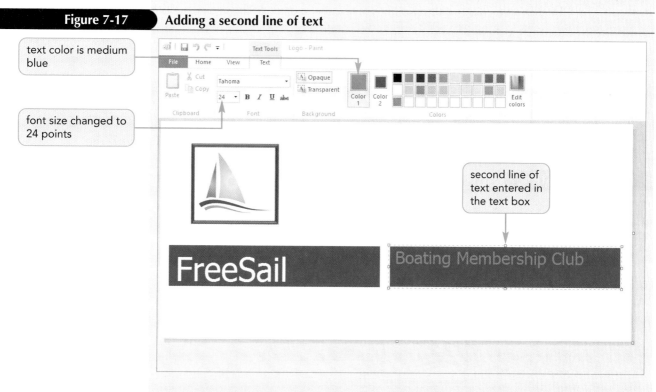

text color is medium blue

font size changed to 24 points

second line of text entered in the text box

Trouble? If the text wraps within the text box or does not fill the text box as shown in the figure, resize the text box.

▶ 8. Click a blank area of the canvas outside the text box to anchor the text.

▶ 9. Click the **Save** button 🖫 on the Quick Access Toolbar to save your work.

Next, you'll show Shawn how to draw a rectangle next to the framed sailboat image. When you finish, you'll move the two lines of text to the new rectangle.

Drawing Shapes

To draw closed shapes, such as squares and circles, you select a shape from the Shapes gallery, and then draw the shape on the canvas. Before or after you draw a shape, you can set the following options:

- Outline—Select a style for the shape's outline. You can use solid color, crayon, marker, oil, natural pencil, watercolor, or no outline.
- Fill—Select a style for the shape's fill, or inside area. You can use solid color, crayon, marker, oil, natural pencil, watercolor, or no fill.
- Size—Select a width for the outline, ranging from thin to thick.
- Color 1—Select a color for the shape's outline.
- Color 2—Select a color for the shape's fill.

TIP

Holding down the Shift key while dragging to create a shape keeps the proportions equal.

For example, to draw a rectangle, click the Rectangle tool in the Shapes group, and then drag the drawing pointer diagonally to create the shape. To draw a square, you hold down the Shift key while dragging. Similarly, you draw an ellipse, or oval, by selecting the Ellipse tool and then dragging to create the shape. To draw a circle, hold down the Shift key while dragging. While the shape is selected, you can select an outline and fill style, an outline size, and an outline and fill color. You can also set these options before you draw.

Now you can draw a dark-blue rectangle next to the framed sailboat graphic. Later, you'll move the two lines of text you created to this rectangle to match the logo's design.

To draw a rectangle:

▶ **1.** In the Tools group, click the **Color picker** tool, and then click the dark-blue background of a text box to change Color 1 to dark blue. Color 2 is already dark blue, which is the color you want for the fill of the rectangle.

▶ **2.** In the Shapes group, click the **Rectangle** tool ▢. See Figure 7-18.

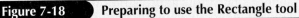

| Figure 7-18 | Preparing to use the Rectangle tool |

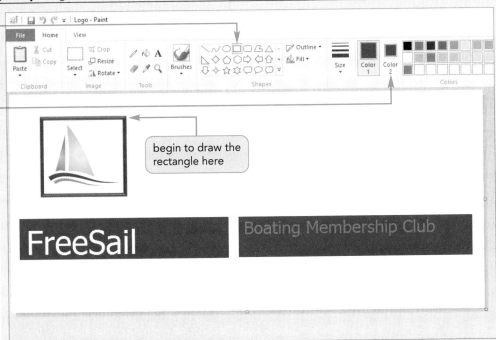

Rectangle tool is selected

Color 2 is dark blue so the outline and fill are the same color

begin to draw the rectangle here

FreeSail

Boating Membership Club

▶ **3.** In the Shapes group, click the **Outline** button, and then click **Solid color** if it is not already selected.

▶ **4.** In the Shapes group, click the **Fill** button, and then click **Solid color**, if necessary.

▶ **5.** Click the **Size** button, and then click the first size to draw a 1-pixel line.

TIP

Watch the sizing coordinates in the second section on the status bar as you draw the rectangle.

▶ **6.** Place the drawing pointer a few pixels to the right of the framed sailboat, drag to draw a rectangle about 400 pixels wide and 165 pixels tall, and then release the mouse button. Figure 7-19 shows the rectangle before releasing the mouse button. Your pixel coordinates may differ.

Figure 7-19   **Drawing a rectangle**

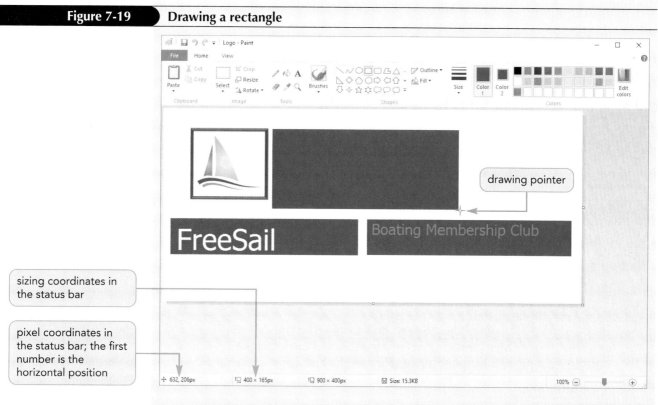

sizing coordinates in the status bar

pixel coordinates in the status bar; the first number is the horizontal position

drawing pointer

Trouble? If the shape you drew is not similar to the one in the figure, click the Undo button ⤺ on the Quick Access Toolbar, and then repeat steps as necessary to redraw the rectangle.

7. Click outside the rectangle to deselect it.

8. Click the **Save** button 🖫 on the Quick Access Toolbar to save your work.

Now you can move the two lines of text you created into the rectangle.

Moving Part of a Graphic

TIP

To delete an area of a graphic, select the area using a selection tool, and then press the Delete key.

To move part of a graphic, you select the area you want to move, and then drag the selection to a new location. You can also move or copy part of a graphic using the options in the Clipboard group on the Home tab: Select an area, click the Cut or Copy button in the Clipboard group, and then click the Paste button to paste the selection into the graphic. The graphic appears in a selection box in the upper-left corner of the canvas until you drag the selected image to the desired location.

Before you move part of a graphic, you might need to change Color 2 so it matches the surrounding area. For example, you would leave Color 2 as dark blue if you wanted to adjust the placement of the text within a text box so the background remains dark blue. However, you would change Color 2 to white before moving the entire text box so the area it occupies changes to white after you move it.

When you move or copy part of a graphic using a selection tool, you can select the image with a solid background (the default) or a transparent background. Choose the Transparent selection command on the Select button list to omit the background color from the selection, so any areas using that color become transparent and allow the colors in the underlying picture to appear in its place when you move or copy the selected image. For example, if you use the Transparent selection command when you select and move a shape with a white background and Color 2 is set to white, the background becomes transparent when you move it to a colored area of the graphic. When the Transparent selection command is selected, it appears with a checkmark on the Select button list. Remove the checkmark to include the background color in your selection when you move or paste it somewhere else in the picture.

Using a Solid or Transparent Background

Using the Transparent selection command in Paint can be an effective way to move an image so it does not appear with a rectangular border. For example, the larger sail in the logo graphic has a curved outline. If you select the sailboat without using the Transparent selection option and move it to a blue area of the graphic, the sailboat image remains in a white rectangle. If you set Color 2 to white and then select the sailboat using the Transparent selection command, however, the sailboat image appears against a blue background when you move it into a blue area, emphasizing the curved outline of the sail. The Transparent selection command works best in a graphic that does not use thousands or millions of colors. A white background in a JPG file, for example, often includes hundreds of shades of white, and only one of those shades is set to be transparent when you use the Transparent selection command.

You'll show Shawn how to move first the "FreeSail" text and then the "Boating Membership Club" text to the dark-blue rectangle. Shawn says that he has a graphic of a life preserver, or lifesaver, that he wants to add to the logo, just to the right of the FreeSail text. You'll move the text to the upper-left part of the dark-blue rectangle.

To move the text into the rectangle:

1. In the Image group, click the **Select button arrow**. If the Transparent selection command appears with a checkmark, click **Transparent selection** to remove the checkmark, and then click the **Select button arrow** again.

2. Click **Rectangular selection**. The pointer changes to ⊹. The Select button displays the Rectangular selection tool and will do so until you change the type of selection.

3. Drag to select all of the **FreeSail** text in the first text box, but only select as much background as necessary.

4. Point to the selected text, and then use the move pointer ✥ to drag the text up to the new rectangle, positioning the text in the upper-left part of the rectangle.

   Trouble? If part of the text remains in its original location, click the Undo button 🔄 on the Quick Access Toolbar, and then repeat Steps 3 and 4.

5. Click a blank spot on the canvas to deselect the text.

6. Select the **Boating Membership Club** text, and then drag the selected text below the "FreeSail" text, positioning the selection so it is close to the first line of text but not overlapping it. See Figure 7-20.

Figure 7-20	Moving text to the rectangle

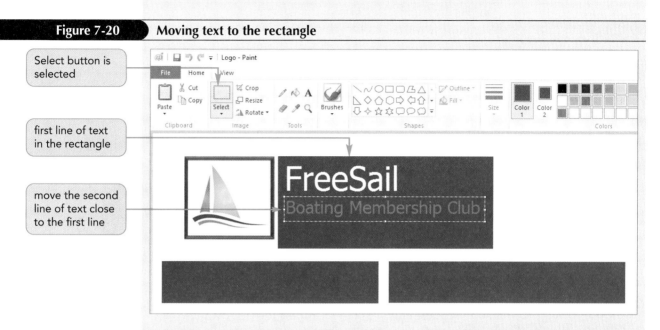

Select button is selected

first line of text in the rectangle

move the second line of text close to the first line

7. Click outside the selection to complete the move. Now both lines of text are part of the rectangle.

8. If you need to adjust the placement of the text, drag to select a line of text, and then use the arrow keys to fine-tune its placement in the rectangle.

Because Color 2 (the background color) is still set to blue, moving the text within the rectangle does not introduce new colors into the text box. Now you want to align the top of the rectangle with the top of the frame, which involves moving the entire rectangle. Before doing so, however, you need to change Color 2 to white so the area the rectangle now occupies doesn't remain blue after you move the rectangle.

To move the text box:

1. In the Colors group, click the **Color 2** button, and then click the **white color box** in the color palette to change the background color to white.

2. If necessary, click the **Select** button in the Image group to use the Rectangular selection tool.

3. Drag to select the rectangle containing the "FreeSail Boating Membership Club" text and as little of the white background as possible. A dashed outline appears around the rectangle.

   Trouble? If the selection box you created contains some of the frame on the left or does not contain all of the rectangle, click outside of the selection, and then repeat Steps 2 and 3.

4. If necessary, use the move pointer ✥ to drag the rectangle so that it appears a few pixels to the right of the frame and aligned with the top edge of the frame. See Figure 7-21.

Figure 7-21 **Moving the rectangle**

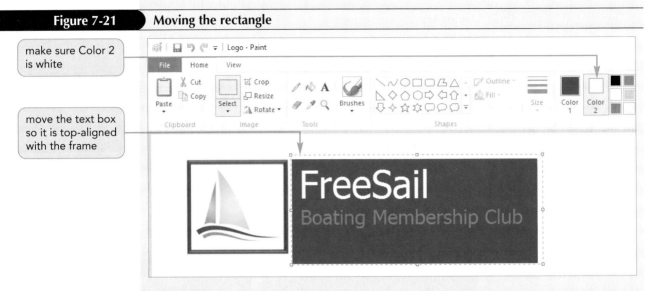

make sure Color 2 is white

move the text box so it is top-aligned with the frame

Trouble? If the rectangle does not move when you drag it, but the selection box changes size, you probably dragged a sizing handle instead of the entire selection. Click the Undo button 🔄 on the Quick Access Toolbar, and then repeat Step 4.

Trouble? If the rectangle is already a few pixels to the right of and top-aligned with the frame, skip Step 4.

5. When the rectangle is in a position similar to the one shown in the figure, click a blank area of the canvas to anchor the text box into place.

6. Click the **Save** button 💾 on the Quick Access Toolbar to save your work.

The entire image is now similar to your original sketch. Shawn wants to add a lifesaver graphic to enhance the logo, but thinks it might be too big for the space. You'll show him how to resize the graphic so it fits in the logo.

Resizing and Rotating Graphics

If an image you want to use is too large or too small for your graphic or design, you can use Paint to resize it. If you are not making drastic changes, such as changing a 10 × 10-pixel image to a 1,000 × 1,000-pixel image, you can usually resize an image in Paint without a noticeable loss of quality. If you want to resize only part of an image, select it first. Otherwise, Paint resizes the entire image. You use the Resize and Skew dialog box to resize images. The Resize section of the dialog box is for changing the width and the height, and the Skew section is for skewing the image. When you **skew** an image, you place it at a slant, which often distorts the image. For example, if you skew a square image horizontally by 45 degrees, its left and right edges are set at 45-degree angles to the top and bottom edges, forming a parallelogram.

You can resize an image horizontally and vertically by percentage or by pixels. Percentage is selected by default in the Resize and Skew dialog box, so if you want to double the size of the image, for example, enter 200 in the Horizontal box in the Resize section. Because the Maintain aspect ratio box is checked by default, Paint enters 200 in the Vertical box for you, and then increases the size of the image by 200 percent when you click the OK button. (Recall that the aspect ratio is the relationship of the width to the height.) If you remove the checkmark from the Maintain aspect ratio box and enter different Horizontal and Vertical percentage values, you change the relationship of width to height, distorting the image. If you are resizing a shape, however, you might want to change one dimension without changing the other. In that case, you can remove the checkmark from the Maintain aspect ratio box before entering a Horizontal or Vertical value.

You can also resize an image by changing the number of pixels in its width or height. For example, if you have an 800 × 600-pixel image and need to fit it in a space that is 650 pixels wide, you can enter 650 pixels as the Horizontal value. If the Maintain aspect ratio box contains a checkmark, Paint automatically enters 487 pixels as the Vertical value to keep the ratio of width to height the same.

Besides resizing and skewing images, you can rotate them. When you rotate an image in Paint, you turn it in 90-degree increments or you flip it horizontally or vertically. For example, if an image of an arrow points to the right, you can flip it horizontally so that it points to the left.

You'll insert the lifesaver graphic in the Logo file, and then show Shawn how to resize it to fit in the design.

To paste the lifesaver image in the Logo file:

▶ **1.** In the Clipboard group, click the **Paste button arrow**, and then click **Paste from**. The Paste From dialog box opens to display the contents of the Module7 > Module folder.

▶ **2.** In the file list, click **Lifesaver** and then click the **Open** button. The lifesaver image appears on the logo picture in a selection box.

▶ **3.** Drag the lifesaver image to the right of the "FreeSail" text. See Figure 7-22. The image is too large for the space and covers part of the text.

| Figure 7-22 | Pasting the lifesaver image in the Logo file |

lifesaver graphic needs to be resized

▶ **4.** With the lifesaver image still selected, click the **Resize** button in the Image group to open the Resize and Skew dialog box.

 Trouble? If you clicked outside of the lifesaver image and anchored it to the Logo graphic, click the Undo button 🔄 on the Quick Access Toolbar to remove the lifesaver image from the logo, and then repeat Steps 1–4.

▶ **5.** If the Maintain aspect ratio box does not contain a checkmark, click the **Maintain aspect ratio** box to have Paint resize the width and height in proportion to each other.

6. In the Resize section, select the value in the Horizontal box, and then type **45** to reduce the size of the selected image to a little less than half its current size. Paint enters "45" in the Vertical box to maintain the aspect ratio.

7. Click the **OK** button to resize the selected image.

8. If necessary, drag the selected image to the right of the "FreeSail" text and above the "Boating Membership Club" text, and then click a blank area of the graphic to deselect the image. See Figure 7-23.

Trouble? If the lifesaver graphic covers part of the "Boating Membership Club" text, click the Undo button 🔙 on the Quick Access Toolbar, and then repeat Steps 1–8. Enter 40 in the Horizontal box, and then click the OK button.

Figure 7-23 **Position of the lifesaver image in the Logo file**

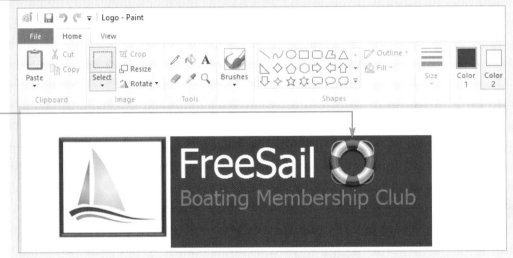

resized lifesaver graphic to the right of the FreeSail text

You and Shawn discuss a few other changes you can make to fine-tune the logo. In particular, you suggest shortening the rectangle containing the text and then adding a row of rectangles below the text box to balance the image. To shorten the large blue rectangle, you can delete part of the shape.

Deleting Part of a Graphic

To delete part of a graphic, you use a selection tool to select the elements you want to remove, and then press the Delete key on the keyboard. Before deleting part of a graphic, check the Color 2 tool on the Home tab. When you press the Delete key, the selected area will be filled with the color displayed on the Color 2 tool.

To create enough white space for the rectangles you want to add to the logo graphic, you need to delete part of the blue rectangle.

To delete part of the blue rectangle:

1. If necessary, click the **Color 2** tool in the Colors group, and then click the **white color square** to set white as the background color.

2. If necessary, click the **Select** button in the Image group to use the Rectangular selection tool.

3. Drag to select a blue area at the bottom of the rectangle that does not contain any text. Your goal is to create about 36 pixels (0.5 inch) of white space from the bottom of the rectangle to the bottom of the frame on the left. See Figure 7-24.

Figure 7-24	Selecting an area for deletion

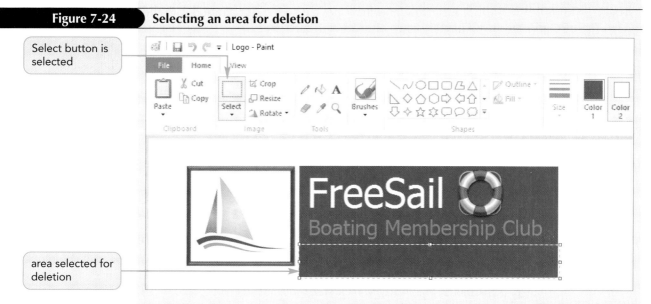

Select button is selected

area selected for deletion

Trouble? If the selection box contains part of the text in the rectangle, or if you did not select enough of the rectangle, click outside of the selection, and then repeat Steps 2 and 3.

4. Press the **Delete** key to delete the selected area.

Now you have enough room to insert the three rectangles below the text box. You want to add three filled rectangles below the text box. You can use the same shade of dark blue as in the large rectangle for the foreground and background colors. You also want to zoom in on the graphic so you can work accurately.

To draw a rectangle:

1. In the Tools group, click the **Magnifier** tool 🔍, and then click below the B in "Boating" to magnify the graphic by 200%.

2. In the Tools group, click the **Color picker** tool 🖊, and then right-click the dark-blue background of the rectangle to change Color 2 to dark blue.

Trouble? If you clicked the background instead of right-clicking it, click the Color picker tool 🖊 again, and then right-click the dark-blue background.

3. In the Shapes group, click the **Rectangle** tool ▢. The settings you chose earlier for the Outline, Fill, and Size buttons still apply, so you don't need to change those settings.

TIP

Refer to the coordinates in the second section from the left on the status bar as you draw the rectangle.

4. Place the drawing pointer ┼ a few pixels below the text box, drag to draw a rectangle about 130 pixels wide and 30 pixels tall, and then release the mouse button.

Trouble? If the shape you drew is not about 130 pixels wide and 30 pixels tall, click the Undo button ↺ on the Quick Access Toolbar, and then repeat Step 4 as necessary to redraw the rectangle.

▶ **5.** Click outside the rectangle to deselect it.

▶ **6.** With Color 2 selected in the Colors group, click the **white square** in the color palette to change the background color to white.

▶ **7.** In the Image group, click the **Select** button, drag to select the rectangle you just drew, and then move it so it is left-aligned with the large blue rectangle and bottom-aligned with the frame.

The element you added is the right size and shape and is in the right position, but repeating the color from the text box doesn't create enough of a contrast. You can change the color of the new rectangle to a different one in the sailboat image to determine if that suits the design of the logo.

Changing Colors

TIP

You can also add color to an image by using a Brush tool and then choosing a style, such as Airbrush.

You can add color to a graphic by choosing colors as you draw or applying color to shapes after you finish drawing them. Before you use a drawing tool, you can select a color for the line or shape, as you did when you drew the rectangles. If you want to add color to an existing image or color a large area of an image, you use the Fill with color tool. When you click a pixel in a graphic with the Fill with color tool, Paint changes the color of that pixel to Color 1. To change the color to Color 2, right-click a pixel with the Fill with color tool. If adjacent pixels are the same color as the one you clicked, Paint also changes those colors to Color 1. In this way, you can use the Fill with color tool to fill any enclosed area with color. Make sure the area you click is a fully enclosed space. If it has any openings, the new color will extend past the boundaries of the area you are trying to color.

REFERENCE

Filling an Area with Color

- Set Color 1 to the color you want to use. (Click the Color 1 button, and then click the desired color in the color palette or click the Color picker tool and then click pixel in the graphic.)
- On the Home tab, in the Tools group, click the Fill with color tool.
- Click inside the border of the area you want to color.

You suggest to Shawn that a contrasting color, such as the aqua that appears in the bottom wave of the sailboat image, would make the rectangles more appealing, and you offer to show him how to quickly change the color of the rectangle you drew.

To change the color of the rectangle:

▶ **1.** In the Tools group, click the **Color picker** tool 🖊, and then click an aqua pixel in the bottom wave of sailboat image to change the foreground color (Color 1) to aqua.

▶ **2.** In the Tools group, click the **Fill with color** tool 🪣, and then move the pointer into the graphic. The pointer changes to a paint can ◇, indicating that any pixel you click will change to the foreground color.

▶ **3.** Click inside the new rectangle to change its color from dark blue to aqua. See Figure 7-25.

Figure 7-25   **Changing the color of the rectangle**

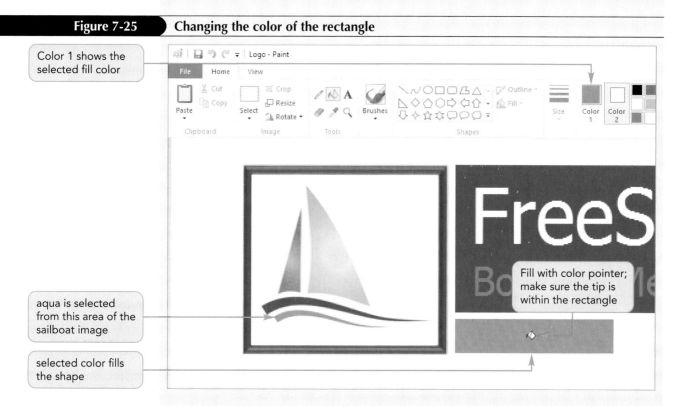

Color 1 shows the selected fill color

aqua is selected from this area of the sailboat image

selected color fills the shape

Trouble? If your rectangle is a different shade of aqua from the one shown in the figure, continue with the steps. If your rectangle is not aqua at all, however, click the Undo button ⤺ on the Quick Access Toolbar, and then repeat Steps 1–3.

Trouble? If the background of the logo graphic turns aqua instead of the rectangle, you clicked the background instead of the rectangle. Click the Undo button ⤺ on the Quick Access Toolbar, and then repeat Step 3, making sure the tip of the paint can pointer is within the border of the rectangle.

▶ **4.** To view the entire image with the new color, click the **Magnifier** tool 🔍 in the Tools group, and then right-click the graphic to return to 100% magnification.

▶ **5.** Click the **Save** button 🖫 on the Quick Access Toolbar to save your work.

Coloring the rectangle aqua creates contrast, which makes that graphic element more interesting. Now you can complete the logo graphic by copying the rectangle so three aqua rectangles appear below the dark blue one.

Copying an Image

Recall that to copy an image, you use a method similar to the one used for moving an image: You select the area you want to copy, copy it to the Clipboard, and then paste it in your graphic. Because the pasted image appears in a selection box in the upper-left corner of the graphic, you must drag the image to a new location. You'll show Shawn how to copy the aqua rectangle and then paste it to create a row of three rectangles below the text box. To create an appealing arrangement, you must make sure that the rectangles are evenly spaced and that their tops and bottoms are aligned. To space and align shapes effectively, you can display gridlines on the canvas to position the shapes accurately. The gridlines do not become a part of the graphic—they are only a visual guide that appears in the Paint window. You'll show Shawn how to display gridlines to aid in positioning the aqua rectangles in a row.

To copy and paste the rectangle:

1. If necessary, click the **Magnifier** tool in the Tools group, and then click the center of the aqua rectangle twice to magnify the image 300%.

2. Click the **View** tab to display options for changing the view of the Paint window.

3. In the Show or hide group, click the **Gridlines** check box to display the gridlines in the Paint window.

4. Click the **Home** tab, in the Image group, click the **Select** button, and then drag to select only the aqua rectangle.

   Trouble? If the selection box includes part of the frame or the dark-blue rectangle, or does not include the entire aqua rectangle, click outside the selection box and repeat Step 4.

5. In the Clipboard group, click the **Copy** button to copy the aqua rectangle to the Clipboard.

6. In the Clipboard group, click the **Paste** button to paste the aqua rectangle in the upper-left corner of the Paint window.

7. Drag the selected rectangle next to the first aqua rectangle, leaving one square of white space on the grid between the two shapes. If necessary, use the arrow keys on your keyboard to adjust the vertical position of the rectangle and its alignment with the first rectangle. The lower edge of the new rectangle should be on the same row of the grid as the lower edge of the first rectangle.

8. Click outside the selection, and then scroll to the right to display the right edge of the second rectangle.

9. In the Clipboard group, click the **Paste** button again to paste another copy of the rectangle in the upper-left corner of the Paint window.

10. Drag the selected rectangle to align its right edge with the right edge of the dark-blue rectangle and its top with the top edges of the other two aqua rectangles. See Figure 7-26.

Figure 7-26   Pasting and positioning copies of the rectangle

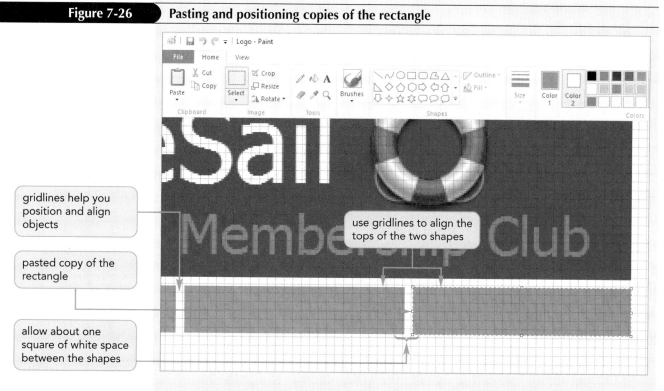

gridlines help you position and align objects

use gridlines to align the tops of the two shapes

pasted copy of the rectangle

allow about one square of white space between the shapes

Trouble? If the three rectangles are not evenly spaced or bottom-aligned, use the Select tool to select a rectangle, and then drag it to change its position so it is evenly spaced and aligned with the other rectangles.

▶ **11.** Click outside the selection to deselect the rectangle.

▶ **12.** To view the entire image with the three rectangles, click the **Zoom out** button ⊖ on the status bar twice to return to 100% magnification.

▶ **13.** Make any other adjustments as necessary to make your graphic similar to the one in Figure 7-27, and then save your work.

Your last task is to position the image on the canvas to minimize the amount of unnecessary white space in the graphic.

Cropping a Graphic

Recall that you can crop an image to remove one or more rows or columns of pixels from the edge of a picture. When you crop a graphic to eliminate unnecessary white space by resizing the canvas, you reduce file size and prevent a border from appearing around your picture when you paste it into another file. You can also crop a graphic using the Crop tool in the Image group on the Home tab. To do so, you select the area you want to retain in the graphic, and then click the Crop tool to remove all parts of the graphic beyond the selection.

To crop the logo graphic:

▶ **1.** If necessary, click the **Select** button in the Image group.

▶ **2.** Using the selection pointer ⊹, drag to select the frame, the dark-blue rectangle with text, and the three aqua rectangles, as shown in Figure 7-27.

Figure 7-27 Selecting the area to crop

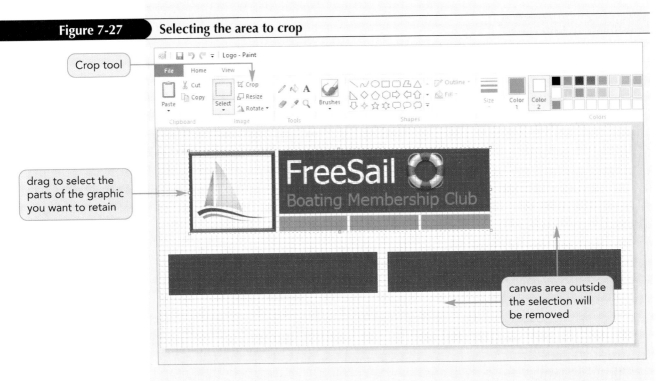

3. In the Image group, click the **Crop** button to remove all of the pixels outside the selected area.

4. Click the **View** tab, and then, in the Show or hide group, click the **Gridlines** check box to remove the checkmark. The gridlines no longer appear in the Paint window. See Figure 7-28. Your graphic doesn't have to look exactly like the figure, but it should look similar.

Figure 7-28 Completed Logo graphic

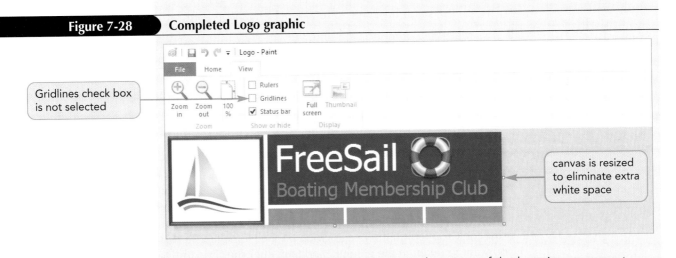

Trouble? If you cropped the image so that parts of the logo image are cut off, click the Undo button on the Quick Access Toolbar, and then repeat Steps 2 and 3.

You've completed the graphic for FreeSail Boat Club, so you can save the Logo file and close Paint.

To save the file and close Paint:

▶ **1.** Click the **Save** button 🖫 on the Quick Access Toolbar.

▶ **2.** Close the Paint window.

Now that you've shown Shawn how to use Paint to create and modify bitmapped graphics, you can get ready to work with Oscar to develop a multimedia presentation.

REVIEW

Session 7.1 Quick Check

1. A(n) _____ is created from rows of colored pixels that together form an image.

2. For what kind of images are vector graphics most appropriate?

3. What command can you use when you want to copy an entire image from another file and paste it in your current image?

4. Name five graphics file formats you can use in Paint.

5. What does it mean to crop a graphic?

6. If you are resizing an image such as a photo, be sure to maintain the _____, or the relationship of the width to the height.

7. If Color 1 is black and Color 2 is white, what happens to a blue rectangle when you right-click it using the Fill with color tool?

Session 7.2 Visual Overview:

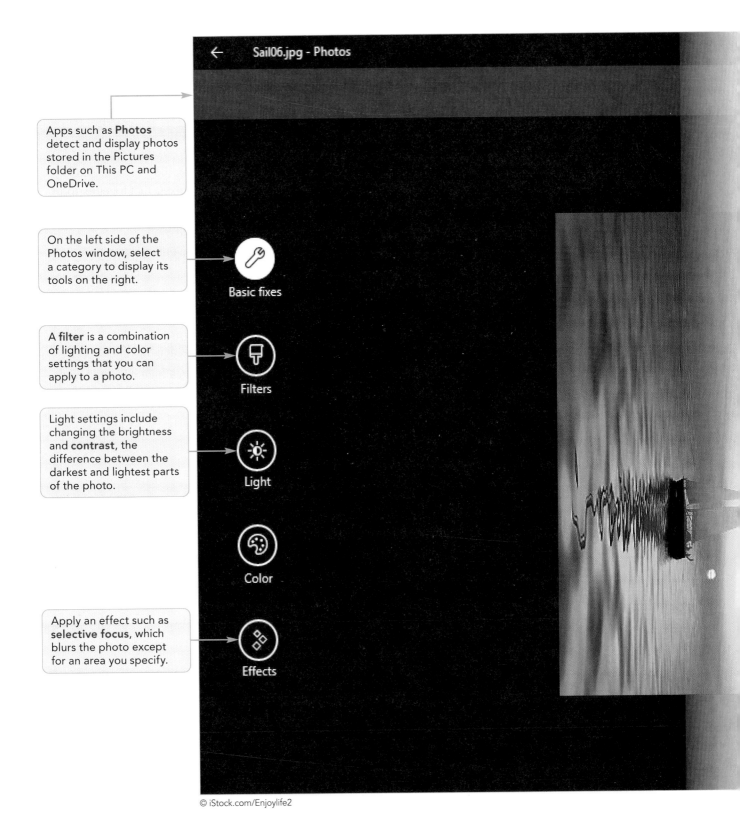

Apps such as **Photos** detect and display photos stored in the Pictures folder on This PC and OneDrive.

On the left side of the Photos window, select a category to display its tools on the right.

A **filter** is a combination of lighting and color settings that you can apply to a photo.

Light settings include changing the brightness and **contrast**, the difference between the darkest and lightest parts of the photo.

Apply an effect such as **selective focus**, which blurs the photo except for an area you specify.

Sail06.jpg - Photos

Basic fixes

Filters

Light

Color

Effects

© iStock.com/Enjoylife2

Editing Photos

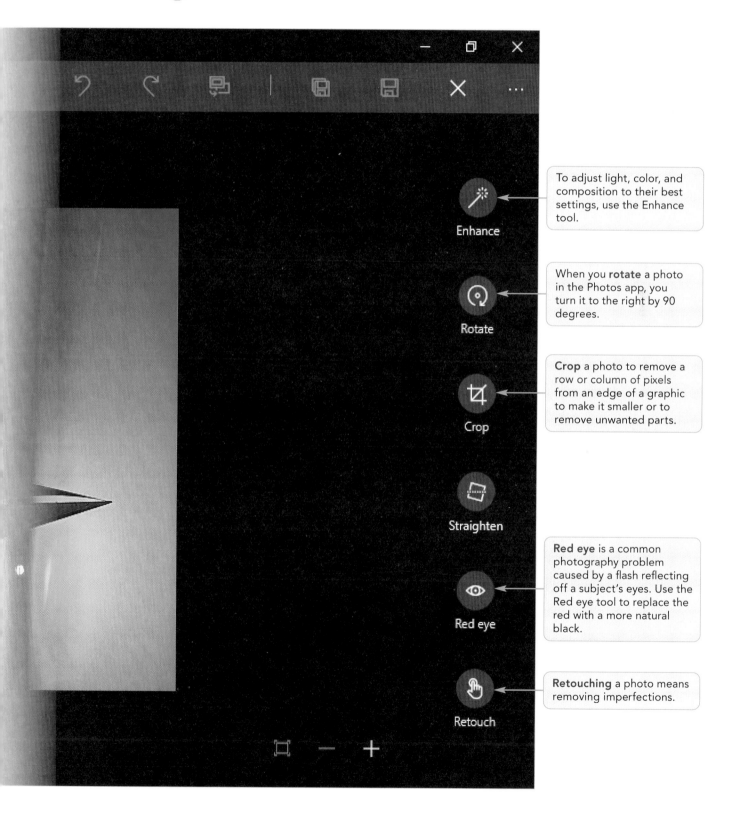

To adjust light, color, and composition to their best settings, use the Enhance tool.

Enhance

When you **rotate** a photo in the Photos app, you turn it to the right by 90 degrees.

Rotate

Crop a photo to remove a row or column of pixels from an edge of a graphic to make it smaller or to remove unwanted parts.

Crop

Straighten

Red eye is a common photography problem caused by a flash reflecting off a subject's eyes. Use the Red eye tool to replace the red with a more natural black.

Red eye

Retouching a photo means removing imperfections.

Retouch

Working with Photos

Innovations in digital cameras and computers have transformed the field of photography, letting anyone edit and print photos without using a darkroom or professional photo lab. Instead, you can take photos with your computer, or transfer them from your digital camera or phone to your Windows computer, where you can fine-tune the images, display them in a slide show, use them as a screen saver or wallpaper, and share them with others.

As an intern for the FreeSail Boat Club, you are preparing to work with Oscar to create a multimedia presentation that FreeSail can use to showcase the boats available to members. In the presentation, he would like to include a slide show of photos with a musical accompaniment. Oscar has already transferred photos of sailboats from his digital camera to his computer. You'll show him how to view, organize, and edit the photos so he can assemble them into a slide show to play in the club's reception area.

Acquiring and Importing Photos

Before you can create a slide show on your computer, you need to acquire and possibly import photos. The most popular way to acquire photos is to use a digital camera to take the photos. The camera can be a single electronic device or part of another device such as a smartphone or computer. (Cameras built into computers are usually called **webcams**.) Cameras store photos as JPG image files, so you can work with them using any photo editor or painting graphics app. Using a digital camera lets you control the subject matter and maintain the legal rights to the images—two notable advantages. Unless you're a trained photographer, the main disadvantage is that your images are not professional quality, though you often can improve them using digital editing tools. If you are using the photos for the enjoyment of family and friends, you might not need to do more than snap the photos on your digital camera or a mobile device with a built-in camera (see Figure 7-29), and then transfer them to your Windows computer.

| Figure 7-29 | Taking photos with a mobile device |

© iStock.com/ivansmuk

If you need professional photos, such as for a product brochure or website, you have a few options. Hiring a photographer to create and prepare the images can be effective, though expensive. You can also purchase photos from stock collections, typically provided online, by paying a licensing fee. These collections usually contain royalty-free images that you can use for any purpose, and cost anywhere from hundreds of dollars to less than a dollar each. You can download photos free of charge and copyright only if the photos are in the public domain and are freely available for use. If you have conventional photographs printed on paper, you can use a scanner to convert the photos into digital pictures if you own the copyright or the photos are in the public domain.

PROSKILLS

Decision Making: Using Copyright-Protected, Royalty-Free, and Public-Domain Photos

Many school and work projects involve graphics. Where and how to acquire graphics is often a decision you need to make early in the project—one that can have legal consequences. Although you can easily copy photos displayed on websites, that doesn't mean that you should. Most photos and other media on the web are protected by copyright law. A copyright gives photographers (and other types of graphic artists and creators) the exclusive right to control their images. They can decide who can copy, distribute, or derive material from their photographs. Before you can use a copyrighted photo, you must receive permission from the photographer.

Some websites and services offer **royalty-free photos**, meaning that the photographers do not receive payment each time their photos are used. However, the photographers still retain the rights to the photos even if they don't receive royalties for each use. Photos in the **public domain** are the only ones not protected by copyright law. These include photos for which the copyright has expired, some government images, and those explicitly identified as being in the public domain.

If you want to copy photos from the web or another digital source, the following guidelines help you respect the photographer's rights:

- Ask the owner of the copyright for permission.
- Find out if the photographer has any stipulations on how the material may be used.
- If explicit guidelines are given, follow them, and credit the source of your material.
- Keep a copy of your request and the permission received.

If you acquire photos from a website or other digital source, you only have to copy them to a folder on your computer so you can edit and organize them. However, if you are using a digital camera, including one in your cell phone, you might need to perform an additional step of importing the photo files from the device to your computer. One way to do this is to connect the device directly to the computer using a cable that plugs into the computer's USB port. Another way is to import pictures using a memory card reader, a device that plugs into your computer's USB port. In either case, Windows 10 should recognize your camera or card (it recognizes most makes and models of digital cameras and cards), and guide you through the steps of importing pictures. After importing the images, Windows 10 stores them in the Pictures folder by default.

If you are taking photos on a Windows device, such as a Windows phone, OneDrive is selected as the default location for storing files. Because OneDrive automatically syncs its content among all of your devices, the photos are available to you on any of your Windows devices. (You need to have a Microsoft account to use OneDrive.)

If you take photos with a mobile device running the iOS operating system, such as an iPhone or iPad, you can use an Apple service called iCloud. As with OneDrive, all the photos you take with your iOS device are stored in the iCloud Photo Library. When you set up iCloud on your mobile device, you can select Photos as an app that can access and sync the files in the iCloud Photo Library. On a Windows 10 computer, start the Photos app to view and manage the photos in the iCloud Photo Library.

TIP

iOS is Apple's proprietary mobile operating system for its handheld devices, such as the iPhone, iPad, and iPod Touch.

Using the Camera App

The Windows 10 Camera app lets you use your webcam to take photos and record videos. The Camera app displays the webcam image in a window. Click the camera icon to capture the image and store it in the Camera Roll folder in the Pictures folder on your computer. You can also use the Camera app to record videos with your webcam. To do so, click the video camera icon in the Camera window to switch to video mode and start recording. As you record, a timer appears so you can keep track of how much video you are recording. When you're finished, click the video camera icon again to stop recording. To see the video, click the left arrow button. You can use the Photos app to display photos you take with the Camera app, and use the Videos app to play videos you record with the Camera app.

Viewing and Organizing Photos

Windows 10 provides a number of tools for working with photos. Although some of these tools have features in common, each one is designed to serve a particular purpose, as explained in the following descriptions:

- File Explorer—When you store photos in the Pictures folder or any other folder, File Explorer provides tools on the Picture Tools Manage tab for manipulating and viewing the photos. For example, you can use the Slide show button to play the photos in the current folder as a full-screen slide show. Other apps, such as the Photos app, detect the photos stored in the Pictures folder so you can quickly create a slide show or share photos with others.
- Photos app—You have already worked with the Windows 10 Photos app to select a photo to display on its Start menu tile. You can also use Photos to organize pictures and videos, edit and enhance photos, play a slide show of photos stored in a single location or display each photo one at a time, and share photos with others.
- Windows Photo Viewer—Although Windows Photo Viewer is not a separate app you can open from the Start menu, it is a full-featured tool you can open from a folder window. If you click a photo file in a folder window and then click the Open button arrow in the Open group on the Home tab, you can select Windows Photo Viewer as the tool you want to use to open the file. You can then view, rotate, and print photos and play a slide show. While File Explorer and Photos are designed to help you find and organize photos by displaying all of them in one place, Windows Photo Viewer lets you concentrate on each photo one at a time. In addition to rotating photos, you can zoom in and view photos at full size.
- OneDrive—If you use the OneDrive app, all of the folders include tools for organizing and sharing photos. For example, you can arrange photos into albums and add tags to photos. You can also invite people you know to access and view the photos.

You might have additional photo-editing tools installed on your computer. These tools are often provided by digital camera and computer manufacturers.

Your first task in developing a presentation with Oscar is to review the photos he has taken of sailboats in Puget Sound and other bodies of water near Seattle. Start by copying the photos in your Module folder to a subfolder of the Pictures folder so that all of the Windows photo tools can access the files easily.

To copy photo files to the Pictures folder:

▶ **1.** Open File Explorer and then click the **Pictures** folder in the navigation pane. You might see other folders on your screen.

2. Create a new folder named **Boats** in the Pictures folder, and then copy the 10 sailboat photos (**Sail01–Sail10**) and the **Sailing Lessons** video from the Module7 > Module folder to the Boats folder. When you're finished, the Boats folder should contain 11 files.

3. If necessary, display the files in the Boats folder, and then resize the Boats folder window to display all of the tools on the Home tab.

Now you can show Oscar how to use File Explorer and Windows Photo Viewer to display, examine, and organize photos.

To examine photos using File Explorer:

1. In the Boats folder window, switch to Details view, if necessary.

TIP

To sort files in alphabetical order or by date, size, or rating, click the column heading.

2. Make sure the Name, Date modified, Type, Size, Tags, and Rating columns are displayed in the Boats folder window. If necessary, right-click a column heading and then click to check or uncheck column names so they match the ones shown in Figure 7-30.

Figure 7-30   Displaying the files in the Boats folder

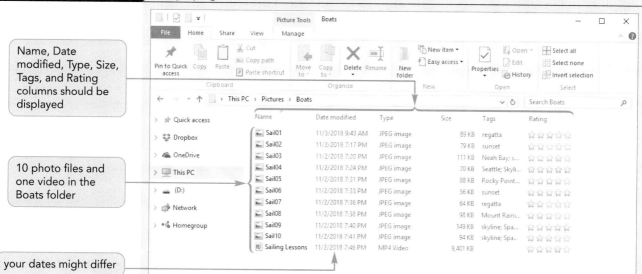

Name, Date modified, Type, Size, Tags, and Rating columns should be displayed

10 photo files and one video in the Boats folder

your dates might differ

3. Click the **View** tab, and then, in the Panes group, click the **Details pane** button to open the Details pane.

4. In the Layout group, click **Large icons** to switch to Large icons view.

Oscar added tags and ratings to these photos when he transferred them to his computer. You can use the tags, ratings, and other details to arrange the photos so they are easier to reference. For example, Oscar sometimes needs to refer to sailboat photos by tag so he can see where they were taken. He might also want to select all of the photos he rated with five stars. You'll show him how to use File Explorer to arrange the photos.

To arrange the sailboat photos:

▶ **1.** In the Current view group, click the **Group by** button, and then click **Rating**. The photos are arranged into four sections: 2 Stars, 3 Stars, 4 Stars, and 5 Stars. See Figure 7-31.

Figure 7-31	Arranging photos by Rating

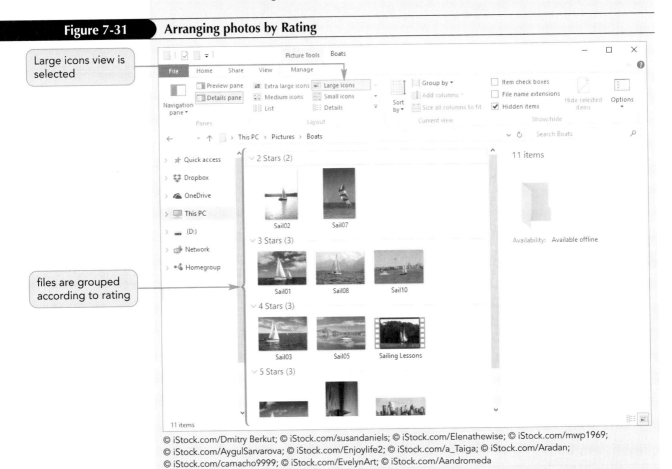

Large icons view is selected

files are grouped according to rating

© iStock.com/Dmitry Berkut; © iStock.com/susandaniels; © iStock.com/Elenathewise; © iStock.com/mwp1969; © iStock.com/AygulSarvarova; © iStock.com/Enjoylife2; © iStock.com/a_Taiga; © iStock.com/Aradan; © iStock.com/camacho9999; © iStock.com/EvelynArt; © iStock.com/Aandromeda

▶ **2.** Click the **Group by** button, and then click **(None)** to return to folder view.

▶ **3.** If the files do not appear in alphanumeric order by name, click the **Sort by** button in the Current view group, make sure the Ascending option is selected, and then click **Name** to sort the files by name.

As you've seen, File Explorer lets you view all of your photos in one place and then arrange them by date, rating, or other criteria. Now you want to show Oscar how to use Windows Photo Viewer so he can compare the two tools.

To view photos using Windows Photo Viewer:

▶ **1.** In the Boats folder window, click the **Sail01** photo, click the **Home** tab, click the **Open button arrow** in the Open group, and then click **Windows Photo Viewer**. The photo opens in Windows Photo Viewer. See Figure 7-32.

Trouble? If the photo opens in a different app, you clicked the Open button instead of the Open button arrow. Close the app window, and then repeat Step 1.

Trouble? If Windows Photo Viewer does not appear in the Open button list, click Choose another app on the menu. Click the More apps link, scroll to and click Windows Photo Viewer, and then click the OK button.

| **Figure 7-32** | **Windows Photo Viewer** |

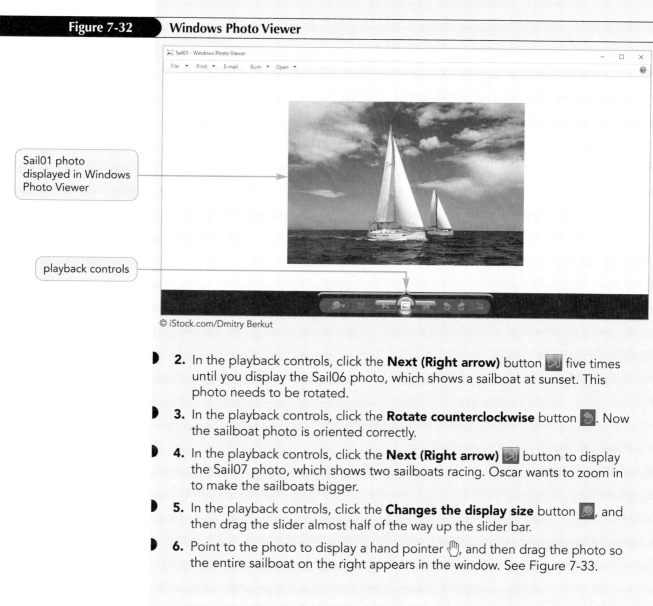

Sail01 photo displayed in Windows Photo Viewer

playback controls

© iStock.com/Dmitry Berkut

▶ **2.** In the playback controls, click the **Next (Right arrow)** button five times until you display the Sail06 photo, which shows a sailboat at sunset. This photo needs to be rotated.

▶ **3.** In the playback controls, click the **Rotate counterclockwise** button . Now the sailboat photo is oriented correctly.

▶ **4.** In the playback controls, click the **Next (Right arrow)** button to display the Sail07 photo, which shows two sailboats racing. Oscar wants to zoom in to make the sailboats bigger.

▶ **5.** In the playback controls, click the **Changes the display size** button , and then drag the slider almost half of the way up the slider bar.

▶ **6.** Point to the photo to display a hand pointer , and then drag the photo so the entire sailboat on the right appears in the window. See Figure 7-33.

Figure 7-33   Magnified view of the Sail07 photo

hand pointer in Windows Photo Viewer; drag the image to scroll

Fit to window button

Changes the display size button

© iStock.com/EvelynArt

> **7.** To display this photo at its original size, click the **Fit to window** button ⊞ in the playback controls.

Besides examining and rotating photos, you can play a simple slide show in Windows Photo Viewer. Oscar wants to play a slide show of sailboats for FreeSail members in the club's reception area.

Playing a Simple Slide Show

You can play a simple slide show in File Explorer by clicking the Slide show button in the View group on the Picture Tools Manage tab; in Windows Photo Viewer by clicking the round Play slide show button in the playback controls; or in the Photos app by clicking the Slideshow button on the toolbar. In any case, the slide show includes all of the photos in the current folder and its subfolders, and plays the photos one after another.

REFERENCE

Playing a Slide Show

- In File Explorer, click a photo and then click the Picture Tools Manage tab.
- In the View group, click the Slide show button.

or

- In Windows Photo Viewer, click the Play slide show button in the playback controls.

or

- In the Photos app, click a photo and then click the Slideshow button on the toolbar.

During a slide show, all three Windows tools automatically display a series of full-screen photos. The slide show plays all of the photos in the current folder, starting with the selected photo. While a slide show is running in Windows Photo Viewer, you can right-click a photo to pause the show, adjust the speed, go forward or backward, and choose whether pictures are shown randomly or sequentially.

To play a simple slide show:

▶ **1.** In Windows Photo Viewer, click the **Play slide show** button ⊙ in the playback controls. The screen darkens, and Windows Photo Viewer displays the current photo for a few seconds, and then displays the next photo.

▶ **2.** To slow the slide show so you can examine the photos, right-click a slide, and then click **Slide Show Speed - Slow** on the shortcut menu.

▶ **3.** After viewing another photo, right-click the slide, click **Slide Show Speed - Medium** on the shortcut menu to return to the default speed, and then press the **Esc** key to end the slide show.

▶ **4.** Close Windows Photo Viewer.

Oscar says that playing only photos in a slide show isn't catchy enough to attract new members. He also wants to play music while displaying the photos. You'll show him how to create such a slide show later. Right now, you want to edit a photo you found to improve its composition. You'll show Oscar how to use the Photos app to edit the photo next.

Editing a Photo

You can use the Photos app to perform photo editing tasks such as rotating, cropping, adjusting the amount of light, adding effects, and retouching photos to remove imperfections. Following are some of the ways you can touch up photos in the Photos app:

- Enhance—If you're not sure how to touch up a photo or want to let Photos adjust settings for you, use the Enhance tool. Photos determines the best corrections to make to light, color, and composition and applies them automatically.
- Red eye—If you used a flash when snapping a photo of one or more people, their eyes might appear red in the picture, a common problem caused by the flash reflecting off the eyes. Use the Red eye tool to reduce or eliminate this effect by replacing the red with a more natural black.
- Color tools—Adjust the **color temperature** to make the photo appear warmer (with more red tones) or cooler (with more blue tones). If one color dominates in the photo and makes the other colors look inaccurate—an effect called **color cast**—adjust the tint by adding or removing a color. If the colors look too vivid or dull, change the **saturation**, which determines the amount of color in the photo.
- Filters—A filter is a combination of lighting and color settings that you can apply to a photo. For example, you can apply a filter to a color photo so it appears in black and white.
- Effects—Apply a **vignette effect**, which fades the corners of the image to black or white, and then set the amount of vignette effect you want to apply. You can also apply a selective focus, which blurs the photo except for an area you specify.

After editing a photo, you can use the Save button on the Photos toolbar to save the photo, which applies the changes to the original photo. If you don't want to alter the original photo, you can use the Save a copy button on the Photos toolbar. The Photos app saves the copy in the Pictures > Saved Pictures folder and adds a number such as "(2)" to the filename so you can distinguish the copy from the original.

Now you can show Oscar how to improve the quality of a couple of sailboat photos. The colors in Sail02 are washed out, which probably means the contrast is unbalanced, and the boat and horizon are tilted slightly. The colors in Sail05 also need to be adjusted. You can fix these problems by using the Photos app to touch up the photos.

To touch up photos:

1. In the Boats folder window, right-click the **Sail02** photo, point to **Open with** on the shortcut menu, and then click **Photos**. The photo opens in the Photos app. See Figure 7-34. Maximize the window if necessary.

   Trouble? If the photo opens in a different app, you clicked the Open command instead of the Open with command. Close the app window, and then repeat Step 1.

Figure 7-34   Photo open in the Photos app

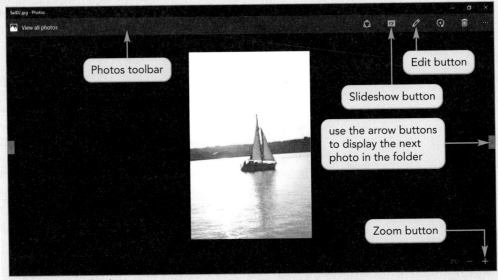

© iStock.com/susandaniels

2. On the Photos toolbar, click the **Edit** button 🖉 to open editing view, which displays editing categories on the left, with the Basic fixes category selected by default. The tools in the selected category appear on the right.

3. Click the **Enhance** button on the right to automatically adjust settings to improve the photo. Photos straightens the image and changes the amount of light in the photo, which improves the clarity.

4. On the Photos toolbar, click the **Save** button 🖫 to save the changes to the photo. Editing view closes and returns to displaying the Sail02 photo and the Photos toolbar.

5. Move the pointer to display left and right arrow buttons, and then click the **right arrow** button ▷ as many times as necessary to display the Sail05 photo.

6. On the Photos toolbar, click the **Edit** button 🖉 to open editing view again.

7. Click the **Color** button on the left to display the tools in the Color category. The blues in this photo are too vivid, so you can reduce the tint.

8. Click the **Tint** button to display a control you use to adjust the saturation. Drag the white balloon counterclockwise to -50 to reduce the tint by 50 percent. See Figure 7-35.

TIP

To save your changes without affecting the original photo, click the Save a copy button on the Photos toolbar.

Figure 7-35   Adjusting the tint

adjust the tint to reduce the amount of color and lighten the photo

drag the white balloon to change the tint

© iStock.com/AygulSarvarova

▶ **9.** Click a blank area of the background to accept and close the Tint setting.

▶ **10.** On the Photos toolbar, click the **Save** button 🖫 to save the changes to the photo.

Oscar wants to apply a filter and an effect to photos to see how these features work. You'll show Oscar how to apply a filter and use the Selective focus feature.

To apply a filter and an effect:

▶ **1.** Use the **right arrow** button ▷ to display the Sail08 photo.

▶ **2.** On the Photos toolbar, click the **Edit** button ✏ to open editing view.

▶ **3.** Click the **Filters** button on the left to display six thumbnails previewing the filters on the right.

▶ **4.** Click the **fifth thumbnail** to apply that filter to the photo. The background fades and darkens slightly, bringing the sailboat into sharper focus. Oscar likes the results.

▶ **5.** On the Photos toolbar, click the **Save** button 🖫 to save the changes to the photo.

▶ **6.** Use the **right arrow** button ▷ to display the Sail09 photo, and then click the **Edit** button ✏ on the Photos toolbar.

▶ **7.** Click the **Effects** button on the left to display the Vignette and Selective focus buttons on the right.

▶ **8.** Click the **Selective focus** button to display a circle with round sizing handles on the photo. The part of the photo in the circle is in focus while the rest of the photo is blurred.

▶ **9.** Drag the circle to the left so that the sailboat with the white sail and the sailboat with the blue-striped sail are within the circle. See Figure 7-36.

Figure 7-36 **Using the Selective focus tool**

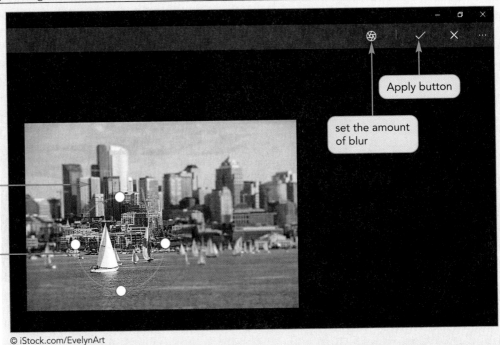

© iStock.com/EvelynArt

> **10.** On the Photos toolbar, click the **Apply** button ☑ to apply the selective focus.

> **11.** On the Photos toolbar, click the **Save** button 🖫 to save the changes to the photo.

Oscar wonders if he could make the photos available to any FreeSail member with a Windows 10 computer. You'll show him how to quickly share the photos with others next.

Sharing Photos

When you share your photos, you make them available for other people to view on their computers. The most popular way to share photos is to post them on a photo-sharing website or another type of site where you have an account, such as Twitter or OneDrive. You can also send photos to others in email messages and text messages. A photo-sharing website lets you share and store pictures, often free of charge. (Check the website's policies before copying your files to an online album.) You can then invite others to visit the website and view your photo albums.

If you're already using the Photos app, the easiest way to share photos is to use the Share button on the Photos toolbar. You can also access OneDrive in File Explorer and then share the files, which is a good alternative if you are organizing photos in a folder window. You'll use both techniques in the following steps.

Sharing Photos from the Photos App

If you have an account set up in the Windows 10 Mail app or the Messaging app, you can use the Share button on the Photos toolbar to share photos via email or text message. Depending on other apps you've installed, you can also use the Share button to send photos to those apps, such as Facebook and Twitter. The Share button also appears on the Share tab in File Explorer. You can use it the same way to share photos from a folder window.

One of Oscar's favorite photos to send to potential members is the photo of sailboats in Puget Sound with the Seattle skyline in the background (Sail09). You'll show Oscar how to share this photo via email.

You must have an account set up in the Mail app to share photos via email. If you do not have an account set up yet, open the Mail app, which will guide you to set up an account.

To share a photo via email:

1. In the Photos window, use the **left arrow** button ‹ or the **right arrow** button › to display the Sail09 photo, if necessary.

2. On the Photos toolbar, click the **Share** button to display the Share menu. See Figure 7-37. Your Share menu might list different apps.

Figure 7-37 | **Share menu for sharing photos**

© iStock.com/EvelynArt

> **Trouble?** If the Photos toolbar isn't displayed, click in the Photos app window.

3. On the Share menu, click **Mail**. If you have more than one email account, click the account you want to use to send the photo. Your email address, the To box, and other controls for sharing the selected photo via email appear in the Mail app window on the right of the screen.

> **Trouble?** If Mail does not appear on the Share menu, read but do not perform the remaining steps.

TIP

To include more than one email address in the To box, insert a semicolon between each email address.

4. Type your email address to send yourself a copy of the photo.

5. Click in the **Subject** box, and then type **Sailboats with Seattle skyline** as the subject of the message.

6. On the Mail toolbar, click the **Send** button to send the photo and message to your email account. The Mail app closes automatically.

7. Close the Photos app.

> **Trouble?** If the "Photos is being used for sharing, some items might not be shared" message appears, click the Close App button **X** to close it.

To share a photo from File Explorer, you can click the photo in a folder window and then click the Share tab. In the Send group, click the Share button to display the same Share menu you used to email the Sail09 photo.

Sharing Photos Using OneDrive

OneDrive is a Microsoft service that provides online, or cloud, storage space for your files. You can open OneDrive from File Explorer or through a browser that takes you directly to the OneDrive website (https://OneDrive.live.com or OneDrive.com) to store files in a secure online location that you can access any time you have an Internet connection. When you access OneDrive with a browser, you are using a full-featured **web app**, an app stored on a server and delivered over the Internet through a browser. As a web app, OneDrive provides more tools for manipulating and sharing files than OneDrive integrated into File Explorer.

The amount of storage space OneDrive provides depends on the type of Microsoft software you use, but a typical amount is 15 GB. You can purchase additional storage space as necessary. As you store files on OneDrive, you can organize them so that some files are private, meaning that only you and others you specify can access them. You can also designate files as public, which means anyone can view and open them. The main advantage of using OneDrive is that you and people you know can use any device to access your OneDrive files, such as a Windows 10 computer, a tablet running a different operating system, or a smartphone.

OneDrive provides a standard set of folders for each user: Documents, Favorites, Shared favorites, and Public. You can add others as you need them. The OneDrive web app provides special tools for organizing and sharing photos. For example, you can arrange photos into albums and add tags to photos. In addition, an online version of the Photos app is integrated into the OneDrive web app so that you can view and edit photos by rotating them or adding captions, for example. You can also play a slide show of photos in a folder.

Oscar wants to post all of the photos in the Boats folder on his OneDrive so that members with a web browser can view them. He can then let members access the photos when they want to select a sailboat to use with their membership. However, he wants only members and potential members to see the sailboat photos, not other people who might access his OneDrive, such as his young children, who might inadvertently change or delete a photo. This means that he should store the photos in a private folder, such as his Documents folder. If he stored the photos in the Public folder, anyone could view them. Because Oscar wants to keep the sailboat photos separate from other files in the Documents folder, you'll create a new folder in the Documents folder on his OneDrive. To do so, you'll use File Explorer to access OneDrive.

To perform the following steps, you need to have a Microsoft account. If you don't have a Microsoft account, use a web browser to go to https://signup.live.com, and then provide the requested information, including a user name (your email address) and password. Note your user name and password so you can use it to access OneDrive.

To copy photos to OneDrive:

▶ **1.** If necessary, navigate to and display the contents of the **Pictures > Boats** folder in File Explorer. If the Details pane is open, close it.

▶ **2.** Right-click the **File Explorer** button 🖿 on the taskbar, and then click **File Explorer** to open a new folder window.

▶ **3.** In the navigation pane, click **OneDrive** to display the default folders and any folders and files you might have already created and stored on OneDrive.

   Trouble? If a window appears requesting your user name and password, enter your user name and password to sign in to OneDrive.

   Trouble? If a window appears asking if you want to change the location of your OneDrive folder, close the window.

4. In the right pane of the OneDrive folder window, double-click the **Documents** folder to open it.

5. On the **Home** tab, in the New group, click the **New folder** button to create a folder for the sailboat photos.

6. Type **OneDrive Boats** as the name of the folder, and then press the **Enter** key.

7. Double-click the **OneDrive Boats** folder to open the folder.

8. Arrange the two windows side by side, select **Sail01–Sail10** in the Boats folder window, and then drag and copy the selected files to the OneDrive Boats folder.

9. Close the OneDrive Boats folder window.

Now members with a web browser can sign in to OneDrive and view the sailboat photos when Oscar invites them to do so. Because you stored the photos in a subfolder of the Documents folder, they are private files. To allow others to access private folders and files, you can use the OneDrive web app to send an email message or a link to other people inviting them to view or edit a file or folder on OneDrive. As you invite people to access your files, you can specify that they can edit the files or only view them with or without a Microsoft account. You'll show Oscar how to send an invitation and then access the files.

As with the previous steps, you need to have a Microsoft account to perform the following steps.

To use the OneDrive web app to share photos:

1. Click the **Microsoft Edge** button e on the taskbar to start the browser, and then maximize the window, if necessary.

2. Click in the **Address bar**, type **onedrive.com**, and then press the **Enter** key. If necessary, click the **Sign in** button and then sign in by providing your user name and password. Your OneDrive opens and displays the default folders and any folders and files you might have already created and stored on OneDrive.

3. Click the **Documents** folder to display its contents, including the OneDrive Boats folder.

4. Click the **OneDrive Boats** folder to display its contents. See Figure 7-38.

Figure 7-38	Photos in the OneDrive web app

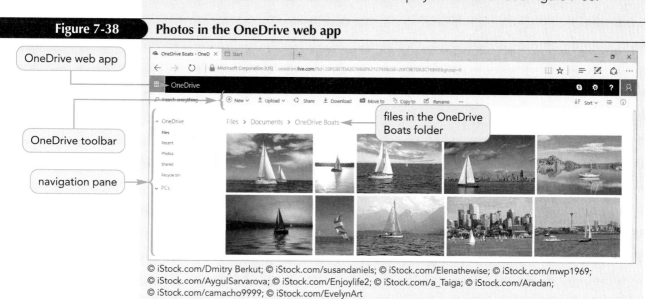

OneDrive web app

OneDrive toolbar

navigation pane

files in the OneDrive Boats folder

© iStock.com/Dmitry Berkut; © iStock.com/susandaniels; © iStock.com/Elenathewise; © iStock.com/mwp1969; © iStock.com/AygulSarvarova; © iStock.com/Enjoylife2; © iStock.com/a_Taiga; © iStock.com/Aradan; © iStock.com/camacho9999; © iStock.com/EvelynArt

▶ 5. On the OneDrive toolbar, click the **Share** button to display the Share dialog box, which you can use to invite people to access the OneDrive Boats folder.

▶ 6. Click in the **To** box, type the email address you use for your email account in the Mail app, click in the **Add a quick note** box, and then type **View the sailboat photos on my OneDrive**.

Trouble? If you do not have an email account in the Mail app, read but do not perform the remaining steps,

▶ 7. Click the **Recipients can only view link** to display options for sharing the files. By default, recipients can only view the files and do not need a Microsoft account to access them. These settings are appropriate for Oscar. If necessary, you could use the arrow button in each box to change the settings.

TIP

If you click "Get a link" in the Share dialog box, OneDrive generates a web address you can copy and paste in an email message, webpage, or other online location.

▶ 8. Click the **Share** button to have OneDrive send a message to your email account, inviting you to access the OneDrive Boats folder.

▶ 9. Click the **Close** button.

▶ 10. Close Microsoft Edge.

Next, you can sync your email to receive the invitation message to find out how your contacts will access the folder you shared.

To respond to the OneDrive invitation message:

▶ 1. Start Mail and then, if necessary, click the **Sync this view** button 🔄 to receive your email messages.

▶ 2. Click the message with the "View the sailboat photos on my OneDrive" subject. The message appears in the Reading pane. See Figure 7-39.

Figure 7-39 | Invitation message in Mail

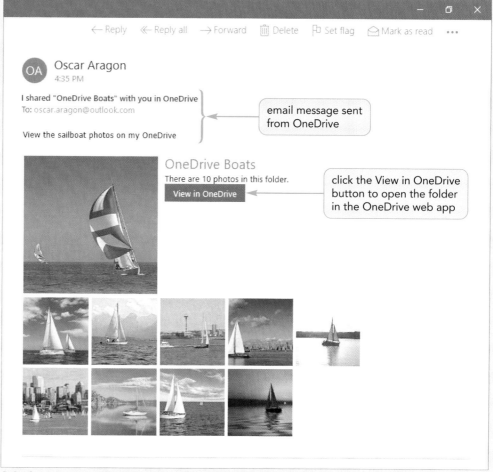

© iStock.com/Dmitry Berkut; © iStock.com/susandaniels; © iStock.com/Elenathewise; © iStock.com/mwp1969;
© iStock.com/AygulSarvarova; © iStock.com/Enjoylife2; © iStock.com/a_Taiga; © iStock.com/Aradan;
© iStock.com/camacho9999; © iStock.com/EvelynArt

> **3.** Point to the **View in OneDrive** button in the message to display a long, complex URL specifying the location of your OneDrive Boats folder, and then click the **View in OneDrive** button. Microsoft Edge starts and displays the OneDrive Boats folder in the OneDrive web app.
>
> **Trouble?** If a window appears requesting your user name and password, enter your user name and password to sign in to OneDrive.

As long as you are viewing the sailboat photos in the OneDrive web app, you offer to show Oscar some of the tools designed for viewing and editing photos. When you select one or more photos using the OneDrive web app, a toolbar appears with buttons for editing photos. For example, you can add a photo to an album, add and modify tags, rotate a photo, and rename the file. An **album** is a collection of photos displayed together, similar to a physical photo album.

To view and edit photos in the OneDrive web app:

> **1.** In the navigation pane, click **Photos**. OneDrive displays the photos in the OneDrive Boats folder and groups them according to date. See Figure 7-40.

Figure 7-40 Grouped photos in the OneDrive web app

OneDrive toolbar has buttons for working with photos

files are grouped by date taken

© iStock.com/susandaniels; © iStock.com/a_Taiga; © iStock.com/Aradan

2. Point to the photo with the October 2018 date. When a white circle appears in the upper-right corner of the photo, click the **white circle** to select the photo. The toolbar now contains buttons for editing the photo.

   Trouble? If you clicked the photo instead of the white circle, click the Back button ← in the Microsoft Edge Address bar to return to the window displaying the grouped photos. The photo is now selected, so you can continue with Step 3.

3. Select the next five photos in the folder so that six photos are selected.

4. On the OneDrive toolbar, click the **Add to album** button. The Add to album pane opens on the right with controls for creating and naming the album.

5. Click in the **New album** box, and then type **2018 Sailboats** to name the album.

6. Click the **Create** button to create an album containing the selected photos.

7. Double-click a blank area of the OneDrive window to deselect the photos, and then click **Albums** on the toolbar to display the photo albums saved on OneDrive.

8. Click the **2018 Sailboats** album to display its photos. See Figure 7-41. The first photo displayed in your album might differ.

Figure 7-41   **2018 Sailboats album**

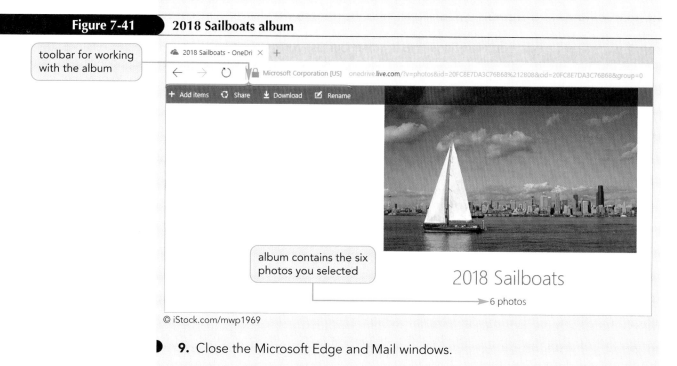

toolbar for working with the album

album contains the six photos you selected

2018 Sailboats

6 photos

© iStock.com/mwp1969

▶ **9.** Close the Microsoft Edge and Mail windows.

Now that you've given Oscar a thorough tour of the Windows 10 photo tools, you are ready to show him how to find and play music to accompany his slide show.

Finding and Playing Music

To play digital music files on your computer, you can use the Groove Music app or the Windows Media Player app. You use Groove Music to play any music files stored in the Music folder on your hard drive or OneDrive. In addition, you can visit the Windows Store, which provides albums and songs for purchase and download. You can generally preview the music free of charge. For music files stored on your computer, you can create **playlists**, which are lists of media files, such as songs, that you want to play in a specified order.

You can also use Windows Media Player to play music stored on your computer, CDs, or websites; download music files you've purchased from online stores; and create your own albums of songs and sync them to a portable music player, such as an MP3 player or your cell phone.

Before you purchase and download music files from an online store using either app, make sure you understand the usage rights that the store grants you. The content that online stores provide is typically protected by media usage rights, which specify what you can do with the content. For example, these rights might set the number of times you can sync the file to a portable music player.

Finding Music Files

You can use Groove Music and the Windows Store to find all types of audio files, including music, speech, and sound effects. All of the music in the Windows Store is available for purchase. Groove Music can also play audio files from other sources as long as their usage rights allow them to be played. The most popular format for music files is the MP3 format, which is short for MPEG-1 or MPEG-2 Audio Layer III. Groove Music plays MP3 files as well as WAV, or Waveform Audio File Format, a common format for other types of sound files.

Oscar wants to find music files he can play during his slide show of sailboat photos, but he's not sure what music would work best. He thinks classical or jazz piano music would appeal to FreeSail members. You suggest using Groove Music to visit the Windows Store where you can preview music free of charge.

Before performing the following steps, make sure that your computer has a sound card and speakers, and that the speakers are plugged into a power source, turned on, and connected to your computer. Also, make sure that the speaker volume is not muted, but is low enough to hear without disturbing others. If you don't have speakers but do have a sound card, you might be able to plug headphones into a headphone jack to listen to music. If your computer does not have the hardware necessary to play music, you can still perform the following steps, though you won't be able to hear the music.

To use Groove Music to preview music:

1. Click in the **Ask me anything** box on the taskbar, type **groove**, and then click **Groove Music** in the search results to open the Groove Music app. Maximize the Groove Music window.

   Trouble? If this is the first time you are running the Groove Music app, you might be requested to sign in to your Microsoft account. Enter the user name and password for your Microsoft account to continue.

2. In the navigation pane, click the **Get music in Store** link to start the Store app with the Music category selected.

3. Scroll down to the Genres section, and then click **Jazz** to display the most popular jazz albums among Store users. The Refine pane on the left lists subgenres, which are categories in the Jazz genre.

4. Scroll the Refine pane, and then click **Smooth Jazz** to display smooth jazz albums on the right.

5. Click a smooth jazz album in the list on the right to display options for playing or purchasing the music.

6. Point to the first song in the Songs list to display the Share and Preview buttons. See Figure 7-42. The album you selected might differ.

| Figure 7-42 | Selecting an album |

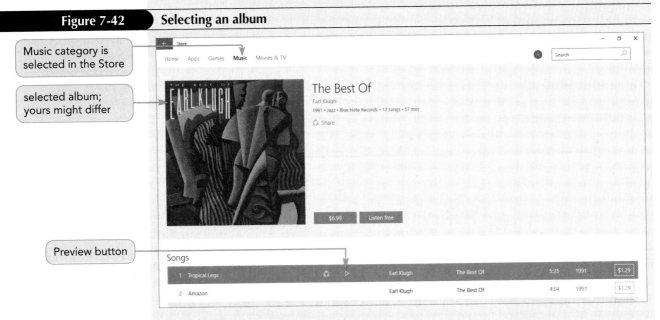

Music category is selected in the Store

selected album; yours might differ

Preview button

7. Click the **Preview** button ▷ to play an excerpt of the song, and then close the Store app.

   Trouble? If you do not hear any music, your speakers might be muted. If you have permission to do so, turn up the speaker volume slightly.

Before purchasing any music at the Windows Store, Oscar wants to play a couple of music files that might work with the slide show. You can copy these files to the Music folder and then use Groove Music to create a playlist of this music to manage the files. You could also use Windows Media Player, but because Groove Music is a Windows 10 app, Oscar can run it on any of his Windows 10 devices, including a tablet, which he will use to play music during the slide show. If he does purchase music from the Windows Store, he can add the music files to OneDrive and then use Groove Music to play the songs on all of his devices at no extra charge.

To use Groove Music to play music files already stored on your computer, you need to specify a location so that Groove Music can find the files. You'll copy the music files from the Module7 > Module folder to a new folder in the Music folder on the hard drive.

To copy music files to Groove Music:

▶ **1.** If necessary, open File Explorer, and then navigate to the **Music** folder on This PC.

▶ **2.** Create a new folder named **FreeSail** in the Music folder.

▶ **3.** Right-click the **File Explorer** button ▢ on the taskbar, and then click **File Explorer** to open a new folder window.

▶ **4.** Navigate to the **Module7 > Module** folder provided with your Data Files, and then copy the **Sailing** and **Waves** files to the FreeSail folder.

▶ **5.** Close the Module folder window, and then minimize the Music folder window.

▶ **6.** In the Groove Music window, click the **Change where we look** link to specify where you stored the music files. Groove Music displays the Build your collection from your local music files dialog box listing the folders from which it plays music. You need to add the Music > FreeSail folder to the list.

   Trouble? If the Change where we look link does not appear in your Groove Music window, click the Settings button ⚙ in the navigation pane to the right of your user icon, and then click the Choose where we look for music link.

▶ **7.** Click the **Add folder** button ⊕ to open the Select Folder dialog box, which contains controls similar to those in an Open dialog box.

▶ **8.** Navigate to the **Music > FreeSail** folder, and then click the **Add this folder to Music** button to add the FreeSail folder to the list of Groove Music folders.

▶ **9.** Click the **Done** button to close the Build your collection from your local music files dialog box.

▶ **10.** In the navigation pane, click the **Songs** link to display the songs in the selected folders, including Sailing and Waves.

TIP

To delete a folder, click the button that displays the location of the folder in Build your collection from your local music files dialog box and then click the Delete button.

Groove Music monitors the locations listed in the Build your collection from your local music files dialog box and updates your collection when you add or remove files. It also adds any music files you purchase from the Windows Store.

Playing Music Files

To play music in Groove Music, double-click a song, an album, or a playlist. While a song is playing, Groove Music provides information and controls at the bottom of the window. A progress bar and timer track the progress of the song, and information such as the song title, album title, and musician name appear in the lower-left corner of the window as the song plays. You can use the playback controls, which are similar to the controls on a portable music player, to play, stop, rewind, fast-forward, mute, or change the volume. You can also shuffle the songs to play them in a random order and repeat the song when it finishes.

You offer to play the two music files in the FreeSail folder so that Oscar can determine whether they are appropriate for the slide show.

As you did earlier, before you perform the following steps, turn down the volume of your computer speakers or use headphones so you do not disturb others in the room. If your computer does not have the hardware necessary to play music, you can still perform the following steps, though you won't be able to hear the music.

To play a song:

1. In the Groove Music window, double-click the **Sailing** song. The song begins to play and playback controls appear at the bottom of the window. See Figure 7-43.

| Figure 7-43 | Playing music in Groove Music |

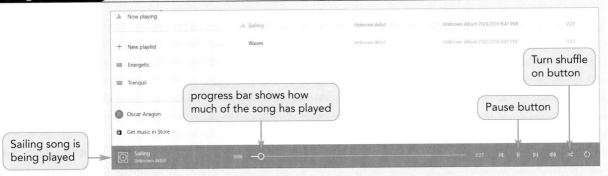

2. In the playback controls, click the **Pause** button ▮▮.

3. Double-click the **Waves** song in the song list. This is not really a song, but a recording of waves on a shore. Wait for the Waves file to finish playing.

Oscar thinks both recordings are good options to use in his slide show, but he wants to play the Waves file before the Sailing song. To organize songs and albums, you create a playlist. You'll show Oscar how to add the songs to a new playlist so he can play them in a certain order.

Creating a Playlist

TIP

To play the songs in a playlist in random order, click the Turn shuffle on button in the playback controls.

A playlist contains one or more digital media files and provides a way to organize files that you want to work with as a group. For example, you can create a playlist of lively songs that you play to wake up in the morning. By default, items in a playlist are played in the order they appear in the list. You can change the order of the items by dragging them within the list, or you can shuffle the items in the list, which means they play in a random order.

Now that you and Oscar have listened to two recordings, you'll add the songs to a new playlist.

To create a playlist:

1. In the Songs list, right-click **Sailing** to display a shortcut menu.

2. Point to **Add to** on the shortcut menu, and then click **New playlist** to display the Name this playlist dialog box.

3. Type **FreeSail Slide Show** as the name of the new playlist, and then click the **Save** button. Groove Music creates the new playlist, includes it in the navigation pane, and displays a message indicating it added a song to a playlist.

Trouble? If Groove Music does not display a message indicating it added a song to a playlist, right-click the Sailing song, point to Add to on the shortcut menu, and then click FreeSail Slide Show.

▶ **4.** Right-click the **Waves** song, point to **Add to** on the shortcut menu, and then click **FreeSail Slide Show**.

▶ **5.** In the navigation pane, click **FreeSail Slide Show** to display the playlist. See Figure 7-44. You want to change the order of the songs so that the Waves recording plays first.

Figure 7-44 **New playlist with songs**

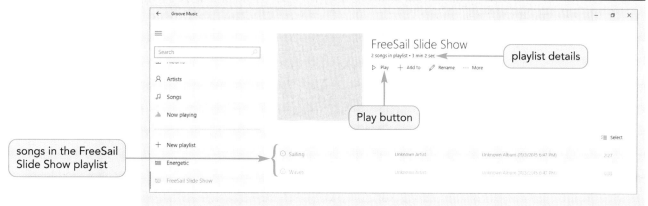

TIP

You can also change the position of a song in the playlist by right-clicking the song and then clicking Move up or Move down on the shortcut menu.

▶ **6.** Drag the **Waves** recording above the Sailing recording to change the order.

▶ **7.** To play the songs in order, display the playlist, and then click the **Play** button near the top of the window.

Now Oscar can start playing the FreeSail Slide Show playlist in Groove Music, make sure the playlist is set to repeat, and then play the sailboat photos as a slide show in the Windows Photo Viewer or Photos app. You'll show Oscar how to play a slide show in the Photos app while playing the FreeSail Slide Show playlist in Groove Music. The Photos app treats videos as moving pictures, so it plays videos along with photos and other pictures in the folder you select.

To play a slide show with music:

▶ **1.** In the Groove Music window, click the **Play** button near the top of the FreeSail Slide Show playlist on the right to begin playing the Waves recording.

▶ **2.** In File Explorer, navigate to the **Pictures > Boats** folder.

▶ **3.** Right-click the **Sail01** file, point to **Open with** on the shortcut menu, and then click **Photos** to display the photo in the Photos app.

▶ **4.** Click the **Slideshow** button 🖵 on the toolbar to begin playing a slide show of the photos in the Boats folder.

▶ **5.** After watching a few photos in the slide show, right-click the slide show to end it.

▶ **6.** Close the Photos app.

▶ **7.** Close the Groove Music app.

Oscar can perform the same steps to play the music and slide show on the computer in the club's reception area. Now that the slide show is complete, Oscar asks you to preview a video of sailing lessons he gave to young boaters. He wants to play the video for members who are interested in lessons. You'll show him how to do so next.

Working with Videos

The Windows 10 Movies & TV app is designed to play videos created in popular video formats—including MPEG-4 (also called MP4), WMV, and WMA. As with Groove Music, you can purchase and rent movies and TV shows from the Windows Store and then play them in Movies & TV, or you can play personal videos in the app and use its tools to watch and share videos. For example, if you have an Xbox connected to a TV, you can wirelessly transfer, or **cast**, the media file to the Xbox and watch the video on the larger, sharper screen of the TV. (You can do the same for other types of media files, such as photos and music, so you can share media content on your home entertainment network.) Windows 10 media casting uses the Miracast wireless display technology, so you can cast videos and other media onto any device that supports Miracast. If your TV does not support Miracast, you can attach a small piece of hardware to the TV so it detects and displays the signals that Windows 10 sends to the TV.

All of the copyright and other rules that apply to downloading graphics and photos from the web apply to videos—you need permission from the video owner to download and use a video unless it's in the public domain or you pay a fee to play the video.

If you store a video file on your hard disk, such as a video you recorded yourself, the easiest way to play it is to right-click the video file in File Explorer, point to Open with on the shortcut menu, and then click Movies & TV. You can then use the playback controls to control the video. Move the pointer to display the playback controls.

Oscar's video is named Sailing Lessons, and you already stored it in the Pictures > Boats folder. In fact, you might have already played this video as part of the FreeSail slide show. You'll show Oscar how to play the video on its own using the Movies & TV app.

To play the Sailing Lessons video:

▶ **1.** Navigate to the **Pictures > Boats** folder, if necessary.

▶ **2.** Right-click the **Sailing Lessons** file, point to **Open with** on the shortcut menu, and then click **Movies & TV** to start playing the file in the Movies & TV app.

   Trouble? If Windows asks you for a user name and password, enter the user name and password you use for your Microsoft account.

   Trouble? If a message appears regarding other apps you can use to play the file, continue with Step 3. The message is just a reminder that will close shortly.

▶ **3.** As the video plays, point to the buttons in the playback controls to display their ScreenTips to identify how you can manipulate the video.

▶ **4.** Close the Movies & TV app.

The playback controls include buttons for casting the video to a compatible device and for changing the aspect ratio. If black bars appeared to the right and left of the video as it played, you can remove these by changing the aspect ratio of the video, so it matches the aspect ratio of your display. You can also remove the title bar and taskbar to play the video on the full screen and set the video to repeat when it's finished playing.

Your tour of the Windows 10 multimedia tools is complete. Oscar is ready to play a slide show with music and share the Sailing Lessons video with FullSail members.

Restoring Your Settings

If you are working in a computer lab or on a computer other than your own, complete the steps in this section to restore the original settings on your computer.

To restore your computer:

▶ 1. Display the contents of the **Module7 > Module** folder. Select all of the files, hold down the **Ctrl** key, and then click the **Logo** file to deselect it. Press the **Delete** key and then click the Yes button to delete all files except for the Logo file.

▶ 2. Navigate to the **Pictures** folder on your computer, and then move the **Boats** folder to the Module7 > Module folder provided with your Data Files.

▶ 3. Navigate to the **Music** folder on your computer, and then move the **FreeSail** folder to the Module7 > Module folder provided with your Data Files. Start Groove Music, click **Albums** in the navigation pane, right-click the **Unknown Album** icon, and then click **Delete**.

▶ 4. If you do not want to store copies of the sailboat photos on your OneDrive, click **OneDrive** in the navigation pane of the open folder window, and then sign in, if necessary. Open the **Documents** folder, right-click the **OneDrive Boats** folder, and then click **Delete** on the shortcut menu.

REVIEW

Session 7.2 Quick Check

1. What does it mean if a photo is protected by copyright?

2. Where does File Explorer provide tools for manipulating and viewing the photos?

3. What is the main difference between viewing photos in File Explorer and in Windows Photo Viewer?

4. In the Photos app, you can adjust the _____ to make a photo appear warmer (with more red tones) or cooler (with more blue tones).

5. How can you let the Photos app automatically determine and apply the best corrections to make to light, color, and composition in a photo?

6. If you store photos in a private folder on OneDrive, how can you invite a friend to view the photos?

7. Why might you want to create a playlist of music files?

8. In Windows 10, you can wirelessly transfer, or _____, a media file from the computer to an Xbox console.

PRACTICE

Review Assignments

See the Starting Data Files section at the beginning of this module for a list of Data Files needed for the Review Assignments.

FreeSail Boat Club is creating a postcard to mail to members to notify them about an upcoming safety clinic. Shawn wants to design a graphic that includes the web address and phone number for the business. Your goal is to create the graphic shown in Figure 7-45. In addition, Oscar is working on a slide show featuring sights near Seattle that club members can easily visit on their boats. He has a few photos and asks you to assemble these into a slide show. He also wants a musical accompaniment to the slide show. Complete the following steps:

Figure 7-45   Completed graphic for the postcard

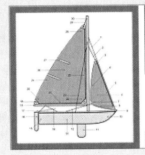

1. Start Paint, open the **Frame** picture from the Module7 > Review folder provided with your Data Files, and then save it as **Postcard** in the same folder. (*Hint:* Accept that transparency will be lost when you save the image.)
2. Paste the **Sailboat Parts** picture into the Postcard picture, and center it within the frame.
3. Increase the size of the canvas to at least 900 × 500 pixels to create a larger work area. Move the graphic down and to the right so that it is easier to work with.
4. Select white as Color 1 and a shade of blue from the frame graphic as Color 2, the background color. (*Hint:* Remember to use the right mouse button to change Color 2.)
5. Using the Text tool with an Opaque background, create a text box of about 450 × 80 pixels below the frame. Choose Tahoma as the font and 30 as the point size. Press the spacebar and then type **FreeSail Safety Clinic** in the text box.
6. Change Color 1 to the same shade of medium blue as used in the sails in the Sailboat Parts picture.
7. Create another text box of about 450 × 80 pixels below the first text box. Choose Tahoma as the font and 18 as the point size. Type **freesail.cengage.com** as the web address. Press the spacebar twice, and then type **(206) 555-7400** as the phone number.
8. Change Color 1 to the same shade of blue as in the background of the text box. To the right of the frame, use a Solid color fill to draw a blue rectangle 450 pixels wide and 100 pixels tall.
9. Move the first line of text to the upper-left part of the rectangle. Move the second line of text below the first line. Adjust the text so its left edge aligns with the text above it. Save your work.
10. Change Color 2 to white and then delete the blue space in the rectangle that does not contain text. Use Figure 7-45 as a guide.

11. Using gridlines, move the text box so its top aligns with the frame and only a few pixels of space separate the text box and the frame, again using Figure 7-45 as a guide. (*Hint:* Zoom out and in on the image as needed so you can work more easily.)

12. Paste the **Shipwheel** picture into the Postcard picture, positioning it directly below the last four digits in the phone number, leaving one or two pixels of space between the text box and the Shipwheel picture.

13. Paste the **Anchor** picture into the Postcard picture, positioning it to the left of the Shipwheel picture below the large rectangle. Save your work.

14. Change Color 1 and Color 2 to the shade of deep red used in the Shipwheel picture.

15. Use the Rectangle tool to draw a red rectangle the same width as the dark-blue rectangle and 20 pixels high. Change Color 2 to white, and then position the red rectangle so it is left-aligned with the dark-blue rectangle and bottom-aligned with the frame. (*Hint:* If the rectangle covers the Anchor or Shipwheel, click the Undo button and repeat the step.)

16. Change Color 1 to the same shade of medium blue as used in the sails in the Sailboat Parts picture.

17. Use the Line tool to draw a 1-pixel vertical line from the top to the bottom of the red rectangle just to the left of the Anchor picture. Make sure no red appears above or below the vertical line.

18. Fill the right side of the vertical line with medium blue. Save your work.

19. If necessary, change Color 2 to white. Crop the graphic to remove the white space around the graphic. Remove gridlines.

20. Compare your graphic with Figure 7-45, make any final modifications as necessary, save your work, and then close Paint.

21. Move the seven photos (Sight1–Sight7) from the Module7 > Review folder provided with your Data Files to a new folder in the Pictures folder named **Seattle Sights**. (*Hint:* Don't copy the Anchor, Frame, Piano1, Piano2, Postcard, Sailboat Parts, and Shipwheel files.)

22. In the Seattle Sights folder window, use a tool on the Picture Tools Manage tab to rotate the Sight3 photo.

23. Use the Photos app to touch up the Sight5 photo by increasing the Contrast setting in the Light category by 50 percent. Save your changes.

24. Use the Enhance tool to improve the Sight7 photo, and then save your changes.

25. Move the Piano1 and Piano2 files from the Module7 > Review folder provided with your Data Files to a new folder in the Music folder named **Background**.

26. Use the Groove Music app to add the Background folder as a music location, and then create a playlist named **Seattle Sights Slide Show** consisting of the Piano1 and Piano2 music (in that order). Start playing the Seattle Sights Slide Show playlist. If necessary, lower the volume of your speakers.

27. Use a Photos app tool to play a slide show of the photos in the Seattle Sights folder.

28. Press the Print Screen key to capture an image of the slide show, and then paste the image in a new Paint or WordPad file. Save the file as **SightsShow** in the Module7 > Review folder provided with your Data Files. Close the Groove Music and Photos windows.

29. Move the Background folder from the Music folder to the Module7 > Review folder provided with your Data Files.

30. Move the Seattle Sights folder from the Pictures folder to the Module7 > Review folder provided with your Data Files.

31. Close all open windows.

Case Problem 1

See the Starting Data Files section at the beginning of this module for a list of Data Files needed for this Case Problem.

Design Exchange   Janie Okupa is the director of the Design Exchange, a website that offers instruction in graphic design and other visual arts. Students subscribe to the online classes, which are taught by professionals in the field. As an associate producer for the Design Exchange, you help Janie promote the online classes. She asks you to complete two tasks. You need to create the Design Exchange logo, shown in Figure 7-46, using a graphic she created. She also wants you to create a slide show of new classes highlighting the kinds of designs potential subscribers might be interested in creating. Janie also wants you to set the slide show to music. Complete the following steps:

Figure 7-46   Completed Design Exchange logo

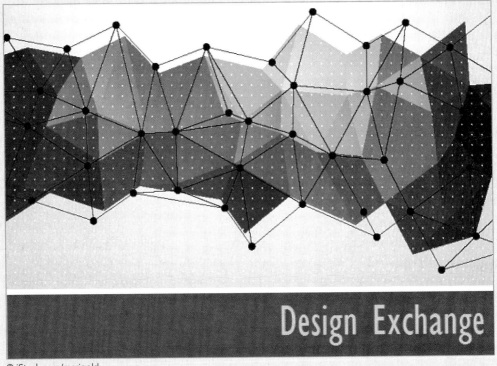

Design Exchange

© iStock.com/marigold

1. Start Paint, open the **Design** picture from the Module7 > Case1 folder provided with your Data Files, and then save it as **DE Logo** in the same folder. (*Hint:* Accept that transparency will be lost when you save the image.)
2. Crop the DE Logo picture to remove the black frame.
3. Increase the size of the canvas to about double its size to create a larger work area, and then move the design down and to the right to work more comfortably.
4. Select a light shade of teal from the picture as Color 1, and then select a medium shade of pink from the picture as Color 2, the background color. Use Figure 7-46 as a guide.
5. Using the Text tool with an Opaque background, create a text box slightly wider than the design and at least 70 pixels high. Choose Gill Sans MT Condensed as the font and 36 as the point size. Press the spacebar, and then type **Design Exchange** in the text box. (If Gill Sans MT Condensed is not installed on your computer, choose another condensed font.)

6. Move the text to right-align it in the rectangle. Save your work.

7. Change Color 2 to white, and then move the pink rectangle so it's about 1 or 2 pixels below the design graphic. Right-align the pink rectangle with the design graphic. If necessary, delete parts of the pink rectangle that extend to the left of the graphic.

8. Crop the graphic so it contains only the design and the text box and no extra white space.

9. Make any final modifications as necessary, using Figure 7-46 as a guide, and then save your work.

10. Open the **Class1** picture from the Module7 > Case1 folder using Windows Photo Viewer, and then use the playback controls to view the Class1–Class8 pictures in the Case1 folder. Each of these pictures represents a design class that the Design Exchange offers. Close Windows Photo Viewer.

11. To provide a class title for the Class2 picture, open the **Class2** picture in Paint. Change Color 2 to a shade of dark blue in the picture, and then increase the height of the canvas by 50 pixels. (*Hint:* Zoom out and in on the image as needed so you can work more easily.)

12. Change Color 1 to white. Using the Text tool, create a text box in the dark-blue rectangle about as wide as the rectangle. Choose Arial Black as the font and 18 as the point size. Press the spacebar, and then type **Pattern Design** in the text box.

13. Move the Pattern Design text to center it in the dark-blue rectangle. Save your work, and then close Paint.

14. Copy the Drums and Swing files from the Module7 > Case1 folder provided with your Data Files to a new folder in the Music folder named **Soundtrack**.

15. In the Groove Music window, add the Soundtrack folder to the music locations. Create a playlist named **Design Exchange** consisting of the Drums and Swing songs. Start playing the Design Exchange playlist, and set the playlist to shuffle.

16. Press the Print Screen key to capture an image of the playlist as a song is playing, and then paste the image in a new Paint or WordPad file. Save the file as **DE Playlist** in the Module7 > Case1 folder provided with your Data Files.

17. On OneDrive in the Documents folder, create a folder named **Classes.** Copy the eight class pictures (Class1–Class8) from the Module7 > Case1 folder provided with your Data Files to the Classes folder on OneDrive.

18. In the OneDrive web app, display the photos in the Classes folder. Rotate the Class4 photo so it appears in the correct orientation. (*Hint:* Select the photo, and then click the Rotate button on the toolbar.)

19. In the OneDrive web app, use the online version of the Photos app to play a slide show of the photos in the Classes folder. (*Hint:* Click a photo in the Classes folder, and then click Play slide show on the toolbar.)

20. Press the Print Screen key to capture an image of the slide show, and then paste the image in a new Paint or WordPad file. Save the file as **DE Slide Show** in the Module7 > Case1 folder provided with your Data Files. Press the Esc key to exit the slide show. Close Microsoft Edge.

21. In File Explorer, move the Classes folder from the Pictures folder to the Module7 > Case1 folder provided with your Data Files.

22. Move the Soundtrack folder from the Music library to the Module7 > Case1 folder provided with your Data Files.

23. Close all open windows.

CHALLENGE

Case Problem 2

See the Starting Data Files section at the beginning of this module for a list of Data Files needed for this Case Problem.

Ascend   Margaret Sobieski owns Ascend in Chicago, Illinois, a consulting company that organizes team-building experiences for companies around the world. As Margaret's assistant, you help her prepare for the team-building events and create promotional materials. You are now preparing a team-building adventure game called Break-Out, in which teams must work together to escape from a hotel room equipped with clues and potential escape tools. Margaret asks you to work with two images to develop a logo for the Break-Out event. She also wants to create a slide show of the clues and tools to promote the event. Your goal is to create the logo shown in Figure 7-47 and the slideshow using jazz music for which Chicago is famous. Complete the following steps:

Figure 7-47   Completed Chicago Break-out Adventure Game logo

1. Start Paint, open the **Chicago** file from the Module7 > Case2 folder provided with your Data Files, and then save it as **BreakOut** in the same folder.
2. Increase the size of the canvas to at least 900 × 500 pixels to create a larger work area.
3. Change Color 1 and Color 2 to Light turquoise in the color palette. Select the Oval shape tool, and then change the Outline and Fill settings to Solid color.
4. Near the top of the canvas and to the right of the skyline, draw a perfect circle about 375 × 375 pixels round with a light turquoise solid outline and a light turquoise solid fill. (*Hint:* Hold down the Shift key as you drag to draw the circle.)
5. Deselect the circle, and then change Color 1 and Color 2 to white.
6. Choose the Transparent selection command, and then use the Select tool to select the skyline.
7. Move the skyline to the circle so that the bottom of the skyline is centered in the middle of the circle. Refer to Figure 7-47 for the correct placement.
8. Delete the part of the blue circle that extends below the skyline.

9. Change Color 1 to a light shade selected from the skyline, and then change Color 2 to a dark shade selected from the skyline.

10. Below the skyline image, create a text box about 380 pixels wide and about 50 pixels tall. Choose an Opaque background and 14-point Broadway font for the text. (If Broadway is not available, select a font similar to the one shown in Figure 7-47, such as Britannic Bold.) Press the Enter key and then type **Chicago Break-out Adventure Game** in the text box. Make sure the text appears centered on one line. Save your work.

11. Change Color 2 to white. If necessary, move the rectangle so it is centered just a few pixels below the skyline.

12. Move the entire image to the upper-left corner of the canvas.

⊕ **Explore** 13. Use the Rectangular selection tool to point to the lower-right corner of the rectangle, and then note its pixel coordinates. Click the File tab on the Paint ribbon, and then click Properties to open the Image Properties dialog box. Enter the pixel coordinates in the appropriate text boxes. Click the OK button.

14. Compare your graphic with Figure 7-47, and then make any final modifications as necessary. Save your work, and then close Paint.

15. Copy the 10 pictures (Game01–Game10) from the Module7 > Case2 folder provided with your Data Files to a new folder in the Pictures folder named **Chicago**.

16. Open the **Game01** picture in Windows Photo Viewer, and then use the playback controls to view each of the other pictures in the Chicago folder. Each of these pictures shows a clue or tool adventure game participants can use.

17. Crop the Game02 picture to remove the red border.

18. Copy the Mystery file to a new folder in the Music folder named **Game**.

⊕ **Explore** 19. Right-click the Mystery file and then play the song using Windows Media Player.

20. Press the Print Screen key to capture an image of the song playing in Windows Media Player, and then paste the image in a new Paint or WordPad file. Save the file as **Mystery Music** in the Module7 > Case2 folder provided with your Data Files.

21. Use Windows Photo Viewer to play a slide show of the photos in the Chicago folder. Change the slide show speed to fast.

22. Right-click the slide show, press the Print Screen key to capture an image of the slide show with the shortcut menu displayed, and then paste the image in a new Paint or WordPad file. Save the file as **Ascend Slide Show** in the Module7 > Case2 folder provided with your Data Files. Close Windows Photo Viewer and then close Windows Media Player.

⊕ **Explore** 23. Share the Game01 picture with your instructor via email. If other apps are set up for sharing on your computer, use one of those apps to share the Game04 picture with your instructor.

⊕ **Explore** 24. Use the Groove Music app to search the Windows Store for jazz songs related to Chicago. (*Hint:* Use **jazz chicago** as the search text, and then refine the results to display songs.) Select a song and then preview it. As the song plays, press the Print Screen key to capture an image of the screen, and then paste the image in a new Paint or WordPad file. Save the file as **Jazz Song** in the Module7 > Case2 folder provided with your Data Files.

⊕ **Explore** 25. In the Store app, search for family movies related to Chicago. (*Hint:* Use **chicago** as the search text, refine the results to display movies, and then refine those results to display the Family genre.) Select a movie and then play the trailer. As the trailer plays, press the Print Screen key to capture an image of the screen, and then paste the image in a new Paint or WordPad file. Save the file as **Chicago Movie** in the Module7 > Case2 folder provided with your Data Files. Close the Store app.

26. Move the Chicago folder from the Pictures folder to the Module7 > Case2 folder provided with your Data Files.

27. Move the Game folder from the Music folder to the Module7 > Case2 folder provided with your Data Files.

28. Close all open windows.

CHALLENGE

Case Problem 3

See the Starting Data Files section at the beginning of this module for a list of Data Files needed for this Case Problem.

Theatrical Costume Guild   Hal Cumby is the owner of the Theatrical Costume Guild in Charlotte, North Carolina. Hal rents costumes to amateur and professional theater productions throughout the southeastern United States. Hal recently hired you as a part-time sales associate at the shop. When he learned that you have some graphic design training, he asked you to help him design a graphic to use on the shop's website to attract interest and new business. Your goal is to create the graphic shown in Figure 7-48. Hal also wants you to develop a slide show highlighting a few of the costumes available for rental. Complete the following steps:

Figure 7-48   **Theatrical Costume Guild graphic**

© iStock.com/burcin tolga kural

1. Start Paint, open the **Mask** picture from the Module7 > Case3 folder provided with your Data Files, and then save it as **Guild** in the same folder.

2. Decrease the magnification of the image so you can see the entire image, and then increase the width of the canvas to at least 900 pixels to create a larger work area. (*Hint:* Zoom out and in on the image as needed so you can work more easily.)

✦ Explore 3. Select the image, and then rotate the image to the right by 90 degrees. (*Hint:* In the Image group, on the Home tab, click the Rotate button, and then click Rotate right 90°.) If necessary, drag the selected image so the entire image appears in the upper-left corner of the canvas. While the image is selected, use the arrow keys to move the selection, making sure that no white space appears to the left or above the image.

✦ Explore 4. Use the Image Properties dialog box to change the size of the canvas so that no white space appears to the right of or below the image. (*Hint:* Click the File menu and then click Properties to open the Image Properties dialog box.)

5. Resize the image by 200 percent. Save your work.

6. Change Color 1 to a shade of white in the mask, and change Color 2 to the same shade of black as in the background of the image.

7. Using the figure as a guide, create a text box of about 520 × 70 pixels, making sure not to cover the mask and leaving room to paste a copy of the bell to the left of the text. Select 36-point Baskerville Old Face for the text. (If Baskerville Old Face is not available, select a font similar to the one shown in Figure 7-48, such as Constantia.) Type **Theatrical Costume Guild** in the text box. Increase the size of the text box, if necessary, to keep the text on one line.

8. Move the text to the right to leave about 1 inch between the beginning of the text and the left edge of the image. See Figure 7-48 for the correct placement. Save your work.

9. Using transparent selection, copy the bell on the left side in the mask image to the blank area to the left of the text. Do not deselect the bell yet. When you selected the bell to copy it, you probably selected some pixels from the mask.

⊕ **Explore** 10. While the bell is selected, flip the bell horizontally. (*Hint:* On the Home tab, in the Image group, click the Rotate button, and then click Flip horizontal.) Use the arrow keys to nudge the image into the correct position. See Figure 7-48.

⊕ **Explore** 11. In the copy of the bell, erase any unnecessary pixels by clicking the Eraser tool in the Tools group, clicking the smallest size in the Size button list, and then clicking the pixels you want to erase from the bell. Increase the magnification to work effectively. Save your work when you finish.

12. Compare your graphic to Figure 7-48, and then make any final modifications as necessary. Save your work, and then close Paint.

13. Move the five costume photos (Costume1–Costume5) from the Module7 > Case3 folder provided with your Data Files to a new folder in the Pictures folder named **Costumes**. Copy the Prelude music file to a new folder in the Music folder named **Theater**.

14. Use a tool of your choice to view each picture in the Costumes folder.

⊕ **Explore** 15. Play the Prelude music file in the Groove Music app, and set the song to repeat so it plays continuously.

16. In the Pictures > Costumes folder, rotate the Costume3 photo.

17. Use the Photos app to enhance each photo in the Costumes folder, saving each change.

18. With the enhanced Costume5 photo displayed in the Photos app, center the Photos window over the Groove Music window, so the playback controls for the Prelude song are displayed. Press the Print Screen key to capture an image of the desktop, and then paste the image in a new Paint or WordPad file. Save the file as **Theatrical** in the Module7 > Case3 folder provided with your Data Files. Close the Photos and Groove Music apps.

19. Move the Theater folder from the Music folder to the Module7 > Case3 folder provided with your Data Files.

20. Move the Costumes folder from the Pictures folder to the Module7 > Case3 folder provided with your Data Files.

21. Close all open windows.

CREATE

Case Problem 4

Data Files needed for this Case Problem: Banner.png, Green.png, Seed.png, and Tree.png

Green Investments Frieda Merriman is the sole proprietor of Green Investments in Bloomington, Indiana. Frieda hired you as her assistant to provide marketing and graphic design services to the business. She asks you to design a logo she can use in print and online. Your goal is to create the logo shown in Figure 7-49. Refer to the figure as you complete the following steps:

Figure 7-49 Creating a logo for Green Investments

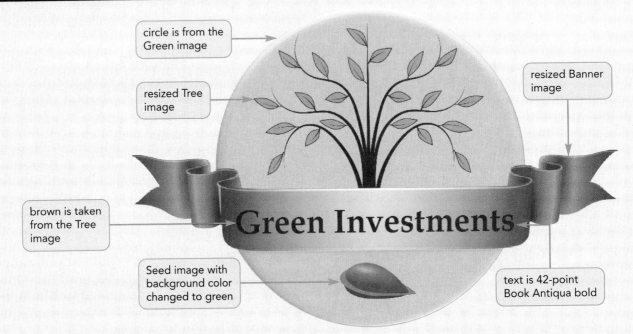

1. Create a logo for Green Investments using the figure and the following information as guides:
    - The ribbon image is named Banner and is stored in the Module7 > Case4 folder provided with your Data Files.
    - The circle image is named Green and is stored in the Module7 > Case4 folder provided with your Data Files.
    - The seed and tree images are named Seed and Tree, respectively, and are stored in the Module7 > Case4 folder provided with your Data Files.
    - The text color is a shade of brown from the tree.
    - The text uses 42-point Book Antiqua bold font. (If Book Antiqua is not available, select a similar font.)
    - The banner and tree images have transparent backgrounds.
    - The banner and tree images have been resized to fit on the circle.
    - The background of the seed image has been filled with the same shade of green as in the circle. (*Hint:* Place the seed image on the circle, change Color 1 to the green from the circle, and then fill the seed's white background with green.)
2. Save the graphic as **GI Logo** in the Module7 > Case4 folder provided with your Data Files.
3. Be sure to save your work after making a significant change to the graphic.
4. Close all open windows.

OBJECTIVES

Session 8.1
- Manage mobile computing devices
- Select and modify power plans
- Present information to an audience
- Explore network concepts
- Manage network connections

Session 8.2
- Set up and use a homegroup
- Access shared network folders
- Synchronize desktop settings
- Allow remote access to your computer

Connecting to Networks with Mobile Computing

Accessing Network Resources

Case | *New Castle Consulting*

Derek Havens is the director of New Castle Consulting (NCC), a firm in New Castle, Delaware, that provides technology services to businesses in the state. NCC helps people set up networks, maintain and repair computers, and solve computer security problems. You have been working for NCC as an assistant for a few months, specializing in helping clients upgrade to Microsoft Windows 10. Derek is preparing to configure a wireless network for the Bravo Law Office, a group of attorneys in Dover providing legal services throughout Delaware, and he asks you to help him. Derek knows how to perform networking tasks in earlier versions of Windows, but is not as familiar with Windows 10. Because Derek often works on his laptop when he travels around the state to visit businesses, he also asks you to adjust mobility settings on his computer so he can use it while traveling without worrying about losing power or disturbing his travel companions.

In this module, you will explore mobile computing, including maintaining power and accessing other computing resources. You will also examine network concepts and learn how to connect two or more computers in a network, and then use the network to share files, folders, and resources.

STARTING DATA FILES

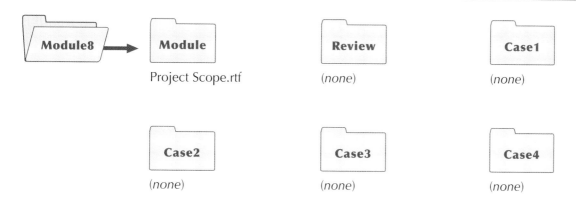

Module8 →	Module	Review	Case1
	Project Scope.rtf	*(none)*	*(none)*
	Case2	Case3	Case4
	(none)	*(none)*	*(none)*

Session 8.1 Visual Overview:

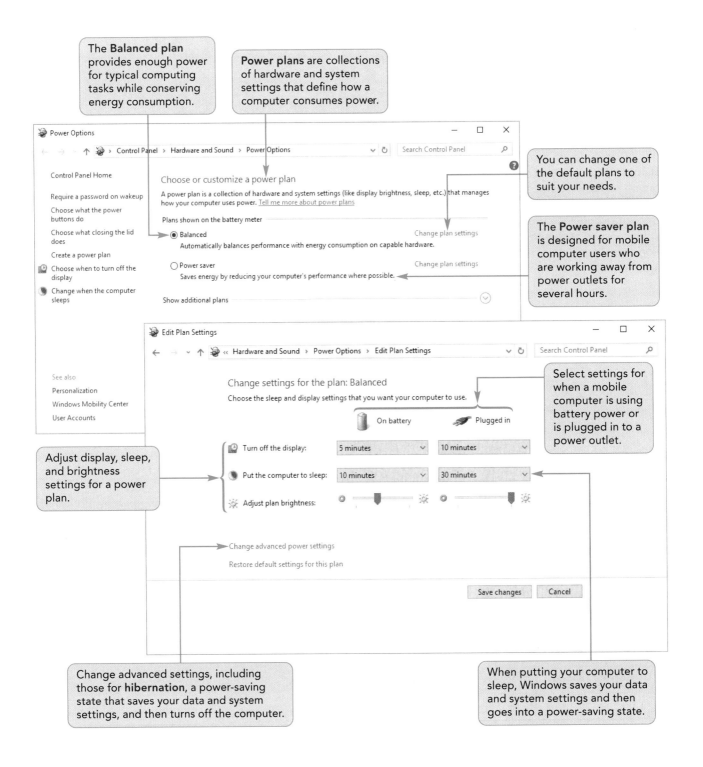

The **Balanced plan** provides enough power for typical computing tasks while conserving energy consumption.

Power plans are collections of hardware and system settings that define how a computer consumes power.

You can change one of the default plans to suit your needs.

The **Power saver plan** is designed for mobile computer users who are working away from power outlets for several hours.

Adjust display, sleep, and brightness settings for a power plan.

Select settings for when a mobile computer is using battery power or is plugged in to a power outlet.

Change advanced settings, including those for **hibernation**, a power-saving state that saves your data and system settings, and then turns off the computer.

When putting your computer to sleep, Windows saves your data and system settings and then goes into a power-saving state.

Mobile Computing Settings

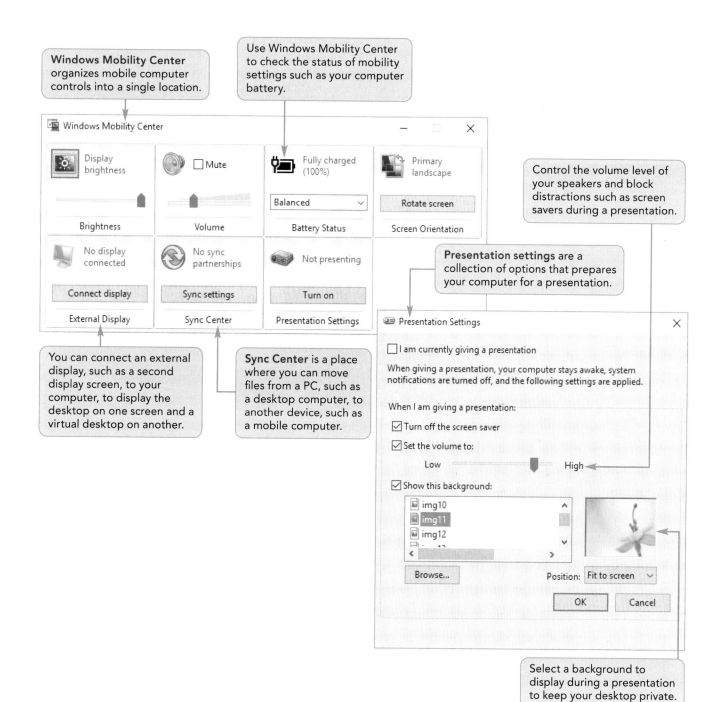

Windows Mobility Center organizes mobile computer controls into a single location.

Use Windows Mobility Center to check the status of mobility settings such as your computer battery.

Control the volume level of your speakers and block distractions such as screen savers during a presentation.

Presentation settings are a collection of options that prepares your computer for a presentation.

You can connect an external display, such as a second display screen, to your computer, to display the desktop on one screen and a virtual desktop on another.

Sync Center is a place where you can move files from a PC, such as a desktop computer, to another device, such as a mobile computer.

Select a background to display during a presentation to keep your desktop private.

Managing Mobile Computing Devices

A **mobile device**, or a **mobile personal computer (PC)**, is a computing device you can easily carry, such as a laptop, tablet, or smartphone. Currently, more people are buying mobile devices, preferring their portability and flexibility, than desktop PCs. Although a desktop PC must always be plugged into a power source and uses cables to connect some of its components and devices, a mobile device contains all of its necessary parts in a single package, including a display screen, processor, and pointing device. Most mobile devices have a touchscreen that lets users select objects and perform other interactions with a fingertip or stylus, including entering text using an **on-screen keyboard**, a keyboard displayed on-screen that includes keys for typing text, numbers, and symbols. See Figure 8-1.

Figure 8-1   Mobile devices

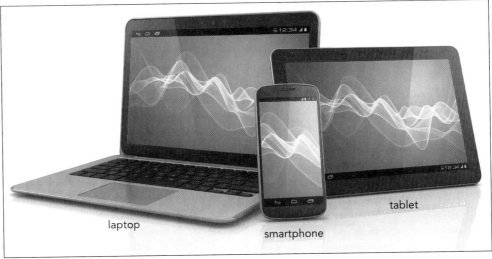

laptop

smartphone

tablet

© iStock.com/mbortolino

The terms **laptop** and **notebook** are often used interchangeably, although laptop is the older term and notebook is sometimes associated with a smaller, lighter computer. (A notebook also refers to a proprietary model of a mobile computer, so this book uses laptop as the more generic term.) Both refer to mobile PCs that are smaller than the average briefcase and light enough to carry comfortably. A laptop has a flat-screen display and keyboard that fold together, and a battery pack that provides power for a few hours so that you don't have to plug the device into a power outlet. A **tablet** is smaller than a laptop and has a touchscreen and sometimes a pointing device, such as a stylus.

Mobile devices are just as powerful as desktop computers; but more importantly, they let you take your computer almost anywhere, including while traveling and meeting with others. However, the portability of mobile devices introduces two problems that desktop computers typically do not have: managing power and keeping your files synchronized. When you're using a mobile device while traveling, for example, you need a way to conserve battery power so you don't lose data or have to shut down unexpectedly. If you do some of your work on a mobile device, such as at a client meeting, and other work at a desktop computer, especially one connected to a network, you need a way to update the files stored on your desktop computer or network with the work you saved on your mobile device, and vice versa.

Windows 10 solves these problems with Windows Mobility Center, power plans, and sync settings. Windows Mobility Center organizes mobile computer controls in a single location. These controls let you view and adjust the settings you use most often on a mobile PC, including the screen brightness, speaker volume, and battery status. From Windows Mobility Center, you can also select a power plan, a collection of hardware and system settings that define how a computer consumes power. For example, you can choose a plan designed to minimize power consumption, maximize system performance, or strike a balance between the two. If you work on more than one computer, you can access Sync Center from Windows Mobility Center to move files from one device, such as a laptop, to another device, such as a desktop computer, network computer, tablet, portable music player, digital camera, or smartphone. By synchronizing the files, Sync Center helps you maintain consistency among two or more versions of the same file stored in different locations, so you don't use an out-of-date file on a mobile device, for example, when you have a more current version on your desktop PC.

Recall that if you have more than one device running Windows 8 or later, Windows can synchronize the desktop backgrounds among all your devices. In the same way, it can sync settings such as the desktop theme, File Explorer preferences, and browser and app settings. By using a Microsoft account and OneDrive, you can also sync files stored in more than one location.

Using Windows Mobility Center

Windows Mobility Center provides a control panel for managing a mobile PC. Although hardware vendors can add and change features in Windows Mobility Center, by default Windows 10 lets you adjust power settings such as the brightness of the computer screen, the speaker volume, and the current power-saving scheme. Windows Mobility Center also lets you manage settings you often need when you are working away from your desk, such as those for synchronizing files, using an external display, and controlling what appears on the screen when you give a presentation. See Figure 8-2.

Figure 8-2	Windows Mobility Center

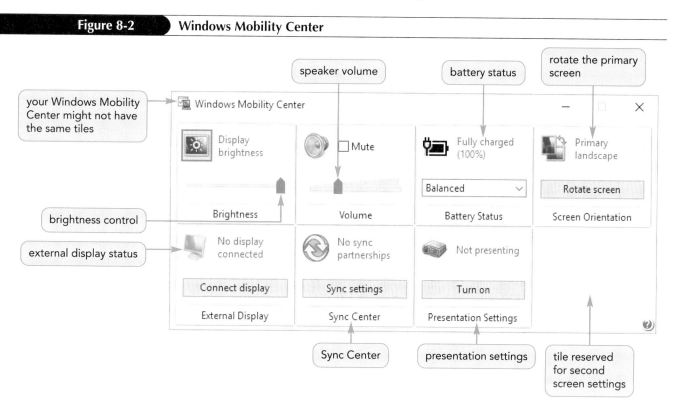

Each control in Windows Mobility Center is represented by a tile and depends on your computer hardware. Figure 8-3 describes the purpose of each tile.

Figure 8-3	Settings in Windows Mobility Center

Tile	Icon	Description
Brightness		Dim or increase the brightness of your screen.
Volume		Use the slider to control the volume of the computer's speakers or mute the speakers to turn off the sound completely.
Battery Status		Select a power scheme that suits how you are working with your computer.
Screen Orientation		Set the screen orientation on a tablet PC to portrait or landscape.
External Display		Connect your computer to another monitor or projector.
Sync Center		Open Sync Center to identify devices containing files to synchronize and then exchange information.
Presentation Settings		Control what appears on a projector when your computer is connected to one.

Setting Speaker Volume

You can set the speaker volume in two ways: using the Volume tile in Windows Mobility Center and using the speaker icon in the notification area of the taskbar. In both cases, you drag a slider to increase or decrease the volume. As you drag the slider to change the volume, a ScreenTip displays the current volume setting, which ranges from a low of 0 to a high of 100. When you stop dragging, Windows plays a sound at the current volume so you can hear how loud or soft it is. You can also use any of these methods to mute sound, which effectively turns off the speakers. You use the same controls to turn the sound back on.

As you help Derek prepare for the trip to the Bravo Law Office in Dover, he reminds you that he wants to work on his laptop during the drive. He is planning to review the presentation he will give to the Bravo Law Office partners and staff. Because the presentation includes audio, he wants to turn off the speakers on his laptop during the trip so that the presentation does not distract anyone else. You'll show Derek how to test the volume of the speakers and then mute them using Windows Mobility Center. Note the original volume setting so you can restore it later.

To perform most of the steps in this session, you must be working on a mobile PC; however, if instructed to do so, you can use a desktop computer on which Windows Mobility Center has been enabled—a process that involves changing Windows registry settings and is beyond the scope of this module (check with your instructor or technical support person). If you are not working on a mobile PC or a desktop computer with Windows Mobility Center, read but do not perform the steps.

To open Windows Mobility Center and adjust the speaker volume:

TIP

You can also right-click the Start button and then click Mobility Center to open Windows Mobility Center.

1. Click in the **Ask me anything** box, type **Mobility Center**, and then click **Windows Mobility Center** in the search results to open Windows Mobility Center.

2. To test the speaker volume, drag the **Volume** slider to 30. Windows plays a sound at that volume.

   Trouble? If your speakers are already set to 30, drag the Volume slider to 40.

▶ **3.** Click the **Mute** check box to insert a check mark. The Volume tile changes to indicate that Windows has turned the speakers off. The Volume icon in the notification area of the taskbar also changes to indicate the Mute setting.

Now that you've shown Derek how to control the volume of his laptop speakers, you'll demonstrate how to keep track of the battery charge by displaying the status of the battery.

Displaying the Battery Status

You can work with mobile PCs anywhere because they get the power they need from a battery, which is installed within the computer case. However, even with recent improvements in battery cell technology, you can use a mobile PC powered by a battery for only a limited time before you need to recharge the battery. To help you manage your mobile PC's power, you can track the status of the battery charge in Windows Mobility Center and in the notification area of the taskbar. Both places display a battery meter icon that shows how much charge remains in the battery. To display the status of the battery charge, click the battery meter icon in the notification area of the taskbar. See Figure 8-4.

Figure 8-4   **Battery status**

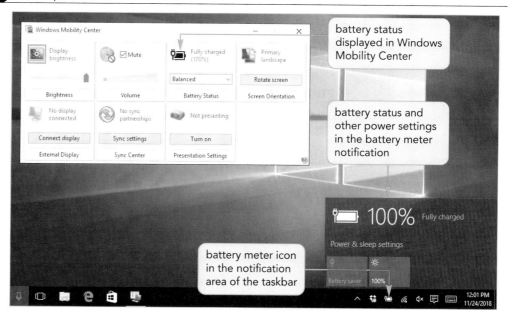

The battery meter notification displays the percentage of battery power remaining. If the percentage is less than 100, the notification also displays the amount of time remaining for the battery charge.

Although a battery meter icon always appears on the taskbar of a mobile PC, it can also appear on a desktop computer that is plugged into an uninterruptible power supply (UPS) or other short-term battery device. If your computer has more than one battery, you can click the battery meter icon in the notification area of the taskbar to display the charge remaining on one battery, click it again to see the charge remaining on the second battery, and so on. Point to the battery meter icon to see the combined charge.

The appearance of the battery meter icon changes to display the current state of the battery so that you can see how much charge remains even when you are not pointing to or clicking the icon. See Figure 8-5.

| **Figure 8-5** | Changes in the battery meter icon in the notification area |

your mobile device is plugged in and the battery is charging	battery is fully charged	your mobile device is running on battery power	battery charge is low	battery charge is critical

When the charge falls below 20 percent, by default, Windows turns on the **Battery saver** feature, which applies a combination of settings, such as lowering the screen brightness, limiting background activities, and delaying notifications.

The Battery saver feature is off by default and turns on automatically when battery power falls below 20 percent unless you are charging the battery. You can change the percentage if you want to have Battery saver turn on when the battery has more or less power than 20 percent. You can also select apps that can run in the background even when Battery saver is on. You'll show Derek how to perform these tasks using the Battery saver category in the System window of the Settings app. The Battery saver settings also let you display how much power system components are using, which apps are running, and how much battery power they are consuming.

To perform the following steps, you need to be working on a mobile PC or a desktop plugged into a UPS. If you are working on a different setup, read but do not perform the following steps.

To turn on Battery saver and check power usage:

1. Click in the **Ask me anything** box, type **battery saver**, and then click **Battery saver** in the search results to open the System window in the Settings app and display the Battery saver category of settings. See Figure 8-6.

Figure 8-6 | Battery saver category of the System window

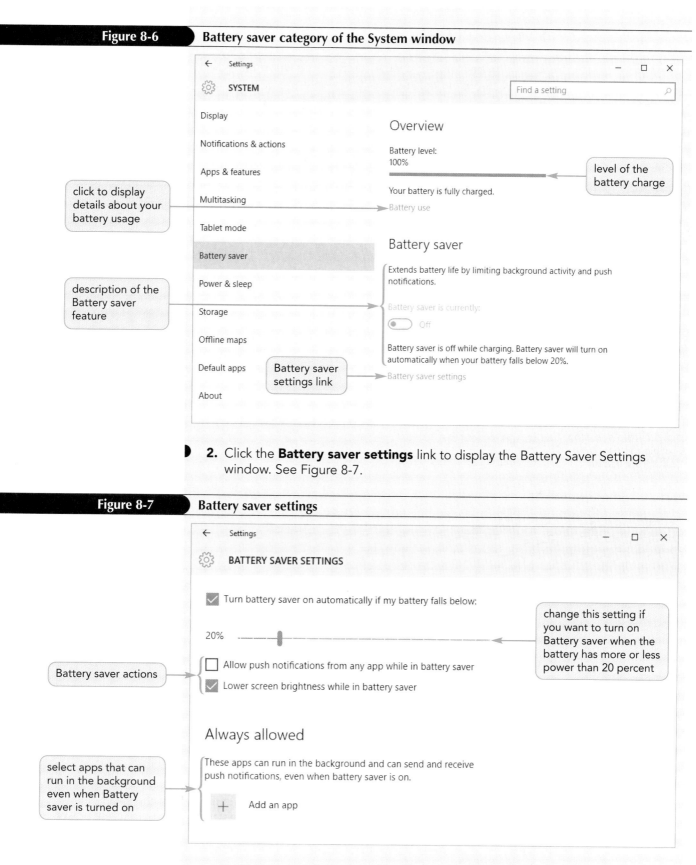

2. Click the **Battery saver settings** link to display the Battery Saver Settings window. See Figure 8-7.

Figure 8-7 | Battery saver settings

You'll show Derek how to allow Mail to run in the background to receive email if he's expecting an important message.

> **3.** Click the **Add an app** button to display a list of apps, and then scroll the list to display the Mail and Calendar item. If Derek wants to allow Mail to run in the background even when Battery saver is turned on, he can select Mail and Calendar in the list, which he won't do at this time.

> **4.** Click the **Back** button ← to return to the Battery Saver Settings window, and then click the **Back** button ← again to return to the Battery saver category of the System window.

> **5.** Click the **Battery use** link to display the Battery Use window. See Figure 8-8.

| Figure 8-8 | Battery usage information |

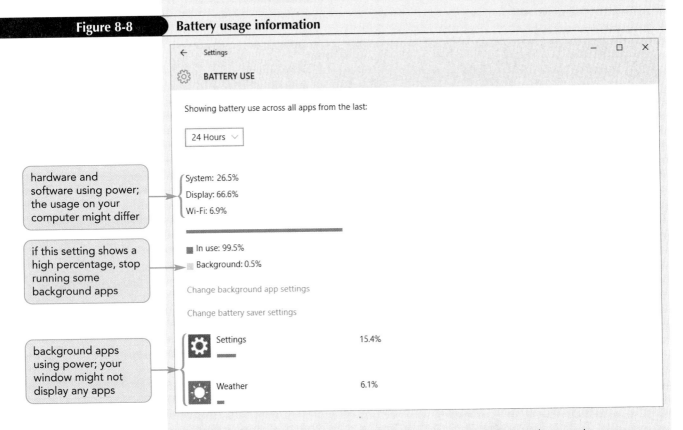

hardware and software using power; the usage on your computer might differ

if this setting shows a high percentage, stop running some background apps

background apps using power; your window might not display any apps

The Battery Use window indicates that during that last 24 hours when Derek has been running his computer on battery power, the display screen consumed about two-thirds of the available battery power. The window also shows which apps are running and how much power they are consuming.

> **6.** Close the Battery Use window.

Now Derek knows how to find battery status information. Next, you'll show him how to manage battery power with power plans.

Selecting a Power Plan

Besides displaying the percentage of charge remaining in the battery, the battery meter icon and the Battery Status tile in Windows Mobility Center display your current power plan. As defined in the Session 8.1 Visual Overview, a power plan is a collection of hardware and system settings that manages how your computer uses and conserves power. To match how you are using your mobile PC with how it consumes energy, you select a power plan. Windows 10 provides three default plans that let you save energy, maximize system performance, or balance energy conservation with system performance. The three default plans are called Balanced, Power saver, and **High performance**, and are described in Figure 8-9. Some computer manufacturers set up other power plans, so different ones might be available on your computer.

Figure 8-9	Default power plans

Power Plan	Description
Balanced	Balances energy consumption and system performance by adjusting your computer's processor speed to match your activity
Power saver	Saves power on your mobile computer by reducing system performance and extending battery life
High performance	Provides the highest level of performance on your mobile computer but consumes the most energy

You can select a power plan by clicking the Battery Status button arrow in Windows Mobility Center, or by right-clicking the battery meter icon in the notification area of the taskbar, clicking Power Options, and then clicking an option button in the Power Options window. (You can also select Power Options in the Hardware and Sound category of the Control Panel.) Most mobile PCs include the kind of hardware Windows 10 expects to support power management settings. However, if your computer does not have the proper kind of hardware or if Windows cannot identify it, the Battery Status button arrow or Power Options window displays only the plans your computer supports.

REFERENCE

Selecting a Power Plan

- Open Windows Mobility Center.
- Click the Battery Status button arrow, and then click a power plan.

or

- Right-click the battery meter icon in the notification area of the taskbar.
- Click Power Options.
- Click a power plan option button.

Because Derek will have to run his laptop computer on battery power during the trip to Dover, he can monitor the battery meter icon in the notification area of the taskbar to keep track of his power consumption. You'll also show him how to change his power plan to Power saver, which is designed for mobile PC users who are working away from power outlets for several hours. Note your original settings so you can restore them later.

To perform the following steps, you must be working on a computer with a battery power source, such as a laptop. If you are not working on such a computer, read but do not perform the steps.

To change the power plan:

▶ 1. In Windows Mobility Center, click the **Battery Status button arrow**, and then click **Power saver**.

Trouble? If your Battery Status is already set to Power saver, skip Step 1.

To extend battery life, the Power saver plan slows system performance (which you might notice only when you are performing a power-intensive task, such as editing a video) and lowers the brightness of the display.

Choosing a Power Plan

When working with computers that are connected to a battery, choose a battery plan that best fits your current activities to conserve battery power and to save energy in general. If you are engaging in activities that don't require a lot of power, such as reading email messages or listening to music, switch to the Power saver plan. If you need a lot of computing power, such as when you are working with complex spreadsheets or creating movies, use the High performance plan. If you are performing a variety of tasks, select the Balanced power plan so that the processor can run at full speed when you are playing a game or watching a video, but slow down to save power when you are checking your email. The Balanced power plan sometimes has the name of the computer manufacturer, such as Dell or HP.

Derek thinks the Power saver plan is perfect for conserving the battery charge while he's traveling. He can then change to the Balanced plan when he arrives in Dover, though he wants to fine-tune that plan to suit his needs. During his presentation, he wants to use power settings that are not offered in any of the default plans, so you'll show him how to modify a default plan.

Customizing Power Options

If the default power plans provided by Windows 10 or your computer manufacturer do not address your power needs, you can change one of the default plans. All of the plans specify how long the computer can be idle before Windows turns off the display and how long to wait before Windows puts the computer to sleep when you are using battery power or a wall outlet.

When putting your computer to sleep, Windows saves your data and system settings in temporary memory and then suspends operations as it goes into a power-saving state. During sleep, the screen is blank and the computer does not perform any activities, which conserves power. In fact, while a mobile PC is asleep, it typically uses 1 to 2 percent of battery power per hour, which is a fraction of what it uses when running on full power. When you wake a computer by moving the mouse or pressing a key, for example, Windows displays the desktop in its presleep state, including open windows and running programs.

Besides changing sleep settings and displaying turn-off times for each default power plan, you can specify advanced settings such as whether to hibernate and how long to wait before hibernating. Hibernation is a power-saving state that saves your work to your hard disk, puts your computer into a low-power state, and then turns off your computer. Of the three power-saving states in Windows 10, hibernation uses the least amount of power. Because the sleep states require some power, Windows automatically puts a mobile PC into hibernation after a specified period of time. Windows also puts a mobile PC into hibernation when the battery charge is critically low. If your computer does not hibernate by default, you can enable hibernation using the power options, which you work with shortly.

Hybrid sleep is an alternative to sleep designed for desktop computers. As its name suggests, hybrid sleep is a combination of sleep and hibernation. Windows saves your open documents and programs to temporary memory and to your hard disk, and then goes into a low-power state without turning off the power. You resume from hybrid sleep in the same way and almost as quickly as from standard sleep. The advantage of hybrid sleep is that if a power failure occurs while your computer is asleep, Windows can restore your documents because it saved them to your hard disk. If you turn on hybrid sleep and click the Sleep option on the Power button menu, Windows puts your computer into hybrid sleep instead of standard sleep.

Windows 10 also has a setting called **hybrid boot**, or fast startup, which starts a computer quickly after it's been shut down. You can manage the fast startup and other shutdown settings, which include sleep, hibernate, and lock, using the Control Panel's System Settings window. By default, the lock screen appears after you restore your computer from sleep or hibernation. You can use the System Settings window to show or hide the lock screen after any type of shutdown.

PROSKILLS

Decision Making: Choosing a Power-Saving State

Sleep, hybrid sleep, and hibernation are three power-saving states Windows uses to conserve power on mobile and desktop computers. Selecting the right option for your computer and your usage style can help you work more efficiently. Keep the following guidelines in mind when choosing a power-saving state:

- Sleep—If you do not plan to use your computer for several hours, Microsoft recommends putting it to sleep rather than turning it off. Sleep is preferable to turning off your computer because when you're ready to use your computer again, it wakes quickly so you can resume your work where you left it. If you put a computer to sleep yourself, be sure to save your data first so you don't lose it in case of a power failure. Even if you let Windows put your computer to sleep after a specified amount of idle time, standard sleep is the best power-saving state for average computing because it resumes operations faster than hybrid sleep or hibernation.
- Hibernation—When you are finished working and know you won't use your mobile PC for up to a day, and that you won't have a chance to recharge the battery on a mobile PC during that time, put the computer into hibernation yourself. Otherwise, you can generally let Windows determine when to use hibernation. If you don't plan to use the computer for more than a day, you save wear and tear on your electronic components and conserve energy by turning the computer off. Hibernation is safer than sleep, but slower to return to a full-power state.
- Hybrid sleep—If you are concerned that you might lose power while your desktop computer is asleep, such as during electrical storms, turn on hybrid sleep so that Windows saves your data on the hard disk before it puts your computer to sleep. Using hybrid sleep, your computer quickly resumes running and avoids the risk of losing data.

Not all computers are set to display Sleep or Hibernate on the Power menu, which is the list of shutdown options that appears when you click the Power button on the Start menu. You can use the Control Panel's System Settings window to include Sleep or Hibernate on the Power button menu. Some computers can use one of these shutdown options but not both, so your System Settings window might display only one of these power-saving options.

Derek wants to make sure that the fast startup, sleep, and hibernate settings are enabled on his mobile PC because each option is useful to him depending on his work environment.

To turn on all shutdown settings:

1. In the Windows Mobility Center window, click the **Change power settings** icon 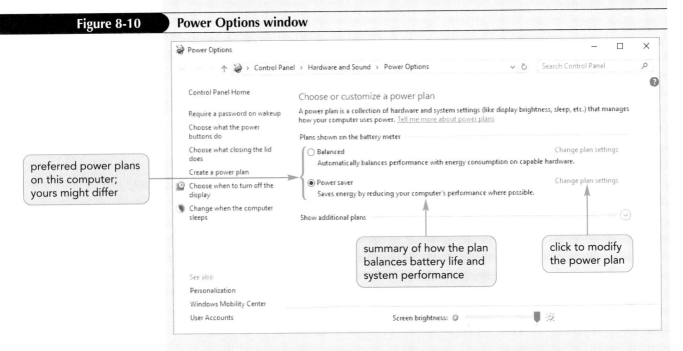 in the Battery Status tile to open the Power Options window. See Figure 8-10.

Figure 8-10   Power Options window

preferred power plans on this computer; yours might differ

summary of how the plan balances battery life and system performance

click to modify the power plan

This window lists power plans and summarizes how each plan balances battery life with system performance.

Trouble? If the message, "Your power plan information isn't available" is displayed in the window, click the Windows Mobility Center link in the lower-left corner of the window, click the Battery Status button arrow and select Balanced, and then double-click the Battery Status icon to return to the Power Options window. Click the Show additional plans link and then select Power saver.

2. Click **Choose what the power buttons do** in the left pane to open the System Settings window.

   Trouble? If the left pane displays a link titled "Choose what the power button does," click that link instead.

3. If some options are inactive (gray), click the **Change settings that are currently unavailable** link to activate the options.

4. Scroll down to display the Shutdown settings section, if necessary. See Figure 8-11. Your settings might differ.

Figure 8-11 System Settings window

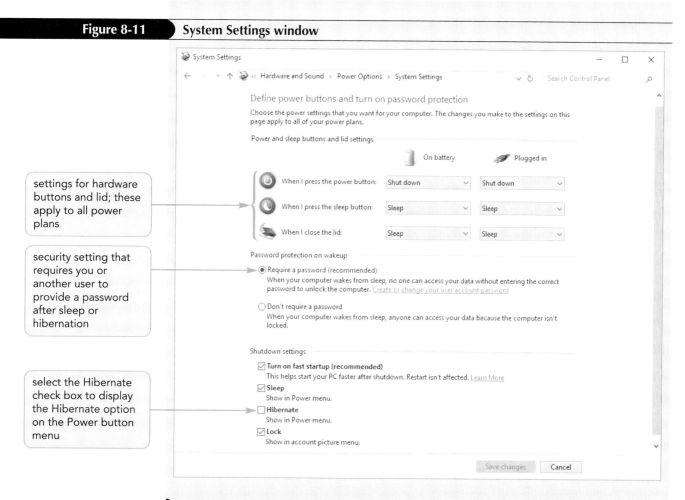

settings for hardware buttons and lid; these apply to all power plans

security setting that requires you or another user to provide a password after sleep or hibernation

select the Hibernate check box to display the Hibernate option on the Power button menu

▶ **5.** Click the check boxes as necessary to select all options in the Shutdown settings section.

▶ **6.** Click the **Save changes** button. Windows saves the new setting and returns to the Power Options window.

▶ **7.** Click the **Start** button ⊞ to display the Start menu, and then click the **Power** button. Hibernate now appears along with the other shut down options.

▶ **8.** Click the **Start** button ⊞ again to close the Start menu.

The System Settings window also determines the settings for the hardware power buttons (one or more buttons included on your computer case) and other items for all power plans. You work with these settings later in this session. To select power settings that affect only one power plan, which is what you want to do for Derek, you modify the power plan.

Modifying a Power Plan

When you modify a power plan, you can adjust up to two basic settings and dozens of advanced settings that apply when your computer is running on battery power and when your computer is plugged into a power outlet. For example, in your Balanced plan, Windows might be set to turn off the display after 5 minutes of idle time if the computer is using battery power and after 10 minutes of inactivity if the computer is plugged into an outlet. You can increase or decrease these times in the Edit Plan

Settings window, which you open from the Power Options window. To change advanced settings, such as whether to use hybrid sleep instead of standard sleep, you use the Advanced settings tab in the Power Options dialog box.

REFERENCE

Modifying a Power Plan

- Open the Power Options window.
- Click the Change plan settings link for the power plan you want to modify.
- For each available option, click its button for a power setting, and then click the amount of time to wait before applying the setting.
- Click Change advanced power settings.
- Expand an advanced setting, change the setting, and then click the OK button.
- Click the Save changes button.

Although Derek uses the Power saver plan while traveling, he uses the Balanced plan when he meets with clients. He wants to make two changes to the Balanced power plan so he can work effectively at client sites. First, he wants Windows to wait for more than 10 minutes of idle time before it turns off the display when his computer is plugged in. For example, during his upcoming presentation at the Bravo Law Office, people might raise questions that lead him to step away from his computer for 20 to 30 minutes of discussion. He wants to keep the display turned on for 30 minutes when it's plugged in, as it will be during the presentation. You'll show Derek how to change this basic setting for the Balanced power plan.

To change basic power plan settings:

▶ 1. In the Power Options window, click the **Change plan settings** link for the Balanced power plan. The Edit Plan Settings window opens for the Balanced plan. See Figure 8-12. Your settings might differ. If you are using a desktop computer, your options might also differ.

Figure 8-12   **Edit Plan Settings window**

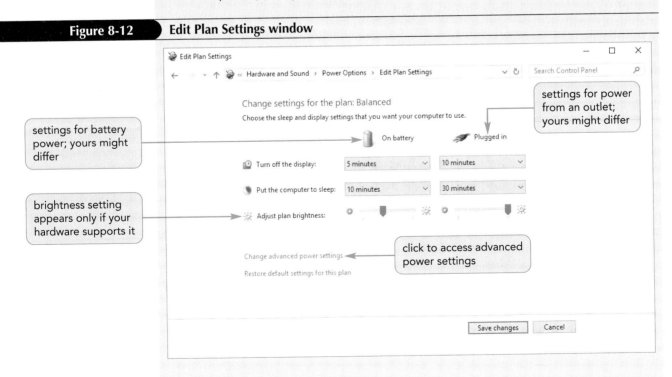

> **Trouble?** If the Balanced plan does not appear in the Power Options window, click the Change plan settings link for the plan other than the Power saver plan.
>
> **2.** For the Turn off the display setting, click the **button** in the Plugged in column, and then click **30 minutes**.
>
> **Trouble?** If you are working on a desktop computer, the window probably includes only one column of settings. Click the button for the Turn off the display setting, and then click 30 minutes.
>
> **3.** Click the **Save changes** button. Windows saves the new setting and returns to the Power Options window.

You can change the other basic power plan settings the same way—click a button for the Turn off the display or the Put the computer to sleep setting while on battery or plugged in, and then select an amount of idle time Windows should wait before activating that setting. You can turn off the setting by selecting Never. For example, if you do not want Windows to put the computer to sleep when it's plugged in, click the button in the Plugged in column for the Put the computer to sleep setting, and then click Never. However, you might lose data if you prevent a mobile PC from sleeping or hibernating and the battery runs out of power.

Next, you'll show Derek how to set multimedia power settings. He occasionally shows videos during client visits. Playing videos can consume a lot of power, so Derek typically plugs his laptop into a power source when he shows videos. In that case, he can use as much power as necessary to optimize video quality. When he plays videos on battery power using the Balanced plan, he is typically just quickly reviewing the video himself, so he can optimize power rather than quality when using battery power. To select these multimedia power settings, you need to change an advanced power option.

To change advanced power plan settings:

> **1.** In the Power Options window, click the **Change plan settings** link for the Balanced power plan to open the Edit Plan Settings window again.
>
> **2.** Click the **Change advanced power settings** link to open the Power Options dialog box. See Figure 8-13.

Figure 8-13   Power Options dialog box

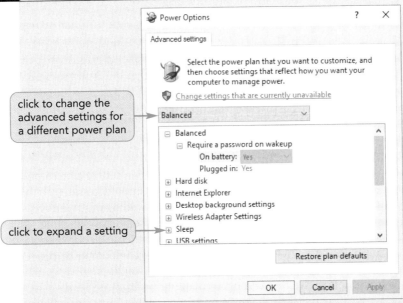

click to change the advanced settings for a different power plan

click to expand a setting

3. Scroll down, click the **expand** button ⊞ for the Multimedia settings option, and then click the **expand** button ⊞ for the When playing video setting. See Figure 8-14. The Plugged in option is already using the setting Derek wants (Optimize video quality), so you only need to change the On battery option.

Figure 8-14   Specifying Multimedia settings

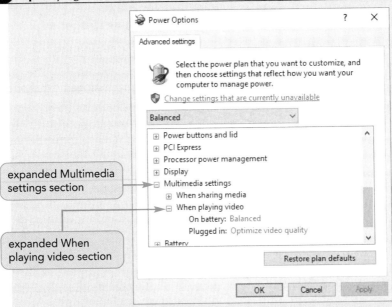

expanded Multimedia settings section

expanded When playing video section

4. In the When playing video section, click the **On battery button arrow**, and then click **Optimize power savings**.

5. Click the **OK** button to close the Power Options dialog box.

6. Click the **Back** button ← to return to the Power Options window.

You've changed basic and advanced settings in Derek's Balanced power plan. Next, you'll show him how to change other power options.

Selecting Other Power Options

Besides using power plans, you can control other power settings, such as what Windows should do when you press a hardware power button or close the lid on your mobile PC. You can apply the following settings to all of your power plans or only to a specific plan.

- Define power button and lid settings. Recall that, by default, Windows puts a mobile PC to sleep when you press a hardware power button or close the lid. It also puts the computer to sleep when you press the hardware sleep button (if your computer has one). You can change the power button, sleep button, and lid settings for all power plans to hibernate, shut down, or do nothing when your computer is running on battery power or is plugged in.
- Require a password on wakeup. If you sign in to your computer by providing a password, Windows locks your computer for security when it sleeps and requires that password to unlock the computer when it wakes from sleep. This is especially helpful if you need to protect confidential information on your computer. However, if you're the only one who uses your computer and you use it at home or another private place, you can change this setting if you don't want to enter a password every time your computer wakes.

Derek is in the habit of using the Sleep command on the Power button menu to put his laptop to sleep and likes having the computer go to sleep when he closes the lid. However, if his computer is running on battery power, he wants to save the battery charge by having the computer hibernate and eventually turn off when he presses the hardware power button on the computer case. In addition, although he wants to maintain password protection during the trip to Dover, he wants to know how to turn off the password protection on wakeup setting so he doesn't need to provide the password when he works from home. You'll show Derek how to change the power button and password protection on wakeup settings. Because he wants these settings to apply no matter which power plan he is using, you'll use the System Settings window to make these selections so they apply system-wide.

To change power options:

▶ **1.** In the Power Options window, click **Choose what the power buttons do** in the left pane. The System Settings window opens.

Trouble? If the left pane displays a link titled "Choose what the power button does," click that link instead.

▶ **2.** For the When I press the power button setting, click the **button** in the On battery column, and then click **Hibernate**.

Trouble? If you are using a desktop computer, your window does not have two columns of buttons. Click the button for the When I press the power button setting, and then click Hibernate.

▶ **3.** Click the **Change settings that are currently unavailable** link, if necessary, to make the Password protection on wakeup settings available.

Trouble? If a dialog box opens requesting an administrator password or your permission to continue, enter the password and then click the Yes button.

▶ **4.** Click the **Don't require a password** option button. This means that when your computer wakes from sleep, it is unlocked and anyone can access your data and settings.

TIP

If you don't have a password, you can click the Create or change your user account password link to create one.

▶ **5.** Click the **Require a password (recommended)** option button. This means that when your computer wakes from sleep, it is locked and you or another user must enter your Windows password to unlock it.

▶ **6.** Click the **Save changes** button.

▶ **7.** Close the Power Options window.

The change you made to the power button now applies to all of the power plans on Derek's computer. To make these changes to only a particular power plan, you use the Advanced settings tab in the Power Options dialog box as you did earlier (that is, by clicking the Change advanced power settings link in the Edit Plan Settings window for the Balanced power plan), and then change the Require a password on wakeup for the Power buttons and lid settings.

If you turn off the setting to require a password to wake your computer from sleep, you should also turn off your screen saver password. (A screen saver password locks your computer when the screen saver is on. The screen saver password is the same as the one you use to sign in to Windows and to wake your computer from sleep.) To turn off the screen saver password, start the Settings app, click Personalization, click Lock screen, scroll down to click Screen saver settings, and then click the On resume, display logon screen check box to remove the check mark.

Now that you've shown Derek how to control the power state of his mobile PC, you and he are ready for the trip to Dover. When you arrive, you can help him prepare his computer for the presentation to the Bravo Law Office.

Presenting Information to an Audience

Giving a presentation is a common practice in business and education. When you use a computer to give a presentation to an audience, you can combine images, text, animation, sound, and visual effects to educate, inform, or train others. You can give a presentation to a small or large group of people while you are all in the same room, or you can present the information remotely to people with whom you share a network connection. To create a presentation, you can use apps such as the slide show feature in the Photos app, Microsoft PowerPoint, or any other presentation app. You can then connect your computer to a projector to broadcast the presentation. To start and control the presentation, you use the keyboard and pointing device on your computer and the tools provided in the presentation app to perform tasks such as switching from one image or slide to another and ending the presentation.

Before you give a presentation, you can use Windows Mobility Center to adjust presentation settings, which are a collection of options that prepare your computer for a presentation. For example, you can control the volume level of your computer and block distractions such as notifications and reminders. You can also use Windows Mobility Center to connect your computer to an external display, such as a larger monitor or projector.

Preparing a Computer for a Presentation

TIP

You can also hide notifications by clicking Notifications & actions in the System window of the Settings app, and then clicking the Hide notifications while presenting slider button to change the setting from On to Off.

Using Windows Mobility Center, you can specify the settings that Windows uses as you are giving a presentation. When you turn on presentation settings, your computer stays awake and Windows blocks system notifications, such as notices about available software updates. You can also choose to turn off the screen saver, adjust the speaker volume, and change your desktop background image. Windows saves these settings and applies them when you turn on presentation settings in Windows Mobility Center. To turn on presentation settings, you can click the Turn on button in the Presentation Settings tile of Windows Mobility Center. Windows also turns on presentation settings when you connect your mobile PC to a projector. To turn off presentation settings, you can click the Turn off button in Windows Mobility Center. Windows also turns off presentation settings when you disconnect your computer from a projector or when you shut down or sign out of Windows.

Now that you and Derek have arrived in Dover, you have some time to prepare for his presentation, which he'll give in a Bravo Law Office conference room. First, you'll customize the presentation settings to turn off the screen saver, turn up the volume, and change the desktop background to black. Then you'll show Derek how to turn the presentation settings on and off. Note your original settings so you can restore them later.

If the Presentation Settings tile does not appear in your Windows Mobility Center, read, but do not perform the next two sets of steps.

To customize presentation settings:

1. In the Presentation Settings tile of the Windows Mobility Center window, click the **Change presentation settings** icon 🖳. The Presentation Settings dialog box opens. See Figure 8-15.

Figure 8-15	Presentation Settings dialog box

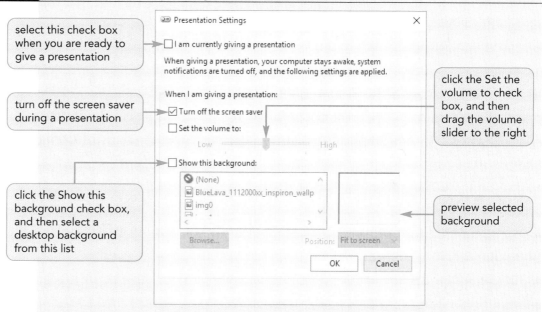

select this check box when you are ready to give a presentation

turn off the screen saver during a presentation

click the Show this background check box, and then select a desktop background from this list

click the Set the volume to check box, and then drag the volume slider to the right

preview selected background

2. If necessary, click the **Turn off the screen saver** check box to insert a check mark.

   Trouble? If you inadvertently click the I am currently giving a presentation check box, click it again to remove the check mark.

3. Click the **Set the volume to** check box, and then drag the slider to **85**. As you drag the slider, numbers appear above it to indicate the volume.

4. Click the **Show this background** check box, and then click **(None)**, if necessary. A preview of the background, in this case, a black background, appears to the right.

5. Click the **OK** button.

TIP

Click the Position button to specify an on-screen background image position, such as Center, Tile, or Fit to screen.

Now Windows will turn off the screen saver, turn up the speaker volume, and display a black desktop background when Derek turns on the presentation settings, which you'll show him how to do next.

To turn presentation settings on and off:

▶ **1.** In the Presentation Settings tile, click the **Turn on** button. The desktop, taskbar, and window borders turn black, and the Turn on button toggles to the Turn off button. See Figure 8-16.

| Figure 8-16 | Turning on presentation settings |

volume is set to 85

black desktop background

Presentation Settings tile indicates that you are presenting

It's not time for Derek's presentation, so you can turn off the settings for now.

▶ **2.** In the Presentation Settings tile, click the **Turn off** button. The desktop returns to its pre-presentation state.

Next, you'll help Derek select display settings when he connects his laptop to a projector.

Displaying Information on an External Display Device

TIP

You can also click the Connect display button in the External Display tile in Windows Mobility Center to select an external projector or monitor.

When you connect a mobile PC to a projector or any other type of additional display device such as an external screen, Windows detects the extra display and recommends the video settings that correspond to that device. To select settings for the additional device, click in the Ask me anything box, type "second screen," and then click Project to a second screen to display the options shown in Figure 8-17.

Figure 8-17 Selecting a display option

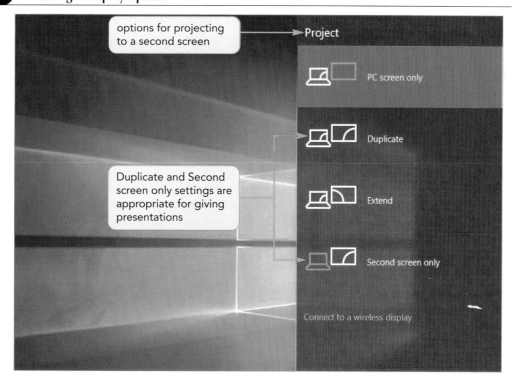

Figure 8-18 describes each option in this panel.

Figure 8-18 Second screen display options

Display Option	Description	When to Use
PC screen only	Does not extend your desktop to another display device	You are using your computer as usual.
Duplicate	Duplicates your desktop on each display device	You are giving a presentation on a projector or a fixed display, such as a TV-type monitor.
Extend	Extends your desktop across all of your display devices	You want to increase your work space, such as by displaying one program window on your primary monitor and another window on a secondary monitor.
Second screen only	Shows your desktop on the external display devices, but not on your mobile computer screen	You want to conserve battery power.

When you disconnect the external display device, Windows restores the original display settings to your main computer monitor. The next time that you connect the same display screen, Windows automatically applies the display settings that you used the last time that you connected that device.

Connecting to an External Display Device

- Connect your mobile PC to an external display device, such as a projector or secondary monitor.
- If Windows does not automatically detect the external display and open a dialog box with display options, open Windows Mobility Center, and then click the Connect display button in the External Display tile.
- Click the appropriate option to duplicate, extend, or show your desktop on the external display only.

Before adding a second display device to your computer, make sure that you have a video card that supports multiple screens or that your computer has more than one video card. A video card that supports multiple screens has two video ports—check the back of your computer to find an available port labeled as "Video" or with an icon of a display device.

When you connect the second display device, Windows should recognize it and open the panel with options for duplicating, extending, or showing your screen on the second screen only. One way to use a second display is to show the main desktop on one screen and a virtual desktop on another.

Derek connects his laptop to the projector in the conference room, clicks the Connect display button in the Windows Mobility Center window, and then selects the Duplicate setting in the list of second screen projection options. Derek's desktop is now displayed on his laptop and is projected on a large white screen in the conference room.

Exploring Network Concepts

As you know, a network is a collection of computers and other hardware devices linked together so they can exchange data and share hardware and software. Networks offer many advantages. Groups of computers on a network can use the same printer, so you don't have to purchase a printer for each computer. Network computers can also share an Internet connection, so you don't need to purchase and install a broadband modem for each computer. Networks also facilitate group projects because one person can save a document in a folder that other users on other computers can access. A network also improves communication in a company because coworkers can easily share news and information.

Large companies that want to connect their computers on a network usually hire a team of network specialists to determine what type of hardware the company should purchase and how to connect the devices to form a **local area network (LAN)**, a network of computers and other hardware devices that reside in the same physical space, such as an office building. Small office and home users can set up a simplified LAN to enjoy the advantages of networking. Like large companies, you also need to decide what type of network technology and hardware you will use if you want to set up a small network. (**Network technology** is the way computers connect to one another.) The most common types of network technology for a small office or home network are wireless, Ethernet, and Powerline. Figure 8-19 compares network technologies.

Figure 8-19 Comparing network technologies

Network Technology	How It Sends Information Between Computers	Pros	Cons
Wireless	Radio waves, microwaves, or infrared light	Because it does not involve cables, setting up the network and moving computers are easy.	Wireless technology is more expensive and often slower than Ethernet. Interference can interrupt wireless connections.
Ethernet	Ethernet cables	Ethernet is a proven and reliable technology, and Ethernet networks are inexpensive and fast.	Ethernet cables must connect each computer to a hub, switch, or router, which can be time consuming and difficult when the computers are in different rooms.
Powerline	Existing home electrical wiring	You don't need hubs or switches to connect more than two computers.	You need an electrical outlet in each room where you want to have a computer. Interference and noise on the line can affect Powerline networks.

Small office and home networks use special network hardware, including the following devices:

- Network adapters—Also called **network interface cards (NICs)**, **network adapters** connect computers to a network. Network adapters are usually installed inside your computer, though you can also plug one into a USB port. See Figure 8-20.

Figure 8-20 Network interface card

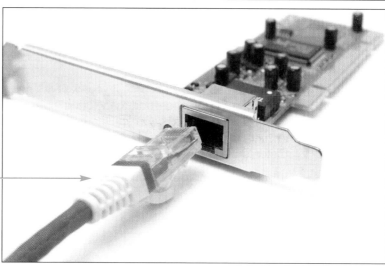

Ethernet cable connects to a network interface card and router

© Bacho/Shutterstock.com

- Network hubs and switches—Used on an Ethernet network, **network hubs** or **network switches** connect two or more computers to the network.
- Routers or access points—**Routers** connect computers and networks to each other and let you share a single Internet connection among several computers. They are called routers because they direct network traffic. An **access point** provides wireless access to a wired Ethernet network. An access point plugs into or is built into a

wired router and sends out a wireless signal, which other wireless computers and devices use to connect to the wired network. Most home networks share access to the Internet by connecting a wireless router to a modem and to a computer with an Internet connection.

- Modems—To connect your computer to the Internet, you need a **modem**, which sends and receives information over telephone or cable lines. Some devices combine a modem with a router.
- Cables—On an Ethernet or Powerline network, **cables** connect computers to each other and to other devices, such as hubs and routers.

Figure 8-21 describes the hardware required for each type of network technology.

Figure 8-21   Hardware needed for each type of network technology

Network Technology	Hardware Required
Wireless	• Wireless network adapter installed on each computer in the network
	• Wireless access point or router
Ethernet	• Ethernet network adapter on each computer in the network
	• Ethernet hub or switch if you only want to connect more than two computers
	• Ethernet router if you want to connect more than two computers and share an Internet connection
	• Ethernet cables
Powerline	• Powerline network adapter for each computer on your network
	• Ethernet router to share an Internet connection
	• One electrical outlet for each computer on your network

Setting Up a Small Office or Home Network

After you determine what type of network you want and acquire the hardware you need, you typically set up a small office or home network by performing the following tasks:

- Install the hardware. Install the network adapters in the computers that need them, if necessary.
- Set up an Internet connection. If you want the network computers to access the Internet, set up a connection to the Internet, usually through a modem.
- Connect the computers. On an Ethernet network, you need a hub, switch, or router to connect the computers. Use a router to share an Internet connection. Connect the router to the computer that is connected to the modem.

If you only want to share an Internet connection on a wireless network, you need to complete two steps:

- Configure the wireless router to broadcast signals.
- Set up Windows 10 on each computer to receive the signals.

In the first step, you install a wireless router and configure it to start broadcasting information to and receiving information from your computer. To have the router broadcast radio signals, you need to run the setup software provided with your router. The steps to run this software vary depending on your router, but usually you provide a network name, or **service set identifier (SSID)**, which is a name you use to identify your wireless network. You'll see this name later when you use Windows 10 to connect to your wireless network. The setup software also lets you turn on security settings to encrypt your data when you transmit it, which helps to prevent unauthorized people from accessing your data or your network. To do so, you need to provide a password so that you can access the network. Figure 8-22 shows a typical setup for a wireless network.

| Figure 8-22 | **Wireless network sharing an Internet connection** |

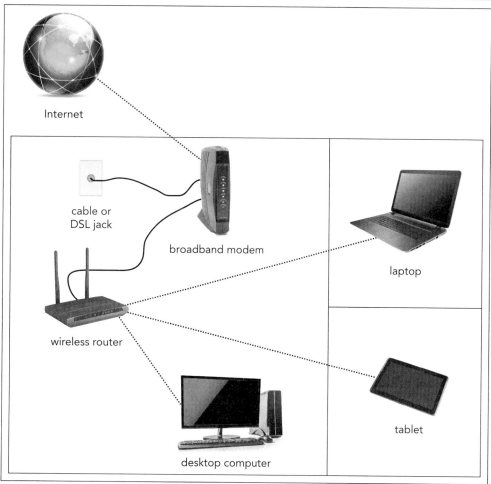

© silver tiger/Shutterstock.com; © Norman Chan/Shutterstock.com; © vipman/Shutterstock.com, © PhotoBalance/Shutterstock.com; © Studio KIWI/Shutterstock.com; © Denis Rozhnovsky/Shutterstock.com

The following section shows you how to set up Windows 10 to receive the wireless signals. If you want to share files and printers as well as an Internet connection on a wireless network, you can set up a homegroup, which is discussed later in this module.

Managing Network Connections

After you connect two or more computers through cables or wireless connections, you can use Windows 10 to monitor and manage your network connections. If your network is set up to share a network printer or an Internet connection, Windows works behind the scenes to organize requests to use these resources. For example, if two people want to print documents at the same time on the network printer, Windows lines up the printer requests in a queue and prints the documents one after the other. It also lets all the network users share a single Internet connection so they can visit websites and exchange email without interrupting each other. Although you can connect to a network using the network icon on the taskbar, to view full network information and change networking settings, you use the Network and Sharing Center window. See Figure 8-23.

Figure 8-23   Network and Sharing Center window

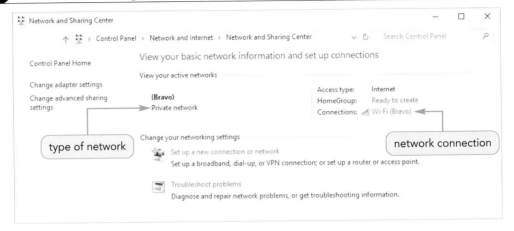

You can now show Derek how to connect his mobile PC to the Bravo Law Office wireless network. He has prepared a Project Scope document for Bravo and wants to copy it to a network folder that the Bravo Law Office partners can access. Derek might also need to retrieve a document stored on their network. Before he can perform those tasks, he needs to connect to the wireless network.

Connecting to a Wireless Network

TIP

You can also connect to or disconnect from a network in the Control Panel's Network and Sharing Center window.

If your computing device has a wireless network adapter, you can display a list of available wireless networks and then connect to one of them, whether it's a private wireless network or a public one. You can display a list of available wireless networks by clicking the network icon in the notification area of the taskbar or by starting the Settings app, and then clicking Network & Internet. Windows displays the following information about each available wireless network:

- Network name—This is the SSID you or someone else provided when the network was set up. Because wireless signals extend past the boundaries of your home or office, the wireless adapter in your computer often detects more than one network within its range.
- Security—Open, or unsecured, networks don't require a password, whereas secured networks do. Secured networks also encrypt data before transmitting it, meaning that unauthorized people cannot intercept sensitive information such as a credit card number when you send it across the network. When you set up a wireless network, you should create a strong password or **passphrase** (more than one word). A strong passphrase has at least 20 characters, including spaces, and is not a common phrase that other people are likely to know. If you don't create a passphrase, the network is protected with a **network security key**, which is usually a series of hexadecimal numbers assigned by Windows.
- Signal strength—Windows displays an icon composed of curved lines that indicate the strength of the signal; the more lines highlighted, the stronger the connection. Having the strongest signal (three lines highlighted) means that the wireless network is nearby or has no interference. To improve the signal strength, you can move your computer closer to the wireless router or access point, or move the router or access point away from sources of interference such as brick walls or walls that contain metal support beams.

If you use a wireless network regularly, you can choose to connect to the network automatically any time your computer is within range. Unless you are accessing a public network, such as in an airport or a hotel, be sure to connect only to the wireless network you are authorized to use, even if you can access an unsecured private network. If you are authorized to connect to more than one wireless network, you should generally use the one with the strongest signal. However, even if an unsecured network has a stronger signal than a secured one, keep in mind that it's safer for your data to connect to the secured network, as long as you are an authorized user of that network.

Bravo Law Office already has a wireless network set up in its offices. Derek asks you to help him perform some basic tasks to manage the Bravo Law Office network by connecting his mobile PC to the company's wireless network. The passphrase to access the network is BravUser12 Dover.

The following steps assume you are equipped to connect to a wireless network named Bravo. Substitute the name of your network and your network password when you perform the following steps. If you are not equipped to connect to a wireless network, read but do not perform the following steps.

To connect to a wireless network:

1. In the notification area of the taskbar, click the **wireless network** icon to display a list of available networks. See Figure 8-24.

Figure 8-24   Available wireless networks

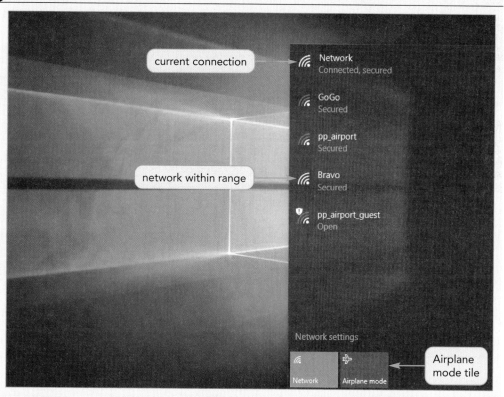

Make sure you are connected to a network to perform the rest of the steps in this module.

2. Click your **network name**, such as Bravo, in the list of available networks, and then click the **Connect** button. If a Disconnect button appears, you are already connected to the network. Read but do not perform the remaining steps.

Trouble? If your network is not listed, the signal strength might be low. Move your computer closer to the wireless router or access point, if possible, click the desktop to close the list of networks, and then repeat Steps 1 and 2.

Trouble? If your network is not listed, but one or more networks appear as "Unnamed network," click an Unnamed network, click the Connect button, and then enter your network name.

▶ 3. If a box opens requesting your network security key, enter your passphrase, such as BravUser12 Dover, and then click the **Next** button. Windows connects to the network.

▶ 4. When asked if you want to turn on sharing between PCs and connect to devices on this network, click the **Yes, turn on sharing and connect to devices** link if you are working on a home or work network.

Trouble? If you are connecting to a network in a public place such as an airport, click No, don't turn on sharing or connect to devices.

▶ 5. If necessary, click the desktop to close the list of networks.

After you connect to a network, you can disconnect by displaying the list of available wireless networks, clicking the network you're using, and then clicking the Disconnect button. On a mobile PC, you can also quickly disconnect from all wireless communications by turning on **Airplane mode**. When you click the wireless network icon in the notification area of the taskbar, the Airplane mode tile appears in the Network settings section below the list of available networks. Click the Airplane mode tile to turn the setting on or off.

Derek's mobile PC is now connected to the Bravo wireless network. Because older cordless phones and other devices can interfere with a wireless connection, you should periodically check the status of the connection. You can do so by opening the Network and Sharing Center, or by using the network icon in the notification area of the taskbar or the Settings menu. You'll show Derek how to check the status using the network icon on the taskbar.

To check the status of a wireless connection:

▶ 1. Point to the **wireless network** icon 📶 in the notification area of the taskbar. A small notification window shows the status of your network connection. For example, the window might display the name of your network and the text "Internet access."

▶ 2. Close all open windows.

Now that you've helped Derek connect to the Bravo Law Office wireless network, you are ready to perform some typical network tasks, which involve connecting to and sharing files with other computers on the network. You'll do that in the next session.

REVIEW

Session 8.1 Quick Check

1. Most mobile devices have a(n) _____ that lets users select objects and perform other interactions with a fingertip or stylus.
2. In what circumstances do you use Windows Mobility Center?
3. Explain how to display the status of the battery charge on a mobile PC.
4. When does Windows turn on the Battery saver feature by default?
5. When should you use the Power saver plan?
6. _____ is a power-saving state that saves your work to your hard disk, puts your computer into a low-power state, and then turns off your computer.
7. How do you turn off the screen saver only when you are giving a presentation?
8. When you display a list of available wireless networks, what three pieces of information does Windows provide?

Session 8.2 Visual Overview:

Use the buttons on the HomeGroup tab to manage and troubleshoot the homegroup.

Other users can **join** a homegroup to make their folders and other resources available to users on the network.

View access lets other homegroup members read but not change shared files.

View and edit access lets other homegroup members read and change shared files.

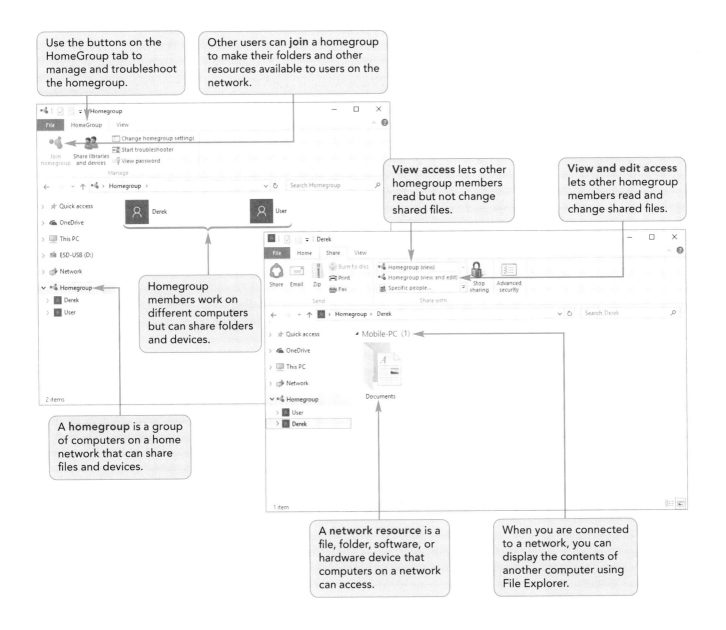

Homegroup members work on different computers but can share folders and devices.

A **homegroup** is a group of computers on a home network that can share files and devices.

A **network resource** is a file, folder, software, or hardware device that computers on a network can access.

When you are connected to a network, you can display the contents of another computer using File Explorer.

Sharing Resources

To use a network file when you are not connected to the network, first make it available offline.

Use commands on the Easy access button menu to manage offline files.

You use Sync Center to identify devices or folders containing files to synchronize and then exchange information.

You can schedule Sync Center to run as frequently as you want, such as daily or weekly, or you can sync files manually.

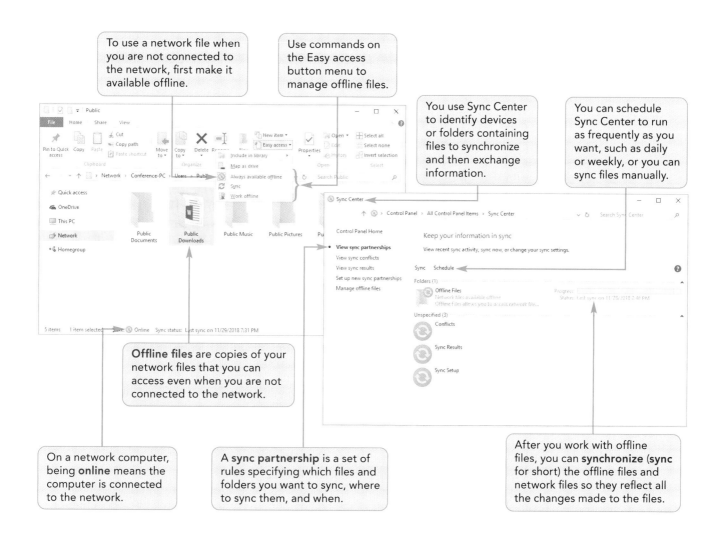

Offline files are copies of your network files that you can access even when you are not connected to the network.

On a network computer, being **online** means the computer is connected to the network.

A **sync partnership** is a set of rules specifying which files and folders you want to sync, where to sync them, and when.

After you work with offline files, you can **synchronize** (**sync** for short) the offline files and network files so they reflect all the changes made to the files.

Using a Windows Homegroup

Like many other people today, you probably have more than one computing device in your home, including laptops, tablets, and smartphones. To make managing those devices easier and to share files and resources among them, you can create a **home network**, a small private network specifically designed for communication among the devices in a home or a small office (usually fewer than 10 people). For example, if all the computers in your house connect to the same wireless network, they form a home network. If you also want to share files and devices, such as a printer, among the users on your home network, you can use a homegroup. Medium or large companies with Windows computers will have a network, but not a homegroup.

INSIGHT

Windows and Homegroups

Windows creates a homegroup for you when you set up a Windows 10 computer. Other user accounts on computers running Windows 10, 8.x, or 7 on your home network can join the homegroup, which is an easy and safe way to share files and printers on a home network. You can let someone connect to your home network to provide access to the Internet, but you don't have to let that user join the homegroup. Only those people with the homegroup password can join the homegroup.

Only computers running Windows 10 or earlier versions up to Windows 7 can participate in a homegroup. Computers running Windows RT, Windows 7 Starter, or Windows 7 Home Basic can join a homegroup, but cannot create one. Computers running Windows Vista or earlier cannot participate in a homegroup.

Creating a Homegroup

Although Windows 10 creates a homegroup when you first set up your computer, you can create one manually if necessary. Now that Derek's laptop is connected to the wireless network at the Bravo Law Office, you suggest he create a homegroup on his laptop, and then, using the desktop computer in the conference room, join the homegroup so he can easily share files between the two computers while working on site. Because Derek's laptop is a member of the NCC homegroup in New Castle, he must first leave that homegroup. (A computer can belong to only one homegroup at a time.) You'll show Derek how to leave the NCC homegroup and then create a homegroup to use at the Bravo Law Office. When he returns to NCC, he can leave the Bravo Law Office homegroup and rejoin the NCC homegroup.

As you create a homegroup for Derek, you can select the folders and devices he can share with other members of the homegroup. In particular, Derek has a document named Project Scope that outlines the services NCC will provide to the Bravo Law Office. He wants to share the Project Scope document with other people at the Bravo Law Office.

After you create the homegroup, users of the Bravo Law Office computers can join Derek's homegroup because their computers are on the same private network as Derek's laptop. As they join, these users also select the folders and devices on their computers to share with other members of the homegroup. Later, they can select individual files and folders to share.

First, copy the Project Scope document from the Module8 > Module folder provided with your Data Files to a new folder on your hard disk.

To copy the Project Scope document to a folder on the hard disk:

▶ **1.** Start File Explorer, and then navigate to the **Documents** folder on the hard disk of your computer.

▶ **2.** On the Home tab, in the New group, click the **New folder** button.

▶ **3.** Type **NCC** as the name of the folder, and then press the **Enter** key.

▶ **4.** Copy the **Project Scope** file from the Module8 > Module folder provided with your Data Files to the NCC folder.

▶ **5.** Close all open folder windows.

Next, leave the homegroup that your computer belongs to so you can create a new one.

To leave a homegroup:

▶ **1.** Click in the **Ask me anything** box, begin typing **homegroup**, and then click **HomeGroup** in the search results. See Figure 8-25.

Figure 8-25 **HomeGroup window**

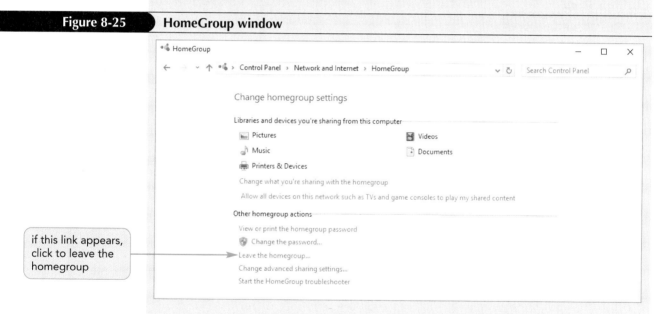

if this link appears, click to leave the homegroup

Trouble? If Windows indicates that your network does not have a homegroup or has a homegroup that you have not joined, read but do not perform the remaining steps.

Trouble? If Windows indicates that you have been invited to join a homegroup, close the HomeGroup window. Read but do not perform the remaining steps.

▶ **2.** Click **Leave the homegroup**. The Leave the Homegroup window opens with options for leaving or remaining in the homegroup.

▶ **3.** Click **Leave the homegroup** to confirm you do not want to belong to this homegroup. Windows removes your computer from the homegroup.

▶ **4.** When Windows indicates that you have successfully left the homegroup, click the **Finish** button.

Now you can create a homegroup on your mobile PC.

If the HomeGroup window now indicates that someone else on your home network has created a homegroup, you can join that homegroup shortly. In that case, your computer is playing the role of a Bravo Law Office user's computer joining Derek's homegroup. Read but do not perform the following steps.

If the HomeGroup window now indicates that the network does not have a homegroup, you can create one. In that case, your computer is playing the role of Derek's laptop. Complete the following steps. You will share the Documents folder and printers and devices connected to your computer so that other members of the homegroup can access the Project Scope document and print it.

To create a homegroup:

▶ **1.** In the HomeGroup window, click the **Create a homegroup** button. A window opens explaining how to use a homegroup.

▶ **2.** Click the **Next** button. A window opens where you select the folders and devices you want to share with the other computers in the homegroup.

▶ **3.** Click the buttons in the Permissions list as necessary to select only the Documents folder and the Printers & Devices resource, as shown in Figure 8-26.

Figure 8-26   **Selecting folders and resources to share**

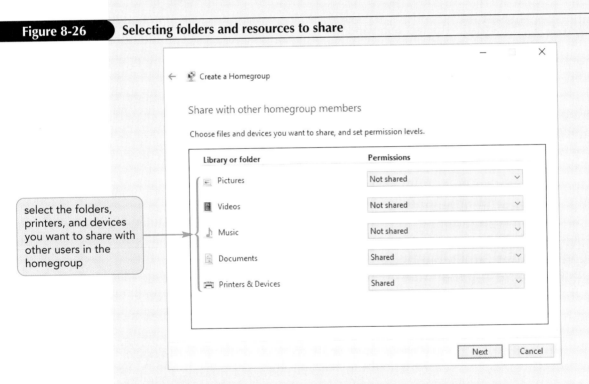

select the folders, printers, and devices you want to share with other users in the homegroup

---

▶ **4.** Click the **Next** button. Windows creates the homegroup and generates a password. Other users on the network need this password to join the homegroup, so you should print it.

▶ **5.** Click the **Print password and instructions** link, and then click the **Print this page** button to print the password, if requested by your instructor.

▶ **6.** Click the **Print** button in the Print dialog box to print the information, and then close the View and print your homegroup password window.

   Trouble? If you cannot print the password, record it in a document or on a sheet of paper. You need to enter the password to access the homegroup from a different computer.

▶ **7.** Click the **Finish** button.

To change the password later to one that's easier to remember, in the HomeGroup window, click the Change the password link, and then follow the steps in the wizard to change the password.

Adding Other Computers to a Homegroup

After you create a homegroup, other computers on your network can join the homegroup. You must give users the homegroup password so they can join. Joining involves using the HomeGroup window to select files and resources for sharing, just as you did when you created the homegroup, and then entering the homegroup password. After other users join the homegroup, you can access the files they've selected for sharing and vice versa.

REFERENCE

Joining a Homegroup

- Open the Control Panel's Network and Internet window, and then click HomeGroup.
- Click the Join now button.
- Click the Next button to start the HomeGroup Wizard.
- Select the folders and devices you want to share, and then click the Next button.
- Type the homegroup password, and then click the Next button.
- Click the Finish button.

If you did not create a homegroup on your computer because someone else already created a homegroup on the network, perform the following steps. You will share only the Documents folder with other members of the homegroup. In the figures, the name of the homegroup creator is Derek and his computer is named Mobile-PC.

If you created a homegroup in the previous set of steps, read but do not perform the following steps.

To join a homegroup:

▶ **1.** Display the HomeGroup window, which includes a message indicating that a user created a homegroup on the network. See Figure 8-27.

Figure 8-27   Joining a homegroup

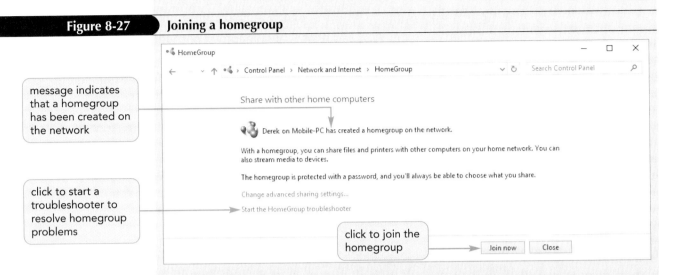

message indicates that a homegroup has been created on the network

click to start a troubleshooter to resolve homegroup problems

click to join the homegroup

If you did not create a homegroup, be sure to click the Join now button so you can perform the rest of the steps in this section.

2. Click the **Join now** button. A window opens describing the benefits of a homegroup.

3. Click the **Next** button. A window opens where you can select the folders and resources you want to share.

4. Click the buttons in the Permissions list as necessary to select only the Documents folder and the Printers & Devices resource, and then click the **Next** button.

5. If a window opens requesting the homegroup password, type the homegroup password you received in the previous set of steps, and then click the **Next** button.

   Trouble? If you do not remember the password, click the Where can I find the homegroup password? link, follow the instructions for retrieving it, and then repeat Step 5.

   Trouble? If you rejoined the homegroup, you do not have to enter the password again. Skip Step 5.

6. When a window appears indicating you successfully joined the homegroup, click the **Finish** button, and then minimize the HomeGroup window.

Next, you'll access the Documents folder available for sharing on the homegroup.

Sharing Files with a Homegroup

After you set up a homegroup with two or more computers, you can share files using File Explorer. First, you can specify which files and folders you want to share in the folder you selected for sharing. You can share files and folders with everyone in your homegroup, with only specific people in your homegroup, or with specified accounts on your computer. You can also prevent a file or folder from being shared with anyone, even if it's stored in a folder you selected for sharing.

When you share files or folders with other people in your homegroup, you can provide two types of access to the file or folder. View access means the homegroup members can read the file(s) but not change them. View and edit access means the homegroup members can read and change the file(s).

You'll share the Project Scope document with all members of your homegroup, but only allow them view access so they don't change the file.

To share a file on the homegroup:

▶ **1.** Click the **File Explorer** button 🔲 on the taskbar to open a folder window.

▶ **2.** Navigate to the **Documents > NCC** folder, and then click the **Project Scope** document to select it.

▶ **3.** Click the **Share** tab on the ribbon to display the options for sharing files.

▶ **4.** In the Share with group, click **Homegroup (view)** to share this file with all homegroup members and allow view access only. See Figure 8-28.

Figure 8-28	Sharing a file with other homegroup members

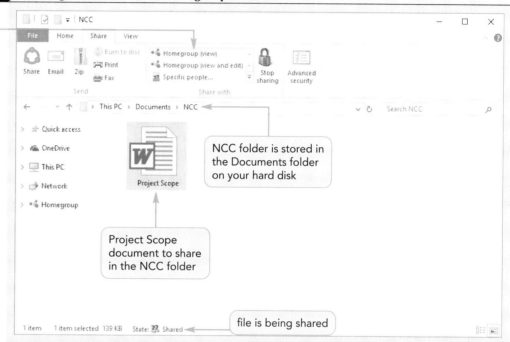

Homegroup (view) in the Share with group

NCC folder is stored in the Documents folder on your hard disk

Project Scope document to share in the NCC folder

file is being shared

Trouble? If the Shared icon does not appear in the status bar, click Specific people in the Share with group. If Homegroup appears in the list of names, click the Cancel button to close the File Sharing dialog box. If Homegroup does not appear in the list of names, click the button arrow, click Homegroup, and then click the Share button.

TIP

Keep in mind that if a homegroup computer is turned off, hibernating, or asleep, it won't appear in the navigation pane.

To access files on a homegroup member's computer, you click or expand Homegroup in the navigation pane to display the other users in your homegroup. Click or expand a user icon to display the folders that the user selected for sharing. Then, navigate the folders as you usually do to find the file you want to access.

When you click Homegroup in the navigation pane, File Explorer displays the HomeGroup tab on the ribbon and the members of the homegroup in the right pane of the window, as shown in the Session 8.2 Visual Overview. You can use the buttons on the HomeGroup tab to manage and troubleshoot the homegroup or you can use the homegroup settings in the Control Panel to control what to share with homegroup members.

If you can work on a homegroup computer other than the one where you just shared the Project Scope file, perform the following steps on that computer, on which the user account is named User. Otherwise, read but do not perform the steps.

In the following steps, the name of the computer you want to access is Mobile-PC and the user account is named Derek. When you perform the following steps, substitute the name of the computer you are using and your user account on that device for Mobile-PC and Derek.

To access shared files on a homegroup:

▶ **1.** On a computer in the homegroup (other than the computer where you shared the Project Scope document), open **File Explorer**.

▶ **2.** In the navigation pane, click **Homegroup**. The navigation pane displays the members of the homegroup.

> **Trouble?** If the homegroup members are not displayed, open the Control Panel, search for "homegroup," and then click the Find and fix problems with homegroup link to run the Homegroup troubleshooter.

> **Trouble?** If you run the Homegroup troubleshooter and still cannot display the homegroup users in the navigation pane, restart all the computers in the homegroup, and then perform these steps again starting with Step 1.

▶ **3.** In the navigation pane, click the **Derek** user (or any user in the homegroup) to display the folders available for sharing on the computer you are using, which is a computer other than Derek's Mobile-PC. See Figure 8-29.

Figure 8-29   **Displaying folders available for sharing**

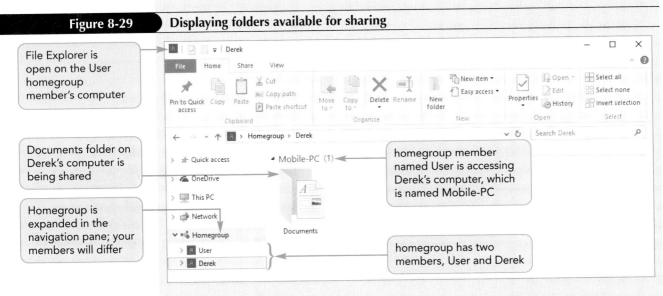

File Explorer is open on the User homegroup member's computer

Documents folder on Derek's computer is being shared

Homegroup is expanded in the navigation pane; your members will differ

homegroup member named User is accessing Derek's computer, which is named Mobile-PC

homegroup has two members, User and Derek

▶ **4.** Navigate to the **Documents > NCC** folder, and then double-click the **Project Scope** document to open it. The document opens in WordPad or another program that can open RTF files, such as Word.

▶ **5.** Type your name at the beginning of the document, and then click the **Save** button on the Quick Access Toolbar to save the document with the same name and in the same location. If you are using WordPad, a dialog box opens indicating that access was denied. If you are using Word, a dialog box asks if you want to replace the existing file. Click the **Yes** button. A Microsoft Word dialog box indicates this file is read-only. In either case, the view access set on the document prevents you from saving changes to the file. If the document had view and edit access, you would be able to save the file with your changes.

▶ **6.** Click the **OK** button to close the dialog box, click the **Cancel** button, if necessary, to close the Save As dialog box, and then close the document without saving your changes.

If you no longer want to share a file or folder on your computer, select the file or folder, and then click the Stop sharing button in the Share with group on the Share tab.

When you click the Stop sharing button, you prevent the file or folder from being shared with anyone in the homegroup. If you want to share the file or folder with some people but not others, then in the Share with group on the Share tab, click Specific people, and then specify the users who can share the file or folder.

Sharing a Printer with a Homegroup

If a printer is connected to a homegroup computer using a USB cable or wireless connection, the printer can be shared with the homegroup. After the printer is shared, you can access it through the Print dialog box in any application, just like any printer directly connected to your computer.

The following steps assume that a printer is connected to a computer in your homegroup but not to your computer directly. If that is not the case, read but do not perform the following steps. Both the printer and the homegroup computer connected to it should be turned on. If you performed the previous steps on a computer other than your own, return to your computer to perform the remaining steps in this section.

To connect to a homegroup printer:

▶ **1.** Display the Control Panel, and then click **View devices and printers** in the Hardware and Sound category. If Windows can automatically connect to the printer, it appears in the Devices and Printers window.

▶ **2.** If the homegroup printer is not listed in the Devices and Printers window, click the **Windows found a homegroup printer** message to connect to the printer.

    Trouble? If the Devices and Printers window does not display a message or the homegroup printer, the printer needs to be installed on the computer hosting the homegroup. Skip Step 2.

▶ **3.** Close the Devices and Printers window.

Derek mentions that he might need to use homegroup files even when he's not connected to the homegroup. You'll show him how to do so next.

Accessing Offline Files

After setting up and sharing files and folders on a homegroup or other network, you might need to work with those files when your network connection is slow or not available. To avoid this problem, you can create offline files, which are copies of your network files that you store on your computer and use when you are not connected to the network.

To create offline files, you first enable offline files on your computer, and then navigate to the folder or file stored on a network computer other than your own. After you choose the network files you want to make available offline, Windows creates copies of these files on your computer.

INSIGHT

Synchronizing Offline Files

If you change the network copies of the offline files, Windows updates, or synchronizes, the offline files so they remain exact duplicates of the network files. When you are not connected to the network, you can open the offline files on your computer knowing that they have the same content as the network files. When you're finished working with the offline files and reconnect to the network, you can use Sync Center to synchronize the offline files and network files yourself, or you can wait for Windows to do it the next time you access the network files.

You can synchronize files whenever you copy and save network files to your computer. When you first create offline files, Windows transfers the files from the network to a specified folder on your hard disk. After that, when you connect to the network folder that contains the files you've also stored offline, Windows makes sure that both the folder containing the offline files and the network folder contain the most recent versions of the files.

You explain to Derek that offline files are especially popular with mobile PC users. You'll show him how to set up his laptop to use offline files, and then you'll make a Public folder on the Bravo Law Office network available to him offline.

Setting Up a Computer to Use Offline Files

Before you specify that a network file or folder should be available offline, make sure that offline files are enabled on your computer. When this feature is turned on, Windows synchronizes the offline files on your computer with the network files as soon as you reconnect to the network.

To make sure offline files are enabled on your computer:

▶ **1.** Open the Control Panel, type **Offline** in the Search box, and then click **Manage offline files** in the Sync Center category. The Offline Files dialog box opens. See Figure 8-30.

Figure 8-30 Offline Files dialog box

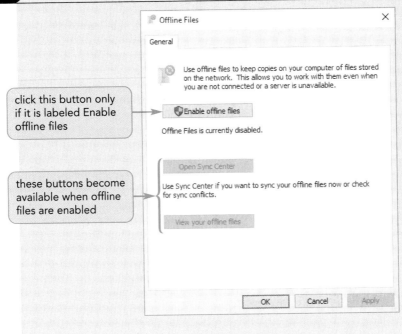

click this button only if it is labeled Enable offline files

these buttons become available when offline files are enabled

> **2.** Click the **Enable offline files** button. The other options to open Sync Center and view your offline files become available.

> **3.** Click the **OK** button to close the dialog box.

> **Trouble?** If a dialog box opens and advises you to restart the computer, restart as instructed, and then open the Control Panel to perform the next set of steps.

Before you share files or folders in one of the Public folders, you should make sure that Public folder sharing is turned on. To do so, you use the Advanced sharing settings window, which you open from the Network and Sharing Center.

To make sure Public folder sharing is turned on:

> **1.** In the Control Panel window, type **Network** in the Search box, and then click **Network and Sharing Center**. The Network and Sharing Center window opens.

> **2.** In the left pane, click **Change advanced sharing settings**. The Advanced sharing settings window opens. See Figure 8-31.

| Figure 8-31 | Advanced sharing settings window |

click to expand the All Networks section

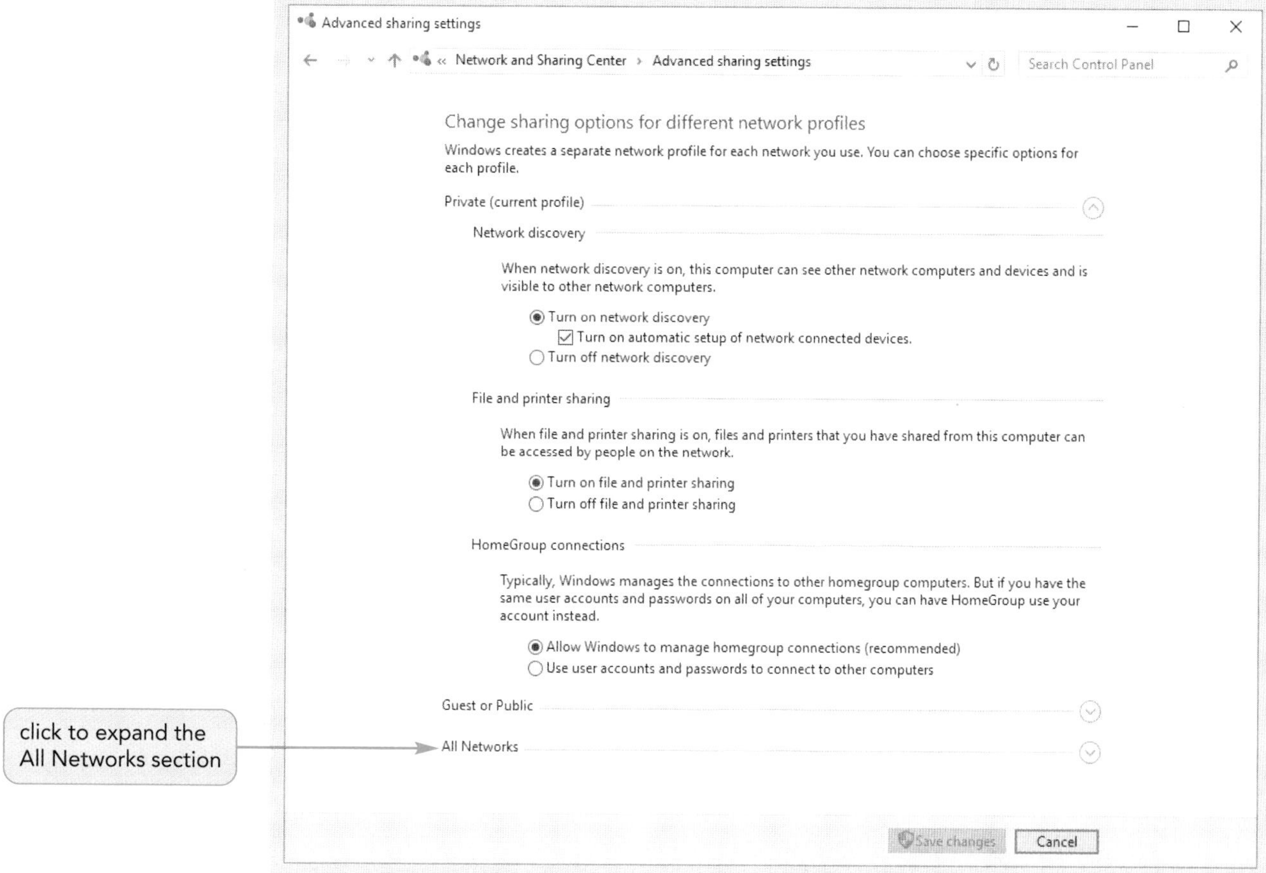

> **3.** Click **All Networks** to expand that section.

> **4.** In the All Networks section, under Public folder sharing, click the **Turn on sharing so anyone with network access can read and write files in the Public folders** option button, if necessary, and then click the **Save changes** button.

Next, you'll access a network folder and make it available to Derek offline.

Making a File or Folder Available Offline

To use a file or folder offline from the homegroup, you specify that it is always available offline using a shortcut menu or the Easy access button menu on the Home tab of a folder window as shown in the Session 8.2 Visual Overview. (When you make a folder available offline, all the files in the folder are also available offline.) Afterwards, you will be able to open the file or folder even if the network version is unavailable. You'll show Derek how to use offline files and folders by making the Public Documents folder on the conference room computer available offline.

The following steps assume that a computer named Conference-PC is connected to your network. If your network does not include a computer named Conference-PC, substitute the name of a different network computer that you can access in the following steps. The steps also assume that you have permission to access the Public Documents folder on the network computer. If you do not have permission to access this folder, ask your instructor which folder you can make available offline. Perform the following steps on a homegroup computer (other than the laptop where you created the homegroup).

To make network files available offline:

▶ 1. In the Address bar of the Network and Sharing Center window, click **Network and Internet** to display the Network and Internet window.

▶ 2. Click **View network computers and devices** to open the Network window.

▶ 3. Double-click the **Conference-PC** computer (or any computer listed on your network) to display the users and resources on the computer.

▶ 4. Double-click the **Users** folder, and then double-click the **Public** folder.

▶ 5. Right-click the **Public Documents** folder, and then click **Always available offline** on the shortcut menu if this command is not checked. Windows prepares the files in the Public Documents folder so they are available offline. Depending on the number of files in the folder, this could take a few minutes.

Trouble? If the Always available offline command does not appear on the shortcut menu, wait for Windows to sync the file, and then repeat Step 5. If the Always available offline command still does not appear, navigate to and right-click a folder you have permission to access offline. If you do not have permission to access any folders offline, read but do not perform the remaining steps.

TIP

To view all of your offline files, open the Offline Files dialog box again, and then click the View your offline files button.

Now you can show Derek how to work with the files in the Public Documents folder offline.

If you made a different folder available offline, substitute that folder for the Public Documents folder in the following steps. If you did not make any folders available offline, read but do not perform the following steps.

To work with offline files:

▶ 1. Click the **Public Documents** folder to select it, if necessary.

▶ 2. On the Home tab, in the New group, click the **Easy access** button, and then click **Work offline**. This option appears only if you have already made this folder available offline.

▶ 3. Close the folder window.

TIP

When you are finished working offline, click the Easy access button in the New group, and then click Work offline to deselect the option and sync the changes you made with the files on the network.

Any changes you make or Derek makes to the files in the Public Documents folder on the Bravo Law Office computer will now be made offline. In addition, if you lose your network connection, Windows turns on offline files and copies to your computer the files you designate as offline files so you can work on them. When you deselect the Work offline option or reconnect to the network, Windows syncs the two copies. You can find out if you're working offline by opening the network folder that contains the file you are working on, and then looking in the status of the folder window. If the status is Offline (working offline), you are working with a copy of the file on your computer. If the status is Online, you are working with the file on the network. You can also use Sync Center to sync all of your offline files at the same time so they match the network copies.

Synchronizing Folders

If you use more than one computer, such as a desktop computer and a mobile PC, it can be difficult to keep track of all your files. To make sure that you have the most recent versions of your files on your mobile PC before you travel, for example, you can synchronize information on your mobile PC, desktop computer, and other devices by using Sync Center. To do so, you create a set of rules that tells Sync Center what files you want to sync, where to sync them, and when. Sync Center makes it easy to move files from a computer to another device, such as another computer or a network server, portable music player, digital camera, or smartphone. Besides copying files from one device to another, Sync Center can maintain consistency among two or more versions of the same file stored in different locations. If you add, change, or delete a file in one location, you can use Sync Center to add, overwrite, or delete an earlier version of the file in other locations.

TIP

To sync only one file or folder, select the file or folder, click the Easy access button in the New group, and then click Sync.

You can also use Sync Center to manage offline files. In this case, Sync Center compares the size and time stamp of an offline file with a network file to see if they are different. For example, suppose you changed an offline file, but have not made the same changes in the network copy. Sync Center copies the offline file to the network so both versions are identical. If Sync Center finds a new file in an offline folder, for example, it copies the file to the network folder. The same is true for deleted files. If Sync Center finds that a file has been deleted from the network folder, for example, it deletes the same file in the offline folder.

Sometimes Sync Center discovers a conflict, which means that both a network file and its offline copy have been changed. A **sync conflict** occurs whenever differences can't be reconciled between a file stored in one location and a version of the same file in another location. A sync conflict stops the sync from being completed. In this case, Sync Center asks you to select the version you want to keep.

INSIGHT

One-way and Two-way Sync

When you are synchronizing a mobile device and your computer, you can use Sync Center to set up a one-way or two-way sync. In a one-way sync, every time you add, change, or delete a file or other information in one location, such as the Music folder on your hard disk, the same information is added, changed, or deleted in the other location, such as your mobile device. Windows does not change the files in the original location, such as the Music folder on your hard disk, because the sync is only one way. In a two-way sync, Windows copies files in both directions, keeping files in sync in two locations. Every time you add, change, or delete a file in either location, the same change is made in the other sync location.

Using Sync Center

You use Sync Center to set up a sync by specifying which files and folders you want to sync, where to sync them, and when. This set of rules—which represents a partnership between two or more sync locations—is called a sync partnership.

To perform the following steps, you must be working on a mobile PC. If you are not working on a mobile PC, read but do not perform the following steps. Perform the following steps on the laptop you used to create the homegroup.

To open Sync Center and sync offline files:

▶ **1.** Open the Windows Mobility Center window.

▶ **2.** Click the **Change synchronization settings** button ⊚ in the Sync Center tile. The Sync Center window opens. See Figure 8-32.

| Figure 8-32 | Sync Center window |

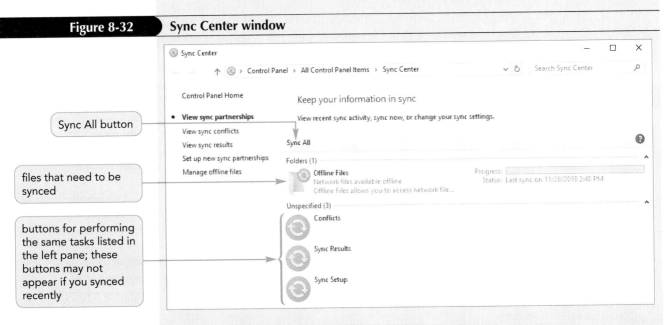

Sync All button

files that need to be synced

buttons for performing the same tasks listed in the left pane; these buttons may not appear if you synced recently

▶ **3.** Click the **Sync All** button. Windows begins to synchronize the files. See Figure 8-33.

| Figure 8-33 | Synchronizing files |

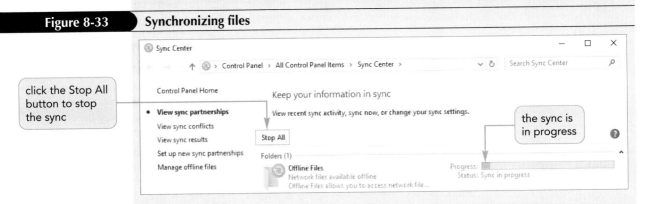

click the Stop All button to stop the sync

the sync is in progress

▶ **4.** When the sync is finished, click **View sync results** in the left pane of the Sync Center window to display the results. See Figure 8-34.

Figure 8-34   **Results of the sync**

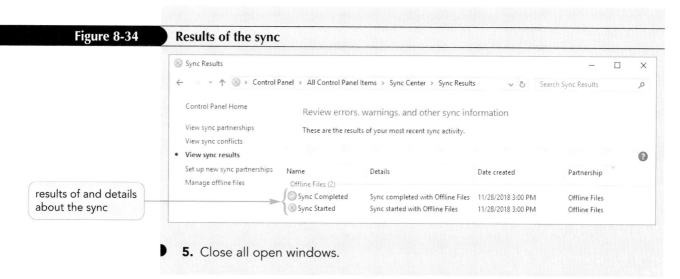

results of and details about the sync

▶ **5.** Close all open windows.

During the sync, if Sync Center finds that the offline file is identical to the network file, Sync Center does nothing because the files are already in sync. If an offline file differs from its network version, Sync Center determines which version of each file to keep and copies that version to the other location. It selects the most recent version to keep unless you have set up the sync partnership to sync differently. If you added a new file in one location but not the other, Sync Center copies the file to the other location. If you deleted a file from one location but not the other, Sync Center deletes the file from the other location. If Sync Center finds a conflict, however, you should know how to resolve it.

Resolving Synchronization Conflicts

If Sync Center finds that a file has changed in both locations since the last sync, Sync Center flags this as a sync conflict and asks you to choose which version to keep. You must resolve this conflict so that Sync Center can keep the files in sync. When Sync Center detects one or more conflicts, it displays a message similar to the one shown in Figure 8-35.

Figure 8-35   **Sync Center shows a conflict**

a yellow progress bar indicates a conflict; a red progress bar indicates an error

click to display details about the conflict

To resolve the conflicts, you click the conflict link, select the offline files, and then click the Resolve button. When you do, the Resolve Conflict dialog box opens for each file in conflict and asks if you want to keep this version and copy it to the other location, or if you want to keep both copies. Click the appropriate option, and then click the OK button.

Problem Solving: Synchronizing Settings and OneDrive Files

If you use more than one Windows 8.x or 10 device, using a different interface on each device can be disorienting. However, if you use the same Microsoft account to sign in to the devices, you can sync your settings such as the theme, Internet Explorer settings, passwords, and Windows settings such as File Explorer preferences. That way, all of your devices will have the same interface. Windows syncs your settings by default. To verify or change the settings, click in the Ask me anything box, start to type "Sync your settings," and then click Sync your settings in the search results to open the Accounts window in the Settings app. In the Sync your settings category, turn on Sync settings, if necessary, and then turn individual sync settings on and off.

If you store files on your OneDrive, they are available to you even when you are not connected to the Internet. For example, suppose you create a Word document named Report and store it on OneDrive when your laptop is online. While you're traveling, you want to work on the Report document, but you're not connected to the Internet. You can still open File Explorer, expand OneDrive in the navigation pane, and then open and edit the Report document offline. If a OneDrive file icon appears with a white X in a red circle, that means the online and offline versions are out of sync. To find out why, click the Show hidden icons button on the taskbar to display hidden notification icons. Right-click the OneDrive icon, which appears as a white cloud, and then click View sync problems.

Using Remote Desktop Connection

Another way to share information among computers is to use **Remote Desktop Connection**, a technology that allows you to use one computer to connect to a remote computer in a different location. For example, you can connect to your school or work computer from your home computer so you can access all of the programs, files, and network resources that you normally use at school or work. If you leave programs running at work, you can see your work computer's desktop displayed on your home computer, with the same programs running.

Suppose you are planning to use a mobile PC at home and want to connect to your computer at work. To use Remote Desktop Connection, the mobile PC and work computer must both be running Windows and must be connected to the same network or to the Internet. Remote Desktop Connection must also be turned on, and you must have permission to connect to the work computer. If you are using a computer at work or school, firewall settings at those locations may prevent you from connecting to another computer using Remote Desktop Connection.

Setting up Remote Desktop Connection is a two-part process. First, you allow remote connections on the computer to which you want to connect, such as your work computer. Next, you start Remote Desktop Connection on the computer you want to connect from, such as your mobile PC. You can allow connections from computers running any version of Remote Desktop Connection, including those in earlier versions of Windows. If you know that the computers connecting to your computer are also running Windows 7, Windows 8.x, or Windows 10, allow connections only if they are running **Remote Desktop with Network Level Authentication (NLA)**. This option provides more security and can protect remote computers from hackers and malware.

After viewing the presentation, the Bravo Law Office partners decide that they want Derek to provide the services described in the Project Scope document. Derek will spend some time in Dover to begin the project. In a private office, Bravo Law Office is providing a desktop computer named Office-PC where Derek can work on the project when he is in Dover. This Office-PC computer is on the Bravo Law Office network, but is not part of the homegroup. Derek anticipates that he will also need to access the Office-PC computer when he is not in Dover. You'll show him how to allow remote connections on the Office-PC computer.

First, you need to determine whether the Office-PC computer is running a version of Remote Desktop with NLA. Perform the following steps on a network computer other than your computer. If you do not have access to such a computer, read but do not perform the following steps.

To see if the computer is running a version of Remote Desktop with NLA:

▶ **1.** Click in the **Ask me anything** box, start typing **Remote Desktop Connection**, and then click **Remote Desktop Connection** in the results. The Remote Desktop Connection dialog box opens. See Figure 8-36.

| Figure 8-36 | Remote Desktop Connection dialog box |

click this icon and then click About

▶ **2.** Click the **Remote Desktop Connection** icon in the title bar, and then click **About**. A window opens describing Remote Desktop Connection. See Figure 8-37. Look for the phrase "Network Level Authentication supported," which indicates whether the computer is running a version of Remote Desktop with NLA.

| Figure 8-37 | About Remote Desktop Connection window |

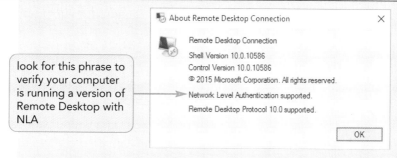

look for this phrase to verify your computer is running a version of Remote Desktop with NLA

▶ **3.** Click the **OK** button to close the About Remote Desktop Connection window.

▶ **4.** Click the **Close** button ☒ to close the Remote Desktop Connection dialog box.

Now you are ready to set up your computer to allow a remote desktop connection from another computer. Before performing the following steps, sign in to your computer as an Administrator. If you are not allowed to use an Administrator account on your computer, read but do not perform the following steps.

To set up Remote Desktop Connection:

▶ **1.** Open the Control Panel, click **System and Security**, and then click **System**. The System window opens.

▶ **2.** In the left pane, click **Remote settings**. The System Properties dialog box opens to the Remote tab. See Figure 8-38.

Figure 8-38 Remote tab in the System Properties dialog box

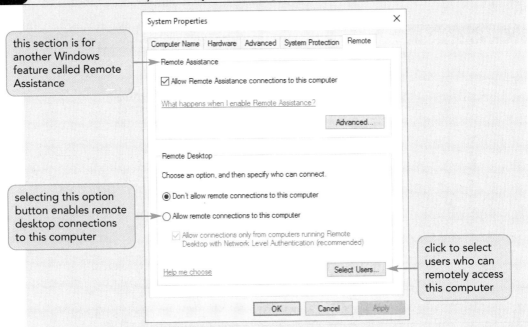

this section is for another Windows feature called Remote Assistance

selecting this option button enables remote desktop connections to this computer

click to select users who can remotely access this computer

Trouble? If you are asked for an administrator password or confirmation, type the password or provide confirmation.

Trouble? If the Remote Desktop section does not appear in your System Properties dialog box, a firewall setting might prevent you from connecting to a remote computer. Close the dialog box, and then read but do not perform the remaining steps.

▶ **3.** Under Remote Desktop, click the **Allow remote connections to this computer** option button, if necessary.

Trouble? If a dialog box opens regarding your power settings, click the OK button.

Trouble? If the check box below the Allow remote connections to this computer option button does not contain a check mark, click the check box.

▶ **4.** Click the **Select Users** button. The Remote Desktop Users dialog box opens.

▶ **5.** Make sure a message indicates that the Administrator account already has access on the computer, and then click the **OK** button to close the Remote Desktop Users dialog box.

▶ **6.** Click the **OK** button to close the System Properties dialog box. Close the System window.

To allow users other than the Administrator to use a remote desktop connection to your computer, click the Add button in the Remote Desktop Users dialog box, enter the name of the user or computer who can access your computer, and then click the OK button. The name you entered appears in the list of users in the Remote Desktop Users dialog box. You can remove any user who should not have remote access.

After you set up Remote Desktop Connection on your remote computer, such as the one at work, you can start Remote Desktop Connection on the computer you want to work from, such as the mobile PC. Before you do, you need to know the name of the computer to which you want to connect. To find the name of a computer, you open the System window by opening the Control Panel, click System and Security, and then click System. The computer name is listed in the Computer name, domain, and workgroup settings section.

The following steps assume that you are set up to connect to a remote computer. To do so, you need to know the name of the computer to which you want to connect. If you are not set up to connect to a remote computer, read but do not perform the following steps. Perform the following steps using the laptop you used to create the homegroup.

To start Remote Desktop Connection to connect to a remote computer:

▶ **1.** Click in the **Ask me anything** box, start typing **Remote Desktop Connection**, and then click **Remote Desktop Connection** in the results to open the Remote Desktop Connection dialog box again.

▶ **2.** In the Computer box, type **Office-PC**. This is the name of the desktop computer Derek will use at Bravo Law Office.

   Trouble? If the name of the remote computer to which you want to connect is not named Office-PC, enter its name instead of Office-PC in the Computer box.

▶ **3.** Click the **Connect** button to connect to that computer on your network.

   Trouble? If a Remote Desktop Connection dialog box opens asking if you want to connect even though the identity of the remote computer cannot be verified, click the Yes button.

▶ **4.** If necessary, enter your user name and password, and then click the **OK** button to establish the connection.

▶ **5.** Click the **Close** button, and then click the **OK** button to disconnect.

Now Derek can access the Office-PC computer at Bravo Law Office when he is working in the NCC offices in New Castle.

Restoring Your Settings

If you are working in a computer lab or on a computer other than your own, complete the steps in this section to restore the original settings on your computer.

To restore your settings:

▶ 1. Open Windows Mobility Center, and then drag the **Volume** slider to its original setting.

▶ 2. If necessary, click the **Mute** check box to remove the check mark and turn the speakers on.

   Trouble? If your speakers were turned off when you originally opened Windows Mobility Center in Session 8.1, skip Step 2.

▶ 3. Click the **Change power settings** icon 🔋 in the Battery Status tile to open the Power Options window, and then click the **Balanced** option button, if necessary.

▶ 4. Click **Change plan settings** for the Balanced power plan, click **Restore default settings for this plan** in the Edit Plan Settings window, and then click the **Yes** button to restore the settings. Close the Edit Plan Settings window.

▶ 5. In the Windows Mobility Center window, click the **Change presentation settings** icon 🖥 in the Presentation Settings tile, and then restore the screen saver, volume, and background controls to their original settings. Click the **OK** button. Close the Windows Mobility Center window.

▶ 6. Open the Network folder window, and then navigate to the **Public** folder on the network. Click the **Public Documents** folder, click the **Easy access** button in the New group on the Home tab, and then click **Work offline** to deselect the option.

▶ 7. Open the Homegroup folder window from the navigation pane. On the HomeGroup tab, in the Manage group, click the **Change homegroup settings** button, click the **Leave the homegroup** link, and then click **Leave the homegroup** to confirm you want to leave. Click the **Finish** button. Close all windows.

▶ 8. On the computer where you set up Remote Desktop, open the Control Panel, click **System and Security**, click **System**, and then click **Remote settings** in the left pane. In the System Properties dialog box, click the **Don't allow remote connections to this computer** option button, and then click the **OK** button.

▶ 9. Delete the **NCC** folder from the Documents folder, and then close all open windows.

In this session, you learned how to create and join a homegroup and then share files with other members of the homegroup. You also learned how to access offline files and then synchronize them with network files. Finally, you learned how to use Remote Desktop Connection to connect to a remote computer.

REVIEW

Session 8.2 Quick Check

1. If you want to share files and a printer among the users on your home network, you can use a(n) _____.
2. What must you do to let other members of your homegroup access a file?
3. What is the difference between a network file and an offline file?
4. When you are connected to a network, you can display the folders on a network computer using _____.
5. To open the Offline Files dialog box so you can enable offline files, you click Manage offline files in the left pane of the _____ window.
6. If Sync Center finds that an offline file is identical to a network file, what does it do and why?
7. If you want to connect from your mobile PC at home to a work computer, the first step is to allow remote connections on the work computer. What is the second step?

PRACTICE

Review Assignments

There are no Data Files needed for the Review Assignments.

You are now working with Derek's partner, Joanne Rose, to help her prepare for a meeting with a client in Wilmington, Delaware—a dental clinic named Wilmington Dental. Joanne asks you to help her prepare her mobile PC for the trip and for a presentation she plans to make to Wilmington Dental when she arrives. Joanne also requests your help with connecting her Windows 10 laptop to the Wilmington Dental wireless network and sharing some of its resources. Complete the following steps, noting your original settings so you can restore them later:

1. Open Windows Mobility Center, and then change the speaker volume to 25.
2. In the Power Options window, change the plan settings for the Power saver plan so that the display turns off after 10 minutes of idle time when running on battery power and after 15 minutes when plugged in. (If you are not using a mobile PC, set the Power saver plan to turn off the display after 15 minutes of idle time.) Save your changes. Use the advanced settings to have the Power saver plan hibernate after 120 minutes of idle time on any type of power. (*Hint*: Use the Change advanced power settings link to open the Power Options dialog box.)
3. Display the settings for the Power saver plan with the Power Options dialog box also clearly visible, and then press the Print Screen key to capture an image of the desktop. Paste the image in a new Paint file, and then save the file as **Power** in the Module8 > Review folder provided with your Data Files.
4. Change what the hardware power buttons do so that when you press a power button when running on battery power, your computer hibernates. (If you are not using a mobile PC, do the same for the default type of power.) Press the Print Screen key to capture an image of the window. Paste the image in a new Paint file, and then save the file as **Hibernate** in the Module8 > Review folder provided with your Data Files. Save your changes, and then close the Power Options window.
5. Change the presentation settings so that when you give a presentation, you turn off the screen saver, set the volume to 75, and show img1 as the desktop background. Press the Print Screen key to capture an image of the dialog box. Paste the image in a new Paint file, and then save the file as **Presentation** in the Module8 > Review folder provided with your Data Files.
6. Connect to an available wireless network, entering a security key or passphrase as necessary. (If you are not equipped to connect to a wireless network, connect to a wired network.) Open the Network and Sharing Center window, and then capture an image of the window. Paste the image in a new Paint file, and then save the file as **Network** in the Module8 > Review folder provided with your Data Files.
7. If necessary, connect to an available homegroup or create a new homegroup. Change the homegroup settings to share all folders, printers, and devices. Press the Print Screen key to capture an image of the window. Paste the image in a new Paint file, and then save the file as **Sharing** in the Module8 > Review folder provided with your Data Files.
8. From the Network window, navigate to the Public Downloads folder on a homegroup computer, if possible, and then make that folder always available offline. As Windows is making the files available, press the Print Screen key to capture an image of the window. Paste the image in a new Paint file, and then save the file as **Offline** in the Module8 > Review folder provided with your Data Files.
9. Copy a file from the Documents folder on your computer to the Public Downloads folder on a homegroup computer, if possible.
10. Open Sync Center and synchronize the offline files. When the sync is finished, view the sync results and then press the Print Screen key to capture an image of the window. Paste the image in a new Paint file, and then save the file as **Sync Results** in the Module8 > Review folder provided with your Data Files.

11. Use the System Properties dialog box to allow connections only from computers running Remote Desktop with NLA. (*Hint*: Select Remote settings in the Control Panel's System window to open the Remote tab in the System Properties dialog box.) Press the Print Screen key to capture an image of the dialog box with this setting. Paste the image in a new Paint file, and then save the file as **Remote Settings** in the Module8 > Review folder provided with your Data Files. Close all open dialog boxes.

12. Restore your original settings. Change the speaker volume to its original setting. Change the Power saver plan to its default settings, and then select your original plan. Restore the original action to the hardware power button. Restore the presentation settings to their original form. Deselect the option to make offline files available for the Public Downloads folder on the network computer. Do not allow remote connections to your computer. Disconnect from the network, if necessary, and then close all open windows.

Case Problem 1

There are no Data Files needed for this Case Problem.

Roving Mechanic   Brent Danielson is the owner of a Roving Mechanic franchise in Austin, Texas. The business sends mechanics around the city and its surrounding areas to perform routine auto maintenance and repairs at the car owner's home. Brent recently hired you to train him and the mechanics in using Windows 10 to perform mobile computing tasks, including managing power options and connecting to wireless networks. Complete the following steps, noting your original settings so you can restore them later:

1. Open Windows Mobility Center, and then mute the speakers.

2. Change the plan settings for the Balanced plan so that the display turns off after 10 minutes of idle time when running on battery power, and after 1 hour when plugged in.

3. Set the Balanced plan to hibernate after 240 minutes whether running on battery or another type of power. Arrange the Power Options dialog box and the Edit Plan Settings window so you can see the settings in both windows, and then press the Print Screen key to capture an image of the desktop. Paste the image in a new Paint file, and then save the file as **Balanced** in the Module8 > Case1 folder provided with your Data Files. Save your changes.

4. Set the computer to require a password when waking from sleep. (*Hint*: In the System Settings window, click the Change settings that are currently unavailable link to access the password options.) Press the Print Screen key to capture an image of the window. Paste the image in a new Paint file, and then save the file as **Password** in the Module8 > Case1 folder provided with your Data Files. Save your changes, and then close the Power Options window.

5. Change the presentation settings so that when you give a presentation, the volume is set to High, the screen saver is turned off, and the background displays img8. Press the Print Screen key to capture an image of the dialog box. Paste the image in a new Paint file, and then save the file as **Img8** in the Module8 > Case1 folder provided with your Data Files. Save your changes.

6. Display a list of wireless networks within range of your computer. Capture an image of the screen. Paste the image in a new Paint file, and then save the file as **Range** in the Module8 > Case1 folder provided with your Data Files.

7. Open the HomeGroup window, and then open the Advanced sharing settings window. Expand the Private section, if necessary. Press the Print Screen key to capture an image of the window. Paste the image in a new Paint file, and then save the file as **Advanced** in the Module8 > Case1 folder provided with your Data Files.

8. Open the Remote Desktop Connection dialog box, and then determine whether your computer supports Network Level Authentication. Press the Print Screen key to capture an image of the window that provides this information. Paste the image in a new Paint file, and then save the file as **NLA** in the Module8 > Case1 folder provided with your Data Files. Close all Control Panel windows.

9. Restore your original settings by turning on the speakers. Change the Balanced power plan to its default settings, and then select your original plan. Remove password protection on wakeup. Restore the presentation settings to their original form. Close all open windows.

CHALLENGE

Case Problem 2

There are no Data Files needed for this Case Problem.

Well Awareness Cassie Levine runs Well Awareness in Nashville, Tennessee, a small business that provides wellness classes to hospitals, clinics, retirement centers, and other places where people want to improve their health and quality of life. Cassie and her staff travel around the Nashville area every day to conduct classes, so she wants to know more about the Windows 10 mobile computing features. During many classes, she demonstrates exercises by playing slide shows that run on a laptop. As Cassie's assistant, you help her with a wide range of tasks, including managing the company's computers. She asks you to help her use Windows 10 to perform mobile computing tasks, including managing power options and giving presentations. Complete the following steps, noting your original settings so you can restore them later:

1. Open Windows Mobility Center and then change the speaker volume to 30.

2. Change the plan settings for the Power saver plan so that the display turns off after 5 minutes of idle time when running on battery power and after 15 minutes when plugged in. (If you are not using a mobile PC, set the display to turn off after 15 minutes of idle time.)

✛ **Explore** 3. For the Power saver plan, enable adaptive brightness, an advanced Display setting, for all types of power. Arrange the Power Options dialog box and the Edit Plan Settings window so you can see the settings in both windows, and then press the Print Screen key to capture an image of the desktop. Paste the image in a new Paint file, and then save the file as **Brightness** in the Module8 > Case2 folder provided with your Data Files.

✛ **Explore** 4. Set the computer to hibernate when you press a hardware power button while using any type of power. Require a password to access your computer when it wakes up. (*Hint*: Click the Change settings that are currently unavailable link to access the password options.) Press the Print Screen key to capture an image of the window. Paste the image in a new Paint file, and then save the file as **Power Button** in the Module8 > Case2 folder provided with your Data Files. Save your changes, and then close the Power Options window.

5. Change the presentation settings so that when you give a presentation, the volume is set to 80, the screen saver is turned off, and a black background is displayed. Press the Print Screen key to capture an image of the dialog box. Paste the image in a new Paint file, and then save the file as **No Background** in the Module8 > Case2 folder provided with your Data Files. Save your changes.

✛ **Explore** 6. Open the HomeGroup window, and then open the Advanced sharing settings window. In the settings for All Networks, display the media streaming options. Press the Print Screen key to capture an image of the window. Paste the image in a new Paint file, and then save the file as **Streaming** in the Module8 > Case2 folder provided with your Data Files.

✛ **Explore** 7. From the HomeGroup window, start the HomeGroup troubleshooter. Follow the steps in the Troubleshooter until the results are displayed, and then view detailed information. Press the Print Screen key to capture an image of the screen. Paste the image in a new Paint file, and then save the file as **Troubleshooter** in the Module8 > Case2 folder provided with your Data Files.

8. Open a window that displays devices on your network. Press the Print Screen key to capture an image of the screen. Paste the image in a new Paint file, and then save the file as **Network Window** in the Module8 > Case2 folder provided with your Data Files.

9. Restore your original settings. Change the speaker volume to its original setting. Change the Power saver plan to its default settings, and then select your original plan. Restore the presentation settings to their original form. Close all open windows.

Case Problem 3

There are no Data Files needed for this Case Problem.

Frontier Farm Group   Jeff Cuevas is an agriculture specialist who consults with small farms about how to sustain farm operations. His company, Frontier Farm Group in Des Moines, Iowa, employs people who often work on mobile PCs at their clients' farms. As an assistant to Jeff, part of your job is to make sure the consultants are using their computers effectively. Jeff asks you to show him how to use Windows 10 to perform mobile computing tasks, including conserving battery power, connecting to networks, using wireless network security, and sharing files. Complete the following steps, noting your original settings so you can restore them later:

1. Start the Settings app and then open its System window. Choose the Power & sleep category, and then click the Additional power settings link. Navigate to where the plan settings are displayed, and then arrange the two open windows so that their settings are visible. Press the Print Screen key to capture an image of the screen. Paste the image in a new Paint file, and then save the file as **Settings** in the Module8 > Case3 folder provided with your Data Files.

2. In the System window, display the Battery saver settings. Show your battery use across all apps, and then press the Print Screen key to capture an image of the screen. Paste the image in a new Paint file, and then save the file as **Battery Saver** in the Module8 > Case3 folder provided with your Data Files.

3. In the Settings app, open the Network & Internet window, and then display a list of Wi-Fi networks. Click a link to display advanced options. Press the Print Screen key to capture an image of the window. Paste the image in a new Paint file, and then save the file as **Wi-Fi** in the Module8 > Case3 folder provided with your Data Files.

4. Return to the Network & Internet window displaying Wi-Fi networks, and then click a link to manage Wi-Fi settings. Click a link to learn more about Wi-Fi Sense. When a webpage appears displaying information about Wi-Fi Sense, look for information about Wi-Fi security. If necessary, click a link to display the security information. Press the Print Screen key to capture an image of the window. Paste the image in a new Paint file, and then save the file as **Security** in the Module8 > Case3 folder provided with your Data Files.

5. Connect to an available wireless network, entering a security key or passphrase as necessary. (If you are not equipped to connect to a wireless network, connect to a wired network.)

⚙ **Troubleshoot** 6. Use the Search box in the Control Panel window to search for troubleshooting computer problems. Start a wizard that troubleshoots Internet connections. When the wizard is finished, click a link to view detailed information. Expand all sections of the Troubleshooting report, and then capture an image of the wizard dialog box. Paste the image in a new Paint file, and then save the file as **Connections** in the Module8 > Case3 folder provided with your Data Files. Close the wizard dialog box.

7. Open the Network window and note the name of a computer other than the one you are using. Open a folder on the computer, and then copy the path in the Address bar.

⚙ **Troubleshoot** 8. Start a troubleshooting wizard that can find and fix problems with accessing files and folders on other computers. Run the wizard. When the wizard requests the network location you want to access, paste the path you copied from the Network window into the box, and then continue the wizard. After Windows finishes detecting problems, view detailed information and show all detection details. Press the Print Screen key to capture an image of the screen. Paste the image in a new Paint file, and then save the file as **Detection** in the Module8 > Case3 folder provided with your Data Files.

⚙ **Troubleshoot** 9. Start a troubleshooting wizard that can improve power usage. After Windows finishes detecting problems, view detailed information to show the potential issues the wizard checked, and then press the Print Screen key to capture an image of the window. Paste the image in a new Paint file, and then save the file as **Power Usage** in the Module8 > Case3 folder provided with your Data Files.

10. Close all open windows.

Case Problem 4

There are no Data Files needed for this Case Problem.

Diprimo Drafting   The managers and staff of Diprimo Drafting in Northfield, Minnesota, are considering connecting their computers on a network. The company has the following characteristics and requirements:

- The company has 14 users—10 on mobile PCs and 4 on desktop computers.
- All computers are running Windows 10.
- Most employees use their computers outside of the office.
- All users often distribute large files to other users.

Tom Diprimo is the owner of the company, and he asks you, an administrative assistant, to help him research small office networks on the web. Complete the following steps:

1. Use Cortana and Microsoft Edge to research appropriate networks for Diprimo Drafting. Choose two types of networks to recommend. Create a document with four column headings: **Network Technology**, **Hardware Requirements**, **Speed**, and **Cost**. Complete the columns according to the following descriptions:

Network Technology	Hardware Requirements	Speed	Cost
List two types of networks.	List devices and other hardware required.	List speed considerations or rates.	List cost considerations.

2. After the table, list the factors that limit Wi-Fi connection speeds.
3. Save the document as **Diprimo** in the Module8 > Case4 folder provided with your Data Files.

WINDOWS

OBJECTIVES

Session 9.1
- Back up and restore files
- Set up a system recovery drive
- Create a system restore point
- Install and uninstall software

Session 9.2
- Maintain hard disks
- Enable and disable hardware devices
- Install and update device drivers
- Install and set up printers

Maintaining Hardware and Software

Managing Software, Disks, and Devices

Case | *Place to Place*

Place to Place, a moving concierge in Lansing, Michigan, provides a full range of services for people and businesses that are moving from one location to another. For example, Place to Place packs, unpacks, hires moving vans and cleaning services, and sets up utilities, electronics, and furnishings. Rachel Grogan is the owner of Place to Place. When she needs to complete office work, she conducts much of her business on a Windows 10 PC. As her assistant office manager, you are responsible for maintaining the hardware and software at the business.

In this module, you will set up the File History feature to back up files and folders automatically and to restore files you've backed up. You will also create a system recovery drive and then learn how to reset Windows 10. After preparing to install new apps, you will install software from the Windows Store and view your updates. You will also learn how employees can work efficiently at home or the office using Windows To Go. To improve system performance, you will check for problems on a hard disk and learn how to maintain the devices attached to a computer, including your display device and printer.

STARTING DATA FILES

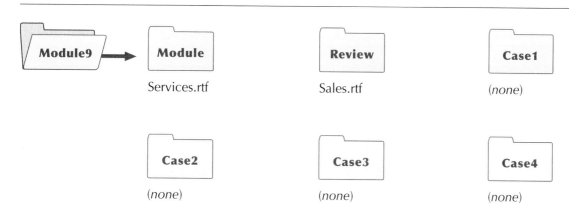

Module9 → Module
Services.rtf

Review
Sales.rtf

Case1
(*none*)

Case2
(*none*)

Case3
(*none*)

Case4
(*none*)

Session 9.1 Visual Overview:

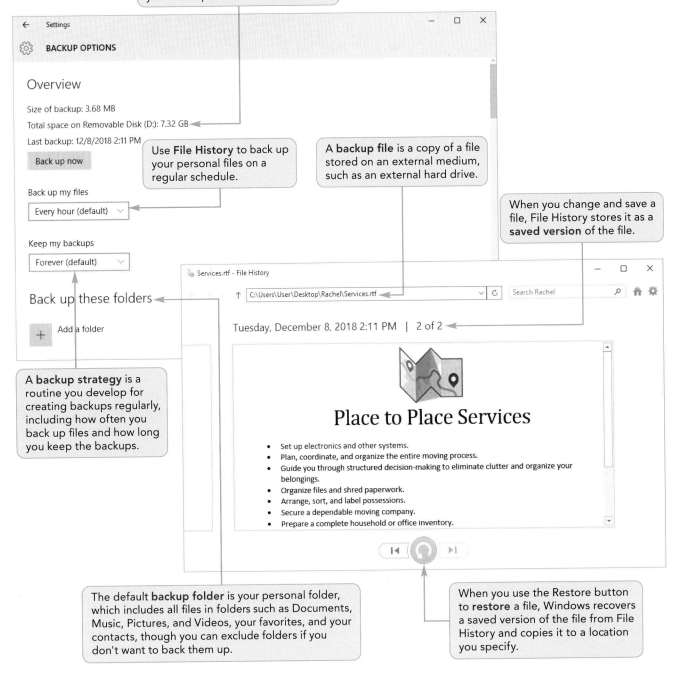

Your **backup medium** can be a USB flash drive, an external hard disk, or a network folder. The **backup location** is the drive or folder where you store your backup files.

Use **File History** to back up your personal files on a regular schedule.

A **backup file** is a copy of a file stored on an external medium, such as an external hard drive.

When you change and save a file, File History stores it as a **saved version** of the file.

A **backup strategy** is a routine you develop for creating backups regularly, including how often you back up files and how long you keep the backups.

The default **backup folder** is your personal folder, which includes all files in folders such as Documents, Music, Pictures, and Videos, your favorites, and your contacts, though you can exclude folders if you don't want to back them up.

When you use the Restore button to **restore** a file, Windows recovers a saved version of the file from File History and copies it to a location you specify.

Settings

BACKUP OPTIONS

Overview

Size of backup: 3.68 MB

Total space on Removable Disk (D:): 7.32 GB

Last backup: 12/8/2018 2:11 PM

Back up now

Back up my files

Every hour (default)

Keep my backups

Forever (default)

Back up these folders

Add a folder

Services.rtf - File History

C:\Users\User\Desktop\Rachel\Services.rtf   Search Rachel

Tuesday, December 8, 2018 2:11 PM | 2 of 2

Place to Place Services

- Set up electronics and other systems.
- Plan, coordinate, and organize the entire moving process.
- Guide you through structured decision-making to eliminate clutter and organize your belongings.
- Organize files and shred paperwork.
- Arrange, sort, and label possessions.
- Secure a dependable moving company.
- Prepare a complete household or office inventory.

Managing Data and Software

Installed apps are apps and programs that have been set up on your computer so that you can run them.

With a trial version, you can try out the software before you buy it.

Uninstalling an app removes it completely from your computer.

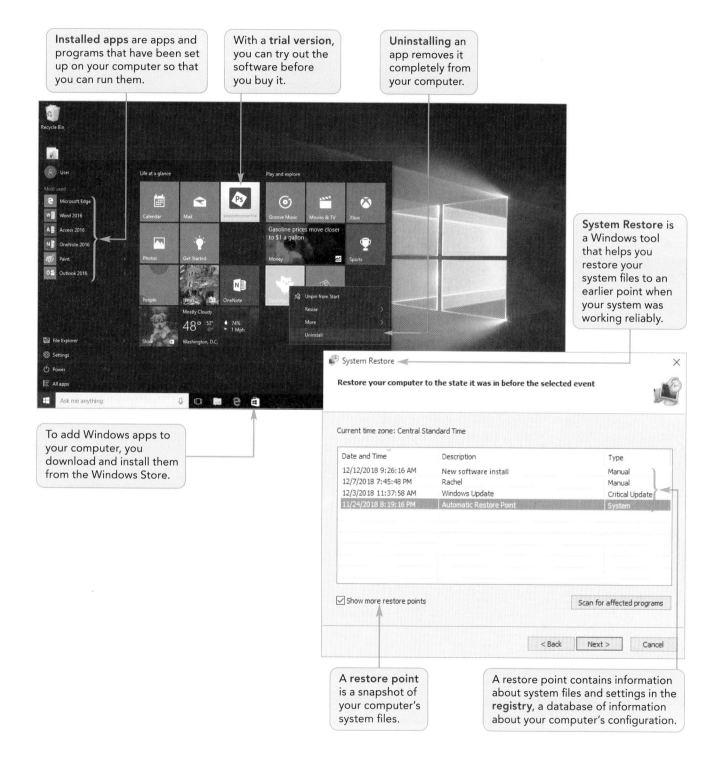

System Restore is a Windows tool that helps you restore your system files to an earlier point when your system was working reliably.

To add Windows apps to your computer, you download and install them from the Windows Store.

A restore point is a snapshot of your computer's system files.

A restore point contains information about system files and settings in the registry, a database of information about your computer's configuration.

Backing Up and Restoring Files

No one is safe from computer problems that result in data loss. Problems such as a power surge, a power loss, a failed section of a hard disk, or a computer virus can strike at any time. Rather than risk disaster, you should make copies of your important files regularly. By doing so, if disaster strikes, you will be able to recover your files and continue working almost without interruption. You have already learned how to copy data to and from your hard disk and removable media. Making a copy of a file or folder on removable media is one way to protect data.

To protect data on a hard disk, however, you should use a backup program instead of a copy procedure. A **backup program** copies files and folders from a hard disk to a specified location and then automatically compresses them. The copied and compressed files are called backup files. The backup program stores backup files on a backup medium (or backup location) such as an external hard disk or a network drive. To back up files in Windows, you use the File History feature.

To illustrate how File History works, suppose you store all of your important files in the Documents folder in three folders named Accounts, Clients, and Projects. Figure 9-1 shows how File History backs up the files in these folders.

Figure 9-1　Backing up data using File History

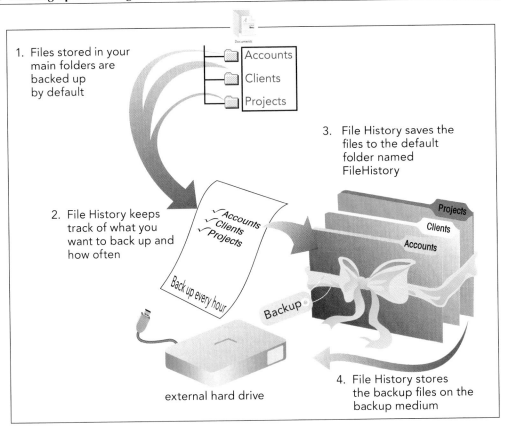

1. Files stored in your main folders are backed up by default

   Accounts
   Clients
   Projects

2. File History keeps track of what you want to back up and how often

   ✓ Accounts
   ✓ Clients
   ✓ Projects

   Back up every hour

3. File History saves the files to the default folder named FileHistory

4. File History stores the backup files on the backup medium

   Backup

   Projects
   Clients
   Accounts

external hard drive

Backing up files is different from copying files because File History compresses the files when it copies them, keeps track of their original locations, and saves changes you've made to the files as different versions. On the other hand, copying simply duplicates the files. Figure 9-2 points out the differences between copying and backing up, showing why backing up files is a faster, easier, and better data-protection method than copying files.

Figure 9-2   Comparing copying and backing up files

Copy	Back Up
Copying your files can be time consuming and tedious because you must navigate to and select each file and folder that you want to copy.	Using File History is faster because you select folders in one step, and File History automatically backs up the files in those folders every hour.
Because a copy of a file occupies the same amount of space as the original file, making a copy of all the files on a hard disk is impractical.	When File History backs up your files, it compresses them so they take up much less space than the original files.
You need to manually track which files and folders have changed since your last backup.	File History keeps track of which files and folders are new or modified, and then backs up only the files that have changed since your last backup.
You need to set reminders on your own to create backups periodically.	File History regularly backs up your files and folders so that you don't have to remember to do it.
If you do lose data because of a computer failure, it is not easy to locate a file you need in your backups.	File History keeps track of the files you have backed up, and makes it easy to find and recover a file.

By using File History to back up your files, you don't have to worry if you lose an important file or damage your hard disk. You can use File History to restore a particular version of a file. For example, suppose you start writing a report on Monday, add information to it on Tuesday and Wednesday, and then complete the report on Thursday. You've saved the report in a folder in the Documents folder. File History is turned on, so Windows is backing up changes to the report file every hour. Several days later, you realize that you accidentally deleted a table of important information that you want to include in the report. Instead of trying to re-create the table, you can use File History to restore a version of the report file that still includes the table. By copying the table from the backup file to the current version of the report, you save a lot of time and anguish.

REFERENCE

Setting Up File History to Back Up Files

- Start the Settings app, and then click Update & security.
- Click Backup.
- If you want to use an external drive for backups, insert the drive in a USB port. If you want to use a network drive, follow the on-screen instructions to specify the drive.
- Click the Add a drive button, and then click a drive to use for backups.

If you backed up files using Windows 7, you can use Windows Backup to back up and restore your files. Windows Backup is considered a **legacy program**, which means it is designed for earlier versions of Windows and is being phased out of use.

Setting Up File History

By default, File History is turned off because it needs information from you before it can start backing up your files. Backing up files with File History involves the following general tasks:

- Selecting a backup location (or medium)
- Selecting folders and files you want to back up
- Specifying how often the backup should occur and how long you want to keep the different versions of the backups

Once you select a backup location, Windows turns on File History so it can back up your files. By default, it backs up every hour, keeps all copies of the files indefinitely, and backs up all the files in your personal folder (the one with your account name), which includes OneDrive and the Contacts, Documents, Downloads, and Favorites folders. You can change the frequency of the backups, the backup location, how long File History keeps the backup files, and the folders to include in the backup.

Selecting the Backup Location

With Windows 10, you can create backups on an external hard drive, a USB drive, or a network folder. To select the location that is best for you, consider the hardware installed on your computer as well as the number and size of files that you want to back up. You can back up files to any of the following locations:

- External hard drive—If your computer has a USB port, you can attach an external hard drive to it and then back up files to the external drive. If you plan to back up all of the folders in your personal folder, use an external hard drive with plenty of free space. The capacity of external hard drives ranges from 320 GB to a few terabytes. (A **terabyte (TB)** is equivalent to 1,000 gigabytes.) Because of its portability, capacity, and ease of use, backing up to an external hard drive is the option experienced computer users prefer.
- USB drive—If you are backing up a limited amount of data, you can use a USB drive. Capacities typically range from 4 GB to 128 GB of data. USB drives are inexpensive and convenient, so they are a good choice for documents and other personal files. However, they are less reliable than external hard disks, so they are not suitable for long-term file storage.
- Network folder—If your computer is on a network, you can create a backup on a network folder. You need to have permission to save files in the folder and set sharing options so that unauthorized users cannot access the backup.

If your computer is not equipped with a USB port or if you are not connected to a network, you can use an Internet-based file backup service instead of File History. These services let you store personal, password-protected backups, usually on a server you can access via the Internet. File History does not support these types of online backup locations.

Selecting Folders to Back Up

By default, File History backs up all the files in your personal folder and its subfolders, including OneDrive, desktop files, browser favorites, and contact records. These locations should include most of your documents, pictures, music, videos, compressed folders, and other personal files. If you have files in other locations, such as another internal hard drive, you can also select those locations for backup. However, File History does not let you back up files that have been encrypted using the Encrypting File System (EFS), which is a Windows feature that allows you to store information on your hard disk in an encrypted format. Furthermore, you can back up only files stored on hard disks formatted with the NT File System (NTFS), not the earlier versions of the file allocation table (FAT) file system. Nearly all hard disks in contemporary computers use NTFS.

Determining Which Files to Back Up

The most valuable files on your computer are your data files—the documents, pictures, videos, projects, and financial records that you create and edit. You should back up any data files that would be difficult or impossible to replace, and regularly back up files that you change frequently. You should also back up browser favorites and contact records, which File History does by default, because this information would be time consuming and difficult to re-create manually. You don't need to back up programs because you can download them from the vendor's website again or use the original product discs to reinstall them, and programs typically take up a lot of space on backup media.

In some cases, you might want to exclude folders from the backup. For example, if you've stored many large files in the Videos folder that you could download from a website, you can conserve storage space by excluding the Videos folder from the backup.

Backing Up Files

After you set up File History by specifying a backup location and selecting folders to back up, you are ready to start backing up files. Before you do so for Rachel, you should copy files to a folder on Rachel's computer so that File History includes them in the backup. You'll store the files in a folder named Rachel so that you can find them easily later.

To copy files to the Rachel folder:

▶ **1.** Open File Explorer and then navigate to and select the **Desktop** folder on the hard disk of your computer.

▶ **2.** On the Home tab, in the New group, click the **New folder** button.

▶ **3.** Type **Rachel** as the name of the folder, and then press the **Enter** key.

▶ **4.** Copy the **Services** file from the Module9 > Module folder provided with your Data Files to the Rachel folder.

▶ **5.** Close all open folder windows.

To back up Rachel's file, your computer needs access to a USB drive. In this module, the USB drive is named Removable Disk on drive D. Substitute the name of your USB drive for Removable Disk (D:) as necessary. Keep in mind that when you use File History to back up your personal files, you can choose an external hard drive or a network folder instead of a USB drive.

To turn on File History:

▶ **1.** Click the **Start** button 🪟 to display the Start menu, and then click **Settings** to start the Settings app.

▶ **2.** Click **Update & security** and then click **Backup** to display the Back up using File History settings option.

▶ **3.** Insert a USB drive in a USB port, and then click the **Add a drive** button to search for and display acceptable locations for the backup, including the USB drive. See Figure 9-3.

Trouble? If a folder window for the USB drive opens, click the Close button ⊠.

Trouble? If a slider button named Automatically back up my files is displayed instead of the Add a drive button, File History is already set up on your computer. Skip Steps 3 and 4.

| Figure 9-3 | Selecting a backup location |

4. Click **Removable Disk (D:)** in the Select a drive list.

Trouble? If the name of your USB drive changes to Recovery or a similar name after you select it, continue to substitute the name of your USB drive for Removable Disk (D:) as necessary in the remaining steps.

Windows turns on File History after you select a backup location. In an hour, File History will start backing up all the files in the subfolders of your personal folder. When you are backing up your own files, you will most likely need a backup medium with more storage space than the USB drive used for Rachel's files.

Changing Backup Options

By default, File History backs up copies of files every hour, which is considered a continuous backup cycle. It keeps saved versions of files forever, so you can restore any saved copy of a document if necessary. In the Back up using File History settings, click the More options link to open the Backup Options window, which you use to change these and other settings as follows:

- Back up my files—Use this setting to set the frequency of backups. If you are working on an important project and can't afford to lose even a few minutes of work, you can change this setting from every hour to every 10, 15, 20, or 25 minutes. If you work at your computer infrequently and notice the system slows during backups, you can increase the amount of time between backups to every 3, 6, or 12 hours or to once a day.
- Keep my backups—Use this setting to set the duration of saved versions. By default, File History keeps saved versions of files forever so you can access every version of a saved file when necessary. However, if the backup location is quickly running out of space, you can change this setting to 1, 3, 6, or 9 months; 1 or 2 years; or until space is needed. You can also click the Clean up versions link and then select which versions to delete, such as those older than 1 year.

- Back up these folders—If you want to back up folders other than those listed in this section, you can click the Add a folder button and then navigate to the folder you want to include.
- Exclude these folders—To bypass a folder so it is not included in the backup, click the Add a folder button and then navigate to the folder you want to exclude.
- Back up to a different drive—If the backup medium is full, click the Stop using drive button in this section, and then attach a new removable drive to your computer, if necessary.

INSIGHT

Using File History with a Homegroup

If you are a member of a homegroup, you can use File History to invite other members of the homegroup to back up files in a central backup location. To do so, click the See advanced settings link in the Backup Options window, click Advanced settings in the left pane of the File History window in the Control Panel, and then select the Recommend this drive link in the Advanced Settings window. File History sends a message to the other members of the homegroup asking if they want to back up their personal files. If they accept the invitation, their files are backed up according to your File History settings.

Rachel wants to back up files only in the Rachel folder for now. You'll show her how to exclude the Documents, Downloads, Music, Pictures, and Videos folders and OneDrive from the backup. Because the Rachel folder is in the Desktop folder, File History will back up the contents of the Rachel folder by default.

To exclude a folder from the backup:

1. Click the **More options** link to display the Backup Options window. See Figure 9-4.

Figure 9-4   **Backup Options window**

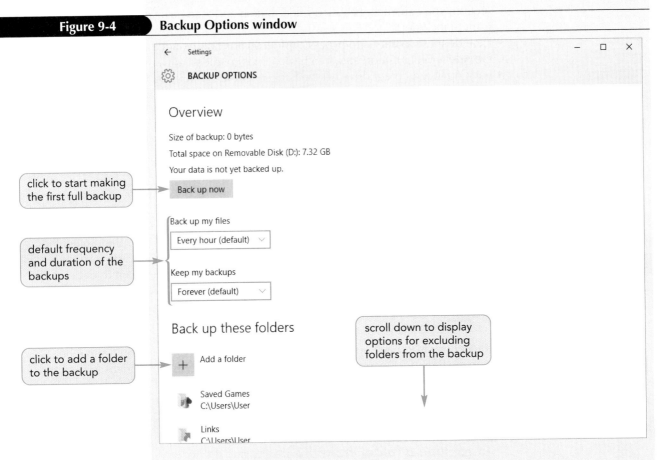

click to start making
the first full backup

default frequency
and duration of the
backups

click to add a folder
to the backup

2. Scroll the window to the Exclude these folders section, and then click the **Add a folder** button to open the Select Folder window, where you select the folders you do not want to include in the backup.

3. If necessary, click **This PC** in the navigation pane. Click the **Documents** folder, and then click the **Choose this folder** button to add the Documents folder to the Exclude these folders list. See Figure 9-5.

Figure 9-5 | **Exclude these folders list**

folder excluded from the backup

click to open a window where you can recommend this drive to other homegroup members

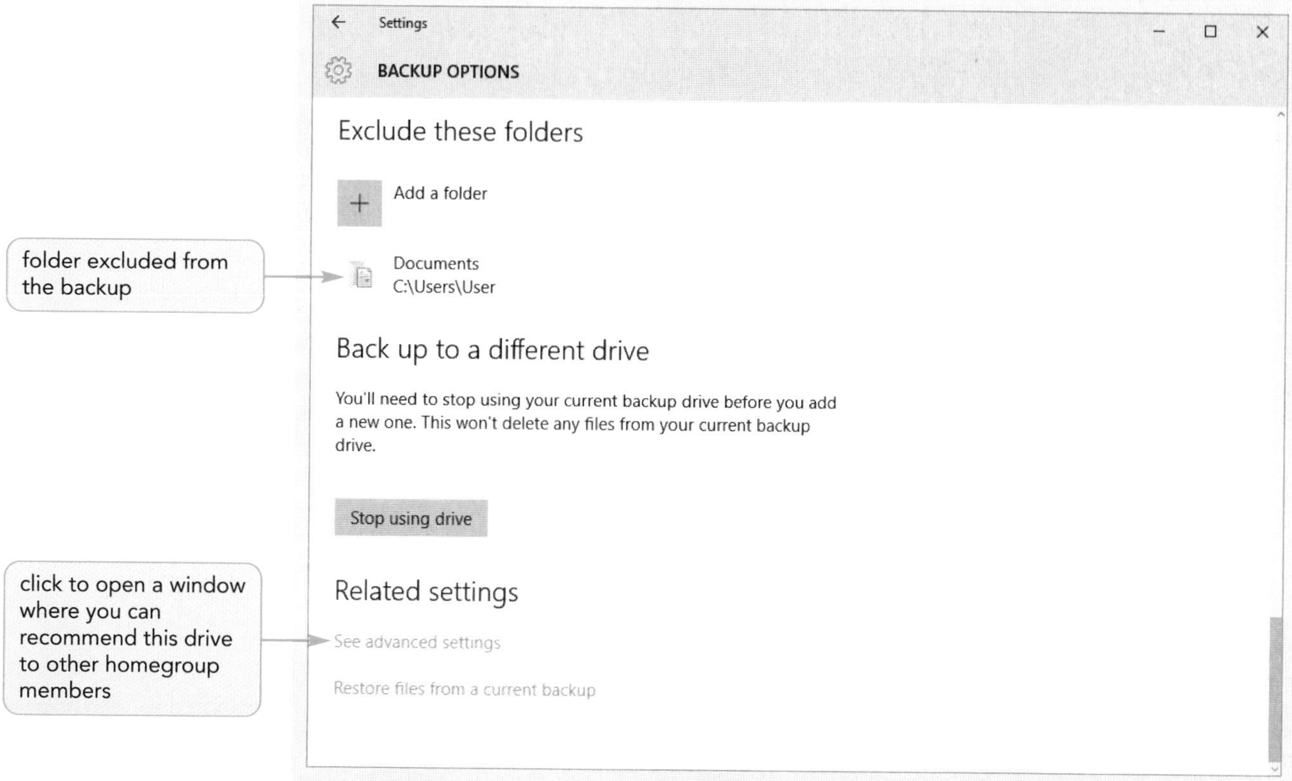

TIP

You can also exclude a folder from a backup by clicking the folder in the Back up these folders list and then clicking the Remove button.

4. Click the **Add a folder** button in the Exclude these folders list, click the **Downloads** folder, and then click the **Choose this folder** button to add the Downloads folder to the Exclude these folders list.

5. Click the **Add a folder** button in the Exclude these folders list, click the **Music** folder, and then click the **Choose this folder** button to add the Music folder to the Exclude these folders list.

6. Click the **Add a folder** button in the Exclude these folders list, click the **Pictures** folder, and then click the **Choose this folder** button to add the Pictures folder to the Exclude these folders list.

7. Click the **Add a folder** button in the Exclude these folders list, click the **Videos** folder, and then click the **Choose this folder** button to add the Videos folder to the Exclude these folders list.

8. Click the **Add a folder** button in the Exclude these folders list, click **OneDrive** in the navigation pane, and then click the **Choose this folder** button to add OneDrive to the Exclude these folders list.

9. If you use another cloud location such as Dropbox, use the same technique as in Steps 4–8 to exclude that location.

10. Review the settings and then change them, if necessary, so that File History excludes all folders except the Contacts, Desktop, and Favorites folders.

Now File History will not back up any files on OneDrive or in the Documents, Downloads, Music, Pictures, or Videos folders. It will back up files stored in the Desktop > Rachel folder along with any favorites and contact files.

PROSKILLS

Decision Making: Creating a Backup Strategy

Before you back up files, develop a backup strategy that you can follow throughout the life of your computer. A backup strategy is a routine you develop for creating backups regularly. The most effective strategy balances security, efficiency, and storage space. Consider the following scenarios:

- Security—If your only concern is security, you could set File History to back up all the files in the default locations more frequently than every hour and store the backup file indefinitely. However, this approach devotes many resources to creating backups and consumes a lot of storage space on the backup medium.
- Efficiency—If your main concern is efficiency, you could save time and money by backing up only your most important files occasionally, such as once a day, and storing them for a limited amount of time. The drawback is that you risk losing many hours of work with this strategy. Instead, you should set a backup routine that secures your data without costing you too much time and money.
- Low computer usage—If you create and modify only a few documents a week, you could back up all of your personal files less frequently than every hour, but store them forever in case you need them.
- High computer usage—If you create and modify many important documents each day, and losing any of those documents would be a hardship, you should back up all of your personal files at least every hour and store them forever.

To show Rachel how File History saves versions of files, you can set File History to back up more often than every hour, and then start backing up files.

To select advanced backup settings:

▶ **1.** Scroll to the top of the Backup Options window, and then click the **Back up my files** box to display a list of time intervals for backing up files. See Figure 9-6.

| Figure 9-6 | Backup frequencies |

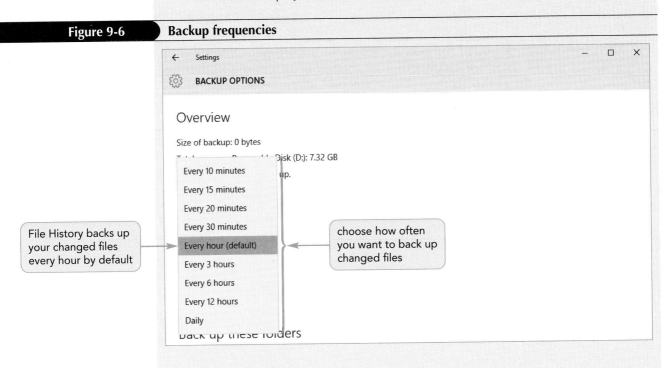

File History backs up your changed files every hour by default

choose how often you want to back up changed files

▶ **2.** Click **Every 10 minutes** to have File History back up files in the specified locations every 10 minutes.

▶ **3.** Click the **Back up now** button in the Backup Options window. File History reports that it is backing up your data. Keep in mind that these are backup copies of your files, not copies you could create yourself using the Copy command.

   Trouble? If a dialog box opens asking if you want to recommend this drive to other members of your homegroup, click the No button.

▶ **4.** Close the Backup Options window, if necessary.

The first time File History backs up your files, it creates a folder named **FileHistory** in your backup location, and then copies all of the files saved in your personal folder, except for those folders you excluded from the backup. This is considered a full backup of your files. Do not delete or move the FileHistory folder in your backup location. If you delete the FileHistory folder, you will lose your backup files. If you move the folder, File History can no longer use it to track the files that have changed on your computer.

After making the first full backup, File History works in the background to back up only files that have changed since your last backup. That means it doesn't need as much storage space to create the subsequent backups. If the backup medium runs out of storage space, File History asks you to replace the drive with a bigger one or change the setting that tells File History how long to keep saved versions. If you replace the drive, File History continues to back up only files that have changed since your last backup. Be sure to store the original drive in a safe place in case you need to restore files it contains.

To demonstrate to Rachel how File History maintains separate versions of backup files, you can change the file stored in the Rachel folder. The Services file lists the services Place to Place offers to its customers. You can research the services of any moving company and then add a service to the list in the Services file.

To modify the Services file:

▶ **1.** Click the **File Explorer** button ▭ on the taskbar to open a folder window, and then navigate to the **Desktop > Rachel** folder.

▶ **2.** Double-click the **Services** document in the Rachel folder to open the document in an app such as WordPad or Microsoft Word, and then scan the list of services.

▶ **3.** Start Microsoft Edge and search for information about moving concierge companies like Place to Place and the services they offer to customers.

▶ **4.** In the Services document, select the text in the first bullet ("Supply boxes and other materials."), and then replace it with text describing a service you found.

▶ **5.** Save the Services document, and then close the app window.

▶ **6.** Close Edge.

When you saved the Services document, you saved a different version of the document. The original version includes "Supply boxes and other materials." as the text for the first bullet, and the updated version contains your replacement text. The next time it backs up files, File History will include the updated version of the Services document and store it separate from the original version.

Restoring Files and Folders

All hard disks eventually fail, even if you maintain them conscientiously. When a hard disk fails, you can no longer access the files it contains. For that reason alone, you should back up your personal files regularly. If your hard disk does fail and a computer maintenance expert believes data recovery is nearly impossible, you'll need to install a new hard disk or reformat the one that you have. Practically everyone who has been using computers for a long time has a data loss story to tell. Many computer owners who now make regular backups learned the hard way how important it is to protect data. Backing up your files is one of the most effective ways to save time and maintain data integrity when you are working on a computer. Create the first backup file, and then let File History regularly create backup copies of updated files. If you do lose data, File History allows you to easily restore the files you lost.

In versions of Windows backup applications before Windows 8, you restored files by first selecting a set of backups created on a certain date. Next, you navigated the backup set to find a folder and then the file you want. To determine the contents of the file, you restored it to the hard disk, and then opened it. If the file you selected was not the version you needed, you closed the file, returned to the backup set, and then restored a different file.

File History makes it much easier to restore the right version of a file because you use File Explorer and its familiar interface to find the file you want. Suppose you created a poster graphic for a presentation on Windows 10 and saved the graphic as a file named Poster in the Presentations folder in the Pictures folder. The Poster file originally included images of the Start menu and the desktop, and then later you removed the desktop image from the file. In the meantime, you saved a few versions of the file. Now you want to restore the version of the Poster file with the Start menu and the desktop. To do so, you use File Explorer to navigate to the Presentations folder in the Pictures folder, which contains only the latest saved copy of the Poster file. Click the History button in the Open group on the Home tab to display the most recent previously saved files in the Presentations folder. See Figure 9-7.

Figure 9-7   **Displaying a folder's history**

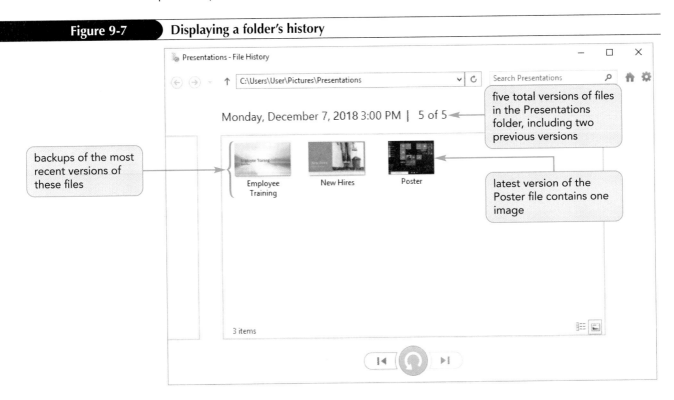

To display the file's history, which comprises all of the previous versions of the file, including the one displaying the Start menu and desktop, you double-click the Poster file. See Figure 9-8.

Figure 9-8   **Displaying a file's history**

You click the Previous version and Next version buttons in the Poster.png - File History window until you find the version you want. When you find the correct version, click the Restore button to restore the file to its original location. File History lets you choose to replace the current file with the backup or to skip the replacement. If you want to save both the older version and the current one, you can move the current version to a different folder or rename it before restoring the older version.

You'll show Rachel how to restore the original version of the Services file.

To restore a file from File History:

▶ **1.** Display the contents of the Rachel folder, if necessary.

▶ **2.** On the Home tab, in the Open group, click the **History** button. If 10 or more minutes have passed since File History made the first backup, the folder window shows the latest version of the file, which is the one you updated based on your research.

   Trouble? If Windows reports that File History is still backing up your files, close the window, wait for the backup to complete, and then repeat Step 2.

▶ **3.** Click the **Previous version** button ◄ to display the previous version of the file. If necessary, continue clicking the **Previous version** button ◄ until you display the original version of the file, which contains "Supply boxes and other materials." as the text for the first bullet. See Figure 9-9.

   Trouble? If your computer does not include an app that can preview the contents of .rtf files, an icon appears for each version of the file instead of the file contents. Double-click the file icon to open the file, and then close the file when you find the correct version.

Figure 9-9   Selecting a file to restore

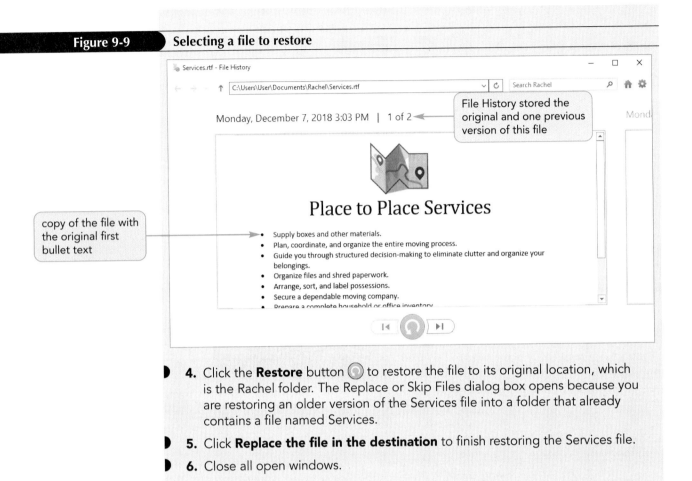

> **4.** Click the **Restore** button ⊙ to restore the file to its original location, which is the Rachel folder. The Replace or Skip Files dialog box opens because you are restoring an older version of the Services file into a folder that already contains a file named Services.

> **5.** Click **Replace the file in the destination** to finish restoring the Services file.

> **6.** Close all open windows.

If you did not want to restore the older file, you could click the Skip this file option in the Replace or Skip Files dialog box. To examine file details more carefully, you could click the Compare info for both files option, also in the Replace or Skip Files dialog box. If you restored the file to a folder that did not already contain a file with the same name, File History would restore the file without opening the Replace or Skip Files dialog box.

Managing System Software

Although your personal files are the most valuable files you have on a computer, they are useful to you only if you have the right software to open, edit, and otherwise enhance those files, including system software. If your hard disk or system suffers damage so that Windows cannot start, you need a **system recovery drive**, which is removable media containing system recovery tools to help restore a computer if a serious system error occurs. If you use an optical disc such as a DVD, this tool is called a **system repair disk**.

If you can start Windows but discover other system problems as you are working on the computer, you can save system files without affecting your personal files by using System Restore, a Windows tool that helps you restore your computer's system files to an earlier point when your system was working reliably. If your system becomes unstable or starts to act unpredictably after installing software, you can try uninstalling the software to see if that solves your problem. If uninstalling does not solve your problem, you can undo system changes by restoring your computer to an earlier date when the system worked correctly.

Windows 10 also provides other recovery tools that can help you avoid problems with the operating system. If your system hasn't been running well for a few days, you can reset the operating system, which means reinstalling Windows. Before you do, Windows lets you choose to keep your files or remove them. Although you can keep your personal files when you reset Windows, you lose your apps and settings. You might want to remove your files, apps, and settings when you are selling, donating, or recycling your computer because resetting in this case removes all traces of your identity. You can also revert to an earlier build of Windows. (A **build** is a version of software, such as an operating system, distributed to users.) When the next build is ready, Windows Update installs it, skipping the problematic build. Figure 9-10 summarizes when to use each Windows 10 recovery option.

Figure 9-10   **Windows 10 recovery options**

Recovery Option	When to Use
System restore point	You recently installed an app, update, or other software, and now the system isn't working well.
Reset Windows	The system isn't working well, and you haven't installed any software recently.
Go back to an earlier build	The system hasn't been working well since a major update.
Recover Windows	The computer won't start and you've created a system recovery drive or a system repair disk.
Reinstall Windows from the original installation files	The computer won't start and you have not created a system recovery drive or a system repair disk.

Creating a System Recovery Drive

To make sure you can start Windows and access recovery tools if something goes wrong with your operating system, you should create a system recovery drive. Most people create a system recovery drive right after they install or upgrade to Windows 10, or when they purchase a new Windows 10 computer. You can use a USB drive, CD, or DVD to create a recovery drive that contains files Windows needs to start and provide you with troubleshooting and system repair tools even when it cannot start as normal. The system recovery drive does not contain a full version of Windows, but only enough files to start your computer.

You'll show Rachel how to create a system recovery drive. To do so, you need a USB drive that can hold at least 8 GB of data and is formatted with the NTFS file system. You check the file system in the following steps. If the drive contains any data, Windows deletes the data as it creates the recovery drive, so be sure to select an unused (or clean) USB flash drive or one that contains files you no longer need. If you do not have a USB flash drive that meets these requirements, read but do not perform the following steps.

To create a system recovery drive:

▶ **1.** Insert a USB drive into a USB port on your computer, making sure the USB drive can hold at least 8 GB of data and does not contain any data you need.

Trouble? If you have a USB drive connected to your computer and do not want to use it as a system recovery drive, click the Show hidden icons button ⌃ on the taskbar, click the Safely Remove Hardware and Eject Media icon ⏏ and then click Eject USB Flash Drive. When Windows displays a Safe to Remove Hardware message, remove the USB flash drive from the computer, and then close the message.

> **2.** Open a folder window, if necessary, right-click the removable drive icon in the navigation pane, and then click **Properties** on the shortcut menu. The Properties dialog box for the removable disk opens.

> **3.** On the General tab, verify that the file system is NTFS, and then click the **OK** button to close the Properties dialog box.
>
> **Trouble?** If the file system is not NTFS, find a different USB flash drive with at least 8 GB of storage space, and then repeat Steps 1–3. If you do not have another USB flash drive, right-click the removable drive icon in the navigation pane, click Format on the shortcut menu, click the File system button, click NTFS, and then click the Start button to format the drive. If necessary, click the OK button to acknowledge the message that all data on the disk will be erased. When the formatting is complete, click the OK button, and then continue with Step 4.

> **4.** Click in the **Ask me anything** box, type **recovery**, and then click **Create a recovery drive** in the search results to start the Recovery Drive Wizard, which guides you through the steps of creating a system recovery drive.
>
> **Trouble?** If a User Account Control dialog box opens requesting a password or your permission to continue, enter the password or click the Yes button.

> **5.** Click the **Back up system files to the recovery drive** check box if it does not contain a checkmark, and then click the **Next** button to display the next wizard dialog box, which lists the removable drives connected to your computer.

> **6.** Click the name of the removable drive, such as D:\Removable Disk, and then click the **Next** button to display a dialog box warning you that Windows will delete everything on the USB drive as it creates the recovery drive.

> **7.** Click the **Create** button. Windows copies utilities and other files to the USB drive so you can use the drive to troubleshoot and repair a start-up problem.

> **8.** When the recovery drive is ready, click the **Finish** button.

TIP

If you use an optical disc instead of a USB drive, you click Create a system repair disk with a CD or DVD instead.

Store the system recovery drive in a safe place. If your computer does not start properly, you can insert the USB drive in a USB port, and then restart the computer to display recovery options, which you'll learn about later in this session.

Creating a System Restore Point

System Restore tracks changes to your computer's system files and uses a feature called System Protection to create a restore point, which is a snapshot of your computer's system files. A restore point contains information about these system files and settings in the registry, which is a database of information about your computer's configuration. If your system becomes unstable, use System Restore to return your computer settings to a particular restore point. System Restore creates restore points at regular intervals (typically once a day) and when it detects the beginning of a change to your computer, such as a Windows Update. You can also create a restore point yourself at any time, such as before playing an online game.

REFERENCE

Creating a System Restore Point

- Click in the Ask me anything box, begin to type Create a restore point, and then click Create a restore point.
- In the System Properties dialog box, click the System Protection tab, if necessary, and then click the Create button.
- Enter a description to help you identify the restore point, and then click the Create button.
- Click the Close button.

Although Windows 10 automatically creates system restore points periodically and before a significant system event such as installing new software, you can create a restore point yourself at any time. To create a restore point, Windows saves images of its system files, programs, and registry settings. It might also save images of files that help to run programs, such as scripts and batch files. Windows can only create restore points on NTFS disks, not FAT disks. To create restore points, you need at least 300 MB of free space on a hard disk that has at least 1 GB of storage space. System Restore might use from 3 to 5 percent of the space on each disk. As this space fills up with restore points, System Restore deletes older restore points to make room for new ones.

Because System Restore reverts to previous system settings without affecting your personal files, it usually cannot help you recover a personal file that has been lost or damaged. Use File History to recover a working version of a personal file.

Rachel's computer is working well right now, so you'll show her how to create a restore point to protect her system. Before you do, you want to make sure that System Protection is turned on for her computer.

To make sure System Protection is turned on:

1. Click in the **Ask me anything** box, begin to type **Create a restore point**, and then click **Create a restore point** in the search results. The System Properties dialog box opens. See Figure 9-11. The Available Drives list shows for which drives System Protection is turned on. Make sure that System Protection is turned on for the system drive, the internal hard drive where Windows 10 is installed on your computer, which is most likely drive C.

| Figure 9-11 | System Properties dialog box |

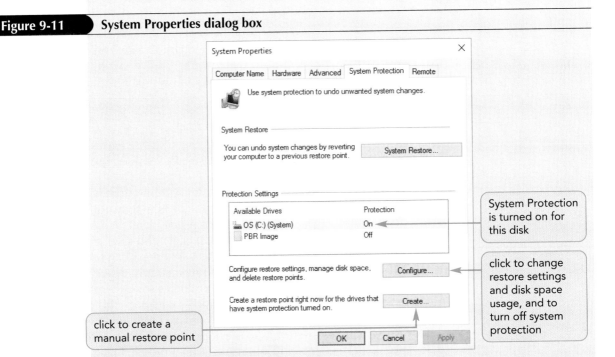

System Protection is turned on for this disk

click to change restore settings and disk space usage, and to turn off system protection

click to create a manual restore point

Trouble? If a User Account Control dialog box opens requesting a password or your permission to continue, enter the password or click the Yes button.

Trouble? If System Protection is turned off for the system drive, click the Configure button, click the Turn on system protection option button, and then drag the Max Usage slider to 3%, if necessary. Click the OK button to accept the settings and return to the System Properties dialog box.

2. In the System Properties dialog box, click the drive for which you want to create the restore point, and then click the **Create** button. The System Protection dialog box opens.

3. Type **Rachel** as the description for this restore point. Windows will add the current date and time automatically.

4. Click the **Create** button. Windows creates a restore point, which might take a few minutes, and then displays a message indicating it was created successfully.

5. Click the **Close** button.

At any point after you or Windows creates a restore point, you can select one to undo changes made to your system up to that restore point. Every time you use System Restore, Windows creates a restore point before proceeding, so you can undo the changes if reverting to a restore point doesn't fix your problem. If you need to restore your computer, Windows recommends using the most recent restore point created before a significant change, such as installing an app. You can also choose from a list of restore points. Select restore points in descending order, starting with the most recent, to minimize the number of system changes. If that doesn't solve your problem, try the next most recent, and so on. Although System Restore doesn't delete any of your personal files, it removes programs installed after the restore point you select, requiring you to reinstall those programs. The System Restore Wizard includes a Scan for affected programs option so you can see which programs will be removed when you restore the system.

You'll show Rachel how to restore her computer in case she has system problems and wants to revert to a previous point. You won't actually restore her computer in the following steps because it doesn't need it right now. You'll work as far as you can through the System Restore dialog boxes, and then click the Cancel button instead of the Finish button. You also inform Rachel that she should always save and close any open files and close any running programs before using System Restore.

To begin restoring a computer:

▶ **1.** In the System Properties dialog box, click the **System Restore** button. The System Restore Wizard starts.

▶ **2.** Click the **Next** button. The next System Restore dialog box opens, where you can choose a restore point. See Figure 9-12.

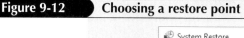

Figure 9-12 **Choosing a restore point**

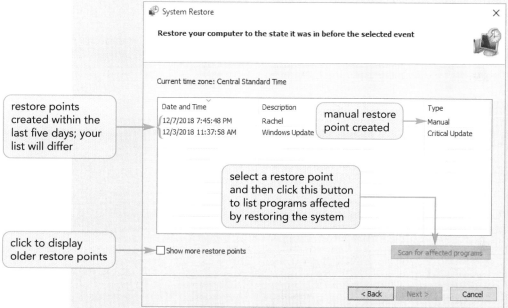

restore points created within the last five days; your list will differ

manual restore point created

select a restore point and then click this button to list programs affected by restoring the system

click to display older restore points

▶ **3.** Click the second restore point in the list, which might be for a recent Windows update, and then click the **Next** button. The last System Restore dialog box opens so you can confirm your restore point.

Trouble? If only one restore point appears in the list, click the Show more restore points check box to display earlier restore points.

▶ **4.** Click the **Cancel** button to close the dialog box without restoring the computer.

Trouble? If you clicked the Finish button instead of the Cancel button, confirm that you want to restore your computer, and then wait until System Restore finishes and restarts your computer. Open the System Properties dialog box, click the System Restore button on the System Protection tab, click the Undo System Restore option button, click the Next button, click the Finish button, and then click the Yes button.

▶ **5.** Close all open windows.

Recall that Windows 10 saves restore points until they fill up the hard disk space reserved by System Restore. (You can change the amount of space allocated for System Restore in the System Protection dialog box.) As you and Windows create new restore points, System Restore deletes old ones. If you turn off System Protection on a disk, Windows deletes all the restore points from that disk. When you turn System Protection back on, Windows starts creating new restore points.

Resetting and Recovering a System

If an electrical storm, a power surge, a virus, or another threat causes system problems severe enough to prevent Windows from running normally, you can reset your installation of Windows. While System Restore returns your system to an earlier state, resetting installs a fresh copy of Windows on your computer and lets you choose whether to retain your data, settings, and apps. To reset, Windows needs to access setup files stored on its installation or recovery medium. You can use the original installation medium (such as the USB drive or DVD containing the setup program and files) or a system recovery drive, such as the one you created in a previous section.

If Windows does not start properly, you can use the system recovery drive to start the system and then display the Troubleshoot screen, which includes the Reset and Advanced options commands. (Your computer manufacturer might add other commands to the Troubleshoot screen.) Select Advanced options to display the Advanced options screen, shown in Figure 9-13.

Figure 9-13   **Advanced options**

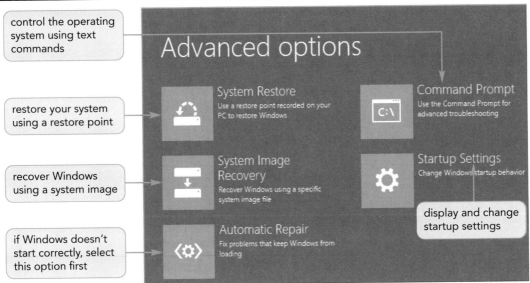

To solve the problem preventing Windows from starting, first select the Automatic Repair option. Windows scans your system and analyzes settings, configuration options, and system files that could prevent the system from starting. If Windows detects any missing or corrupt files or settings, it attempts to repair them. If it can fix the problem, it does so automatically and then restarts.

If the Automatic Repair option does not solve the problem, it displays the Advanced options again. Now you can try to solve the startup problem by using a restore point to restore Windows or recovering the operating system from a system recovery drive. You can also contact a Microsoft technical support expert who might guide you through entering commands at the command prompt. In that case, you can select the Command Prompt option in the Advanced options. You can also use the Startup Settings option if the support expert wants to examine and change the startup settings.

As mentioned earlier, you can choose to use the Reset option on the Troubleshoot screen, which appears after you start your computer using the system recovery drive. You can also access the Reset option by pressing and holding the Shift key and then clicking Restart on the Power button menu or by using the Settings app. You'll show Rachel how to learn about the Reset option using the Settings app.

If you are in a computer lab, you probably cannot access the Reset option. In that case, read but do not perform the following steps.

To learn about resetting your system:

▶ **1.** Click in the **Ask me anything** box, type **reset**, and then click **Reset this PC**. The Settings app starts and opens the Update & Security window with the Recovery category selected. See Figure 9-14.

Figure 9-14 **Reset and recovery options**

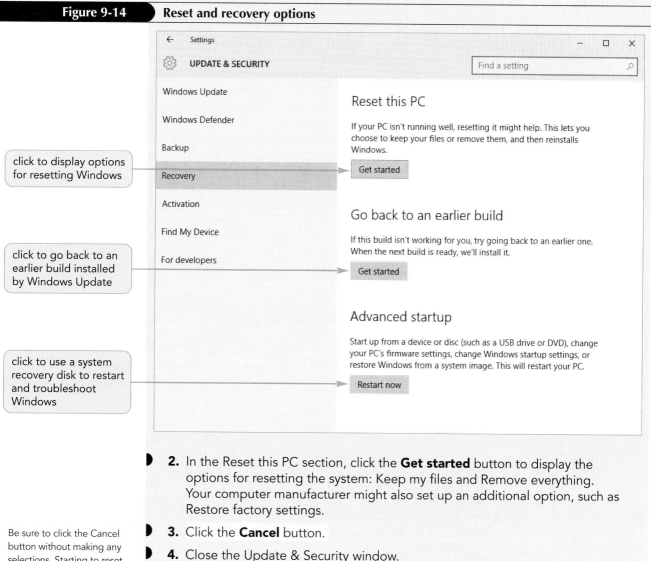

click to display options for resetting Windows

click to go back to an earlier build installed by Windows Update

click to use a system recovery disk to restart and troubleshoot Windows

▶ **2.** In the Reset this PC section, click the **Get started** button to display the options for resetting the system: Keep my files and Remove everything. Your computer manufacturer might also set up an additional option, such as Restore factory settings.

Be sure to click the Cancel button without making any selections. Starting to reset your PC could make your system unusable.

▶ **3.** Click the **Cancel** button.

▶ **4.** Close the Update & Security window.

If you decide to reset your system, make sure you have been creating backups with File History, and have the File History drive or network folder handy so you can restore your files.

Managing Application Software

When you buy a new Windows 10 computer, it comes with the operating system and other system software already installed, along with a few useful Windows 10 apps. The computer manufacturer might also install apps such as entertainment or utility software. To add other software to your system, you **install** it, which means you copy files from a website, a hard disk, or removable media to your system to make the software ready to run and use. To install Windows 10 apps, you must download them first from the Windows Store. You can also install apps from the publisher's website or by using removable media. When you no longer need or want the software, you can uninstall it, which removes the software from your system.

Installing Apps from the Windows Store

If you want to install a Windows 10 app on your system, you can visit the Windows Store, the online marketplace for Windows 10 apps and tools. By providing apps in the Windows Store, Microsoft can enforce strict guidelines to make sure that Windows 10 apps are secure, perform reliably, work as advertised, and protect your privacy. The Windows Store features three types of apps: free, paid, and trial versions of paid apps. (A trial version lets you try the software before you buy it. Usually, without any initial cost, you can install and use the software for a limited time or you can use only some features.) These apps are organized into categories such as Social, Entertainment, Games, and Productivity.

Rachel has mentioned that she wants to improve her Spanish language speaking skills so she can communicate effectively with her Spanish-speaking customers. You know that the Windows Store has an app called Duolingo that provides language instruction. You'll show Rachel how to download and install this free app from the Windows Store.

To perform the following steps, make sure you have permission to download and install software from a website. If your school does not allow you to download files or install software, read but do not perform the following steps. You also need a Microsoft (or Xbox) account to download and install apps from the Windows Store.

To install an app from the Windows Store:

▶ 1. On the taskbar, click the **Store** button 🔳 to visit the Windows Store.

▶ 2. On the menu bar at the top of the window, click **Apps** to display featured apps and a customized selection of apps based on other items you have downloaded from the Windows store, if any.

▶ 3. Click in the **Search** box, type **duolingo**, and then click **Duolingo – Learn Languages for Free** in the search results. The Duolingo page opens in the Store window. See Figure 9-15. Your Duolingo page might differ.

Figure 9-15	Duolingo page in the Windows Store

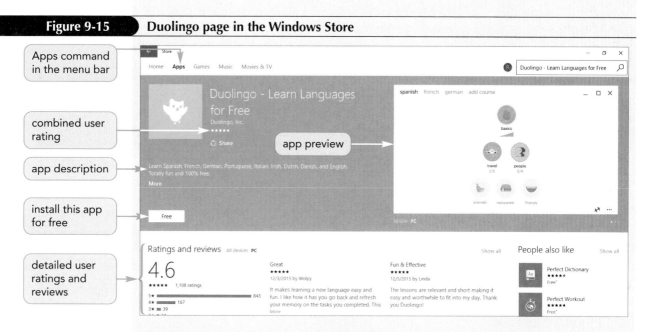

Apps command in the menu bar

combined user rating

app description

install this app for free

detailed user ratings and reviews

> **4.** Click the **Free** button. Windows downloads and installs Duolingo on your computer.
>
> **Trouble?** If Duolingo is already installed on your computer, skip Step 4.
>
> **Trouble?** If Windows does not download and install the app, close the Store window and then repeat Steps 1–4.

Microsoft and other developers often continue to improve apps in the Windows Store even after you've installed them. By default, the Store downloads updates to its apps during a Windows update. You can check for updates yourself by visiting the Store. Click your user icon next to the Search box, and then click Downloads and updates on the menu. On the Downloads and updates page, click the Check for updates button. Windows lists any updates to your apps so you can select the one you want, and then click the Update all link to update all the listed apps or click the update icon (a down arrow) to update only a single app.

When you first install an app from the Windows Store, you can click the Open button on the app's page to start the app. Afterwards, you can start the app as you do any other Windows 10 app: using the Start menu or the Ask me anything box on the taskbar. After starting Duolingo, you can demonstrate it to Rachel and see if she wants to keep it on her computer.

To start the Duolingo app:

> **1.** On the Duolingo page in the Store window, click the **Open** button to display a setup window.
>
> **2.** Click the **get started** button, if necessary, and then click **spanish**.
>
> **3.** Follow the instructions to set up a profile by selecting a language and providing user information.
>
> **Trouble?** If you have already set up a profile on Duolingo, close the setup window, and then close the Store window.

▶ **4.** Click the **Start tour** button to begin Duolingo. Follow the instructions on each page, and then click the **Continue** button.

Trouble? If the Start tour button does not appear, read but do not perform Step 4.

▶ **5.** Close Duolingo.

▶ **6.** Close the Store window.

Rachel isn't sure that she would use the new app, so you'll show her how to uninstall it.

Uninstalling Software

You can uninstall software from your computer if you no longer use it. Doing so frees up space on your hard disk, sometimes a significant amount of space, depending on the app. To uninstall Windows 10 apps, you right-click the appropriate item on the Start menu or the Cortana search results, and then click Uninstall on the shortcut menu. If a shortcut menu does not open when you right-click an app on the Start menu or Cortana search results, you use the Apps & features window in the Settings app to uninstall a Windows app or use the Programs and Features window in the Control Panel to uninstall a desktop app. In either case, uninstalling removes the program's files and any changes made to Windows system settings.

To use the Apps & features window, type "uninstall" in the Ask me anything box, and then click Apps & features in the search results. The Apps & features window lists installed apps in alphabetic order. Click the app you want to uninstall, and then click the Uninstall button. If a Modify button appears when you click an app, you can use it to change the way the app and its features are set up on the computer. If a Move button appears, you can use it to move the app to another drive.

To use the Programs and Features window, type "uninstall" in the Ask me anything box, and then click Programs and Features in the search results. The Programs and Features window lists all the desktop applications and other software tools installed on your computer. Click an application and then click the Uninstall button on the toolbar to uninstall the application. If a Change or Repair button appears on the toolbar, you can click it to change the program's configuration.

You'll show Rachel how to uninstall the Duolingo app and remove it from the Start menu.

To uninstall a Windows 10 app:

▶ **1.** Click in the **Ask me anything** box, begin typing **duolingo**, and then right-click **Duolingo** to display its shortcut menu. See Figure 9-16.

| Figure 9-16 | Preparing to uninstall an app |

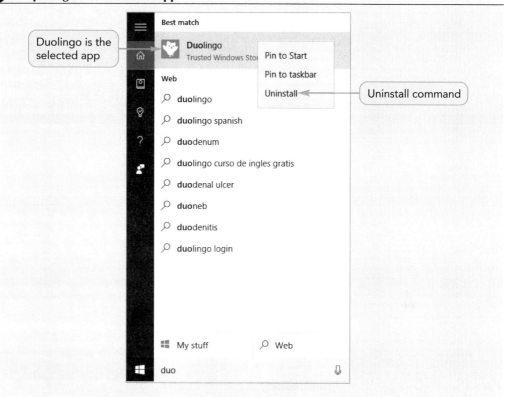

2. Click **Uninstall** on the shortcut menu. Windows removes the app from the computer, which could take a few minutes.

Besides installing and uninstalling software, you can maintain software by making sure it runs as designed in Windows 10. You'll show Rachel how to do so next.

Setting Up a Program for Compatibility

If you install programs written for earlier versions of Windows, such as Windows 7 or Windows Vista, chances are that they will run properly. However, some older programs might run poorly or not run at all. When you run an older program, the Program Compatibility Assistant dialog box might open if it detects known compatibility issues. The dialog box notifies you about the problem and offers to fix it the next time you run the program.

If the Program Compatibility Assistant dialog box does not appear when you run an older program, you can use the Program Compatibility Troubleshooter to select and test compatibility settings that might fix the problems in the older program. You can let Windows apply recommended settings or you can troubleshoot the program manually. When you troubleshoot manually, you can choose an operating system recommended for the program or one that previously supported the program correctly. After you apply recommended settings or select an operating system, you can start the older program to see if the new settings solve the problem. If they don't, you can return to the troubleshooter and try other settings.

Microsoft advises that you should not use the Program Compatibility Troubleshooter on older antivirus programs, disk utilities, or other system programs because it might remove data or create a security risk.

Rachel installed a Windows Vista program called E-Organizer on her Windows 10 computer, and it has not displayed menus or title bars correctly since she installed it. You'll run the Program Compatibility Troubleshooter, select the E-Organizer program to run it with compatibility settings, and see if that solves the problem.

The following steps select compatibility settings for a program named E-Organizer. Ask your instructor to identify a program on your computer that you can use instead of E-Organizer. The program should not be an antivirus program, a disk utility, or another system program. Substitute the name of that program for E-Organizer when you perform the following steps.

To use the Program Compatibility Troubleshooter:

1. Click in the **Ask me anything** box, start typing **Run programs made for previous versions of Windows**, and then click **Run programs made for previous versions of Windows** to start the Program Compatibility Troubleshooter.

2. Click the **Next** button. The troubleshooter scans your computer, lists installed programs, and instructs you to select the program that is causing problems.

3. Click **E-Organizer** (or the program name recommended by your instructor), and then click the **Next** button. The troubleshooter gives you two options: Try recommended settings or Troubleshoot program.

   Trouble? If the troubleshooter indicates that a paid upgrade is available, click the Continue troubleshooting the program option.

4. Click **Try recommended settings**. Windows detects which operating system the program is designed for and then applies settings, if possible. See Figure 9-17.

Figure 9-17   Program Compatibility Troubleshooter window

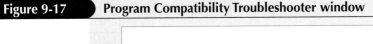

5. Click the **Test the program** button. If a User Account Control dialog box opens, click the **Yes** button. E-Organizer (or the other program) starts.

   Trouble? If the older program does not start or run correctly, close the program window, and then read but do not perform the following steps.

▶ **6.** Close the program, and then click the **Next** button. The next wizard dialog box asks if the program has been fixed.

▶ **7.** Click **Yes, save these settings for this program**. Windows saves the settings, generating a report that provides a summary.

▶ **8.** Click the **Close** button to close the Program Compatibility Troubleshooter window.

▶ **9.** Close all open windows.

Exploring Windows To Go

Windows To Go is designed for businesses and other organizations to use with their employees. These groups often use Windows computers on a network and specify the appearance and content of the desktop on each computer, including security policies and custom applications developed or modified specifically for the organization. Employees who travel or work from home want to replicate the setup on their office computers so they can work in a familiar environment even when they are out of the office. At the same time, businesses might discourage employees from connecting their personal computers to the company network because they don't want to risk introducing malware to the network.

Windows To Go solves these problems by allowing businesses to install all of the software employees need on a certified USB drive. (To see a list of certified USB drives, visit the technet.microsoft.com website, and then search for Windows To Go.) The Windows To Go drive includes Windows 10 and the organization's settings, security policies, and software. Employees can then plug the Windows To Go drive into a computer that they use away from the office to access Windows 10 and the computing environment they use at work, including applications and settings. They can store files on the organization's network folders. When employees remove the Windows To Go drive from their computers, the computers resume their original state, which might be a personalized Windows 7, Windows 8.x, or Windows 10 environment.

Creating a Windows To Go drive involves advanced computing tasks that are typically performed by a technical expert.

You're finished showing Rachel how to back up and restore files and manage her software. In the next session, you'll examine how to maintain hard disks and monitors and work with device drivers.

Session 9.1 Quick Check

REVIEW

1. Explain how using File History to back up files differs from copying files.

2. When you _____ a file, you use Windows to recover a saved version of the file from File History and copy it to a location you specify.

3. How often does File History back up files by default?

4. Why should you not delete or move the FileHistory folder in your backup location?

5. When should you use a system recovery drive?

6. In what conditions should you return your computer settings to a restore point?

7. Select the _____ option on the Advanced options screen to have Windows scan your system and analyze settings, configuration options, and system files that could prevent the system from starting.

8. What is the advantage of downloading and installing apps from the Windows Store?

Session 9.2 Visual Overview:

Hardware is any physical piece of equipment, called a **device**, that is connected to your computer and controlled by your computer.

A **local disk** is installed in your computer.

Windows 10 must be installed on a disk using the **NT file system (NTFS)**, which is the underlying structure a computer uses to organize data on the hard disk.

As part of a regular maintenance program, you should be familiar with the properties of your hard disk, including how much free space it has.

The **Disk Cleanup tool** frees disk space by deleting unnecessary files such as temporary files.

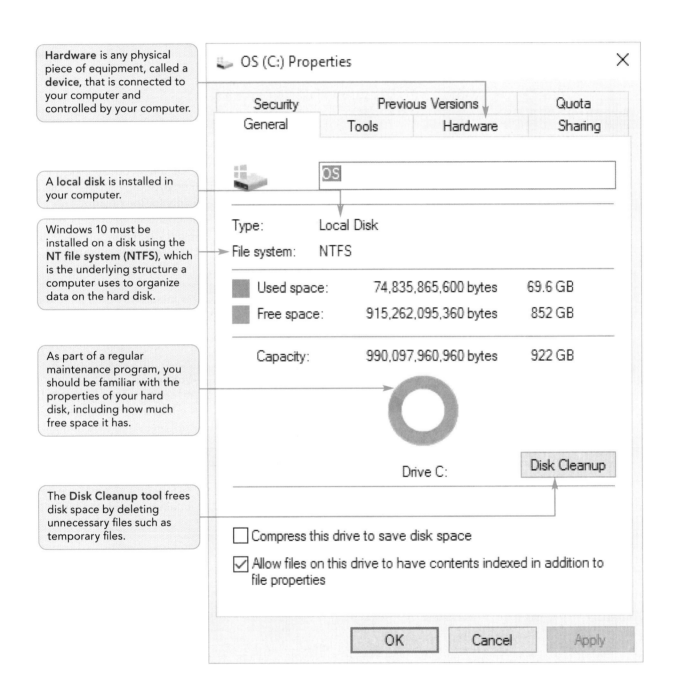

OS (C:) Properties   ✕

| Security | Previous Versions | Quota |
| General | Tools | Hardware | Sharing |

OS

| Type: | Local Disk |
| File system: | NTFS |

| ■ Used space: | 74,835,865,600 bytes | 69.6 GB |
| ■ Free space: | 915,262,095,360 bytes | 852 GB |

| Capacity: | 990,097,960,960 bytes | 922 GB |

Drive C: Disk Cleanup

☐ Compress this drive to save disk space

☑ Allow files on this drive to have contents indexed in addition to file properties

OK   Cancel   Apply

Managing Hardware

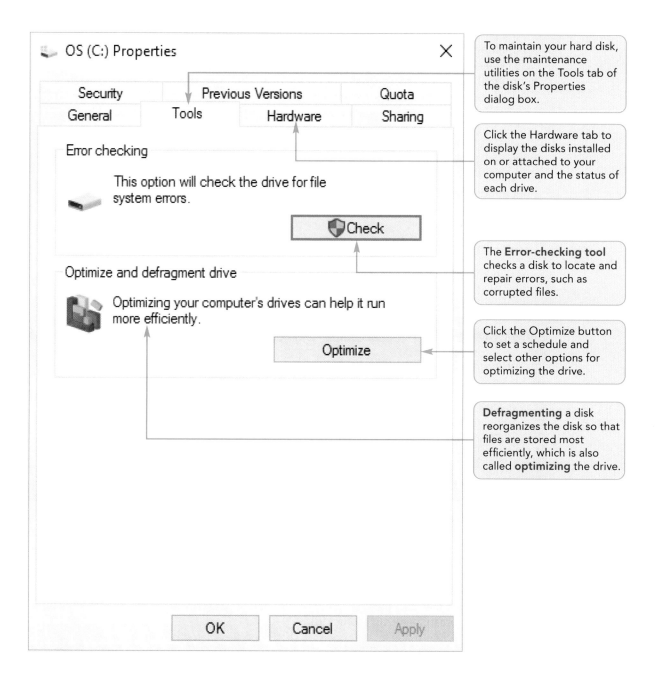

Maintaining Hard Disks

As a computer owner, one of your most important responsibilities is to maintain your hard disk by keeping it free of problems that could prevent you from accessing your data. The failure of a hard disk can be a headache if you have backups of your data, and a disaster if you don't. Windows helps you prevent disk failure from occurring in the first place by providing some valuable disk maintenance accessories.

As part of a regular maintenance program, you should become familiar with the properties of your hard disk, including whether it is partitioned. Next, you should check each disk on your computer to locate and repair errors, such as parts of corrupted files and damaged sections on the disk. Then you should defragment each disk. If you are responsible for maintaining a computer that is used all day, you should probably run these maintenance procedures on a weekly or even daily basis. On the other hand, if you use your computer less frequently—for example, you use a home computer only for correspondence, games, and maintaining your finances—you might only need to run disk maintenance procedures once every month or so.

Rachel has not performed any maintenance tasks on her computer, so you'll guide her through the cleanup tasks and show her how to make sure they are completed on a regular basis.

Viewing Hard Disk Properties

As you know, all of the applications and system files on your computer are stored on your hard disk. You should periodically check the amount of free space on your hard disk to make sure you have enough room for your data and software.

REFERENCE

Viewing Hard Disk Properties

- Open File Explorer.
- Click the This PC icon in the navigation pane.
- Right-click a hard disk in the This PC window.
- Click Properties on the shortcut menu.
- Click the General tab to display general details about the hard disk.
- Click the Hardware tab to display the disks attached to your computer.

View the properties of your hard disk to learn the following information:

- File system—Recall that Windows 10 must be installed on a hard disk using the NTFS file system. NTFS supports file system recovery (in the case of a hard disk failure) and can access disk drives up to 2 TB in size. NTFS is the preferred file system if your disk drive is larger than 32 GB. Your computer might also be able to access a disk that uses the FAT32 file system, which employs an older, less efficient method of organizing data on the disk.
- Used space, free space, and capacity—The Properties dialog box for your hard disk shows the amount of space that files and other data use, the amount of free space remaining, and the total capacity of the disk.
- All disk drives—The Hardware tab of a disk's Properties dialog box lists all of the disks installed in or attached to your computer. If you are having trouble with a disk, you can view more details about it, such as its status, which indicates whether it is working properly.

You'll start your maintenance session with Rachel by viewing the properties of her hard disk. In the following steps, the hard disk is named OS (C:). Substitute the name of your hard disk if it is different.

To view the properties of a hard disk:

▶ 1. Click the **File Explorer** button ▨ on the taskbar, and then click **This PC** in the navigation pane to open the This PC window.

▶ 2. Right-click **OS (C:)** and then click **Properties** on the shortcut menu to open the OS (C:) Properties dialog box. See Figure 9-18. The space details on your computer will differ.

Figure 9-18 | OS (C:) Properties dialog box

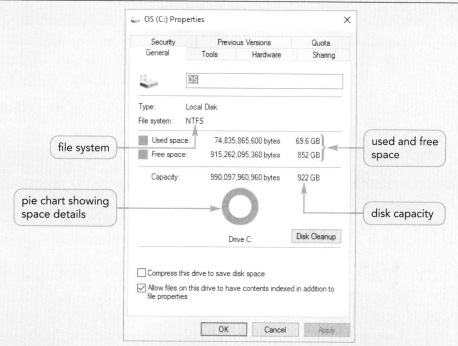

Trouble? If the hard disk where Windows is installed has a different name, right-click that disk icon and then click Properties on the shortcut menu.

▶ 3. Click the **Hardware** tab to display the disks attached to your computer. See Figure 9-19. Your details will differ.

Figure 9-19 ⟩ **Hardware tab of the OS (C:) Properties dialog box**

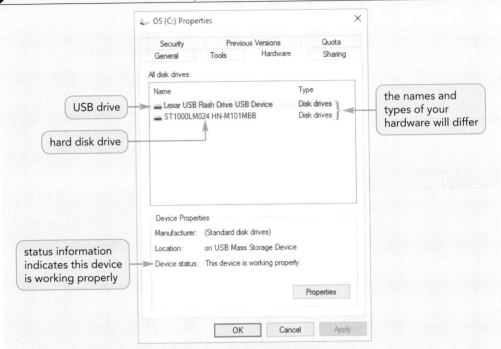

4. Click a disk in the list, if necessary, and then click the **Properties** button. The Device Properties dialog box for that disk opens, displaying details about the selected device.

5. Click the **OK** button to close the Device Properties dialog box.

6. Close the This PC window, but leave the OS (C:) Properties dialog box open.

You want to show Rachel another way to learn more about her hard disk.

Checking for Partitions

A **partition** (sometimes called a **volume**) is part of a hard disk that works like a separate disk—it can be formatted with a file system and identified with a letter of the alphabet. A hard disk needs to be partitioned and formatted before you can store data on it. Computer manufacturers usually perform this task for you, and set up the hard disk as a single partition that equals the size of the hard disk. You are not required to partition a hard disk into several smaller partitions, but you can do so if you want to use partitions to organize data on your hard disk or if you want to install more than one operating system on your computer. Some users prefer to have separate partitions for Windows operating system files, apps, and personal data.

You can use Disk Management, which is an Administrative tool, to view the partitions on your system. Windows computers must have a **system partition**, which contains the hardware-related files that tell a computer where to find the files that start Windows. They must also have a **boot partition**, which contains the Windows operating system files. These files are located in the Windows folder. Usually, the system partition files and boot partition files are located in the same main (or primary) partition, especially if you have only one operating system installed on your computer. If you have more than one operating system on your computer, such as Windows 10 and Windows 7 (called a **dual-boot** or **multiboot computer**), you have more than one boot partition. In this case, a single system partition remains and serves as the primary partition. The other partitions are for your programs and data.

You'll show Rachel how to view the partitions on her hard disk and identify the system partition in the Disk Management window. Usually, only experienced computer administrators work in this window, but you can open it to view basic information about your hard disk and any other disks attached to your computer. The easiest way to open the Disk Management window is to use the Start button shortcut menu, also called the Power User menu, which you open by right-clicking the Start button. The Start button shortcut menu includes commands for managing and maintaining your computer.

You need to sign in to Windows using an Administrator account to perform the following steps. If you are not allowed to sign in as an Administrator, read but do not perform the following steps.

To view the partitions on a hard disk:

1. Right-click the **Start** button ⊞ on the taskbar, and then click **Disk Management** on the shortcut menu to open the Disk Management window. See Figure 9-20. You can resize or scroll the window to see information for all the disks on your computer. The information in your Disk Management window will differ.

Figure 9-20   Disk Management window

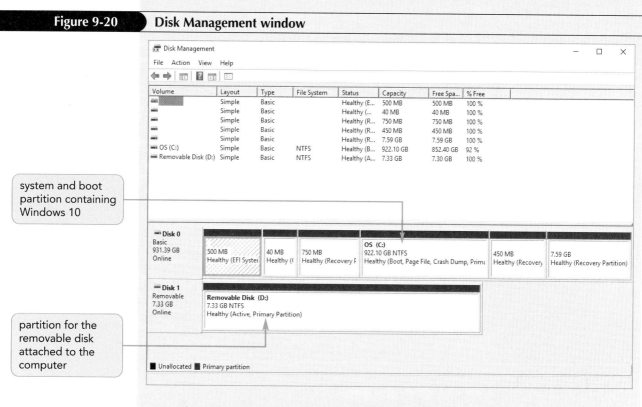

system and boot partition containing Windows 10

partition for the removable disk attached to the computer

The recovery partitions are areas where Windows stores recovery files. If Windows can't start from the primary partition, which is OS (C:) in this figure, it uses the files in the recovery partitions to display the Advanced options, for example, and the files that perform a system repair.

2. Close the Disk Management window.

Now that you and Rachel are acquainted with her hard disk, you can start performing maintenance tasks. The first task is to remove unnecessary files using Disk Cleanup.

Deleting Unnecessary Files with Disk Cleanup

When you work with apps and files in Windows 10, unnecessary files, such as temporary Internet and setup files, accumulate on your hard disk and impair system performance. The Disk Cleanup tool helps you free disk space by permanently deleting these files. When you start Disk Cleanup, it searches your disk for unnecessary files, and then lists the types of files it found in the Disk Cleanup dialog box. Figure 9-21 describes the typical types of files Disk Cleanup can remove when you choose to clean your files to free space on your hard disk. Your Disk Cleanup dialog box might include a different set of files depending on your computer activity.

Figure 9-21   Typical types of files to remove when using Disk Cleanup

Category	Description
Downloaded Program Files	Program files downloaded automatically from the Internet when you view certain webpages
Temporary Internet Files	Webpages stored in the Temporary Internet Files folder on your hard disk for quick viewing
Offline webpages	Webpages stored on your computer so you can view them without being connected to the Internet
Hibernation File Cleaner	Information about your computer stored in the Hibernation file if your computer is set to hibernate; removing this file disables hibernation
Recycle Bin	Files you deleted from your computer, which are stored in the Recycle Bin until you remove them permanently from the Recycle Bin
Setup Log Files	Files Windows created during system setup
Temporary files	Files generated by programs and used temporarily; usually these are deleted when you close the program, but if the program isn't shut down properly, the temporary files remain on your disk
Thumbnails	Copies of your picture, video, and document thumbnails if you are using file and folder thumbnails

You can also choose to clean files for all users on a computer if you are using an Administrator account. In that case, the Disk Cleanup dialog box includes an additional tab named More Options. Using the More Options tab, you can uninstall programs that you no longer use and delete all but the most recent restore point on the disk.

You can clean internal and external hard disks. You'll clean Rachel's hard disk by starting the Disk Cleanup tool from the OS (C:) Properties dialog box.

To use Disk Cleanup:

▶ 1. In the OS (C:) Properties dialog box, click the **General** tab.

▶ 2. Click the **Disk Cleanup** button. If you have more than one partition on your hard disk for storing data files, a dialog box opens asking which files to clean up.

TIP

You can also start Disk Cleanup by typing "Disk Cleanup" in the Ask me anything box, and then clicking Disk Cleanup in the search results.

3. If necessary, click the **Drives arrow button**, click the drive where Windows 10 is installed, such as OS (C:), and then click the **OK** button. Disk Cleanup calculates how much space you can free (which takes a few minutes), and then opens the Disk Cleanup for (C:) dialog box. See Figure 9-22. The information in your Disk Cleanup dialog box will differ.

Figure 9-22	Disk Cleanup for (C:) dialog box

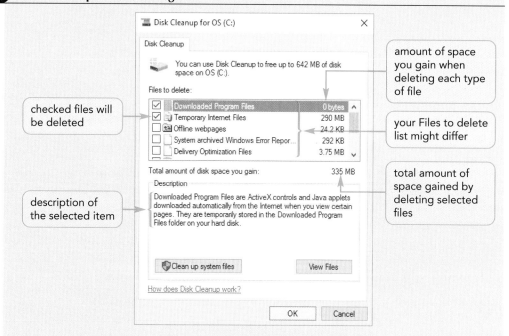

checked files will be deleted

description of the selected item

amount of space you gain when deleting each type of file

your Files to delete list might differ

total amount of space gained by deleting selected files

Rachel wants to delete only downloaded program files and temporary Internet files.

4. If the Downloaded Program Files and Temporary Internet Files check boxes are not selected, click to select them.

5. Scroll the list and then click to remove checkmarks from any other boxes.

6. Click the **OK** button. A dialog box opens asking if you're sure you want to permanently delete these files.

7. Click the **Delete Files** button. It might take a few minutes to clean the files from your hard disk.

Next, you'll check Rachel's hard disk for errors and other problems.

Checking a Hard Disk for Errors

Most PCs have a magnetic hard disk, which is a storage device that contains one or more metal platters that are usually sealed in the computer. Sections of the magnetic surface of a disk sometimes get damaged. Regularly scanning your disks for errors can be an effective way to prevent potential problems that would make data inaccessible. The Windows Error-checking tool not only locates errors on a disk, but attempts to repair them. If it can't repair them, the tool marks the defective portions of the disk so that Windows doesn't try to store data there. In some earlier versions of Windows, the Error-checking tool was called Check Disk or ScanDisk.

To understand what problems the Error-checking tool looks for and how it repairs them, you need to understand the structure of a disk. A hard disk is organized as a concentric stack of disks or platters. Each platter has two surfaces, and each has its own read/write head, which are the small parts of a disk drive that move above the disk platter and read and write data magnetically on the surface of the platters. The data is stored on concentric circles called **tracks** on the platter surfaces. An individual block of data is one **sector** of a track, as shown in Figure 9-23.

Figure 9-23	Single platter on a hard disk

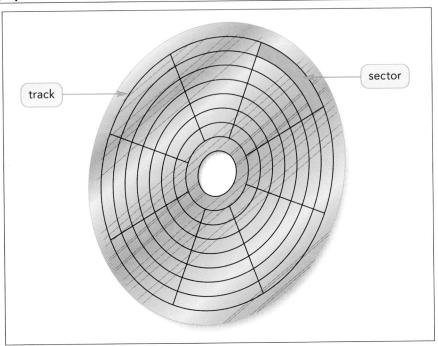

Corresponding tracks on all surfaces on a drive, when taken together, make up a **cylinder**. The number of sectors and tracks depends on the size of the disk. A 400 GB hard disk, for example, has 160,384 cylinders. Each cylinder has 80 heads, with one head per track. Each track has 63 sectors, with 512 bytes per sector. That makes more than 400 billion bytes, which is about 400 GB.

Although the physical surface of a disk is made up of tracks and sectors, a file is stored in clusters. A **cluster** is one or more sectors of storage space—it represents the minimum amount of space that an operating system reserves when saving the contents of a file to a disk. Most files are larger than 512 bytes (the size of one sector). That means a file is usually stored in more than one cluster. A file system error known as a **lost cluster** occurs if Windows loses track of which clusters contain the data that belongs to a single file. The Error-checking tool identifies file system errors and can repair them if necessary.

Checking for Errors After Power Failures

INSIGHT

If your computer suffers a power surge, a power failure, or any problem that locks it up or causes it to shut down unexpectedly, Windows might lose one or more clusters from a file that was open when the problem occurred. This means that you could lose the data stored in those clusters. The presence of lost clusters on a disk is not damaging, but lost clusters do take up valuable space. Having too many lost clusters can lead to other types of file system errors. To prevent an accumulation of file system errors, you should check your hard disk for errors immediately after a power failure. The Error-checking tool can remove lost clusters and their data automatically.

When you use the Windows 10 Error-checking tool to scan your disk for errors, you can specify whether you want it to automatically repair file problems that the scan detects, such as lost clusters, or only report problems and not fix them. You can also perform a thorough disk check by scanning for and repairing physical errors on the hard disk itself, including **bad sectors**, which are areas of the disk that do not record data reliably. Performing a thorough disk check can take much longer to complete.

You'll show Rachel how to check her hard disk for file system errors. Because her computer is still relatively new, it's unlikely the hard disk has any bad sectors. After using her computer for a while, she should check the hard disk on a regular basis for bad sectors and file system errors. To perform the following steps, you must be using an Administrator account. If you are not using an Administrator account, read but do not perform the steps.

To check the hard disk for errors:

▌ **1.** In the OS (C:) Properties dialog box, click the **Tools** tab. See Figure 9-24.

| **Figure 9-24** | **Tools tab of the OS (C:) Properties dialog box** |

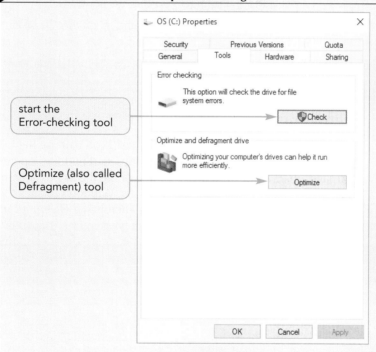

start the Error-checking tool

Optimize (also called Defragment) tool

▌ **2.** Click the **Check** button to open the Error Checking (OS (C:)) dialog box. See Figure 9-25. Even though Windows tells you that you don't need to scan the drive, you might want to scan in case an error appeared since the last scan.

Figure 9-25   **Error-Checking (OS (C:)) dialog box**

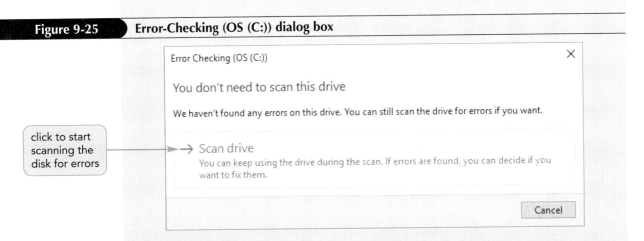

click to start
scanning the
disk for errors

3. If instructed to scan the drive, click **Scan drive** to scan the selected drive for errors, which might take a few minutes.

   Trouble? If your instructor doesn't want you to scan the drive, click the Cancel button, and then skip this step and Step 4.

4. When Windows is finished scanning, click the **Close** button.

If Windows found file system errors, it would fix them automatically or advise you how to proceed.

Defragmenting a Disk

After correcting any errors on your hard disk, you can use the Optimize Drives tool to improve the disk's performance so that apps start and files open more quickly. When you save a file, Windows stores as much of the file as possible in the first available cluster. If the file doesn't fit into one cluster, Windows locates the next available cluster and puts more of the file in it. Windows attempts to place files in contiguous clusters whenever possible. The file is saved when Windows has placed all of the file data into clusters. Figure 9-26 shows two files named Address and Recipes saved on an otherwise unused platter on a hard disk.

Figure 9-26 | Two files saved on a hard disk

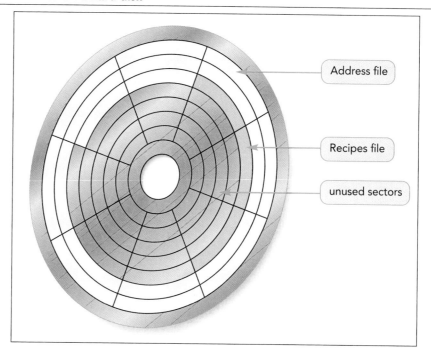

Address file

Recipes file

unused sectors

As you create and save new files, Windows uses more clusters. If you delete a file or two, Windows frees those clusters. Figure 9-27 shows the disk after you save a new file named Memo and then delete the Recipes file.

Figure 9-27 | Adding one file and deleting another file

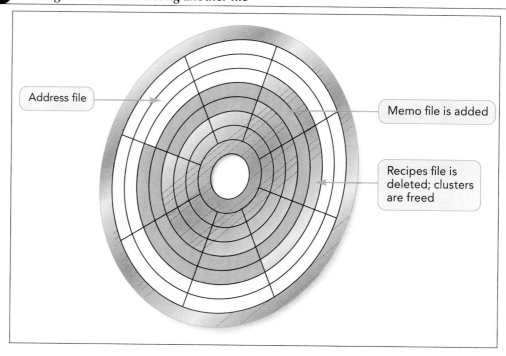

Address file

Memo file is added

Recipes file is deleted; clusters are freed

The next time you save a file, Windows searches for the first available cluster, which is now between two files—the orange sectors between the white and blue ones. Figure 9-28 shows what happens when you save a fourth file named Schedule—it is saved to clusters that are not adjacent.

Figure 9-28 Adding a new file in fragmented clusters

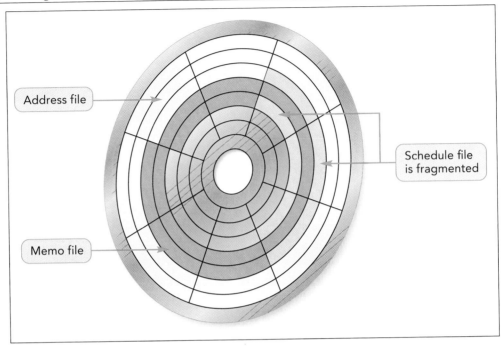

The more files you save and delete, the more scattered the clusters for a file become. A disk that contains files whose clusters are not next to each other is said to be **fragmented**. The more fragmented the disk, the longer Windows takes to retrieve the file, and the more likely you are to have problems with the file. Figure 9-29 shows a fragmented disk. When an app tries to access a file on this disk, file retrieval takes longer than necessary because the app must locate clusters that aren't adjacent.

Figure 9-29 Fragmented files

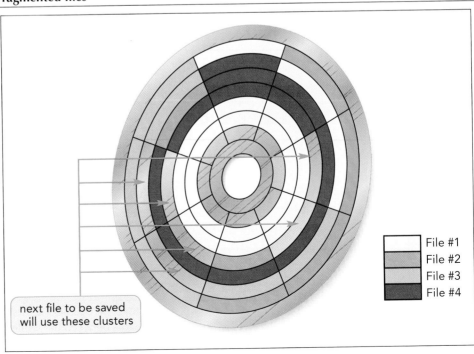

Whenever a disk has been used for a long time, it's a good idea to defragment it. Defragmenting rearranges the clusters on the disk so each file's clusters are adjacent to one another. When a disk is in this state, it is considered optimized. To defragment a disk, you use the Optimize Drives tool, which rearranges the data on your hard disk and reunites fragmented files so your computer can run more efficiently. In Windows 10, the Optimize Drives tool runs on a schedule so you don't have to remember to run it, although you can still run it manually or change the schedule it uses.

You'll show Rachel how to start the Optimize Drives tool and examine its schedule. Because defragmenting a hard disk can take a long time and you must close all apps, including antivirus software, before defragmenting, you won't defragment now.

To start the Optimize Drives tool:

▶ **1.** On the Tools tab of the OS (C:) Properties dialog box, click the **Optimize** button. The Optimize Drives dialog box opens. See Figure 9-30.

> **Trouble?** If a dialog box opens with a message that Optimize and defragment drive was scheduled using a different program, click the Cancel button, and then read but do not perform the remaining steps.

| Figure 9-30 | Optimize Drives dialog box |

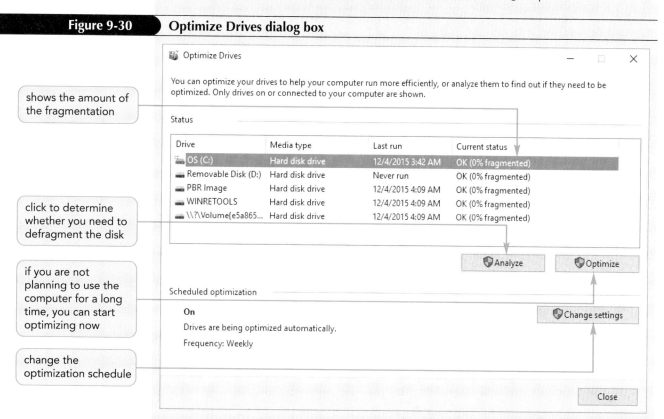

shows the amount of the fragmentation

click to determine whether you need to defragment the disk

if you are not planning to use the computer for a long time, you can start optimizing now

change the optimization schedule

▶ **2.** Click the **Change settings** button to examine the defragmenting schedule. Another Optimize Drives dialog box opens showing the optimization schedule. See Figure 9-31.

Figure 9-31   Optimization schedule

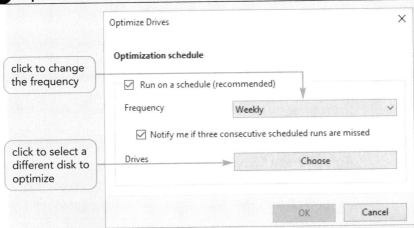

click to change
the frequency

click to select a
different disk to
optimize

This schedule is frequent enough for Rachel's computer, so you don't need to change it.

▶ **3.** Click the **Cancel** button to close the Optimize Drives dialog box showing the schedule.

▶ **4.** Click the **Close** button to close the first Optimize Drives dialog box.

▶ **5.** Close the OS (C:) Properties dialog box.

By default, the Optimize Drives tool is set to run every week if necessary to make sure your disk is defragmented.

Working with Devices and Drivers

Hardware devices include external equipment such as printers and scanners, which remain outside the case of the computer, and internal equipment, such as disk drives, modems, and network adapter cards, which are placed inside the case of the computer.

External devices are connected to your computer through a **port**, which is a physical connection that is visible on the outside of the computer. Windows 10 supports serial, parallel, and USB ports for external devices, though USB ports are the most common. A **USB port** is a thin, rectangular slot that accommodates a high-speed connection to a variety of external devices, such as removable drives, additional displays, video conferencing cameras, and printers. To use USB technology, your computer must have a USB port, and the device you install must have a USB connector, which is a small, rectangular plug. See Figure 9-32. Even if you use a wireless device, such as a wireless mouse, you plug a USB connector in a USB port to communicate with the computer. The location of ports varies depending on the device and its manufacturer. Some tablet computers might not include USB ports because they rely on wireless network technology to transfer data.

Figure 9-32 USB ports on a laptop

USB ports

ports for a
microphone and
headphones

USB connector

© iStock.com/Robert Kirk

When you plug the USB connector into the USB port, Windows recognizes the device and allows you to use it immediately. The current version of USB technology is USB 3.1, which is faster and more efficient than earlier versions (USB 1.1, USB 2.0, and USB 3.0).

You can also **daisy-chain** up to 127 devices together, meaning that you plug one device, such as a scanner, into the USB port, and then plug a second device, such as a microphone, into the scanner, so you are no longer limited by the number of ports on your computer. Instead of daisy-chaining devices, you can also connect multiple devices to a single inexpensive **USB hub**. A hub is a box that contains many USB ports—you plug the hub into your computer, and then plug your USB devices into the hub. USB devices communicate with your computer more efficiently—a USB port transfers data many times faster than other types of ports. You can also connect and disconnect USB devices without shutting down or restarting your computer.

- Internal devices are connected to the **motherboard**, a circuit board inside your computer that contains the **microprocessor** (the "brains" of your computer), the computer memory, and other internal devices. Internal devices such as the microprocessor and memory chips are connected directly to the motherboard. Desktop computers have the option of connecting additional internal devices via a socket in the motherboard called an **expansion slot**. You can insert devices such as network adapter cards or sound cards into expansion slots. Devices that you insert into expansion slots are often called **expansion cards** or **adapter cards** because they "expand" or "adapt" your computer, and they look like large cards. See Figure 9-33.

Figure 9-33　**Motherboard for a desktop computer**

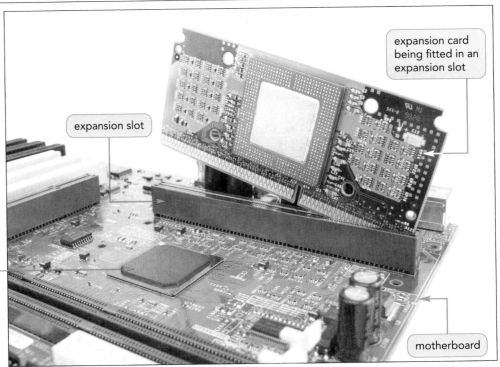

© Piotr Zajc/Shutterstock.com

Understanding Device Resources

Windows assigns each device a set of system resources to help it work with the computer. Windows can assign up to four resources to a device: an IRQ, a DMA channel, an I/O address, and a memory range. When two devices share a particular resource, a **device conflict** can occur, rendering one or both of the devices unusable.

A hardware device often needs to use the microprocessor in the computer to send or receive information. When you are trying to complete several computer tasks at once (for example, when you search for a webpage while you are printing a document and playing music from an online source), Windows needs a way to handle these simultaneous requests. It does so by assigning each device an **interrupt request (IRQ) line** number that signals the microprocessor that the device is requesting an action. Windows 10 makes available 16 IRQ numbers, numbered from 0 to 15, to hardware devices. Lower numbers have higher priority and receive attention first. Occasionally, Windows has to handle more devices than available IRQs, resulting in an IRQ conflict. If you use USB devices, however, Windows 10 only uses one set of resources for all USB devices, meaning it doesn't have to resolve these types of IRQ conflicts.

If the device does not need to use the microprocessor, information can be transferred directly between the device and the system's memory. This channel for transferring data is called the **direct memory access (DMA) channel**. Most computers have four DMA channels, numbered from 0 to 3, available for your devices.

When the computer receives information from one of its devices, it needs a place to store that data in the computer's memory. It does this by reserving a specific section of the computer's memory for each device. The section of the computer's memory devoted to the different devices on a computer is called the **I/O address**. Each device requires a different I/O (input/output) address.

Finally, some devices, such as video cards, require additional computer memory for their own use (not related to communicating with the microprocessor). For example, a video card needs additional memory to manage video and graphics that are not essential to the operating system. This resource is called the **memory address**, or **memory range**.

Your computer uses all four types of system resources—IRQs, DMA channels, I/O addresses, and memory addresses—to communicate between hardware and software.

Understanding Device Drivers

Each hardware device requires a **driver**, a software file that enables Windows to communicate with and control the operation of the device. In most cases, drivers come with Windows. If not, you can find them by using Windows Update to check for updates. If Windows doesn't have the driver you need, you can find it on the manufacturer's website. Hardware manufacturers update drivers on a regular basis to improve device performance and speed. If you are having trouble with a device, you can use Windows Update or check the manufacturer's website to download and install an updated driver.

A **signed driver** is a device driver that includes a digital signature. Recall that a digital signature is an electronic security mark that identifies the publisher of the software and whether someone has changed the original contents of the driver package. If a publisher signed a driver by verifying its identity with a certification authority, you can be confident that the driver actually comes from that publisher and hasn't been altered. Windows alerts you if a driver is not signed, was signed by a publisher that has not verified its identity with a certification authority, or has been altered since it was released.

Installing a Device

Before installing new hardware, check the instructions included with the device to determine whether you need to install a driver before you connect the device. Typically, Windows detects a new device after you connect it and then installs the driver automatically. However, some devices require you to install the driver before plugging the device in. Although most devices that have power switches should be turned on before you connect them, others require that you turn them on during the installation process. Because of differences like this one, it is a good idea to read the instructions included with a new device before you connect it.

To install new devices of any type, you typically can plug the device into a port, and then Windows detects the hardware, automatically installs the correct driver, and notifies you when installation begins and when it's complete. The first time you plug a USB device into a USB port, for example, Windows installs a driver for that device. After that, you can disconnect and reconnect the device without performing additional steps.

Enabling and Disabling Devices

Device Manager is a Windows tool that lets you manage the external and internal devices your computer uses. Using Device Manager, you can determine which devices are installed on your computer, update driver software for your devices, check to see if hardware is working properly, and modify hardware settings.

Enabling and Disabling Devices

- Click in the Ask me anything box, begin to type Device Manager, and then click Device Manager in the search results. If you are prompted for an administrator password or confirmation, type the password or provide confirmation.
- Expand the list of devices as necessary, and then click a device.
- If the device is disabled, click the Enable button on the toolbar to enable it. If the device is enabled, click the Disable button on the toolbar to disable it.

You can use Device Manager to change how your hardware is configured and how it interacts with your programs. Advanced users can use the diagnostic features in Device Manager to resolve device conflicts and change resource settings. Typically, however, you use Device Manager to update device drivers and troubleshoot problems by checking the status of your devices. Suppose you occasionally do not hear sounds from your computer's internal speaker. You can check the status of the speaker in Device Manager and try to repair it by disabling the device and then enabling it. When troubleshooting, you might also disable a device instead of uninstalling it to see if that device is causing a larger system problem. If the problem persists, you can enable the device and disable a different device. When you disable a device, you turn it off. When you enable a device, you turn it on.

You'll start Device Manager and show Rachel how to disable and then enable a USB drive.

To perform the following steps, you need to log on using an Administrator account. You also need a USB drive, such as the one you used to create backups in Session 9.1. Disabling a USB drive does not affect any existing data on the drive. If you cannot sign in using an Administrator account or if you do not have a USB drive, read but do not perform the following steps.

To disable a USB drive:

▶ 1. If necessary, plug a USB drive into a USB port on your computer. Close any dialog boxes that open.

▶ 2. Click in the **Ask me anything** box, start to type **Device Manager**, and then click **Device Manager** in the search results. The Device Manager window opens. See Figure 9-34.

Module 9 Maintaining Hardware and Software | Windows

Figure 9-34 Device Manager window

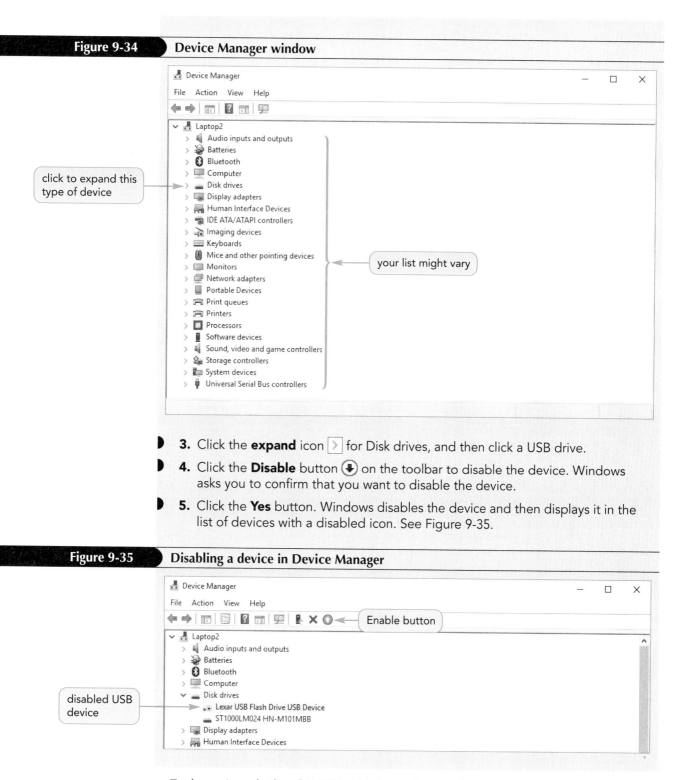

click to expand this type of device

your list might vary

3. Click the **expand** icon ⧉ for Disk drives, and then click a USB drive.

4. Click the **Disable** button ⊕ on the toolbar to disable the device. Windows asks you to confirm that you want to disable the device.

5. Click the **Yes** button. Windows disables the device and then displays it in the list of devices with a disabled icon. See Figure 9-35.

Figure 9-35 Disabling a device in Device Manager

disabled USB device

To determine whether this USB drive is causing problems with your system, you could troubleshoot to see if your system now works properly with this device disabled. Rachel is not having any problems with this USB drive, so you can enable it again.

To enable a disabled device:

▶ **1.** In the Device Manager window, click the disabled USB device, if necessary.

▶ **2.** Click the **Enable** button on the toolbar to enable the device. Windows turns on the device so you can use it.

   Trouble? If an AutoPlay dialog box or a folder window opens, close it.

Another way to troubleshoot a hardware problem is to install or update device drivers.

Installing and Updating Device Drivers

If a hardware device isn't working properly, or if an application that you're installing indicates that it requires newer drivers than you currently have installed, first check Windows Update for updated drivers. Windows Update automatically installs the device drivers you need as it updates your computer. In some cases, such as when technical support personnel ask you to install drivers from the device manufacturer's website, you can also manually update drivers for your device using Device Manager.

To install or update a device driver, you can use the Properties dialog box for the hardware device. The Driver tab in this dialog box lets you update the driver, roll it back to a previous version, disable it, or uninstall it. You can also find out if a driver is signed. If you want to update a driver, you can have Windows search your computer and the Internet for the appropriate files. If you have removable media that contains the updated driver, you can navigate to and install the driver files yourself.

PROSKILLS

Problem Solving: Installing Device Drivers on Your Own

Sometimes you install a device and find that it works well. Then, when you visit the manufacturer's website, you notice that it has provided a newer driver that you can download and install. However, if you're not having any problems with the device, you might not need to download and install that updated driver. Newer drivers are not necessarily better. They might not include any improvements to help your hardware run better. Device drivers that are not available when you use Windows Update typically add support for new products or technologies you don't have. For example, a manufacturer might provide new drivers when it releases new high-speed USB devices. One of the drivers might also support the older USB flash drive that you purchased from the manufacturer. Unless you have one of the new USB flash drives, you probably won't benefit from the new driver. If the driver hasn't been fully tested with your older USB flash drive, it might even cause problems with the hardware.

You'll show Rachel how to check for and manually install an updated driver in case she needs to update a device driver on her own.

To perform the following steps, you need to sign in to Windows using an Administrator account. The USB drive that you worked with in the preceding set of steps should also be available and plugged into a USB port. If you cannot sign in using an Administrator account or if you do not have a USB drive, read but do not perform the following steps.

To update and install a device driver:

▶ **1.** In the Device Manager window, double-click the USB drive to open its Properties dialog box. See Figure 9-36.

Figure 9-36   **Properties dialog box for a USB device**

Driver tab provides driver details and lets you update a driver

device type, manufacturer (if provided), and location

current status of the driver

▶ **2.** Click the **Driver** tab. You can use this tab to find out if a driver is signed, update the driver, roll it back, disable it, or uninstall it. See Figure 9-37.

Figure 9-37   **Driver tab in the device's Properties dialog box**

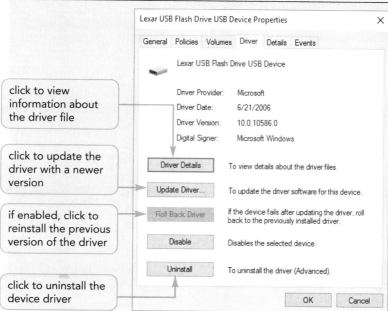

click to view information about the driver file

click to update the driver with a newer version

if enabled, click to reinstall the previous version of the driver

click to uninstall the device driver

▶ **3.** Click the **Driver Details** button. The Driver File Details dialog box opens, displaying the name, location, and other details about the driver file.

▶ **4.** Click the **OK** button to close the Driver File Details dialog box.

▶ **5.** Click the **Update Driver** button. A dialog box opens asking how you want to search for driver software.

▶ **6.** Click **Search automatically for updated driver software**. Windows searches your computer and the Internet for the latest version of the driver software. For Rachel's USB drive, it determines that the best driver software for the device is already installed.

Trouble? If Windows determines that you need to update the driver software for your device, it asks if you want to install the software now. Click the No button.

▶ **7.** Click the **Close** button to close the Update Driver Software dialog box.

▶ **8.** Close all open windows.

Sometimes, installing an updated driver can cause more problems than it solves. In that case, you can restore the driver to a previous version.

Rolling Back a Driver to a Previous Version

If your computer or device has problems after you upgrade a driver, try restoring, or rolling back, the driver to a previous version. In many cases, that solves the problem. To roll back a driver, you use the Roll Back Driver button on the Driver tab of the device's Properties dialog box. (If this button is not available, that means no previous version of the driver is installed for the selected device.) Windows restores the previous version of the driver.

Safely Removing Devices

You can remove, or unplug, most USB devices whenever you like. When unplugging storage devices, such as USB drives, make sure that the computer has finished saving any information to the device before removing it. If the device has an activity light, wait a few seconds after the light stops flashing before unplugging the device.

You know you can remove a USB device when you see the Safely Remove Hardware icon in the notification area of the taskbar. This means that all devices have finished all operations in progress and are ready for you to remove. Click the icon to display a list of devices, and then click the device you want to remove.

Maintaining Your Display Device

When your display device is installed, Windows chooses the best settings for it, including screen resolution, refresh rate, and color. If you start having problems with your display screen or want to improve the quality of its images, you can change the following settings or restore them to their defaults:

- Brightness and contrast—For the best results, you can use a calibration device to adjust brightness, contrast, and color settings. You usually attach the device to the front of your monitor to read light and color levels, and then use a program that came with the device to optimize your monitor's display. You can also adjust brightness and contrast manually (though not as precisely) by using the hardware controls, which are usually available on the keyboard, such as on the function keys.
- Color settings—The number of colors determines how realistic the images look. However, the higher the resolution and color setting, the more resources your display needs; the best settings for your computer balance sharpness and color quality with computer resources. Windows colors and themes work best when you have your display set to 32-bit color.
- Display resolution—You can adjust the screen resolution to improve the clarity of the text and images on your screen. Recall that at higher resolutions, computer images appear sharper. They also appear smaller, so more items fit on the screen. At lower resolutions, fewer items fit on the screen, but they are larger and easier to see. At very low resolutions, however, images might have jagged edges. Recall that for an LCD device, you should use its native resolution.

• Screen refresh rate—To reduce or eliminate flicker, you can adjust the screen refresh rate. If the refresh rate is too low, the images can flicker. Most display device manufacturers recommend a refresh rate of at least 75 Hertz.

Rachel already knows how to adjust the brightness, contrast, and screen resolution. You'll show her how to maintain her display device by adjusting the screen refresh rate and selecting color settings.

Adjusting the Screen Refresh Rate

A flickering screen can contribute to eyestrain and headaches. You can reduce or eliminate flickering by increasing the **screen refresh rate**, which determines how frequently the display device redraws the images on the screen. The refresh rate is measured in Hertz. A refresh rate of at least 75 Hertz generally produces less flicker.

REFERENCE

Adjusting the Screen Refresh Rate

• Right-click the desktop and then click Display settings on the shortcut menu.
• Click the Advanced display settings link.
• Click the Display adapter properties link.
• Click the Monitor tab.
• Click the Screen refresh rate button, and then click a refresh rate.

You might need to change your screen resolution before changing the refresh rate because not every screen resolution is compatible with every refresh rate. The higher the resolution, the higher the refresh rate should be. Recall that to change your screen resolution, you can right-click the desktop, click Display settings on the shortcut menu, click the Advanced display settings link, click the Resolution button, and then click a resolution.

Rachel recently increased the screen resolution on her monitor from 1280 × 720 to 1366 × 768 to improve the clarity of her icons. However, the screen flickers slightly since she changed that setting. You'll show her how to increase the screen refresh rate to reduce monitor flicker.

To change the screen refresh rate:

1. Right-click the **desktop** and then click **Display settings** on the shortcut menu. The System window opens in the Settings app.

2. Click the **Advanced display settings** link to open the Advanced Display Settings window.

3. In the Related settings section, click the **Display adapter properties** link. The Properties dialog box for your display opens.

4. Click the **Monitor** tab to display the monitor settings. See Figure 9-38.

TIP

You can also open the Properties dialog box for your display by opening the Control Panel, clicking Adjust screen resolution, and then clicking Advanced settings.

| Figure 9-38 | Monitor tab in the display's Properties dialog box |

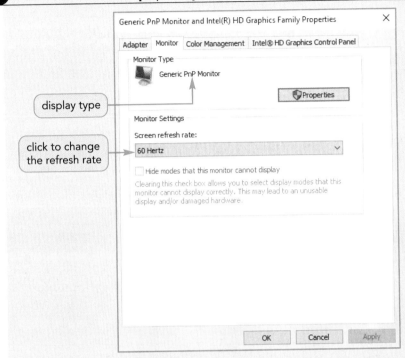

5. Click the **Screen refresh rate** button, and then click **75 Hertz**.

   Trouble? If your list of refresh rates does not include 75, click any other refresh rate that is higher than your current refresh rate.

   Trouble? If you cannot change the screen refresh rate, click a blank spot in the dialog box to close the Screen refresh list, and then skip Steps 5, 6, and 7. Leave the monitor's Properties dialog box open.

6. Click the **Apply** button to apply the new setting. Windows asks if you want to keep these display settings.

7. Click the **Keep changes** button and leave the display's Properties dialog box open.

Next, you'll show Rachel how to manage the color settings on her computer. She is planning to update and print a four-color ad for Place to Place, and she wants to make sure the colors she sees on her monitor are the same colors that print in the ad.

Selecting Color Settings

You can use the Properties dialog box for your display device to make sure that the colors on your monitor match the colors produced on a color printer, for example. To do so, you use the Windows color management settings.

Hardware devices that produce color, such as displays and printers, often have different color characteristics and capabilities. Display screens don't have the same set of colors that a printer can print because each device uses different techniques to produce color on a screen or on paper. Scanners and cameras also have different color characteristics. Even two devices of the same type can display color differently. For example, the LCD screen built into a laptop computer might display shades of color that are different from those displayed on the LCD monitor attached to a desktop computer.

To overcome these differences, Windows uses color management settings and color profiles to maintain consistent colors no matter which device produces the color content. Hardware manufacturers can create a **color profile**, which is a file that describes the color characteristics of a device. Profiles can also define viewing conditions, such as low light or natural light. When you add a new device to your computer, the color profile for that device is included with the other installation files, so you don't need to add or remove a color profile. In addition, the default color management settings almost always produce the best results; therefore, only color professionals, such as compositors and typographers, should change them. However, you can use the Properties dialog box for your display device to verify that your computer is using the default color management settings.

Before Rachel updates and prints her four-color ad for Place to Place, you'll show her how to make sure her computer is using the default settings for color management.

To verify the color management settings:

1. In the Properties dialog box for your display device, click the **Color Management** tab and then click the **Color Management** button. The Color Management dialog box opens to the Devices tab, which identifies your hardware display and lists its color profiles, if any.

2. Click the **Advanced** tab to display the color management settings. See Figure 9-39, which shows all of these settings set to the system default. Your settings might differ.

Figure 9-39	Advanced tab in the Color Management dialog box

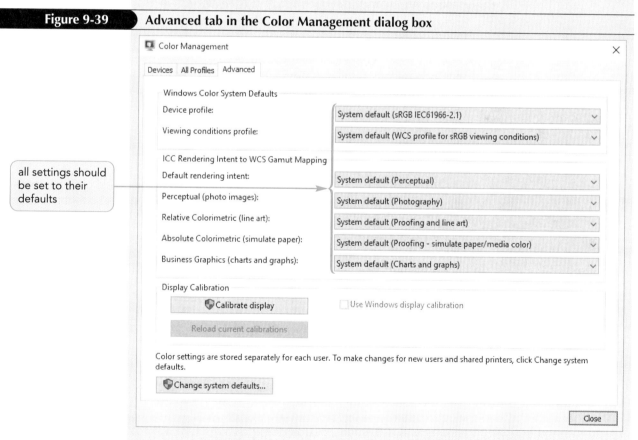

all settings should be set to their defaults

3. Click the **Close** button to close the Color Management dialog box.

4. Click the **OK** button to close the Properties dialog box for your display device, and then close the Advanced Display Settings window.

Now you can turn to the final hardware task: installing and setting up a printer.

Installing and Setting Up a Printer

Before you can print anything from your computer, you need to connect a printer directly to your computer, making it a **local printer**, or create a connection to a network or shared printer. Before using Windows to install a printer, check the installation instructions for your printer. For some printers, you plug the printer into your computer, usually using a USB port, and then Windows detects the new printer and installs its driver. For other printers, you need to install their software first, and then plug in and turn on the printer.

Most printers that you buy today are USB printers, meaning you connect them by plugging the printer's cable into a USB port on your computer. Most also have wireless capabilities, so you can share a printer on your homegroup or wireless Internet connection. Older printers use a parallel cable that connects to your computer's printer port (also called the LPT1 port). If you are installing a second or third printer, you might need to use a parallel cable if you are using the computer's USB ports for other devices.

Installing a Local Printer

Using the printer manufacturer's directions, you attach or connect a local printer to your computer using a cable. In most cases, Windows installs the printer without further action from you. If Windows does not recognize the printer, you can install it yourself.

REFERENCE

Installing a Local Printer

- Follow the printer manufacturer's instructions to connect the printer to your computer.
- If Windows does not automatically detect the printer and install its drivers, click in the Ask me anything box, start to type Printers & scanners, and then click Printers & scanners in the search results.
- Click the Add a printer or scanner button.
- When Windows finds the printer, click its name, and then click the Add device button.

Rachel already uses a laser printer that is connected to her network, and she needs to connect a color printer to her computer using a USB cable plugged into the printer port. You'll show Rachel how to install her Hewlett-Packard color laser printer, which is called HP Color LaserJet 2700 PCL6.

If you are working on a school or organizational network, you probably cannot install a printer on your computer. In that case, read but do not perform the following steps. If you have a printer you can install, substitute the name of the printer, the manufacturer, and printer model as needed in the following steps.

To install a local printer:

▶ **1.** Physically connect your printer to your computer.

   Trouble? If you plugged the printer into a USB port, Windows might detect the printer and install the drivers automatically. In that case, the printer is ready to use. Read but do not perform the following steps.

▶ **2.** If Windows does not detect the printer, click in the **Ask me anything** box, start to type **Printers & scanners**, and then click **Printers & scanners** in the search results. The Devices window opens in the Settings app. See Figure 9-40.

Figure 9-40 | Devices window in the Settings app

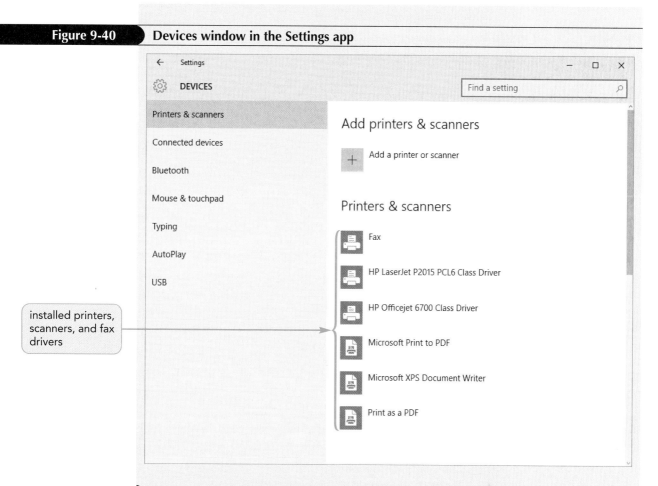

installed printers, scanners, and fax drivers

3. Click the **Add a printer or scanner** button. Windows searches for the connected printer, but does not find the HP Color LaserJet 2700 PCL6 printer.

   Trouble? If Windows finds the printer you connected to your computer, click the printer name, and then click the Add device button. Windows installs the printer. Read but do not perform the following steps.

4. Click **The printer that I want isn't listed**. The Add Printer wizard starts and opens a dialog box that lets you find a printer by other options.

5. Click the **Add a local printer or network printer with manual settings** option button, and then click the **Next** button. The next wizard dialog box opens, where you can choose a printer port.

6. Make sure the Use an existing port option button is selected, and then click the **Next** button. The next wizard dialog box opens, where you can select the manufacturer and model of your printer. See Figure 9-41.

Figure 9-41   **Installing the printer driver**

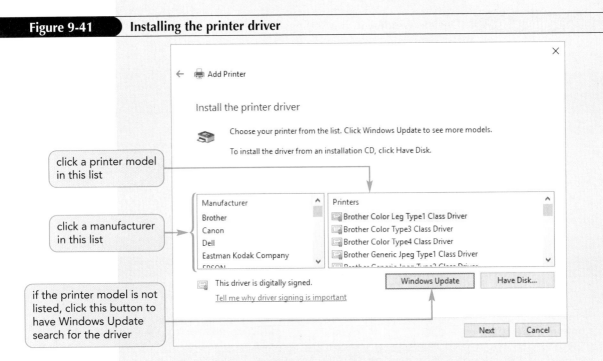

click a printer model in this list

click a manufacturer in this list

if the printer model is not listed, click this button to have Windows Update search for the driver

7. Scroll the Manufacturer list, click **HP**, scroll the Printers list, and then click **HP Color LaserJet 2700 PCL6 Class Driver**.

   Trouble? For the printer you are installing, select the appropriate manufacturer and printer driver from the list.

8. Click the **Next** button. The next wizard dialog box asks you to confirm the printer's name or enter a different one.

9. Click the **Next** button to accept the default name. The final wizard dialog box confirms that the printer is installed and lets you print a test page, if necessary.

   Trouble? If the Printer Sharing window opens, click the Do not share this printer option button, and then click the Next button.

10. Click the **Finish** button.

TIP

To verify that the printer works correctly, click the Print a test page button before clicking the Finish button.

Windows manages the default printer, which is the printer used to print all documents and other files. Windows sets the last used printer as the default printer. If you want to manage the default printer yourself, click the When turned on, the default printer is the last used printer button in the Printers & scanners settings. To change the default printer, click the printer you want to use in the Printers & scanners list, and then click the Set as default button.

Restoring Your Settings

If you are working in a computer lab or on a computer other than your own, complete the steps in this section to restore the original settings on your computer. If a User Account Control dialog box opens requesting an Administrator password or confirmation after you perform any of the following steps, enter the password or click the Yes button.

To restore your settings:

▶ 1. Click in the **Ask me anything** box, type **backup**, and then click **File History settings** in the search results.

▶ 2. In the Back up using File History settings, click the **Automatically back up my files** slider button to turn off File History.

▶ 3. Click the **More options** link, click each location in the Exclude these folders list, and then click the **Remove** button to remove the location from the list. Close the Backup Options window.

▶ 4. Move the **Rachel** folder from the desktop to the Module9 > Module folder provided with your Data Files.

▶ 5. Right-click the **desktop** and then click **Display settings** on the shortcut menu.

▶ 6. Click the **Advanced display settings** link, click the **Display adapter properties** link, and then click the **Monitor** tab.

▶ 7. Click the **Screen refresh rate** button, and then click your original refresh rate, such as 60 Hertz. (Your refresh rates might differ.) Click the **OK** button, and then click the **Keep changes** button to close the Properties dialog box for your display device. Close the Advanced Display Settings window.

▶ 8. Click in the **Ask me anything** box, start to type **Printers & scanners**, and then click **Printers & scanners** in the search results. Click the extra printer you installed in this module, and then click the **Remove device** button. Click the **Yes** button to confirm that you want to remove the device.

▶ 9. Close all open windows.

In this module, you learned how to use the File History feature to back up files and folders automatically and to restore files you've backed up. You created a system recovery drive and then learned how to reset Windows 10. You installed software from the Windows Store and learned how to uninstall an app. To improve system performance, you learned how to check for problems on a hard disk and maintain the devices attached to a computer, including your display device and printer.

REVIEW

Session 9.2 Quick Check

1. How can you display the file system of your hard disk?
2. A computer with more than one operating system is called a(n) _____ computer.
3. What are temporary Internet files?
4. What tool do you use to check a hard disk for file system errors such as bad sectors?
5. A disk that contains files whose clusters are not next to each other is said to be _____.
6. What is a port?
7. Each hardware device requires a(n) _____, a file that enables Windows to communicate with and control the device.
8. In most cases, how do you install a local printer?

PRACTICE

Review Assignments

Data File needed for the Review Assignments: Sales.xlsx

You are now working with Jon Grunwald, the sales manager of Place to Place. He has recently acquired a new Windows 10 computer, and he asks you to show him how to maintain its hardware and software. He is particularly concerned about protecting the photos he uses to advertise the company and its services. Complete the following steps, noting your original settings so you can restore them later:

1. Use File Explorer to create a folder named **Jon** in the Desktop folder on your computer, and then copy the **Sales** file from the Module9 > Review folder provided with your Data Files to the Jon folder.

2. Attach a USB flash drive or an external hard drive you can use for backups by plugging the drive into a USB port on your computer.

3. Display the Backup settings in the Settings app, and then turn on File History, using the USB flash drive or external hard drive you attached in Step 2 as the drive to use for backups.

4. Exclude all locations from the backup except the Desktop, and then set File History to make backups every 10 minutes.

5. Back up your files now. Press the Print Screen key to capture an image of the screen. Paste the image in a new Paint file, and then save the file as **File History** in the Module9 > Review folder provided with your Data Files.

6. Open the **Sales** document, add your name to the beginning of the document, format your name in red, save the document, and then close the application window.

7. Download and install the free StumbleUpon app from the Windows Store. When a notification appears indicating the app has been installed, press the Print Screen key to capture an image of the screen. Paste the image into a new Paint file, and then save the file as **New App** in the Module9 > Review folder provided with your Data Files. Close the Store window.

8. Create a system restore point named **Jon**. Open the System Restore window, navigate to the dialog box displaying the restore points on your computer, and then press the Print Screen key to capture an image of the screen. Paste the image in a new Paint file, and then save the file as **System Restore** in the Module9 > Review folder provided with your Data Files. Close all open windows.

9. Display the amount of free space and used space on your hard disk. With the dialog box open showing this information, press the Print Screen key to capture an image of the screen. Paste the image in a new Paint file, and then save the file as **Free Space** in the Module9 > Review folder provided with your Data Files.

10. Open the Disk Cleanup dialog box for your hard disk, and then choose to clean up only your temporary files (not temporary Internet files). Press the Print Screen key to capture an image of the dialog box with Temporary files selected for clean-up. Paste the image in a new Paint file, and then save the file as **Temp Files** in the Module9 > Review folder provided with your Data Files. Close the Disk Cleanup dialog box without deleting files.

11. Display the schedule for defragmenting your hard disk. Press the Print Screen key to capture an image of the screen. Paste the image in a new Paint file, and then save the file as **Schedule** in the Module9 > Review folder provided with your Data Files. Close all open windows.

12. Open the Device Manager window and expand devices as necessary to display the drives attached to your computer. Disable the USB flash drive. With the Device Manager window open, press the Print Screen key to capture an image of the screen. Paste the image in a new Paint file, and then save the file as **Disable** in the Module9 > Review folder provided with your Data Files. Enable the USB flash drive. Close all open windows.

13. Open the **Sales** document in the Jon folder, add your school's name to the beginning of the document, format your name and the school's name in blue, save the document, and then close the application window.

14. Display the refresh rate of your display device. With the Monitor tab open in the Properties dialog box for your display device, press the Print Screen key to capture an image of the screen. Paste the image in a new Paint file, and then save the file as **Refresh Rate** in the Module9 > Review folder provided with your Data Files. Close the System Restore window without restoring your system. Close all open windows.

15. Install a local printer named **Office** using the Printers & scanners settings in the Settings app. (*Hint*: You can install a local printer even if it is not connected to your computer. Choose any printer driver in the Add Printer wizard.) Do not share the printer or set it as the default. Select the new Office printer, and then press the Print Screen key to capture an image of the screen. Paste the image in a new Paint file, and then save the file as **Office Printer** in the Module9 > Review folder provided with your Data Files.

16. Display the history of the files in the Jon folder. Restore the file that displays your name in red (and does not include your school's name) to the Jon folder.

17. Turn off File History, and then move the Jon folder to the Module9 > Review folder provided with your Data Files.

18. Restore your settings by removing the Office printer from the Printers & scanners list. Open the Start menu, and then uninstall StumbleUpon. Close all open windows.

Case Problem 1

There are no Data Files needed for this Case Problem.

Esprit Dance Academy   Lauren Millard is the owner of the Esprit Dance Academy, which has three studios in Dallas, Texas. She recently hired you to help her automate the academy's business operations and marketing efforts. Lauren has been using a Windows 10 mobile computer for a few months, and she asks you to help her properly maintain its hardware and software. Complete the following steps, noting your original settings so you can restore them later:

1. Start Microsoft Edge, display the Bing home page at bing.com, and then press the Windows+Print Screen keys to capture an image of the Bing window. (*Hint*: The Windows key is the one displaying the Windows logo.) The image is automatically saved in the Screenshots folder in the Pictures folder as a file named Screenshot (x), where x is a number, as in Screenshot (1). You can open File Explorer and navigate to the Pictures folder to make sure the file has been saved. Close Microsoft Edge.

2. Attach a USB flash drive or an external hard drive you can use for backups by plugging the drive into a USB port on your computer.

3. Display the Backup settings in the Settings app, and then turn on File History, selecting the USB flash drive you attached in Step 2 as the drive to use for backups.

4. Exclude all locations from the backup except the Pictures folder. Press the Print Screen key to capture an image of the screen. Paste the image in a new Paint file, and then save the file as **Pictures Backup** in the Module9 > Case1 folder provided with your Data Files.

5. Download and install a free photo-editing app from the Windows Store. When a notification appears indicating the app has been installed, press the Print Screen key to capture an image of the screen. Paste the image in a new Paint file, and then save the file as **Photo App** in the Module9 > Case1 folder provided with your Data Files.

6. Create a restore point named **Lauren**. With the System Restore window open and displaying the restore points on your computer, press the Print Screen key to capture an image of the screen. Paste the image in a new Paint file, and then save the file as **Lauren Restore** in the Module9 > Case1 folder provided with your Data Files. Close the System Restore window without restoring your system.

7. Open the Properties dialog box for your local hard disk. Display all of the disk drives attached to your computer. With the dialog box open showing this information, press the Print Screen key to capture an image of the screen. Paste the image in a new Paint file, and then save the file as **Drives** in the Module9 > Case1 folder provided with your Data Files.

8. Use Device Manager to check for an updated driver for any device on your computer. After checking, press the Print Screen key to capture an image of the dialog box showing the results. Paste the image in a new Paint file, and then save the file as **Update Driver** in the Module9 > Case1 folder provided with your Data Files. If Windows found an updated driver, do not install it.

9. Open the Properties dialog box for your display device, and then display the Color Management settings. Click the All Profiles tab in the Color Management dialog box to display the color profiles installed on your system. Press the Print Screen key to capture an image of the screen. Paste the image in a new Paint file, and then save the file as **Color Profiles** in the Module9 > Case1 folder provided with your Data Files.

10. Display the printers installed on your computer. Select the printer you use most often to display the Set as default button. Press the Print Screen key to capture an image of the screen. Paste the image in a new Paint file, and then save the file as **Default Printer** in the Module9 > Case1 folder provided with your Data Files.

11. Turn off File History, and then move the Screenshot (x) file from the Screenshots folder in the Pictures folder to the Module9 > Case1 folder provided with your Data Files.

12. Restore your settings by uninstalling the photo app you installed in Step 5. Close all open windows.

Case Problem 2

There are no Data Files needed for this Case Problem.

Lightning Delivery   Jake Cermak is the operations manager of Lightning Delivery, a delivery service company in Chapel Hill, North Carolina. You are an office assistant for the company and primarily help Jake perform computer tasks using his Windows 10 computer. Jake recently lost some data during a power failure, so he asks you to help him back up the files. He is also concerned about maintaining the software on his computer. You'll show him how to complete these maintenance tasks. Complete the following steps, noting your original settings so you can restore them later:

1. Attach a USB flash drive or an external hard drive you can use for backups by plugging the drive into a USB port on your computer.

2. Display the Backup settings in the Settings app, and then turn on File History, selecting the USB flash drive you attached in Step 1 as the drive to use for backups.

3. Set File History to back up files every 3 hours. Press the Print Screen key to capture an image of the screen. Paste the image in a new Paint file, and then save the file as **Backup** in the Module9 > Case2 folder provided with your Data Files.

Explore 4. At the bottom of the Backup Options window, click the See advanced settings link to open the File History window in the Control Panel. Press the Print Screen key to capture an image of the window. Paste the image in a new Paint file, and then save the file as **Control Panel** in the Module9 > Case2 folder provided with your Data Files.

Explore 5. At the bottom of the File History window, click the System Image Backup link to open the Backup and Restore (Windows 7) window in the Control Panel, and then click the Create a system image link. After Windows finishes scanning for a backup location, press the Print Screen key to capture an image of the window. Paste the image in a new Paint file, and then save the file as **System Image** in the Module9 > Case2 folder provided with your Data Files. Close all open windows without creating a system image.

6. Open the Store app, and then click a link that displays categories of apps. Select the Navigation & maps category. Press the Print Screen key to capture an image of the screen showing navigation apps. Paste the image in a new Paint file, and then save the file as **Navigation Apps** in the Module9 > Case2 folder provided with your Data Files.

⊕ **Explore** 7. Open the System Restore window, and then choose to show more restore points. Select the first automatic restore point in the list. With the System Restore window open and displaying the restore points on your computer, press the Print Screen key to capture an image of the window. Paste the image in a new Paint file, and then save the file as **Auto Restore** in the Module9 > Case2 folder provided with your Data Files. Close the System Restore window without restoring your system.

8. Open the Programs and Features window in the Control Panel. (*Hint*: Use the Ask me anything box.) Select the first application in the list. Press the Print Screen key to capture an image of the screen. Paste the image in a new Paint file, and then save the file as **Installed** in the Module9 > Case2 folder provided with your Data Files.

9. If you can sign in using an Administrator account, display the partitions on your computer. Press the Print Screen key to capture an image of the page. Paste the image in a new Paint file, and then save the file as **Partitions** in the Module9 > Case2 folder provided with your Data Files.

⊕ **Explore** 10. Start a wizard that allows you to calibrate the color on your display device. (*Hint*: Use the Ask me anything box to open the Display Color Calibration window.) Follow the instructions to calibrate color, read the definition of gamma, and then display a screen where you can adjust gamma. Press the Print Screen key to capture an image of the screen. Paste the image in a new Paint file, and then save the file as **Gamma** in the Module9 > Case2 folder provided with your Data Files.

11. Close all open windows.

Case Problem 3

There are no Data Files needed for this Case Problem.

Silver Spring Kennels Julia Woo is the owner of Silver Spring Kennels in Salem, Oregon. Julia and her staff provide day care and grooming services to dogs and cats in the Salem area. Julia hired you to help her maintain the computer hardware for her company. They frequently use USB drives to save and exchange information about clients and their pets. Complete the following steps, noting your original settings so you can restore them later:

1. Install a USB flash drive or an external hard disk on your computer.

2. Display the amount of free space and used space on the removable disk. With the dialog box open showing this information, press the Print Screen key to capture an image of the window. Paste the image in a new Paint file, and then save the file as **Disk Space** in the Module9 > Case3 folder provided with your Data Files.

3. Open the Error Checking dialog box for the removable disk. Choose to scan the drive even if Windows has not found any errors on the drive. When Windows finishes scanning the drive, press the Print Screen key to capture an image of the screen. Paste the image in a new Paint file, and then save the file as **Scan** in the Module9 > Case3 folder provided with your Data Files.

⊕ **Explore** 4. Display the Optimize Drives dialog box, select your removable disk, and then click the Analyze button. When the analysis is complete, press the Print Screen key to capture an image of the window. Paste the image in a new Paint file, and then save the file as **Analyze** in the Module9 > Case3 folder provided with your Data Files.

⊕ **Explore** 5. Click the ReadyBoost tab in the Properties dialog box for the removable disk. Settings on this tab let you use a USB flash drive to boost your available memory. Test the device, if possible. Even if you cannot test the device, press the Print Screen key to capture an image of the screen. Paste the image in a new Paint file, and then save the file as **ReadyBoost** in the Module9 > Case3 folder provided with your Data Files.

⊕ **Explore** 6. Open the Device Manager window, and then view all of the devices by connection. (*Hint*: Click View on the menu bar, and then click Devices by connection if it is not selected.) Press the Print Screen key to capture an image of the screen. Paste the image in a new Paint file, and then save the file as **Device Connections** in the Module9 > Case3 folder provided with your Data Files. Return the view to Devices by type.

CHALLENGE

⊕ **Explore** 7. Open the Control Panel, and then display the System and Security window. Click Schedule tasks in the Administrative Tools category to explore the settings you can use to start a program according to a schedule (rather than manually from the Settings app, for example). Press the Print Screen key to capture an image of the screen with the Task Scheduler window open. Paste the image in a new Paint file, and then save the file as **Scheduler** in the Module9 > Case3 folder provided with your Data Files.

⊕ **Explore** 8. Open the Devices and Printers window in the Control Panel. Click the Add a printer button on the toolbar. When Windows finishes scanning for printers to install, press the Print Screen key to capture an image of the Devices and Printers window and the Add a printer wizard. Paste the image in a new Paint file, and then save the file as **Printers** in the Module9 > Case3 folder provided with your Data Files.

9. Restore your settings by removing the USB device from your computer. Close all open windows.

Case Problem 4

There are no Data Files needed for this Case Problem.

Van Buren Vision   Darryl Pierce is the manager of Van Buren Vision, an optometry service business with six stores throughout the state of Arkansas. Darryl needs to back up many files for his stores and is interested in online backup services. You work part-time for Van Buren Vision and usually perform data entry, computer hardware maintenance, and other computer-related tasks. Darryl asks you to research online backup services that he can use with the store's Windows 10 computers. Complete the following steps:

1. Use your favorite search engine to research online backup services. Look for answers to the following questions:
    - What tasks do online backup services perform?
    - What types of backups do they create?
    - How do you use an online backup service?
    - How can you access a backup file created by an online backup service?
2. Create a document that provides the answers to the questions in Step 1. Write the answers in two or three paragraphs.
3. In the same document, create a table of popular online backup service providers. Include three columns: Online Backup Service, Web Address, and Notes. Research four online backup services and list them in the table. Add their web addresses to the Web Address column. In the Notes column, describe any services that might set the provider apart from other providers.
4. Save the paragraphs and table in a document named **Online Backups** in the Module9 > Case4 folder provided with your Data Files.

OBJECTIVES

Session 10.1
- Examine system information
- Optimize computer performance
- Monitor system tasks
- Increase memory capacity with ReadyBoost

Session 10.2
- Use the Action Center to respond to notifications
- Troubleshoot typical computer problems
- Use the Steps Recorder
- Manage Remote Assistance

Improving Your Computer's Performance

Enhancing Your System and Troubleshooting Computer Problems

Case | *HealthWeb*

HealthWeb in Tempe, Arizona, develops a mobile app that provides a social network for people with particular chronic diseases and conditions, such as heart disease and arthritis. HealthWeb connects participants to a personal health trainer and a group of other people with the same condition. The health trainer gives fitness and nutrition lessons, group members offer encouragement and advice based on personal experience, and the app provides incentives, tracking tools, and a forum for exchanging information. You work for the HealthWeb Training Department as a computer specialist, and your supervisor is Ryan Kapoor, the company's system administrator. Your job is to help Ryan keep the computers in the HealthWeb Training Department running at peak performance. Ryan is familiar with system maintenance and troubleshooting tools in earlier versions of Windows, but he is new to Windows 10.

In this module, you will improve your computer's performance by optimizing system settings and increasing memory capacity. You'll monitor system performance, respond to notifications in the Action Center, and diagnose and repair computer problems using the Steps Recorder and Remote Assistance.

STARTING DATA FILES

There are no starting Data Files needed for this module.

Session 10.1 Visual Overview:

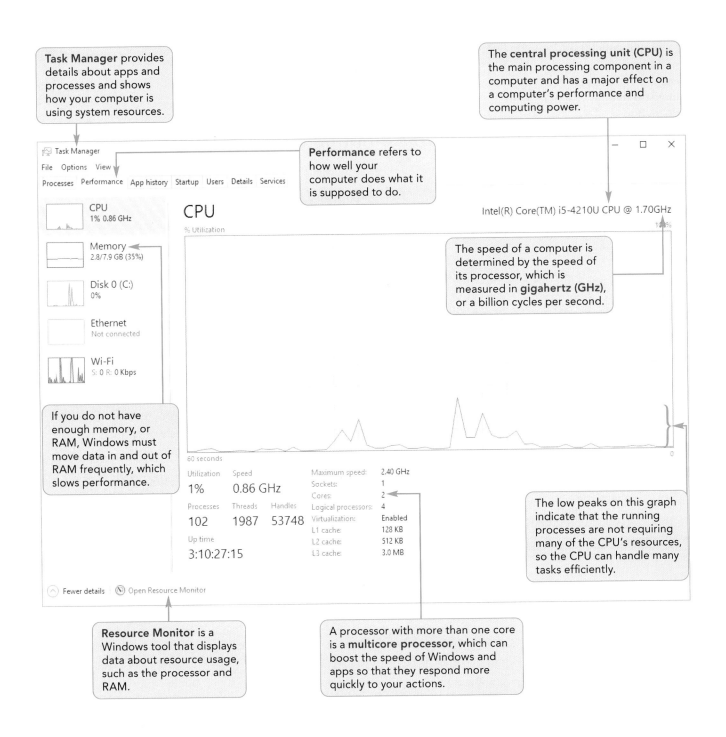

Task Manager provides details about apps and processes and shows how your computer is using system resources.

The **central processing unit (CPU)** is the main processing component in a computer and has a major effect on a computer's performance and computing power.

Performance refers to how well your computer does what it is supposed to do.

The speed of a computer is determined by the speed of its processor, which is measured in **gigahertz (GHz)**, or a billion cycles per second.

If you do not have enough memory, or RAM, Windows must move data in and out of RAM frequently, which slows performance.

The low peaks on this graph indicate that the running processes are not requiring many of the CPU's resources, so the CPU can handle many tasks efficiently.

Resource Monitor is a Windows tool that displays data about resource usage, such as the processor and RAM.

A processor with more than one core is a **multicore processor**, which can boost the speed of Windows and apps so that they respond more quickly to your actions.

Task Manager window

Intel(R) Core(TM) i5-4210U CPU @ 1.70GHz

CPU
% Utilization

CPU	1% 0.86 GHz	
Memory	2.8/7.9 GB (35%)	
Disk 0 (C:)	0%	
Ethernet	Not connected	
Wi-Fi	S: 0 R: 0 Kbps	

60 seconds

Utilization	Speed		Maximum speed:	2.40 GHz
1%	0.86 GHz		Sockets:	1
			Cores:	2
Processes	Threads	Handles	Logical processors:	4
102	1987	53748	Virtualization:	Enabled
			L1 cache:	128 KB
Up time			L2 cache:	512 KB
3:10:27:15			L3 cache:	3.0 MB

Fewer details | Open Resource Monitor

Tracking System Performance

The tasks the processor handles are called **processes**.

The CPU column shows the percentage of processing resources each app and background process requires from the CPU to run, with the total percentage at the top of the column.

Memory, or **random access memory (RAM)**, is short-term memory Windows and apps use to temporarily store data.

The Processes tab shows the current resource usage for each running app and process.

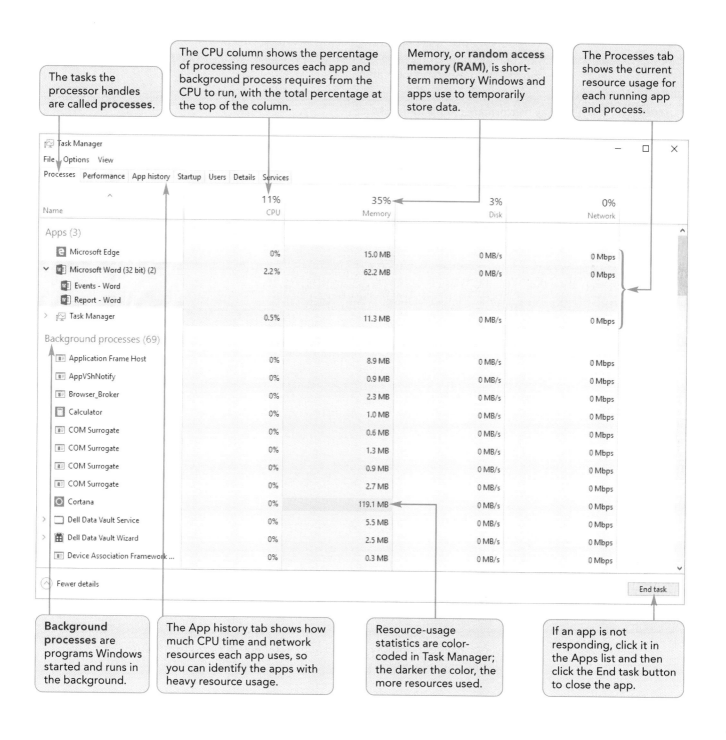

Background **processes** are programs Windows started and runs in the background.

The App history tab shows how much CPU time and network resources each app uses, so you can identify the apps with heavy resource usage.

Resource-usage statistics are color-coded in Task Manager; the darker the color, the more resources used.

If an app is not responding, click it in the Apps list and then click the End task button to close the app.

Improving System Performance

After using your computer for a while, and especially after installing software or saving and deleting files, you might notice changes in your system performance. These changes usually mean that your computer is not as quick to respond to your actions or to perform system tasks as it was when Windows was first installed. In that case, you can improve system performance by identifying the problem, upgrading system components, and completing maintenance tasks. Figure 10-1 describes these tasks and the tools you use to perform them.

Figure 10-1   Performance tools and tasks

Task	Description	Tool
Review system basics	Display basic information about your computer.	System window
View system details	Display information about hardware and software components.	System Information window
Set performance options	Modify how Windows displays visual effects and uses processor and memory resources.	Performance Options dialog box
Identify performance problems	Display details about apps, processes, and system resources such as RAM.	Task Manager dialog box
Track performance details	Display graphs of system performance.	Performance Monitor window
Track resource usage	Collect data about resource usage.	Resource Monitor window
Increase memory	Add memory for Windows and apps using ReadyBoost.	USB drive Properties dialog box

In this module, you explore these tools to help improve the performance of your computer.

Displaying Basic System Information

The speed and performance of individual components determines the overall performance of your computer. The components that affect performance the most are the **processor**, random access memory (RAM), and system type. The first step in maintaining or improving computer performance is becoming familiar with these components and their specifications.

In Windows 10, you can find basic system information in two places: the About settings in the System window of the Settings app and the System window in the Control Panel. Both windows provide the system information described in Figure 10-2.

| Figure 10-2 | Basic system information |

Component or Detail	Description
PC name and organization	Identifies your computer on a network
Windows information	Displays the Windows edition, version, build, and product ID
Processor	Indicates the type and speed of the processor
Installed RAM	Provides the amount of installed RAM
System type	Identifies the operating system as a 32-bit or 64-bit operating system
Pen and touch	Indicates how Windows interacts with a touchscreen if the computer has one

Although Ryan knows his laptop is running Windows 10 Professional, he doesn't know what type of processor the computer uses, how much RAM is installed, or what the system type is. You'll show Ryan how to find basic information about his computer and operating system.

To view system basics:

1. Click in the **Ask me anything** box on the taskbar, type **about**, and then click **About your PC** in the search results. The Settings app starts and displays the About settings in the System window. See Figure 10-3. Your settings will differ.

| Figure 10-3 | About settings in the System window |

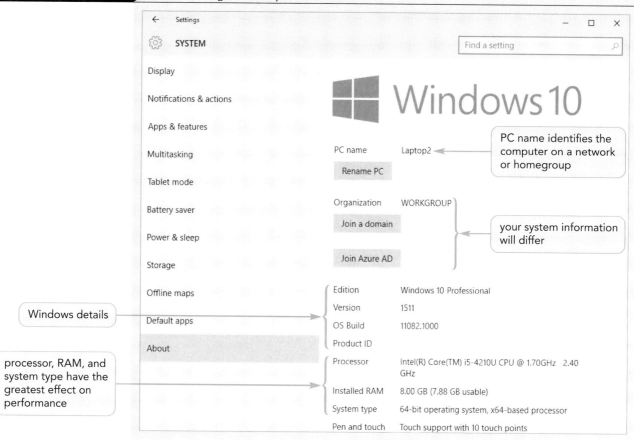

Windows details

processor, RAM, and system type have the greatest effect on performance

▶ **2.** Review the settings, scroll the window to the Related settings section, and then click the **System info** link. The System window in the Control Panel opens. See Figure 10-4.

| Figure 10-4 | System window in the Control Panel |

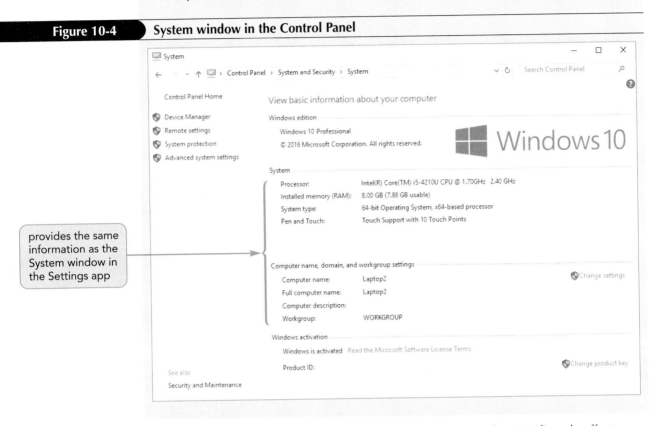

provides the same information as the System window in the Settings app

Both windows provide details about the three components that significantly affect performance. The processor, also called the microprocessor or the central processing unit (CPU), is the main processing component in a computer. Because it contains all the electronic circuitry a computer needs to process data and instructions from the operating system, it has a major effect on a computer's performance and computing power.

The speed of a computer is determined by the speed of its processor, which is called the **clock speed** and indicates the number of instructions the CPU can process per second. Clock speed is measured in megahertz (MHz), or a million cycles per second, and gigahertz (GHz), or a billion cycles per second. (A Hertz is one cycle per second.) A CPU that runs at 2 GHz completes 2 billion clock cycles in one second. Ryan's processor shown in Figures 10-3 and 10-4 is an Intel Core i5 processor running at a minimum of 1.7 GHz with the capacity to run at 2.4 GHz, which provides midrange processing power for contemporary computers.

RAM is short-term memory, also called main memory and primary memory. Data and instructions from apps and Windows are stored temporarily in RAM, which is usually several chips on a circuit board plugged into the motherboard. The amount of RAM in your computer has a significant effect on performance. If you have plenty of RAM, Windows can easily provide RAM as the CPU and apps request it. If you do not have enough RAM, Windows must move data in and out of RAM frequently, which slows performance.

Ryan's computer has 8 GB of RAM. The amount of RAM he needs depends on the types of apps he runs and tasks he performs. A complex multimedia app, for example, uses more RAM than a simple text editor. A computer with 2–4 GB of RAM can handle basic tasks such as browsing the web and exchanging email. A computer with 16 GB of RAM can perform more complex tasks such as video editing and intensive, high-resolution photo editing. The type of tasks Ryan performs falls between those two extremes, so 8 GB of RAM is appropriate for his computer.

In addition to processor speed, the system type also indicates how well the processor performs. The system type is determined by its **bit size**, which indicates how many bytes of data the CPU can retrieve from RAM at once. A byte of data is roughly equivalent to one character, such as x. An 8-bit CPU can process 1 byte at a time, while a 16-bit CPU can process 2 bytes at a time. Modern CPUs are 32-bit (4 bytes at once) and 64-bit (8 bytes at once) processors. An operating system and other software can be designed to take advantage of the processor's bit size. For example, the 64-bit version of Windows handles large amounts of RAM more effectively than the 32-bit version. Ryan's computer is running a 64-bit version of Windows for a 64-bit processor, which is an ideal system type.

After reviewing the basic system information on Ryan's computer, you realize the best way for him to improve performance is to upgrade to a faster processor. Because changing the processor on a laptop can be difficult, you recommend he continue exploring other ways to improve performance on his current computer until he's ready to purchase a new one.

Reviewing Detailed System Information

While the About settings and System window in the Control Panel provide basic system information, the System Information window collects detailed information about your computer system. Advanced users often find it more convenient to use the System Information window to learn additional details about hardware resources, internal components, and software such as drivers and background programs. Computer administrators and technical support experts sometimes need to know these details to troubleshoot a computer problem. You'll show Ryan how to use the System Information window to view hardware information and other system details.

To examine detailed system information:

▶ **1.** Minimize the Control Panel's System window and then close the Settings app.

▶ **2.** Click in the **Ask me anything** box, type **system information**, and then click **System Information** to open the System Information window. By default, this window opens to show a system summary. See Figure 10-5.

Figure 10-5	System Information window

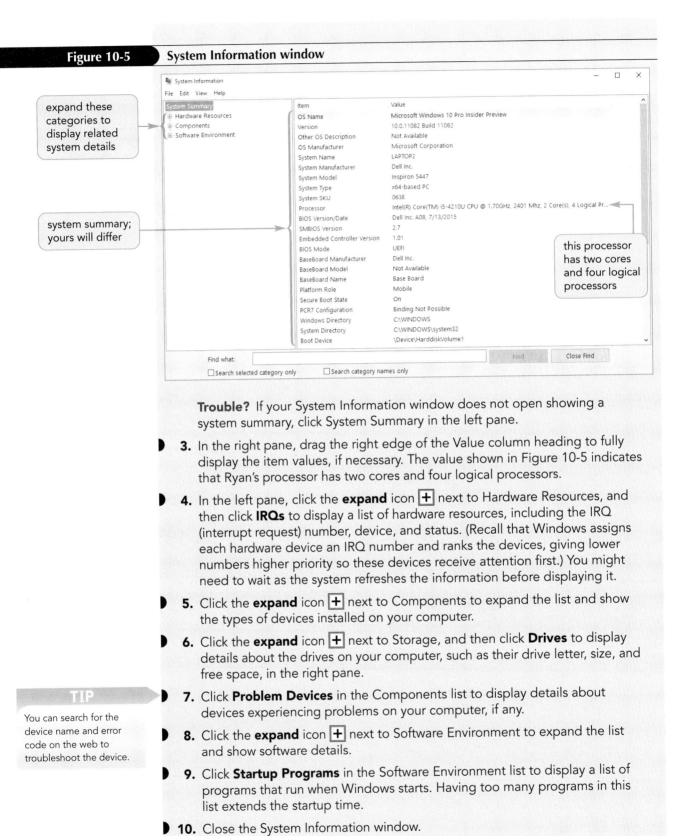

expand these categories to display related system details

system summary; yours will differ

this processor has two cores and four logical processors

Trouble? If your System Information window does not open showing a system summary, click System Summary in the left pane.

3. In the right pane, drag the right edge of the Value column heading to fully display the item values, if necessary. The value shown in Figure 10-5 indicates that Ryan's processor has two cores and four logical processors.

4. In the left pane, click the **expand** icon ⊞ next to Hardware Resources, and then click **IRQs** to display a list of hardware resources, including the IRQ (interrupt request) number, device, and status. (Recall that Windows assigns each hardware device an IRQ number and ranks the devices, giving lower numbers higher priority so these devices receive attention first.) You might need to wait as the system refreshes the information before displaying it.

5. Click the **expand** icon ⊞ next to Components to expand the list and show the types of devices installed on your computer.

6. Click the **expand** icon ⊞ next to Storage, and then click **Drives** to display details about the drives on your computer, such as their drive letter, size, and free space, in the right pane.

TIP

You can search for the device name and error code on the web to troubleshoot the device.

7. Click **Problem Devices** in the Components list to display details about devices experiencing problems on your computer, if any.

8. Click the **expand** icon ⊞ next to Software Environment to expand the list and show software details.

9. Click **Startup Programs** in the Software Environment list to display a list of programs that run when Windows starts. Having too many programs in this list extends the startup time.

10. Close the System Information window.

Instead of selecting items in the left pane of the System Information window, you can also use the Find what box to search for a component such as "startup programs" to display details about that component or process.

The System Information window provides much more information than the System windows. For example, the System Information window indicates that Ryan's processor has two cores and four logical processors. This means that Ryan's processor is a multicore processor, a single chip that contains more than one processor. Specifically, the processor has two cores that can act like four cores when necessary. A multicore processor can boost the speed of Windows and apps so that they respond more quickly to your commands, especially when you are running multiple programs at the same time.

Optimizing Visual Effects

Windows uses visual effects to enhance your computing experience. For example, it shows thumbnails instead of icons to help you identify files in a folder window. It also fades menu items after you click them to reinforce your selection. However, these visual effects consume system resources related to memory and graphics components. If Windows pauses before showing the contents of a folder or displaying a thumbnail for a taskbar button, your computer might be working especially hard to display visual effects. In that case, you can improve performance by displaying some effects and not others using the Visual Effects tab in the Performance Options dialog box. This tab lists settings for visual effects such as animating windows when minimizing and maximizing. It also provides the following four option buttons:

- Let Windows choose what's best for my computer—Allow Windows to select the visual effects to balance appearance and performance for your computer hardware.
- Adjust for best appearance—Use all of the visual effects listed.
- Adjust for best performance—Use none of the visual effects listed.
- Custom—Select only the visual effects you want to use.

Selecting one of the first three options automatically selects or deselects the features listed in the box under Custom.

You'll show Ryan how to turn off window animation to improve performance. You need to be signed in using an Administrator account to adjust visual effect settings. If you cannot sign in with an Administrator account, read but do not perform the following steps.

To adjust visual effect settings:

1. Click the **Control Panel** button 🔲 on the taskbar to display the Control Panel's System window.

2. In the left pane, click **Advanced system settings** to open the System Properties dialog box.

   Trouble? If a User Account Control dialog box opens requesting a password or your permission to continue, enter the password or click the Yes button.

3. On the Advanced tab in the Performance section, click the **Settings** button to open the Performance Options dialog box. See Figure 10-6. Be sure to note the original settings.

Figure 10-6   Performance Options dialog box

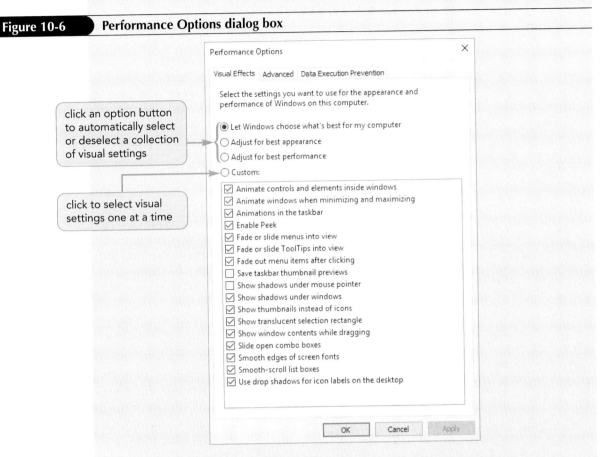

click an option button to automatically select or deselect a collection of visual settings

click to select visual settings one at a time

▶ **4.** Click the **Animate controls and elements inside windows** box to remove the checkmark. This automatically selects the Custom option button at the top of the Visual Effects tab.

▶ **5.** Click the **Animate windows when minimizing and maximizing** box to remove the checkmark.

▶ **6.** Click the **OK** button to change the visual effects Windows uses.

▶ **7.** Close all open windows.

Next, you'll show Ryan how to examine system information and determine how efficiently Windows and apps use the CPU and RAM, important performance indicators.

Using Task Manager to Examine System Information

You can use Task Manager, shown in the Session 10.1 Visual Overview, to view information about the apps and processes running on your computer. For example, you can use Task Manager to monitor your computer's performance or to close an app that is not responding. When you start Task Manager, it shows only the apps running on your computer. You can expand the Task Manager window to display more details, as shown in Figure 10-7.

Figure 10-7   Expanded Task Manager window

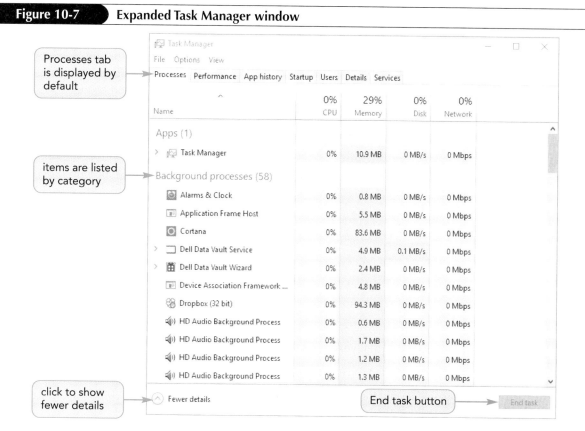

Processes tab is displayed by default

items are listed by category

click to show fewer details

End task button

The expanded Task Manager window contains the tabs described in Figure 10-8.

Figure 10-8   Tabs in the Task Manager window

Task Manager Tab	Description
Processes	Lists the apps and processes running on your computer, including apps that are not responding, and provides resource-usage statistics, which are color coded (the darker the color, the more resources used)
Performance	Provides graphs and statistics about how your computer is using system resources, such as memory and the CPU
App history	Lists details about how apps have used resources such as CPU time and network bandwidth in the past few days
Startup	Lists programs that start when Windows starts and allows you to enable or disable the programs
Users	Identifies the users that are currently signed in to the computer and their status
Details	Provides details about the running apps and processes
Services	Lists current services, which are the background programs or processes that support other programs

You can use some of the tabs in the Task Manager window to troubleshoot system problems and improve performance. For example, the Processes tab displays each active application, background process, and Windows process and groups them by type. If "Not Responding" appears next to an app name on the Processes tab, you can close the app by clicking it and then clicking the End task button or the Restart button. However, closing an application this way discards any unsaved changes you made with that app.

Although viruses and other malware rarely appear as apps or processes on the Processes tab, they sometimes appear as processes on the Details tab. To learn more about a process, you can right-click it on the Details tab, and then click Properties on the shortcut menu. Click the Details tab in the Properties dialog box to view a description of the file, the program with which it's associated, and its copyright information. Often, the Details tab for malware files does not provide any information. You can also search the web for more information about the files listed on the Processes tab and the Details tab. To do so, right-click the file, and then click Search online on the shortcut menu. If you are certain a process is associated with malware, click the file, and then click the End task button. If you don't know the purpose of a process, don't end it. If you end a process associated with an open program, such as a word-processing program, the program closes without saving your data. If you end a process associated with a system service, some part of the system might not function properly.

A **service** is a program or process running in the background that supports other programs; currently running services appear on the Services tab in the Task Manager window. If a process is associated with a service, you can right-click a service on the Services tab, and then click Go to details on the shortcut menu. (This command is available only for services associated with an active process.) The Details tab opens and selects the process associated with that service.

The Performance tab displays graphs to illustrate how your computer is using system resources, including CPU and RAM. If the CPU Usage percentage appears frozen at or near 100%, a program might not be responding. In that case, you should open the Processes tab and end that app as previously described.

You'll explore Task Manager with Ryan to show him the kinds of information it provides. First, start an application so you can track information about it.

> **TIP**
>
> Right-click a column heading in the Task Manager window, and then click Status on the shortcut menu to display the status column, which displays the status of a process or app.

To start and use an application:

▶ 1. Start Microsoft Edge and then go to **bing.com**.

▶ 2. Next, open the Task Manager window.

▶ 3. Right-click the **taskbar** and then click **Task Manager** on the shortcut menu to open the Task Manager window.

▶ 4. If the Task Manager window includes a More details button, click the **More details** button to display all of the tabs, options, and information in a larger Task Manager window. See Figure 10-9. The Apps section lists running apps, including Microsoft Edge and Task Manager. Your list of apps might differ.

Figure 10-9   **Processes tab in the Task Manager window**

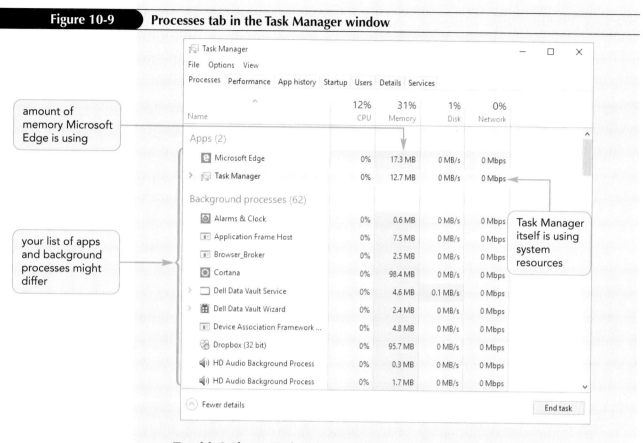

amount of memory Microsoft Edge is using

your list of apps and background processes might differ

Task Manager itself is using system resources

Trouble? If your Task Manager window does not group processes in sections such as the Apps and Background processes, click View on the menu bar, and then click Group by type to select the option.

TIP

Click a column heading to sort the list by that detail.

5. In the Memory column, note the background color and the value for Microsoft Edge, and then scroll down to see background processes and Windows processes using a similar amount or more memory. If you have many high-memory processes running and apps respond slowly to your commands, your computer probably needs more RAM.

6. Click the **Performance** tab to display system performance information, including a graph. By default, this tab displays a CPU graph and statistics. The graph shows how much processing power the system is using every second. See Figure 10-10. Your performance details might differ.

| Figure 10-10 | Tracking CPU usage in the Task Manager window |

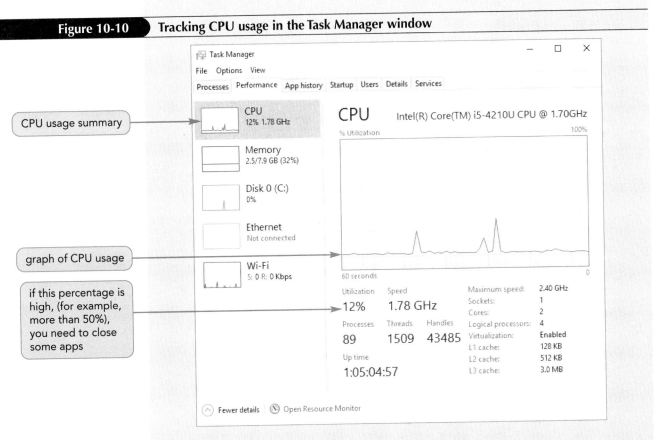

CPU usage summary

graph of CPU usage

if this percentage is high, (for example, more than 50%), you need to close some apps

Typically, CPU usage should not exceed 50 percent for more than a few seconds unless you are running resource-intensive apps such as video games or media-editing programs.

7. Click **Memory** in the left pane to display memory details. Note the amount of memory in use and available.

8. In Edge, open a new tab and go to **microsoft.com**. In the Task Manager window, watch the change in the Memory usage graph and corresponding statistics. See Figure 10-11.

Figure 10-11   Memory details on the Performance tab

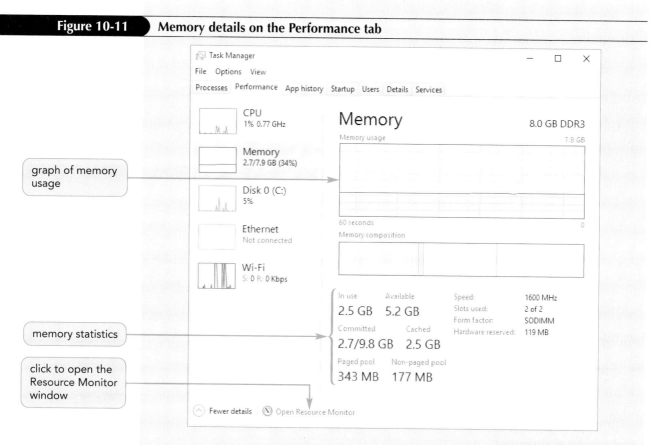

graph of memory usage

memory statistics

click to open the Resource Monitor window

▶ **9.** Close Edge, and then click the **Processes** tab to view the total amount of memory that apps and processes are using, which is smaller than the total amount used when Edge was open.

▶ **10.** Scroll down to the Windows processes section, right-click **Desktop Window Manager**, and then click **Go to details** on the shortcut menu. The Details tab opens and highlights the dwm.exe file. This file helps to manage the desktop and its windows. If you ended this task, your desktop would become unstable. Therefore, you should not disable this process, even if it uses a lot of memory.

▶ **11.** Close the Task Manager window.

Before ending a task or process, research the filename on the web to learn its purpose and whether it's safe to end manually.

Although Task Manager provides information about software running on your computer and displays some resource information, you can track more system performance details using a different tool.

Monitoring System Performance

A common complaint from computer users is that their computer seems to be running more slowly than usual. If you are experiencing this same symptom, too many programs might be running at the same time, causing a loss of performance, or the computer might be low on memory or require an upgrade to a faster processor. To determine the cause, you need to measure the performance of the system in numerical terms. Some of this information is provided in Task Manager. However, you can use **Performance Monitor** to find more detailed performance information and to track it using customized graphs and reports.

REFERENCE

Monitoring System Performance

- Click in the Ask me anything box, type "performance monitor," and then click Performance Monitor in the search results.
- Expand the Monitoring Tools folder in the left pane, if necessary.
- Click Performance Monitor to graph system performance.

When you open the Performance Monitor window, it displays an overview describing the Performance Monitor tool. A system summary provides statistics and other information about memory, your network interface, your physical disk (or hard disk), and processor performance. You can also use Performance Monitor to produce a graph that reflects system performance. See Figure 10-12.

Figure 10-12 Performance Monitor tracking performance indicators

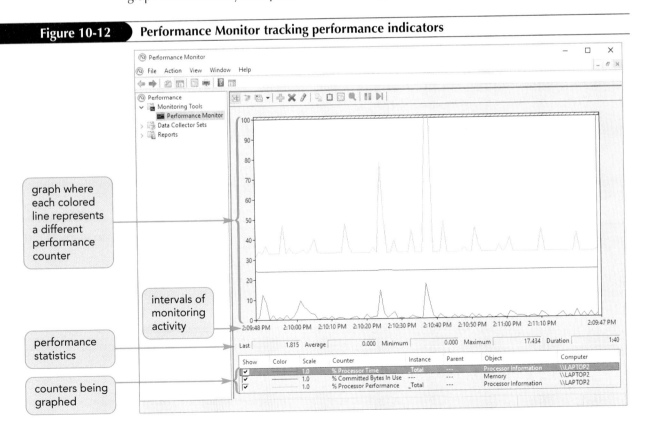

graph where each colored line represents a different performance counter

intervals of monitoring activity

performance statistics

counters being graphed

By default, Performance Monitor tracks the percentage of time your processor is working, which is one measure of how busy your system is. You can also track other performance indicators, such as how fast your computer retrieves data from the hard disk. Tracking performance information can locate the source of trouble in a slow system, and can help you determine what to do to speed up the system.

To track performance indicators other than processor time, you add an item, called a **counter**, to measure a particular part of the system performance and track the values of the counter in the graph. The counter is updated at intervals you specify—usually every few seconds. To add a counter to the graph, you click the Add button on the Performance Monitor toolbar or right-click a counter below the graph and then click Add Counters on the shortcut menu to open the Add Counters window. This window lists performance counters that are included with Windows.

Another common problem that affects performance is low memory. All programs use RAM; so if you have many programs running or are using a program that requires a lot of RAM, Windows might not have enough RAM to run a program. In that case, Windows temporarily moves information that it would normally store in RAM to a file on your hard disk called a **paging file**. The paging file is a hidden file on the hard disk that Windows uses to hold parts of programs and data files that do not fit in RAM. Windows moves data from the paging file to RAM as needed and moves data from RAM to the paging file to make room for new data. Because Windows swaps data in and out of the paging file, it is also known as a swap file. The amount of information temporarily stored in a paging file is called **virtual memory**. Using virtual memory—in other words, moving information to and from the paging file—frees up enough RAM for programs to run correctly.

INSIGHT

Preventing and Solving Low Memory Problems

If you try to open a dialog box or make a selection in an app and the app responds slowly or seems to stop working, your computer is probably low on memory. You can prevent or solve low memory problems by observing the following guidelines:

- Run fewer apps at the same time, especially those that run at startup and those that require lots of memory, as shown in Task Manager.
- Increase the size of the paging file. Windows increases virtual memory the first time your computer becomes low on memory, but you can increase it up to the amount of RAM installed. However, this might cause your apps to run more slowly overall.
- Determine if an app uses too much memory. Track the paging file usage in Performance Monitor or Task Manager when you are running a particular application. If these tools show frequent activity, check for updates to the app and install them.
- Install more RAM. Open the System window to view the amount of RAM your computer has installed, and then look on the computer manufacturer's website to find out if you can install more. Because this solution involves purchasing and installing RAM, try the other solutions first.

You'll show Ryan how to use Performance Monitor to track processor time. In this case, the graph in the Performance Monitor window measures the percentage of time that the processor is not idle. A value near 100% suggests that the processor is almost never idle. If so, that indicates the processor might be so busy that it can't perform tasks efficiently. If a HealthWeb employee reports that a computer is working slowly, you can track the processor time to see if the employee is running too many apps or processes at the same time.

Besides tracking processor time on Ryan's computer, you'll also track the paging file usage to diagnose memory problems. If a HealthWeb employee indicates that a program is responding slowly or that Windows reports a low memory problem, you can track the paging file usage and increase its size, if necessary. (You'll learn how to increase the size of the paging file shortly.)

To perform the following steps, you must be signed in to Windows using an Administrator account. If you are not signed in as an Administrator, read but do not perform the following steps.

To track processor time:

▶ **1.** Click in the **Ask me anything** box, begin typing **performance monitor**, and then click **Performance Monitor** in the search results. The Performance Monitor window opens.

▶ **2.** In the left pane, expand the Monitoring Tools folder, if necessary, and then click **Performance Monitor**. The Performance Monitor graph appears in the right pane, tracking the percentage of time that the processor is in use each second. See Figure 10-13. The graph on your computer will show different activity.

Figure 10-13	Tracking processor time

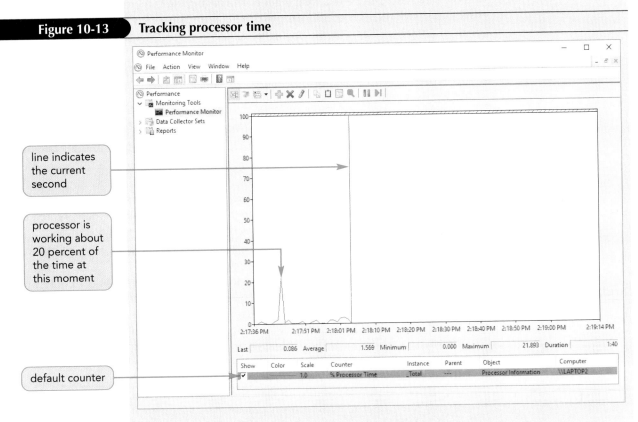

line indicates the current second

processor is working about 20 percent of the time at this moment

default counter

▶ **3.** Below the graph, right-click the **% Processor Time** counter, and then click **Add Counters** on the shortcut menu. The Add Counters dialog box opens. See Figure 10-14.

Figure 10-14 | Adding a counter to the Performance Monitor

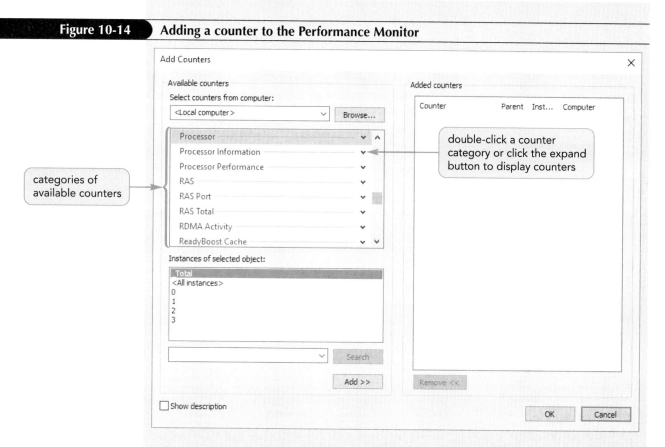

4. Scroll the Available counters list, and then double-click **Paging File**. Details you can track appear below the Paging File entry.

5. Click **% Usage** and then click the **Add** button to use that counter.

6. Click the **OK** button. The Performance Monitor begins tracking paging file usage.

The graph shows that the paging file usage on Ryan's computer is steady. This number usually increases when you start a program that uses many system resources, such as a Microsoft Office program. If the paging file usage does not decrease by that same amount when you close the program, the program leaves temporary files or processes open in memory, which can cause problems. Windows usually recovers that memory after a few minutes of idle time. If it does not, a temporary solution is to restart your computer to clear everything from RAM and make the maximum amount of memory available to your computer. The long-term solution is to install updates to the program that is not handling memory efficiently.

The Performance Monitor on Ryan's computer is tracking two system indicators, but both lines in the graph are red. You'll show Ryan how to change the % Usage counter to a contrasting color so he can distinguish one counter from the other.

To change the color of the % Usage counter:

1. Below the graph, right-click the **% Usage** counter, and then click **Properties** on the shortcut menu. The Performance Monitor Properties dialog box opens to the Data tab.

2. Click the **Color** button and then click **blue** (the third color from the top of the list).

3. Click the **OK** button. The % Usage indicator line is now displayed in blue. See Figure 10-15. Because Windows does not need to use the paging file often on Ryan's computer, the % Usage indicator line is difficult to see, indicating that Ryan has plenty of RAM for the current tasks.

| Figure 10-15 | Tracking paging file usage |

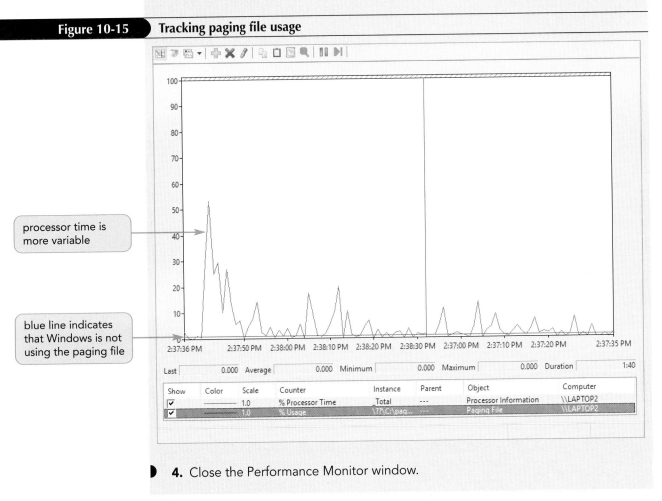

processor time is more variable

blue line indicates that Windows is not using the paging file

4. Close the Performance Monitor window.

You'll use the Performance Monitor window again later in this session to generate a System Diagnostics report.

Decision Making: Selecting a Tool to Solve Performance Problems

A computer's performance normally decreases over time as you install programs and save files. However, if a computer is performing so slowly that it significantly affects your productivity, you need to know how to identify and solve the problem. You might need to add memory, remove a troublesome device driver, or replace the entire system. How do you know what to do to fix the problem? Start by using Performance Monitor and Task Manager. Each one is designed to provide certain types of information.

Performance Monitor is the main tool you use to diagnose problems with system performance. System administrators typically use Performance Monitor with a new system to set **baselines**, which are starting points used for comparisons. System administrators select key counters for memory, the network interface, the paging file, the physical disk, and the processor. They graph them a few times during a typical day and then save the graph and data. You can also set baselines to create a record of your computer when it is performing well. If you notice your computer is working more slowly than normal, select the same counters and graph them again. Then, compare the baseline information to the new information to diagnose the problem. For example, the **Pages/Sec counter** shows how often the system accesses the paging file. In a high-performing system, this value is zero or close to zero. Having consistently high values probably means that your system does not have enough RAM, so adding RAM could solve the performance problem. Performance Monitor's drawback is that it includes hundreds of counters. Although you can search online for information about each one, you need to understand what each counter measures to accurately interpret the data, which takes time and technical knowledge.

Task Manager provides a simplified version of Performance Monitor. Although Task Manager does not save information so you can compare it later, the Performance tab provides immediate and clear information related to system performance. For example, when you click Memory on the Performance tab, the Committed values show how many demands programs and files are making on available memory resources. If the first Committed value is close to the second one, close applications and large files to improve performance. As with the Performance Monitor counters, you can search online for more information about the values on the Performance tab.

Windows provides another advanced tool for tracking system performance, which is called Resource Monitor.

Using Resource Monitor

Another tool you can use to measure system performance is Resource Monitor. On the Overview tab of the Resource Monitor window, you can view four graphs to track the usage of the CPU, disk, network, and memory as your computer is using these resources. The Overview tab also includes four bars—one for each system resource. You can click a bar or an expand button to display details about each resource. For example, click the CPU bar to display a summary of processor usage. See Figure 10-16.

Figure 10-16   Overview tab in the Resource Monitor window

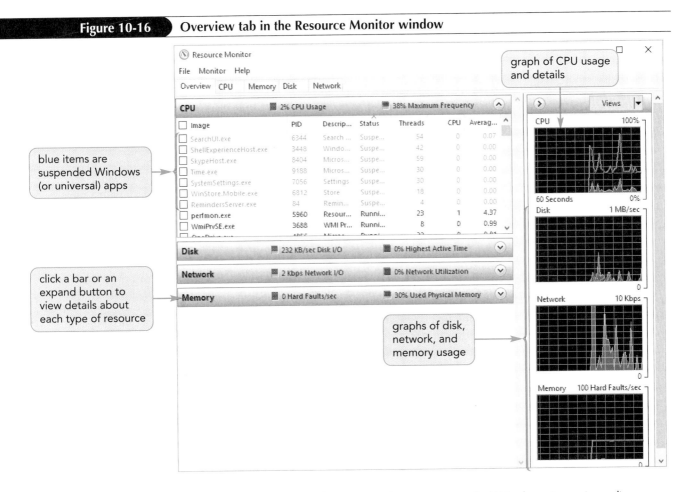

blue items are suspended Windows (or universal) apps

click a bar or an expand button to view details about each type of resource

graph of CPU usage and details

graphs of disk, network, and memory usage

The blue items listed in the CPU section are suspended Windows (or universal) apps. Windows suspends these apps so that they do not use CPU resources unless they are active, which is especially useful on a mobile device.

The CPU graph shows how much of the CPU is being used. A high percentage of CPU usage means that the currently running apps or processes are consuming most of the available CPU resources, which can slow the performance of your computer. If the CPU usage appears frozen at or near 100%, look for apps that are not responding. Click the CPU bar to view the processes, or images, that are using CPU resources.

The Disk graph and bar reflect program activity on your hard disk, measured by the number of times a program reads (retrieves) data from the hard disk or writes (stores) data on the hard disk. Click the Disk bar to see which files are reading or writing data to your hard disk.

The Network graph and bar indicate the amount of network activity your computer is experiencing, measured in kilobytes per second (Kbps). Click the Network bar to see the network address of the programs exchanging information with your computer.

The Memory graph and bar display the percentage of RAM currently being used and the number of hard faults occurring per second. A **hard fault**, or **page fault**, occurs when a program retrieves data from RAM and stores it in virtual memory, which is an area on the hard disk. If a program is responding slowly to your commands, look in the Memory graph and bar for a high number of hard faults, which indicates that the program is continually reading data from disk rather than RAM.

Ryan wants to know what to do if HealthWeb employees report that their computers are suddenly running more slowly than normal. You'll show him how to open the Resource Monitor window and view the resources Windows is currently using to diagnose the problem with an employee's computer.

TIP

You can use Task Manager to stop nonresponsive apps by clicking the app and then clicking the End task button.

To perform the following steps, you must be signed in to Windows using an Administrator account. If you are not signed in to Windows as an Administrator, read but do not perform the following steps.

To examine an overview of resource usage:

▶ **1.** Click in the **Ask me anything** box, type **resource monitor**, and then click **Resource Monitor** in the search results. Click the **Overview** tab, if necessary, to display an overview of system resources.

▶ **2.** Click the **Memory** bar to display details about memory usage. For example, explorer.exe is File Explorer, which typically uses more memory than other processes. It should appear near the top of the Memory list.

▶ **3.** Close the Resource Monitor window.

The resources on Ryan's computer do not indicate any performance problems. However, you and Ryan can track these resources to diagnose problems for the HealthWeb employees when necessary.

Next, you'll show Ryan how to use another advanced tool to diagnose system problems—a System Diagnostics Report.

Generating a System Diagnostics Report

To have Windows collect data about your system and diagnose any problems, you can generate a report titled "System Diagnostics Report." This report includes a number of sections. The first section identifies the computer, the date of the report, and the length of time Windows spent collecting the data for the report. The second section, Diagnostic Results, is especially helpful to system administrators. This section has two subsections: The Warnings section lists problems found on the computer, if any, and assigns them a severity level, such as Critical or Warning. The Performance section shows the results of basic system checks, such as a survey of the attributes of the operating system, and a resource overview, such as CPU and network usage. The Software Configuration and Hardware Configuration sections provide details about these checks. Also included are the CPU, Network, Disk, and Memory sections, with Report Statistics, the last section, listing details about the computer, files, and events.

Because Ryan's system is performing well right now, you'll generate and save a System Diagnostics Report to use as a baseline so he has a snapshot of the computer's performance when it's running at a normal level. When the system has problems, Ryan can generate another System Diagnostics Report to compare to the baseline report. Using baseline reports, he can anticipate and then prevent problems.

Because the System Diagnostics Report collects performance data, you generate the report using the Performance Monitor window.

To generate a System Diagnostics Report:

▶ **1.** Click in the **Ask me anything** box, type **performance monitor**, and then click **Performance Monitor** in the search results to open the Performance Monitor window.

▶ **2.** In the left pane, expand the **Reports** folder, expand the **System** folder, and then expand the **System Diagnostics** folder.

Trouble? If you receive the message "There is nothing displayed in this view," expand the Data Collector Sets folder, expand the System folder, right-click Systems Diagnostics in the right pane, and then click Start on the shortcut menu. The name of your computer should now appear in the System Diagnostics folder. Continue with Step 3.

TIP

To create a hard copy of the System Diagnostics Report, click the **Print** button on the toolbar.

3. In the System Diagnostics folder, click the name of your computer. The Performance Monitor window displays a progress bar as Windows collects data about your system for 60 seconds. When it's finished collecting data, Windows generates and displays the System Diagnostics Report. See Figure 10-17.

Figure 10-17	System Diagnostics Report

4. Close the Performance Monitor window.

You now want to show Ryan useful ways to increase memory capacity by adjusting the size of the paging file and using a feature called ReadyBoost with a USB drive.

Increasing Memory Capacity

If you receive system warnings that your virtual memory is low, you can increase the minimum size of your paging file. Windows sets the initial minimum size of the paging file to the amount of RAM installed on your computer plus 300 MB. It sets the maximum size at three times the amount of RAM installed on your computer. If you see warnings at these recommended levels, then increase the minimum and maximum sizes.

Although Ryan has not been receiving messages about virtual memory, you'll show him how to increase the minimum and maximum size of the paging file for future reference. To do so, you use the Performance Options dialog box, which is the same dialog box you used to select visual effects.

To increase the size of the paging file:

1. Click in the **Ask me anything** box, type **advanced system**, and then click **View advanced system settings** in the search results to open the System Properties window.

2. In the Performance section, click the **Settings** button.

3. Click the **Advanced** tab to display paging file information. See Figure 10-18.

Figure 10-18 Advanced tab in the Performance Options dialog box

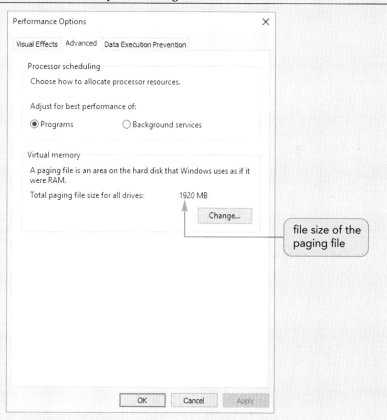

file size of the paging file

4. Click the **Change** button to open the Virtual Memory dialog box. See Figure 10-19.

Figure 10-19   **Virtual Memory dialog box**

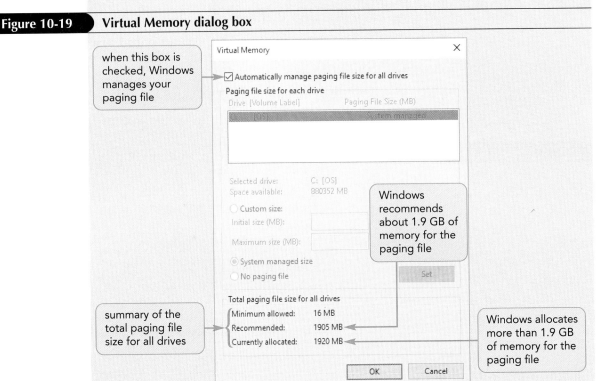

If Ryan wanted to manage the paging file size himself, he could click the Automatically manage paging file size for all drives box to remove the check mark, click the drive he wants to manage, click the Custom size option button, enter the initial (minimum) and maximum size for the paging file, and then click the Set button. However, managing the size of the paging file manually can make the system unstable, so it's best to let Windows manage the file.

▶ 5. Click the **Cancel** button to close the Virtual Memory dialog box without making any changes.

▶ 6. Click the **OK** button to close the Performance Options dialog box, and then click the **OK** button to close the System Properties dialog box.

The Virtual Memory dialog box shows that Ryan has slightly more space for the paging file than Windows recommends. If Windows needs more space for the paging file on all drives due to patterns of computer usage, it will increase the size of the paging file.

Using ReadyBoost to Increase Memory Capacity

ReadyBoost is a Windows tool that can use storage space on some removable media devices, including USB drives, to speed up your computer. When you insert a device with this capability, the AutoPlay dialog box offers you the option to speed up your system using ReadyBoost. If you select the ReadyBoost option, you can then choose how much memory to use for this purpose, up to a maximum of 32 GB of additional memory on a single removable media device.

In some situations, you might not be able to use all of the memory on your storage device to speed up your computer. If your computer has a hard disk that uses solid-state drive (SSD) technology, it might be too fast to benefit from ReadyBoost. In this case, the

AutoPlay dialog box does not provide a ReadyBoost option. Some USB storage devices contain both slow and fast flash memory, and Windows can only use fast flash memory to speed up your computer. If your device contains both slow and fast memory, keep in mind that you can only use the fast memory portion for this purpose. USB drives eventually wear out after a certain number of uses, so using ReadyBoost can wear out the USB drive, although it generally takes a few years.

Keep in mind that ReadyBoost is not a replacement for an adequate amount of system memory. Investing in additional RAM is a sure way to improve computer performance. In addition, ReadyBoost is not a replacement for the paging file. ReadyBoost works with the paging file to maximize the amount of memory your computer can use. For certain types of tasks, ReadyBoost provides extra memory that the computer can access much more quickly than it can access data on the hard drive. For other types of tasks, Windows uses the paging file more efficiently.

The recommended amount of memory to use for ReadyBoost acceleration is one to four times the amount of RAM installed in your computer. For instance, if your computer has 2 GB of RAM and you plug in an 8 GB USB flash drive, dedicating from 2 GB to 6 GB of that drive to ReadyBoost offers the best performance boost. If you reserve less than the total capacity of the removable drive for ReadyBoost, you can use the remaining space for storing files.

You can turn ReadyBoost on or off for a USB drive or other removable storage device, as long as the removable media device contains at least 256 MB of space to work with ReadyBoost. The USB drive must also support USB 2.0 or higher. Windows indicates whether the USB drive you want to use is suitable for ReadyBoost.

You will show Ryan how he can use ReadyBoost to access extra memory when he needs it. To perform the following steps, you need a USB drive that has at least 1 GB of free space. If you do not have such a device, read but do not perform the following steps.

To use ReadyBoost:

1. Plug a USB drive into an available USB port on your computer. A notification appears asking what should happen with removable drives. See Figure 10-20.

Figure 10-20   Removable drive notification

click the notification to select what you want to do with your USB drive

Removable Disk (D:)
Tap to choose what happens with removable drives.

6:52 PM
12/29/2018

Trouble? If a notification does not appear, open File Explorer, right-click the USB drive, click Properties, and then click the ReadyBoost tab. Skip Steps 2 and 3.

2. Click the notification, and then click **Open File Explorer** to open File Explorer with the USB drive selected in the navigation pane.

▶ **3.** Right-click the USB drive in the navigation pane, and then click **Properties** on the shortcut menu to open the Properties dialog box for the USB drive. If necessary, click the ReadyBoost tab. See Figure 10-21.

Figure 10-21 ▶ **ReadyBoost tab in the Properties dialog box for a USB drive**

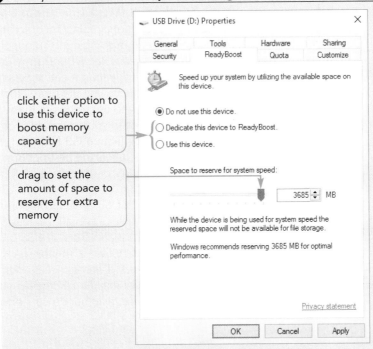

click either option to use this device to boost memory capacity

drag to set the amount of space to reserve for extra memory

▶ **4.** Click the **Use this device** option button to turn on ReadyBoost.

▶ **5.** Drag the slider to the far right, if possible, to select the maximum amount of available space on your USB drive to reserve for boosting your system speed.

▶ **6.** Click the **OK** button. A ReadyBoost icon, indicating the size of the increased memory, appears in the File Explorer window.

▶ **7.** Close all open windows. Keep the USB drive attached to your computer until you restore your system.

Each time Ryan attaches that USB drive to his computer, he will have more than 3 GB of extra memory that Windows can use to improve system performance. The settings you select on the ReadyBoost tab apply to that USB drive until you change them.

REVIEW

Session 10.1 Quick Check

1. What are the three components that most affect computer performance?
2. The speed of a CPU is called the _____ and indicates the number of instructions the CPU can process per second.
3. Which version of Windows handles large amounts of RAM more effectively, the 32-bit version or the 64-bit version? Explain why.
4. What is the drawback of closing an unresponsive app in Task Manager using the End task button?
5. The _____ is a hidden file on the hard disk that Windows uses to hold parts of programs and data files that do not fit in RAM.
6. Why would you use Performance Monitor to set baselines for counters when your computer is performing well?
7. What is ReadyBoost?

Session 10.2 Visual Overview:

Microsoft Support is a website that provides step-by-step instructions, videos, and articles about using Microsoft products.

The **Microsoft Community** is a website that hosts forums of users and Microsoft experts where you can search, browse, and post questions and answers.

Action Center collects notifications that request a response.

Security and maintenance notifications also appear in the Security and Maintenance window.

Respond to a notification by clicking it; Windows opens the appropriate app or setting for fixing the problem.

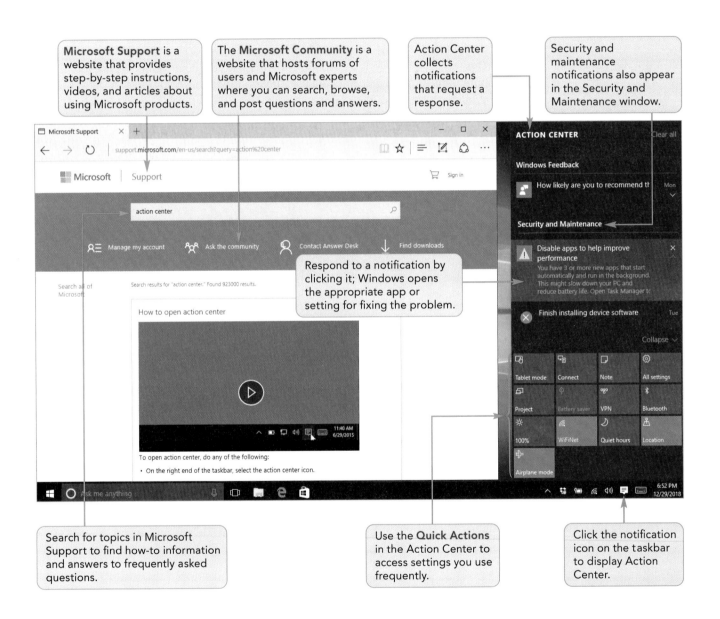

Search for topics in Microsoft Support to find how-to information and answers to frequently asked questions.

Use the **Quick Actions** in the Action Center to access settings you use frequently.

Click the notification icon on the taskbar to display Action Center.

Solving System Problems

Click to choose the types of system problems for which Windows sends Microsoft a **problem report**, a set of technical information about the problem.

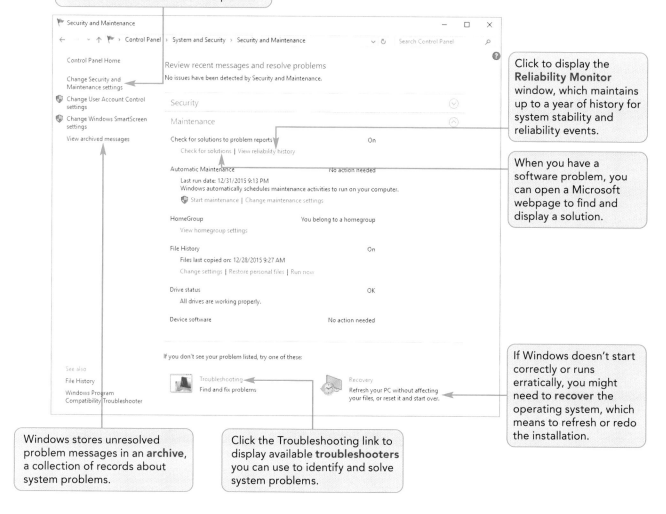

Click to display the **Reliability Monitor** window, which maintains up to a year of history for system stability and reliability events.

When you have a software problem, you can open a Microsoft webpage to find and display a solution.

If Windows doesn't start correctly or runs erratically, you might need to **recover** the operating system, which means to refresh or redo the installation.

Windows stores unresolved problem messages in an **archive**, a collection of records about system problems.

Click the Troubleshooting link to display available **troubleshooters** you can use to identify and solve system problems.

Responding to Notifications

When your computer system wants your attention, Windows displays a notification, a small message that appears in the lower-right part of the desktop. When you plugged a UBS drive into a port in the previous session, a notification probably appeared. If you do not have a chance to respond to the notification and it requests a response, Windows stores it in the Action Center, a panel that appears on the right side of the desktop when you click the notification icon on the taskbar. See Figure 10-22.

Figure 10-22   Action Center

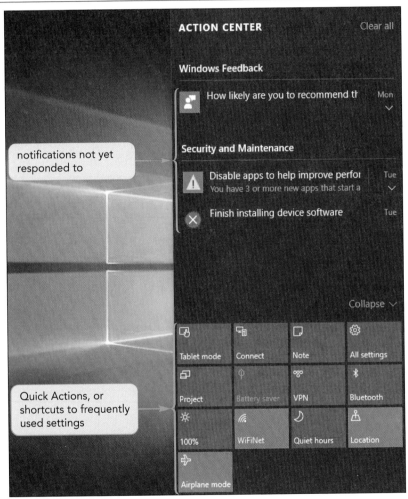

To expand a notification, click its arrow button, as shown in Figure 10-23. To respond to a notification, click it in the Action Center. Windows opens the app or setting that lets you respond appropriately. For example, if you click the notification shown in Figure 10-23, which recommends changing startup settings to improve performance, Windows opens the Task Manager with the Startup tab displayed so you can disable the startup apps as the notification recommends. To close a single notification, click its Close button. To close all notifications, click the Clear all link.

Figure 10-23 Managing a notification

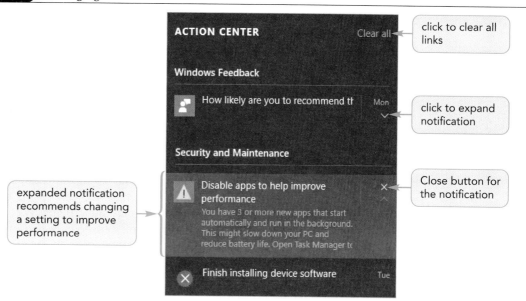

Although you always receive notifications from Windows about potential problems, the app notifications you receive vary depending on the app. For example, the News app displays headlines for breaking news stories and Calendar displays appointment details. Your response depends on the content. Some notifications, such as those that appear when you insert a USB drive, require only an immediate response, so they are not stored in Action Center if you don't respond to them. In the System window of the Settings app, you can choose whether to receive notifications from apps, and if so, which apps. You can also choose notification settings for a particular app. For example, you can have Mail play a sound when a new message arrives, which is the default, or you can turn off the sound.

You use the Quick Actions in the Action Center to access settings you use frequently. For example, you can control the brightness of the display, connect to a network, or use **Quiet hours**, a setting that temporarily disables notifications, which you might want to do while you are watching a movie or concentrating on a computer project, for example. Click the Quiet hours tile again to turn it on so you can continue to receive system notifications.

Finding Troubleshooting Information

Receiving a notification is usually the first sign that Windows encountered a problem with its apps and settings, your computer, or other hardware. If clicking the notification and changing a setting according to the notification's recommendation does not solve the problem, look for troubleshooting information. You can find troubleshooting information in at least two resources: the Troubleshooting window in the Control Panel and the Microsoft Support webpage. You have already used a troubleshooter to identify and solve power problems. You can use similar troubleshooters if you have problems with programs, hardware devices, networking and the Internet, and system and security tools.

REFERENCE

Using a Troubleshooter

- Click in the Ask me anything box on the taskbar, start to type "troubleshooting," and then click Troubleshooting in the search results.
- In the list of troubleshooters, select a troubleshooter; or click a category, and then select a troubleshooter.
- Follow the instructions in the troubleshooter dialog boxes.

The Microsoft Support webpage includes links to the Answer Desk, which provides information about common questions, and to the Microsoft Community website, which hosts forums for users and Microsoft experts where you can search, browse, and post questions and answers. The Microsoft Community site provides access to support articles and videos that provide troubleshooting steps to help you solve or identify a problem. You need a Microsoft account to participate in the Microsoft Community website, though you can read questions and answers without one. You can also use a search engine to search the web for troubleshooting advice. Look for information from established experts, and never download a file unless you know and trust the source.

PROSKILLS

Problem Solving: Troubleshooting System Problems

When you suspect a problem on your computer, take a systematic approach to solving it. Complete the following problem-solving steps so you can troubleshoot problems thoroughly and consistently.

- Define the problem—Describe the trouble that you observe, being as specific as possible. For example, if you are having trouble printing, note when the trouble occurs, such as when you try to print from a particular program or with a certain print setting.
- Identify possible causes—Look for obvious causes first, such as a loose cable connecting a printer to your computer. Next, determine when the system was last performing normally and what has changed since then. Did you download and install a new driver from Windows Update? Did you install new hardware? These are possible causes of the problem.
- Test the causes—For each cause, determine what you can do to see if it is the source of the problem. For example, if you suspect a loose cable is causing printing problems, reconnect the cable. If you installed a new printer driver, try reverting to a previous version. You can solve most computer problems by systematically testing each cause.
- Find additional help—If the problem persists, refer to other resources for solutions. For example, does the Devices and Printers window or the Device Manager window display a message about the printer? Does Windows Help and Support provide information about the problem or a similar one? Can you find possible solutions on the printer manufacturer's website?
- Apply solutions—As you did when testing causes, try each solution you find, starting with the solutions that affect your system the least. For example, try installing a new printer driver before using System Restore to restore your system. Before you make any major changes to your computer, set a system restore point and back up your data so you don't lose important work.

Using Troubleshooters to Find and Fix Computer Problems

Windows provides a collection of automated troubleshooters for detecting and solving dozens of computer problems. When you run a troubleshooter, it might ask you some questions or reset common settings as it works to fix the problem. If the troubleshooter fixes the problem, you can close the troubleshooter dialog box. If it can't fix the problem, you can display options and then go online to find an answer. In either case, you can display a complete list of changes the troubleshooter made.

The first dialog box in each troubleshooter includes an Advanced link. Click this link to display a selected Apply repairs automatically check box. You can clear this check box to select a solution from a list of fixes instead of applying them automatically.

Ryan wants to train HealthWeb employees to troubleshoot typical computer problems, such as those involving the computer system, network connections, and security. One particular problem employees have experienced involves searching for files. When using Cortana to search for files, some employees report that Cortana is not finding a file, though the employee is certain the file is stored on the hard disk. This problem is most likely related to search and indexing settings.

Recall that you can set indexing options to help you find files on your computer. When Windows indexes a folder, it keeps track of details for the files the folder contains. Windows can then scan the indexed information rather than the file contents so it can find files quickly. However, HealthWeb employees notice that indexing sometimes slows the computer as it runs in the background. You'll show Ryan how to run a troubleshooter that can detect and fix problems with searching and indexing.

To troubleshoot search and indexing problems:

▶ **1.** Click in the **Ask me anything** box, start to type **troubleshooting**, and then click **Troubleshooting** in the search results to open the Troubleshooting window.

▶ **2.** Click **System and Security** to display a list of system and security troubleshooters. See Figure 10-24.

Figure 10-24	**Troubleshooters for solving system and security problems**

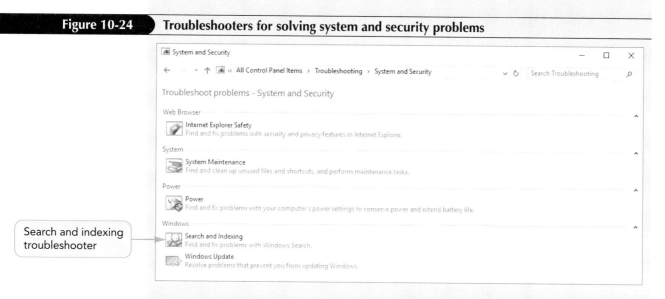

Search and indexing troubleshooter

▶ **3.** Click **Search and Indexing** to start the Search and Indexing wizard.

Ryan wants to review changes and repairs before Windows applies them, so you need to display an advanced option. You also recommend that he run the troubleshooter with administrator permissions.

▶ **4.** Click the **Advanced** link to display advanced options. See Figure 10-25.

| Figure 10-25 | Troubleshooter for search and indexing problems |

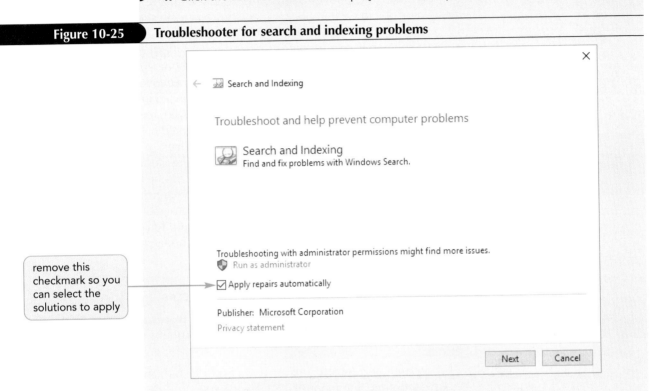

remove this checkmark so you can select the solutions to apply

▶ **5.** Click the **Apply repairs automatically** check box to remove the checkmark, click the **Run as administrator** link, and then click the **Next** button. The next dialog box displays possible searching and indexing problems that need troubleshooting. See Figure 10-26.

Trouble? If you do not have administrator permissions, click the Next button without clicking the Run as administrator link.

Figure 10-26   Possible problems

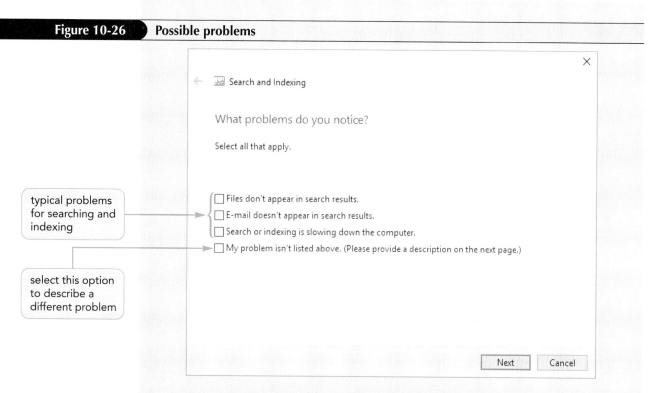

typical problems for searching and indexing

select this option to describe a different problem

6. Click the **Files don't appear in search results** check box and the **Search or indexing is slowing down the computer** check box, and then click the **Next** button. Windows finds a problem and displays a description.

7. Click the **View detailed information** link to generate a troubleshooting report. See Figure 10-27. Your Troubleshooting report might differ.

Figure 10-27   **Troubleshooting report**

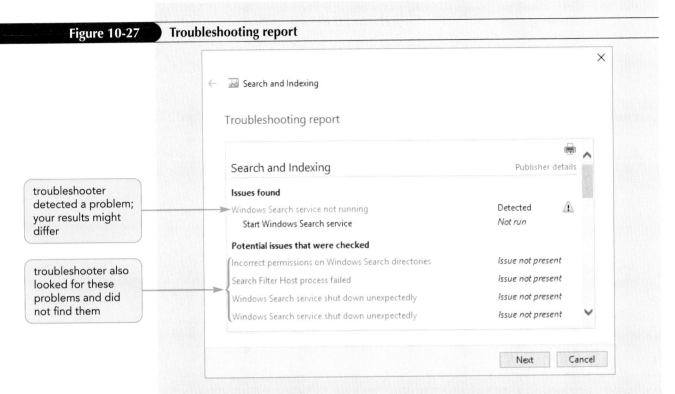

troubleshooter detected a problem; your results might differ

troubleshooter also looked for these problems and did not find them

▶ **8.** Click the **Next** button to display the repairs Windows can make automatically.

▶ **9.** Click the **Next** button to resolve the problem, and then click the **Close** button to close the troubleshooter.

   Trouble? If Windows does not find any issues with search and indexing, you do not need to click the Next button. Click the Close button to finish using the wizard.

▶ **10.** Close all open windows.

You'll show Ryan the next step to take if employees can't find solutions to their problems using a troubleshooter.

Searching the Microsoft Community

The Microsoft Community is a website that provides support information for Microsoft product users. Because the Microsoft Community supports all Microsoft software products, it is a valuable resource when you are troubleshooting computer problems. However, it can sometimes be difficult to pinpoint the answer to your question. Just as you search for information on the Internet, you can search the Microsoft Community for answers by entering one or more keywords. The webpage then displays the answer or support articles associated with those keywords.

New HealthWeb employees sometimes have problems when they sign up for a Microsoft account, such as being unable to verify their identities. You'll show Ryan how to use the Microsoft Community website to find answers to questions other users have about Microsoft accounts so he is prepared to guide new employees appropriately.

To find information on the Microsoft Community website:

▶ **1.** Start Edge, type **answers.microsoft.com** in the Address bar, and then press the **Enter** key. If a sign in window appears, enter your username and password. Edge opens the Microsoft Community webpage.

▶ **2.** In the Browse the Categories section, click **Windows** and then click **Windows 10** to restrict the questions to Windows 10. The webpage displays all the questions and discussions related to Windows 10 sorted in descending order by date. You can filter the results to find topics about Microsoft accounts only.

▶ **3.** In the left column of the webpage, click the **Windows topics** box, click **Security, privacy, & accounts**, and then click the **Apply** button. The webpage displays questions and answers related to security, privacy, and accounts.

▶ **4.** Click in the search box, type **verify identity windows 10**, and then press the **Enter** key. The results include questions and answers about verifying your identity in Windows 10. See Figure 10-28. Information on the web changes frequently, so your results might differ from those shown in the figure.

Figure 10-28 **Microsoft Community results**

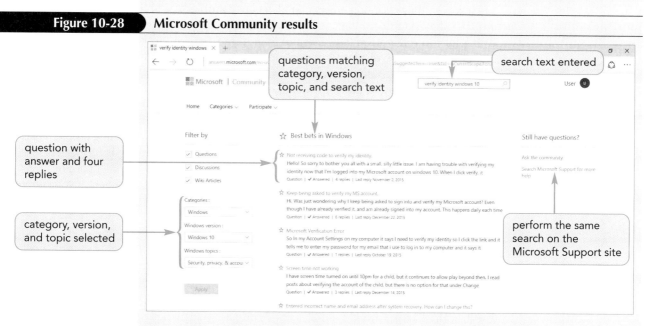

▶ **5.** Click the first result with an answer, such as the first result shown in Figure 10-28. The first part of the result is the original question. Links appear below the question so you can report that you are experiencing the same problem, reply to the question yourself, report an abuse of the forum, or subscribe to updates, which means you receive an email message when someone answers or replies to the question. Scroll down to read the complete question and any answers or replies.

▶ **6.** In the Still have questions? section on the right, click the **Search Microsoft Support for more help** link to search for the same topic on the Microsoft Support website. The results include other questions and answers from the Microsoft Community (these links begin with "answers.microsoft.com"), related help topics, and topics from the Microsoft Support website. Scroll the results to display Help and support topics, which include links beginning with "windows.microsoft.com" and often include "Microsoft Help" in the topic title.

▶ **7.** Click a Help or support topic. The help topic opens and provides an explanation and steps, if appropriate, for performing the task.

▶ **8.** Close Edge.

Now Ryan can help the employees at HealthWeb find answers to their Windows questions online.

Troubleshooting Printing Errors

You have already learned how to use the Devices and Printers window to install a printer and select the default printer to use with Windows applications. Besides using a troubleshooter to detect and repair problems for you, you can also use the Devices and Printers window to troubleshoot some typical printing errors, such as problems with print quality. You need to address certain printing problems, such as running out of paper or clearing a print jam, directly at the printer. For example, when the printer runs out of paper, you need to restock the paper tray with printer paper. To clear a jam, you need to follow the printer manufacturer's recommendations, which might involve pressing a button to clear the jam or opening the printer to remove paper.

However, these printing errors can also cause problems with the **print queue**, which is the list of documents waiting to be printed. While you clear a printer jam, for example, you might need to pause and then restart the print jobs in the print queue. The print queue also displays information about documents that are waiting to print, such as the printing status, document owner, and number of pages to print. You can use the print queue to view, pause, resume, restart, and cancel print jobs.

Ryan has not been able to print with a laser printer installed on his system. You'll try printing to the laser printer, and then show Ryan how to troubleshoot the problem using the Devices and Printers window and the print queue. To simulate a printing problem and perform the following steps, turn off the printer to which your computer is connected, if possible. The following steps use "Laser Printer" as the name of the printer causing problems. Substitute the name of the printer you turned off for "Laser Printer." If you cannot turn off a printer connected to your computer, read but do not perform the following steps.

To troubleshoot printing errors:

▶ **1.** Turn off your printer, start Notepad, and then type your name in the Notepad document.

▶ **2.** Click **File** on the menu bar, click **Print** to open the Print dialog box, click **Laser Printer** in the Select Printer list, and then click the **Print** button.

▶ **3.** In the Notepad window, press the **Enter key** and type today's date.

▶ **4.** Repeat Step 2 to print the document, and then minimize the Notepad window.

▶ **5.** Click in the **Ask me anything** box, start to type **devices and printers**, and then click **Devices and Printers** in the search results to open the Devices and Printers window.

   Trouble? If a notification appears indicating that the printer cannot print, close the notification.

▶ **6.** If necessary, right-click a blank spot in the window, point to **View** on the shortcut menu, and then click **Details** to display the window in Details view. Scroll down to display the Printers category, if necessary, and then click **Laser Printer** to display printer information in the status bar. If necessary, drag the border of the status bar up to display the printer status. See Figure 10-29.

Figure 10-29 Devices and Printers window in Details view

click to open the print queue for the selected printer

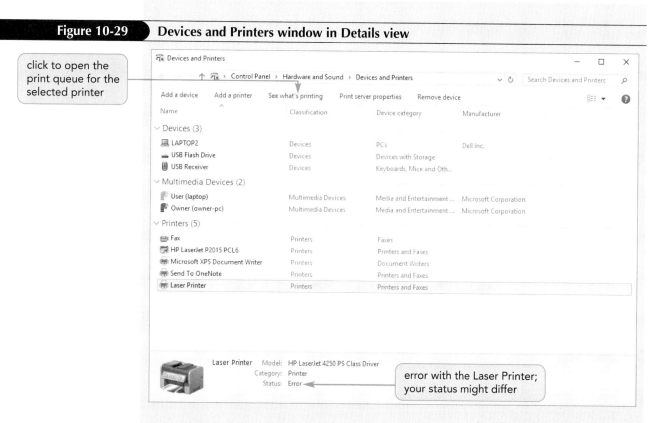

error with the Laser Printer; your status might differ

7. Click the **See what's printing** button on the toolbar to display the print queue. See Figure 10-30.

Figure 10-30 Laser Printer print queue

details about the print jobs

print jobs

number of documents waiting to print

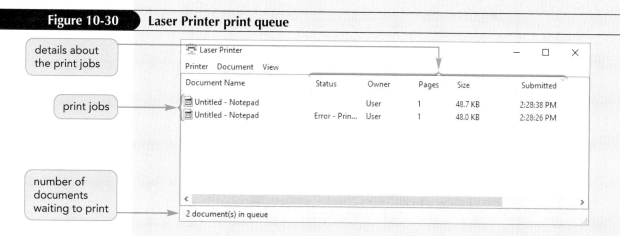

8. Right-click the second **Untitled – Notepad** print job in the queue, and then click **Pause** on the shortcut menu. This pauses the print job so you can solve the printer problem.

9. Right-click the first **Untitled – Notepad** print job in the queue, and then click **Cancel** to prevent this print job from printing and to delete it from the print queue. Click the **Yes** button when asked if you are sure you want to cancel the document.

▶ **10.** Reconnect the printer to your computer and turn it on, if necessary.

TIP

If a print job is interrupted for some reason before it can finish printing, click Restart on the shortcut menu.

▶ **11.** In the Laser Printer print queue, right-click the paused **Untitled – Notepad** print job, and then click **Resume** on the shortcut menu. The Notepad document prints on the Laser Printer.

▶ **12.** Close all open windows without saving any changes.

Software errors also cause occasional problems for HealthWeb employees. You'll now show Ryan how to report software problems to Microsoft and find and apply solutions.

Recovering from Software Errors

To keep your computer running at peak performance, you need to know how to recover from two types of software errors: those produced by programs, such as an app closing unexpectedly, and those produced by Windows itself, including Edge and Internet Explorer. You have already learned to use Task Manager to respond to an application that stops working or responding to your actions. Recall that you can open the Processes tab in Task Manager to identify unresponsive apps and then click the End task button to close the app. Another way to recover from software errors is to use the Apps & features settings in the System window of the Settings app or the Control Panel's Programs and Features window to change the installed features of a program or to try to repair the installation. (To do so, you open the appropriate window, click the troublesome program, and then click the Modify button or the Repair button.) After Windows reports software problems to Microsoft, you can check for a solution, which indicates the steps you should take to prevent or solve the problem, or whether Microsoft needs more information to find or create a solution.

REFERENCE

Checking for Solutions to Software Problems

- Click in the Ask me anything box on the taskbar, start to type "security and maintenance," and then click Security and Maintenance in the search results.
- Expand the Maintenance section, if necessary.
- If a message appears in the Maintenance section, click a button or a link to respond to the message and remove it from the Security and Maintenance window.
- Click the Check for solutions link.
- Follow any steps Windows provides.

In addition to reporting problems and checking for solutions, you can use the Security and Maintenance window to view archived messages about computer problems, change maintenance settings, and produce a reliability report, which gives you a history of the stability of your computer so you can pinpoint when software errors occurred.

Reporting and Solving Software Errors

If your computer is connected to the Internet, Windows can report software problems to a secure part of the Microsoft website. When an app closes unexpectedly, for example, a Windows dialog box appears indicating the app stopped working. Depending on your maintenance settings, Windows will send a problem report to Microsoft, check for problems with the app, and notify you if a solution is available. See Figure 10-31.

| Figure 10-31 | Problem with an app |

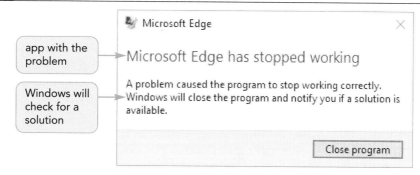

app with the problem

Windows will check for a solution

> **Microsoft Edge**   ✕
>
> Microsoft Edge has stopped working
>
> A problem caused the program to stop working correctly. Windows will close the program and notify you if a solution is available.
>
> Close program

The report Windows sends to Microsoft includes the name and version of the app, the date and time the problem occurred, and other technical information that can help diagnose the problem. Microsoft collects and reviews problem reports even for Windows software produced by companies other than Microsoft.

When Microsoft receives a problem report, it checks for a solution, which might be a link to a Help article, a file to download, or steps to perform. When a solution is available, Microsoft sends the solution to your computer and displays a notification, which you can find in the Action Center if you don't respond to it immediately. You can also use the Control Panel's Security and Maintenance window to check for solutions yourself.

You'll show Ryan how to use the Security and Maintenance window to see what types of software problems Windows tracks and to check for solutions to software problems:

To check for solutions to software problems:

1. Click in the **Ask me anything** box, start to type **security and maintenance**, and then click **Security and Maintenance** to open the Control Panel's Security and Maintenance window, which you have used before to monitor security settings.

2. Click **Maintenance** to expand the maintenance section, if necessary. See Figure 10-32. In this case, the Security and Maintenance window displays a message regarding a problem with device software, which is most likely a driver on Ryan's computer. Ryan can solve the problem by clicking the Install button to install the software, which he can do at a more convenient time.

| Figure 10-32 | Problem message in the Security and Maintenance window |

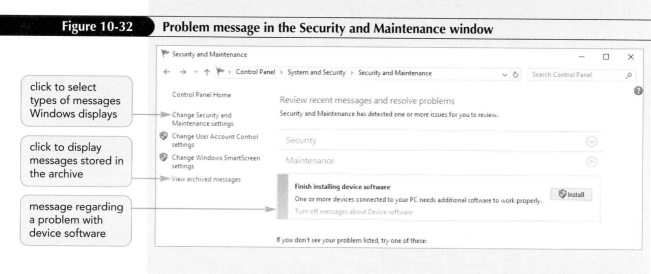

click to select types of messages Windows displays

click to display messages stored in the archive

message regarding a problem with device software

TIP

After responding to a problem message and removing it from the Maintenance section, click the Check for solutions link to search for solutions to previous problems.

3. In the left pane, click the **View archived messages** link. If you have reported any problems to Microsoft, they are listed in the Archived Messages window.

4. Click the **Change Security and Maintenance settings** link to display lists of security and maintenance problems for which Windows notifies you by sending a message to the Action Center and the Security and Maintenance window. See Figure 10-33. By default, all types of problems are selected, which is appropriate for Ryan's computer.

Figure 10-33	Change Security and Maintenance settings window

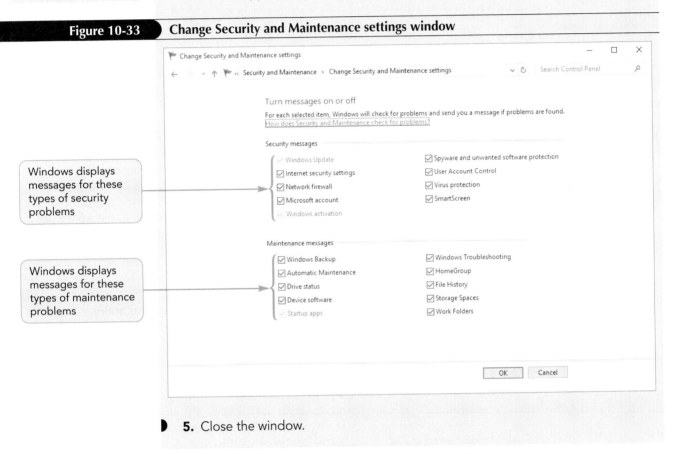

Windows displays messages for these types of security problems →

Windows displays messages for these types of maintenance problems →

5. Close the window.

Now Ryan is sure he will receive solutions to any software problems his computer experiences. You'll show him how to use another tool to track software problems: the Reliability Monitor.

Viewing the Reliability History

TIP

If no maintenance messages appear in the Security and Maintenance window, you can click View reliability history in the Maintenance section to open the Reliability Monitor window.

The Reliability Monitor window includes information about the performance of your system. It includes a chart tracking the stability of your computer, and it maintains up to a year of history on your system's stability and reliability events. For example, this tool tracks software failures, such as a program shutting down unexpectedly, and problems with the hard disk and memory. It also records whether your computer successfully installed updates to keep the system running reliably. The Reliability Monitor window displays these events on a chart, assigning each event a number from 1 (least stable) to 10 (most stable). The Reliability Monitor window also displays an icon for each event. A **critical event** indicates that a failure has occurred from which the application or component cannot automatically recover. A **warning** is an event that indicates a potential problem. An **information event** indicates that a program, driver, or service performed successfully.

You'll show Ryan how to use the Reliability Monitor window to identify events that have affected the stability and reliability of his computer.

To view the reliability history chart:

▶ **1.** Click in the **Ask me anything** box, start to type **reliability**, and then click **View reliability history** in the search results to open the Reliability Monitor window. See Figure 10-34. The chart and other system information on your computer will differ.

| Figure 10-34 | **Reliability Monitor window** |

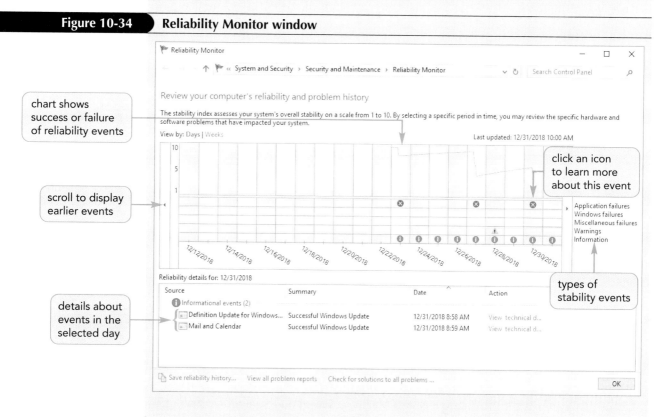

chart shows success or failure of reliability events

scroll to display earlier events

details about events in the selected day

click an icon to learn more about this event

types of stability events

▶ **2.** Click an **Information** icon 🛈 on the chart. Details about that event appear in the Reliability details list. See Figure 10-35. Your details will differ.

Figure 10-35 Viewing details about information errors

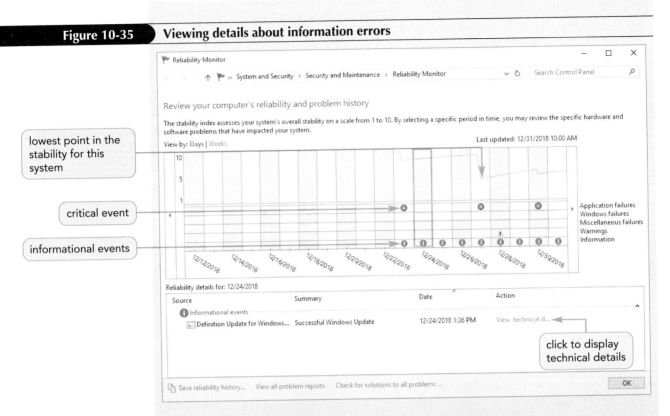

3. If possible, click the first **View technical details** link in the Action column to view details about the problem or event.

4. Click the **OK** button to return to the Reliability Monitor window.

5. If possible, click a **Critical** icon 🛑 in the chart.

6. In the Action column, click **Check for a solution** for a critical event. The Problem Reporting dialog box opens and checks for solutions online. If Windows does not find a solution, it reports that solutions will appear in Security and Maintenance when they are available.

   Trouble? If the Action column does not include a Check for a solution link, click any link in the Action column.

7. Close the dialog box to return to the Reliability Monitor window.

8. At the bottom of the window, click the **View all problem reports** link. The Problem Reports window opens and displays all the problem reports that Windows has sent for software and settings.

9. Double-click a problem report in the list to display details about the problem. See Figure 10-36, which shows the details about a problem with Cortana. Your problem details will differ.

Figure 10-36	Problem Details window

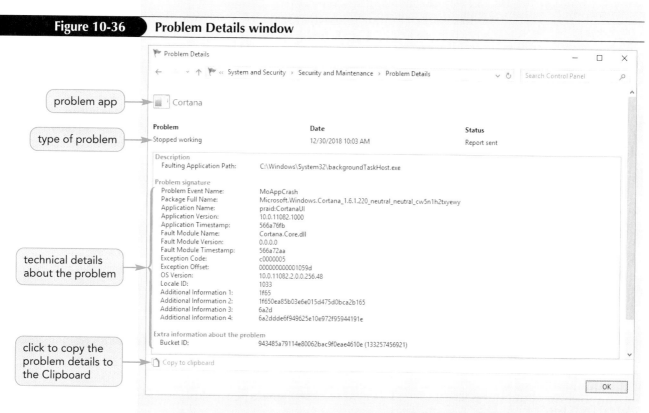

problem app

type of problem

technical details about the problem

click to copy the problem details to the Clipboard

▶ **10.** Click the **OK** button to return to the Problem Reports window, and then click the **OK** button to return to the Reliability Monitor window.

The chart shows that the stability of Ryan's computer is usually between 7 and 10, though it has dipped as low as 4. Overall, this means his system has been fairly stable and reliable over the period shown in the chart.

▶ **11.** Close all open windows.

When you display details about reliability problems, you can copy the technical details and paste them in an email message or document to send to technical support professionals. Windows provides another tool that records technical details about software errors and other system events, which you'll show Ryan next.

Viewing Details About System Events

As you saw when viewing the reliability history, it is helpful to view details about system events, such as a program closing unexpectedly, especially when you are troubleshooting problems with Windows and other programs. Windows records these system events in an **event log**, a special text file that contains details about the event. You can read event logs by using **Event Viewer**, an advanced performance tool that tracks system events, including the following types:

• Program events—As in the Reliability Monitor window, Event Viewer classifies the severity of each program event as critical, warning, or information. In addition, Event Viewer records **errors**, which indicate a significant problem, such as loss of data.

• Security events—These events are called **audits** and are either successful or failed. For example, when you sign in to Windows, Event Viewer records that as a successful audit.

• System events—Similar to program events, Windows classifies each system event as critical, error, warning, or information.

To view details about an event, double-click the event listed in the Event Viewer window to open the Event Properties window, which describes the event and provides details that are helpful to a PC professional. You can copy the event properties to the Clipboard, and then paste them in a text file or an email message to send to a computer technician, for example.

You'll show Ryan how to open the Event Viewer window and find information about critical events.

To perform the following steps, you must be signed in to Windows using an Administrator account. If you are not signed in as an Administrator, you can only change settings that apply to your user account, and you might not be able to access some event logs. However, you can still complete the following steps.

To use Event Viewer:

▶ 1. Click in the **Ask me anything** box, type **event viewer**, and then click **Event Viewer** in the search results. A message might appear indicating that Windows is adding a snap-in, which is a tool installed in a window, and then the Event Viewer window opens.

▶ 2. In the left pane, expand the **Windows Logs** folder, and then click **System**. Event Viewer lists system events in the middle pane in descending order by date. See Figure 10-37. The layout of your Event Viewer window might differ.

Figure 10-37	System events in Event Viewer

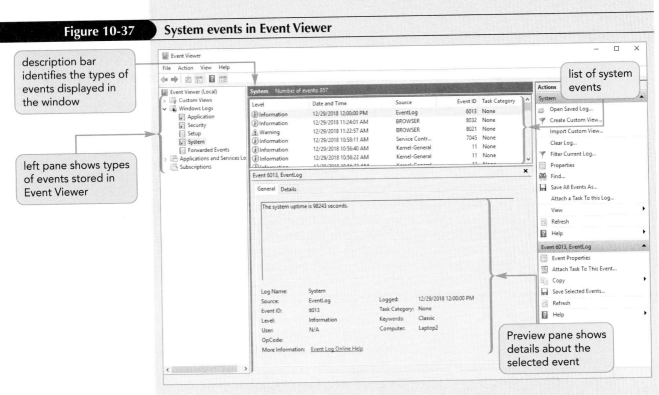

▶ 3. If necessary, scroll the list of events, and then double-click a **Warning**. The Event Properties window opens. See Figure 10-38. Note that this particular event has an Event ID of 8021 and is associated with the browser. If necessary, you could provide the Event ID to a PC technician or search for the Event ID on the Microsoft website to troubleshoot your computer.

Figure 10-38   **Event Properties window**

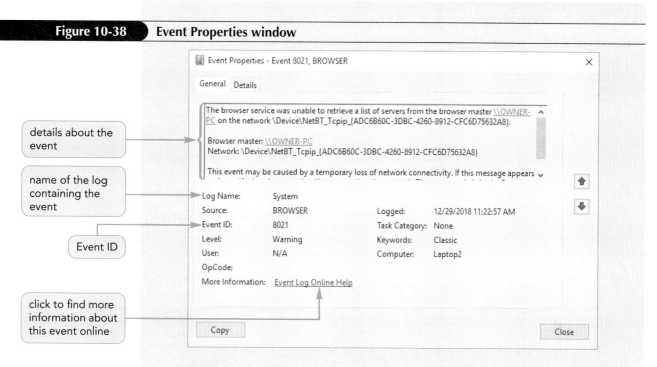

details about the event

name of the log containing the event

Event ID

click to find more information about this event online

Trouble? If no Warnings are listed in your Event Viewer window, double-click any type of event.

▶ **4.** Click the **Close** button to close the Event Properties window.

▶ **5.** Close the Event Viewer window.

If you experience a system problem that interrupts your computing activities, open Event Viewer and look for Errors and Critical events for the current date and time. Most likely, the problem is listed in Event Viewer. You can search online for the event by its ID number to find information about solving the problem.

Recovering the Operating System

If Windows 10 doesn't start correctly or runs erratically, you can try the troubleshooting steps provided in Figure 10-39 to solve the problem. These solutions are listed in order of complexity, with the simplest solution listed first.

The correct key to display the Advanced Boot Options menu on your computer appears onscreen when the computer starts. If necessary, substitute the correct key name for the F8 key in Figure 10-39.

Figure 10-39   Recovering the operating system

Tool	Description	How to Access
System Restore	Use System Restore to restore your computer's system files to an earlier point in time.	1. Open the Control Panel, click System and Security, click System, click System protection, and then click System Restore. 2. Click the Next button, click the most recent restore point, and then click the Next button. 3. Click the Finish button.
Last Known Good Configuration	This advanced startup option starts Windows using the registry settings and drives that were in use the last time the computer started successfully.	1. Restart your computer. 2. Press and hold the F8 key before the Windows logo appears. 3. On the Advanced Boot Options screen, select Last Known Good Configuration, and then press the Enter key.
Safe mode	If the Last Known Good Configuration option doesn't work, use safe mode to try to identify and fix the problem. If your computer starts only in safe mode, try disabling recently installed hardware or programs.	1. Restart your computer. 2. Press and hold the F8 key before the Windows logo appears. 3. On the Advanced Boot Options screen, select Safe Mode, and then press the Enter key.
Startup Repair	In extreme cases, you can use Startup Repair to fix missing or damaged system files that might prevent Windows from starting.	1. Insert the Windows installation media. 2. Restart your computer. 3. Select your language settings, and then click the Next button. 4. Click Repair your computer. 5. Select the operating system to repair, and then click the Next button. 6. On the System Recovery Options menu, click Startup Repair.
Reinstall Windows	If your system has been severely damaged, you might need to reinstall Windows. A custom, or clean, installation of Windows permanently deletes all of the files on your computer and reinstalls Windows, so only use this option if all other recovery options have been unsuccessful. After the installation, you must reinstall your programs and restore your files from backup copies.	1. Insert the Windows installation media. 2. Open the Settings app, click Update & security, click Recovery, and then click the Get started button in the Reset this PC section. 3. Click an option to keep or remove your files. 4. Follow the instructions that appear on your screen.

Last Known Good Configuration, Safe mode, and Startup Repair are advanced startup options that let you select settings before Windows 10 starts. **Last Known Good Configuration** uses the most recent system settings that worked correctly. Every time you turn your computer off and Windows shuts down successfully, it saves important system settings in the registry. If those new settings cause system problems, you can bypass the settings when you restart the computer by selecting the Last Known Good Configuration option on the advanced startup menu. When you do, Windows loads the settings it saved the second-to-last time you shut down the computer (the time before you shut down the computer after selecting the faulty new system settings). You can then disable a device or uninstall a program that is causing problems. Be sure you select the Last Known Good Configuration option before you sign in to Windows—you must press the F8 key right after the computer starts and before Windows does. If you sign in to Windows or start and wait for the desktop to appear, the Last Known Good Configuration will include the faulty new settings.

Safe mode is a troubleshooting option for Windows that starts your computer with only basic services and functionality. If a problem you experienced earlier does not reappear when you start Windows in safe mode, you can eliminate the default settings and basic device drivers as possible causes. While in safe mode, you can use Device Manager to disable a problematic device or restore a driver to its previous version. You can also restore your computer to an earlier point using System Restore.

Startup Repair is a Windows recovery tool that can fix problems such as missing or damaged system files, which might prevent Windows from starting. This tool is provided on the Windows installation media and, depending on how Windows was installed, might also be stored on your hard disk.

INSIGHT

Selecting a Restore Point or the Last Known Good Configuration

If your operating system is running erratically, the two least disruptive solutions to try are reverting to a restore point and using the Last Known Good Configuration. These two options are often confused. Choose System Restore when you notice your system behaving strangely and Windows is still running. Then you can select a restore point to return the system to an earlier point in time when things worked correctly. Unlike Last Known Good Configuration, you can undo the changes made with System Restore, so you can troubleshoot operating system problems by selecting a restore point first. Choose the Last Known Good Configuration option if you can't start Windows, but it started correctly the last time you turned on the computer.

Using the Steps Recorder

If you are having trouble performing a task in Windows, you can use the Steps Recorder to record the steps you take on a computer. The Steps Recorder captures the screen each time you click, saves the screen image, and then includes a text description of where you clicked. Then, as part of the process, you can save the captured images and text in a zipped file and send it to a support professional or someone else helping you with a computer problem.

When you record steps on your computer, anything you type is not recorded. If what you type is an important part of re-creating the problem you're trying to solve, use the Add Comment feature in the Steps Recorder to highlight where the problem is occurring and to provide other types of explanations or descriptions.

Ryan has been having trouble installing a Windows update. Each time he tries, Windows reports that the update failed. You'll show him how to use the Steps Recorder to record the steps he takes to install the update. He can then send the report to other system experts at HealthWeb or Microsoft to see if they can help him troubleshoot the problem.

To use the Steps Recorder:

► **1.** Click in the **Ask me anything** box, begin typing **steps recorder**, and then click **Steps Recorder** in the search results. The Steps Recorder window opens. See Figure 10-40.

Figure 10-40   Steps Recorder window

red light blinks when Steps Recorder is recording

click to start recording

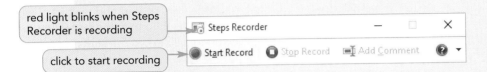

2. Click the **Start Record** button. The Steps Recorder starts recording your steps.

   Trouble? If a warning dialog box opens indicating you might need to run the Steps Recorder as an administrator, click the OK button.

3. Click in the **Ask me anything** box, type **updates**, and then click **Check for updates** in the search results. While the Steps Recorder is recording, a small red dot appears in the title bar of the recorder.

4. Click the **Advanced options** link, and then click the **View your update history** link.

5. If possible, click a link to reinstall an update that failed, and then wait while Windows prepares and then installs the update or fails to do so.

   Trouble? If no updates have failed, skip Step 5.

6. In the Steps Recorder window, click the **Stop Record** button. The Steps Recorder window opens. Scroll down to display a green rectangle indicating the first step you performed. See Figure 10-41.

Figure 10-41   Captured steps

text identifies the step and describes the current action

pointer is captured to show where you clicked

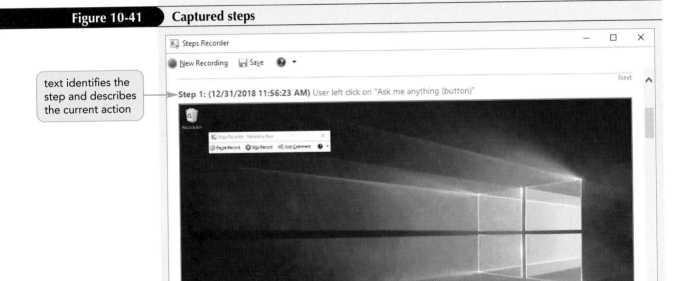

7. Scroll to review the remaining recorded steps, click the **Save** button at the top of the window, and then save the recorded steps as a ZIP file named **Windows Update** in the Module10 > Module folder provided with your Data Files.

8. Close all open windows.

Ryan will email this file containing the recorded steps to a technical support specialist later.

Requesting and Managing Remote Assistance

If you are experiencing a computer problem and can't find a solution yourself, you can use Remote Assistance to have someone show you how to fix a problem. Remote Assistance is a convenient way for someone you trust, such as a friend, coworker, or technical support person, to connect to your computer and step you through a solution—even if that person isn't nearby. To help ensure that only people you invite can connect to your computer using Remote Assistance, all sessions are encrypted and password protected.

To request Remote Assistance, you can send an email message to invite someone to connect to your computer. After connecting, that person can view your computer screen and chat with you about what you both see on your computer screen. With your permission, your helper can even use a mouse and keyboard to control your computer and show you how to fix a problem. You can also help someone else in the same way.

Before you can use Remote Assistance to connect two computers, you must enable the feature. You'll show Ryan how to enable Remote Assistance connections so that he can request help from you and vice versa.

To enable Remote Assistance connections:

1. Click in the **Ask me anything** box, type **remote**, and then click **Allow remote access to your computer** in the search results. The System Properties dialog box opens and displays the settings on the Remote tab.

2. If necessary, click the Allow Remote Assistance connections to this computer box to insert a check mark.

To disable Remote Assistance invitations, you remove the check mark from the Allow Remote Assistance connections to this computer box on the Remote tab in the System Properties dialog box. You can also use the Remote tab in the System Properties dialog box to access advanced Remote Assistance settings, such as how much time you want to enable Remote Assistance and how long invitations will be available.

When you allow Remote Assistance connections to your computer, you can send and receive Remote Assistance invitations using email or an option called Easy Connect. **Easy Connect** is a technology that connects two computers on a network so one computer can access the desktop and other resources of another computer.

You want to show Ryan how to limit the amount of time that a Remote Assistance invitation is available, so that an unauthorized person cannot control your computer without your knowledge.

To select advanced Remote Assistance settings:

▶ **1.** On the Remote tab in the System Properties dialog box, click the **Advanced** button. The Remote Assistance Settings dialog box opens. See Figure 10-42.

Figure 10-42 **Remote Assistance Settings dialog box**

remove this checkmark if you want others to only view but not control your computer using their mouse and keyboard

change this number to increase or decrease the amount of time invitations are open to others

click to limit invitations to computers running Windows Vista or later

---

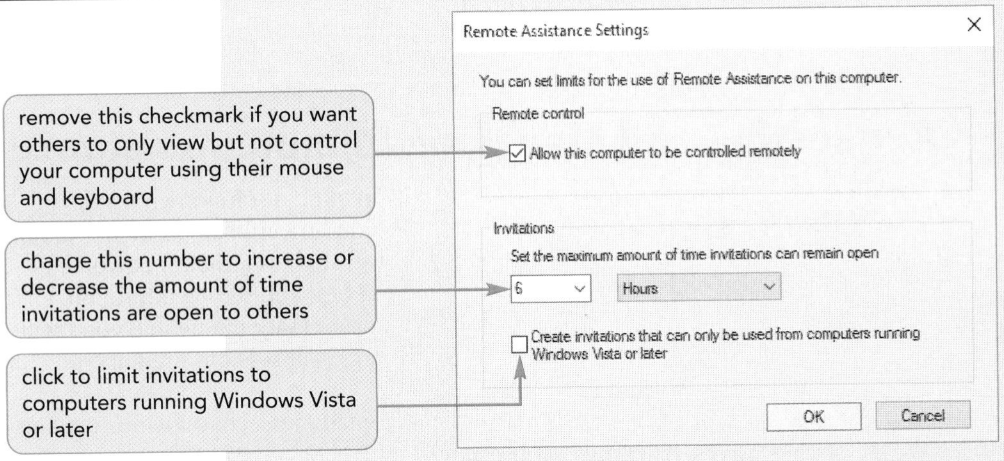

▶ **2.** In the Invitations section, click the box on the left, which contains 6 by default, to select the time that invitations can remain available, and then type **4** to reduce the amount of time a Remote Assistance invitation is available. Leave the Hours option set.

▶ **3.** Click the **OK** button to close the Remote Assistance Settings dialog box.

▶ **4.** Click the **OK** button to close the System Properties dialog box.

You can also use the Remote Assistance Settings dialog box to create invitations only for computers running Windows Vista or later, which protects the security of your computer. Although Ryan doesn't need to establish a Remote Assistance session now, you'll show him how to request assistance using the Windows Remote Assistance Wizard.

Requesting Remote Assistance

When you need help from someone else, you can request Remote Assistance using the Windows Remote Assistance Wizard. You'll show Ryan how to use this wizard to send an email message inviting you to help him troubleshoot a problem on his computer. When you perform the following steps, substitute the email address of a friend or classmate for the email address used in the steps.

To request Remote Assistance:

▶ **1.** Click in the **Ask me anything** box, begin typing **remote assistance**, and then click **Invite someone to connect to your PC and help you, or offer to help someone** in the search results. The Windows Remote Assistance Wizard starts. See Figure 10-43.

Figure 10-43 Starting the Windows Remote Assistance Wizard

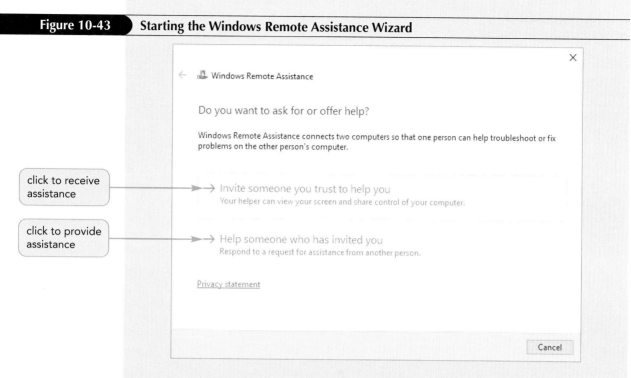

click to receive assistance

click to provide assistance

2. Click **Invite someone you trust to help you**. The next wizard dialog box opens, asking how you want to invite someone to help you.

3. Click **Use email to send an invitation**. Remote Assistance opens an invitation email in your default email program and fills in the subject and content of the message for you. See Figure 10-44.

Trouble? If you do not have a default email program set up on your computer, Windows asks you to select an email program to use. Select the program and wait for the invitation email to open, and then continue with Step 4.

Trouble? If a message appears regarding creating an email profile, close the message and then read but do not perform the remaining steps.

Trouble? If the Use email to send invitation option is grayed out, click Save this invitation as a file, use your email software to open a new email message, attach the file you just saved, and continue with the remaining steps.

Figure 10-44 **Email message with Remote Assistance invitation**

type an email address here

recipient double-clicks the attachment to accept the invitation

standard invitation message

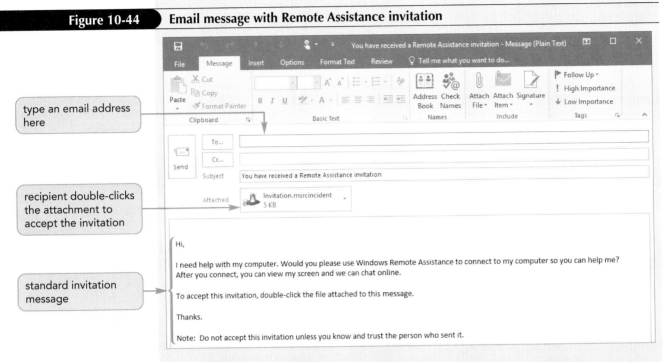

4. Enter the email address of a friend or classmate, such as **Helper@healthweb. cengage.com**, in the To box, and then click the **Send** button. A window opens displaying a connection password. Wait for your helper to receive and open the invitation, which might be an email attachment. If necessary, tell your helper the password in whatever way is convenient for you, such as a phone call. Your helper should start Remote Assistance on his or her computer, and then enter the password to connect to your computer. A Remote Assistance dialog box opens on your computer, asking if you want to allow your helper to connect to your computer.

5. Click the **Yes** button to allow the connection. Your helper can now see your desktop and can click the Request control button on the toolbar in the Windows Remote Assistance window on your helper's computer. You then see the Windows Remote Assistance window shown in Figure 10-45. During a Remote Assistance session, Windows usually changes your desktop background to black to conserve power.

Figure 10-45 **Remote Assistance in action**

click when you are ready to stop sharing

you are sharing your computer with a helper

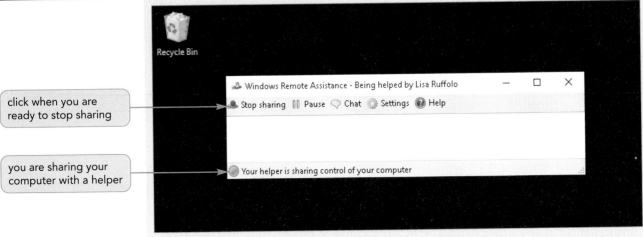

You can now perform the steps with which Ryan is having trouble. You can see Ryan's computer screen because you are playing the role of helper, and you and he can chat using the online Chat tool. With permission granted, you can control Ryan's computer to show him how to fix the problem. Right now you will just show him how to end the Remote Assistance session.

To end the Remote Assistance session:

▶ **1.** If your helper clicked the Request control button in the Remote Assistance window on his or her computer, click the **Stop sharing** button. Your helper no longer has access to your computer.

▶ **2.** Close the Remote Assistance window to end the Remote Assistance session.

▶ **3.** Close all other open windows.

Now that you're finished helping Ryan improve his computer's performance and troubleshoot system problems, you should restore your system settings.

Restoring Your Settings

If you are working in a computer lab or on a computer other than your own, complete the steps in this section to restore the original settings on your computer. If a User Account Control dialog box opens requesting an Administrator password or confirmation after you perform any of the following steps, enter the password or click the Yes button.

To restore your settings:

▶ **1.** Click in the **Ask me anything** box, start to type **advanced system settings**, and then click **View advanced system settings** in the search results to open the System Properties dialog box with the Advanced tab displayed.

▶ **2.** Click the **Settings** button in the Performance section.

▶ **3.** Restore your original settings, and then click the **OK** button to close the Performance Options dialog box.

▶ **4.** Open File Explorer, right-click the USB drive, and then click **Properties** on the shortcut menu.

▶ **5.** Click the **ReadyBoost** tab, and then click the **Do not use this device** option button. Click the **OK** button to close the Properties dialog box.

▶ **6.** In the System Properties dialog box, click the **Remote** tab.

▶ **7.** In the Remote Assistance section, restore your original setting, if necessary.

▶ **8.** Click the **Advanced** button, and then restore your original setting for the maximum amount of time Remote Assistance invitations can stay open, which is 6 hours by default. Click the **OK** button to close the Remote Assistance Settings dialog box.

▶ **9.** Click the **OK** button to close the System Properties dialog box.

▶ **10.** Close all open windows, and then eject the USB drive.

In this session, you learned how to respond to notifications and find troubleshooting information on your computer and online to identify and correct system problems. You used tools, including the Reliability Monitor and Event Viewer, to respond to system errors. You also used the Steps Recorder and Remote Assistance to work with other people to solve system problems.

Session 10.2 Quick Check

REVIEW

1. What happens when you click a system notification in the Action Center?
2. What does the Action Center's Quiet hours setting do?
3. What is the advantage of running a troubleshooter when you have a computer problem?
4. The _____ is a list of documents waiting to be printed.
5. How can you view solutions to problems that Windows has reported to Microsoft?
6. In the Reliability Monitor window, a(n) _____ event indicates that a program, driver, or service performed successfully.
7. When must you select the Last Known Good Configuration to recover from a system error?

PRACTICE

Review Assignments

There are no Data Files needed for the Review Assignments.

Now that you've helped Ryan improve system performance and troubleshoot hardware and software problems on his computer, he asks you to show another HealthWeb manager, Joelle Robinson, how to optimize her computer. Complete the following steps, noting your original settings so you can restore them later:

1. In the Settings app, display the name of your computer, the edition of Windows you are running, and other basic system information such as the processor name and speed. Press the Print Screen key to capture an image of the screen. Paste the image in a new Paint file, and then save the file as **Basic** in the Module10 > Review folder provided with your Data Files.

2. Use the System Information window to display a system summary that shows details about the display device component on your computer. Press the Print Screen key to capture an image of the screen. Paste the image in a new Paint file, and then save the file as **Display Device** in the Module10 > Review folder provided with your Data Files.

3. To improve performance, adjust the visual effects on your computer. Do not animate controls and elements inside windows. In addition, do not allow animations in the taskbar. With the Performance Options dialog box open to the appropriate tab, press the Print Screen key to capture an image of the screen. Paste the image in a new Paint file, and then save the file as **Visual Effects** in the Module10 > Review folder provided with your Data Files.

4. Open the Task Manager window and display the current apps and processes running on your computer. (*Hint*: To make sure that Task Manager groups processes by type, click View on the menu bar. If the Group by type option is not selected with a check mark, click Group by type.) Start an app of your choice, and then make Task Manager the active window. Press the Print Screen key to capture an image of the screen. Paste the image in a new Paint file, and then save the file as **Task Manager** in the Module10 > Review folder provided with your Data Files.

5. Open File Explorer, and then display a graph of CPU usage in the Task Manager window. Press the Print Screen key to capture an image of the window. Paste the image in a new Paint file, and then save the file as **CPU** in the Module10 > Review folder provided with your Data Files. Close all open windows.

6. Open the Performance Monitor and then add a counter for % Idle Time. Change the color of the % Idle Time counter to blue. Press the Print Screen key to capture an image of the window. Paste the image in a new Paint file, and then save the file as **Performance** in the Module10 > Review folder provided with your Data Files.

7. Display the System Diagnostics report for your computer. Expand the Performance section, if necessary, and then scroll to display all the information in the Performance section. Press the Print Screen key to capture an image of the window. Paste the image in a new Paint file, and then save the file as **Diagnostics** in the Module10 > Review folder provided with your Data Files.

8. Open the Resource Monitor and then expand the Disk section, if necessary. Press the Print Screen key to capture an image of the window. Paste the image in a new Paint file, and then save the file as **Resources** in the Module10 > Review folder provided with your Data Files. Close all open windows.

9. Display the size of the paging file on your computer. Press the Print Screen key to capture an image of the dialog box. Paste the image in a new Paint file, and then save the file as **Paging Size** in the Module10 > Review folder provided with your Data Files. Close the Performance Options dialog box.

10. Attach a USB flash drive to your computer, and then increase the memory capacity of your system by turning on ReadyBoost. Select the maximum amount of available space on your USB flash drive to reserve for boosting your system speed. Press the Print Screen key to capture an image of the screen. Paste the image in a new Paint file, and then save the file as **USB ReadyBoost** in the Module10 > Review folder provided with your Data Files.

11. Display the Action Center and then expand a notification, if possible. Press the Print Screen key to capture an image of the screen. Paste the image in a new Paint file, and then save the file as **Action Center** in the Module10 > Review folder provided with your Data Files.

12. Display the Windows 10 category of questions and answers at the Microsoft Community website. Show questions and answers on the Performance & system failures topic. Select a recent question with an answer, a reply, or both, and then press the Print Screen key to capture an image of the screen. Paste the image in a new Paint file, and then save the file as **Community** in the Module10 > Review folder provided with your Data Files.

13. Use the Security and Maintenance window to view the archived problem messages on your computer. Press the Print Screen key to capture an image of the screen. Paste the image in a new Paint file, and then save the file as **Archived Messages** in the Module10 > Review folder provided with your Data Files.

14. Display your computer's reliability and problem history. Select a critical event or a warning, and then press the Print Screen key to capture an image of the screen. Paste the image in a new Paint file, and then save the file as **Reliability** in the Module10 > Review folder provided with your Data Files.

15. Open the Event Viewer window, select the Windows Logs folder, and then display application events. Display details about an error event. If your Event Viewer window does not list any error events, display details about a critical event or a warning. Press the Print Screen key to capture an image of the window. Paste the image in a new Paint file, and then save the file as **App Event** in the Module10 > Review folder provided with your Data Files. Close all open windows.

16. Use the Steps Recorder to record the steps for opening an accessory on your computer, such as Notepad. (*Hint*: Scroll the All apps list to the Windows Accessories folder, and then open the folder.) Save the steps in a Zip file named **Accessory Steps** in the Module10 > Review folder.

17. Set the maximum amount of time Remote Assistance invitations can stay open to 5 hours. Press the Print Screen key to capture an image of the screen. Paste the image in a new Paint file, and then save the file as **Invitation** in the Module10 > Review folder provided with your Data Files.

18. Restore your settings by completing the following tasks:
    - Adjust the visual effects on your computer by letting Windows choose what's best for your computer.
    - Turn off ReadyBoost.
    - Return the maximum amount of time Remote Assistance invitations can stay open to its original setting, which is 6 hours by default.

19. Close all open windows.

Case Problem 1

There are no Data Files needed for this Case Problem.

Dockery Musical Therapy   Michelle Dockery owns a small business called Dockery Musical Therapy in Oakland, California, which works with school-age children to improve their abilities to concentrate and express themselves. Michelle hired you as a part-time computer specialist and is particularly interested in getting your help to improve the performance of her company's computers. She also wants to know how to find troubleshooting information for problems with Windows Media Player. Complete the following steps, noting your original settings so you can restore them later:

1. Open the Control Panel and then display basic information about your computer. Press the Print Screen key to capture an image of the screen. Paste the image in a new Paint file, and then save the file as **System** in the Module10 > Case1 folder provided with your Data Files.

2. In the System Information window, display a list of running tasks in the software environment. Press the Print Screen key to capture an image of the screen. Paste the image in a new Paint file, and then save the file as **Running Tasks** in the Module10 > Case1 folder provided with your Data Files.

3. Adjust the visual effects on your computer for best performance. With the Performance Options dialog box open to the appropriate tab, press the Print Screen key to capture an image of the dialog box. Paste the image in a new Paint file, and then save the file as **Best Performance** in the Module10 > Case1 folder provided with your Data Files.

4. Open the Task Manager window and display the apps and processes running on your computer. Display the Details tab and then sort the list of details in descending order by CPU usage. (*Hint*: Click the CPU column heading.) Press the Print Screen key to capture an image of the screen. Paste the image in a new Paint file, and then save the file as **Details** in the Module10 > Case1 folder provided with your Data Files.

5. Open Resource Monitor and display a resource overview, including graphs of CPU, Disk, Network, and Memory usage. Expand all sections, and then press the Print Screen key to capture an image of the screen. Paste the image in a new Paint file, and then save the file as **Resource Overview** in the Module10 > Case1 folder provided with your Data Files.

6. Attach a USB flash drive to your computer, and then increase the memory capacity of your system by turning on ReadyBoost. Select the minimum amount of available space on your USB flash drive to reserve for boosting your system speed. Press the Print Screen key to capture an image of the dialog box. Paste the image in a new Paint file, and then save the file as **Minimum** in the Module10 > Case1 folder provided with your Data Files.

7. Use a Windows troubleshooter to find troubleshooting information about common problems with settings in the Windows Media Player program. In the wizard, do not have Windows apply repairs automatically and, if possible, run as an administrator. After Windows detects potential problems, view detailed information about the configuration settings. Press the Print Screen key to capture an image of the wizard listing a suggested fix for Windows Media Player settings. Paste the image in a new Paint file, and then save the file as **WMP Settings** in the Module10 > Case1 folder provided with your Data Files.

8. Use the Microsoft Community website to find solutions to problems with Windows Media Player settings. Use the Search box as necessary. Display a question with an answer, scroll to the answer, and then press the Print Screen key to capture an image of the screen. Paste the image in a new Paint file, and then save the file as **Answer** in the Module10 > Case1 folder provided with your Data Files.

9. Search Microsoft Support for help on Windows Media Player settings. Press the Print Screen key to capture an image of the screen. Paste the image in a new Paint file, and then save the file as **Support** in the Module10 > Case1 folder provided with your Data Files.

10. Open the Event Viewer window and display details about a system warning. Press the Print Screen key to capture an image of the screen. Paste the image in a new Paint file, and then save the file as **Warning** in the Module10 > Case1 folder provided with your Data Files.

11. Start the Windows Remote Assistance Wizard and prepare to send an email invitation to your instructor. Press the Print Screen key to capture an image of the open email invitation. Paste the image in a new Paint file, and then save the file as **Remote Invitation** in the Module10 > Case1 folder provided with your Data Files.

12. Restore your settings by adjusting the visual effects so that Windows chooses what's best for your computer. Turn off ReadyBoost.

13. Close all open windows.

Case Problem 2

There are no Data Files needed for this Case Problem.

Pacific Forestry   Doug Curran and Brad Lutz are partners in Pacific Forestry, a forestry service company in Yakima, Washington. Doug and Brad upgraded their computers to Windows 10 a few months ago, and they have noticed that the computers are not running as efficiently as they were when Windows 10 was first installed. As the office manager of Pacific Forestry, you share responsibility for optimizing the computers. Doug asks you to help him improve the performance of his computer and to troubleshoot problems he's having playing training videos on the company's WiFi network. Complete the following steps, noting your original settings so you can restore them later:

1. In the System Information window, display details about Video Codecs, which are multimedia software components that compress or decompress digital video files. Press the Print Screen key to capture an image of the window. Paste the image in a new Paint file, and then save the file as **Video Codecs** in the Module10 > Case2 folder provided with your Data Files.

2. Find more information about video codecs at the Microsoft Community website. Display a question and answer about a video codec, scroll to show as much of the answer as possible, and then press the Print Screen key to capture an image of the window. Paste the image in a new Paint file, and then save the file as **Codec Answer** in the Module10 > Case2 folder provided with your Data Files.

3. Search Microsoft Support for information about video cards. Display a topic that provides answers to frequently asked questions about video cards, and then press the Print Screen key to capture an image of the screen. Paste the image in a new Paint file, and then save the file as **Video Card** in the Module10 > Case2 folder provided with your Data Files.

4. Open Task Manager to display a list of running apps and processes. Sort the list by memory, with the app or process requiring the most amount of memory at the top of the list. (*Hint*: Click the Memory column heading.) Press the Print Screen key to capture an image of the dialog box. Paste the image in a new Paint file, and then save the file as **High Memory** in the Module10 > Case2 folder provided with your Data Files.

⊕ **Explore** 5. On the Performance tab of the Task Manager window, chart the performance of the Wi-Fi network. Press the Print Screen key to capture an image of the dialog box. Paste the image in a new Paint file, and then save the file as **Wi-Fi** in the Module10 > Case2 folder provided with your Data Files.

⊕ **Explore** 6. Open the Resource Monitor window and monitor network activity. (*Hint*: Click the Network tab.) Expand the Processes with Network Activity section and the Network Activity section. Press the Print Screen key to capture an image of the screen. Paste the image in a new Paint file, and then save the file as **Network Monitor** in the Module10 > Case2 folder provided with your Data Files.

7. Open the Reliability Monitor and then view all problem reports. Press the Print Screen key to capture an image of the window. Paste the image in a new Paint file, and then save the file as **Problem Reports** in the Module10 > Case2 folder provided with your Data Files.

⊕ **Explore** 8. Return to the Reliability Monitor window and then check for solutions to all problems. When the results are displayed, press the Print Screen key to capture an image of the screen. Paste the image in a new Paint file, and then save the file as **All Solutions** in the Module10 > Case2 folder provided with your Data Files.

9. Use a Windows troubleshooter in the Programs category to troubleshoot problems with playing DVDs in Windows Media Player. In the wizard, do not have Windows apply repairs automatically and, if possible, run the wizard as an administrator. Press the Print Screen key to capture an image of the screen listing the results. Paste the image in a new Paint file, and then save the file as **DVD** in the Module10 > Case2 folder provided with your Data Files.

10. Use the Steps Recorder to record the steps for starting the Windows 10 Movies & TV app, selecting a video or movie, and then playing it, if possible. Save the recorded steps as a Zip file named **Video Steps** in the Module10 > Case2 folder provided with your Data Files.

11. Close all open windows.

Case Problem 3

There are no Data Files needed for this Case Problem.

Home Repair Connections   Tanya Subio manages Home Repair Connections in Lexington, Kentucky, to provide repair and maintenance services to home owners. Recently, she noticed that new software runs erratically on her Windows 10 computer. In addition, after she shuts down her computer, Windows is slow to start. As her office assistant, you offer to help her solve these problems. Complete the following steps, noting your original settings so you can restore them later:

Explore 1. Open the System Properties dialog box and then display Startup and Recovery settings. (*Hint*: Click the Settings button in the Startup and Recovery section.) Press the Print Screen key to capture an image of the screen. Paste the image in a new Paint file, and then save the file as **Startup** in the Module10 > Case3 folder provided with your Data Files.

2. In the System Information window, display a list of running tasks. Note the filename of one task listed in the right pane.

Explore 3. Open Task Manager to display details about the currently running processes on the Details tab. Sort the processes alphabetically by Name. Click a filename you displayed in the previous step. Arrange the windows on the desktop so you can see the System Information and Task Manager windows clearly. Press the Print Screen key to capture an image of the desktop. Paste the image in a new Paint file, and then save the file as **Running Tasks** in the Module10 > Case3 folder provided with your Data Files.

Explore 4. Display the apps and processes that run at startup. (*Hint*: Click the Startup tab.)

5. In the System Information window, display information about Startup Programs in the software environment on your computer. Arrange and resize the Task Manager window and the System Information window on the desktop so you can see startup information in both windows. Press the Print Screen key to capture an image of the desktop. Paste the image in a new Paint file, and then save the file as **Startup Tasks** in the Module10 > Case3 folder provided with your Data Files. Close the Task Manager window.

6. Open the Reliability Monitor and select a day when the reliability index is less than 10. Display details about an event that occurred that day. Press the Print Screen key to capture an image of the screen. Paste the image in a new Paint file, and then save the file as **Details** in the Module10 > Case3 folder provided with your Data Files.

Explore 7. Open the Performance Monitor window and graph the percentage of time your processor is working. Add a Memory counter to graph the percentage of committed bytes in use (% Committed Bytes In Use). Change the color of the % Committed Bytes In Use counter to green. After the Performance Monitor graphs the two counters for a few seconds, press the Print Screen key to capture an image of the screen. Paste the image in a new Paint file, and then save the file as **Memory Counter** in the Module10 > Case3 folder provided with your Data Files.

8. On the Microsoft Community website, display questions and answers for the Power on or off a device topic for Windows 10. Display a question in this list related to startup problems. Press the Print Screen key to capture an image of the screen. Paste the image in a new Paint file, and then save the file as **Startup Question** in the Module10 > Case3 folder provided with your Data Files.

9. Search Microsoft Support for information about safe mode in Windows 10. Display the steps for starting Windows in safe mode, and then press the Print Screen key to capture an image of the screen. Paste the image in a new Paint file, and then save the file as **Safe Mode** in the Module10 > Case3 folder provided with your Data Files.

10. Close all open windows.

Case Problem 4

There are no Data Files needed for this Case Problem.

High Security Storage   Ton Kang owns High Security Storage in Galveston, Texas. Ton's company provides portable storage containers to businesses that want to store documents and other items in a secure location. He recently set up a small network in his office so he and his staff can share computer resources. Everyone at High Security Storage has Windows 10 installed on their computers. Ton uses a broadband digital subscriber line (DSL) to connect to the Internet, but the connection is frequently interrupted. He also sometimes receives a message that the connection is limited. As the office manager, you offer to research how to solve Ton's Internet connection problems. Complete the following steps:

⚙ **Troubleshoot** 1. Use Microsoft Support to find information about and suggested solutions for Ton's Internet connection problems.

⚙ **Troubleshoot** 2. Search the Microsoft Community website for similar troubleshooting information, including articles about limited connections.

3. Use your favorite search engine to find troubleshooting information for DSL connections.

4. Based on your research, write one to two pages recommending how Ton can solve his problem. List the possible causes along with suggested steps to solve his problem. Save the document as **Connection Troubleshooting** in the Module10 > Case4 folder provided with your Data Files.

5. Submit the results of the preceding steps to your instructor, either in printed or electronic form, as requested.

INDEX

A

About Remote Desktop Connection window (fig.), WIN 423

About settings, System window, WIN 500–501

accent colors, changing, WIN 98–100

access, controlling your computer's, WIN 249–250

access points, WIN 399–400

accessing
CD drives, WIN 29
Cortana, WIN 10–11
DVD drives, WIN 29
offline files, WIN 415–419
OneDrive, WIN 29
shared files on homegroups, WIN 414–415

accounts
Microsoft, WIN 4, WIN 192
switching, WIN 248
synchronizing, WIN 241
user. See user accounts

Action Center
described, WIN 98, WIN 528–529
displaying, WIN 526
Quick Actions, WIN 526, WIN 529

active objects, WIN 7

active window, WIN 14

ActiveX controls, WIN 158, WIN 228

adapter cards, WIN 477–478

Add a field button, People app, WIN 192

Add Comment feature, Steps Recorder, WIN 547

Address bar, WIN 50
described, WIN 24
navigating with, WIN 54–55

addresses, email, WIN 179, WIN 181

Administrator accounts, WIN 240, WIN 480

Advanced Boot Options, WIN 545

Advanced Display Settings window, WIN 107–108

Advanced link, troubleshooters, WIN 531

Advanced options, WIN 454–455

Advanced Options window, Windows Update (fig.), WIN 216

advanced search criteria, WIN 284–288

Advanced tab, Color Management dialog box (fig.), WIN 487

Advanced tab, Performance Options dialog box (fig.), WIN 521

adware, WIN 220

Airbrush style, Brush tool, WIN 334

Airplane mode, WIN 404

albums, WIN 357

alert messages, WIN 210

All apps command, WIN 10

Allowed apps window, Windows Firewall, WIN 213–214

American Job Center home page (fig.), WIN 159

AND Boolean filter, WIN 284–285, WIN 287–288

annotating webpages, WIN 166–168

annotations on webpages, Microsoft Edge, WIN 149

Answer Desk, Microsoft Support, WIN 530

antimalware programs, WIN 221

antispyware, WIN 221

antivirus software, WIN 218–219

App history tab, Task Manager, WIN 499

application software, managing, WIN 456–461

applications
See also apps
described, WIN 4
starting and using, WIN 508–511
switching between, WIN 14–15

appointments, scheduling, WIN 194–195

apps
See also applications or specific app
adding to Start menu, WIN 129–131
closing, WIN 20–22
closing unnecessary, WIN 22
hiding, WIN 15
installed, WIN 435
installing from Windows Store, WIN 456–457
pinned to taskbar (fig.), WIN 116
pinning to taskbar, WIN 119–120
purchasing, adding, WIN 129
running multiple, WIN 13–17
searching for, WIN 261–263
solving problems with, WIN 538–540
starting, WIN 457–458
taskbar buttons to access, WIN 2

tiles, WIN 7
two open (fig.), WIN 14
uninstalling, WIN 458–459
viewing running, WIN 14
web, WIN 151
Window, WIN 5
Windows, universal, desktop, WIN 11

arranging photos by rating, WIN 345

arrow buttons, WIN 42

arrow-shaped pointer, WIN 6

Ask me anything box, WIN 260–261, WIN 289, WIN 458, WIN 503

attaching files to email messages, WIN 188–189

attachments, not opening unexpected email, WIN 220

audio
See also media, music
speaker volume (mobile computing), WIN 377, WIN 380–381

audits, WIN 543

AutoComplete, WIN 155

Automatic Repair option, WIN 454–455

AutoPlay dialog box, WIN 522

B

Back location button, WIN 42, WIN 50

Background, adding to Start menu, WIN 130–131

background colors, WIN 307, WIN 320

Background processes, Task Manager, WIN 499, WIN 509

background programs, WIN 117, WIN 119

backgrounds
changing desktop, WIN 96–98
desktop, WIN 91
settings (fig.), WIN 97
using solid or transparent, WIN 328

backing up
vs. copying files, WIN 437
creating backup strategy, WIN 444–445
files, WIN 436–440
files using File History, WIN 437–445
selecting backup location, WIN 438

backup files, WIN 434

backup folder, WIN 434

backup medium, WIN 434

backup options, changing, WIN 440–445

Backup Options window (fig.), WIN 442

backup programs, WIN 436

backup strategy, WIN 434

backups, WIN 64

Balanced plan, WIN 376, WIN 386

batteries settings (mobile computing), WIN 376, WIN 381–384

Battery saver feature (mobile computing), WIN 382

Battery saver settings (fig.), WIN 383

battery status (fig.), WIN 381

Bcc lines, email, WIN 184

Best match section, Cortana settings, WIN 264

Better Business Bureau, WIN 239

Bing
    described, WIN 282
    Help page, WIN 293
    highlights, WIN 283
    using search expressions, WIN 293–294
    weather search results in (fig.), WIN 290

bing.com, WIN 100

biometric security, WIN 242

Birthday calendar, WIN 193

bit size, WIN 503

bitmap graphics, WIN 306
    described (fig.), WIN 308
    file formats, WIN 314
    saving in different file type, WIN 315
    selecting, WIN 309

bitmap-editing programs, WIN 308

black hat hackers, WIN 208

blocking
    cookies, WIN 235–236
    malware, WIN 232–233
    pop-up windows, WIN 233–234

BMP files, WIN 314

bolding text, WIN 18

Boolean filters
    combining search criteria, WIN 285–286
    combining with file properties, WIN 288
    described, WIN 284

boot partitions, WIN 466

brightness, display setting, WIN 484

broadband connection, WIN 152

browsers, WIN 148
    See also Microsoft Edge
    accessing the web, WIN 152
    web, WIN 151–152

Brush tool, WIN 334

Bureau of Labor Statistics website, WIN 155

buttons
    See also specific button
    moving taskbar, WIN 120–121
    taskbar. See taskbar buttons
    window (fig.), WIN 15

C

cables, WIN 400

cached data and files, WIN 236

Calendar app
    closing, WIN 21
    currency conversion, WIN 262–263
    displaying Calendar details on lock screen, WIN 195–196
    illustrated (fig.), WIN 13
    managing your schedule with, WIN 193–195
    sharing information with Mail app, WIN 178
    starting, WIN 12, WIN 194

Camera app, WIN 344

cameras, WIN 342

canvas
    described (fig.), WIN 307
    in Paint window (fig.), WIN 311
    resizing, WIN 317–319

cases
    Crafted Quilts, WIN 89
    FreeSail Boat Club, WIN 305
    HealthWeb, WIN 497
    Ithaca Imports, WIN 257
    Miami Trolleys, WIN 41
    New Castle Consulting, WIN 375
    For Pet's Sake, WIN 1
    Place to Place, WIN 433
    Snap Home Association, WIN 205
    Step Up career coaching agency, WIN 147

cast, WIN 364

Cc lines, email, WIN 184

CD drives, accessing, WIN 29

central processing unit (CPU)
    See also CPU (central processing unit)
    described, WIN 498

certificates, WIN 230

Change Security and Maintenance settings window (fig.), WIN 540

Check Disk, WIN 469

clicking, WIN 6, WIN 8

clip art
    described, WIN 310
    images websites, WIN 310

Clipboard, WIN 59, WIN 335

clock speed, WIN 502

clocks, different time zones, WIN 264–266

Close button, WIN 8, WIN 34

closing
    apps, WIN 20–22
    apps with End Task, WIN 499
    Hub, Microsoft Edge, WIN 177
    Mail app, WIN 191
    Paint, WIN 339
    windows, WIN 118
    Windows 10, WIN 33–34

cloud, WIN 45

cloud computing, WIN 151

Cloud-based protection, WIN 224

Collapse button, WIN 13

collapse icon, WIN 24, WIN 48

color cast, WIN 349

color management settings, WIN 486–487

color palette, WIN 307

color profiles, WIN 487

color settings, display devices, WIN 484

color temperature, WIN 349

colors
    accent, in windows and Start menu, WIN 90
    background. See background colors
    changing accent, WIN 98–100
    changing desktop, WIN 98–100
    changing graphic's, WIN 334–335
    filling area with, WIN 334
    foreground. See foreground colors
    selecting in Edit Colors dialog box (fig.), WIN 324
    tinting, WIN 350–351
    tools, WIN 349

Colors group's color palette, WIN 307

combining
    Boolean filters and file properties, WIN 288
    search criteria, WIN 285

commands
    See also specific command
    selecting, performing action, WIN 18

compatibility, setting up program for, WIN 459–461

compressed (zipped) folders, WIN 64

compressed files
    extracting, WIN 83
    working with, WIN 81–82

compressing files, folders, WIN 81–83

computer graphics, WIN 308–310

Computer icon, WIN 110

computers
    adding to homegroups, WIN 411–412
    connecting to Internet (fig.), WIN 150
    controlling access to your, WIN 249–250
    drives and disks (fig.), WIN 44
    exploring your, WIN 26–30
    multiboot, WIN 466
    preparing for presentations, WIN 394–396
    protecting from malware, WIN 214–220
    resetting, recovering a system, WIN 454–455
    restoring, WIN 453–454
    restoring your settings, WIN 490–491
    setting up to use offline files, WIN 416–417
    speed of, WIN 498
    synchronizing, WIN 240

connecting
    to external display devices, WIN 398
    to wireless networks, WIN 402–404

connections, managing network, WIN 401–404

contacts, adding to People app, WIN 191–193

contents, searching for files by, WIN 269–270

contextual tabs, WIN 27

contrast, display setting, WIN 340, WIN 484

Control Panel, WIN 92
    categories (fig.), WIN 93
    opening, WIN 92–93
    searching for, WIN 266
    System window, WIN 500

controls, WIN 18
    dialog box, WIN 19
    types on ribbon (fig.), WIN 19

Conversation view, WIN 178

cookies, WIN 227, WIN 235

Copy command, WIN 61–62

copying, WIN 58
    compared with backing up files, WIN 437
    drag files for, WIN 62
    files using Clipboard, right-drag technique, WIN 61–62
    images, WIN 335–337
    and pasting to create graphic, WIN 315–317
    photos to OneDrive, WIN 354–355

copyrighted
    photos, WIN 343
    webpage content, WIN 176

Cortana, WIN 2, WIN 10, WIN 11
    accessing, WIN 10–11
    activating, WIN 162–163
    finding instant result, WIN 163–164
    finding webpages and topic details, WIN 164–165
    pane, Microsoft Edge, WIN 148
    searching for apps and information, WIN 261–263
    searching for files, WIN 267–270
    searching for online information using, WIN 162–165
    searching the web, WIN 288–290
    searching with, WIN 260

counters for tracking performance, WIN 513–515

CPU (central processing unit)
    See also central processing unit (CPU)
    column, Task Manager, WIN 499
    percent used, Resource Monitor, WIN 518
    usage, Task Manager, WIN 510

crackers, WIN 208

Create an account for this PC window (fig.), WIN 244

creating
    backup strategy, WIN 444–445
    compressed folders, WIN 82
    desktop shortcuts, WIN 112–115
    email messages, WIN 184–186
    files, WIN 68–69
    folders, WIN 56–58
    graphics by copying and pasting, WIN 315–317
    graphics in Paint, WIN 310–312
    homegroups, WIN 408–411
    local-only user accounts, WIN 242–243
    music playlists, WIN 362–363
    PINs, WIN 245–246
    Reading list, Microsoft Edge, WIN 169–170
    screenshots of Start menu, WIN 137–138
    and sending email messages with attachment, WIN 188–189
    shortcuts, methods of (fig.), WIN 113
    subfolders, WIN 58
    System Diagnostics Report, WIN 519–520
    system recovery points, WIN 449–450
    text boxes, WIN 322–323

critical errors, WIN 543

critical events, WIN 540

cropping
    graphics, WIN 337–338
    photos, WIN 341

Ctrl+Alt+Del keys, WIN 5

currency conversion, WIN 262–263

Customize Settings window, Windows Firewall, WIN 212

customized folder window (visual overview), WIN 64–65

customizing
    folder windows, WIN 76–81
    navigation pane, WIN 80–81
    New tab, WIN 159
    power options, WIN 386–389
    presentation settings, WIN 395–396

D

daisy-chain, WIN 477

daisy-chaining devices, WIN 477

data
    cached, WIN 236
    managing (visual overview), WIN 434–435

Data Files
    described, WIN 42
    navigating to, WIN 52–53

Date and time dialog box (fig.), WIN 266

date modified, searching for files by, WIN 274–275

dates, sorting files by (fig.), WIN 74

Date/Time control, WIN 2

decision making
    creating backup strategy, WIN 444–445
    selecting bitmap or vector graphics, WIN 309
    selecting performance tools, WIN 517
    using copyright-protected, royalty-free, and public-domain photos, WIN 343

default settings, WIN 6

defragmenting disks, WIN 463, WIN 472–475

deleting
    See also removing
    area of graphic, WIN 327
    cookies, browsing history, WIN 236–237
    email messages, WIN 190–191, WIN 191
    files and folders, WIN 67–68
    unnecessary files with Disk Cleanup, WIN 468–469

deprecated, WIN 158

desktop
    adding shortcuts to, WIN 110–111
    changing background, WIN 96–98
    changing colors, WIN 98–100
    customized, visual overview, WIN 90–91
    described, WIN 5
    icons, personalizing, WIN 109–110

interacting with, WIN 6
managing with taskbar tools, WIN 123–128
settings, saving as theme, WIN 106
touring the, WIN 6–9
two windows open on (fig.), WIN 5
using virtual, WIN 127–128
visual overview, WIN 2–3

desktop apps, WIN 11

desktop icons, WIN 109, WIN 111–112

Desktop Icons Settings dialog box (fig.), WIN 111

desktop shortcuts, creating, WIN 112–115

desktop theme, WIN 2

Details pane, WIN 65, WIN 77, WIN 78, WIN 277

Details tab, Properties dialog box, WIN 508

Details view
described, WIN 24, WIN 28
sorting and filtering files, WIN 73

device conflict, WIN 478

device drivers
described, WIN 479
installing, updating, WIN 482–484

Device Manager, WIN 480–482

Device Manager window (fig.), WIN 481

devices
See also specific device
daisy-chaining, WIN 477
enabling, disabling, WIN 479–482
installing, WIN 479
maintaining display, WIN 484–487
removing, WIN 484
resources, WIN 478–479
working with, WIN 476–478

Devices and Printers window in Details view (fig.), WIN 537

devices described, WIN 462

Devices window, Settings app (fig.), WIN 489

diagnosing system, WIN 519–520

dialog boxes
described, WIN 19
using, WIN 19–20

digital cameras, WIN 342

digital signatures
described, WIN 228
detecting, WIN 232
and Microsoft Edge, WIN 228

direct memory access (DMA) channel, WIN 478

disabling, enabling devices, WIN 479–482

disk, WIN 44

Disk Cleanup dialog box (fig.), WIN 469

Disk Cleanup tool, WIN 462, WIN 468–469

Disk Management window (fig.), WIN 467

display devices, maintaining, WIN 484–487

display options, WIN 397

display settings, changing, WIN 106–109

displaying
See also showing, viewing
Action Center, WIN 526
basic system information, WIN 500–503
Calendar details on lock screen, WIN 195–196
contents of another computer, WIN 406
Favorites bar, WIN 173
file history, WIN 446–447
filename extensions, WIN 65
filename extensions in folder windows, WIN 79–80
file's properties, WIN 258
folders available for sharing, WIN 414–415
gridlines, WIN 306
History list, WIN 170–171, WIN 238
images in live Photos tile, WIN 134
images of vintage art, WIN 294–295
information on external display device, WIN 396–398
pictures on desktop background, WIN 96–98
quarantined files, WIN 222
shortcut menus, WIN 8–9
standard desktop icons, WIN 110–111
webpages in Internet Explorer, WIN 158

Do Not Track requests, Microsoft Edge, WIN 238–239

.doc files, WIN 271

documents, printing, WIN 19–20

Documents folder
displaying contents of, WIN 51
opening, WIN 29–30, WIN 50–51

.docx, WIN 71

domain names, WIN 154

double-clicking, WIN 7

downloading
files safely, WIN 231–232
themes, WIN 105

Downloads list, using, WIN 176, WIN 231–232

dragging
described, WIN 16
to move and copy files (fig.), WIN 62

drawing shapes, WIN 325–327

drive, WIN 44

drive Properties dialog box (fig.), WIN 465

Driver tab, device's Properties dialog box (fig.), WIN 483

drivers
described, working with, WIN 479
installing printer, WIN 490
working with, WIN 484

drives, creating shortcut to USB, WIN 113–114

dual-boot computers, WIN 466

DVD drives, accessing, WIN 29

E

East access button menu, WIN 407

Easy Connect, WIN 549

Edit colors button, WIN 307

Edit Colors dialog box (fig.), WIN 324

Edit Plan Settings window (fig.), WIN 390

editing
appointments, WIN 195
photos, WIN 349–352
photos (visual overview), WIN 340–341
photos in OneDrive, WIN 357–358
pictures, WIN 71
text files, WIN 71

effects
See also specific effect
applying, WIN 340
for editing photos, WIN 349

email
See also Mail app
addressing, WIN 181
compressing files to transfer, WIN 82
defending against viruses, WIN 225
etiquette, WIN 190
getting started with, WIN 180–181
messages. *See* email messages
sending and receiving (fig.), WIN 180
sending and receiving using Mail app, WIN 183–188
setting up, WIN 181–183
sharing photos via, WIN 353–354

email app, WIN 180

email messages
attaching files to, WIN 188–189
creating, sending, reading, WIN 184–186
deleting, WIN 190–191, WIN 191
described (fig.), WIN 179
replying to, WIN 187–188
and viruses, WIN 189

email relay, WIN 225

email server, WIN 180

enabling, disabling devices, WIN 479–482

Encrypting File System (EFS), WIN 438

End Task button, WIN 499

Enhance tool, WIN 341, WIN 349, WIN 350

Error-Checking (OS (C:)) dialog box (fig.),
WIN 472

Error-checking tool, WIN 463

errors
    checking hard disks for, WIN 469–472
    information, viewing details about (fig.),
    WIN 542
    recovering from software, WIN 538–547
    reporting and solving software,
    WIN 538–540
    troubleshooting printing, WIN 536–538

Ethernet technology, WIN 398–400

etiquette, email, WIN 190

Event Properties window (fig.), WIN 545

Event Viewer, WIN 543–545

events
    adding to Calendar, WIN 194
    critical, information, WIN 540
    viewing details about system, WIN 543–545

Exchange email accounts, WIN 181

Exclusion list, Windows Defender, WIN 224

Exit command, WIN 21–22

exiting
    See also closing
    apps, WIN 21–22
    Microsoft Edge, WIN 177

expand icon, WIN 24, WIN 30, WIN 52

expansion slots, WIN 477–478

external display devices
    connecting to, WIN 398
    displaying information on, WIN 396–398

external hard drives, WIN 438

extract, WIN 82

extracting compressed files, WIN 83

F

facial scans, WIN 242

family and other user settings, user accounts,
WIN 243

FAT32 file system, WIN 464

Favorites list
    adding webpages to, WIN 172–174
    adding webpages to folders in, WIN 174
    displaying, hiding, WIN 173
    links to webpages in (fig,), WIN 174

in Microsoft Edge, WIN 149
    organizing, WIN 175
    quick access to webpages, WIN 169

file allocation table (FAT) file system, WIN 438

File Explorer, WIN 5
    accessing from Start menu, WIN 10
    deleting files, WIN 231
    displaying contents of another computer,
    WIN 406
    examining photos using, WIN 345
    exploring files, folders, WIN 48–55
    illustrated (fig.), WIN 43
    navigating with, WIN 26–27
    playing slide shows, WIN 348–349
    viewing, organizing photos, WIN 344
    visual overview, WIN 24–25

file formats
    bitmap file, WIN 308
    graphics (fig.), WIN 314
    MP3, WIN 359
    video, WIN 364

File History, WIN 434
    backing up data using (fig.), WIN 436
    saved versions of files, WIN 434
    setting up to back up files, WIN 437–445
    using with homegroups, WIN 441

file icons, WIN 43

file path, WIN 42

file system, WIN 45

file types
    compressed, WIN 82
    .docx files, WIN 71
    searching for files by, WIN 270–271
    .txt, WIN 66, WIN 71

FileHistory folder, WIN 445

filename extensions
    described, WIN 66
    displaying in folder windows, WIN 65,
    WIN 79–80

filenames
    anatomy of, WIN 66
    described, WIN 43

files, WIN 5
    accessing offline, WIN 415–419
    adding tags to, WIN 278–281
    attaching to email messages, WIN 188–189
    backing up, WIN 436–440
    backup. See backup files
    cached, WIN 236
    compressed. See compressed files
    compressing, extracting, WIN 81–83
    copying vs. backing up, WIN 437
    creating, WIN 68–69
    creating and saving, WIN 72

deciding where to store, WIN 48
    deleting, WIN 67–68
    deleting unnecessary with Disk Cleanup,
    WIN 468–469
    Details view of, WIN 24
    determining which to back up, WIN 439
    downloading safely, WIN 231–232
    dragging to move and copy (fig.), WIN 62
    exploring, WIN 48–55
    extract described, WIN 82
    finding music, WIN 359–361
    finding using Search box, WIN 55–56
    in folder window (visual overview),
    WIN 42–43
    in folders, viewing, WIN 48–49
    fragmented (fig.), WIN 474
    hidden, WIN 79
    making available offline, WIN 418–419
    managing, WIN 56–62
    moving, WIN 58–60
    naming, renaming, WIN 66–67
    offline, WIN 407
    opening and editing, WIN 71
    opening digital picture, WIN 71
    opening image, WIN 313
    organizing, WIN 45–48, WIN 72–76
    pathnames, WIN 154
    preparing to manage your, WIN 44–48
    preventing lost file problems, WIN 73
    quarantined, WIN 222
    renaming, WIN 64
    restoring, WIN 446–448
    saving, WIN 69–70, WIN 339
    saving graphics, WIN 314–315
    searching for, WIN 267–277
    searching for (visual overview), WIN 258–259
    selecting multiple, WIN 61
    sharing with homegroups, WIN 412–413
    sorting and filtering, WIN 72–76
    storing on OneDrive, WIN 45
    viewing contents, WIN 68

filling area with color, WIN 334

filter, WIN 72

filtering
    to display files modified today (fig.), WIN 75
    and grouping files in folders, WIN 75–76
    search results, WIN 282
    search results by size, WIN 272
    vs. searching, grouping, sorting, WIN 272
    and sorting files, WIN 73–76

filters, WIN 340
    Boolean. See Boolean filters
    for editing photos, WIN 349,
    WIN 351–352
    search, WIN 258, WIN 273–274

Find toolbar, WIN 283

finding
See also searching
music files, WIN 359–361
troubleshooting information, WIN 529–538

fingerprint readers, WIN 242, WIN 246

firewall. *See* Windows Firewall

first-party cookies, WIN 235, WIN 236

flag icons, email, WIN 187–188

flicker, screen refresh rate, WIN 485–486

flights, finding information about, WIN 289–290

Folder Options dialog box, WIN 65, WIN 80

folder windows, WIN 48
changing layout of, WIN 77–79
customized (visual overview), WIN 64–65
customizing, WIN 76–81
Zip button, Send group, Share tab, WIN 82

folders, WIN 5, WIN 24
backup, WIN 441–443
changing views of, WIN 53
compressed (zipped), WIN 64
compressing, WIN 81–83
contents grouped (fig.), WIN 64
creating, WIN 56–58
customized window (visual overview),
WIN 64–65
deleting, WIN 67–68
displaying history, WIN 446–448
dragging to move and copy (fig.), WIN 62
exploring, WIN 48–55
in Favorites list, adding webpages to,
WIN 174
FileHistory, WIN 445
finding files using Search box, WIN 55–56
in Mail app, WIN 178
making available offline, WIN 418–419
managing, WIN 56–62
moving, WIN 58–60
naming, renaming, WIN 66–67
OneDrive, WIN 354
organizing, WIN 45–48
pinning to Start menu, WIN 131
Quick access, WIN 26
restoring, WIN 446–448
saving files to, WIN 70–71
selecting multiple, WIN 61
selecting to share, WIN 410
selecting which to back up, WIN 438–439
sorting and filtering files in, WIN 75–76
synchronizing, WIN 419–421
viewing contents, WIN 49–50
windows. *See* folder windows
zipped. *See* compressed (zipped) folders

foreground colors, WIN 307, WIN 320

Forward location button, WIN 42, WIN 50

FreeSail Boat Club (case), WIN 305

Frequent folders list, WIN 26

G

GB, WIN 44

Get Started app
starting, WIN 31
viewing Get Started topics, WIN 32

GIF files, WIN 314

gigabytes, WIN 44

Gmail, WIN 181, WIN 182

Google Advanced Search page, WIN 292–293

Google email, WIN 181

Google search engine, WIN 291, WIN 293

graphics, WIN 308
adding text to, WIN 320–325
copying and pasting to create, WIN 315–317
creating in Paint, WIN 310–312
creating in Paint (visual overview),
WIN 306–307
cropping, WIN 337–338
exploring computer, WIN 308–310
file formats (fig.), WIN 314
magnifying, WIN 320
moving part of, WIN 327–330
opening in Paint, WIN 312–314
resizing, rotating, WIN 330–332
saving bitmap, in different file type, WIN 315
saving files, WIN 314–315
selecting area for deletion, WIN 332–333,
WIN 338
vector, WIN 308, WIN 309

graphics apps, WIN 306

graphics files, saving, WIN 313–314

graphics images, WIN 308

gridlines, displaying, WIN 306, WIN 336

Groove Music
described, WIN 359–361
playing music in (fig.), WIN 362

grouping
described, WIN 72
and filtering files in folders, WIN 75–76
vs. searching, WIN 272

groups described, WIN 18, WIN 64

H

hackers, WIN 208, WIN 218

Halo series of games, WIN 11

hard disks, WIN 44
checking for errors, WIN 469–472
defragmenting, WIN 472–475

maintaining, WIN 463, WIN 464
organizing folders, files on (fig.), WIN 47
partitions, checking for, WIN 466–468
platter on (fig.), WIN 470
viewing properties, WIN 464–466

hardware, WIN 462
managing (visual overview), WIN 462–463
needed for types of network technology
(fig.), WIN 400
working with devices, drivers, WIN 476–484

Hardware tab, WIN 463

Hardware tab, OS (C:) Properties dialog box
(fig.), WIN 466

HealthWeb (case), WIN 497

Help
Bing, WIN 293
getting, WIN 31
Microsoft Support, WIN 222, WIN 526

Hey Cortana setting, WIN 289

hibernating webpages, WIN 34

hibernation, WIN 376, WIN 386

hidden files, WIN 79

Hide Folders button, Save As dialog box,
WIN 70

hiding
filename extensions in windows, WIN 79–80
navigation pane, WIN 76
notifications, WIN 394
Task View button, WIN 121

High performance power plan, WIN 385,
WIN 386

History list, WIN 169
revisiting webpages from, WIN 171–172
using, WIN 170–171

hits, WIN 282

home networks
described, WIN 408
setting up, WIN 400–401

home page, Microsoft Edge, WIN 152–153

Home tab, WIN 18, WIN 24

HomeGroup tab buttons, WIN 406

homegroups, WIN 406
accessing shared files on, WIN 414–415
capabilities of, WIN 406
creating, WIN 408–411
File History, using with, WIN 441
joining, WIN 411–412
leaving, WIN 409
sharing files with, WIN 412–413
sharing printers with, WIN 415
Windows and, WIN 408

Hub, Microsoft Edge, WIN 149, WIN 169, WIN 176

hubs
    network, WIN 399
    USB, WIN 477

hybrid sleep, WIN 386–387

hyperlinks, WIN 148

Hypertext Transfer Protocol, WIN 154

I

iCloud, WIN 343

iCloud email, WIN 182

icons
    adding to desktop, WIN 110–111
    Cortana, WIN 162
    on desktop, WIN 2
    desktop, WIN 90
    flag, email, WIN 187–188
    lock, WIN 226
    microphone, WIN 289
    padlock, WIN 239
    personalizing desktop, WIN 109–110
    security, WIN 206
    shortcut, WIN 110

images
    See also photos, pictures
    changing on desktop icons, WIN 111–112
    copying, pasting, WIN 335–337
    displaying in search results, WIN 294–295
    graphics, WIN 308
    inserting, WIN 331
    magnifying, WIN 320–321
    moving, WIN 316–317, WIN 317–319
    open in Paint (fig.), WIN 313
    pasting in files, WIN 315–316
    resizing, rotating, WIN 330–332
    of vintage art, displaying, WIN 294–295

importing
    contact information to People app, WIN 192
    photos, WIN 342–344

indexed locations, WIN 276

information, presenting to audience, WIN 394–398

information events, WIN 540

InPrivate Browsing, WIN 226–227, WIN 237–238

inserting images in files, WIN 331

install described, WIN 456

installed apps, WIN 435

installing
    apps from Windows Store, WIN 456–457
    devices, WIN 479

local printers, WIN 488–489
software on USB drives, WIN 461
and updating device drivers, WIN 482–484

Internet, WIN 150
    exploring, WIN 150–151
    metered connections, WIN 215
    searching the (visual overview), WIN 282–283

Internet Explorer, displaying webpages in, WIN 158

Internet service providers (ISPs), WIN 152, WIN 181

interrupt request (IRQ) line, WIN 478

I/O address, WIN 478

IP address, WIN 154

IRQ conflicts, WIN 478

J

joining homegroups, WIN 411–412

.jpg files, WIN 271, WIN 273

JPG picture files (.jpg, .jpeg), WIN 82, WIN 314

Jump List, WIN 119

junk email, WIN 191, WIN 225

Junk folder, Mail app, WIN 178, WIN 191

K

keyboard shortcuts, WIN 15

keywords, WIN 291, WIN 294

L

laptops, WIN 378

large icons, WIN 25

Large icons view, WIN 28

Laser Printer print queue (fig.), WIN 537

Last Known Good Configuration, WIN 546, WIN 547

layout of folder windows, changing, WIN 77–79

LCD display screen settings, WIN 107

Library of Congress webpage (fig.), WIN 151

license agreements for software, WIN 220

Life at a glance group of apps, WIN 128

links
    adding to webpages in Favorites list, WIN 173–174
    navigating with, WIN 155–157
    verifying, WIN 241

live tiles, WIN 7

local area networks (LANs), WIN 398

local disks, WIN 462

local printers, WIN 488

local-only user accounts, WIN 240, WIN 242–243

lock icon, WIN 226

lock screen, WIN 4, WIN 36
    displaying Calendar details on, WIN 195–196
    personalizing, changing picture, WIN 100–102
    settings, adding to Start menu, WIN 130–131

logos
    cropping graphic, WIN 337–338
    design for (fig.), WIN 313

M

Magnifier tool, Tools group, Home tab, WIN 320

Mail app
    See also Calendar app, email
    closing, WIN 191
    sending and receiving email using, WIN 183–188
    sharing photos via email, WIN 353–354
    tools and components, WIN 184
    visual overview, WIN 178–179

Mail tile, WIN 134

Maintain aspect ratio box, WIN 330, WIN 331

maintaining
    display devices, WIN 484–487
    hard disks, WIN 463, WIN 464–476

Make a Web Note tools, Microsoft Edge, WIN 149, WIN 168

malicious software, WIN 208

malware, WIN 208
    blocking, WIN 232–233
    protecting your computer from, WIN 218–220
    recognizing types of, WIN 218
    and Unified Extensible Firmware Interface (UEFI), WIN 250

managing
    application software, WIN 456–461
    data and software (visual overview), WIN 434–435
    desktop with taskbar tools, WIN 123–128
    downloaded files, WIN 231–232
    files and folders, WIN 56–62
    hardware (visual overview), WIN 462–463
    Microsoft Edge security, WIN 228–234
    mobile computing devices, WIN 378–379
    network connections, WIN 401–404
    system software, WIN 448–455

webpages with Microsoft Edge, WIN 158–161

Windows Firewall, WIN 210–214

your schedule with Calendar, WIN 193–195

manipulating windows, WIN 15–17

Maps app, and Cortana, WIN 11

Maximize button, WIN 16, WIN 31

media
multimedia settings, Power Options dialog box, WIN 392
music. See music
videos, WIN 364

Medium Icon view, WIN 53

memory
address, memory range, WIN 479
increasing capacity, WIN 520–522
increasing capacity using ReadyBoost, WIN 522–524
low memory problems, preventing and solving, WIN 513
space, WIN 464
virtual, WIN 513

Memory details, Performance tab (fig.), WIN 511

Memory, Task Manager, WIN 498, WIN 499

Memory usage graph, Task Manager, WIN 510

menu commands, WIN 7

menus, WIN 7
See also specific menu
shortcut. See shortcut menus

metered Internet connection, WIN 215

microphone icon, WIN 289

microprocessors, WIN 477–478

Microsoft accounts, WIN 4, WIN 45, WIN 192, WIN 240
for apps from Windows Store, WIN 456
obtaining, WIN 354

Microsoft Community, WIN 526, WIN 530, WIN 534–536

Microsoft Edge, WIN 32
adding search engines, WIN 296
Cortana. See Cortana
default home page (fig.), WIN 153
exiting, WIN 177
Favorites list. See Favorites list
getting started with, WIN 152–153
managing security, WIN 228–234
managing webpages with, WIN 158–161
privacy settings, WIN 234–237
Reading list, WIN 169–170
searching the web, WIN 291–292
security features, visual overview, WIN 226–227

tools, navigating with, WIN 158
visual overview, WIN 148–149
as Windows app, WIN 152

Microsoft Report a website webpage (fig.), WIN 230

Microsoft Support webpage, WIN 222

Microsoft Support website, WIN 526

Microsoft website, searching for help on, WIN 32–33

Microsoft Windows 10, WIN 4

Microsoft Word .docx files, WIN 71

Minimize button, WIN 15–16

Miracast wireless display technology, WIN 364

mobile computing, Balanced plan, WIN 376

mobile computing devices, managing, WIN 378–379

mobile computing settings (visual overview), WIN 376–377

mobile devices, WIN 378
displaying information on external display device, WIN 396–398
syncing one- and two-way, WIN 419
taking photos with, WIN 342–344

modems, WIN 400

Monitor tab, display's Properties dialog box (fig.), WIN 486

monitoring system performance, WIN 512–517

motherboard, WIN 477–478

mouse, WIN 6
clicking, WIN 6
double-clicking, WIN 7
right-clicking, WIN 8

Movies & TV app, WIN 364

moving
described, WIN 58
files, folders, WIN 58–60
images, WIN 316–317, WIN 317–319
part of graphic, WIN 327–330
taskbar buttons, WIN 120–121
text boxes, WIN 329–330
text in shapes, WIN 328–329

multiboot computer, WIN 466

multicore processor, WIN 498

music
creating playlists, WIN 362–363
finding files, WIN 359–361
playing files, WIN 361–362
playing slide shows with, WIN 363–364

Music folder, WIN 51

N

name, searching for files by, WIN 267–269

naming
See also renaming
files and folders, WIN 66–67
folders, WIN 56–57
groups of tiles, WIN 133
image files, WIN 314–315
user names, WIN 241–242

National Park Service (NPS), WIN 165

native resolution, WIN 107

navigating, WIN 26
with Address Bar, WIN 54–55
with File Explorer, WIN 26–27
hierarchy of folders, drives, WIN 54
with links, WIN 155–157
with Microsoft Edge tools, WIN 158
to your Data Files, WIN 52–53

navigation area, Microsoft Edge, WIN 153

navigation bar, Microsoft Edge, WIN 148

navigation buttons, WIN 55

navigation pane, WIN 25
customizing, WIN 80–81
in folder window, WIN 77–78
hiding, WIN 76
using, WINI 29–30, WIN 48–49

network adapters, WIN 399

Network and Sharing Center window (fig.), WIN 402

Network folder as backup location, WIN 438

network hubs, WIN 399

network interface cards, WIN 399

Network Level Authentication (NLA), WIN 422

network resources, WIN 406

network security key, WIN 402

network technologies
comparing (fig.), WIN 399
described, WIN 398

networks, WIN 45
concepts, WIN 398–400
connecting to wireless, WIN 402–404
home. See home networks
managing connections, WIN 401–402
private and public, WIN 211
setting up small office or home, WIN 400–401

New Castle Consulting (case), WIN 375

New Folder button, WIN 24

news feed, WIN 153

NOT Boolean filter, WIN 284–285, WIN 293

Notebook
  Cortana's use of, WIN 163
  described, WIN 11

Notepad, creating and saving files, WIN 68–71

notification area, WIN 2, WIN 117
  battery meter icon (fig.), WIN 382
  illustrated (fig.), WIN 117
  monitoring, WIN 119

Notification bar, Microsoft Edge, WIN 227

notifications
  hiding, WIN 394
  Quiet hours, WIN 529
  responding to, WIN 528–529
  security and maintenance, WIN 526

Notifications icon, WIN 210

NT File System (NTFS), WIN 438, WIN 450,
WIN 462, WIN 464

O

objects
  active, WIN 7
  changing size of, WIN 108–109
  clicking, WIN 6
  dragging, WIN 16
  right-clicking, WIN 9
  selecting, opening, WIN 7–8

office networks, setting up small, WIN 400–401

offline files, WIN 407
  accessing, WIN 415–419
  making available, WIN 418–419
  synchronizing, WIN 416
  syncing, WIN 420–421

OneDrive, WIN 29, WIN 47, WIN 48, WIN 182,
WIN 343
  responding to invitation messages,
  WIN 356–357
  saving, opening files location, WIN 70
  sharing photos using, WIN 354–359
  stored pictures on, WIN 101
  storing files on, WIN 45
  synchronizing files, WIN 422
  website, WIN 354

OneDrive app, WIN 344, WIN 355–356

OneNote, WIN 169

online, WIN 407

Opaque button, Text Tools Text tab, Background
group, WIN 322

Open command, WIN 71

Open dialog box, WIN 71

opening
  See also starting
  apps, WIN 457–458

Control Panel, WIN 92–93
  dialog boxes, WIN 19
  drives, folders, WIN 49–50
  email messages with attachments,
  WIN 189
  File Explorer, WIN 26
  files, WIN 71–72
  folders, WIN 27
  graphics in Paint, WIN 312–314
  image files, WIN 313
  objects, WIN 7–8
  Personalization window, WIN 95
  Recycle Bin, WIN 7
  Screen Saver Settings dialog box, WIN 103
  Security and Maintenance window,
  WIN 208–209
  Start menu, WIN 7
  Sync Center, WIN 420
  webpages, WIN 154–158
  webpages on new tabs, WIN 159–160
  Windows Mobility Center, WIN 380

operating system, recovering, WIN 527,
WIN 545–547

Optimize button, WIN 463

Optimize Drives dialog box (fig.), WIN 475

Optimize Drives tool, WIN 472, WIN 475–476

optimizing drives, WIN 463

OR Boolean filter, WIN 284–285, WIN 287,
WIN 288

organizing
  Favorites list, WIN 175
  files, folders, WIN 45–48, WIN 72–76
  tiles on Start menu, WIN 132–133
  and viewing photos, WIN 344–348

Outlook.com, WIN 180
  setting up email accounts, WIN 181,
  WIN 182–183
  signing up for email account, WIN 179

Overview tab, Resource Monitor window (fig.),
WIN 518

P

padlock icon, WIN 239

paging file, WIN 513, WIN 516

Paint, WIN 310
  closing, WIN 339
  creating graphics in, WIN 310–312
  creating graphics in (visual overview),
  WIN 306–307
  images. See images
  opening graphics in, WIN 312–314
  resizing, rotating images, WIN 330–332
  starting, WIN 310

tools (fig.), WIN 312
  Transparent selection command, WIN 328
  window, WIN 15–17, WIN 311

Paint app
  closing, exiting, WIN 21–22
  pinning to taskbar, WIN 119–120
  running multiple, WIN 13–14

painting programs, WIN 308

panes
  See also specific pane
  described, WIN 9, WIN 48
  of Start menu (fig.), WIN 10

Panes group options, WIN 64

partitions, checking for hard drive, WIN 466–468

passphrases, WIN 402

passwords, WIN 4
  for backups, WIN 438
  requiring on wakeup, WIN 393–394
  selecting for user accounts, WIN 241–242
  strong, WIN 227, WIN 241

Paste command, WIN 62

pasting images in files, WIN 315–316

pathnames, WIN 154

PDF files, WIN 129

Peek, keeping track of windows with,
WIN 125–126

Peek taskbar tool, WIN 116

People app
  adding information to, WIN 191–193
  and Cortana, WIN 11
  turning on Start menu live tiles,
  WIN 134–135

People Search, Yahoo!, WIN 181

performance
  improving system, WIN 500–520
  measuring system, WIN 517–519
  monitoring system, WIN 512–517
  selecting tool to solve problems, WIN 517
  tools and tasks (fig.), WIN 500
  tracking system (visual overview),
  WIN 498–499

Performance, Task Manager, WIN 498

Performance Monitor
  described, WIN 512
  monitoring system performance,
  WIN 512–517

Performance Options
  dialog box, Advanced tab, WIN 520–521
  dialog box (fig.), WIN 506

Performance tab, Memory details (fig.),
WIN 511

Personal calendar, WIN 193

personal folder, WIN 90

personal information number (PIN), WIN 241, WIN 245–246

personalization tools, WIN 90

Personalization window, WIN 91, WIN 95

personalized assistant. *See* Cortana

personalizing
 desktop icons, WIN 109–110
 lock screen, WIN 100–102
 Mail app's appearance, WIN 185
 Start menu, WIN 128–138
 taskbar, WIN 118

phishing, WIN 210, WIN 225, WIN 229

photos
 acquiring, importing, WIN 342–344
 albums, WIN 357, WIN 358
 copyright-protected, royalty-free, and public-domain, WIN 343
 cropping, WIN 341
 editing, WIN 349–352
 editing (visual overview), WIN 340–341
 retouching, WIN 341
 rotating, WIN 341
 saving, WIN 349
 searching for, WIN 273–274
 selecting, WIN 340, WIN 351
 sharing from Photos app, WIN 352–354
 sharing generally, WIN 352
 sharing using OneDrive, WIN 354–359
 storing in specific locations, WIN 134
 touching up, WIN 349–350
 viewing, organizing, WIN 344–348
 working with, WIN 342

Photos app, WIN 340, WIN 344
 sharing photos from, WIN 352–354
 slide show feature in, WIN 394

Photos tile, making live, WIN 135

picture passwords, WIN 241–242, WIN 247–248

Picture Tools Manage tab, WIN 27

pictures
 See also images, photos
 changing desktop background, WIN 96–98
 changing lock screen, WIN 100–102
 changing user account, WIN 136–137
 displaying on lock screen, WIN 91
 opening digital files, WIN 71
 personalized lock screen (fig.), WIN 102

Pictures folder, WIN 51, WIN 340
 copying photos to, WIN 344–345
 displaying contents of, WIN 30
 in File Explorer, WIN 27

Pinned items on taskbar, WIN 118

pinning, WIN 80
 apps to taskbar, WIN 119–120
 folders to Quick access list, WIN 80–81
 tiles on Start menu, WIN 129–130
 webpages to Start menu, WIN 160–161

pixel coordinates, WIN 306

pixels, WIN 106

Place to Place (case), WIN 433

platter on hard disk (fig.), WIN 470

Play and explore group of apps, WIN 128

playing
 music files, WIN 361–362
 slide shows, WIN 348–349
 slide shows with music, WIN 363–364
 videos, WIN 364

playlists, creating, WIN 362–363

PNG files, WIN 314

point, WIN 6

pointer, WIN 2

pointing device, WIN 6

pop-up ads, WIN 220

Pop-up Blocker, WIN 226, WIN 228, WIN 233–234

pop-up windows, blocking, WIN 233–234

ports, WIN 476

positioning windows, WIN 17

Post Office Protocol (POP) accounts, WIN 182

Power command, WIN 10, WIN 34, WIN 35

power failure, error-checking after, WIN 470

Power menu options, WIN 35–36

power options, WIN 393
 customizing, WIN 386–389
 selecting other, WIN 393–394

Power Options dialog box (fig.), WIN 392

Power Options window (fig.), WIN 388

power plans, WIN 376
 default (fig.), WIN 385
 modifying, WIN 389–393
 selecting, WIN 384–386

Power saver plan, WIN 385, WIN 386

Power saving plan, WIN 376

Powerline network technology, WIN 398–399, WIN 400

Presentation Settings dialog box (fig.), WIN 395

Presentation settings (mobile computing), WIN 377

presentations
 background to keep desktop private, WIN 377
 customizing settings, WIN 395–396
 preparing computer for, WIN 394–396

Preview pane
 described, WIN 77
 in folder window, WIN 77–78

previewing
 documents before printing, WIN 19
 images before printing, WIN 319
 windows with Peek (fig.), WIN 126

previews, windows corresponding to taskbar buttons, WIN 118

Previous Locations button, Address bar, WIN 54

Print command, WIN 19

Print dialog box, working with, WIN 20

Print Preview, WIN 319

print queue, WIN 536

printers
 setting up, WIN 488–490
 sharing with homegroups, WIN 415

printing
 documents, WIN 19–20
 errors, troubleshooting, WIN 536–538
 Quick Print, WIN 19
 webpage content, WIN 176–177

privacy
 protecting with InPrivate Browsing, WIN 237–238
 settings, Microsoft Edge, WIN 234–237

private networks, WIN 211

Problem Details window (fig.), WIN 543

problems
 sending problem reports, WIN 527
 solving system (visual overview), WIN 526–527
 troubleshooting and fixing computer, WIN 531–534
 troubleshooting system, WIN 530

processes, WIN 499

Processes tab, Task Manager, WIN 499, WIN 509, WIN 538

processor, WIN 500

processor time, tracking, WIN 514

Program Compatibility Assistant dialog box, WIN 459

Program Compatibility Troubleshooter, WIN 459–461

programs, WIN 4
  background, WIN 117, WIN 119
  for compatibility, setting up, WIN 459–461
  at Windows Store, WIN 129

properties
  adding to files, WIN 277
  displaying file's, WIN 258
  of objects, changing, WIN 92
  setting taskbar, WIN 122–123
  using file, as search criteria (fig.),
  WIN 284–285

Properties dialog box (fig.), WIN 278

Properties dialog box for device driver (fig.),
WIN 483

protocols, WIN 154

public domain described, WIN 343

Public folder, turning sharing on, WIN 417

public networks, WIN 211

public-domain photos, WIN 343

Q

quarantined, WIN 222

Quick access
  changing window view, WIN 28
  folders, WIN 26

Quick access list, WIN 48, WIN 60
  pinning, unpinning folders, WIN 80–81
  returning to, WIN 30

Quick Access Toolbar, WIN 42

Quick Actions, Action Center, WIN 526,
WIN 529

Quick Print, WIN 19

Quiet hours, WIN 529

quotation marks, in searches, WIN 293

R

RAM (random access memory), WIN 502–503
  increasing capacity, WIN 520–524
  low memory problems, preventing and
  solving, WIN 513

ratings, photo, WIN 345

Reader app, pinning to Start menu,
WIN 129–130

reading
  email messages (fig.), WIN 186
  webpages, WIN 166–168

Reading list, Microsoft Edge, WIN 149,
WIN 169–170

Reading view, WIN 149, WIN 166–168

ReadyBoost, increasing memory capacity using,
WIN 522–524

Real-time protection, WIN 223

Recent locations button, WIN 42, WIN 50

recording steps on your computer,
WIN 547–549

recovering
  operating system, WIN 527, WIN 545–547
  from software errors, WIN 538–547
  a system, WIN 454–455

recovery options, Windows 10 (fig.), WIN 449

Rectangle tool, WIN 326–327, WIN 333–334

rectangles, drawing, WIN 325–327,
WIN 333–334

Rectangular selection tool, WIN 318

Recycle Bin, WIN 2, WIN 7
  deleting files, folders, WIN 67
  two appearances, WIN 110
  viewing contents, WIN 8

Red eye tool, WIN 341, WIN 349

redisplaying minimized windows, WIN 16

refresh rate, screen, WIN 485–486

registry, and restore points, WIN 435

reinstalling Windows, WIN 546

Related searches list, WIN 283

Reliability Monitor
  described, WIN 527
  viewing, WIN 540–543

Remote Assistance
  in action (fig.), WIN 552
  ending sessions, WIN 553
  requesting, managing, WIN 549–552
  Settings dialog box (fig.), WIN 550

remote connections, now allowing, WIN 426

Remote Desktop Connection
  described, setting up, WIN 422–425
  dialog box (fig.), WIN 423

Remote Desktop with Network Level
Authentication (NLA), WIN 422

Remote tab, System Properties dialog box (fig.),
WIN 424

removable disks
  creating shortcuts to, WIN 114–115
  searching for files on, WIN 276

removing
  See also deleting
  devices, WIN 484
  viruses, WIN 220

Rename command, WIN 66, WIN 67

renaming
  See also naming
  files, WIN 64
  files and folders, WIN 66–67
  folders, WIN 81
  groups of tiles, WIN 133
  renaming, WIN 81
  shortcut icons, WIN 113

replying to email messages, WIN 187–188

reporting software errors, WIN 538–540

reports
  sending problem, WIN 527
  "System Diagnostics Report," WIN 519–520

reputation checking, WIN 228

requesting Remote Assistance, WIN 549–553

resetting, recovering a system, WIN 454–455

Resize and Skew dialog box, WIN 330

resizing
  graphics, WIN 330–332
  Paint canvas, WIN 317–319
  windows, WIN 17

resolution
  changing screen, WIN 107–108, WIN 318
  display, WIN 484
  native, WIN 107

Resolve Conflict dialog box, WIN 421

Resource Monitor, WIN 498
  Overview tab, Resource Monitor window
  (fig.), WIN 518
  using, WIN 517–519

resources
  examining overview of usage, WIN 519
  network, WIN 406
  selecting to share, WIN 410
  sharing (visual overview), WIN 406–407
  usage in Task Manager, WIN 499

Restore button to restore files, WIN 434

Restore Down button, WIN 13, WIN 16

restore points, WIN 435
  creating, WIN 450–454
  selecting, WIN 547

restoring
  computers, WIN 453–454
  files and folders, WIN 434, WIN 446–448
  your settings, WIN 83–84, WIN 138–139,
  WIN 196–197, WIN 250–251, WIN 365,
  WIN 426, WIN 490–491

retouching photos, WIN 341

Review Assignments
  Module 1, WIN 37
  Module 2, WIN 85–86

ribbon, WIN 18
  changes to provide appropriate buttons, WIN 25
  examples of controls (fig.), WIN 19
  Mail, WIN 179
  Paint (fig.), WIN 311
  tabs on, WIN 26
  using, WIN 18–19
  View tab, WIN 64

right mouse button, moving files, WIN 59

right pane, WIN 25, WIN 48

right-clicking, WIN 8

right-drag, WIN 42

rolling back drivers to previous version, WIN 484

root directory, WIN 45, WIN 46

rootkits, WIN 218

rotating
  graphics, WIN 330–332
  photos, WIN 341

routers, WIN 399

royalty-free photos, WIN 343

S

Safe mode, WIN 546, WIN 547

sandbox, WIN 228

saturation, WIN 349

Save As dialog box, WIN 68, WIN 69–71

Save command, WIN 69

Saved Pictures folder, WIN 27

saving
  annotated webpages to Reading list, WIN 169–170
  bitmap graphics in different file type, WIN 315
  files, WIN 69–71, WIN 339
  graphics files, WIN 314–315
  image files with new name, WIN 314–315
  photos, WIN 349
  searches, WIN 276–277
  themes, WIN 105–106
  webpage content, WIN 176–177
  work before shutting down, WIN 34

ScanDisk, WIN 469

scanners, WIN 309

scanning
  your computer with Windows Defender, WIN 221–222
  your fingerprint, WIN 247

scheduling appointments, WIN 194–195

screen refresh rate, adjusting, WIN 485–486

screen resolution, WIN 5, WIN 106, WIN 107–108, WIN 318

Screen Saver Settings dialog box, WIN 103

screen savers, WIN 5, WIN 90
  activating, WIN 102–104
  presentation settings, WIN 394

screenshots
  creating of Start menu, WIN 137–138
  of webpages, WIN 168

ScreenTips, WIN 6, WIN 156, WIN 166

Search box, WIN 43, WIN 50, WIN 272, WIN 284–285
  finding files using, WIN 55–56
  using, WIN 260–261

search criteria, WIN 259
  advanced, WIN 284–288
  combining, WIN 285
  combining (fig.), WIN 284
  typical (fig.), WIN 267

search engines, WIN 151
  See also specific search engine
  additional search criteria, WIN 283
  choosing, WIN 296–298

search expressions, WIN 282, WIN 292

search results, WIN 259
  evaluating webpages in, WIN 294
  examining, WIN 275–276

Search the web and Windows box, WIN 10, WIN 18

Search Tools Search tab, WIN 56, WIN 258

searches, saving, WIN 276–277

Searches folder, WIN 276

searching, WIN 288
  See also finding
  for apps and information with Cortana, WIN 261–263
  developing search strategies, WIN 260–261
  for files, WIN 267–277
  for files (visual overview), WIN 258–259
  for files using Search box, WIN 55–56
  for help on Microsoft website, WIN 32–33
  the Internet (visual overview), WIN 282–283
  keywords, WIN 291
  for Microsoft Community, WIN 534–536
  Microsoft Support topics, WIN 526
  narrowing your search, WIN 292–295
  for online information using Cortana, WIN 162–165
  for photos, WIN 273–274
  search tools (fig.), WIN 260
  for settings, WIN 264–266
  vs. sorting, filtering, grouping, WIN 272
  suggestions on New tab (fig.), WIN 164

using advanced search criteria, WIN 284–288
  the web, WIN 33, WIN 288–292
  with wildcards, WIN 271
  Windows How-to webpages, WIN 33–34

sector (of hard disk), WIN 470

Secure Boot, WIN 250

security
  biometric, WIN 242
  events (audits), WIN 543
  features (fig.), WIN 209
  features of Microsoft Edge, WIN 226–227
  message in Microsoft Edge (fig.), WIN 231
  screen savers and, WIN 103
  websites, deciding whether to trust, WIN 239

Security and Maintenance window, WIN 206, WIN 208, WIN 539

security tools
  See also specific tool
  Microsoft website, WIN 220
  using, WIN 208–214
  visual overview, WIN 206–207

Select a Clip button, WIN 168

selecting
  backup location, WIN 438
  battery plan (mobile computing), WIN 384–386
  color settings, WIN 486–487
  commands, WIN 18
  graphics area for deletion, WIN 332–333, WIN 338
  multiple files and folders, WIN 61
  objects, WIN 7–8
  other power options, WIN 393–394
  power plan (mobile computing), WIN 385
  restore points, WIN 547
  tags for files, WIN 281
  themes, WIN 104–105
  tool to solve performance problems, WIN 517
  views, WIN 27

selective focus, WIN 340, WIN 351

sending and receiving email using Mail app, WIN 184–186

Sent Items folder, Mail app, WIN 178

server addresses, WIN 154

servers, WIN 29

service pack (SP), WIN 214

service set identifier (SSID), WIN 400

services described, WIN 508

Services file, File History, WIN 445

setting up
    printers, WIN 488–490
    program for compatibility, WIN 459–461
    Remote Desktop Connection, WIN 424–425
    small office or home networks, WIN 400–401
    user accounts, WIN 240–248
    Windows Hello, WIN 246–247
    Windows Update, WIN 215–216

settings
    changing display, WIN 106–109
    for Photos app (fig.), WIN 135
    pinned to Start menu (fig.), WIN 131
    presentation, WIN 394–396
    Reading view, WIN 167–168
    restoring your, WIN 83–84, WIN 138–139,
        WIN 196–197, WIN 250–251, WIN 298–299,
        WIN 365, WIN 426, WIN 490–491
    searching for, WIN 264–266
    setting Windows 10, WIN 92–106
    Windows Firewall, WIN 212

Settings app
    categories (fig.), WIN 94
    Devices window (fig.), WIN 489
    Personalization window, WIN 91
    starting, WIN 93–94
    System window, WIN 500

Settings command, WIN 10

Shake
    illustrated (fig.), WIN 117
    minimizing and restoring with, WIN 127

shapes
    changing color of, WIN 334–335
    drawing, WIN 325–327
    moving text in, WIN 328–329

Shapes group (fig.), WIN 311

Share menu for sharing photos (fig.), WIN 353

sharing
    files with homegroups, WIN 412–413
    Internet connection over wireless network
        (fig.), WIN 401
    photos, WIN 352–359
    printers with homegroups, WIN 415
    resources (visual overview), WIN 406–407

shortcut icons, WIN 90

shortcut menus
    described, WIN 9
    displaying, WIN 8–9

shortcuts, adding to desktop, WIN 110

Show hidden icons button, WIN 117, WIN 119

showing
    See also displaying, viewing
    filename extensions in windows, WIN 79–80
    Task View button, WIN 121

Shut down option, WIN 34

shutdown settings, WIN 387–388

shutting down, or sleep, or signing out, WIN 35

signal strength for wireless networks, WIN 402

signed drivers, WIN 479

sign-in options, user accounts, WIN 244–248

signing in to Windows 10, WIN 4

signing out of Windows 10, WIN 35

Silverlight, WIN 158

size, filtering search results by, WIN 272

sizing
    Start menu, Start menu tiles, WIN 134
    text, objects, WIN 108–109

sizing coordinates, WIN 306, WIN 327

sleep, WIN 34, WIN 35, WIN 36, WIN 391,
    WIN 393

Sleep command, WIN 393

slide shows, playing, WIN 348–349

small office or home network, setting up,
    WIN 400–401

SmartScreen filter, checking websites with,
    WIN 228–230

Snap
    arranging windows with, WIN 123–125
    illustrated (fig.), WIN 117

Snap Assist, WIN 123

Snipping Tool, WIN 310

software, WIN 448–455
    See also specific program
    application, managing, WIN 456–461
    license agreements for, WIN 220
    managing (visual overview), WIN 434–435
    problems, WIN 527
    recovering from errors, WIN 538–547
    system. See system software
    uninstalling, WIN 458–459

solid background, WIN 328

sorting, WIN 72
    files by date (fig.), WIN 74
    and filtering files, WIN 73–76
    vs. searching, filtering, grouping, WIN 272

spam, WIN 225

spammers, WIN 225

speaker volume (mobile computing), WIN 377,
    WIN 380–381

special characters, WIN 57

speed of computers, WIN 498

spoofed website, WIN 228

spyware
    defending against, WIN 220–225
    described, WIN 220

SSID (service set identifier), WIN 400

Standard accounts, WIN 240

Start and Cortana search area on taskbar,
    WIN 118

Start button, WIN 2

Start menu
    adding apps to, WIN 129–131
    creating screenshots of, WIN 137–138
    display options, WIN 128–129
    exploring, WIN 9–11
    modifying tiles on, WIN 133–136
    opening, WIN 7
    organizing tiles on, WIN 132–133
    personalizing, WIN 128–138
    pinning tiles on, WIN 129–130
    pinning webpages to, WIN 160–161
    testing tiles on, WIN 131–132
    visual overview, WIN 116–117

starting
    apps, WIN 12–13, WIN 457–458
    Calendar app, WIN 194
    Disk Cleanup tool, WIN 468
    Get Started app, WIN 31
    Mail app, WIN 183–184
    Microsoft Edge, WIN 152–153
    Optimize Drives tool, WIN 475
    Paint, WIN 310
    Remote Desktop Connection, WIN 425
    Settings app, WIN 93–94
    and using applications, WIN 508–511
    Windows 10, WIN 4–5
    WordPad, WIN 18

Startup Repair, WIN 546, WIN 547

status bar, WIN 24, WIN 26, WIN 306, WIN 327

status of wireless network, checking, WIN 404

stemming, WIN 285

Steps Recorder, WIN 547–549

storage devices, identifying, WIN 29

store-and-forward technology, WIN 180

strong passwords, WIN 227, WIN 241

stylus, WIN 153

subfolders, WIN 29, WIN 58

switches, network, WIN 399

switching
    accounts, WIN 248
    between applications, WIN 14–15

sync, WIN 240

sync, one-way and two-way, WIN 419

Sync Center, WIN 377, WIN 407
    managing offline files, WIN 419
    resolving sync conflicts, WIN 421
    synchronizing offline files, WIN 416
    using, WIN 420–421

sync conflicts, WIN 419, WIN 421

sync partnerships, WIN 407, WIN 420

synchronize, WIN 240

synchronize (sync), WIN 407

synchronizing
    folders, WIN 419–421
    offline files, WIN 416, WIN 420–421
    settings and OneDrive files, WIN 422

System Diagnostics Report,
WIN 519–520

system events
    in Event Viewer (fig.), WIN 544
    viewing details about, WIN 543–545

system files, WIN 79

system information
    displaying basic, WIN 500–503
    examining using Task Manager,
    WIN 506–511
    reviewing detailed, WIN 503–505

System Information window, WIN 504–505

system notifications. See notifications

system partitions, WIN 466

system performance
    improving, WIN 500–520
    measuring, WIN 517–519
    monitoring, WIN 512–517
    tracking (visual overview), WIN 498–499

system problems
    solving (visual overview), WIN 526–527
    troubleshooting, WIN 530

System Properties dialog box (fig.), WIN 452

System Protection
    turning on, WIN 451–452
    using, WIN 454

system recovery drive, WIN 448

system recovery points, creating,
WIN 450–454

system repair disk, WIN 448

System Restore, WIN 435, WIN 448, WIN 454,
WIN 546

System Restore Wizard, WIN 452

System Settings window (fig.), WIN 389

system software
    described, WIN 12
    managing, WIN 448–455

System window
    Battery saver category (fig.), WIN 383
    in Control Panel (fig.), WIN 502
    Settings app, WIN 502

T

tabbed browsing in Microsoft Edge, WIN 149

tablets, WIN 378

tabs, WIN 18
    contextual, WIN 27
    on ribbon, WIN 26
    in Task Manager window (fig.), WIN 507
    using in tabbed browsing, WIN 158

tags, WIN 259, WIN 277
    adding to files, WIN 278–281
    for photos, WIN 345
    selecting for files, WIN 281

Task Manager
    examining system information,
    WIN 506–511
    visual overview, WIN 498–499
    window, tabs in (fig.), WIN 507

Task View button, WIN 14, WIN 116

Task view (fig.), WIN 15

taskbar, WIN 2
    modifying, WIN 118–123
    moving buttons, WIN 120–121
    pinning apps to, WIN 119–120
    sections of, WIN 118
    setting properties, WIN 122–123
    visual overview, WIN 116–117

Taskbar and Start Menu Properties dialog box,
WIN 122–123

taskbar buttons, WIN 2
    redisplaying minimized windows,
    WIN 16
    switching between apps with, WIN 15

tasks, ending, WIN 499

temporary files, WIN 79

text
    adding to graphics, WIN 320–325
    bolding, WIN 18
    changing size of, WIN 108–109
    moving in shapes, WIN 328–329

text boxes
    creating, WIN 322–323
    moving, WIN 329–330

text files, searching for, WIN 285

text passwords, WIN 241

Text tool, WIN 320, WIN 323

theme packs, WIN 106

themes, WIN 2
    described, selecting, changing,
    WIN 104–105
    desktop background, WIN 91
    saving, WIN 105–106

third-party cookies, WIN 235

This PC
    contents (fig.), WIN 51
    icon, WIN 42

thumbnails, WIN 14, WIN 43

TIF, TIFF files, WIN 314

tiles, WIN 7
    live, turning on, WIN 134
    modifying on Start menu, WIN 133–136
    naming groups of, WIN 133
    organizing on Start menu, WIN 132–133
    pinning on Start menu, WIN 129–130
    testing on Start menu, WIN 131–132

Tint button, WIN 350–351

To box, Mail app, WIN 184

toggle button (fig.), WIN 19

toolbar, Mail, WIN 179

Tools tab, OS (C:) Properties dialog box (fig.),
WIN 471

touching up photos, WIN 349–350

touchscreen
    described, WIN 4
    pointing to objects, WIN 7

tracking
    processor time, WIN 514
    protection, requesting, WIN 238–239
    system performance (visual overview),
    WIN 498–499

transparent background, WIN 328

Transparent selection command, Paint,
WIN 328

trial versions, WIN 435

Trojan horses, WIN 218

troubleshooters, WIN 527, WIN 530–534

troubleshooting
    and fixing computer problems,
    WIN 531–534
    information, finding, WIN 529–530
    printing errors, WIN 536–538
    reports, WIN 534
    system problems, WIN 530

TRUSTe, WIN 239

"Trusted Windows Store app," WIN 261

trusting, WIN 241

turning off Windows 10, WIN 34–36

turning on
SmartScreen filter, WIN 229–230
System Protection, WIN 451–452

.txt, WIN 66, WIN 71

U

Undo button, Quick Access Toolbar, WIN 316

Unified Extensible Firmware Interface (UEFI), WIN 250

uniform resource locator. *See* URL (uniform resource locator)

uninstalling
apps, WIN 435
software, WIN 458–459

universal apps, WIN 5, WIN 11

unpinning folders from Quick access list, WIN 80–81

Update & Security window, WIN 207

Update and shutdown option, WIN 36

updates, WIN 207
antivirus software, WIN 219–220
displaying installed, WIN 217
windows. *See* Windows Update
from Windows Update, WIN 215–216

updating device drivers, WIN 482–484

URL (Universal Resource Locator)
display in Microsoft Edge, WIN 148
opening webpages using, WIN 154–155
parts of a, WIN 154

USB devices, removing, WIN 484

USB flash drives, WIN 44, WIN 47, WIN 52
accessing, WIN 29
as backup location, WIN 438, WIN 439
certified for Windows To Go, WIN 461
creating shortcuts to, WIN 113–114
deleting files, folders, WIN 67
ReadyBoost tab, Properties dialog box (fig.), WIN 524

USB hub, WIN 477

USB ports, WIN 476–477

USB printers, setting up, installing, WIN 488–490

User Account Control (UAC), WIN 249–250

user accounts
changing sign-in options, WIN 244–248
icon, changing, WIN 136–137
setting up, WIN 240–248
switching, WIN 248

user IDs, WIN 181

user names, WIN 4

V

vector graphics, WIN 308
described (fig.), WIN 309
selecting, WIN 309

verifying that User Account Control is turned on, WIN 249–250

videos, working with, WIN 364

view access, view and edit access, WIN 406

view buttons, WIN 25, WIN 43

View tab
described, WIN 25, WIN 64
displaying contents of, WIN 18

View tab options (fig.), WIN 77

viewing
See also displaying, showing
basic system information, WIN 500–503
details about system events, WIN 543–545
display settings, WIN 109
files by groups, WIN 75–76
file's contents, WIN 68
files in folders, WIN 48–49
folders, WIN 49–50
Get Started topics, WIN 32
hard disk partitions, WIN 467
hard disk properties, WIN 464–466
My Documents folder contents, WIN 29–30
and organizing photos, WIN 344–348
photos in OneDrive, WIN 357–358
photos using Windows Photo Viewer, WIN 345–346
Recycle Bin contents, WIN 8
Reliability Monitor, WIN 540–543
ScreenTips, WIN 6
update history, WIN 217

views
changing folder, WIN 53
changing Quick access, WIN 28
Conversation, WIN 178
Reading, WIN 149, WIN 166–167
selecting, changing, WIN 27–28

vignette effects, WIN 349

virtual desktops, WIN 15, WIN 127–128

virtual memory, WIN 513

viruses, WIN 189, WIN 206, WIN 208
avoiding, removing, WIN 220
checking for protection on your computer, WIN 219–220
defending against email, WIN 225

Visual Effects tab, Performance Options dialog box, WIN 505–506

visual overviews
creating graphics in Paint, WIN 306–307
editing photos, WIN 340–341
managing data and software, WIN 434–435
managing hardware, WIN 462–463
mobile computing settings, WIN 376–377
sharing resources, WIN 406–407
solving system problems, WIN 526–527
tracking system performance, WIN 498–499

voice search, Cortana, WIN 289

volume, WIN 466

volume of speakers (mobile computing), WIN 377

W

wallpaper, WIN 96

warnings, WIN 540

WAV files, WIN 359

Waveform Audio File Format, WIN 359

weather information, finding, WIN 289–290

web, WIN 150
opening pages on, WIN 154–158
searching the, WIN 33, WIN 288–292

web app, WIN 354

web browsers
described, WIN 151–152
Microsoft Edge, WIN 32–33

web mapping services, WIN 151

webcams, WIN 342

webpages
adding links to, in Favorites list, WIN 173–174
adding to Favorites list, WIN 172–174
adding to Favorites list folders, WIN 174
adding to Reading list, WIN 169–170
displaying in Internet Explorer, WIN 158
displaying in Reading view, Microsoft Edge, WIN 149
evaluating in search results, WIN 294
illustrated (fig.), WIN 148
managing with Microsoft Edge, WIN 158–161
opening on the web, WIN 154–158
pinning to Start menu, WIN 160–161
printing, saving content, WIN 176–177
reading, annotating, WIN 166–168
using Cortana to learn more about topics on, WIN 162

websites
checking using SmartScreen filter, WIN 228–230
deciding whether to trust, WIN 239
spoofed, WIN 228

webTrust, WIN 239

Wikipedia online encyclopedia, WIN 296–297

wildcards, WIN 271

Window apps, WIN 5

windows, WIN 5, WIN 75–76
    active, WIN 14
    arranging with Snap, WIN 123–125
    closing, WIN 118
    controls, WIN 18
    customized folder window (visual overview), WIN 64–65
    folder. See folder windows
    Get Started, WIN 31–32
    keeping track of with Peek, WIN 125–126
    manipulating, WIN 15–17
    minimizing and restoring with Shake, WIN 127
    Paint (fig.), WIN 311
    previewing with Peek, WIN 126
    resizing, WIN 17

Windows 10
    browser. See Microsoft Edge
    changing settings, WIN 92–106
    closing, WIN 33–34
    desktop (visual overview), WIN 2–3
    and homegroups, WIN 408
    introducing, WIN 4
    Mail app. See Mail app
    Movies & TV app, WIN 364
    ports, WIN 476–477
    recovery options (fig.), WIN 449
    reinstalling, WIN 546
    searching for help on Microsoft website, WIN 32–33

security tools, WIN 208–214
    turning off, WIN 34–36
    videos from, WIN 364

Windows apps, WIN 11

"Windows as a Service," WIN 1

Windows Defender, WIN 207, WIN 218–219
    scanning your computer with, WIN 221–222
    setting options, WIN 223–225

Windows Error-checking tool, WIN 469–472

Windows file hierarchy (fig.), WIN 46

Windows Firewall, managing, WIN 210–214

Windows Hello, WIN 242, WIN 244, WIN 246–247
    option for fingerprint verification (fig.), WIN 246

Windows Help, WIN 31

Windows homegroups. See homegroups

Windows Media Player, WIN 213, WIN 359

Windows Mobility Center (mobile computing), WIN 377
    described (fig.), WIN 379
    displaying battery status, WIN 381–384
    opening, WIN 380
    power plan, selecting, WIN 384–386
    presentation settings, WIN 394–396
    using, WIN 379–386

Windows Photo Viewer, WIN 344, WIN 345–346

Windows spotlight, WIN 91

Windows Store, WIN 129
    finding music files, WIN 359–361
    installing apps from, WIN 456–457

Windows To Go, WIN 461

Windows Update
    described, WIN 207
    setting up, WIN 214–217

wireless
    network sharing Internet connection (fig.), WIN 401
    networks, checking status, WIN 404
    networks, connecting to, WIN 402–404
    technology, WIN 398–399

Word
    documents, searching for, WIN 285
    .docx files, WIN 71

WordPad
    closing, WIN 21
    creating files, WIN 68
    described, starting, WIN 18

Work calendar, WIN 193

World Wide Web, exploring, WIN 150–151

worms, WIN 218

Y

Yahoo! People Search, WIN 181

YahooMail, WIN 182

Z

Zip button, Send group, Share tab, folder window, WIN 82

zipped folders. See compressed (zipped) folders

zooming
    on images, WIN 321
    in Paint, WIN 307